Film

THE BETTMANN ARCHIVE

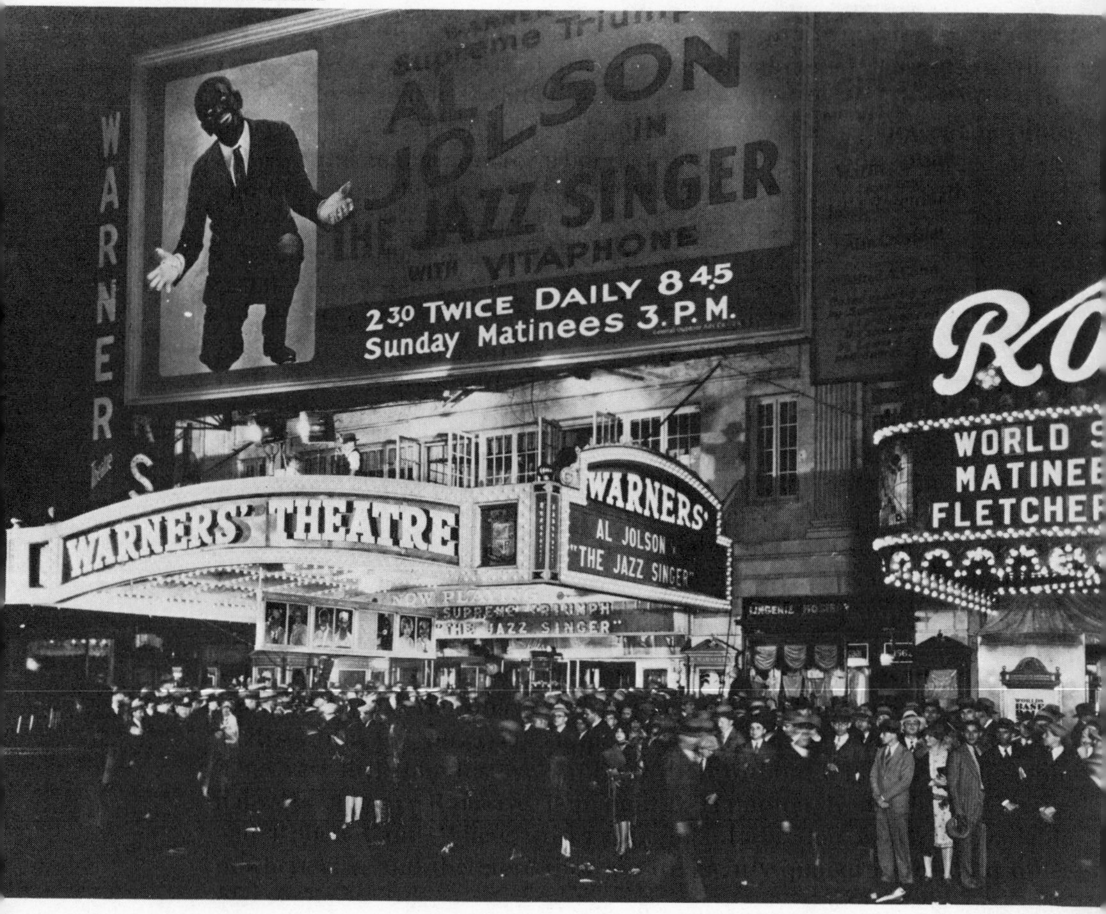

Film

The Democratic Art

GARTH JOWETT

FOR THE AMERICAN FILM INSTITUTE

Little, Brown and Company — Boston – Toronto

FIRST EDITION

T 03/76

The author is grateful to the following for permission to reprint from previously published materials:

Doubleday & Company, Inc., for excerpts from *Memoirs of Will Hays* by Will Hays. Copyright © 1955 by Doubleday & Company, Inc.

Simon & Schuster, Inc., for excerpts from *A Million and One Nights* by Terry Ramsaye. Copyright 1926, renewed 1954 by Simon and Schuster.

Teacher's College Press, for selections from *The Rise of the American Film* by Lewis Jacobs, Copyright 1939, 1948, © 1967 by Lewis Jacobs.

Little, Brown and Company, Publishers, for quotations from *Hollywood: The Dream Factory* by Hortense Powdermaker. Copyright 1950 by Hortense Powdermaker.

University of Illinois Press, for a table from *Hollywood Looks at Its Audience* by Leo A. Handel. Copyright 1950 by the University of Illinois Press.

Prentice-Hall, Inc., for a table from *The Press and America*, 2nd edition, by Edwin Emery. Copyright © 1962 by Prentice-Hall, Inc.

John A. Sargent, for a table from his unpublished dissertation "Self-Regulation: The Motion Picture Production Code, 1930–1961," University of Michigan, 1963.

Fredric Stuart and Arno Press, Inc., for a table from *The Effects of Television on the Motion Picture and Radio Industries*. Copyright © 1960 by Fredric Stuart.

The Regents of the University of California, for tables from "Motion Picture Economics" by Anthony Dawson, *Hollywood Quarterly*, Vol. 3, No. 3; copyright 1948 by The Regents of the University of California. From "Movie Attendance of the Art House Audience" by Dallas W. Smythe, et al., *Quarterly of Film, Radio and Television*, Vol. 8, No. 1; copyright 1954 by The Regents of the University of California. From "Portrait of a First-Run Audience" by Dallas W. Smythe, et al., *Quarterly of Film, Radio and Television*, Vol. 9, No. 4; copyright 1955 by The Regents of the University of California.

Motion Picture Association of America, Inc., for tables from the 1957 study "The Public Appraises Movies," conducted by The Opinion Research Corporation.

LIBRARY OF CONGRESS CATALOGING IN PUBLICATION DATA

Jowett, Garth.
  Film: the democratic art.

  (The American Film Institute series)
  Bibliography: p.
  Includes index.
  1. Moving-pictures — United States. 2. Moving-pictures — Social aspects. I. Title. II. Series: American Film Institute. The American Film Institute Series.
  PN1993.5.U6J67   791.43'0973   75-32411
  ISBN 0-316-47370-7

Designed by Susan Windheim

*Published simultaneously in Canada
by Little, Brown & Company (Canada) Limited*

PRINTED IN THE UNITED STATES OF AMERICA

For Miriam and Adam

It has come then, this new weapon of men, and the face of the whole earth changes. In after centuries its beginning will be indeed remembered.

It has come, this new weapon of men, and by faith and a study of the signs we proclaim that it will go on and on in immemorial wonder.

Vachel Lindsay, *The Art of the Moving Picture*

Acknowledgments

The preparation of this volume took six years, and while its final shape is solely my own responsibility, many people influenced my decisions about what to examine, include and even exclude. While it would be impossible to acknowledge all those who read various sections and drafts of the manuscript, I would like to single out the following for special thanks:

The Faculty of the Graduate History Department of the University of Pennsylvania, who collectively encouraged my interest in the history of communications.

Professor Seymour Mandelbaum, who directed the dissertation which formed the basis of the first half of this book, and who provided me with the intellectual stimulus to dig beneath the surface issues.

Dean George Gerbner of the Annenberg School of Communications, University of Pennsylvania, for his continual encouragement and interest in this project.

Professor Ian Jarvie, whose own work provided inspiration, and whose advice and encouragement were most welcome.

Sali-Ann Kriegsman, formerly of the American Film Institute, for her faith and enthusiasm in seeing this project through to publication.

Sam Kula of the Public Archives of Canada, for his interest from the very first.

Richard McDonough, my editor, for his patience, advice and most of all encouragement when most needed.

Monica Schouten and Havilah Eichenberg for their help in compiling bibliographical material.

Professor Mark A. May for permission to quote from a letter regarding the Payne Fund Studies.

While many typists worked on the manuscript, I owe special thanks to Gail Driscoll and Doreen Truant for their patience and assistance.

The Canada Council, Carleton University and the University of Windsor for financial support at various times.

Preface

At the outset, I think that I should admit that it is impossible to write anything like a complete social history of the motion picture. For a period of over fifty years the movies were such an important and pervasive part of American society that no one study can possibly do justice to describing their place in the American scene. The book that follows is my attempt to chronicle and analyze some of the ways in which the motion picture affected the lives of the American people, and those forces, both positive and negative, which shaped the final product seen on the screen.

As a historian, I became aware of how little attention most historians pay to the influence of the mass media as major factors in social change. I was particularly interested to discover that not since Margaret Thorp in 1939 had anyone attempted to write a book examining the motion picture as an integral part of the American social fabric. My curiosity unsatisfied, I attempted some preliminary research as a graduate student, which only served to convince me of the impossibility of writing a complete social history of the American movies. The task is simply too large for one individual. Nevertheless, this was a story which needed telling, and no matter how incomplete it might be, I was anxious that historians be made more aware of the necessity to examine such facets of the material culture.

While film studies have made great strides in recent years, there has been an unfortunate tendency to concentrate on the aesthetic or biographical aspects at the expense of the sociological or psychological. The reason for this is clear; the introduction of television caused all interest in the study of media "influence" to be focused to the newer, and certainly more pervasive, smaller screen. In this process the rich legacy of material available to historians and others on the subject of motion picture influence and impact has been largely ignored by all but the most diligent film scholars. The importance of the motion picture as a major socializing agency in the first half of this century has never received the serious attention it deserves, and American social and cultural history has suffered as a result.

The book that follows is not aimed entirely at historians — hopefully its readership will be wider than that — but, in honesty, it was written with the needs of the social historian as a guiding perspective. If the book succeeds in stimulating more serious inquiry into the historical importance of the motion picture, then it will have achieved its primary purpose.

Regarding bibliographic sources for this study, it was my deliberate intention to avoid the use of movie trade publications, except where absolutely unavoidable. My reasoning was that I could obtain a more accurate perception of the general public's attitude toward the movies by the use of nonindustry sources. (Still, *Variety* proved invaluable.) I also used, where these were available, as much material generated by social scientists and other empirical investigators on the "effects of the movies" as possible. Some of this material is incorporated into the text; some is added at the end of certain chapters as "Special Studies." The quality of this research varies widely, but most of it is interesting for what it tells us about the perceived role of the movies at specific points in time.

The source material for any history of the motion picture industry in America is a paradox. While an enormous number of books, articles and other materials are available, there are very few primary sources which really come to grips with the problem of the medium's impact upon national life. A further problem is that most of the major secondary sources do not contain the thorough documentation required by scholarly research, but instead rely upon conjecture and anecdote. The continued reluctance of the motion picture industry to give its support to any form of research in the past now means that reliable industry statistics, and other relevant information, are generally not available. Thus the film historian is forced to fall back upon unsubstantiated material, or imprecise approximations.

Because so much that occurred in the film industry was of a "private" nature, film historians have had to place great reliance on the subjective analyses of a few observers supposedly intimate with the circumstances. Thus very little film history can be written without reference to the seminal work of Terry Ramsaye, Benjamin B. Hampton, Kenneth MacGowan, and Robert Grau. These works contain information which is available nowhere else, and therefore they are frequently quoted in this and other film studies.

In specialized areas of film history it is also necessary to rely upon a few standard works. The work of Raymond Moley, even though obviously biased in favor, is essential in examining the history and development of the Hays Office, as is the autobiography of Will H. Hays. The Catholic Legion of Decency never received the examination its importance warranted, and the work of Paul Facey, S.J., is therefore indispensable. Similarly, the work of Ruth Inglis is based upon primary research in industry files, and is extremely valuable in considering the effectiveness and methods of motion picture control.

No discussion of secondary sources would be complete without paying homage to the important work of Lewis Jacobs, who has performed those broad analyses of shifts in content that allow historians to relate the movies to the larger historical context. Without Jacobs's monumental research to rely upon, this study would have been incomplete.

It is an unfortunate fact that the publication of *The New Film Index* by Richard Dyer MacCann and Edward S. Perry occurred precisely at the time that this manuscript was in the copyediting stage. Had it been available three years earlier, this magnificent work of scholarship would have saved me a great deal of time and effort, and provided me with sources I may have missed.

Anticipating certain criticisms, I want to point out that it was never my intention to write a book about the history of the motion picture as an art form. There are many such histories available, and I have no pretensions about my abilities in this direction. However, this is an examination of "movie-going," and I have concentrated my research efforts on this aspect of motion picture history. Doubtless some will suggest that one cannot write a social history of movie-going without analyzing the product on the screen; nevertheless, it is my personal belief that this approach can be justified.

May I also suggest that the interested reader pay particular attention to the chapter notes, which are designed to be an integral part of the text as a whole.

Finally, I would appreciate hearing from those who wish to challenge or correct what I have written here. This is the first attempt to comprehensively examine this topic, and hopefully future editions could incorporate such suggestions for improvement.

GSJ
Windsor, Ontario

Contents

Tables

Film

Introduction

The Agents of Change

HISTORIANS HAVE TRADITIONALLY SHOWN a reluctance to interpret social and cultural changes as a function or result of innovations in the technology of communication. The reasons for much of this reluctance include, on the one hand, an outdated conception of which social and cultural forces are really of historical significance, and, on the other, a definite lack of substantive empirical research material for use as guidelines to gauge the effects on a society of long-term exposure to various forms of communication. However, in recent years we have begun to witness the development of a body of scholarship, both empirical and theoretical, which has indicated that various forms of communication have indeed played a significant role in shaping the long-term development of societies.[1]

The central problem confronted by communications historians is what takes place when a new medium of communication is introduced into a social system. What social, cultural, economic and political adjustments are necessary to accommodate this new force? What institutional changes will have to be made, and what are the long-term psychological effects on the population? In a more abstract vein, what changes occur in the collective sharing of symbols in that society? These vital questions have seldom been examined systematically, and the whole of social history has suffered as a result.

This study is an attempt to answer a small part of some of these large questions, by examining the dramatic alterations in both the communications infrastructure and the leisure patterns of the American people when the motion picture was introduced into the United States. The primary objective is to gain a more acute understanding of some of the adjustments necessary for the social and cultural integration of the motion picture, as both a communications medium and a primary entertainment form, and

3

its eventual acceptance and elevation to the role of a major social institution. In order to assess these overall changes as a result of this innovation it is necessary to first examine the "time-place" setting in which it occurred.[2]

The Changing Face of America

Between 1890 and 1930, the spatial organization of American society was dramatically transformed. This transformation was the result of three developments of the late nineteenth century: first, the increasing population growth in urban areas; second, the location of large-scale industrial complexes in close proximity to these growing urban centers; and third, the invention and adoption of revolutionary new communications media such as the telegraph and telephone. These three developments, inextricably linked and constantly acting as impetuses to one another, created a new social and economic order with dramatically enlarged spatial boundaries. Stretching out from the industrial cities of the Northeast, important communications and transportation links restructured all previous concepts of time and distance, and encouraged the development of economic control of industry from centralized locations mainly in the Northeast.[3]

The "old" America with a predominantly rural-based population was transformed into a nation whose population lived mainly in cities, and while the more traditional rural culture would continue to play an important vestigial role in American life, eventually it too was forced to yield some of its hold under pressure from the more widely disseminated urban culture inherent in the new communications media. This battle was not easily won, and the strength of rural America as a symbol of "good and virtue" persists, and has become a part of the accommodation process toward urbanization.[4] Historians have generally seen this change from a rural to an urban culture with new values and ideals as a major aspect of the modernization of the United States, and the source of much of the social and cultural tension evidenced in the early years of the twentieth century.[5]

The migration of people into urban areas had long been a feature of American life, but this movement reached its zenith in the two decades between 1890 and 1910, when internal movement from American farms combined with massive immigration from Europe to increase the urban population by nearly twenty million.[6] The interaction of the newcomers with those already established in the urban centers created a volatile mixture which made the American city an exciting if not terrifying place to some.

4

TABLE 1
POPULATION IN URBAN AND RURAL TERRITORY,
1870–1950
POPULATION IN MILLIONS

YEAR	RURAL (Under 2,500)	URBAN (Above 2,500)	% URBAN
1870	28.7	9.9	25.5
1890	40.8	22.1	35.1
1910	50.0	42.0	45.6
1920	51.6	54.2	51.4
1930	53.8	69.0	56.4
1940	57.2	74.4	56.5
1950	54.2	96.5	64.0

Source: Historical Statistics of the United States
(Washington: Bureau of the Census, 1961),
Series A 195–209, p. 14.

The importance of industrial development in encouraging the growth of urban centers in the period after the Civil War cannot be overlooked. Whereas American cities had long been major centers of commerce, the transformation from the commercial to the industrial city was a feature of post–Civil War urban development.[7] The improvement made in transportation, especially railroads, opened up vast new fields of raw materials to these growing industries. In the decade of the eighties, over 71,000 miles of new railway lines were built, and the entire Northeast was laced with a dense and complex network of railroad systems.[8] Not only did the railroads make new markets accessible for industry by bringing the various geographic and economic sectors of the country into much closer contact than ever before, but they also helped considerably in the extension of the concept of a "national American community."

It was, however, the development of new forms of communications media which did the most to bring about this national community. This fact is made clearer if we accept Francis E. Merrill's definition of community as a "permanent group of persons, occupying a common area, interacting in both institutional and non-institutional roles, and having a sense of identification with the entity (the community) that arises from this interaction."[9] While this definition of community is synonymous with society, it does stress the importance of social interaction as the basis for the development of national interests and emotional bonds which can create a geographically extended common culture. The ability of the communications media to bring about the creation of a national identity is well documented, and it has been noted that "the structure of social communication reflects the structure and development of society."[10] It is

5

communication which can overcome the development of a vast number of unique cultural identities caused by wide geographic separation — a danger which was all too real in the United States.

The new communications media that were developed, such as the cheap, daily newspaper in the 1830s; the telegraph in 1844; the telephone in 1876; commercial, projected motion pictures in 1896; and commercial radio in the 1920s, were all part of this total communications revolution that would so radically transform many aspects of American life. No longer was the individual confined to local interaction; his environmental horizons were greatly expanded, as was his sphere of political interests. The stage was now set for the development of a new national consciousness among the American people.

While even today, after much examination, the degree and direction of association between the development of new forms of communication and the nature of social change are not completely clear, certain definite links can be indicated in the case of the United States. That important social document, the President's Report on *Recent Social Trends,* published in 1933, examined in detail the changes brought about by innovations in the fields of communication and transportation and synthesized the major effects into four areas:

1. The problems of coordination and competition, which "because of their public aspects . . . have involved to an unusual degree, planning, regulation and control."
2. The problems of mobility: "The transmission of goods, of the voice and possibly of vision may act as a retarding influence on human mobility in the future and may cause a development of more remote and impersonal directions and controls."
3. The centralization of human life caused by "the effectual shortening of distances and the increasing size of the land area which forms the basis or unit of operation for many organized activities."
4. The problems arising from the greater ease and diffusion of the media: "Regional isolation is being broken down all over the world. . . . The agencies of mass communication increase the possibilities of education, propaganda and the spread of information. . . . The developments bring problems of mass action, of mass production and standardization."[11]

The men drafting this report further noted that these new forms of communication, and especially the mass media and their cultural manifestations of mass entertainment, had helped to bring about what Henry Commager has called "a greater uniformity of character and habit than had been common in the nineteenth century."[12] Even then the final results were not clear and the report indicated that "the surface picture is one of chaos and conflict . . . however certain tendencies appear. There has developed a partially integrated system whereby contacts are established between individuals with a maximum of ease over an area of ever-increasing radius."[13] America was growing smaller as the system of social interaction grew larger!

There is no doubt that the series of changes brought about by the formidable combination of urbanism, industrialism and the communications revolution generated myriad tensions in turn-of-the-century America. Various historians have attempted to analyze the effects of these tensions, and different labels have been created to explain society's reactions, such as: "the status revolution"; "the search for order"; "the response to industrialism"; or even "the end of innocence." Whatever the most apt description might be, each of these three forces for change generated a similar set of problems and responses.

First, each indicated new possibilities for the centralization of power and control; this in turn presented a very real threat to the existing sources of power and authority and resulted in the inevitable struggle for ultimate social control. Thus the city eventually superseded the rural areas in political and economic control; large corporations, such as the monopolistic trusts, gained an ever-increasing share of the American economy to the detriment of small business; while the new forms of communication became an integral and indispensable part of the social and cultural infrastructure, capable of wielding immense power with their unrivaled ability to disseminate symbols and messages to large segments of the American population within a very short time period.

Second, the deep and rapid changes that resulted from this three-pronged attack on traditional society left in their wake a dazed population that was uncertain about which social and cultural norms it was to follow. In societies undergoing such rapid changes, new norms are constantly created and old ones abandoned. The established patterns of organized relationships constituting the family, church, school and government were all subjected to severe stress that could be stabilized only by a major social and cultural reorientation which could accommodate the new order. The internalization of these new norms, together with their social significance, was not easily achieved by large segments of the population.

The third reaction to these changes was the direct result of their combined assault on the existing social order. So vast and far-reaching were the transformations they set in motion that ultimately they were considered by many to be the cause of all the harmful, antisocial influences that threatened to destroy the basis of traditional American society. Thus for a great many Americans the city had always been symbolic of all that was evil. The sociologist Anselm Strauss has noted that this attitude had two

7

related, but different, aspects: "The city destroyed people who were born or migrated there. The city also imperiled the nation itself. Especially after the Civil War . . . and . . . the cities were replete with crime, vice, immorality, and poverty — the city served to threaten its own citizens, those still living in the countryside, and the very fabric of the nation itself."[14] In 1885, the Reverend Josiah Strong in his attack on the changes in American society observed that "the city has become a serious menace to our civilization, because in it . . . each of the dangers we have discussed is enhanced, and all are focalized."[15]

In much the same way the technological and economic changes brought about by development of large-scale industry caused the American people to revise their basic ideas concerning the nature of their society, themselves, and their role in the world. But here, too, there were deep suspicions of the end results of industrialization which were all too easily reinforced by the sights of smoke-filled skies, long, dark rows of workers' homes, dreadful living conditions and filthy city streets, and the conspicuous inequality in the distribution of wealth. The machine had long created conflicts in the American psyche, but these tensions reached a peak at the turn of the century when mechanization threatened to bring about the total depersonalization of the individual and thus destroy a basic tenet of faith in everything the New World had stood for.[16] It took the combined efforts of religious and social groups, with the assistance of stringent legislative action, to ensure that the final products of industrialization were to be used to enhance the development of a new society for all segments of the population.

However, it is in assessing the reactions and prevailing attitudes toward the new communications media that we find the greatest paradox. Certainly initial reactions were mixed, and much depended on the immediate social and economic utility of the particular form of communication. The telegraph and the telephone were of obvious benefit to society, and to industry in particular, and thus were the objects of praise and promise. On the other hand, the forms of communication which we now call mass communication, that is, newspapers, motion pictures, radio and ultimately television, have all been both praised and damned as being either "cornerstones of democracy" or "agents of the devil." Of the three agents of change that we have examined, the mass media have been the most unsuccessful in fully integrating themselves into the structure of American society, and their acceptance or rejection at any one time was dependent upon a wide variety of criteria relating to their social utility, content and cost. There were also wide regional variations in their pattern of acceptance or rejection which must be considered.

It is clear that the accommodation process to certain forms of communications media was not as successful as in the case of urbanization or industrialization.[17] The question remains, why? We can only suggest a few possible answers. First, while all three agents of change experienced similar problems, the communications revolution was in fact quite different from the other two in that its end product was more abstract, less substantive, and yet ultimately influenced a larger number of people over a longer period of time. (In fact its influence has not yet reached a peak, and the information explosion is only now making itself felt on the population as a whole.) Second, while the communications media gained much faster initial acceptance than either industrialization or urbanization, in the long run, because of their inherent characteristics and capabilities, they have experienced much more difficulty in finding their proper social or cultural niche. The real or imagined fears associated with the media's ability to induce attitude changes or to convey certain antisocial modes of behavior, together with their capability of transcending local and traditional influences, have made total acceptance difficult. This in essence is the central theme of this social history — an examination of how one of these media, in its institutional form as the motion picture industry, attempted to gain social and cultural acceptance, and the problems encountered in the accommodation process.

NOTES

1. There is still a definite lack of material which systematically examines the historical significance of the media of communication. The best theoretical works are Harold Innis, *The Bias of Communication* (Toronto: University of Toronto Press, revised edition 1972); and Marshall McLuhan, *Understanding Media* (New York: McGraw-Hill Book Company, 1964). Much of the work done by communications theorists can be considered in a historical light, particularly the research concerning the development of mass media systems in emerging countries. Thus many of the developmental models contained in Lucien Pye, ed., *Communications and Political Development* (New Haven: Princeton University Press, 1963), are useful and provocative for considering the role of the mass media in the development of Western society.

2. The importance of considering the "time-place setting" is based upon the theories of innovation contained in Homer G. Barnett, *Innovation: The Basis of Cultural Change* (New York: McGraw-Hill Book Company, 1953). While this study does not attempt to examine the introduction of the motion picture strictly within the theories suggested by Barnett, his categories of factors conducive to both innovation and acceptance have been influential in the formulation of the overall approach to the problem of the introduction of the motion picture.

3. There are several good sources which examine the growth and importance of metropolitan regions: Seymour J. Mandelbaum, *Boss Tweed's New York* (New York: John Wiley and Sons, 1965), examines the entire concept of new forms of communication as centralizing forces, concentrating on New York City in the last half of the nineteenth century; Allan R. Pred, *The Spatial Dynamics of U.S. Urban-Industrial Growth, 1800–1914* (Cambridge: M.I.T. Press, 1966), develops theoretical models to describe this process; Beverly Duncan and Stanley Lieberson, *Metropolis and Region in Transition* (Beverly Hills: Sage Publications, 1970), covers the historical framework and develops

economic models; while Ralph Thomlinson, *Urban Structure: The Social and Spatial Character of Cities* (New York: Random House, 1969), is a broad overview of the ecology of urban life.

4. The persistence of the agrarian myth in American culture has been discussed in many books and articles, the best of which are Henry Nash Smith, *The Virgin Land* (New York: Random House, Vintage Books, 1950); and Leo Marx, *The Machine in the Garden* (New York: Oxford University Press, 1967), which discusses the relationship between technology and the pastoral ideal in America.

5. The best expositions of the changes in America at this time are found in Robert H. Wiebe, *The Search for Order* (New York: Hill and Wang, 1967); Richard Hofstadter, *The Age of Reform* (New York: Random House, Vintage Books, 1955); and Samuel P. Hays, *The Response to Industrialism* (Chicago: University of Chicago Press, 1957).

6. *Historical Statistics of the United States* (Washington: Bureau of the Census, 1961), Series A 195-209, p. 14.

7. Pred, *Spatial Dynamics*, contains a useful model of the relationship between established centers of commerce and the emergence of industrial complexes, based upon the concept of "initial advantage." See pp. 12–41.

8. John F. Stover, *American Railroads* (Chicago: University of Chicago Press, 1961), p. 145.

9. Francis E. Merrill, *Society and Culture* (Englewood Cliffs: Prentice-Hall, 1969), p. 310.

10. Wilbur Schramm, "Communication Development and the Development Process," in Pye, p. 34.

11. *Recent Social Trends in the United States*, vol. 1 (New York: McGraw-Hill Book Company, 1933), pp. xxvi–xxvii. This study included changes in transportation as part of the overall alteration in communications networks.

12. Henry Steele Commager, *The American Mind* (New Haven: Yale University Press, 1950), p. 408.

13. *Recent Social Trends*, p. 167.

14. Anselm Strauss, *The American City: A Sourcebook of Urban Imagery* (Chicago: Aldine Publishing Company, 1968), p. 125.

15. Quoted in Strauss, p. 127.

16. For a detailed discussion of the problem of the conflict between the development of technology and the agrarian myth see Marx, *Machine in the Garden*.

17. The concept of "accommodation" has usually been defined within the context of personal conflict and adaptation. However, it can also be seen as a means of coping with social change. For a good description of how societies do adapt to such changes see Robin M. Williams, Jr., *American Society* (New York: Alfred A. Knopf, 1970), chapter 14 — "The Integration of American Society."

I

The Recreation Revolution

The New "Mass" Media

Starting with the first large-circulation daily newspapers in the 1830s, followed by the motion picture in 1896, and radio and then television in the twentieth century, the mass media have had a profound influence on American life, and created a vast new audience eager to consume whatever content they had to offer. The nature and characteristics of these new media and their emerging audiences created a form of social interaction which was entirely new.[1]

These new media were directed primarily toward large audiences which were essentially heterogeneous in composition. Members of the audience had to share a common interest in the content of the media and a common set of cultural understandings and values. Communication now took place over great distances, and the relationship between the audience and the communicator was relatively impersonal, as the flow of communication was basically in one direction, from the source to the audience. (The establishment of a two-way interaction, or "feedback," was one of the major aims of groups interested in social control of the media, while its absence proved to be an important barrier to total acceptance.) Finally, as Denis McQuail notes, "the audience for these new media was a collectivity unique to modern society." It was basically an aggregate of individuals "united by a common focus of interest, engaging in an identical form of behaviour, and open to activation towards common ends; yet the individuals involved are unknown to each other, have only a restricted amount of interaction, do not orient their actions to each other and are only loosely organized or lacking in organization."[2]

These characteristics and their implications created social conditions which were so totally new that their existence brought about fundamental changes in the structure and interaction within American society. The

11

new communications media gave rise to totally new complexes of activity concerned with the manipulation of symbols and personalities, and in the process the mass media inevitably acquired their own status and authority, and were placed in the position of being able to confer prestige and legitimacy on those issues or personalities to which they turned their attention.

Almost from the first, the mass media were dominated by the idea of providing entertainment for their large audiences. (This presumes that news has an intrinsic entertainment value.) This emphasis can be attributed to a combination of circumstances. First, the media needed to secure relatively large audiences to provide a strong economic base, and this could only be obtained by providing what a significant segment of the population seemed to want. Second, the rapid transformation of social and cultural conditions, especially urbanization, had created large potential audiences who were searching for inexpensive entertainment as a form of recreational activity. Third, the communications media proved to be ideally suited for carrying entertainment previously available only in the larger centers into the smaller cities and towns. Fourth, in the case of the motion picture and television, both of these innovations were originally conceived and introduced as an extension of an extant entertainment industry.[3] Finally, although some forms of the mass media were widely used for purposes other than public entertainment, such as military use of radio, or government use of motion pictures, such utilitarian uses failed to catch the public's imagination in quite the same manner as did their more "glamourous" entertainment content. It was mainly in this entertainment role that the mass media were able to permeate all segments of society, and to become an important source for establishing trends in such areas as leisure, personal consumption and even courting behavior.

A major aspect of the introduction of the mass media, and one that was particularly important to the future of the motion picture industry, was their ability to bypass the existing channels of social communication and authority structures in the spheres of politics, religion, education, kinship and economics, and to establish direct contact with the individual.[4] Particularly in the areas of education and religion, parents and teachers became concerned because they felt powerless to prevent the influence of these new communications forms, which seemed to be so readily accessible to the young. Thus many of the mass media's inroads into existing institutions were initially resisted, but eventually there was a gradual move toward greater accommodation, and finally each of the affected institutions came to use these media for its own purposes.

The motion picture exemplifies this pattern of "accommodation by adoption," for once it was established as a commercial success and more than just a passing fad, political, educational and religious institutions quickly adopted it while offering a great deal of praise for its potential in their particular spheres of interest. The paradox, therefore, was that the motion picture was accepted, utilized and praised on the institutional level, while at the same time the commercial-entertainment film was viewed with a great deal of suspicion.

The awareness of the potential of these new media to reach vast audiences across great distances with a sense of immediate impact was a cause of genuine concern, for there were no established mechanisms of cultural or social control. This resulted in a strong movement toward greater political or formal control.

The fears surrounding the lack of controls were especially relevant in the development of the commercial film industry, because the motion picture quickly demonstrated an amazing ability to attract large audiences once it became generally available in its projected form. The public's strange fascination with the "moving image" has been well chronicled, and the commercial "movies" were the end product of centuries of innovative activity.[5] Nevertheless, the tremendous attraction which the unknown medium held for its early audiences was viewed with trepidation in many quarters. Two other factors contributed to these fears. First, the initial industry structure was so decentralized and fragmented that early attempts to centralize control were ineffective. Also, the actual production of the films was remote from the exhibition sites and thus the focus of critical attention was for a long time directed to the local exhibitor, who, in fact, had very little control over the product he had contracted to exhibit. As wider and more effective controls were forced on the industry the more centralized its structure would become. Eventually, for a period of over thirty-five years the control of the entire industry would essentially be under one authority and in the hands of only a few men.

Second, there was a strong fear associated with the introduction of the mass media which indicated a concern for the possible detrimental influences they would have in lowering the overall standards of culture set by the intellectual elite. The controversy surrounding high culture and low culture and the suspected role of the mass media in the dilution of cultural standards has a long and incomplete history.[6] In a society pervaded by mass communications there is a strong tendency toward a semblance of uniformity, because the population generally receives the majority of its messages from a relatively small number of authoritative sources. Denis McQuail has pointed out that this uniformity differs from the cultural consensus previously obtained from the traditional internalized values and attitudes, because it depends on a sustained flow of information and is therefore in some sense unstable. It is, however, precisely this unstable quality which allows modern societies to undergo the rapid social and economic changes required of them. In this manner the media of mass communications can in fact have a positive integrative role in a period of differentiation and fragmentation of relationships.[7]

13

The motion picture played just such an integrative role in helping to shape many of the ideas, concepts and values of its audience, and when scientific studies were undertaken in later years to determine the nature and degree of such influence, the results tended to indicate the film medium's inherent ability to suggest, disseminate and sometimes to establish acceptable norms in certain areas of social behavior. This was especially true of such areas as fashion, courtship, and even attitudes toward foreign nations.

The question remains to be answered as to how these various new media forms were adopted and integrated into American society, and why some of them experienced so much difficulty in the process. We have already noted the "acceptance by use" concept utilized by institutions, but total social and cultural acceptance required a greater measure of accommodation by both the medium and its audience. Thus as each of the mass media spread throughout the country, certain definite adjustments had to be made to ensure that these technological innovations and their content would conform, as far as possible, to the existing local system of values and social norms. These adjustments were not easy, for the wide dissemination of a single set of values by the mass media could not possibly satisfy all segments of a highly pluralistic society, and localized values thus came into conflict with the national content of the media.

Particularly in the case of motion pictures and later radio, the problems raised by the economic requirement to provide a large and therefore national audience base were almost insurmountable. As Wilbur Schramm has suggested, the wide dissemination of such content raised questions, "which were never very important in the relatively restricted arts of theater, circus, and vaudeville, or the relatively indigenous folk art."[8] The introduction of television has, of course, extended the boundaries of this problem beyond all hope of settlement.[9]

The question of centralization and size became important, for within a very few years of their introduction motion pictures, radio and television, and to a lesser extent newspapers, grew to become large business organizations as well as great agencies of communications. How could these centralized institutions continue to be representative of, and sensitive to, local interests and values, especially as the intense competition of the marketplace quickly reduced their numbers? This question was partly answered by the Commission on Freedom of the Press in 1947, when the commissioners noted: "If modern society requires great agencies of mass communication, if these concentrations become so powerful that they are a threat to democracy, if democracy cannot solve the problem simply by breaking them up — then those agencies must control themselves or be controlled by government."[10] It is a fact, nevertheless, that, except for certain specific actions taken by the Federal Communications Commission with regard to radio and television, the major mass media have never been made accountable for "representativeness" toward their audiences. The motion picture in particular was, and is, continually criticized for its inability or unwillingness to serve large minority segments of its audience by catering to a wider variety of tastes and values.

Recreation and Entertainment at the Turn of the Century

A major aspect of the immense social and cultural changes taking place in America in the period after the Civil War was a growing interest and participation in many new forms of recreation and entertainment. Eventually these new mass recreational forms would alter the pattern of American social and cultural life away from an emphasis on local interests and activities to a more national outlook. Traditional forms of recreation had taken place mainly at the local level, with individual groups participating in similar, but disassociated and decentralized, activities. While many of these groups maintained contact with similar organizations in other communities (baseball teams from different localities played against each other, or touring theatrical troupes gave local performances), still the basis of support and interest in recreational activity was largely on the local community or city level.

While each of the mass media played a significant role as both an impetus to, and a component of, the increase in recreational opportunities, the major contribution of the print media during the nineteenth century must be emphasized. In the period after the Civil War new journalistic practices and concepts emerged which abruptly altered the pattern of media usage. Helped by the rapid mechanization of the printing industry, and the favorable postal regulations under the 1879 act, some new publishers indicated their willingness to risk their capital in a bid to capture a mass readership. Cyrus H. Curtis started the *Ladies' Home Journal* in 1883, and with Edward W. Bok as his editor he soon achieved a half million circulation. Curtis also purchased and revitalized the *Saturday Evening Post* in 1879 and proceeded to make its circulation close to two million. These two publications, together with *Collier's,* founded in 1888, dominated the low-cost weekly field. The older high-quality monthlies, such as *Harper's,* the *Century,* and *Scribner's,* found it difficult to compete with the cheap illustrated monthlies, such as *McClure's Magazine* (1893), *Cosmopolitan Magazine* (1886), and *Munsey's Magazine* (1889), which sold for ten to fifteen cents.[11] Edwin Emery, the historian of American journalism, has noted that "it was these magazines circulating more extensively than any of their predecessors, which were to open the minds of more readers to social and cultural trends."[12]

It was during the period 1880–1890 that the first true mass urban newspapers appeared on the streets of America's cities and towns. Although the cheap daily newspaper had first appeared in the 1830s it was limited in terms of its printing technology, distribution, and especially the geographic extent of its news gathering. Improvements in technology such as high-speed presses and Linotype, the introduction of the telegraph and telephone, and the development of news-gathering agencies with far-flung offices all contributed to making the newspaper more attractive to a larger number of readers. Improvements in transportation also increased the distribution range of individual newspapers, while the news agencies telegraphed their stories from all over the nation, and even the world, into all corners of the country, from the large metropolitan areas to the smaller cities and towns. Thus with the aid of these new wire services the daily newspaper assumed the important role as the centralized supplier of national and world news to the local community.[13]

The growth of the large mass newspaper was dependent upon more than just the innovations indicated above, for without a significant increase in the potential circulation base publishers would not have been willing to risk further capital expenditures. The rapid influx of immigrants and rural Americans into the expanding urban areas had provided the necessary population base, but this alone did not account for the tremendous increase in newspaper readership during the period 1870–1910. There were other less tangible reasons for this growth, ascribed to the air of excitement generated by the important transformations then taking place in America. "The daily newspaper was the chronicler of the national scene and interpreter of the new environment," suggests Emery, and "the city reader ... was the eager customer of the publisher who met successfully the new challenge to journalism."[14] The increase in newspapers and newspaper readership can be seen in the following table:

TABLE 2

GROWTH OF NEWSPAPERS AND POPULAR
PERIODICALS, 1870–1930[a]

	1870	1900	1914–15	1930–31
POPULATION (MILLIONS)[b]	39,905	76,094	100,549	124,149
DAILY NEWSPAPERS (ENGLISH)	489	1,967	2,358	2,109
DAILY NEWSPAPERS (FOREIGN)	85	148	156	159
NEWSPAPER CIRCULATION (MILLIONS)	2,602	15,102	28,777	39,589
PERIODICALS (MONTHLIES)	n.a.	2,328	n.a.	3,804

[a] *Source:* Edwin Emery, *The Press in America* (Englewood Cliffs: Prentice-Hall, 1962), p. 345.
[b] *Source: Historical Statistics,* p. 7.

However, these figures do not indicate the large circulations that individual newspapers and periodicals had achieved. In New York, the *World* in 1892 had a daily circulation of 375,000, while in the same year the *Ladies' Home Journal* had a monthly circulation of 700,000.[15]

The circulation of daily newspapers increased 400 percent between 1870 and 1900, while the population grew by only 95 percent. This discrepancy between population growth and circulation can be accounted for in part by the decrease in illiteracy, which fell in this same period from 20 to 10.7 percent, and by a general raising of educational standards. The percentage of children attending public schools in the United States rose from 57 to 72 percent between 1870 and 1900. Further, the number of high schools grew from only 100 in 1860 to 800 by 1880, and then increased dramatically to 6,000 in 1900.[16]

There were still other factors which contributed to the increasing importance of reading and the growth of large publications. The publishers of the urban dailies quickly became aware of the type of reading matter which would appeal to the new urban populace, and these new periodicals were deliberately created to be low-priced, aggressive, easily read and sensationalist, a formula which greatly enhanced their popularity. The growing desire for reading matter was further satisfied by publications aimed specifically at women and children, while specialty technical journals aimed at professionals and amateurs alike found their way onto the newsstand.

However, the single most important factor favoring the growth of all recreational activity was the increase in available leisure time. The decline in the workweek of American workers meant more time for reading and other forms of self-improvement, which in turn led to greater efficiency and productivity and more available leisure hours. Thus in nonagricultural industries the workweek declined by about ten hours between 1850 and 1900 — from sixty-six to fifty-six hours. In the next four decades reductions were even sharper than in the previous half century. Between 1900 and 1940 the workweek in nonagricultural industries declined from fifty-six hours to forty-one hours, with the sharpest declines occurring between 1900 and 1920, when the average workweek in nonagricultural industries dropped about five hours every ten years.[17] An examination of the decrease in the workweek of certain types of workers between 1890 and 1928 indicated the amount of extra leisure time available.

The increase in available leisure time would encourage the creation and use of all recreational forms, especially commercial amusements such as the motion picture, which required a more definite and specific commitment of free time, unlike books, newspapers or periodicals, which could be read in the home with greater ease.

17

TABLE 3
AVERAGE HOURS OF LABOR PER WEEK
IN ELEVEN INDUSTRIES, 1890–1928

	AVERAGE HOURS PER WEEK		PERCENT DECREASE DURING PERIOD
	1890	*1928*	
Bakeries	64.7	47.4	26.7
Boot and shoe	59.5	49.1	17.5
Building	52.0	43.5	16.3
Cotton goods	62.8	53.4	14.9
Foundry and machine shops	59.8	50.4	15.7
Blast furnaces	84.6	59.8	29.3
Marble and stone	54.7	44.0	19.6
Millwork	52.0	44.8	13.8
Book and job printing	56.4	44.3	21.5
Newspaper printing	48.2	45.1	6.5
Woolen goods	58.9	49.3	16.3

Source: Recent Social Trends, p. 829.

The Development of Recreational Activity

The combination of more available leisure time, the decrease in illiteracy and the growth of the mass circulation press resulted in a wider dissemination of interest in sports and recreational activities on a national level. Professional baseball was the first of these new nationwide interests to take hold, and by 1871 a professional league encompassing teams from major cities and towns was already in existence.[18] While baseball would remain the major spectator sport it was by no means the only one to capture the public's imagination. Prizefighting reached its "golden age" with the new media's attention being focused on men such as John L. Sullivan and "Gentleman" Jim Corbett, while thoroughbred horse racing enjoyed great prosperity. College football was also just coming into its own as a spectator sport. This rise in interest in sports and the continued growth of commercial amusements contributed to a breaking down of the gospel of hard work as man's sole ethic, and this credo was tempered by an increased understanding of the need for recreational activity, a philosophy that was reflected in the newspapers and magazines of the time. In the summer of 1886 the *New York Tribune* devoted approximately five hundred columns to sports, compared to minimal coverage before 1870, while in 1896 William Randolph Hearst began an important innovation in the *New York Journal* with a page entitled "In the World of Professional and Amateur Sports."[19]

The arrival and growing influence of the mass media caused American recreational interest to divide into two distinct layers of participation. On the bottom was the continued local participation in all forms of recreational opportunities, including sports, excursions and even urban commercial amusements such as penny arcades, burlesque, ethnic theater and the male specialties of the saloon and billiard parlor. All of these were organized within the control of the local community, and as such were subject to local tastes and preferences.

The top layer in this schema consisted of the vast, vicarious participation in national sports, news, and recreational interests, fostered particularly by the support given to them by the mass media, and consisting of an audience of millions stretching over a wide area. The sources for these activities were more centralized, and therefore beyond the control of any one local group, other than by outright suppression. Many of the motion picture's particular problems can be attributed to the fact that it depended upon both local and national support. The movies were in effect a national medium which was in turn susceptible to local pressures and preferences. It was for this reason that local control of the motion picture became a key issue.

The growth of the mass spectator sports has already been mentioned, but other more personal recreational activities were also becoming more popular, and tennis, archery, canoeing and even croquet became very much in vogue among those who could afford to participate. Roller-skating, which had been introduced in 1863 as an amusement for the "educated and refined class," soon surrendered to democracy and rinks were built in every town and city.[20] It remained for bicycling to become the most spectacular craze of all, and by 1887 there were some one hundred thousand confirmed cyclists in the country.[21] As popular as cycling was, it was still available only to those who could afford the price of $100 to $125 for a machine, which obviously excluded a very large proportion of the American public.[22]

While recreation in all forms took a firm hold in America in the 1890s, nevertheless, the old American ethic which praised the virtues and rewards of "hard work" and which was taught so assiduously in the famous *McGuffey Readers* was still very much in evidence, and the increased leisure time made available by the shorter workweek was seen by some as a frivolous waste of human resources. It was especially in the city that this traditional view would meet its strongest opposition, while in the rural sectors the old prejudices against amusement would continue to hold fast for some time to come.[23] City children found outlets for their pent-up energies in the various activities created specifically for them by well-meaning social organizations conscious of their needs. The Boy Scouts, the Girl Scouts and the Camp Fire Girls were all created to supply city children with some knowledge and understanding of the outdoors. Toward

19

the end of the century urban needs led to large-scale planning of public parks, reaching a peak in the 1890s and resulting in such achievements as Chicago's beautiful Lincoln Park along the lake front and the metropolitan park systems of Boston, Cleveland and other cities.[24] Old favorites such as the circus, the theater, burlesque, vaudeville and the melodrama continued to thrive in the growing urban environment.

These entertainment forms sometimes had a social significance which was not immediately apparent, but which went deep into the social fabric of the new emerging urban culture. Albert F. McLean, in a provocative study, *American Vaudeville as Ritual*, examined this entertainment form and suggested that vaudeville was, "for at least four decades, not only a significant social institution but also a mythic enactment, through ritual of the underlying aspirations of the American people."[25] Much of what McLean claims for vaudeville could also be said for the movies, with the added factor that movies had a much larger audience, appealed to a wider range of immigrant groups, and were especially welcomed by those in the lower social-economic segment. In the final analysis the two entertainments were essentially different, in that vaudeville was a highly stylized, artificial and ritualistic form, with recognized and repetitive actions which were expected by the audience, while the film medium relied more on elements of surprise and visual effects in an attempt to be as realistic as possible.

What was certain is that the demand for urban recreational activities seemed insatiable, and sharp-witted entrepreneurs were not slow to exploit this need by supplying myriad entertainment forms, such as the dime museum, dance halls (which, while extremely popular, were also a great source of consternation to many city authorities), shooting galleries, beer gardens, bowling alleys, billiard parlors, saloons, and other more questionable social activities. F. R. Dulles indicated that even the electric trolley, when first introduced, provided a Sunday or holiday substitute for many of these amusements, and yet another means of occupying the increased leisure time. The trolley ride proved to be an outstanding feature of weekend recreation and the new rapid-transit companies even advertised special trolley carnivals in the evening, complete with multicolored lights and popular band music.[26] However, while entertainment in the city was available in these varied forms, there were still many segments of the population which were unable to partake of any amusements on a regular basis because of economic considerations, long working hours, or problems with the English language. It was from this group that many of the initial adherents to the motion picture would come, for the movies could satisfy all of these problems in one way or another — they were cheap, easily accessible and required very little proficiency in the English language.

NOTES TO CHAPTER I

1. Much of the theory on the nature and functions of the mass media in this study is based upon the outline proposed by Denis McQuail in *Towards a Sociology of Mass Communication* (London: Collier-Macmillan, 1969). McQuail's theories have been modified to reflect the historical dimension with which this study is concerned. For a summary of the characteristics of the mass media see pp. 11–17.

2. McQuail, pp. 9–10.

3. The introduction of the telephone also corroborates this contention. When first made available the new invention was foreseen to have a great future as an entertainment medium. Alexander Graham Bell always included music as well as voice in his demonstrations. The perfection of the radio, of course, destroyed this aspect of telephonic communication. For a fuller description of the use of the telephone as an entertainment medium see Erik Barnouw, *A Tower In Babel* (New York: Oxford University Press, 1966), pp. 7–9.

4. McQuail, p. 12.

5. The best treatments of the "prehistory" of the medium are Martin Quigley, Jr., *Magic Shadows: The Story of the Origin of Motion Pictures* (Washington, D.C.: Georgetown University Press, 1948); and C. W. Ceram, *Archaeology of the Cinema* (New York: Harcourt, Brace and World, 1965).

6. While there are no answers to this argument, there is a great deal of interesting material on both sides. The best examinations of the whole concept of "mass culture" are found in Raymond Williams, *The Long Revolution* (New York: Harper and Row, 1965); Bernard Rosenberg and David Manning White, eds., *Mass Culture* (Glencoe: Free Press, 1957), and *Mass Culture Revisited* (New York: Van Nostrand Reinhold Company, 1971); while the results of a symposium on the subject containing many important viewpoints are in Norman Jacobs, ed., *Culture for the Millions?* (Boston: Beacon Press, 1961).

7. McQuail, p. 13.

8. Wilbur Schramm, *Responsibility in Mass Communication* (New York: Harper and Brothers, 1957), p. 4.

9. The difficulties encountered in trying to evolve programming that will appeal to the largest number of people, while also taking into account their demographic variations, are found in a recent book, Les Brown, *Television: The Business Behind the Box* (New York: Harcourt Brace Jovanovich, 1971).

10. The Commission on Freedom of the Press, *A Free and Responsible Press* (Chicago: University of Chicago Press, 1947), p. 5.

11. Edwin Emery, *The Press in America* (Englewood Cliffs: Prentice-Hall, 1962), pp. 351 ff.; and Frank Luther Mott, *American Journalism* (New York: Macmillan Company, 1962), pp. 590–591.

12. Emery, p. 352.

13. This interpretation owes much to the theories formulated in Melvin De Fleur, *Theories of Mass Communication* (New York: David McKay Company, 1970), chapter 11.

14. Emery, p. 346.

15. Mott, p. 507.

16. Emery, p. 346.

17. This summary is taken from Joseph S. Zeisel, "The Workweek in American Industry, 1850–1956," in Eric Larrabee and Rolf Meyersohn, eds., *Mass Leisure* (Glencoe: Free Press, 1958), pp. 145–153.

18. Foster Rhea Dulles, *A History of Recreation: America Learns to Play* (New York: Appleton-Century-Crofts, 1965), p. 193.

19. *Ibid.*, p. 201.

20. *Ibid.*, p. 193.

21. *Ibid.*, p. 194. See also Gary Allan Tobin, "The Bicycle Boom of the 1890's," in *Journal of Popular Culture*, vol. 7, no. 4 (1974), pp. 838–849.

22. Dulles, p. 196.

23. Dale A. Somers, "The Leisure Revolution: Recreation in the American City, 1820–1920," in *Journal of Popular Culture*, vol. 5, no. 1 (1971), pp. 125–143. This article indicates the degree and direction of the opposition to new recreational forms.

24. Harvey Wish, *Society and Thought in Modern America* (New York: David McKay Company, 1962), p. 281.

25. Albert F. McLean, *American Vaudeville as Ritual* (Lexington: University of Kentucky Press, 1965), p. 2.

26. Dulles, pp. 221–222.

II

Enter the Movies!

IN THE 1890s IT WAS OBVIOUS that America was in the throes of a dramatic social transformation, and nowhere was this more evident than in the busy streets of the growing cities. Millions of new city dwellers had congregated in these urban locations in order to live, work and play, and the cities were straining to provide the housing, jobs and recreational opportunities necessary to fulfill their ever-growing needs. In all, these new "urbanites" adjusted very quickly to living in the much more restricted space of the city, and they were helped by concurrent developments in technology, politics and social welfare. New forms of communication such as the telephone and telegraph improved intracity information channeling, while innovations in mass transit relieved congestion in city streets.[1] Political reforms and new methods of scientific city management had made city governments more responsive and efficient. The churches, and later the newly emerged professional social workers, attempted to reorder the spiritual and social life of the city, and while their interest was mainly concentrated on the immigrants and others of the working class, eventually their efforts would improve the lives of most city residents.

One of the more severe adjustments required of the new city dweller was the change in the nature of the recreational or leisure activities available to him. The social and physical conditions of the city altered the traditional sense of community and created a new set of relationships, which "rendered the simpler, unorganized, and often spontaneous diversions of rural America unsatisfactory or inaccessible."[2] Most of the new urban-based recreational forms discussed in the first chapter were introduced largely in response to the vacuum created by the absence of these traditional leisure-time pursuits. And of all the commercial amusements spawned by the particular needs of the city, none would become as powerful, or have such far-reaching appeal, or cause as much controversy as would the motion picture.

The Search for Pictorial Realism

The development of the motion picture camera and projector was the end product of an extraordinarily large and complex cultural inventory, incorporating the wishes, ideas and practical inventions of a society which had long sought the means with which to capture the living and moving image for the purposes of visual entertainment. Martin Quigley, Jr. claimed that a direct line can be traced from the "magic lantern" of Athanasius Kircher, first exhibited in 1644, to the modern motion picture apparatus.[3] However, other motion picture historians are more skeptical about the motion picture's lineage, and the prehistory of the medium is the subject of much controversy.[4] Cinema historian Raymond Fielding has noted that "we begin conceding that we know more about the Greco-Roman civilizations of antiquity than we do about the first fifteen years of the motion picture."[5] It is nevertheless well established that mankind had long derived much pleasure from various forms of visual entertainment and stimulation. The important question is, what set of conditions — social, cultural or economic — encouraged and facilitated the development and perfection of the motion picture apparatus at this specific point in American history?

Nicholas Vardac, in his important book *From Stage to Screen,* suggested that in the nineteenth century there were three periods of technological development discernible in the evolution of the motion picture projector.[6] The first period (1824–1832) resulted in the production of crude and animated pictures; the second (1853–1861), making use of the new development of still photography, allowed the production of animated photographs; while the third (1864–1895) finally saw the perfection of a series of machines which continuously projected objects photographed in motion, or true motion pictures.[7]

The development of the motion picture apparatus is an excellent example of how the desires and needs of a society can both encourage an innovation and facilitate its acceptance.[8] Vardac's thesis leads him to conclude that the increasing desire to create greater pictorial realism in the live theater acted as an impetus to the perfection of a projected mechanism. This spirit of reality, beginning with the new stage realism of David Garrick in England, was pervasive all through the nineteenth century, and the motion picture can be considered the ultimate aesthetic expression of realistic-pictorial theatrical production.[9]

John L. Fell has also noted this continuity between the melodrama and the early motion picture, but he goes even further in suggesting that not only Victorian theater but "its contemporary photography, graphics, prose, even the comic strip" all shared a common impulse toward the solution of similar narrative problems — how to render pictorially time and space.[10] Fell indicated not only that the motion picture was the "logical extension of the theater's inclination to place real objects on the stage," but that movie houses were deliberately modeled after legitimate theaters, when in fact there was no real need for such elaborate architecture.[11]

In America, stage realism reached its zenith in the form of the melodrama, especially in the New York productions of David Belasco in the late 1890s.[12] However, as the century wore on, the realistic limitations of the melodrama became more and more obvious, for the basic staging methods then in use had not changed much from those in use during the seventeenth century.

Dialogue in many melodramas of this later period was of secondary importance, and, as in the silent film, pictorial action, pantomime and "business" dominated. Rahill observed that while "dialogue was an ingredient of the mixture . . . the talk was accessory to the central business of hubbub and spectacle."[13] Actors too were unwittingly being trained for the silent motion picture, and this subsequently enabled many of them to make the transition to films when melodrama lost its popularity. Rahill has also indicated that the triumph of the movies had a much more disastrous effect on the popular theater than on melodrama, for "what melodrama did when the crisis came was simply to drift over into the ranks of the enemy, taking along its gaudy accoutrements, its raffish sideshow manners, and its bag of tricks . . . which were no small windfall for a new and ill-regarded art [the movies] that had to scrounge for its raw material."[14] The melodrama techniques of acting and directing, not to mention the stories and themes, were of immense value to the new medium, which had not yet acquired a style or voice of its own.

The melodrama had also received a stunning blow from an unexpected source with the introduction of electricity into theaters. (A rather ironic development, and certainly not one that Edison had planned.) The new lighting source drew attention to the obvious frauds of conventional scenic practice, and the two-dimensional settings, deprived of the soft lights and mysterious shadows of gas-lighting, lost all semblance of reality in the garish glow of the incandescent bulb. No wonder that much later, D. W. Griffith's successful experiments with realistic lighting effects for the screen met with so much approval.[15]

The promise of the motion picture as a visual entertainment superior to the live theater was quickly noticed by those intimately concerned with the theater arts. Reviewing the spectacular melodrama *Ben Hur* in the *New York Herald* of December 3, 1899, Hilary Bell made a prophetic observation: "In the play we see merely several horses galloping on a moving platform. They make no headway, and the moving scenery behind them does not delude the spectators into the belief that they are racing. . . . The only way to secure the exact scene of action for this incident in a theater *is to represent it by Mr. Edison's invention."*[16] (*Ben Hur* has of course had three very successful film productions in the last fifty years.)

The introduction of the motion picture with its ability to provide greater pictorial realism freed the live theater to return to more traditional pursuits. W. P. Eaton, the New York drama critic, recognized this possibility in 1914 when he stated: "Because the camera can be carried so far afield . . . the pasteboard stage of the theater can never hope to depict with a thousandth part of the camera's realism, [and] it is more likely that the old fashioned spectacular play will fall more and more into disrepute. . . ."[17]

The desire to capture reality on the stage was without doubt a potent and precipitating force in the eventual emergence of the cinema apparatus. The more elaborate the stage spectacle, with its trains, its holdups, explosions, gunfights, Indian chiefs, galloping chariots and real live bears, sheep and cows, the more successful the production seemed to be, and the more excited the audience became. However, this type of theater sowed the seeds of its own demise, and proved to be a glorious but futile parting gesture. It was therefore no coincidence that the motion picture finally emerged at the precise time when stage productions were no longer capable of satisfying this aspect of the audience's desires. Only the movies with their greater reproduction of reality and improved visual sensation could successfully continue the trend.

The Origins of an Industry

The crucial developments in the perfection of the motion picture apparatus in the United States were those associated with Thomas Edison, although Gordon Hendricks's important research has conclusively indicated that Edison's personal contribution to the invention of the apparatus was minimal.[18] In 1887 a young Scotsman named W. K. L. Dickson joined the Edison Laboratories in West Orange, New Jersey, bringing with him a strong interest in photography. With the excellent facilities of the laboratory at his disposal, by the end of 1892 Dickson had perfected both a camera and a projecting apparatus known as the Kinetoscope.[19] Although the Kinetoscope became commercially very successful as a basic form of viewing mechanism in the penny arcades, it was still confined to a special boxlike viewing apparatus, and only one viewer at a time was able to see the moving picture. In 1895, Thomas Armat projected an Edison Kineto-scope film upon a screen with his machine, the Vitascope, which he had developed together with Francis C. Jenkins in Washington, D.C.[20] Edison, having persuaded Armat to join him, in 1895 exhibited an improved form of the Vitascope which incorporated some of the mechanics of his own Kinetoscope. It was this Vitascope-Kinetoscope, with its many subsequent modifications, which finally achieved the long-awaited dream of the pro-jection of photographic images that appeared to move — the first true moving pictures.

The first Edison Kinetoscope peep-show machines were exhibited on April 14, 1894, at 1155 Broadway, New York, by the Holland brothers. These ten machines had been purchased from Edison for a total of $2,500 while the films were an extra $10 each.[21] (By 1895 this basic unit price had been reduced to $127.50, while secondhand machines were available for $100 to $150.)[22] The Broadway show was an immediate sensation, and long lines of patrons stood waiting to look into the peephole machines to see the pictures that lived and moved. The cost of entrance was surpris-ingly high — twenty-five cents — but this entitled the viewer to view one row of five machines.[23] Later, special coin boxes were devised which al-lowed individuals to select their own choices for five cents, and this became the standard practice.

As he had previously done with the phonograph, Edison made the Kinetoscope available through local agencies, to whom he sold the machines. Through this successful merchandising technique the Kineto-scope was soon spread across the country, and had even found its way into Mexico by January, 1895.[24] Almost all the subjects featured on these early short films were performances by vaudeville artists, while boxing also became very popular. The success of these nickel-parlors indicated the commercial potential of moving pictures, and acted as an incentive to enterprising inventors and businessmen to devise a machine that would project the moving pictures on a screen where they could be viewed by a larger number of people at one time.

Spurred on by this promise of large financial rewards, the search for a suitable projection mechanism continued. Eventually, through the com-bined efforts of many individual inventors and the marketing expertise of the Edison Laboratories, a suitable projection mechanism was perfected.[25] By the spring of 1896, projected motion pictures were being presented publicly in New York, Paris and London. The tremendous speed with which the transition was made from peep show to projected motion pic-ture exhibition was a direct result of the combination of entrepreneurship and invention which Edison represented, and it was undoubtedly the magic and past triumphs of the Edison name which inspired the confidence of the large number of investors anxious to obtain projection equipment.[26] Thus, while Edison's claim to have "invented" the motion picture apparatus is no longer valid, without the use of his name its distribution would undoubtedly have been delayed, and its reception by a skeptical public would have been slowed.

The first important public exhibition of the projected motion picture by a machine billed as "Thomas A. Edison's Latest Marvel — THE VITASCOPE," took place on April 23, 1896, at Koster and Bial's Music Hall, Herald Square, New York City.[27] Following this introduction the motion picture was featured by the Keith Theater Circuit as one of their major attractions, a move which was of tremendous importance in popularizing the commercial potential of the medium throughout the country, and an unofficial signal for other theater managers to include motion pictures in their own vaudeville programs.

The diffusion of the projected motion picture throughout the United States in the years before 1905 was accomplished mainly through well-established distribution channels. Vaudeville had added movies as merely another act on the bill, theatrical booking agents and amusement parlor owners acquired distribution rights, and traveling road showmen added the new invention to their current stock of magic lanterns. The importance of this fact is that, initially, the invention was made widely available without creating heavy additional costs in capital investment or new construction, the major investment being the cost of the projection equipment and films.

Another important marketing development was Edison's decision to make his projector available for outright sale through his various agents. While the cost of the individual machines was approximately $250, the "state's rights" for the Vitascope were sold for prices ranging from $1,500 for lesser territories to $5,000 for the state of New York.[28] The owners of state's rights to distribute Edison's invention in turn either sold or leased the machines to individual exhibitors. However, Edison's machine was not the only projector on the market, and within a period of months after its introduction several competing models were being sold or leased. The death of the Vitascope market was finally assured when Edison himself brought out the Projecting Kinetoscope, and merchandised it "as a mere piece of machinery, available to any purchaser, regardless of territory or intended use."[29]

The steady stream of new entries into the moving picture business continued undeterred by threats of lawsuits from Edison, who insisted that all inventors and manufacturers of projection equipment were operating in violation of his patents. However, the film industry had entered its first boom stage and the vision of quick profits offset the dangers of possible litigation and, besides, the demand for machinery far exceeded the supply.

The result was chaos, with numerous small manufacturers trying to compete with larger, more financially secure organizations. Terry Ramsaye has noted of this early period that "trouble and the motion picture business became synonymous. There was safety and assurance nowhere for anyone engaged in the affairs of the screen — but there was always ahead the vision of vast profits."[30]

Regardless of the chaotic situation surrounding the manufacturing and distributing aspects, by 1898 the motion picture had become established as a staple item in vaudeville shows, although there was a low period when films were used as "chasers" to force patrons to leave the theaters to make room for the next audience. The relegation of the medium to this lowly status was primarily due to the rather dull nature of the films then being turned out. These consisted mainly of scenic shots or fake reproductions of current and historical events, and audiences soon grew tired of having to watch the same type of film over and over again.

In 1901, there occurred one of those fateful incidents which historians love so much. On February 21, 1901, all vaudeville performers in New York suddenly went on strike to combat the formation of a vaudeville trust aimed at keeping down wages. The performers organized a union, called the "White Rats" after the London actors' union, and this union had decided upon strike action. The vaudeville managers, faced with the alternatives of closing down or finding a substitute, immediately turned to the motion picture as their principal attraction. The response from the public was clear, and Jacobs observes that, "to the theater managers' great astonishment, people came — and came again."[31]

Robert Grau was particularly enthusiastic about the results of this scablike action of the motion picture. Writing about the "White Rat Strike" he noted:

Some of the play houses closed temporarily, others were enabled to open solely through the help of the camera man. At last, the latter, had come into his own. The day of the "chaser" had passed for all time as far as he was concerned. Showmen all over the country were brought to realize that a new manner of presenting an entire "show" was now possible without any need for worry as to whether the "ghost could walk" on salary day.[32]

If Grau's comments are correct then the motion picture must have had a much stronger hold on the public than its use as a chaser might have led theater managers to believe.[33] The "White Rat Strike" incident clearly indicated the potential for the motion picture as a public entertainment in its own right.

Certainly the exploitation of movies by the vaudeville houses was the lowest point in motion picture history, and almost succeeded in killing off the young medium before it had completely matured and attained its full commercial potential. Luckily, the development of motion pictures did not have to depend on their success in enthralling vaudeville audiences. Their use as chasers was not a true gauge of their inherent popularity, for the bulk of the future audience for the movies did not entirely come from those who frequented this form of entertainment. The "real movie devotees," noted Benjamin Hampton, were "the customers of the arcades, parlors, and dime museums . . . they could not see them often enough, and they wandered from one place to another, searching for films they had not seen before."[34] It was the excitement caused by these eager patrons that motivated exhibitors to buy or rent more projectors and films and to find larger rooms or halls where they could set up in business.[35]

Where or when the first "true" motion picture house came into being is still not certain, nor is it of vital importance.[36] We do know that Harry Davis and John P. Harris of Pittsburgh, who had a history of being the first to launch novelties in that city, "discovered that they had an unused portion on the ground floor of one of their playhouses on the main street, and they constructed there a bijou auditorium with what is believed to have been the forerunner of the 'Nicolet' in that nearly all of the thousands of store theaters that came afterward were apparently modelled after [their] unique idea."[37] They opened their "nickelodeon" the day before Thanksgiving, 1905, with less than two hundred seats in their auditorium, and fortuitously decided to use Edwin S. Porter's *The Great Train Robbery* as their opening show — the first great narrative film, and the box-office and artistic sensation of 1903.[38] The first day they collected $22.50, while the next day the profits jumped to $76. Within two weeks the show was starting at eight o'clock in the morning and running until midnight.

The vacant store, turned theater, was after a few weeks producing for its proprietors a profit of nearly a thousand dollars a week. It was the success of this venture which brought about a drastic alteration of the basic exhibition format, from the back rooms of penny arcades, or just another act on the vaudeville bill, to the development of true picture houses devoted solely to the showing of motion pictures. It was in this form that the industry would literally sweep across the nation, for with a "trivial investment in a projection machine and a few chairs anyone could become a showman and prosper."[39] Davis and Harris had conclusively demonstrated that extensive and costly new construction was not necessary, and that success lay in cheap conversion and a constant supply of new films which held the audience's attention.

Benjamin Hampton has given us a graphic description of how many of these store-front conversions were made:

Parlors and arcades were remodelled at moderate cost into nickelodeons by removing the peep-show cabinets and the partition across the back end of the room, and filling the entire store with kitchen chairs. If the front of the building had been taken out to make a wide-open entrance, the arcade owner now built a new front some distance back from the sidewalk line, thus making a large lobby in which posters could be displayed. The ticket booth was placed at the centre of one side or the back, and when crowds besieged the theaters — as they usually did each evening — patrons could wait in the lobby or the mob could overflow to the sidewalk in the long lines that ever since then have been typical of movie theaters.[40]

It is difficult to estimate the exact number of nickelodeons at any one time, but Ramsaye and Hampton both seem to agree that within a year of the opening of the Harris and Davis theater, a thousand or more were scattered across the country, and within four years there were eight to ten thousand.[41] Robert Grau has pointed out that the success of the Harris and Davis project and others like it was so great "that it awakened the vaudeville managers of the country to the necessity of entering this new field in one way or another, or else be confronted with endless competition...."[42]

It was not only the vaudeville theaters which had reason for concern, for the penny arcades or "peep shows" were also affected by this new development. Marcus Loew was one entrepreneur whose quick perception of the shifting winds eventually made him one of the great movie moguls. Loew was operating penny arcades in Ohio, Kentucky and New York in 1905–1906, when he observed that a newly opened nickelodeon diagonally opposite to one of his New York locations was "attracting large crowds while he began to lose money. Within a month Loew dismantled all of his arcades and transformed them into the new moving picture shows, with auditoriums much superior to those then in existence." Grau comments that Loew's success "was truly remarkable," for he then proceeded to convert a half dozen of New York's unsuccessful playhouses "into gold-laden temples of the silent drama," with the result that by 1914 Loew's empire was the largest in the entire entertainment field.[43]

It was the dramatic, almost overnight growth of the nickelodeon that led to the development of a motion picture industry which consisted of three basic segments — production, distribution and exhibition. With the establishment of a more stable exhibition process, in the form of movie houses, the production companies could now proceed to invest in better and longer films. Similarly, the development of film exchanges had to await the establishment of reliable clients who required regular change of product on a consistent, and therefore commercially feasible, basis. The establishment of a stable exhibition venue also allowed the public the opportunity to develop definite tastes which could now be more accurately gauged than in the past. This in turn meant that film producers could make films which they were reasonably assured would receive favorable reception. As North has indicated, "With the rise of the nickelodeon, the the producer who could merely crank a camera and develop film was no longer adequate. The new motion picture audiences were no longer satisfied with episodic comedy and newsreel films alone; they also wanted long comedy and drama subjects, and in quantity."[44] While the new nickelodeons were springing up all over the country, several companies were busy in New York, New Jersey and Chicago working at top speed to supply films for a seemingly insatiable, entertainment-hungry public. Everyone wondered how long the "picture craze" would last. The expansion which took place during 1907 and 1908 when the motion picture moved out from the large eastern cities into the country was almost without parallel in American business history. Premier locations were soon gone in most large cities and towns, and a new prospective owner had to make up his mind from the outset that he would be facing stiff competition for the customer's nickel or dime.

The economics of operating a nickelodeon were fairly simple, and the weekly operating costs in 1907 were estimated by Joseph Medill Patterson in a *Saturday Evening Post* article to be about $175 to $200 a week, divided as follows:[45]

Wage of manager	$ 25
Wage of operator	$ 20
Wage of doorman	$ 15
Wage of porter or musician	$ 12
Rent of films (two reels changed twice a week)	$ 50
Rent of projecting machine	$ 10
Rent of building	$ 40
Music, printing, "campaign contributions," etc.	$ 18
TOTAL	$190

Patterson continued: "Merely to meet expenses, then the average nickelodeon must have a weekly attendance of 4,000. This gives all the nickelodeons 16,000,000 a week, or over 2,000,000 a day. Two million people a day are needed before profits can begin, and two million are forthcoming. It is a big thing, this new enterprise."[46]

The exhibitor's desire for a quick and constant turnover of customers created a demand for an ever-ready supply of new films. Thus in a very short time the production end of the fledgling industry became the most important segment — a situation that was to endure and become the reason for most of the industry's problems in later years. The demand for a constant supply of fresh material also led to the formation of film exchanges, so that exhibitors were no longer required to purchase films outright but now had access to an almost unlimited supply on a rental basis. By 1907 there were 125 to 150 film exchanges spread through the country.

As the number and competitiveness of the nickelodeons grew, the importance of obtaining the rights to the first run became greater, for the first showing of a picture had the greatest entertainment and commercial value and often commanded ten to twenty times the rental it could command at a later showing. Howard T. Lewis, the economist, has noted that this led to "reckless price cutting, violation of release dates, and many other forms of unfair practice on the part of competing exchanges in order to swell their volume of business."[47]

The confusion surrounding patent rights continued to hinder the smooth expansion of the motion picture industry, for while the Edison Company was still the largest producer of projectors and films, it was unable to meet the great demand for equipment and films now pouring in from all across the country. Edison was prepared to sell projectors, but he would neither sell nor lease cameras in the vain hope that he could continue to control the production and sale of films. Within three years other thinly disguised versions of the Edison camera were widely available, claiming real or purported improvements on the original design to circumvent legal restrictions, and this opened the way for a number of competing film suppliers. Because each of the competing manufacturers of equipment was concerned with selling or providing films to the greatest number of permanent installations possible, it was common practice to insert a clause in the contract of sale requiring that an exhibitor use in conjunction with his machine only those films produced by the seller or lessor. Clearly this provision was unenforceable, especially since the demand for films far exceeded the supply. Fortunately, most of the equipment on the market was technically compatible, and this prevented any independent advantage falling to one manufacturer as cameras, projectors and films were more or less interchangeable.

The next step was inevitable. Given the success of the large trusts in other commercial areas, a giant step toward stabilization of the industry was taken in 1908, when six independent producers of equipment and films licensed under the Edison patents, two French producers, together with George Kleine, a Chicago film importer-distributor, and the Edison Company itself, joined to form the Motion Picture Patents Company. The Eastman Kodak Company, the largest producer of raw film stock, contracted with the Patents Company to sell raw film only to its licensees. Under the terms of the agreement entered into by these interests, all patent rights and claims were surrendered by the several companies and

33

pooled with the newly organized Patents Company. Each individual producer, however, retained the right to make any picture he saw fit and to
distribute it through any channel he chose. Only 116 independent exchanges were issued distribution licenses to handle films produced by the
Patents Company, and they in turn had to agree to sell only to licensed
exhibitors. The exhibitors were required to pay two dollars weekly for a
projection license.[48]

The Motion Picture Patents Company, by its firm grip on the industry
in this early period, was, in fact, a force for stabilization. Unfortunately,
it created an exhibition system tied to films of one reel, or about fifteen
minutes in length, and thus for a normal two-hour show, eight reels were
required. Conant points out that, "for a daily program change, the rental
charge was $100 to $125 a week for theaters in the best locations, graduated
down to $15 for smaller, poorly situated ones."[49]

The move to license exchanges and exhibitors did not fully solve the
control problems, and unlicensed producers and independent exchanges
continued their profitable operations because of the tremendous demand
for films made by the ever-increasing number of exhibitors. The exchanges
were the major violators of the agreement, so it seemed that the only way
to maintain greater control was to secure a consolidation of the exchanges
themselves. In 1910, the General Film Company was organized by the
members of the Patents Company for the purpose of distributing its films.
This move was highly profitable, for the Patents Company succeeded "under threat of revocation of license, in buying fifty-seven of the fifty-eight
exchanges then operating throughout the country."[50] (The minor exchanges were driven out of business.) This was also the first stage in the
process of vertical integration which would eventually lead to a reorganized film industry where production, distribution and exhibition
were all integrated, and in the hands of a few large companies.[51] It was at
this point that control of the "film trust" reached its zenith.

In the meantime, the independents, led by such men as William Fox,
who operated the fifty-eighth exchange, and producer Carl Laemmle,
opened "war" on the Patents Company and its attempt to control the industry.[52] After a long and sometimes bitter struggle the independents
triumphed, and in 1915 the General Film Company was dissolved by the
order of the federal courts. The success of the government's antitrust
action against the film trust served to encourage the entry of new producers, while dissatisfied members left to go their own way. The long
series of litigations, commencing as early as 1897, failed to diminish the
tremendous attraction the medium exerted on the public's imagination,
and in spite of the lack of concern being given to the artistic quality of
the product being turned out, audiences had continued to grow while the
industry was undergoing this spasm of self-destruction.

The First Motion Picture Audiences

The exact composition and characteristics of the first motion picture audiences has always been something of a historical mystery. While the classic histories of the movies all attempt to describe the makeup of the initial devotees of this new entertainment, they are seldom able to go beyond a cursory analysis of the type found in Benjamin Hampton's *A History of the Movies* (1931), where the author simply noted that "a new class of amusement buyer sprang into existence as quickly and apparently as magically as screen pictures themselves appeared."[53] Only Lewis Jacobs in his seminal work, *The Rise of the American Film* (1939), goes into the kind of detail which is useful to film and social historians.[54]

The question remains — who were this audience, and where did they come from? And why were they attracted to this new entertainment form in such vast numbers in such a short period of time? Only now are some of these answers beginning to appear as film and social historians start to piece together the early years of the motion picture industry. It is becoming more and more obvious that the movies were no lucky innovation, arriving merely at a propitious time, but that they answered a deep social and cultural need of the American people.

But what was the nature of this "new" audience that so eagerly embraced this welcomed digression in their lives? Part of the answer can be found in a brief examination of the religious, social and economic conditions of the period. The motion picture's first audience appears to have been made up from three groups: First, those from the middle class who had never previously attended the theater or other amusements because of religious beliefs, and who were now free to explore new entertainments. Benjamin Hampton observed that the motion picture was perfected at a time when "more and more people, mainly the young, broader-minded and more daring than their forebears, crept through the barriers which had been erected by religious prejudice."[55] Once freed from religious strictures this group began to enjoy theatrical presentations of local or professional repertory groups. Among the plays which helped break down the religious objections to this type of entertainment were *Uncle Tom's Cabin* and *Ten Nights in a Bar Room*.[56] As church restrictions were relaxed, informally at first, then later by popular assent, more and more Americans began seeking new diversions, with the major criteria being moral acceptability, accessibility and low cost. It was many of these same people who also welcomed the phonograph, Kinetoscope parlors and arcades, and then later the dime museums, trolley rides and amusement

35

parks. However, most of them turned to the movies as a principal source of entertainment, slowly at first and then with an increasing fervor which caught the whole country by surprise.

The second group of early movie adherents came from those patrons of the live theater or vaudeville who for one reason or another decided that motion pictures were more suited to their tastes. The effect of the introduction of the motion picture on the live theater was in the long run disastrous, and ultimately resulted in the almost total destruction of regional live stage productions in America. There is strong evidence to show that a significant segment of the live-theater-going public turned to the movies in ever-increasing numbers as movie houses were built across the country.[57] Soon after the arrival of the new entertainment it became apparent that the galleries of theaters, which catered mainly to an audience of low income, including many members of the working class, were not as filled as they used to be. Jack Poggi has pointed out that "the reason for the immediate attraction of the movies is obvious enough," and because of the price differential, "a person who wanted to see one legitimate play might have to forego five movies."[58] We have already seen that Vardac's thesis suggests that the movies were the natural extension of the desire for *pictorial realism* exhibited by the audiences that frequented the melodramas.

Then too, as a commercial offering, the theater suffered from the many serious deficiencies found in the majority of provincial theaters, which were not technically equipped to handle the very complex machinery used for the realistic productions in New York or other large eastern cities. Most towns with a population of less than ten thousand possessed inadequate equipment for the presentation of road shows which might have competed with the realism and sensationalism available in the motion picture melodrama.[59]

In the cities the live theater, although a very popular and well-publicized entertainment, was still not able to reach all the people. Benjamin Hampton estimated that "perhaps a million, possibly two million people were regular patrons of the various forms of theater entertainment — opera, spoken drama, musical comedy, vaudeville and burlesque — and perhaps another million enjoyed the stage occasionally. . . . However, ninety percent of the American population was not reached by any method of story-telling and character delineation by play-acting."[60]

In 1909, a special study commissioned by the Twentieth Century Club of Boston on "The Amusement Situation in the City of Boston" supported Hampton's contention that the live theater did not reach as many people as the movies were able to later.[61] The exhaustive survey indicated that in 1909 the weekly seating capacity (calculated by multiplying each theater's seating capacity by the number of weekly performances) of the various segments of the entertainment industry was as follows:

TABLE 4
SEATING IN BOSTON PLACES OF
AMUSEMENT, 1909

AMUSEMENT	WEEKLY SEATING CAPACITY
Opera	13,590
First class theaters	111,568
Popular theater	17,811
Stock house	21,756
Vaudeville houses	45,744
Burlesque houses	80,700
Vaudeville and moving pictures	79,362
Moving picture theaters	402,428

The population of metropolitan Boston at this time was estimated at 625,000. The study noted that of the entertainment seating total, vaudeville and moving picture shows accounted for 85.4 percent, legitimate performances, 13.5 percent, and grand opera, 1.1 percent. The average attendance prices were:

Moving picture shows	$ .10
Vaudeville and moving pictures	.15
Vaudeville	.50
Regular theater	1.00
The Boston opera	2.00

The authors of this study noted with some alarm the "overwhelming preponderance of cheaper and less desirable forms of entertainment," but realistically commented that "these theaters evidently appeal more and more strongly to their habitués. The great growth of new houses of this type indicates not only a rapidly increasing following, but also a tremendous and growing tendency toward a lower and less desirable form of recreative amusement."[62]

The relatively high cost of the theater also proved to be prohibitive to its wide acceptance and use, especially among the lower, working classes. The price of tickets ranged from $1.50 to $2 for orchestra seats, to $.50 for the gallery in metropolitan areas, and $1.50 to $.25 in smaller areas.[63] At this time the average workman's pay was approximately $2 a day, and the relatively high cost of the gallery seats could not have been a great inducement considering the noise of the gallery mob. However, after 1880, the presentation of drama and melodrama at popular prices in second-class theaters in the larger cities had achieved some success in attracting new groups of entertainment buyers. Many of these same companies also later toured county seats and larger provincial towns, appearing in opera houses, which, as we have seen, remained dark between these infrequent engagements. Nevertheless, all the live theatrical entertainment available could not satisfy the special and growing needs of a very large segment of the American population.

In his examination of the impact of economic forces on the live theater in America, Poggi succinctly described the end result of the introduction of the movies: "When the movies came along, this is what probably happened: the 'first-class' theaters lost part of their audience (at first mostly the patrons of the galleries) to the movies; the 'popular-priced' theaters were wiped out altogether; and the group that had rarely gone to either, now found a home in the movie houses."[64] It is interesting to note that initially the motion picture was not viewed as being much of a direct threat to the legitimate theater, because the nature of the clientele seemed so different. It was for this reason that vaudeville was the first form of live entertainment to feel the direct effects of the growing legion of nickelodeons springing up all over the country, because its patrons most closely matched those of the movie audience.

The third and most important group which made up the first movie audiences came from the large urban working class who seldom went anywhere near live entertainment. For them the movies proved to be the ideal form of recreation. Especially for the immigrant worker, the movies provided more than just an idle way of filling in time, but also acted as a guide to the newcomer on the manners and customs of his new environment. It was somewhat ironic that while the workers formed by far the largest segment of the nickelodeon audience in the early years, the owners of these establishments very quickly coveted the patronage of the more prestigious middle class.[65] Russell Merritt has pointed out that, from the first, the nickelodeon "catered to him [the worker] through necessity, not through choice. The blue-collar worker and his family may have supported the nickelodeon. The scandal was that no-one connected with the movies much wanted his support — least of all the immigrant film exhibitors who were working their way out of the slums."[66] However, whether he liked it or not, the exhibitor had to contend with the working class, and especially the immigrant, as the backbone of his support.

There is no doubt that the movies were indeed an important factor in the social life of the urban working class, and this is graphically confirmed in the following extracts taken from one of the studies forming the Pittsburgh Survey, an in-depth social study of the workers in that city completed in 1907–1909. One researcher reported:

I shall not soon forget a Saturday evening when I stood among the crowd of pleasure seekers on Fifth Avenue, and watched the men and women, packed thick, at the entrance of every picture show. My companion and I bought tickets for one of the five cent shows. Our way was barred by a sign, "Performance now going on." As we stood near the door, the crowd of people waiting to enter filled the long vestibule and even part of the sidewalk. They were determined to be amused, and this was one of the things labeled, "Amusement." They were hot and tired and irritable, but willing to wait until long after our enthusiasm was dampened, as we had left them standing in line for their chance to go in.

It was an incident not without significance, this eagerness with which they turned toward leisure after a working week of unmeaning hours. . . .[67]

The lack of available recreational opportunities for many workers is amply demonstrated in the findings of the Pittsburgh Survey. Discussing the role of recreation in the lives of working women, the survey pointed out that of the 22,185 working women surveyed in Pittsburgh in 1907, only 258, or less than 2 percent, were in touch with a center for social development and recreation.[68] While the importance of the motion picture in filling this leisure gap was obvious, the social workers involved in doing the survey were still somewhat skeptical about its ultimate value. The report continued: "Nickelodeons and dance halls and skating rinks are in no sense inherently bad, but so long as those maintained for profit are the only relief for nervous weariness and the desire for stimulation, we may well reckon leisure a thing spent, not used."[69]

A few of the reasons for the immense popularity of the movies have already been suggested, but the extra relief they provided in a dreary, work-laden life must be emphasized. The survey only alluded to this when it continued: "In so far as hours of work tend to dull and stupefy the worker, they are longer than the community can afford. Dulled senses demand powerful stimuli; exhaustion of the vital forces leads to a desire for crude, for violent excitation. . . . Craving for excitement is the last symptom of a starved imagination. . . ."[70] However, the fact that some forms of recreational stimuli were needed was not lost on the social workers; their only doubts concerned the medium's social utility. The report continued: "Any excitation, destructive or not, is acceptable, if only it be strong; the effect of it is to create a desire for stronger stimulation. Roller-skating rinks, dance halls, questionable cafes, may figure only temporarily in the worker's life or by increasing the demand for excitement, may lead to sexual license."[71] Even at this early stage it was becoming ominously clear; the motion picture, although a major source of entertainment and recreation for a large portion of the working class, was already being classified as "destructive," "unsocial," and the cause of "sexual license."

The whole problem of leisure and recreation was of great concern to the newly emerging professional social workers, who were anxious that all

Americans should make maximum use of their spare time in constructive ways. Unfortunately, the movies' origins as an adjunct of both vaudeville and the rather seamy arcades had saddled it with an unsavory reputation. While there certainly were unscrupulous motion picture house operators, and store-front theaters that were both unsanitary and morally unsafe, by far the majority of nickelodeons provided their ever-increasing clientele with a form of recreation and entertainment which was vastly superior in moral tone and low cost to that available in many other urban leisure activities such as saloons, vaudeville or burlesque.

The important fact is that in many working-class districts the motion picture was the only source of amusement available, and certainly the only form of commercial entertainment which many working-class families could afford to attend together as a family unit. In a survey of the mill town of Homestead one researcher reported:

Practically the only public amusements in Homestead, during my stay there, were the nickelodeons and skating rinks. Six of the former, all on Eighth Avenue, sent out their penetrating music all evening and most of the afternoon. There was one ten-cent vaudeville house, but others charge five cents for a show consisting of songs, moving pictures, etc., which lasts fifteen minutes or so.

The part these shows play in the life of the community is really surprising. Not only were no other theatrical performances given in Homestead, but even those in Pittsburgh, because of the time and expense involved in getting there, were often out of the reach of working men and their families. . . . Many people, therefore, find in the nickelodeons their only relaxation. Men on their way from work, stop for a few minutes to see something of life outside the alternation of mill and home; the shopper rests while she enjoys the music, poor though it be, and the children are always begging for five cents to go to the nickelodeon. In the evening the family often go together for a little treat. . . . In many ways this form of amusement is desirable. What it ordinarily offers does not educate but does give pleasure. . . . As the nickelodeon seems to have met a real need in the mill towns, one must wish that it might offer them a better quality of entertainment.[72]

The expense of entertainment was therefore a major consideration for most working-class families, and the study indicated that with a weekly budget of between $12 and $15, the average allowed for "sundries" was $1.23. The social worker commented, "We see how small an amount can be free at this and lower levels for what could be called amusements. Ten cents a week for the nickelodeon or for candy, a car ride to the country once in a while — these are the possibilities which seem open to mothers and children depending on a day-laborer's pay."[73]

It was, however, the lack of alternative recreational opportunities which was the major factor accounting for the popularity of the motion picture among the entire urban working-class population, of which the immigrants were, of course, a significant segment. We have already noted the relatively high cost of other forms of commercial amusements, and the expense and other difficulties encountered in attending the live theater. Alternative forms of recreation were either too expensive or not widely available in the working-class districts of cities. Very few public playgrounds were in existence at this time, and by 1910 the playground movement had just began to make a little headway. The report on recreation in the U.S. government study *Recent Social Trends* indicated that in 1910 only 17.6 percent of the playgrounds reported were operating on a year-round schedule, and that organized playground activities formed only a small part of the regular recreational program of the urban community.[74] It is little wonder, therefore, that the motion picture appealed to the working class, and especially to the children with time on their hands. The new medium of entertainment had no difficulty in finding a ready-made and eager audience among this segment of the urban population.

As the moving picture evolved from its early exposure in arcades, to vaudeville theaters, and then in store-front theaters, it passed into the mainstream of American life. For the price of five to ten cents a patron could partake of an entertainment experience that was demonstrably more realistic than anything he would find on the stage. Initially at least, this low cost was a great inducement for the entertainment seeker to sample the new experience, and was an important reason for its quick success. However, once established as a permanent and highly desirable attraction, the price of film-going increased commensurate with the increasing length and improved quality of the product being offered.

What was it like to attend a moving picture show? We have several accounts which indicate that attendance at a nickelodeon was certainly not the dignified social occasion we associate with attendance at the live theater. The crowd went expecting to interact volubly with the screen, and each other, and this they did — sometimes to excess. They were attracted initially by colorful posters and bright lights, with a promise of "Thrills of a Lifetime," while the theaters themselves were often small, uncomfortable and dirty. The show itself usually consisted of a sing-along featuring popular ballads or patriotic songs of the day, followed by a series of fifteen-minute films lasting an hour or two. Before the audiences became completely familiar with the medium, there would often be a lecture to describe the action on the screen. Often inexpensive vaudeville acts were also included as part of the entertainment. (A practice which caused some alarm, as we shall see on pages 79–83.)

The films were, of course, silent, and this was just as well considering the army of vendors which tramped up and down the aisles selling popcorn, peanuts, soft drinks and candy. Often the program was interrupted by slides requesting, "Will the Women with Hats Please Remove Them so that Others May See," or "Please Do Not Stamp — The Floor May Cave In." There were also frequent interruptions while the fragile film of these early years was repaired — to the accompaniment of a chorus of clapping, whistles and foot-stamping. Yet despite what seems to us an intolerable series of distractions, for the price of admission, the audience was indeed entertained.[75]

The motion picture, it must be concluded, filled a vacuum in the lives of many Americans, bringing pleasure where none had existed before or increasing the frequency with which such pleasure could be obtained. To the majority of the non-theater-going public the larger than life moving pictures were not merely a novelty, they were also a marvel that held an elusive promise of something vague, indefinite, but full of encouraging possibilities. The anonymous author of an article in the *American Magazine* for July, 1913, was able to eloquently describe the meaning of the movies to their audience:

This is the marvel of the motion pictures: it is art democratic, art for the race. It is in a way a new universal language, even more elemental than music, for it is the telling of a story in a simple way that children are taught — through pictures. . . . There is no bar of language for the alien or the ignorant, but here the masses of mankind enter through the rhythm of vivid motion the light that flies before and the beauty that calls the spirit of the race. For a mere nickel, the wasted man, whose life hitherto has been toil and sleep, is kindled with wonder; he sees alien people and begins to understand how like they are to him; he sees courage and aspiration and agony and begins to understand himself. He begins to feel a brother in a race that is led by many dreams.[76]

The Content of Early Motion Pictures

The first peep-show films had used vaudeville acts and similar entertainments for their public offerings, with boxing matches added as a special attraction. In order to produce these films in sufficient quantity and as cheaply as possible, Edison built the world's first studio specifically for motion picture production in New Jersey in 1893. This stark, black structure became known affectionately as the "Black Maria."[77] It was in this studio that most of the films for the Kinetoscope were made before being shipped out to parlors across the country. By the end of 1894, the Edison studios had committed to film such diverse subjects as Buffalo Bill's *Sioux Indian Ghost Dance;* a "pickaninnies" dance from *The Passing Show,* a popular Broadway musical; and four "Arab" numbers from the *Wild West Show*.[78] It was also in 1894 that Carmencita, called the first "queen of the movies," danced before the Kinetoscope cameras in West Orange.[79]

When the motion picture moved into the vaudeville houses the emphasis was still on filmed theatrical turns, but by now travel films had been added in order to demonstrate the visual superiority of the new medium. The films shown that fateful first night on Broadway in 1896 included such items as: *Sea Waves; Umbrella Dance; Burlesque Boxing; Venice, Showing Gondolas; Kaiser Wilhelm, Reviewing His Troops;* and a patriotic rouser entitled *Cuba Libre*.[80] This type of content continued with very little variation until 1903, except for individual items of interest such as the Corbett-Fitzsimmons fight in 1897.

In 1900, Edwin S. Porter joined the Edison Studios, where he was responsible for all Edison productions until 1909. Porter's first important film, produced in 1903, was *The Life of an American Fireman,* which can be considered the first true innovation in the development of the American story motion picture. In 1903, Porter also filmed *Uncle Tom's Cabin* and *The Great Train Robbery*. The latter, based upon a live melodrama stage production, proved to be the artistic and thematic impetus needed to raise the motion picture from the mediocrity to which it had sunk while in the custody of the vaudeville circuits. It was also this film — the first of the Westerns — which was of immense assistance in establishing many of the early nickelodeons. (See page 30.)

After Porter's success with story films, other producers followed with their own variations and innovations. Lewis Jacobs in analyzing the content of these early films noted:

The Americans rarely left their own backyards and streets even when they were technically able to do so. Fairy tales, fantasies, storybook romances, were far removed from their immediate interests. Subject matter was derived from American life — from the exploits of the policeman and burglar, cowboy and factory worker, farmer and country girl, clerk and politician, drunkard and servant girl, store keeper and mechanic.[81]

Alexander Walker has suggested that there were valid social reasons for the wholehearted acceptance of much of this morbid content:

It is worth emphasizing that the sentimentality of the plots, which jars today, was then very much a fact of life for nickelodeon audiences from the backstreets or immigrant ghettos where drunkenness bred brutish parents, long-lost off-spring were the common price of having to leave one's homeland, and the dying babies of melodrama had their statistical reality in the infant mortality rate.[82]

It was, however, precisely this type of motion picture content which seemed to bother the growing army of detractors of the medium. In an article published in the *Review of Reviews* in 1908, an anonymous critic complained:

One's regret for such exhibitions is deepened by the reflection that just as much time and effort have been spent in preparing the films for these pictures, as would have been in producing others of a more desirable character. . . . And all the thought, time and energy have been expended for the portrayal of the realism of bloodshed, crime and brutality.

There are, of course, many exhibitions in the moving picture line that give praiseworthy entertainments; but there are very many more that pander to low passions and have nothing but the film that will draw the biggest crowd without actually pulling the house into the policecourt.[83]

Not all the early motion pictures were sordid and melodramatic, as comedies and chase films of all types were immensely popular. Certain conventions quickly developed. Fads were exploited; domestic tribulations were ridiculed; sympathy was always on the side of the worker, although attempts were made to show the boss as a "regular guy"; and "a lively and popular subject for films, both comic and serious, was the various racial and national minorities in America."[84] The Western became immediately and permanently popular after the success of *The Great Train Robbery,* and more so after film companies began to move to California to seek a better light for filming. (And also in an attempt to get as far away as possible from legal entanglements regarding patent infringement.)

The insatiable public demand for films led to a ransacking of the available literature from stage and fiction. Every possible source was examined for suitable material; "short stories, poems, plays, operas, popular best-sellers, and classics were all condensed into one-reel screen presentations." Jacobs listed some of these early pioneer works: *Parsifal, Uncle Tom's Cabin, Ben Hur, As You Like It, Hiawatha, Evangeline, Dr. Jekyll and Mr. Hyde, The Scarlet Letter,* and *The Merry Widow.*[85] The adoption of well-known plays and stories quickened during the censorship flare-up after 1907–1908, in the hopes that material taken from accepted literary works would remove the basis of attack on motion picture content.

By 1908, the content of the early motion pictures had changed considerably in the five years since the first story films. The initial concern with sensation, scenic wonders, everyday life and squalid melodrama had given way to American history, the early West, more pretentious literary works and morality dramas. The film still, however, represented a means of escapism for its audiences, and it was this kind of escapist material that was to emerge as the single most popular form. As the film industry grew and attempted to make its financial investments more secure, it tended to concentrate on those content forms which were the most acceptable to the general audience. This in turn led to a concept of the formula plot; a series of dramatic conventions that would dictate the quality of the American film up to the present day. Even at this early stage, the emergence of the motion picture as a major American industry resulted in the development of marketing practices much like those in other consumer industries. (Many of the early film producers had in fact come out of the clothing and other highly competitive industries.) The films themselves were always seen by the producers and their studios (if not the actual makers — the writers and directors) as products to be licensed or wholesaled to exhibitors. The exhibitors in turn viewed films as so much merchandise to be sold finally to the customer-viewer. The American motion picture industry had no serious pretensions about its ability or desire to bring art to the people. It was strictly a commercial venture and each film was expected to show a profit for the studio.

However, before the industry could consider itself securely established, it was forced to undergo a series of examinations and evaluations, for the rapidity with which the medium had found its way into the hearts and minds of the American public was also the cause for alarm among the guardians of the public morality, and the "custodians of culture."[86]

Special Studies and Statistics

Accurate statistics on the growth and development of the motion picture industry have always been difficult to find. While many such collections of statistics exist, few have any basis in reality, but are usually estimates, or sometimes wishful thinking. This is especially true of the early chaotic years in the industry's growth. However, even during the period of Hollywood's greatest hold on the American public such statistics were seldom made public. What follows is an attempt to pull together statistics which appear in many diverse sources, but which are useful in indicating growth trends and patterns of attendance.

• In 1907, Barton W. Currie in an article in *Harper's Weekly* estimated that there were 500 moving picture houses in New York City, and that over 200,000 people a day were attending these.[87]

• In September, 1910, an article in *Review of Reviews* gave the following comprehensive figures on the number of theaters and seating capacity in major American cities:[88]

TABLE 5
SEATING CAPACITIES IN MAJOR AMERICAN CITIES

CITIES	POPULATION	MOTION PICTURE THEATERS	SEATING CAPACITY
New York	4,338,322	450 (est.)	150,000
Chicago	2,000,000	310 "	93,000
Philadelphia	1,491,082	160 "	57,000
St. Louis	824,000	142 "	50,410
Cleveland	600,000	75 "	22,500
Baltimore	600,000	83 "	24,900
San Francisco	400,000	68 "	32,400
Cincinnati	350,000	75 "	22,500
New Orleans	325,000	28 "	5,600

• In 1909, Edward H. Chandler, secretary of the Twentieth Century Club of Boston, noted the results of surveys conducted in that city which indicated that of 235 boys from ten to fourteen years of age, 65 of these went to the movies twice a week or more, while nearly all were regular patrons.[89]

• In 1912, Joseph R. Fulk, superintendent of schools, Seward, Nebraska, presented to the annual meeting of the National Education Association statistics on attendance in his home state. Thirty-five percent of those attending such shows were children under the age of fifteen, while the total attendance in the thirty-six towns reporting was 40,000 a week.[90]

• In 1915, a study in Portland, Oregon, indicated that only 9.5 percent of the children examined did not attend the movies; 28.4 percent attended twice a week, while 5.6 percent attended three times a week. Boys attended more frequently than girls, while 63.7 percent of these children attended at night.[91]

NOTES TO CHAPTER II

1. Mandelbaum discusses this problem in chapters 1–4 of *Boss Tweed's New York*; while Blake McKelvey, *The Urbanization of America* (New Brunswick: Rutgers University Press, 1963), also deals with the same problem in a less analytical manner, but with greater narrative detail.

2. Somers, "Leisure Revolution," p. 126.

3. Quigley, *Magic Shadows*, p. 9.

4. Ceram, *Archaeology of the Cinema*, notes that "the prehistory of cinematography begins at a perfectly specific time, the year 1832, with Plateau's Phenakistiscope and Stampfer's Stroboscope" (see pp. 15–17).

5. Raymond Fielding, *A Technological History of Motion Pictures and Television* (Berkeley: University of California Press, 1967), p. i.

6. Nicholas Vardac, *From Stage to Screen* (Cambridge: Harvard University Press, 1949), pp. xv ff. Vardac also indicates on page xix the interrelationship between the developments in photography and the perfection of the apparatus of the motion picture. Melvin De Fleur, *Theories of Mass Communication*, makes a strong case for considering the development of photography and the motion picture apparatus as essentially being subject to different social needs. He indicates that the tremendous growth and popularity of photography in the United States was due to the great mobility of the populace, which caused frequent separation of families. The portrait photograph obviously had an important social function in these conditions. De Fleur also suggests that family portraits might have served as a status symbol in place of the traditional painted portrait. The motion picture, as we have seen, has its origins more in the need for recreational opportunity.

7. Vardac, p. xviii.

8. For the theoretical considerations behind this concept of social tensions and needs see Barnett, *Innovations*, pp. 39–96.

9. Vardac, p. xxi.

10. John L. Fell, "Dissolves by Candlelight," *Film Quarterly*, vol. 23, no. 3 (1970), p. 23.

11. *Ibid.*

12. Frank Rahill, *The World of Melodrama* (University Park: Pennsylvania State University Press, 1967), pp. 265–268. Both Fell and Vardac also examine this history in detail.

13. Rahill, p. 297.

14. *Ibid.*

15. Vardac, p. 9.

16. *New York Herald*, December 3, 1899. (Italics added.)

17. W. P. Eaton, "A New Epoch in the Movies," *American Magazine*, October, 1914, pp. 44–45.

18. Gordon Hendricks, *The Edison Motion Picture Myth* (Berkeley: University of California Press, 1961).

19. Gordon Hendricks, *The Kinetoscope* (New York: Beginnings of the American Film, 1966), pp. 1–2.

20. The controversy which developed between these two over the ownership of the patent to the apparatus is complicated and unclear as to the result. The best account is found in Terry Ramsaye, *A Million and One Nights* (New York: Simon and Schuster, 1926), pp. 142–143.

21. Hendricks, *Kinetoscope*, pp. 56–57.

22. *Ibid.*, p. 13.

23. *Ibid.*, p. 58.

24. *Ibid.*, p. 66.

25. For a useful account of this early period see Joseph H. North, *The Early Development of the Motion Picture, 1887–1909* (New York: Arno Press, 1973).

26. Ramsaye, pp. 224–225.

27. *New York Daily Tribune*, April 23, 1896, p. 9.

28. Ramsaye, p. 235.

29. *Ibid.*, p. 327.

30. *Ibid.*, p. 310.

31. Lewis Jacobs, *The Rise of the American Film* (New York: Teacher's College Press, 1939), p. 5.

32. Robert Grau, *The Theatre of Science* (1914; reprinted New York: Benjamin Blom, 1969), pp. 26–27.

33. The nature of public reception of the motion picture during the years 1900–1903 is the subject of much debate. Joseph H. North has indicated that each of the major film historians has his own interpretation (pp. 184–191). From the evidence, it seems likely that the public was indeed more interested in films than the vaudeville managers perceived. However, because of the general lack of creativity in many early offerings, the public was not as encouraged as it would be after 1903.

34. Benjamin Hampton, *A History of the Movies* (New York: Covici-Friede Publishers, 1931), p. 17.

35. It should be noted that Ramsaye claims that "the vaudeville screen continued to be the principal avenue to the public for almost a decade (1896–1905)," p. 264.

36. Each of the major histories of the motion picture has its own "favorite" for the title of the first permanent motion picture house, but they all agree that the Harris and Davis operation was the first one to gain national prominence, or to have any significant influence on the entire industry.

37. Grau, p. 17.

38. Hampton claims that the theater had only ninety-six seats, pp. 45–46. It was Ramsaye who used the phrase "less than 200 seats," on p. 430.

39. Ramsaye, p. 430.

40. Hampton, p. 45.

41. Hampton, p. 46; Ramsaye, pp. 430–431.

42. Grau, p. 17.

43. *Ibid.*, pp. 19–20.

44. North, p. 256.

45. Joseph Medill Patterson, "The Nickelodeons, the Poor Man's Elementary Course in the Drama," *Saturday Evening Post*, November 23, 1907, pp. 10–11, 38.

46. *Ibid.*, p. 38.

47. Howard T. Lewis, *The Motion Picture Industry* (New York: D. Van Nostrand Company, 1933), p. 5.

48. The best accounts of the economics of the Patents Company are found in Michael Conant, *Antitrust in the Motion Picture Industry* (Berkeley: University of California Press, 1960), pp. 18–21; and in Mae D. Huettig, *Economic Control of the Motion Picture Industry* (Philadelphia: University of Pennsylvania Press, 1944), pp. 14–16.

49. Conant, p. 19.

50. Lewis, p. 6.

51. The concept of vertical integration in American industry is examined in detail in the work of Alfred Chandler, particularly "The Beginnings of 'Big Business'" in Richard M. Abrams and Lawrence W. Levine, eds., *The Shaping of America* (Boston: Little, Brown and Co., 1965), pp. 62–92; and in *Strategy and Structure* (New York: Doubleday and Co., 1966), pp. 1–94. For a description of vertical integration in the film industry see Conant; Huettig; and Lewis.

52. For details on this "war" see Upton Sinclair, *Upton Sinclair Presents William Fox* (Los Angeles: Published by the author, 1933).

53. Hampton, p. 17.

54. While very little work has been done in this area of film studies, an important article on this topic has recently been published. See Russell Merritt, "Nickelodeon Theaters: Building an Audience for the Movies," *AFI Report*, May, 1973, pp. 4–8. This short article contains many interesting ideas, particularly on the nature of the early "movie-going experience."

55. Hampton, p. 15.

56. *Uncle Tom's Cabin* was one of the many theatrical presentations which found their way into early film scripts, thus creating a further bond of continuity. For a detailed examination of the career of this play as a motion picture see William L. Slout, " 'Uncle Tom's Cabin' in American Film History," *Journal of Popular Film*, vol. 2, no. 2 (Spring, 1973), pp. 137–152.

57. There are two important studies of the interrelationship between the legitimate theater and the motion picture. Jack Poggi, *Theater in America: The Impact of Economic Forces, 1870–1967* (Ithaca, N.Y.: Cornell University Press, 1968), is more concerned with the entire decline of live theater in America, but clearly identifies the movies as a major factor in this decline. R. G. McLaughlin, *Broadway and Hollywood: A History of Economic Interaction* (New York: Arno Press, 1974), examines much of the same material, but goes into much greater detail about the exact nature of this relationship. Both are highly critical of the motion picture industry's methods in actively seeking to destroy the legitimate theater because it was seen as competition for the same entertainment dollar. Both offer evidence that theaters were deliberately purchased and changed into movie houses to prevent the continuation of live stage performances. Paradoxically, of course, the motion picture industry also relied upon the legitimate theater to a great extent for actors, producers, directors and thematic material.

58. Poggi, p. 42.

59. In their classic study of the Middletown community, the Lynds point out how meager were the offerings of the provincial theaters in the 1890s:

Like the automobile, the motion picture is more to Middletown than simply a new way of doing an old thing; it has added new dimensions to the city's leisure. To be sure, the spectacle watching habit was strong upon Middletown in the nineties. Whenever they had a chance people turned out to a "show," but chances were relatively fewer. Fourteen times during January, 1890, for instance, the Opera House was opened by performances ranging from *Uncle Tom's Cabin* to *The Black Crook*, before the paper announced that "there will not be any more attractions at the Opera House for nearly two weeks." In July there were no "attractions"; a half dozen were scattered through August and September; there were twelve in October [p. 263].

In a footnote, the Lynds add that there were fewer than 125 performances, including matinees, for the entire year. By 1923, however, there were nine motion picture theaters in Middletown (which was, of course, the city of Muncie, Indiana), operating from 1:00 to 11:00 P.M. seven days a week, summer and winter, with a total of over 300 cinematic performances available to the residents every week of the year. These observations clearly indicate that by the time of the introduction of the film as a commercial entertainment, the extensive provincial audiences were being offered nothing more than conventional staging, while the more realistic productions were limited in circulation to a few large eastern cities. This is further evidenced by the remarkable growth in the number of motion picture houses in those outlying areas once they had been spawned and found acceptance in their urban birthplace. Robert S. Lynd and Helen Merrell Lynd, *Middletown* (New York: Harcourt, Brace and World, 1929), p. 263.

60. Hampton, p. 14.

61. "The Amusement Situation in the City of Boston," a report prepared by the Drama Committee of the Twentieth Century Club, Boston, 1910, pp. 10–11.

62. *Ibid.*, pp. 6–7.

63. Hampton, p. 14.

64. Poggi, p. 266.

65. Merritt cites a Russell Sage study which indicated that 78 percent of the audience in New York nickelodeons were members of the "working class." See Merritt, p. 5.

66. *Ibid.*

67. Elizabeth Beardsley Butler, *Women and the Trades: Pittsburgh 1907–08* (New York: Charities Publication Committee, 1909), p. 333.

68. *Ibid.*, p. 332.

69. *Ibid.*, p. 333.

70. *Ibid.*, p. 356.

71. *Ibid.*

72. Margaret F. Byington, *Homestead: The Households of a Mill Town* (New York: Charities Publication Committee, 1910), pp. 110–111.

73. *Ibid.*, p. 89.

74. *Recent Social Trends in the United States*, pp. 916–917.

75. The best accounts of the early nickelodeons are found in Edward Wagenknecht, *The Movies in the Age of Innocence* (New York: Random House, Ballantine Books, 1971), pp. 8–24; and Jacobs, pp. 56–57.

76. "The Ubiquitous Moving Picture," *American Magazine*, July, 1913, p. 105.

77. Hendricks, *Kinetoscope*, p. 21.

78. *Ibid.*, p. 80.

79. Ramsaye, p. 115.

80. *Ibid.*, p. 236.

81. Lewis Jacobs, *The Rise of the American Film*, p. 67.

82. Alexander Walker, *Stardom* (New York: Stein and Day Publishers, 1970), p. 61.

83. Editorial in *Review of Reviews*, December, 1908, pp. 744–745.

84. Jacobs, *American Film*, pp. 73–74.

85. *Ibid.*, p. 76.

86. For a discussion of the role of the "custodians of culture" in American history during this period see Henry May, *The End of American Innocence* (New York: Alfred A. Knopf, 1959), p. 336.

87. Barton W. Currie, "The Nickel Madness," *Harper's Weekly*, August 24, 1907, pp. 1246–1247.

88. "The Moving Picture and the National Character," *American Review of Reviews*, September, 1910, pp. 315–320.

89. "How Much Children Attend the Theater," *Proceedings of the Child Conference for Research and Welfare* (New York: G. E. Stechert and Co., 1909), p. 56.

90. Joseph R. Fulk, "The Effect on Education and Morals of the Moving Picture Shows," *Proceedings of the National Education Association Annual Meeting*, 1912, p. 460.

91. "How Children Are Entertained," *Journal of Education*, February 25, 1915, pp. 207–212.

III

The Development
of an Industry, 1909–1918

BY 1915 THE MOTION PICTURE HAD ACQUIRED a recognition in the community that many early film pioneers would have thought impossible. In a period of a little over ten years the medium had progressed from the back rooms of penny arcades through dreary store fronts into the magnificent picture palaces on the main streets of American cities. Now there was no turning back, and the skeptics who had doubted that the industry could ever attain respectability as an acceptable family entertainment had long since disappeared. Also, the audience for the movies was no longer made up primarily of the urban working class. Several far-reaching developments in the ten years since the first nickelodeons had caused a change in the composition of the audience. The industry stabilized, the quality of films improved, the exhibition sites became more comfortable, and the price of admission rose. While movie houses continued to do a thriving low-cost admission business in working-class districts, the emphasis and glamour of the industry had shifted to the new first-run, luxurious film theaters, where admission could run as high as $2.50 depending on the film or its stars. These important industry innovations had resulted in the attraction of a more affluent middle-class audience, and the new audience had in turn increased the desire of the theater owners to become more respectable in the eyes of the community.

The change in the audience from largely working class to a more middle-class mixture created several additional problems for the industry, for this new group was far more critical and intolerant of the inconveniences to which the original movie fans had been subjected. Lewis Jacobs has pointed out that "they had no patience with broken films; they disliked waiting while reels were changed. Movie houses had to be comfortable and sanitary, with upholstered seats, polite ushers, carpeted floors, clean lounging rooms."[1] Thus as the films themselves became more sophisticated and refined so did the customers. This in turn led to a greater demand for better-quality productions, and the cycle of improvement was set in motion.

More important for the motion picture industry in its attempt to gain acceptance and respectability was the interest and influence which came with this new audience. They not only criticized their physical surroundings and the quality of the productions, but they also lost no time in criticizing the role that the motion picture was playing within the community, and they seemed to be particularly concerned with its unfulfilled promise as an educational and entertainment medium. These new voices carried more weight with the industry for several reasons: first, they were actually paying customers of the movies and thus were able to make firsthand criticisms of any dubious content; second, they genuinely had the interest of the industry at heart, and were obviously not out to destroy it; third, they brought some sophistication and suggestions to their criticisms, in contrast to the often wild, unsubstantiated generalities offered by other groups; and finally, their power at the box office gave them much greater leverage on the exhibitor as a means of maintaining local standards.

Ultimately it would be many of these new viewers, themselves "fans" of the medium, who would constitute the most intelligent and also the most dangerous segment of all groups clamoring for greater public control over the motion picture industry. Conversely, members of this new audience also became the most eloquent spokesmen in favor of greater freedom, for they saw the motion picture as the "art of the people" — the dramatic expression of democracy, which should be left free to communicate to the masses without social or political restraints.

We have seen that after 1909, and the establishment of the Patents Company with the larger independents as its major competitors, the motion picture industry achieved a certain degree of stability. The early exhibition forms had been left far behind in only five short years since the first nickelodeon, and movie houses were now found in almost every town in America. *Variety* magazine reported in 1907 that "between 4,000 and 5,000 were running and solvent, and the number is increasing rapidly. This is the boom time in the moving-picture business." The magazine also noted that most of the new show places were called "family theatres" and that vaudeville was reported to be suffering as a result of the "cheap movie opposition."[2]

Certainly the growth and diffusion of the medium had been beyond the wildest expectations of the original nickelodeon operators, and film producers. Terry Ramsaye, using the records of the General Film Company, indicated that on October 31, 1910, there were 9,480 picture theaters in the United States — and this after only seven years. The Patents Company served 5,281 of these, leaving 4,199 to the independents. Only twenty months later, on July 12, 1912, the number of movie houses had increased to 12,869.[3]

The bitter competition between the independents and the trust continued during these early years with an intense ferocity as both groups were locked in a deadly struggle to attain control of an immensely profitable and growing market. This struggle did, however, have five important positive results for the development of the whole motion picture industry.[4] (1) The independents improved the quality of their films in contrast to the standardized low-cost product of the trust. (2) Carl Laemmle, Adolph Zukor and several other major independents introduced the star system, which gave unprecedented publicity to leading players, thus introducing a whole new element into the social influence of the medium. (3) The production center for motion pictures was shifted from New York and Chicago to Hollywood. The independents were forced to move to evade attacks — both legal and physical — by the Patents Company, and southern California provided several immediate benefits, such as accessibility to Mexico, and the very obvious climatic and geographic advantages. (4) The keen competition resulted in the introduction of the multireel, or feature, film in place of the traditional one-reelers. It was this longer film, usually a European import at first, and later American-produced, that did much to gain prestige for the motion picture as a recognized entertainment form, and proved to be a major factor in attracting middle-class audiences. (5) The attraction of more affluent audiences in turn necessitated the building of lavish new "movie palaces" (copied after the best of the live theaters), a sure sign that the motion picture had achieved some form of legitimate social status.

Integration of the Movie Industry[5]

Outmaneuvered at every turn, the Patents Company had by 1914 lost its importance as the major factor in the film industry, but the era of perfect competition was still far from realization, for the independents, growing more and more powerful, soon developed their own fierce intrarivalry. This race for dominant economic power culminated in 1917, when Paramount (the leading distributor), Famous Players–Lasky (the major producer), and twelve lesser producers combined under producer Adolph Zukor in an attempt to dictate terms to exhibitors. Except for the films of the extremely popular Charlie Chaplin and Mary Pickford, Paramount dominated the production field. Taking advantage of this control over the other popular figures of the screen, Zukor instituted the practice of block-booking — a marketing technique which was to survive to plague the industry as late as the mid-1950s. This practice had been used before, but Zukor's ability to provide films that the public seemed to want made his version much more effective. (The practice of block-booking consisted of using the films of the more popular stars as levers to push the sales of less spectacular merchandise; thus the good was rented with the bad in one package. This industry practice will be examined in Chapter VIII.) By 1918 Zukor was distributing some 220 features a year to over 5,000 theaters.[6]

The exhibitors were obviously upset at the necessity of buying unwanted films from the large distributors, so to protect their own bargaining position against the producer-distributors, they combined into circuits to obtain films at lower rental scales. In 1917, First National Exhibitors Circuit was created to act as purchasing agent for twenty-six of the largest first-run exhibitors in the country. This was the second important industry consolidation in this period, and was another major step in the vertical integration of the industry. By 1920, First National serviced 639 member theaters.[7]

The final result of these industry moves was complete vertical integration of producers, distributors and exhibitors. To guarantee their own supply of films, First National contracted with stars of the first magnitude, such as Chaplin and Pickford, to supply their own pictures. Not to be outdone, Paramount extended its control into the final link in the industry chain — the exhibition business — and by 1921 Zukor had acquired 303 theaters. Such was the success of this integration movement that other independent producers experienced a great deal of difficulty in obtaining first-run releases for their own films. Eventually, faced with a difficult situation, the other big producers, such as Goldwyn Pictures Corporation, decided to secure or build their own first-run movie houses, a move followed in due course by almost all the major film studios. In the chronicle of the development of the film industry this phase is known as the "Battle for Theaters," and as Mae D. Huettig has suggested in her perceptive study of the economic history of the film industry, "the intensity of the drive against resisting theater owners was out of all proportion to the value of the objective."[8] In fact, many of these theaters were ultimately returned to their original owners when centralized operation on such a large scale proved to be both unprofitable and illegal.

The Star System

The establishment of the motion picture star as a hero in American popular culture, and the industry's adoption of the star system, was an important outcome of the patents war. It has already been noted that the mass media have the ability to impart a great deal of prestige and legitimacy to certain subjects and individuals. There existed a precedent for this public reception of the film star in the idolization of actors and actresses who appeared on the legitimate stage, but their reputations were not widely known outside the large eastern cities, except for the few who had achieved national recognition or had toured widely. However, the motion picture was in a unique position to create an entirely new form of hero in American society. The sociologist Orrin E. Klapp has referred to this new social symbol as "the hero of surfaces" — men and women who "are basically showmen who play to the crowd, specialize in impression, and never muff their parts." As such, says Klapp, "They fit peculiarly well into a society where mass communication, audience acceptability and role playing skill — not being a 'whole man' — are the new obligations of greatness." Klapp's conclusion is that the proliferation of these new hero types has resulted in an orientation in American society which he calls "audience-directed."[9]

In order to gain a measure of immediate respectability for the new medium, early attempts were made to use well-known stage personalities in motion pictures. But this experiment was unsuccessful because most of the first film audiences were unfamiliar with these actors and actresses, except for a few outstanding public personalities such as Sarah Bernhardt, whose film debut was a spectacular box-office success, even if not exactly an artistic triumph. The failure of the top stage personalities on the screen proved to be an important psychological boost to the struggling neophyte film actors, who soon realized that they had the potential to attain tremendous drawing power in their own right. It seemed as if the younger, more flexible actors and actresses were more adaptable to the new medium than the older, more experienced, but stylized stage performers.[10]

As early as 1910, it became obvious that patrons of movie houses favored certain players and had begun to express their preferences. This was in spite of the fact that actors' identities were kept anonymous by the producers, who went to great pains to maintain this anonymity, having correctly surmised that public recognition and clamor would result in a demand for higher salaries.[11] It was Carl Laemmle, the head of Independent Motion Pictures Company (IMP), the leading independent at the time, who was responsible for consciously creating the first star. In 1910, he built a unique "premature death" publicity campaign around the actress Florence Lawrence, whose exclusive services he had just acquired.[12] Other independents soon realized the tremendous value of the free publicity that could be obtained from a news-hungry press, and began to turn their own performers into public figures. The licensed companies of the patents trust continued to fight this trend for as long as they could, and suffered a mortal blow as a result. Many of their top performers, attracted by the promise of fame and fortune offered by the more progressive independent companies, left to join the upstart group. For a while the trust even tried to blacklist those who had made the change, but this trend toward the star system as an essential ingredient in the marketing of motion pictures was unstoppable.

Of course, the more public attention and favor a performer received the more money he or she could command, and the motion picture industry's economic structure was peculiarly suited to providing the larger salaries demanded and received by its performers. Whereas the number of stage stars and their appearances were limited, the film's stars and their performances could be mechanically reproduced and repeated almost endlessly, cheaply, and, most important of all, simultaneously in hundreds of places at the same time. For the motion picture actor, time and place were removed and the size of the potential audience enormously increased. Also of significance was the fact that the performance could be made more permanent than ever before — a fact not unnoticed by the bankers who were increasingly being asked to finance the growing cost of making feature films. Captured on film, the star could be placed in a portable can and used as collateral for a bank loan. A unique development was thus taking place in American entertainment: the actors and the public following they could command were being turned into concrete negotiable objects.

The arrival of the film star as an idolized public figure receiving an excessive salary only added to the criticisms already aimed at the industry, and reports that actors like Chaplin were earning $10,000 a week in 1915 caused a great deal of dissension in many quarters. Nevertheless, the ever-increasing film audience, now also becoming more sophisticated in its preferences, took these new American heroes to its heart and lavished a great deal of attention on every facet of their professional and also their private lives. Eventually a whole new form of subliterature was established to cater to the public demand for information about the movie stars, and to provide a voyeuristic view of their every action. In 1911, the first fan magazine, *Motion Picture Story Magazine,* was established, and it became an instant success. By 1914, it had acquired circulation of 270,000 and was quickly followed by the *Photoplay Magazine* in 1912, and *Motion Picture Stories* in 1913.[13] Initially these publications featured the plot outlines of the films, but as the popularity of the individual stars grew the magazines began to devote more and more space to articles on their life-styles, and biographies. The newspapers and other mass periodicals were not far behind in sensing this new development of public interest, and starting in March, 1914, the *New York Herald* began a series of full-page illustrated articles on the movie industry in its Sunday magazine section, which, Robert Grau claimed, "has projected the photoplayers more intimately and quite seriously to the general public."[14]

The Feature Film

The reluctant acceptance of the multireel feature film as the standard industry offering was an anomaly in what had always been a highly dynamic industry. This particular innovation was resisted by many producers to the point where they found themselves unable to compete with the suppliers of the more demanded longer films. The one-reel feature film had evolved as the standard product because of the misguided belief, based on the vaudeville experience, that the audience would not sit still for any film longer than ten or fifteen minutes. However, as audiences became more sophisticated in their tastes for motion pictures and were able to distinguish the good from the bad, they demanded longer films, with more sustained story lines. It was the remarkable Adolph Zukor, once again, who assumed the role of innovator, when in 1912 he imported a four-reel French film — *Queen Elizabeth,* starring Sarah Bernhardt. It was the unprecedented box-office and publicity success of this film which really opened the eyes of the industry to the immense commercial possibilities the medium offered. Exhibited first on July 12, 1912, at the prestigious Lyceum Theater, the Bernhardt film proved to be an immediate hit, and Zukor himself commented on the significant fact that "the audience had not been restless despite the hour and a half running time."[15] At first exhibitors objected strongly to paying fifty dollars a day for rental of this film, but this opposition soon vanished when the exhibitors found to their delight that the carriage trade now appeared at their box offices to view the Divine Sarah. Zukor claimed that it was this film which indicated to others in the industry the possibility that a higher class of trade would be attracted to movie houses by full-length feature films.[16]

Despite this success and others that followed, the General Film Company operated by the trust obstinately refused to distribute full-length feature films. The independents, who had set up their own distributorship in the interim, were thus able to make further gains. Europe was still the main source of supply for feature films, and in 1913 the movement toward longer films was given yet another boost by the success of the Italian film *Quo Vadis,* which was a then unheard-of eight reels in length. This epic, imported by George Kleine, a charter member of the Patents Company, was not distributed by the trust but was exhibited in large legitimate theaters rented especially for the occasion. Terry Ramsaye said of *Quo*

Vadis that it "startled the amusement world by playing a run of twenty-two weeks on Broadway with a top admission price of one dollar. It achieved a similar success in most of the larger cities. The profits were tremendous."[17] Not only were film producers convinced, and audiences enthralled, but those who ran legitimate theaters were now also forced to sit up and take notice, and the theater critics were suddenly made aware of a "new epoch" in the meteoric career of the motion picture.

Writing in *American Magazine* in October, 1914, Walter Pritchard Eaton, the noted theater critic, discussed what the coming of this longer film meant to the stage and the motion picture industry. Eaton's ideas are worth examining, for as far back as 1907 he had been one of the first recognized theatrical experts to take the film seriously. He saw several possible developments. First, the longer film required better production qualities, higher admission prices, and therefore an enlarged seating capacity in theaters. These new conditions acted as a means of "natural selection" and thus many of the smaller and shabbier movie houses gave way to larger and more prosperous ones. The "attendant increase in comfort for the audience" meant a "general rise in dignity" for the entire medium. Second, the film would become more artistically acceptable, especially after it was able to fully utilize its greatest asset — its mobility. Eaton also correctly forecast that each competing medium (theater and film) would find its own means of expression, and "when the movies settle down to a normal level we shall find that they have risen to a higher level of artistic worth, and that they fill a useful and by no means to be despised place in the life of the people."[18] Surprisingly, Eaton was not able to foresee any success for the "talking" feature film, for, as he noted, "what will become of pictorial interest when you photograph two persons sitting in chairs indulging in a twenty minute intellectual discussion?"[19] He was optimistic about the future of the legitimate theater, because the motion picture could never hope to provide its audience with "the deep emotional glow, the keen intellectual zest, the warm esthetic satisfaction, which come from living, vital acting," and therefore "the living drama will not perish."[20]

The industry and the public had accepted the feature film as the norm by 1914. Even the trust now decided that its future lay in producing longer films, but this decision was made too late to ensure its survival. The market for full-length films was insatiable, and in 1915 the Paramount group made 104 features, while the contributions from other companies such as Triangle, Fox, Universal, and Biograph grew to the point where 687 new features were available in 1917, and 841 in 1918.

It was, of course, D. W. Griffith's magnificent *The Birth of a Nation* which had finally convinced the film industry that the public would pay relatively high admission prices to see well-made, intelligent and visually exciting spectacles on the screen. The coming of the feature film did, however, create new financial problems for the industry. Kenneth MacGowan in his history of the film industry noted that the actual length of a film had very little to do with cost or profit. In 1913, George Loane Tucker had spent $5,700 making the six reels of *Traffic in Souls,* while Edwin S. Porter spent between $40,000 and $50,000 on his four-reeler *The Prisoner of Zenda.* Tucker's film had no star but it grossed almost $500,000, while it was doubtful that Porter's film made as much, despite the $5,000 salary paid to Broadway actor James K. Hackett as the star.[21]

The thematic content of a film was as much a factor as star appeal in its success, and the industry soon began paying large sums of money for plays and novels with proven appeal. Lasky paid $5,000 for *The Squaw Man,* while by 1918 a magazine story called *Virtuous Wives* was sold for $15,000. Griffith, it was claimed, paid $175,000 in 1920 for the play *Way Down East,* which had not been on Broadway for fifteen years.[22]

The Motion Picture Palace

The feature film's encouraging public reception and the growing attentions of a middle-class audience created a need for better exhibition facilities. Increased prices were also called for as the rapid-turnover principle of the nickelodeon was no longer applicable with the longer program time. The exhibitor became much more conscious of and concerned about the quality of the films presented and the surroundings in which they were presented. No longer were potted palms in the foyer sufficient to offset dismal interiors and a lack of toilet facilities. In 1913, Mitchell L. Mark, who had built up a chain of theaters in Buffalo and other eastern cities, startled the motion picture world (and without doubt the owners of legitimate theaters as well) by beginning to build the Strand Theater in Longacre Square, New York City. This theater, devoted entirely to motion pictures, had nearly three thousand seats on only two floors and was the first of the great motion picture palaces. Benjamin Hampton commented on Mark's announcement that "a scattered few applauded his judgement and courage, but otherwise he was regarded as an over-optimistic enthusiast."[23]

The day after the Strand opened on April 1, 1914, Victor Watson, the drama critic of the *New York Times,* wrote:

Going to the new Strand Theatre last night was very much like going to a Presidential reception, a first night at the opera or the opening of the horse show. It seemed like everyone in town had simultaneously arrived at the conclusion that a visit to the magnificent new movie playhouse was necessary.

. . . when I saw the wonderful audience last night in all its costly togs, the one thought that came to my mind was that if anyone had told me two years ago that the time would come when the finest looking people in town would be going to the biggest and newest theatre on Broadway for the purpose of seeing motion pictures, I would have sent them down to visit my friend, Dr. Minas Gregory at Bellevue Hospital. The doctor runs the city's bughouse you know.[24]

Managed by the legendary movie-house impresario S. L. Rothapfel ("Roxy"), the Strand offered the audience a full-length film, and music played by the "Strand Celebrated Concert Orchestra," all for the price of fifteen cents in the balcony, fifty cents in the loges or boxes. A handbill distributed by the theater contained a social note which is indicative of the change in audience composition: "Physicians (or others) anticipating phone calls will please notify the Captain of the Ushers so that location of their whereabouts may be known."[25]

The Gaumont-Palace in Paris was larger than the Strand, but the New York theater was the largest building specifically designed for exhibiting films. The Strand was designed, claimed Mark, to be a " 'National Institution' which would stand for all time as the model of Moving Picture Palaces."[26] The debut of the picture palace in America began auspiciously when the opening feature *The Spoilers* played to forty thousand patrons the first week,[27] even though *Variety* was reported to have been skeptical about the exclusive use of this type of theater. The magazine suggested that "the Strand would not continue with pictures, but would take on a legitimate attraction by next season, probably musical comedy."[28] The old traditions die hard, and even in 1914, the motion picture was still considered to be the poor cousin of the legitimate theater!

By April, 1914, a second elaborate movie house — the Vitagraph — had opened in the heart of the Broadway theatrical district. The news of the success of these "million dollar palaces," devoted exclusively to the exhibition of the motion picture in surroundings of style and comfort, swept the country, and within a short time many of these new specialty theaters were being built in cities in every part of the United States and Canada. Hampton estimated that between 1914 and 1922 some four thousand new motion picture theaters opened. However, this resulted in the closing down of so many smaller nickelodeons that the total number of movie houses declined.[29] These new "palaces of the people" completed the first movie revolution, for combined with the feature film and the growing public popularity of the stars, the motion picture was on its way to becoming an accepted and respectable form of amusement for people from all walks of life.

These new film theaters soon became important advertisers in local newspapers, and the newspapers responded to their new clients' wishes and the growing public interest by giving movies and movie stars a great deal of publicity. In this way films released for their first runs in large metropolitan areas were given publicity buildups which later created a demand in the outlying areas. It quickly became obvious to the film studios that a film which had not received such first-run publicity did not do as well when released directly to neighborhood or suburban theaters. Eventually the prestige of first-run presentation became essential to the profitable production and distribution of major features, and it was imperative to the film producers that they have available to them a sufficient number of first-run outlets in key cities. It was this crucial need for exhibition sites which prompted the move toward vertical integration of the industry.

The building of motion picture houses in residential areas started in Chicago and Los Angeles and spread across the country. These neighborhood theaters brought the motion picture into direct conflict with local interests and were to be the cause of much of the criticism aimed at the industry. Comfortable and attractively decorated, and with a seating capacity of six hundred to one thousand, thousands of these theaters suddenly became important centers of activity in local neighborhoods.[30] The movie houses not only took over from the local vaudeville and burlesque houses, but they exceeded them in size as well. This architectural innovation was possible because now there were no limiting factors of audibility, and the screen was large enough to allow the transmission of minute details of facial expression and other close-up actions even to those in the back-row seats.

Thus these new developments — the star system, the feature film, and the new motion picture theaters — greatly facilitated and encouraged the commercial expansion of the industry. Once the public accepted or demanded these important innovations several new factors became significant, all of which had direct bearing on the problems associated with local control of the medium. First, the quality of the product had improved markedly and acquired an individuality, of both story and star; thus the exhibitor and the audience now had specific choices as a basis for selection. No longer was the emphasis merely on a regular supply of films, but on a particular story and a popular star. Second, this new differentiation in the product led to price variations based upon the value of a particular property to a specific theater, and depending upon the status of the film's run (first, second, third, etc.). Third, the exclusive licensing agreements then in force with certain theater chains, meant that wide geographic distribution was absolutely necessary in order to achieve maximum revenue for the studios. This national distribution also had to take into account regional variations in value and price and provide for careful servicing and reshipping. As a result of these requirements the studios placed an overemphasis on efficient distribution and aggressive sales promotion. It was these aspects of the industry's marketing procedures which led to the abuses associated with block-booking and advertising, and ultimately to the failure to provide any reasonable measures of local control or responsiveness.[31]

The Content of Motion Pictures, 1909–1918

In the years before 1915 the motion picture was still essentially a working-class entertainment, but few films of the period reflected this. Instead the values contained in most films of this era tended to reflect those of a population whose ideals and beliefs lay in the nineteenth century. It seemed as if the film makers, themselves products of an earlier period, had absorbed these ideas to such an extent that they were unable to make the content of their product reflect some of the more important cultural and social changes then taking place. In those early years there were very few films which dealt specifically with the problems of immigrants or ethnic groups, and theatrical conventions still proved to be the dominant force in deciding content.

Lewis Jacobs has indicated that in the period 1908 to 1914 the motion picture "preached." He suggested that "current events underwent moral and often sentimental inspection, and the outlines of facts tended to become blurred by the enthusiasm of the movie makers. Literary works were shaded to emphasize the rightness of current popular doctrines."[32] Even when the motion picture did start to face the twentieth century it continued to preach. Jacobs continued: "Behind these more 'modern' films was the producer's conviction that entertainment must be stressed no more than enlightenment — a conviction in keeping with the new age of mass production in books and newspapers [and] with earnest persistence the movies pointed their moral lessons, exposed corruption, pleaded causes, elaborated their sociological and religious sermons."[33] No matter what twists these plots took the essential theme was the battle between good and evil, and almost every film ended with "sin punished and virtue rewarded." Even the ever-popular Western became a morality play particularly attuned to the American scene, with the frontier serving to remind the mass of city dwellers of the simple and clear-cut differentiation between "good" and "evil" found in the country. In an age of changing values there were no confused virtues in the cowboy, who had a highly developed sense of right and wrong.

Russell Merritt has indicated the importance of the "New American Woman" as both patron and protagonist in these early years: "We can see the special attention the woman received in the films themselves.

Original screenplays in particular reflected a steady courtship of the woman's attention. Female protagonists far outnumbered males, whether combatting New York gangsters, savage Indians, oversized masters, or 'the other woman.' "[34] The choice and shaping of content expressly to attract female viewers became an accepted industry practice even at this early stage. In later years many studios operated on the credo that "movies that don't appeal to women, don't make money."

In the period immediately before the World War military patriotism was also a popular subject, and a large number of films explored this theme, teaching reverence for flag and country. After 1912, other topical subjects were also examined, and America's film makers at long last turned to rather controversial themes, such as the woman's suffrage movement, white slavery, political corruption, capital-labor issues and the tribulations of immigrants and racial minorities.[35]

While the exploration of these themes was commendable in that it exposed large segments of the relatively uninformed public to relevant social issues of the day, the depth and sincerity of the treatment accorded these issues left a great deal to be desired. As an example, in 1913, after several years of merely hinting at sex (but enough to infuriate reformers), the motion picture industry finally made a film which openly used sex as its major ingredient. Called *Traffic in Souls,* and made by director George Loane Tucker for the IMP studios of Carl Laemmle, this film was blatantly exploitive and became an immediate financial success. Although the film was steeped in the Victorian sense of morality and had the conventional "evil is punished" ending, it was nevertheless an extremely risqué topic for its time.[36] The advertising for the film gave further evidence of its wholly commercial intentions:

TRAFFIC IN SOULS — The sensational motion picture dramatization based on the Rockefeller White Slavery Report and on the investigation of the Vice Trust by District Attorney Whitman — A $200,000 spectacle [the film actually cost $5,700 to make] in 700 scenes with 800 players, showing the traps cunningly laid for young girls by vice agents — Don't miss the most thrilling scenes ever staged, the smashing of the Vice Trust.[37]

Ramsaye noted that the film attracted an audience of 30,000 spectators the first week in New York, with a flat admission charge of twenty-five cents. Within a very short time the film had moved to twenty-eight theaters in greater New York, and gross receipts totaled over $450,000.[38] The incredible success of this film has been credited by many film historians with ensuring that sexual themes became an industry staple.[39] Alexander Walker, in his study *The Celluloid Sacrifice,* has pointed out that this film was followed by several others on the same theme, and that "it is undeniable that these films popularized sex as a subject for the screen by exploiting its social abuses." However, Walker also noted of these films that "none of them projected sex in a way that would set social fashions."[40]

The film treatments of other important social issues were less exploitive, and perhaps more sincere, but they were also not as commercially successful as was the use of sexual themes. Lewis Jacobs, in his exhaustive and unique analysis of film content in this era, indicated that as the medium became more secure, "progressivism began to appear in the movies' treatment of minority groups in the nation. A genuine effort was exerted to represent most minorities, native and foreign, by more human and realistic interpretation instead of conventional vaudeville comic caricatures."[41] Much of this change can be attributed to the increasing importance of minorities in the community, and the gradual change in the composition and sophistication of the audience for motion pictures.

It was also at this time that increasing evidence was being gathered that the motion picture as a social force was capable of such great influence that its thematic explorations bore close watching. The earliest example offered by supporters and critics alike of these "persuasive capabilities" was the successful use of a film, *Escape from the Asylum* (1907), to argue sympathetically on behalf of Harry Thaw, the convicted murderer of architect Stanford White. It was therefore no surprise when the movement of the motion picture into the field of social commentary was considered by many critics to be yet another unwelcome and dangerous intrusion. Obviously the prospect of widely disseminating these more insidious influences on the screen caused alarm in a society then experiencing some difficulties with labor and social unrest.[42]

While exploring these new themes, the American film industry was also becoming a powerful worldwide influence. Critics now claimed that the medium was responsible for creating a false image of America in other countries. (This particular complaint would reach its peak in the period after the First World War.) The image of America presented to recent immigrants was also attacked, as can be seen from the view expressed in an article in *Outlook* in 1916, which noted with alarm that "the version of life presented to him [the immigrant child] in the majority of moving pictures is false in fact, sickly in sentiment, and utterly foreign to the Anglo-Saxon ideals of our nation."[43] It is important to realize, however, that there was almost no attempt by film producers to create and distribute deliberately contrived propaganda, and that these films utilized their excursions into the exploration of current social issues purely as box-office devices.

The motion picture continued to mature both technically and thematically after 1914, and a number of significant content trends emerged which dramatically altered the focus of the industry and which in turn caused still greater apprehension among those groups concerned with the medium's "capacity for evil." Jacobs noted that during these years the subject matter of films was broadened and the selection and manipulation of material became more purposeful and self-conscious as "the morality of the nineties was being transformed into the new progressivism."[44] The new middle-class audience, more used to the broader and relevant themes of popular novels or even the live stage, necessitated a profound change in film content if their interest was to be maintained. The preaching and obvious morality of the movies became less pronounced, while the philosophic and financial outlook of the industry moved upward into the middle classes. Films no longer told the workingman of his problems, but instead attempted to divert his attention and sought to entertain him by showing the world of the more fortunate.

The combination of the new middle-class audience and America's entry into the war pushed the motion picture toward a greater sophistication, and the "moralism and religiousness" of the prewar period was transformed into the more sophisticated fare offered to postwar audiences. Jacobs pointed out:

As the poor became less important as the mainstay of the movies, as theatres began opening on main streets, as admission prices greatly increased — particularly during 1918, with the addition of the war tax — the ideals and tribulations of the masses lost some of their importance as subject matter for the motion picture. Patrons of the better-class theatres had more critical standards, more security in life, and different interests. . . . Pictures began now to be devoted almost exclusively to pleasing and mirroring the life of the more leisured and well-to-do citizenry.[45]

The Movies and the First World War

In the period from 1914 to 1917, while America remained outside the war then raging in Europe, the motion picture industry was presented with an ideal opportunity to consolidate its role in American society. The eventual entry of American forces into the war, and the inconclusive result of the war itself, had a profound effect on the American people. The motion picture played no small part in the transformation which took place in the years 1914 to 1919, and the war made the movie industry and the American public acutely aware of the movies' influence both as an entertainment and as a propaganda medium.

At the outbreak of the fighting in Europe in 1914, one of the great frustrations of the motion picture industry was the inability to get sufficient footage of the actual fighting to satisfy the demands of the American audience. The movies were obviously the ideal medium for conveying the excitement of battle scenes, and movie audiences had previously been conditioned to such scenes by the dramatic footage of the Mexican revolution, which had been shown in the new newsreels.[46] Unfortunately, the military and civilian authorities in Europe were not as cooperative as the Mexican general Pancho Villa had been, when he signed a contract with Mutual Film Corporation for exclusive rights to film his campaigns.[47] What film could be smuggled from the European front lines was eagerly snapped up, while "faked" material was quite common.

It was, however, in the realm of the popular fictional movie that the American public became aware of the "horrors of War." At first such films as *Behind the German Lines, The Great War in Europe,* and *The Cruise of the M* used existing footage which had been reassembled to make some sort of story. Producers were soon made aware that the public wanted something more than documentaries, and the war provided the ideal background for both action and romance. In the face of American neutrality, producers made no attempt to be impartial, and the movie industry soon began an obvious attempt to influence the thinking of the American public.[48] There is, in fact, much evidence to indicate that the motion picture was an important influence in molding American opinion in favor of the British position.[49]

J. Stuart Blackton, one of the founders of the Vitagraph Company, was the foremost of the patriotic producers, and released *The Battle Cry of Peace* in September, 1915, just in time to play on public sympathies already aroused by the sinking of the *Lusitania.* This film, based upon Hudson Maxim's book *Defenceless America,* portrayed an unnamed enemy (obviously German) besieging New York from the sea, and reducing the city skyline to blackened ruins. Blackton himself stated that the aim of the film was ". . . to arouse in the heart of every American citizen a sense of his strict accountability to his government in time of need — and to bring to the notice of the greatest number of people in the shortest possible time the fact that there was a way to insure that peace for which all Americans so earnestly prayed."[50] Certainly the cinemas were mobilized against Germany well before Wilson led the nation into war.[51]

It was the growing awareness of the importance of the motion picture and other mass media by the government which led President Wilson to establish the Committee on Public Information (C.P.I.) on April 14, 1917, just eight days after America entered the war. The C.P.I. was given the task of providing news, information and a general attitude to the American public. The chairman of this committee, George Creel, was a forceful individual whose personality dominated the work of the group.[52] Creel quickly enlisted the services of the motion picture industry in his efforts to "sell the War to the American public." However, it was not until

September 25 that the Division of Films was formed, and most of the really important film work was accomplished only in the last months of the war. The C.P.I. was responsible for arranging to have released to the public such documentary films as *Labor's Part in Democracy's War, The 1917 Recruit,* and *Woman's Part in the War,* using film made by the signal corps. These films were distributed free to "patriotic societies and state councils of defense."[53]

It soon became obvious that in order to reach the large audiences necessary for success in the war effort commercial channels would have to be used. The C.P.I. financed the production of three full-length films, and a large number of short films, all made by private interests. Toward the end of the war the C.P.I. was just starting to get into production for itself. Finding little unity or cooperation among existing distributors, the government proceeded to distribute its own films to metropolitan first-run theaters, and contracted out distribution to outlying areas. Terry Ramsaye claimed that the special war films reached about one-third of the movie houses — about the same as a Chaplin comedy — "an excellent showing considering the slight entertainment value of the war."[54] The C.P.I.'s film program died together with the committee when wiped out by a congressional enactment on June 30, 1919. However, the significance and effectiveness of the medium's use as a propaganda tool was not lost on those groups then pressing for stricter and more effective social restraints on commercial films.[55]

Once America showed signs of entering the war the commercial film producers forgot their pacifist outlook of 1914–1915, and quickly jumped on the bandwagon of patriotism. In a very short time they produced such stirring and anti-German dramas as *A Daughter of France, War and Woman, The Kaiser,* and *Beast of Berlin,* while even Charlie Chaplin in *Shoulder Arms* heaped ridicule on the German military. The American public's taste was fickle, however, and by 1918 the horrors of the real war, contrasted with the "mock heroics" being shown on the screen, caused a shift in audience preferences. The gradual realization that the war would have no satisfactory conclusion, and the diminishing patriotic fervor and the loss of life, created a definite antipathy to war films. Benjamin Hampton, after noting that in late 1918 practically every theater was showing a war film, re-created the following Armistice Day scene:

A cluster of three boys and three girls pushing slowly through the mob that packed Longacre Square, stopped at the entrance of a movie palace, and read the title of the play. "Oh! It's a war picture!" said one of the girls. "We're fed up on war — and it's over anyway. Let's go somewhere and see a *real* picture."[56]

The war had another and more important effect on the growth of the American film industry, for the devastation caused by the conflict had almost completely destroyed European film production capability, and the American studios were not slow in filling the vacuum this caused. Thomas Guback, in his study *The International Film Industry,* has pointed out that the studios lost little time in turning out the additional prints for export, and by 1925 "American films had captured 95 percent of the British market and 70 percent of the French market."[57] This complete domination of foreign markets gave both European and American critics yet another reason to object to the influence of the movies, this time citing the dangers of "cultural imperialism." (See pages 203–205 for a fuller examination of the attitude toward the American film's influence in foreign countries.)

By the end of the war the motion picture industry had become extremely big business, and it was frequently referred to as "America's Fifth Industry," a description which it in fact did not warrant.[58] Wall Street investment houses began to pour money into the expanding film companies as the search for capital became ever wider. Productions were now more lavish, more costly and more controversial. When the studios began to list their stocks on the New York Stock Exchange in 1919, this increased the already intense rivalry for the customer's entertainment dollar, and the fierce competition that resulted was a prime factor in motivating the producers to explore themes which gave the audience greater and greater thrills. We have already seen some of the consequences of this competitive rivalry, in that stars' salaries climbed dramatically, and the once inexpensive story properties were bid up by the studios anxious to secure exclusive rights to best-selling novels and hit plays. These properties were in turn produced with expensive settings and costumes, and each major production and its star was accompanied by costly, but necessary, audience-building publicity campaigns.

The motion picture had now acquired a new status in the entertainment hierarchy, and the industry was anxious to secure this newfound respectability in order to protect its investment. In 1915, one studio — Essaney — offered a twenty-five-dollar prize to anyone coming up with a more acceptable pseudonym for the rather vulgar term "movies." The winning entry was "photoplay," and Kenneth MacGowan noted that "so great was the desire [for respectability] of the movie-makers — and the movie critics — that everyone decided to accept the winning word."[59] Although the oldest of the motion picture fan magazines had borne that same title (the *Photoplay*) since 1912, the "movies" continued to remain the "movies" to millions of Americans.

The entire period 1914–1918 saw a definite shift away from any attempt at serious social commentary by the commercial film industry. While a few films examined themes such as temperance, political chicanery, capital punishment and the "evils of dope," the major emphasis was now on either the lighter, sophisticated side of life, or on controversial subjects hitherto considered taboo — divorce, birth control and "educational" sex dramas. The industry made no secret of the audience it now coveted, and in his examination of the content trends of this period Lewis Jacobs observed:

In keeping with this new-found realistic outlook went a loss of respect for spiritual values and an increased regard for material ones. The philosophy of self-aggrandizement, the regard for elegant clothes and polished manners, the veneration of the successful businessman and wealth, and the fashion of high-pressure salesmanship — all of which were to become dominant in films of the post-war period — now began receiving favorable attention on the screen.[60]

The basic ingredients now existed for the emergence of the sex star — the relatively sophisticated audiences, the star system and the gradual shift in content toward more mature themes. Added to this was the vision of the potential financial rewards that sexual themes promised, evidenced by the success of the "white slave" films. An important milestone was reached in January, 1915, when producer William Fox released *A Fool There Was*, starring the mysterious and sensational Theda Bara (her real name was Theodosia Goodman), and the word "vamp" was introduced into the English language. Surrounded by a phalanx of publicity men throughout her brief career, Miss Bara made about forty films over the next three years, including *Eternal Sin, Purgatory, The Forbidden Path,* and *She-Devil.* Alexander Walker noted of her films that they were "redolent of damnation, transgression, fall from grace, profane worship and the rest of the folklore and topography of heaven and hell." It was these films and others like them which Walker indicated deliberately set out "to make sex fascinating to the growing middle-class audiences."[61] It would be up to Cecil B. De Mille to elevate the use of "sex appeal" in the motion picture to a true art. (See Chapter VIII.)

This analysis of the shifting content of the motion picture provides the necessary background for a more complete understanding of the emergence of official censorship legislation in the period after 1909. The major area of concern was with the perceived decline of the old moral codes and the emergence of new life-styles and values based largely on the urban experience. The critical attacks concentrated on two areas — sex and crime, separately or linked — as the major sources of motion picture evils, and it was primarily toward the control of these moral issues that censorship was proposed. While there were isolated examples of the use of censorship to prevent the dissemination of political ideas or themes, there is no sustained evidence during this period that the political censorship of the motion picture was ever a stated aim of the groups advocating "social" control.

By 1918 the motion picture had become an integral part of American life — as normal as going to church on Sunday. However, the medium was still a long way from being totally accepted, and the social and cultural accommodation process was still far from complete. The relationship between the film industry and many influential segments of American society continued to be unsatisfactory and subject to a great deal of tension. Those bent on reforming or controlling the medium were still a small minority of the total movie-going public, but they worked tirelessly, had prestige and influence, and their activities kept the entire industry alert to the dangers inherent in their proposals.

However, while many institutions such as the church and the school were still searching for suitable means of coping with this new phenomenon, the majority of the American public showed absolutely no reticence in taking the movies to their hearts. They were completely captured by what they saw on the screen, and by their new heroes — the movie stars. The demand for new films was one of the economic and cultural marvels of the period.

It was precisely this tremendous hold the new medium had on the American public which troubled so many "reformers," for the ultimate effects of uncontrolled movie-going were the subject of much speculation. These speculations would continue, even until the present, and would result in an outcry for public control unknown in previous American history.

NOTES TO CHAPTER III

1. Lewis Jacobs, *Rise of the American Film,* p. 108.

2. Abel Green and Joe Laurie, Jr., *Show Biz: From Vaudeville to Video* (New York: Henry Holt and Co., 1951), p. 50.

3. Ramsaye, *A Million and One Nights,* p. 528.

4. This outline owes much to the concept proposed in William F. Hellmuth, Jr., "The Motion Picture Industry," in Walter Adams, ed., *The Structure of American Industry* (New York: Macmillan Company, 1967), p. 396. For a detailed examination of the early years in Hollywood see Richard Dale Batman, "The Founding of the Hollywood Motion Picture Industry," in *Journal of the West,* vol. 10 (October, 1971), pp. 609–623.

5. The best examinations of the complex issues involved in the economic history of the motion picture industry are Michael Conant, *Antitrust in the Motion Picture Industry* (1960); Mae D. Huettig, *Economic Control of the Motion Picture Industry* (1944); Howard T. Lewis, *The Motion Picture Industry* (1933); and William Marston Seabury, *The Public and the Motion Picture Industry* (New York: Macmillan Company, 1926).

6. Hellmuth, p. 397.

7. Huettig, pp. 33–34.

8. *Ibid.*, p. 37.

9. Orrin E. Klapp, *Heroes, Villains and Fools* (Englewood Cliffs: Prentice-Hall, 1962), p. 103. The historical significance of the emergence of the film star in American society has received several treatments. Among the best are Edgar Morin, *The Stars* (New York: Grove Press, 1960); Richard Griffith, *The Movie Stars* (New York: Doubleday and Co., 1970); Richard Schickel, *The Stars* (New York: Bonanza Books, 1962); and Alexander Walker, *Stardom* (New York: Stein and Day, 1970).

10. Walker, pp. 47–48.

11. Lewis Jacobs, p. 86.

12. *Ibid.;* also Walker, pp. 31–36.

13. Grau, *Theatre of Science*, p. 254.

14. *Ibid.*, p. 243.

15. Adolph Zukor, *The Public Is Never Wrong* (New York: G. P. Putnam's Sons, 1953), p. 71.

16. *Ibid.*, p. 72.

17. Ramsaye, p. 607.

18. Walter P. Eaton, "A New Epoch in the Movies," p. 44.

19. Walter P. Eaton, "The Menace of the Movies," *American Magazine*, September, 1913, p. 55.

20. *Ibid.*, p. 55.

21. Kenneth MacGowan, *Behind the Screen* (New York: Dell Publishing Company, 1965), pp. 179–183.

22. *Ibid.*, pp. 180–181.

23. Hampton, *History of the Movies*, p. 117.

24. Quoted in Ben M. Hall, *The Best Remaining Seats* (New York: Bramhall House, 1961), p. 39.

25. *Ibid.*, p. 41.

26. It should be noted that an earlier neighborhood "picture palace," the Regent, had been built in 1913, on the corner of 116th Street and Seventh Avenue. However, the owner, Henry N. Marvin, had overestimated the neighborhood's desire for a fancy movie house. While downtown critics were enthusiastic, the largely immigrant audience stayed away. Only after S. L. ("Roxy") Rothapfel took over and made numerous changes did the Regent show signs of being a financial success (Hall, pp. 30–35).

27. Hampton, p. 127.

28. Quoted in Hall, p. 41.

29. Hampton, p. 204. He notes that because of the increase in size, it was possible that "16,000 theaters in 1922 could hold as many people as 40,000 houses of the types existent in 1914."

30. Russell Merritt, "Nickelodeon Theaters," has described how movie theaters gradually moved into the suburbs in the period after 1910. Reluctant suburban communities finally allowed movie houses to open only after considerable pressure (pp. 7–8). For an excellent history of movie houses see Dennis Sharp, *The Picture Palace* (New York: Frederick A. Praeger, 1969).

31. See Lewis, chapter 1. It should be noted that regional variation in taste was also a factor, but this was adhered to only in extreme cases. The inability of the industry to cope with such taste variations was one of the major reasons for local censorship pressure.

32. Lewis Jacobs, p. 137.

33. *Ibid.*, p. 138.

34. Merritt, p. 6.

35. Lewis Jacobs, pp. 139–147.

36. The complete story of the production of this film and the intrigues involved in its final exhibition are chronicled in Ramsaye, pp. 612–619.

37. Ramsaye, p. 617.

38. *Ibid.*, p. 617.

39. Lewis Jacobs, p. 148; Ramsaye, p. 617; Alexander Walker, *The Celluloid Sacrifice* (London: Michael Joseph, 1966), p. 20; Richard Schickel, *Movies: The History of an Art and an Institution* (New York: Basic Books, 1964), p. 61.

40. Walker, *Celluloid Sacrifice*, p. 20. Walker also claims that one good reason that sex was not the major content form at this time was that no real "sex stars" had emerged in the early period.

41. Lewis Jacobs, p. 153.

42. For a description of the serious labor problems experienced in America in the period 1909–1919, see Henry Pelling, *American Labor* (Chicago: University of Chicago Press, 1960), pp. 226–290.

43. *Outlook*, July, 1916, p. 695.

44. Lewis Jacobs, p. 156.

45. *Ibid.*, p. 271.

46. The history of the American newsreel is brilliantly described in Raymond Fielding, *The American Newsreel, 1911–1967* (Norman: University of Oklahoma Press, 1973). The section on the Mexican revolution and the role of the newsreel in World War I is found on pp. 109–126.

47. *Ibid.*, p. 112.

48. Curiously enough, only one film presenting the German position to the neutral American public was a success. This film, entitled *The German Side of the War*, opened on September 20, 1915, in New York. Terry Ramsaye notes: "It was an opening with a bang. No attraction before or since has the record of such a sensation in so short a time. The lines awaiting the attention of the box office extended for four blocks. . . . It was the first chance that the German population of New York had to see anything on the screen that admitted there were two sides to the war. It was also the last chance" (p. 686).

49. Timothy J. Lyons, "Hollywood and World War I, 1914–1918," *Journal of Popular Film*, vol. I, no. 1 (Winter, 1972), pp. 15–29, offers a new view of the importance of the movies in creating a mood favorable to America's entry into the war. Lyons clearly shows that the motion picture had indeed become an important social influence by 1914. For other articles on the subject see Creighton Peet, "Hollywood at War, 1915–1918," *Esquire*, September, 1936, pp. 60–63, 109; for a contrary view of Hollywood's role in the First World War see Peter A. Soderbergh, " 'Aux Armes': The Rise of the Hollywood War Film, 1916–1930," *South Atlantic Quarterly*, vol. 65 (1966), pp. 509–522.

50. Quoted in James R. Mock, *Censorship 1917* (Princeton: Princeton University Press, 1941), p. 173.

51. For a somewhat jaundiced view of World War I propaganda activities in the motion picture industry see Lief Furhammar and Folke Isaksson, *Politics and Film* (New York: Praeger Publishers, 1971), pp. 7–12. They quote a letter from the German chief of staff, General Ludendorff, to the Imperial Ministry of War in Berlin, in which he said: "The war has demonstrated the superiority of the photograph and the film as means of information and persuasion. Unfortunately our enemies have used their advantage over us in this field so thoroughly that they have inflicted a great deal of

damage . . . films should be made to work with the greatest possible effect wherever any German persuasion might still have any effect" (pp. 11–12).

52. For further information on the C.P.I. see James R. Mock and Cedric Larson, *Words that Won the War: The Story of the Committee on Public Information* (Princeton: Princeton University Press, 1939); George Creel, *How We Advertised America* (New York: Harper, 1920); Richard Dyer MacCann, *The People's Films* (New York: Hastings House, 1973), pp. 120–123; and Fielding, *Newsreel,* pp. 123–125.

53. MacCann, p. 121.

54. Ramsaye, p. 784.

55. Lyons notes that "in this period, the Hollywood film had its first opportunity to participate in a 'real' and contemporaneous war. And in doing so, the efforts of the motion picture defined the medium as a socializing force capable of shaping public opinion to varying degrees. . . . By reducing the situation to that of a melodramatic scenario, Hollywood presented the war in terms that the American public could not only understand but, more importantly, absorb" (p. 27).

56. Hampton, p. 201.

57. Thomas H. Guback, *The International Film Industry* (Bloomington: Indiana University Press, 1969), p. 8.

58. See Gertrude Jobes, *Motion Picture Empire* (Hamden, Conn.: Archon Books, 1966), in which the author has an entire section called "America's Fifth Industry." This assessment of the industry's relative size was frequently mentioned in other places, particularly by spokesmen for the industry itself. The best refutation, because it is based upon a sound analysis of U.S. government statistics, is found in Mae D. Huettig, who notes that measured by dollar volume of business, the motion picture industry was not among the first forty American industries in 1937 (pp. 55–57). However, she also points out that in the entire field of commercial amusement, the movies accounted for 78 percent of the gross income and 92 percent of the total net income of the group (p. 58).

59. MacGowan, p. 185.

60. Lewis Jacobs, p. 275.

61. Walker, *Celluloid Sacrifice,* p. 28.

IV

The Initial Response

WHEN THE MOTION PICTURE WAS FIRST INTRODUCED to the American public, there was little realization of how far its impact would carry. Considered at first a mere diversion for an entertainment-hungry working class, the movies soon became an important social and cultural force in American society, which in turn required the creation of specific means to cope with this phenomenon. First critical reactions to the new entertainment were very mixed, and there was little agreement on what mechanisms should be established to ensure the most advantageous use of the medium's obvious abilities to communicate to (and therefore educate) large numbers of people with seeming ease. Everyone from clergymen to private detectives offered advice on how to "improve the movies," while the more zealous appealed to their political representatives for action to prevent what they considered to be a gross and dangerous misuse of the medium's innate potential. Only one thing was certain — the movies were not the passing fad that many had predicted they would be, for by 1915, they had acquired an enormous group of devoted followers and, possibly more important, a large capital investment.[1]

Progressivism and the Movies

While it was in the growing American cities that the motion picture had achieved its greatest success, it was here too that the motion picture ran up against the myriad forces of Progressivism, and the battle was joined. The "Progressives," a group which has proven difficult for historians to define collectively, were dedicated to the principle that history was rooted in a sense of progress by stages, and that new developments in all spheres

74

of human endeavor should be utilized where possible to improve the quality of life. More basically, Progressivism was bound up with urbanization and industrialism as the agrarian idealism of the nineteenth century confronted the anxieties of the more complex urban community.[2] As historian Robert Wiebe has suggested, "what had served to explain a community-centered society proved increasingly inadequate to comprehend America late in the nineteenth century."[3] The crowding of the cities, the development of greater bureaucracies, and the introduction of the mass media all meant that it became much more difficult for the individual to isolate himself, for, as Wiebe has noted, "as more of the previously distant world intruded upon community life, it grew more difficult to untangle what an individual did and what was done to him, even to distinguish the community itself from the society around it."[4]

Many scholars have observed the emergence at this time of a new professional middle class who would "form the bulwark of those men and women who dedicated themselves to replacing the decaying system of the nineteenth century."[5] Their training and urban orientation gave them the insight to recognize that the old ways and old values would no longer suffice; but paradoxically many of their urban ideals were still based upon those of traditional rural America. While they were obsessed with the development of viable bureaucracies, they also indicated a concern for the individual which tended to continue the domination of traditional village values. To do this they altered the concept of Spencerian Social Darwinism to emphasize the individual's ability and right to control his own destiny in this "higher social evolution."

The Progressives placed a great deal of faith in "science" and the use of rational, scientific reasoning as an answer to the many social ills of the day. This led to important ideological changes in the new science of psychology, away from the study of one individual's "faculties" toward a greater concern for how mankind was acting collectively. Sociology also emerged as an important new social science for the study of human interaction, and economics and political science were both given greater academic and public recognition. It was, however, in the field of education that Progressivism best manifested its love of scientific methodology, and this resulted in a major reorientation in American educational philosophy.[6] No longer was the school seen as a form of intellectual discipline merely to "train the power of the mind," and while many competing theories of education fought to replace this outmoded system, they all basically emphasized a technique which adapted the subject matter to the everyday world and needs of the child. "Learning by doing" became the key phrase, and in John Dewey the Progressives found their educational champion. Essential to Dewey's philosophy was his contention that "we cannot overlook the importance for educational purposes of the close and intimate acquaintance got with nature at first hand, with real things and materials, with the actual processes of their manipulation, and the knowledge of their social necessities and uses."[7] The school was to reflect the life of the larger society, thereby removing its traditional isolation from reality; but even more important, Dewey's theories cast the school into the role of a lever of social change, and the educator also became a social reformer.[8] This last ideological shift is of significance because when it became evident that the motion picture was increasingly becoming a major social influence in the life of the child, educators took a prominent part on both sides of the debate on the "evils of the movies."

Progressivism also manifested itself in the emergence of highly trained, professional social workers, who, disentangling themselves from their bonds of philanthropy, became established as a distinct field within the new social sciences. This dedicated group of young men and women organized America's first concerted attack on urban poverty, but they went beyond merely eradicating the visible social ills. Using the settlement house as a base of operations, they attempted to diagnose and combat all urban problems.[9] Operating at the most local of all levels, they saw that many of the problems of the city were interrelated, and that the urban dweller needed to be made aware of all the possible dangers, as well as the benefits, offered by his environment. While the settlement house movement was not an unqualified success, the leaders of the movement quickly learned that major changes could not be effected by action on the neighborhood level alone. Society had grown so large and complex that cooperation on all political levels, including that of many outside agencies, was needed to bring about some of the most fundamental changes.

It was only natural that the motion picture house, fast becoming a standard and popular item in the neighborhood, would receive attention from the social workers, and they soon discovered that this form of entertainment and its content were beyond their immediate control. Few, if any, city ordinances were available at this early date to regulate the content of the films shown, and while there might be some building codes and health regulations governing the conditions of the exhibition sites, these were usually loosely enforced. It was, however, the film's ability to entertain, inform and influence such a vast audience, especially the uninitiated minds of the immigrant and the young, that led many local community workers to want to know more about the effects of this form of recreation. The more perceptive among them soon realized that this entertainment was not as innocuous and innocent as it may have initially seemed. The results of these "investigations" by social workers are among the first important comments made about the movies and their influence on American society.

The Moral and Social Issues

Almost from the moment of its first appearance the motion picture found itself under close scrutiny from not only social workers but also other institutions which had a vested interest in any new communications medium indicating an ability to educate and influence its audience. However, while attacks on the motion picture industry were frequent in the period before 1922, no organized groups of any significance were specifically formed for this purpose. Instead, the suggestions, criticisms, and finally condemnations came from many different sources, each with its own particular solution to the problem of the "menace of the movies." These diverse and diffused criticisms can be more conveniently examined in four broad categories: (1) the child and the influence of the motion picture; (2) the problem of health; (3) the problem of "movie morals and manners"; and (4) education and religious responses. Almost all the negative reactions to the new medium coalesced around these four central social and cultural issues.

The Child and the Motion Picture

Much of the attention paid to the motion picture during the earliest period of its diffusion and establishment was due to its extreme attractiveness and accessibility to children, and the nature of the relationship between the child and the medium became the dominating factor in all discussions of motion picture influence. This concern for the future of the child was not unusual, for as Robert Wiebe suggested, "if humanitarian progressivism had a central theme, it was the child. He united campaigns for health, education and a richer city environment, and he dominated much of the interest in labor legislation."[10] The child symbolized all that the Progressives held sacred, for his innocence and freedom made him receptive to the scientific, rational concepts of men like John Dewey, and he held the positive future of society in his development. It was toward this development of the child, by the most beneficial and constructive method possible, that much of progressive social activity was directed. The interests of progressive educators and social workers intersected at this point, and Roy Lubove noted of this joint interest that "both viewed the child as a key to the problem of urban social control . . . and the public school assumed special significance as an instrument of acculturation."[11]

77

It is within this context that the motion picture was scrutinized by social workers, educators and clergymen, for its undenied appeal to the young proved to be an obtrusive force in the total scheme of scientific educational development. Beyond the immediate control of the local community, dispensing messages sometimes at odds with accepted social norms and values, and obviously competing with the school for the child's attention, the movies needed to be correctly "placed" within the total environmental experience of the child.

The famous director of Hull House, Jane Addams, was among the first to comment on the possible influences of the motion picture on the child's development and she devoted an entire chapter in her book *The Spirit of Youth and City Streets* (1909) to an analysis of what she poetically called "The House of Dreams." Her attitude toward the motion picture show was most ambivalent. While recognizing the recreational role of the movies for the city child, she also voiced considerable alarm at the possible harmful effects that this "unreal" world had. She noted that " 'going to the show' for thousands of young people in every industrial city is the only place where they can satisfy that craving for a conception of higher life than that which the actual world offers them."[12] Thus children were attracted to the movies in ever-increasing numbers as a means of counteracting their dreary surroundings, and the theater became to them a "veritable house of dreams," which was "infinitely more real than the noisy streets and crowded factories."[13] Further, the motion picture provided a "transition between the romantic conceptions which they vainly struggle to keep intact and life's cruelties and trivialities which they refuse to admit."[14]

In fact, Jane Addams argued, the child's pleasure in "the House of Dreams" was but a cruel illusion, and she cited several examples of the kinds of films that she felt filled "their impressionable minds with these absurdities which certainly will become the foundation for their working moral codes and the data from which they will judge the proprieties of life."[15] She claimed to know of many cases where children had stolen in an attempt to obtain money for tickets; but for her the greatest harm lay in the differences between what was contained in the content of the five-cent theater and the moral code of life as "prescribed by the church." Further, she commented that "the five-cent theater is also fast becoming the general social center and club house in many neighborhoods."[16] Thus Jane Addams was concerned that whole families now made use of the motion picture house as a center for recreational activity — a fact confirmed earlier by the Pittsburgh Survey. Whether or not she was jealous of this usurpation of the function of the settlement house is difficult to say, but it was most certainly a factor in shaping her attitude toward the motion picture.

The entire chapter devoted to "The House of Dreams" was a broad mixture of naïve amazement at the medium's ubiquity coupled with a fear of the powerful influence it seemed to have on its audience ("forming the ground pattern of their social life") and an attack on the dangers it presented — neurosis, delinquency, sexual license, antisocial behavior, bad health, and even "attempted murder." Jane Addams's attitude was basically one of disapproval and genuine concern over the overwhelming appeal of the medium, and the chapter ended with a survey of the alternative, and for her more attractive, forms of recreation then being implemented in American cities such as Boston, New York and Chicago. She concluded:

To fail to provide for the recreation of youth is not only to deprive all of them of their natural form of expression, but is certain to subject some of them to overwhelming temptation of illicit and soul-destroying pleasures. To insist that young people shall forecast their rose-colored future only in a house of dreams, is to deprive the real world of that warmth and reassurance which it so sorely needs and to which it is so justly entitled. . . .[17]

Jane Addams was not alone in her concern with the growing importance of the motion picture as a socializing influence in the lives of American children. In July, 1909, at the Conference on Child Welfare, Edward H. Chandler, the secretary of the Twentieth Century Club in Boston, presented a paper on the subject of children's attendance at the "theatre" and its effects upon them. Chandler likened the coming of the motion picture to "a new and curious disease [that] had made its appearance in our cities, selecting for its special victims only boys and girls from ten to fourteen years of age. . . ." Warming to his theme, he went on to inquire whether it was not "possible that a social force may become so insidious in its influence as to sap the mental and moral strength of the young people in a similar way?" Continuing with his disease analogy, Mr. Chandler wanted to know if it would not "be reasonable to expect the same excited public sentiment and the same eager efforts to overcome the evil at its source?"[18] Citing the results of a pioneering study made by settlement houses in Boston in 1908, Chandler indicated that the motion picture was already an essential part of urban recreational activity for youth.[19]

Chandler's comments and criticisms did not go unnoticed in the press. Two years later, in 1911, he wrote an article for *Religious Education* in which he indicated a dramatic alteration of his original position. By now he fully recognized the social importance of the medium, noting that "for the first time in the history of the world the theater, in this form, has become established and supported by the mass of the people and they have accepted it as an essential social factor."[20] This time, however, he directed his attack toward "that strange hodge podge of anything that can be done on the stage in five or ten minutes to interest an audience, which goes under the name of *vaudeville*." The crudity and vulgarity that accompanied moving pictures now became the danger, for "moving pictures in themselves do not produce these demoralizing results. They may be and in most instances are, both informing or wholesomely entertaining."[21] He offered a solution to this new problem of mixed entertainment: "As for popular entertainment it is not unreasonable to ask why there may be not established municipally-conducted popular theatres, under the direction of boards as able and high minded as the present school boards, where not only the character of the program but the attendance can be regulated and where every provision [can be] made for health and comfort."[22] Chandler's was one of the first important negative evaluations of the motion picture and its possible harmful effects on children. The problems he outlined were essentially the same problems that would be cited time and time again in the future by those concerned with the growing influence of this mass medium.

At the next Child Welfare Conference in 1910, John Collier, an important member of the National Board of Censorship (see pages 126–135), presented a paper entitled simply "The Motion Picture." The social workers of America were obviously anxious to find out more about the movies, and Chandler's earlier presentation followed by this one from Collier was an indication of their growing awareness of the need to understand the role and function of the medium in the community and its influence on the American people, especially the child. Collier's position was more favorable to the motion picture, as his opening remarks indicated:

I wish to present motion pictures as one of the most important and most practical problems and opportunities now confronting social workers and students of the child. It is a problem which because it is a new problem as well as a large problem, especially calls for careful investigation and patient, scientific thought.

The motion picture show is one of the silent, unregarded, and largely misunderstood agencies which are making history today. . . . The motion picture is the foremost art influence among the wage-earners of our country. . . . It speaks directly to the sentiments, the prejudices, passions, the romantic and social interests of more than a million American middle-class and laboring families.[23]

Collier then presented his audience with statistics which graphically indicated the extent of the medium's diffusion:

There are about ten thousand motion picture theatres in the country, as against about 1,400 theatres of all other kinds. The motion picture audience is four times the total audience of all other theatres. This means that the audience reached by dramatic art has been quadrupled through the agency of motion pictures. . . . Economic conditions debar the vast majority in America from the regular theatre. The motion picture theatre is within the reach of all.[24]

Collier, who was also a theater critic, pointed out that unlike the live theater, which was dominated by the New York "leisure class and travelling public out for a good time," the movies were largely patronized by family groups.[25] For this reason he was anxious that a representative public opinion should emerge from movie house patrons themselves, and not be forced on them by those who more regularly attended the live theater. In this respect he was stating the philosophy of the newly formed National Board of Censorship, namely, that the public would eventually censor its own amusements.[26]

While Collier's bias in favor of the motion picture and its future possibilities was obvious and predictable, his emphasis on the positive aspects was a welcomed defense of the beleaguered medium. In the years following 1910, the National Board of Censorship, and later its successor the National Board of Review, would form a close working relationship with child welfare workers. Also, the annual Child Welfare Conferences were always receptive to further addresses on motion picture topics, and the film industry made maximum use of this platform to improve its public image.

With children making up a very high proportion of the daily audience at picture shows it was only natural that the medium would be accused of encouraging criminal behavior. While many other "movie habits" were also condemned, the presentation of detailed criminal behavior on the screen was the most constant source of complaint. As early as 1912, Robert Grau quoted William J. Burns, the "celebrated detective," as saying that he deplored the fact that pictures tended to show crime as being easily committed and to emphasize the "genius of the criminal."[27] While many films did in fact show criminal acts ranging all the way from murder and robbery to stealing apples as a plot device in order to start a "chase" sequence, crime was by no means the major content form. It was, however, the inability at this early stage to accurately gauge the effects of the individual film on the individual child which led to the broad generalizations which condemned almost all films for all children.

To compound the problem, some of the warnings against the harmful effects of the motion picture came from highly reputable and influential sources. William Healy, the pioneer in the study of juvenile delinquency, in his seminal work *The Individual Delinquent,* published in 1915, included several case studies concerning children who he alleged had been "influenced" by moving pictures into committing criminal acts. Regarding movies and crime Healy observed: "The strength of the powers of visuali-

zation is to be deeply reckoned with when considering the springs of crim-
inality. . . . It is the mental representation of some sort of pictures of
himself or others in the criminal act that leads the delinquent onward in
his path."[28] Healy's description of the psychology involved in the "movie
experience" gave way to a more subjective analysis of the "evils of the
cinema." He claimed that he had "much evidence" that "movies may be
stimulating to the sex instinct," and that the real danger lay in the dark-
ness of the hall where the pictures were shown. "Under cover of dimness
evil communications readily pass and bad habits are taught. Moving picture theaters are favorite places for the teaching of homosexual practices."
Healy did, however, recognize that some children may be more susceptible
than others to "pictorial suggestions," and that the main hope for preventing these undesirable effects was to be found "in rigorous censorship of
perverting pictures, and in radical prosecution of those who produce and
deal in obscene and other demoralizing pictorial presentations."[29]

Healy's fear of the darkened movie theater as a source of moral and
even physical danger to the child was not an unusual concern. In an age
when lip service was still paid to certain conventions of courtship and
sexual behavior, the sight of a darkened room where the sexes mixed
freely and without supervision was sufficient to arouse much moral indignation. The sociologist Donald R. Young commented that "the undoubted
effect on standards of conduct resulting from the fact that the audience,
often young boys and girls, are packed in narrow seats, close together, in
a darkened room" would be to increase the possibility of undesirable
sexual behavior. Young's fears were not entirely without some foundation,
for he correctly pointed out that new words and phrases had been coined
to meet these new situations, and "movie masher" and "knee flirtation"
were added to the American vocabulary at this time.[30]

It was not only criminal or sexual behavior that was of concern. The
influence of the film in areas such as everyday behavior, sense of humor,
sadistic tendencies and the acquisition of misinformation was considered
to be a major fault with motion picture socialization, and therefore a
problem that needed to be controlled. One critic even suggested that
movie "English" was detrimental to the child, although here he was referring to silent film captions.[31] Even when the film producers attempted
to upgrade their product by filming the literary "classics," they were condemned for their efforts because "the effect upon the young mind is too
often an assimilation of facts that are not facts and the acceptance of
adulterated versions of literature."[32]

These early attempts to assess the nature and intensity of the influence
of the motion picture upon the undeveloped personality of the child were
relatively unsophisticated and largely based upon unsubstantiated generalization. However, these strong attacks did indicate the importance

placed on this problem by those concerned for the moral welfare of the American child, and this concern continued to be the major motivation behind the more sophisticated and empirically based studies of motion picture influence and its social role undertaken in the years after 1918. In the meantime the criticism of the new entertainment continued unabated with the child remaining the pivotal focus of these attacks.

The Motion Picture and Health

The problem of unsanitary conditions in the motion picture theater was one of the first and most tangible major criticisms aimed at the new entertainment. In an age of deliberate emphasis on outdoor activity and the development of organized recreational opportunities, the motion picture house was viewed by many social reformers as the complete antithesis of all that they had struggled for. While more and better outdoor facilities were being made available to urban youth, it was indeed ironic that the darkened theaters attracted them in even greater numbers. To many, especially the social workers and the clergy, and also the new breed of public health workers, the motion picture house thus represented a complete negation of all that they had worked so hard to eradicate.

In many instances this fear was not unfounded, for the first nickelodeons were constructed hastily in vacant stores or converted penny arcades with little regard for safety or sanitary conditions. While this situation would correct itself in due course with the adoption of new local regulations and eventually the building of specially designed movie theaters, it nevertheless represented a major stumbling block to the complete acceptance of the motion picture. The concern in this early period was mainly directed toward the physical dangers presented by the converted buildings, although some attention was given to the "health problems" caused by viewing too many films, especially the danger of eye damage.

An editorial in the *Independent* in March, 1910, summed up the feelings on the subject of "moving pictures and health." It pointed out that there was scarcely a village of more than two thousand inhabitants in America that did not have a moving picture show, and although "it is probable that the fad will die out in the course of a few years," it was still evident that "great harm to health may be worked by them, for they are maintained as a rule under the worst possible hygienic conditions and nearly everything about them favors the spread of disease." If this rhetoric seems strong, it should be remembered that in 1910 tuberculosis was still a major urban problem, and these older buildings with bad ventilation, sputum on the floor, and dusty conditions must have represented a serious challenge to health workers. The article continued: "We would not think for a moment of permitting schoolrooms to get into the condition in which most of the moving picture halls are, yet it must not be forgotten that a great many children spend hours each week in these places and that no precautions at all are taken. . . ."[33] Thus, once again the public's attention was directed toward the possible physical dangers that the motion picture constituted for the child.

Movie Morals and Manners

The nature and extent of the film's influence on the minds and behavior of the American people is a subject that has had a tumultuous history, sparked by claim and counterclaim, examined in hundreds of formal and informal studies, and debated in every form of legislative assembly, including the U.S. Senate, all without ever reaching a satisfactory conclusion. As early as 1916, a student at the University of Iowa wrote a master's thesis on "A Social Study of the Motion Picture" in which he stated, "The development of the motion picture has been so phenomenal that its social significance has not been realized. Any form of entertainment or amusement which attains the proportions of the motion picture business, must be considered a potent factor in moulding the minds and morals of a nation, and treated accordingly. . . ."[34]

There were obvious reasons why the motion picture had achieved such vast popularity — it was cheap, entertaining, and accessible to nearly all who wanted to attend. While recognizing these overt reasons, many of the motion picture's detractors, and also a few of its champions, continued to search for more covert, perhaps deeper psychological, reasons for the medium's popularity. How much of this search for deeper meaning was the result of the influence of the work of Sigmund Freud is difficult to estimate, but it could have been a factor. Although Freudianism did not reach its height of popularity in America until the 1920s, the great Austrian's influence on American thought had begun in 1909, and his writings had been translated into English in 1911.

The earliest, and still one of the most important, psychological studies of the motion picture was Hugo Munsterberg's *The Photoplay: A Psychological Study*, which appeared in 1916.[35] The well-known Harvard psychologist's attention to the motion picture was an important step forward in obtaining academic recognition of the medium's innate abilities to influence and educate its audience. Unfortunately Munsterberg died in 1916, and was therefore never able to fulfill his major ambition to actually produce suitable educational motion pictures. Munsterberg's analysis of the effects and social role of the motion picture was somewhat unusual, being quite optimistic in tone, for he saw in the film a unique opportunity for "aesthetic cultivation."[36] The motion picture had the potential to instruct the masses as to the nature of beauty — "the moral impulse and the desire for knowledge are, after all, deeply implanted in the American crowd, but the longing for beauty is rudimentary; and yet it means harmony, unity, true satisfaction and happiness in life."[37]

Munsterberg was acutely aware of the powerful influence that the film could have on its audience:

The intensity with which the plays take hold of the audience cannot remain without strong social effects. It has even been reported that sensory hallucinations and illusions have crept in; neurasthenic persons are especially inclined to experience touch or temperature or smell or sound impressions from what they see on the screen. The associations become so vivid as realities, because the mind is so completely given up to the moving pictures.[38]

His theories were primarily aimed at providing a strong aesthetic philosophy for the film, but he did not ignore the more pressing social issues which were then becoming so evident. Turning his attention to the claim that the motion picture was a prime influence in criminal activities, he noted:

. . . it is evident that such a penetrating influence must be fraught with dangers. The more vividly the impressions force themselves on the mind, the more easily must they become starting points for the imitation and other motor responses. The sight of crime and vice may force itself on the consciousness with disastrous results. The normal resistance breaks down and the moral balance, which would have been kept under the habitual stimuli of the narrow routine life, may be lost under the pressure of the realistic suggestions.[39]

Munsterberg admitted that "the possibility of physical infection and destruction cannot be overlooked"; however, he also claimed that "no psychologist can determine exactly how much the general spirit of righteousness, of honesty, of sexual cleanliness, and modesty, may be weakened by the unbridled influence of plays of low moral standard."[40] The motion picture was not entirely a bad influence, however, and it could also become a social force for positive results. Munsterberg offered this advice:

. . . while the sources of danger cannot be overlooked, the social reformer ought to focus his interest still more on the tremendous influences for good which may be exerted by the moving picture. The fact that millions are daily under the spell of the performances on the screen is established . . . any wholesome

85

influence emanating from the photoplay must have an incomparable power for remolding and upbuilding the national soul.[41]

While recognizing the need for educational films, designed for specific purposes, the psychologist was perceptive enough to note that the largest contribution had to be made by the local movie houses where the public was exposed to films without being conscious of the educational significance of what they saw there. After all, "the teaching of the moving pictures must not be forced on a more or less indifferent audience, but ought to be absorbed by those who seek entertainment and enjoyment. . . ."[42]

Munsterberg's brilliantly perceptive, and eminently fair, analysis of the motion picture's function was for some reason almost completely ignored, and after the initial publicity surrounding the book, his work was seldom referred to in the subsequent literature on the subject. It may be speculated that his views on the effects of the medium were too "soft" and therefore his usefulness to groups opposing the film and its antisocial influence was limited. It is far more difficult to explain why the motion picture industry and its supporters never made more use of his theories, although for several years prior to the publication of his work he had contributed articles to the *Paramount Pictograph,* a "house" fan magazine, and in 1916 he had presided over the Motion Picture Ball.[43] The film historian Richard Griffith suggested Munsterberg's rather indiscreet wartime activities (involving attempts to prevent an Anglo-American alliance) and early death in December, 1916, contributed to the general ignorance of his work. Griffith further suggested that, "if we who concern ourselves with the fundamentals of film art have neglected this book through the years, that can only be because we have neglected its subject — its indispensable and challenging subject [the social impact of the motion picture]."[44]

While Munsterberg's work lay largely forgotten or ignored, there were other less reasoned viewpoints which became only too prevalent. Two years before the publication of *The Photoplay,* an editorial in the *Dial* had examined some of the same questions that inspired Munsterberg, but had arrived at quite different answers. This editorial compared the popularity of motion pictures to the growth of photographic illustrations which "disfigure our newspapers," and suggested further that "it shows in a very striking way the demoralizing modern tendency to seek lines of least resistance in every form of activity, to convert education into amusement, and work into play, without giving the least thought to the way in which the process softens the mental fibre and saps the character." Obviously concerned for the future of the printed word, the writer of the editorial had viewed the motion picture as a further step in the decline of "culture." The film destroyed man's powers of analysis demanded by reading and listening, with the result that "the opportunities offered . . . for ministering to vulgar and depraved tastes are so obvious, and so attested by reports from countries in which license is unchecked, that some sort of censorship is demanded in the interests of public morality."[45] This was the more common type of reaction to the motion picture in the years before the First World War, especially in the smaller "literary" magazines, or publications of social concern.

Not all the literary critics, however, were enemies of the movies. In 1912, William Dean Howells, then the editor of *Harper's*, wrote a long and influential column on the motion picture as an increasingly important aspect of American life. Howells suggested that attacks on the motion picture had "been too exaggerated in [their] expression," and that "the lurid imagination of the public has been invoked without the specifications, and the moving-picture show dropped to zero in the esteem of most self-respecting persons." The noted editor's reasoned and positive approach to the motion picture was rather surprising, and certainly out of step with that of most of his fellow "patriarchs" of American culture. Howells did admit some danger in that the motion picture habit "tends in both old and young to lethargy of mind and inertness of body." This problem he felt would be solved by improved content as the medium matured. It was, however, in the field of education that Howells saw the greatest potential for the medium, and he suggested that authorities waste no time in introducing moving pictures into school curricula. Failing this, he made the rather startling suggestion that local movie house managers be asked to work in cooperation with the school systems. This would answer many of the motion picture problems faced by school authorities, because:

They may be assured that in any conflict with these managers they will be beaten; for the managers will have all the children on their side; clandestinely, we fear, they will have the parents, too. But by inviting the managers to cooperate with them, they will have a fair chance of winning them over and at the same time sugar-coating the pill of learning so that the youth of this fair land of ours will eagerly swallow it.[46]

Howells clearly saw the motion picture problem as essentially one of local control, but he condoned the setting up of competing, school-board-owned movie houses only as a last resort, as "this would savour of socialism, and socialism is the last thing we would advise."[47]

The fact that the motion picture had evolved as a commercialized means of disseminating entertainment and information had never sat well with certain groups of social reformers. While anti-Semitic sentiments were never openly voiced, it seemed as if there was a basic resentment that this "art of the people" should be in the hands of "Jewish ex-clothing merchants" who sold their product like so many cheap garments. The stigma of the movies' early origins was difficult to eradicate, especially in the period before the great movie palaces made "going to the movies" a respectable middle-class activity. Therefore, a constant attitude evident in many of the criticisms of the growing influence of the medium was that it was too powerful or potentially useful to remain exclusively in the hands of these commercial interests. An example of this sentiment, more specific and articulate than most, is contained in an article by Frederic C. Howe, the great urban reformer, in which he attacked the whole concept of the commercial exploitation of leisure:

. . . commerce has had no concern for the boy and the girl, the mother and the father. It has split up the family and in the cities at least has sent the girl to the dance hall, the boys to the pool room, the father to the saloon. Occasionally the whole family goes to motion picture shows. These with the streets and theaters, are the melting pot of our city population in the hours when they neither work nor sleep. And commercialized leisure is moulding our civilization — not as it should be moulded, but as commerce dictates.[48]

Howe's wrath at commercialized amusements as the "moulders of civilization" was a familiar expression, and he too turned to the school as the answer to his problem. The schools, he suggested, should be turned into local "leisure centers" where the neighborhood could congregate; the same should be done with museums, public libraries and even colleges — all should be available to the local community when not serving their primary function. Howe's ideas about using schools and other public buildings were echoed by other social reformers, but the "school center movement," as this concept was called, was not a complete success.[49] In many areas there were just not enough public buildings to properly accommodate all proposed community functions, and commercial entertainments proved to be the only alternative recreational forms available. This, as we have previously seen, was a major factor in accounting for the quick success of the movie houses in working-class districts.

The saloon too was recognized by many social workers as a natural social center in most neighborhoods. Allen Davis, in his study of settlement workers, noted that "they saw the saloon as a refuge for the derelict, the street gang, the prostitute and the pimp. . . . Most of all they saw the saloon as leading to the downfall of the young. . . ."[50] It is therefore somewhat ironic that in the evaluation of the motion picture's social worth there was frequent mention of the possibility that, handled in the "proper manner," the movies could replace the saloon as the major form of neighborhood recreation. Howe hinted at this in his article, and the social workers who conducted the Pittsburgh Survey had also alluded to this possibility. In the period after 1912 several articles on this precise topic appeared in the popular press, one of which, in 1916, observed: "Nothing in social and recreational life is doing more to furnish a saloon substitute than the motion picture house. And furnishing a saloon substitute isn't the comparatively easy task that most people think it to be."[51]

In the period before 1914 the exhibition of such films as the *Saloon Dance* and *The Saloon-Keeper's Nightmare,* in 1908, and *The Saloon Next Door* in 1910, preached the cause of dry propaganda. Andrew Sinclair in his social history of Prohibition, *Era of Excess,* noted that the brewing industry was quick to denounce the motion picture houses as both false prophets and trade rivals, while the mayor of Cleveland was advised, "If you want to see the motion-picture business flayed alive and its skin hung up to dry, talk to a saloon-keeper. . . ."[52]

The motion picture house did in fact present certain similarities to the saloon, among which were the free, normal atmosphere for men; the lack of social pressure; the fact that there was no need to dress for the occasion; and a certain degree of independence maintained by the customer-viewer. In an article in the *Independent* in 1916, the writer listed the advantages in choosing the movies over the saloon. He pointed out that a man could take his family with him, and it cost about the same as an average evening alone in the saloon, and "he feels a lot better for it in the morning after." Also, the positive educational aspect of the movies was not to be ignored, for it "comes in a form that is palatable and easily digested. The mind isn't taxed unduly."[53]

The poet Vachel Lindsay, in his literary treatment of film, *The Art of the Moving Picture,* published in 1915, included a chapter entitled "Substitute for the Saloon" in which he suggested that the movie house did indeed have a detrimental effect on the saloon: "Often when a moving picture house is set up, the saloon on the right hand or the left declares bankruptcy."[54] Lindsay too claimed that movies had "reunited" lower-class families, and "no longer is the fire-escape the only summer resort for big and little folks. . . . Here, under the wind of an electric fan, they witness everything. . . ."[55] Prophesying the coming of national prohibition, Lindsay looked to the motion picture (the "first enemy of King Alcohol") to provide a substitute activity so that "the people will have a shelter where they can readjust themselves."[56] He called upon the temperance forces and the motion picture industry to "ask each other to dinner," as they had much in common. The manager of the local cinema came in for particular praise, and Lindsay made this suggestion:

So, good citizen, welcome the coming of the moving picture man as a local social force. What ever his private character, the mere formula of his activities makes him a better type . . . he will make himself the centre of more social ideals than

89

the bar-tender ever entertained. And he is beginning to have as intimate a relation to his public as the bar-tender.[57]

The only real evidence that the appearance of the movie houses did have a deleterious effect on the saloon is found in an article in the *Independent* of February 13, 1913. The writer suggested that the battle between the motion picture house and the saloon was a real one, and one "in which the saloon seems to be losing." He cited the example of the Excise Board in Washington, D.C., which issued 513 saloon licenses in 1911, whereas by 1912 the number had declined to less than 200, and indicated that this reduction "was attributed by a large number of dealers to this new and better form of entertainment." The article continued: "A more distressing tale for the bartender comes from Pottsville, Pa., where in the first ten months of 1912 the picture houses drove almost exactly one hundred saloons [out] of business."[58] While the examples cited are provocative, there is no corroborative evidence that this exchange of entertainments was in any way a national trend during these years. Joseph Gusfield in his examination of Prohibition, *Symbolic Crusade,* indicated that in fact the consumption of alcohol in urban areas reached a peak in 1911–1915.[59] Thus, while this rather naïve wish to see the movie house replace the saloon had its merits, it is doubtful that at this stage very many people permanently deserted the public bar for the privacy of the picture palace.[60]

There were other evaluations of the motion picture's ability to become a positive socializing influence, but outside of optimistic pronouncements from educational authorities, these were infrequent and seldom had the same news value as the more dramatic denuciations of the medium's critics. In one of the more articulate positive evaluations of the motion picture, the Reverend Herbert A. Jump, of New Britain, Connecticut, examined the role of films in the lives of his congregation, which had a large immigrant component. After several years' work he concluded that "a new form of entertainment for the people has grown up which appeals to all races, all ages, all stages of culture. The motion picture today is one of the most democratic things in modern life, belonging in a class with the voting booth and the electric car." Jump praised the efforts of the National Board of Censorship for helping to make "the motion picture the cleanest form of popular entertainment being given indoors today." He concluded his analysis of the role of the film in American society by claiming that "in three aspects its significance looms conspicuously": (1) it added immensely to the general intelligence of the common people; (2) it had a positive effect in the immediate home surroundings by creating "higher ideals of home aesthetics"; and (3) it had a good influence on the moral standards of the community, because the audience received an "approved," or censored, version of the film. Thus, according to his examination of the problem, "decent moral standards are being taught by the motion picture much more than by the regular drama." Jump ended his analysis by asking a question that would become a standard one for movie reformers: "Why may not the motion picture be used deliberately for moral education?"[61]

The Motion Picture in Education and Religion

Ironically, it was in the field of education that the motion picture would receive most of its early support; ironic because it was the sanctity of the emergent "scientific-progressive" educational system that was most threatened by the arrival of the motion picture as a counterproductive social and educational force. Faced with the obvious, but undetermined, influence of the movies as a competitor, educators were soon convinced that the medium would better serve as an ally and therefore a useful tool with which to further the goals of progressive education. After all, its inherent appeal and latent potential made it ideal for educational use.

Addressing the National Education Association (N.E.A.) in 1912, Joseph R. Fulk, the superintendent of schools in Seward, Nebraska, made the rather dramatic statement: "The public school and the moving picture now seem to be the only truly democratic institutions in the United States." Fulk pleaded for more and better use to be made of films for educational purposes, because "under the most favorable circumstances the public motion picture theater has very little educational value . . . and [is] often detrimental to education."[62] Fulk's comments were the first official words on the subject heard at the N.E.A. annual convention, but they were by no means the last, for, like the National Conference on Social Work, this association would endure many presentations on all aspects of the motion picture and its uses. The film industry especially used the N.E.A. as a convenient forum for presenting its views on the major issue of self-regulation. The N.E.A. also appointed several committees at various times to examine methods for the proper utilization of the visual medium for educational purposes.

Thomas Edison himself had always visualized educational usage as a prime function of the motion picture. In 1913, in an interview he articulated his views on "catching them young":

I have noticed that the time to make good moral citizens is when the children are between eleven and twelve years, or round there. Then they are interested in everything. Their minds are awake. They want to know about everything. Then you can impress them, mold them for all their lives and make them moral. This is one of the highest things I hope for from this moving picture teaching.[63]

John Dewey, too, was intrigued by the possibilities of using the motion picture for educational purposes. On a visit to Edison's laboratory in 1913, he was enthusiastic, but tempered this with some reservations about how the film would be conducive to his educational philosophy of "learning by doing." Dewey agreed with Edison's convictions that children and adults learn best from matters in which they are interested, but he added:

. . . there is some danger . . . that a widespread adoption of motion pictures in schools might have a tendency to retard the introduction of occupations in which children actually do things. . . . A closely associated danger is that their use will, for a time at least, strengthen the idea, already much too strong, that the end of instruction is the giving of information and the end of learning its absorption.[64]

Dewey's fears were somewhat unfounded, for although motion pictures were quickly adopted by American school systems, they would remain a relatively ineffective educational tool for a long time. For the next thirty years the educational system would struggle to find ways and means of utilizing the film to its maximum potential with very limited success; and all the while the commercial film would continue to attract ever-larger audiences. The inability of American education to successfully counter the effects of the commercial film was an important pedagogical issue, and many writers in educational journals and popular periodicals voiced their apprehensions at this growing problem. Whether children were really getting more "education at the local movie house than in the classroom" was difficult to measure, but this was the popular view. Writing in the *Review of Reviews* in 1914, one educator commented:

Indeed the educator *must* use it; for at the present time the film manufacturers are educating about five million American children a day along undesirable lines. . . . But in the schools themselves nobody seems to have ventured yet to take the first step towards getting the full benefit of this new force; substituting for some less-effective book the stimulating reality of the motion picture.[65]

The United States government was not as slow in adopting the use of motion pictures for educational purposes. In 1907 the U.S. Reclamation Service had exhibited films at the Jamestown Exposition, showing the work of the government in reclaiming arid lands. The Department of Agriculture soon followed and was the first branch of the government to establish a laboratory of its own for the production of educational films. Films were also made by the Bureau of Mines; the navy; the Children's Bureau of the Department of Labor; and the Bureau of Standards. Apparently these films were in great demand and the various departments were unable to provide enough copies for circulation owing to the lack of available funds for this purpose. Also, as we have seen, during World War I, George Creel's Committee on Public Information (C.P.I.) established a film division which was second only to the newspaper division in spreading information at home and abroad.[66]

The film was also used as an educational medium by many other social agencies such as the church, local health authorities, agricultural organizations, and correctional institutions. The use of films in religious activities is of particular interest because so much of the opposition to the commercial motion picture came from organized religion. This did not obscure the fact that the film could be put to use to work its wonders in favor of the church's teachings, and not against them, and there were many reports of individual clergymen instituting film programs in their church basement. There seemed to be no lack of "religious" films, either made by church groups, or offerings from commercial film producers. (Religious themes were among the earliest explored in the commercial cinema, with the *Passion Play* a big hit as early as 1907, while *Ben Hur* and *Quo Vadis* were among the most popular early films.) By 1916, religious films had become more sophisticated, preaching Christian morality with a clarity and impact sadly lacking in many live pulpit sermons. One writer noted: "It is this very ability of cinematography to expose injustice, cruelty, and suffering in all their naked ugliness that has impressed the clergymen and church workers with the importance of this marvelous invention of the last decade." This same writer also noted that Professor Milton Fairchild of Baltimore in a lecture to the teachers of Topeka, Kansas, had advocated the appointment of a "moral instructor" by the University of Kansas to go about the state with a motion picture projector giving "visual instruction" in the effects of "wickedness and righteousness."[67] It was the motion picture's inherent ability to visually stimulate where mere words could not suffice that proved to be the key factor in the church's decision to make such extensive use of the medium. The motion picture soon became an indispensable part of the foreign missionary's equipment, and "religious instruction" film production became a major subindustry.

The church was naturally very concerned with the new recreational forms then emerging, not only for moral reasons, but also because the time devoted to increased recreational activity was beginning to eat into time devoted to worship. In an interesting book, *The Church and People's Play,* published in 1915, the author Henry A. Atkinson assessed the role of the Protestant church in the newly evolving recreational system. While he was critical of many popular forms of amusement, particularly dancing in dance halls, he took a rather realistic view of the motion picture's influence and status in society, and the church's position relative to this new

93

entertainment. Atkinson's comments on the motion picture are worth examining in some detail, for they represent a mature evaluation of an important social influence which was uncommon in religious circles at this
time. He observed:

The motion picture shows have done more to redeem the theater than any
other one thing, simply because they have presented the best in drama and literature in a pleasing form and at a price that is within the reach of all the
people. . . .[68]

The Church instead of being critical and suspicious of the people's motives,
must be sympathetic with every endeavour to find right kinds of play, and ready
to help provide those things that are good and make it possible for people to
follow their best inclinations. . . . The way to strike a proper balance is not by
prohibiting all pleasures, nor by indiscriminate condemnation, but by giving
such persons other things to think about and worthy tasks to do, so that recreation and amusement will naturally fall in to their proper place in the ordered
scheme of life.[69]

Finally, Atkinson advocated that the churches themselves consider providing motion pictures and other forms of popular entertainment. "Outside of their own specialized field the churches in every community ought
to feel that they are a part of the national movements which are recon-
structing the play life of the people, helping them secure more of the joy
of living which is the birthright of every individual."[70] This is in fact what
many churches did do, but in their efforts to become part of the new recreation they were loath to relinquish their moral responsibilities, and in this
fashion they justified their right to comment on, and if necessary to attack,
the commercial film industry for its activities. The power of the church
on the local level was strong, particularly the Catholic church, and many
congregations would find themselves at some future date "forbidden" to
attend certain films, or subjected to all-encompassing diatribes against
Hollywood — the "New Babylon."

A close examination of the criticisms aimed at the motion picture in the
period before 1918 reveals that, although these come from a wide variety
of sources, there were no apparent variations from region to region, or
even among the various social or vocational groups such as social workers,
educators, clergymen and politicians. Each group, in every part of the
country, attacked the same problems — crime and delinquency, sexual
license, false information, physical dangers and antisocial behavior. The
significance of this homogeneity of response is that the opposition to the
medium was based upon a very clearly defined sense of the "evils" it
could cause, even though these attacks were without much "scientific"
validity.

The Motion Picture as Symbol

There were, of course, those who saw the motion picture in a much more positive light. Introduced at a time when the traditional culture was being challenged by rigorous onslaughts of change, the motion picture became an important symbol for many American intellectuals who saw in the new medium the emergence of an art that would symbolically reflect the concept of a democratic American nation. Myron Lounsbury, in his important study " 'Flashes of Lightning': The Moving Picture in the Progressive Era," noted that "the moving picture captured the Progressive imagination, for it suggested numerous opportunities for human freedom without encouraging a condition of anarchy; it inspired a sense of communal responsibility without acquiring the stigma of socialism."[71]

No sooner were the basic industry structures established in 1909 than the motion picture was being asked to perform a social and cultural task for which its commercial origins did not equip it. The attacks upon the medium were countered by a small but committed group who were anxious to stress the positive benefits to be gained from the new medium. This group sought to explain the moving picture in an "egalitarian" context, and attempted to thrust upon it the impossible role of becoming a social bond for the American people. They made constant references to the motion picture as the "art of the masses" or "the democratic art." It was this alternative assessment of the medium's potential which its defenders, and especially the industry, hoped would stem the tide of continuous criticism, and counter the fear that the film was an instrument for encouraging and disseminating mass antisocial behavior. By emphasizing the medium's ability to educate informally, this group made a strong, if not futile, case for considering the motion picture a means for encouraging in the lower classes an appreciation of those concepts of art and beauty which had traditionally been the domain of the upper or intellectual classes. Hugo Munsterberg, whose work we have examined, was one of the foremost proponents of this use of the medium.

As early as 1908, in an article in the *Independent* entitled "Moving Picture Drama for the Multitude," the author had made a strong plea for considering the motion picture an opportunity for the mass public to participate in the "pictorial drama."[72] An editorial in the same publication in September, 1910, entitled "The Drama of the People," contained a much stronger and pragmatic plea for reevaluating the social utility of the medium. The editorial noted that "the cinematograph is doing for the drama what the printing press did for literature, bringing another form of art into the daily life of the people. Plays are now within the reach literally of the poorest, as are good books and pictures." The favorable economics of the "mass production" of films were also considered to be an ideal means of making good art available to the general population: "The secret of cheapness in art as in other things is mechanical multiplication ... once on celluloid a spectacle can be reproduced indefinitely, the good as cheaply as the poor, and superiority no longer handicapped." The writer considered motion pictures superior "both artistically and morally" to the vaudeville and melodrama they had replaced and concluded by observing that their success was not due only to their low price of admission, but that "they gave the spectator a run for his money."[73]

While the critics of the new entertainment continued to attract the most attention, especially in their increasing attempts to obtain official censorship legislation, other prominent observers of the American scene were more concerned with understanding the nature of the grip the film held on its audience, and channeling this toward more positive influences. A prime example was Joseph Medill Patterson, a successful journalist, who eventually became coeditor and publisher of the *Chicago Tribune* from 1914 to 1925. Patterson was one of the more influential writers who visualized a great future for the motion picture, and he had also been among the first to examine the commercial viability of the nickelodeon (see page 32). In 1907, after a close examination of the entertainment, he wrote: "Few people realize the important part these theaters are beginning to play in city life. They have been looked upon largely as places of trivial amusement, not calling for any serious consideration. They seem, however, to be something that may become one of the greatest forces for good or evil in the city."[74] Later that same year in an important article in the *Saturday Evening Post* Patterson noted:

Civilization, all through the history of mankind, has been chiefly the property of the upper classes, but during the past century civilization has been permeating steadily downward. The leaders of the democratic movement have been general education, universal suffrage, cheap periodicals and cheap travel. Today the moving picture machine cannot be overlooked as an effective protagonist of democracy. For through it the drama, always a big factor in the lives of the people at the top, is now becoming a big fact in the lives of the people at the bottom. Two million of them a day have found a new interest in life. . . . The sentient life of the half-civilized beings at the bottom has been enlarged and altered, by the introduction of the dramatic motif, to resemble more closely the sentient life of the civilized beings at the top.[75]

Patterson's insight at this stage was clearer than that of any other student of the subject, and his positive attitude presented in this popular magazine must have had some influence on his middle-class readers. He also accurately foresaw the growing controversy surrounding the movies:

Those who are "interested in the poor" are wondering whether the five-cent theater is a good influence, and asking themselves gravely whether it should be encouraged or checked (with the help of police).

Is the theatre a "good" or a "bad" influence? The adjectives don't fit the case. Neither do they fit the case of the nickelodeon, which is merely the theatre democraticized.[76]

Patterson's observations went beyond a mere analysis of the nickelodeon's current status, or a defense of its offerings. He also eloquently described the limitless opportunities which the motion picture presented for the improvement of lower-class life:

. . . the moving picture machine, uncouth instrument though it be, has enlisted itself on especial behalf of the least enlightened, those who are below the reach even of the yellow journals. For although in the prosperous vaudeville houses the machine is but a toy, a "chaser," in the nickelodeon it is the central, absorbing fact, which strengthens, widens, vivifies the subjective life, which teaches living other than living through senses alone. . . .

The nickelodeons are merely an extension course in civilization, teaching both its "badness" and its "goodness." They have come in obedience to the law of supply and demand, and they will stay as long as the slums stay, for in the slums they are the fittest and must survive.[77]

Surprisingly, Patterson was not able to recognize the possibility of the motion picture becoming an entertainment which would appeal to all classes of American society.

After 1912, there was a subtle shift away from praising the educational possibilities of the motion picture. The emphasis then switched to a deeper examination of the medium's artistic or aesthetic capabilities and how these could be improved and presented to the masses. Myron Lounsbury has indicated in his research how film criticism developed as a separate branch of theatrical journalism in this period.[78] While film criticism seldom influenced the preferences of the general movie-going public, these early attempts to establish meaningful criteria contributed to the development of the aesthetic and technical improvement of the American film. More important, the development of film criticism, and the prominence given to film journalism of all types, was a major factor in the expansion of the industry by attracting to the movie house a different class of patrons curious to see this "new art" for themselves.

The popularity of the motion picture presented a problem for the emerging group of American intellectuals then active in redefining the "uniqueness of the American experience." Almost as a reaction to the conservative attacks on this popular entertainment many of them sought to justify its existence as a means of bringing fresh ideas, concepts and

97

even art into the lives of the ordinary people. (Holding such a positive attitude took courage, considering the quality of the average film then being produced in American studios.) These defenders of the movies were well aware that the medium represented the major entertainment opportunity for millions of people of all ages. The idea of bringing art to the masses by breaking the hold of the traditionalists was foremost in their plans, and they were particularly set on cutting away from the blind allegiance owed to European aesthetic influences. A major problem they faced was how to dispel the myth that the movies were contributing to the creation of a "mass society" in America. Lounsbury's examination of the small magazines published by members of these avant-garde groups has caused him to note that "in the sympathetic atmosphere provided . . . the moving picture acquired a new prominence; rather than being a symbol of the dehumanization of modern existence, it embodied a life-giving spirit which might overwhelm the rigid standards of European cultural tradition."[79] These champions of the moving picture cautioned the young medium to discover its own modes of expression, and to avoid imitation of the traditional aesthetic codes, which were generally associated with European tastes and styles.

The recognition of the motion picture as an "art form" became more prevalent after 1912, largely due to the development of the full-length feature film, and the work of the small band of theater-film critics who by their reevaluation of the medium had contributed to its cultural elevation. An example of this new attitude is seen in an editorial which appeared in the *Independent* in 1914. Entitled "Birth of a New Art," this editorial is particularly significant because it was one of the first admissions by a major publication that the "entertainment of the people" was to be considered a serious form of artistic endeavor. The editorial observed that recent censorship activities had cleaned up most of the "objectionable features," and the emphasis should now be placed on evaluating "artistic merit." What remained was to select "the best rather than further suppression of the worst. . . . The way to do it is doubtless the same as . . . in the case of books, pictures and plays, independent and conscientious criticism from the standpoint of the public." The publication then announced that its new policy was to "describe and criticize films" which were deemed to be of "educational value, or religious interest, or historical or special social interest." And furthermore, the publication would attempt to be as fair as it had been "in the criticism of books and plays."[80] This equation of the movies with literature and the legitimate theater was a definite step forward.

The most eloquent praise of the film as the "democratic art" appeared in 1915, when the poet Vachel Lindsay published his volume *The Art of the Moving Picture,* a paean to the plastic art that aroused both controversy and praise.[81] In his analysis of the medium, Lindsay noted that his "platform" was based on the premise that "The Motion Picture Art is a Great High Art, Not a Process of Commercial Manufacture." His stated aim was to "convince" three important cultural groups of this fact. These were: (1) the great art museums of America and all their patrons, students, organizers; (2) the departments of English, of drama, and art history in all American universities; and (3) the critical and literary world generally. Lindsay continued sardonically: "Somewhere in this enormous field, piled with endowments mountain high, it should be possible to establish the theory and practice of the photoplay as a fine art."[82]

The Art of the Moving Picture was in many ways an unsatisfactory document, in that Lindsay's analogies tended to be esoteric and unclear, and it is doubtful that it made any serious contribution to furthering the aesthetic appreciation of films or film criticism.[83] The book did, however, receive a significant amount of publicity. The importance of the volume lay in its "aggressive confidence" about the future of the medium as a "people's art." Lindsay was particularly anxious to defend the film against the criticisms of those theatrical critics who berated the new entertainment as being merely an inferior extension of the stage. He called for the development of a cinematic art separated from the stage, for only in this way could the full potential of the motion picture be achieved. Comparing the stage and the screen he noted that "the Supreme photoplay will give us things that have been but half expressed in all other mediums allied to it."[84] Lindsay also noticed that while the two forms of entertainment could continue to "live in each other's sight in fine and friendly contrast," the situation at present was that "they are in blind and jealous warfare."[85]

While Vachel Lindsay's role in giving to the film a mantle of "respectability" in the intellectual-academic community cannot be ignored, nevertheless, historians of the movies continue to disagree about the importance of his influence. Terry Ramsaye's assessment was that Lindsay's contribution was slight — "capable for its day and pleasant, but neither professing nor possessing penetration."[86] Kenneth MacGowan considered Lindsay to have "gone overboard in praising it [the film] as a pictorial art, and analyzing it into categories."[87] Paul Rotha, however, considered him to have been one of the "pioneers in discovering aesthetic virtues in the primitive films of the early century,"[88] while Lounsbury noted that "Lindsay's terminology now seems crude, but it served the valuable function of bestowing identity on a relatively new art form. . . ."[89]

The concept of the motion picture as the "democratic art" received a great deal of attention in the United States, but the realization of this dream was never achieved through the commercial film industry; perhaps it was unrealistic to have expected it in the first place. The experience in Soviet Russia, where the motion picture became an ideological arm of the government, was that the relationship between the state, the film makers, and the audience was always a tenuous one based on compromise. This conscious attempt to create a "people's art" was not a success and John Rimberg in his examination of the Soviet film industry has indicated that production declined whenever the state pressured for greater political content.[90] In America, however, Hollywood felt that it had an accurate gauge of the public's desires, and judging from the success of its product, both domestically and in foreign markets, it was difficult to argue with the industry's position. The use of the motion picture by the American people as a true "art of the masses" would have to wait until the development and perfection of inexpensive equipment, capable of greater mobility. A major stumbling block was the strong grip the commercial industry held on public taste, for this was enough to prevent widespread popular interest in an alternative product of a more "experimental" nature. Film appreciation societies, and other groups dedicated to fostering the elevation of the medium as an artistic expression of American democratic principles, never made much impression on the content preferences of the industry or the public. Even film critics, who had done much to give the motion picture some cultural recognition, were seldom able to influence the tastes of the audience or the quality of the product.

The majority of the American people enjoyed the slick, stylized commercial offerings featuring popular stars, even though these were conventional and "middle class." Where the movies did succeed was in providing cheap and accessible entertainment geared to the new urban life-style of a large segment of the American population. This in itself was sufficient to ensure the industry's growth.

The Movies in Print

In the period before 1907 the motion picture was all but ignored in the periodical press. This is somewhat strange considering the tremendous popularity the entertainment had already achieved. However, after 1907, when the whole issue of the effect on the nation, and especially on the malleable minds of the young, came to the fore, the movies suddenly became an important topic. The first attempts at censorship served to accelerate this interest.

Prior to 1907, a close examination of the print media reveals little real interest in motion pictures, except as a "scientific curiosity." *Scientific American* and *Popular Mechanics* were among the only publications that recognized the important possibilities in the moving picture and, as Grau pointed out, they "revealed to the layman persistently almost every development, illustrating the articles appropriately and presenting the text in non-technical language."[91] However, this interest was essentially in the mechanics of the apparatus, and not in the development of the industry or the consequences for American society.

After 1908, publications like *Literary Digest* summarized the activities of the film industry from the trade press, and the larger urban newspapers began to give the phenomenon some notice — but little advertising! Publications such as *Harper's*, the *Atlantic*, the *Independent*, the *Dial*, the *Saturday Evening Post*, and *Scribner's* also featured occasional articles on the "motion picture craze." Eventually the growing complexity of the industry itself, and the need for more professional information, led to the development of trade publications, the first of which was *Views and Film Index*, which appeared in 1906. This was soon followed by *Moving Picture World* and *Moving Picture News*, which established the basic format containing reports of camera and projection equipment, of competition among manufacturers and legal arguments over patent rights. The next development in the motion picture literature was the acceptance of film advertising and news items by such publications as *Billboard, Variety*, and the *New York Dramatic Mirror*. These last publications even began to provide brief "reviews" of new films as a service to their newly acquired film trade readership.[92]

The change in the press's attitude after 1908 was as dramatic as that in the medium itself, and the movies and all their facets became so popular that many newspapers in the United States, in small and large cities, started full-page departments devoted to motion picture news and advertising. In 1914, Robert Grau, who was intimately acquainted with the value of publicity, observed of these newspapers that "in many . . . more space is given over to motion pictures than to opera, drama, and vaudeville combined, while in the majority of the smaller cities the newspapers used syndicated matter. . . ."[93] Kenneth MacGowan recollected that in 1915 he was made editor of an eight-page amusement tabloid included in the *Philadelphia Public Ledger*, which carried advertising for well over fifty movie theaters.[94] Surprisingly, New York was the last of the large cities to have major coverage of the motion picture, and not until 1914 did any of the dailies inaugurate regular film pages.[95] The motion picture had, however, begun to receive a great deal of attention by 1912, and the entertainment medium and its "stars" quickly became a major source of news and interest for the American public.[96]

The "Birth of a Nation" Controversy

In the period before World War I both the accusers and the defenders of the motion picture thrashed about for evidence to support their conflicting views. Where such evidence was lacking, as indeed it was in most cases, they relied upon "instinctual" feelings about what they thought the motion picture was doing, or capable of doing, to the American public. Occasionally, however, certain significant incidents would occur to lend credence to all the misgivings voiced by reformers. Just such an occasion was furnished by the dramatic events precipitated by the exhibition of D. W. Griffith's great film masterpiece *The Birth of a Nation* in 1915.[97] Certainly, no single cinematic event in this early period did more to emphasize to the movie's detractors and defenders the power wielded by the medium than the furor surrounding the release of this film.

Griffith's personal interpretation of the Reconstruction period in American history had been adapted from Thomas Dixon, Jr.'s popular, if crude, novel *The Clansman*. The film was not only the first of the "great" American motion picture epics, but was also one of the first to deal with a social issue of national importance — the role of the Negro in American society.

While it remains difficult to accurately assess the impact of this film in altering public attitudes toward the Negro, the mere existence of the film was sufficient to cause an uproar, attesting more to the influential powers ascribed to the cinematic medium than to the actual content of the film itself. It is of significance to note that the publication of Dixon's book had caused no outcry whatsoever (except from the literary critics), although it was widely read. Most of the controversy associated with the film stemmed from Griffith's portrayal of the Negro with all the usual stereotypes — lazy, shiftless, sexually immoral, rapacious, and so on. It was the fear that the mass dissemination of this image through the potent visual medium would undo years of patient struggle that aroused organized opposition to the exhibition of the film.

In his excellent biography of Griffith, Robert M. Henderson notes that it is difficult to understand through contemporary eyes what the fuss was all about. However, to an audience still relatively unsophisticated in the power of the visual experience, the ingredients put together by Griffith must have had a powerful effect. Henderson suggests:

It is a film of emotional excess with the immediacy of the close-up. The same situation would have less impact on a remote theatre stage. Griffith played on the fears of his white audience, appealed to their prejudices, and perpetuated the Southern myth of Reconstruction that had grown since the 1890's. Above all Griffith showed that an audience would accept fiction as reality. Griffith also demonstrated that an audience became most involved with the "truth" of a motion picture when they were involved in the lives of "real" people.[98]

Within four days of the opening of the film in 1915, the National Association for the Advancement of Colored People announced in the *New*

York Times that they intended to wage a fight to have the film either stopped or censored.[99] The film, however, was an immediate box-office and critical success, with tickets selling for two dollars on Broadway, where it stayed for a "solid" forty-four weeks.[100] In New York City it was estimated that over 825,000 people saw the film in 1915.[101]

When *The Birth of a Nation* was first exhibited in Boston, ten days after its run had begun a crowd estimated at three thousand marched to the capitol of Massachusetts and demanded that exhibition of the film be stopped. President Charles E. Eliot of Harvard charged the film "with a tendency to perversion of white ideals," while Jane Addams was "painfully exercised over the exhibition." Film historian Terry Ramsaye pointed out that "the roaring denunciations from the high places sent the whole public to the theatre to see what the row was about."[102] (Thus further reinforcing the Hollywood adage, "there is no such thing as 'bad' publicity!") Griffith himself responded to the outcry by publishing at his own expense a booklet entitled *The Rise and Fall of Free Speech in America,* in which he attempted to uphold the right of the screen to freedom of speech, a right which the Supreme Court of the United States would emphatically deny to the medium in the same year. Griffith's next major film was pointedly entitled *Intolerance!*

Lewis Jacobs in his history of the American film has noted of this incident that "the raging controversy awakened the nation to the social import of moving pictures. But this realization was overshadowed by the great acclaim for the picture's artistry, its rich imagery and powerful construction."[103] Other opinions were harsher; writing retrospectively in 1949, Seymour Stern suggested that "it cannot be denied that the effect of *The Birth of a Nation* on Negro-white relations was prolonged and damaging in the extreme."[104] The film nevertheless was a benchmark, not only in the development of American cinematic art, but also in the public acknowledgment of the motion picture as an important influence on American society and culture.

NOTES TO CHAPTER IV

1. W. P. Lawson, "The Miracle of the Movie," *Harper's Weekly,* January 2, 1915, pp. 7–9. Lawson estimated the capital invested in the movie industry to be over $500 million; with 250,000 employees; 1914 receipts to December 1 were $319 million. (These figures appear to be somewhat inflated.)

2. For a detailed examination of the relationship between the moving picture and the mind of the Progressives see Myron O. Lounsbury, " 'Flashes of Lightning': The Moving Picture in the Progressive Era," *Journal of Popular Culture,* vol. 3, no. 4 (1970), pp. 769–797. This is a brilliant examination of the imagery that emerged with the introduction of the motion picture and the resulting changes in the social and cultural system.

3. Wiebe, *The Search for Order*, p. 133. This book also contains a fine analysis of the breakdown of individualized community structure and the emergence of a new, more centralized society in America during the period 1875–1920.

4. *Ibid.*

5. *Ibid.*, p. 129.

6. The best study of the transformation of education in the United States, and the incorporation of progressive ideals, is Lawrence A. Cremin, *The Transformation of the School* (New York: Random House, Vintage Books, 1964).

7. Quoted in Cremin, p. 117.

8. *Ibid.*, p. 118.

9. There are two fine histories of the social work profession, both of which examine the settlement house movement: Allen F. Davis, *Spearheads for Reform* (New York: Oxford University Press, 1967); and Roy Lubove, *The Professional Altruist* (Cambridge: Harvard University Press, 1965).

10. Wiebe, p. 169.

11. Lubove, p. 38.

12. Jane Addams, *The Spirit of Youth and City Streets* (New York: Macmillan Company, 1909), pp. 75–76.

13. *Ibid.*, p. 76.

14. *Ibid.*, p. 77.

15. She specifically cites two stories: one involving a robbery and murder, with a ten-year-old boy avenging his father's death; the other involving a robbery and murder of a Chinese laundryman by two young boys in order to feed their starving mother and younger sister. This last murder, Miss Addams claimed, ended with "a prayer of thankfulness for this timely and heaven-sent assistance." Addams, pp. 78–80.

16. *Ibid.*, p. 86.

17. *Ibid.*, p. 103.

18. Edward H. Chandler, "How Much Children Attend the Theatre," *Proceedings of the Child Conference for Research and Welfare* (New York: G. E. Stechert and Co., 1909), p. 55.

19. The study revealed that nearly every child between ten and fourteen attended movies occasionally. Over 10 percent of them went as often as once a week. These studies indicated that one prime reason for the popularity of the movies was the low admission price, in contrast to the "live" theater. Regarding the effects of the films themselves, the consensus seemed to be that they had a decidedly negative influence on both boys and girls. Chandler's remedy for the "problem of the motion picture" was seen strictly in terms of pressure exerted at the local level. Specifically his suggestions were, first, a change in the conception of the child's amusement requirements toward more "self-directed" activities. Second, while recognizing that improvements had been made in regulating the content of films, he advocated that parents and teachers should exercise a censorial function because "mental and moral contagion are far more fatal than physical contagion." Last, he suggested the establishment of a proper form "of public dramatic amusement for children."

20. Edward H. Chandler, "The Moving Picture Show," *Religious Education*, October, 1911, p. 345.

21. *Ibid.*, p. 347.

22. *Ibid.*, p. 348.

23. John Collier, "The Motion Picture," *Proceedings of the Child Conference for Research and Welfare* (New York: G. E. Stechert and Co., 1910), p. 108.

24. *Ibid.*, p. 109.

25. With a rather devious bit of logic — the precursor of the industry's credo, "We give the public what they want" — Collier pointed out, "Whether or not you accept my assurances that motion pictures are the cleanest form of theatrical amusement in our country, you will admit that the nature of its audience here pointed out must tend to make it wholesome and clean." There is, in fact, very little evidence to substantiate his contention that audiences were largely family groups. Collier, "The Motion Picture," p. 109.

26. He estimated that in 1910, between 500,000 and 600,000 children attended picture shows every day in the U.S. However, he also noted that the motion picture was only one of the influences that "play upon the child," and that children were being over-protected from the normal process of socialization. Collier, "The Motion Picture," p. 115.

27. Grau, *Theatre of Science*, p. 89.

28. William Healy, *The Individual Delinquent* (Boston: Little, Brown and Co., 1915), p. 307.

29. *Ibid.*, p. 308.

30. Donald R. Young, *Motion Pictures: A Study in Social Legislation* (Philadelphia: Westbrook Publishing Company, 1922; reprinted New York: Jerome S. Ozer, 1971), p. 6.

31. "Movie Manners and Morals," *Outlook,* July 26, 1916, p. 694.

32. *Ibid.*, p. 695.

33. Editorial in the *Independent*, March 17, 1910, pp. 591–593.

34. Ray Leroy Short, "A Social Study of the Motion Picture" (M.A. thesis, Iowa State University, 1916), p. 11.

35. Hugo Munsterberg, *The Photoplay: A Psychological Study* (1915; reprinted New York: Dover Publications, 1970). For an excellent and detailed examination of Munsterberg's work in film theory, see Donald L. Frederickson, "The Aesthetic of Isolation in Film Theory: Hugo Munsterberg" (Ph.D. dissertation, University of Iowa, 1973).

36. *Ibid.*, p. 99.

37. *Ibid.*

38. *Ibid.*, p. 95.

39. *Ibid.*

40. *Ibid.*

41. *Ibid.*, p. 96.

42. *Ibid.*, p. 97.

43. *Ibid.*, introduction by Richard Griffith, p. ix.

44. *Ibid.*

45. Editorial in the *Dial,* February 16, 1914, pp. 129–130.

46. William Dean Howells, "The Editor's Easy Chair," *Harper's,* September, 1912, pp. 634–637.

47. *Ibid.*, p. 637.

48. Frederic C. Howe, "Leisure for the Millions," *Survey,* vol. 31 (1914), pp. 415–416.

49. For more information on the "school center movement," see Davis, pp. 76–83.

50. *Ibid.*, p. 82.

51. Charles Stelzle, "Movies Instead of Saloons," *Independent,* February 28, 1916, p. 311.

52. Andrew Sinclair, *Era of Excess* (New York: Harper Colophon Books, 1962), p. 320. This study gives important information on the motivation of the temperance reformers, and has much bearing on the subject of pressure for motion picture reform.

53. Stelzle, p. 311.

54. Vachel Lindsay, *The Art of the Moving Picture* (1915; reprinted New York: Liveright Publishing Company, 1970), p. 235.

55. *Ibid.*, p. 236.

56. *Ibid.*, p. 242.

57. *Ibid.*, pp. 243–244.

58. Carl Holliday, "The Motion Picture and the Church," *Independent*, February 13, 1913, pp. 353–356.

59. Joseph R. Gusfield, *Symbolic Crusade* (Urbana: University of Illinois Press, 1963), p. 101.

60. This does not mean that there was no connection or interchange between the audience for the motion picture and the patron of the saloon; however, in this early period there is little evidence to support the claims of proponents of the movie houses. There is strong indication that Prohibition did have a positive influence on movie attendance in the 1920s. This is developed in chapter 8.

61. Rev. Herbert A. Jump, "The Child's Leisure Hour — How it Is Affected by the Motion Picture," *Religious Education*, October, 1911, pp. 349–354.

62. Fulk, "The Effect on Education and Morals of the Moving Picture Shows," pp. 456–461.

63. The *Survey*, September 6, 1913, p. 684.

64. *Ibid.*, p. 691.

65. Henry W. Lanier, "The Educational Future of the Moving Picture," *American Review of Reviews*, December, 1914, pp. 725–729.

66. Don Carlos Ellis and Laura Thornborough, *Motion Pictures in Education* (New York: Thomas Y. Crowell Company, 1925), pp. 17–20. Because this study will not deal with the documentary film, except where it touches upon the development of the commercial motion picture, the use of motion pictures by the U.S. government and other agencies will not be examined in any detail. The full history of such governmental use is found in Richard Dyer MacCann, *The People's Films*.

67. Holliday, pp. 353–356.

68. Henry A. Atkinson, *The Church and People's Play* (Boston: Pilgrim Press, 1915), p. 137.

69. *Ibid.*, p. 138.

70. *Ibid.*, pp. 202–203.

71. Lounsbury, " 'Flashes of Lightning,' " p. 777.

72. George E. Walsh, "Moving Picture Drama for the Multitude," *Independent*, February 6, 1908, pp. 306–310.

73. "The Drama of the People," editorial in the *Independent*, September 29, 1910, pp. 713–715.

74. Joseph Medill Patterson, "Nickelodeons," *Moving Picture World and View Photographer*, May 4, 1907, p. 149.

75. Patterson, "The Nickelodeons," *Saturday Evening Post*, November 23, 1907, p. 10.

76. *Ibid.*, p. 11.

77. *Ibid.*, pp. 11–12.

78. Myron Lounsbury, *The Origins of American Film Criticism* (New York: Arno Press, 1973). This is the best source for an understanding of the development of critical attitudes toward the motion picture in America.

79. Lounsbury, " 'Flashes of Lightning,' " p. 780.

80. "The Birth of a New Art," *Independent*, April 6, 1914, pp. 8–9.

81. The best analysis of Lindsay's motion picture criticism is contained in Glen J. Wolfe, *Vachel Lindsay: The Poet as Film Theorist* (New York: Arno Press, 1973).

82. Lindsay, p. 45.

83. In characteristic fashion, Lindsay himself saw his book as having had a profound influence on the film industry. Wolfe has detailed Lindsay's thoughts on this issue on pp. 12–20.

84. Lindsay, p. 197.

85. *Ibid.*, p. 198.

86. Ramsaye, *A Million and One Nights*, p. viii.

87. MacGowan, *Behind the Screen*, p. 203.

88. Paul Rotha, *The Film Till Now* (London: Spring Books, 1949), p. 416.

89. Lounsbury, " 'Flashes of Lightning,' " pp. 783–784.

90. John Rimberg, *The Motion Picture in the Soviet Union, 1918–1952: A Sociological Analysis* (New York: Arno Press, 1973).

91. Grau, p. 232.

92. *Ibid.*, pp. 252–253.

93. *Ibid.*, p. 253. Also, Ramsaye has a whole section on what he calls the "Screen and Press Conspiracy," in which he details the use of serials in newspapers "dovetailed" with screen offerings. These were apparently very successful both in increasing newspaper circulation and in attracting patrons to movie houses. See pp. 656–669.

94. MacGowan, p. 184.

95. Grau, p. 236.

96. An interesting way to illustrate the growth of interest in motion pictures in the periodical press is to examine the number of articles listed in the *Reader's Guide to Periodical Literature*. Before 1905 the number of articles listed was minimal. The growth after 1905 is as follows:

PERIOD	NUMBER OF ARTICLES LISTED
1905–1910	33
1912–1915	249
1916–1918	381
1925–1928	500 approximately
1932–1935	640 approximately

97. The best account of this incident is Thomas R. Cripps, "The Reaction of the Negro to the Motion Picture *Birth of a Nation*," *Historian*, vol. 25, (1963), pp. 344–362. For an excellent account of the continued fight against the showing of this film in one state see Goodwin Berquist and James Greenwood, "Protest Against Racism: 'The Birth of a Nation' in Ohio," *Journal of the University Film Association*, vol. 26, no. 3 (1974), pp. 39–44. The authors note that as a result of serious pressure from both white liberals and black organizations, backed by a sympathetic governor (Frank B. Willis), the film was officially banned from Ohio for two years.

98. Robert M. Henderson, *D. W. Griffith: His Life and Work* (New York: Oxford University Press, 1972), p. 158. This biography is an excellent account of Griffith's life and the influences on his work.

99. *New York Times*, March 7, 1915, p. 13.

100. Green and Laurie, *Show Biz*, p. 150.

101. Henderson, p. 160.

102. Ramsaye, pp. 643–644.

103. Lewis Jacobs, p. 178.

104. Seymour Stern, "The Birth of a Nation," *American Mercury*, March, 1949, p. 308.

V

The Movies Censored

AS EARLY AS 1894, the fledgling motion picture industry was embroiled in fighting threats of censorship. During the next sixty years the industry would devote a large part of its energy, and a great deal of money, to resisting all threats of censorship or other forms of legal restriction. While some of these battles were successful, many others were not, and in the end American film makers were never allowed to exercise the artistic freedom accorded to other forms of creative expression. Nor were they allowed to express ideas with the same degree of freedom from prior censorship as guaranteed by the Constitution to "the press." For this situation the industry was partly to blame, for it had chosen to be considered primarily a supplier of a consumer commodity, and not as part of the artistic community. As such its product was subjected to evaluative procedures essentially different from those applied to the stage, to books, to paintings, or even to still photography, all of which had a much more limited audience exposure.

The introduction of the motion picture, and its immediate popularity, was an important issue for those who were concerned with the changing standards of morality and shifts in social and cultural values. Obviously a part of the processes of urbanization and industrialization, the movies dramatically symbolized the diminishing power of localized control as a factor in American society. It was this reluctance to relinquish control over their own lives, and especially the lives of their children, that motivated many individuals and groups to agitate against the medium's pervasive influence in the community. These various fears, which we have already examined, brought together many diverse groups in their opposition to the motion picture. Collectively they had one basic aim — greater control over the content of this visual product then being consumed in such large quantities throughout America. While each group formed its own ideas about the most functional role for the movies and how this could be best achieved, they all agreed that the first step was to place the medium under more stringent control, and to make it more responsive to local standards of morality.

The struggle over motion picture censorship took place on three different political levels — local or municipal government; state government; and in the halls of Congress. Each of these three levels of political control became directly involved in the regulation of motion pictures, with the local and state governments concerning themselves with the problem of maintaining acceptable standards of morality for their immediate communities, while the federal government concentrated more on trade regulation and antitrust legislation. Despite the concentrated attacks on the industry, the imposition of complete federal censorship of motion picture content was never achieved, although there were several occasions when the industry had every reason to fear the worst. The "problem of the movies" was in the final analysis a struggle for local control, and it was here that the censorship battle would be fought the hardest.

The First Attempts at Motion Picture Censorship[1]

No sooner had the first prototypes of the movies been introduced than they were under attack for being "immoral and offensive to public taste." Even during its first month as a "peep show" the motion picture had found itself subjected to censorship and condemnation when, in 1894, Senator James A. Bradley, the well-known founder of Asbury Park, condemned the display of ankles shown by the Spanish dancer Carmencita in one of Edison's Kinetoscopes.[2] The first official court case involving a movie was *People v. Doris* in 1897, in which the presiding judge ruled that a pantomime of a bride's wedding night was "an outrage upon public decency."[3] This was but the forerunner of many such rulings as the long struggle for control of the content of the motion picture began.[4]

One of the favorite subjects for early film fans, especially in the parlors and arcades, was the "fight film," which showed the pugilistic talents of many of the top boxers of the day.[5] This exhibition of prizefighters as a popular public entertainment did not meet with unanimous approval and ultimately proved to be an important obstacle in gaining respectability for the new medium. The *New York Times* in 1897 stated its position on these films quite clearly:

It is not very creditable to our civilization perhaps that an achievement of what is now called the "veriscope" that has attracted and will attract the wildest attention should be the representation of the prizefight. Moralists may deplore the fact that the fight in question "sold more extras" than would a presidential election. But they will have to eradicate a great deal of human nature before they can alter it.[6]

The continued interest in prizefight films eventually resulted in federal legislation to prevent the interstate transportation of such films.

However, it was not until the motion picture houses had become an accepted feature of the urban scene that the first official attempt was made to place the movies under a form of permanent local control. In 1907, an editorial appeared in the *Chicago Tribune* which attacked the city's motion picture houses. This editorial noted of the current films then being exhibited:

[They are] . . . without a redeeming feature to warrant their existence . . . ministering to the lowest passions of childhood . . . proper to suppress them at once . . . should be a law absolutely forbidding entrance of boy or girl under eighteen . . . influence is wholly vicious. . . . There is no voice raised to defend the majority of five-cent theatres, because they cannot be defended. They are hopelessly bad.[7]

At this time Chicago already had 116 nickelodeons, 18 ten-cent vaudeville houses, and 19 penny arcades, peep and screen, showing motion pictures. The daily attendance at these shows was estimated at 100,000 patrons. The editorial triggered a barrage of comments — pro and con — on the worthiness of the new entertainment. Ramsaye cited a list of the films showing in Chicago at the time:[8]

Cupid's Barometer	*Old Man's Darling*
A Seaside Flirtation	*The Bigamist*
Beware, My Husband Comes	*Gaieties of Divorce*

Unfortunately, there is no indication of how these films compared in content with the stage melodrama or burlesque shows then available to Chicago entertainment seekers.

On May 2, Jane Addams, then active in Hull House, presented a resolution advising regulation rather than suppression of the picture theaters, but apparently to no avail, because on November 4, 1907, the Chicago City Council passed an ordinance of censorship which was to be effective on November 19 of that year. The ordinance empowered the general superintendent of police to issue permits for the exhibition of motion pictures. In a legal contest the ordinance was held valid in 1909 by the Supreme Court of Illinois, and yet later by the Supreme Court of the United States.[9] Chicago had taken the bold and somewhat "un-American" step of instituting official prior censorship, something no other medium of communication had been subjected to since the drafting of the Constitution.

New York City, where the largest number of motion picture houses and patrons were to be found, was not far behind Chicago in officially expressing its opinion on the moral safety of the new medium. In May, 1907, one theater proprietor was arraigned for showing *The Great Thaw Trial* to an audience "largely composed of children under fifteen."[10] In June, Mayor George B. McClellan received a rather condemnatory report from his police commissioner which recommended the cancellation of *all* licenses of nickelodeons and penny arcades. The issue then smoldered for eighteen months, while the movie houses became more and more ubiquitous and popular, and thus a greater source of social concern. Mayor McClellan, without much advance warning, called for a public hearing for the afternoon of December 23, 1908, to discuss in general the condition of movie theaters, and in particular the possibility of closing them all down. The mayor stated that he had received many complaints from clergymen, "who are indignant at some of the plots shown, and are protesting that they spread demoralization among the children. Many complain too that they keep children away from Sunday Schools. . . ."[11]

It was in connection with this incident that Canon William Sheafe Chase of Christ Church, Brooklyn, first appeared on the scene as one of the chief movers behind this crusade to "clean up" the movies, a cause to which he devoted the rest of his life. A group called the Interdenominational Committee for the Suppression of Sunday Vaudeville was also an interested party, as were several prominent Catholic clergymen.

The *New York Times* claimed that at this time there were eight hundred moving picture shows and fifty theaters in operation in New York on Sundays. There was obvious widespread public interest in the future of the motion picture, and this was confirmed by the fact that the meeting on the afternoon of December 23 was "one of the biggest public hearings ever held in City Hall." The mayor listened to arguments against the motion picture houses from clergymen of almost every denomination (Catholic groups, if present at this meeting, made no official statements), and Mr. Frank Moss of the Society for the Suppression of Vice gave evidence and made an elaborate case against the movies. The argument for the other side was vigorously presented by the theater owners and film manufacturers whose livelihoods were being threatened. It was Canon Chase, however, who drew most of the attention as he noted of the exhibitors that "these men who run these shows have no moral scruples whatever. They are simply in the business for the money there is in it." The newspaper accounts indicated that evidence was given (they did not say what kind) that motion picture shows encouraged degeneracy "and in some cases, actual crime." The major defense for the entertainment was offered by Mr. Charles Sprague Smith of the People's Institute, who expressed the view that there were other things in the city that needed cleaning up more than the picture shows, and this comment was greeted by wild applause from the gallery, only to be silenced by a stern admonition from the mayor. A letter was read from Bishop Greer, who said that the city was spending millions of dollars to take children from bad environments and yet it permitted them to be exposed "to material of this nature."[12]

During the hearing it became obvious that the New York motion picture house owners were willing to consider prior censorship along the lines of the Chicago model, but that they steadfastly refused to consider closing on Sundays, the day when they did the largest part of their total weekly business. The exhibitors were also willing to accept institution of stricter building code ordinances to cover their establishments. The film manufacturers, through their spokesman, J. Stuart Blackton of the Vitagraph Company, indicated that they would refrain from making "any disagreeable films" and would keep out foreign importations of this type. A petition signed by thousands of patrons of the movie houses had hastily been put together and was presented to the hearing. The *Times* noted that the entire hearing went on for over five hours.[13]

What process of logic or legality Mayor McClellan used to arrive at his decision is not known. However, his order to close all movie houses in the city of New York, made public on December 24, was of enough importance to receive the first front-page mention of motion pictures in the *New York Times,* when on December 25 the headline read, "Picture Shows all put out of Business." The article detailed the mayor's decision to revoke the license of every movie house in New York City, and the newspaper estimated that a total of 550 such establishments would be affected by the order. The mayor gave as his main reason for this unprecedented action the safety hazards present in the movie houses and theaters, citing as proof an affidavit to this effect presented by the chief of the fire department. The Bureau of Licenses was ordered to inspect every site making reapplication and report "directly" to the mayor, while these new licenses were to be issued only on condition that the licensees agreed in writing to close on Sundays. The mayor also threatened to revoke the licenses of all exhibitors who exhibited films "which tend to degrade or injure the morals of the community." A letter from the mayor's office to the chief of police ordering him to "read the Mayor's notice to all managers regarding Sunday operations" was released to the newspapers, together with the statement that prosecutions would begin immediately. (It was never made clear who was to be prosecuted and for what reason.)[14]

The result of the mayor's precipitous action was absolute and total confusion throughout the motion picture and vaudeville industries, and no one knew or understood exactly what would happen next, how it was going to happen, what the legality of the mayor's actions was, and if the proposed regulations could actually be enforced. From this morass of indecision and legal entanglements it was finally made clear that only the five-cent theaters would be affected, and not the ten-cent shows. (The reasons for this were interesting: the ten-cent houses received their licenses from the police commissioner, and paid $150 a year; while the five-cent houses received their licenses directly from the mayor's marshal, and paid only $25 a year. The five-cent theaters had to have a seating capacity of less than 300 patrons to qualify for the lower license fee.)[15]

The industry's reaction was predictable, and a mass meeting of theater owners and film producers was called with producer William Fox in charge. Fox told the assembled group that the industry's investment, now in jeopardy, exceeded $50,000,000 and that 40,000 people (employees and families) would be directly affected by the closing of the motion picture houses.[16] At this meeting, held at the Murray Hill Lyceum, a "committee of thirty" was formed, and it was agreed that their lawyer, Gustavus A. Rogers, was to seek an injunction against the mayor's actions. An injunction restraining the mayor from any further actions against the movie houses was subsequently obtained on Saturday, December 26, from Justice Gaynor. The *Times* in reporting this whole affair noted that the Interdenominational Committee of the Clergy of Greater New York wrote a letter thanking the mayor for his prompt action in the matter.[17]

This New York fiasco was the first and last serious attempt to bring about a total legal restriction of the motion picture industry in any one locality. The failure to impose more stringent controls, and the strength of public support for the exhibitors, indicated that the mayor and the religious and other pressure groups behind the action had grossly underestimated the importance of the motion picture house as a recreational activity for the ordinary people of New York City. The aldermen did, however, pass an ordinance on January 6, 1909, that barred children under sixteen from motion picture houses unless accompanied by an adult. This law proved to be almost impossible to enforce successfully. The theater owners even cheated by employing "surrogate" parents to escort children into the theaters. It also took several more years of bickering before the city council would pass meaningful laws regarding the physical conditions of the picture houses.

Local or Municipal Censorship

The first form of official and continuous motion picture censorship was the result of the ordinance passed by the Chicago City Council in 1907 requiring police inspection and licensing of all films that were shown in that city. The police chief was given the authority to withhold a permit if in his judgment the film was "immoral" or "obscene." This law was tested in the Illinois Supreme Court in 1909 in the case of *Block v. Chicago,* the first movie censorship controversy to be adjudicated in the courts.[18] Professor Richard Randall in his study of film censorship has noted that the court agreed that the purpose of the ordinance was to "secure decency and morality in the motion picture business," and that the standards of "immoral" and "obscene" were adequate, since "the average person of healthy and wholesome mind" knew what the words meant.[19]

City or municipal censorship of motion pictures in various forms became the most common type of control in use in the United States. Those cities in the home-rule states had the power to establish local boards of censorship. Even where cities were incorporated under general charter, the authority granted was broad enough to authorize cities to pass general censorship ordinances. In some states, such as Louisiana, power to establish censorship was delegated specifically to the cities.[20] Thus, although many states established full or partial forms of censorship, many cities continued to exercise their options for more localized control.

Relatively few cities, however, took advantage of their legal powers to enact censorship legislation. In his 1929 survey, Ford H. MacGregor estimated that less than 100 of 2,500 incorporated cities of over 2,500 population in the United States provided censorship boards or officials.[21] An examination of these cities reveals no discernible pattern or common reason for their having chosen to adopt municipal motion picture censorship. They ranged in size from Green Bay, Wisconsin, to Chicago, Illinois; from Pasadena, California, in the West to Washington, D.C., in the East; and from Worchester, Massachusetts, in the North to Birmingham, Alabama, in the South. Their administrations covered almost the entire spectrum of city government styles. Chicago was the first to adopt censorship in 1907, while Portland, Oregon, waited until 1923 to introduce a comprehensive censorship package. This wide range indicated the pervasiveness of the medium and the importance of the problem of movie control to communities of all sizes. Further, the need for local censorship seemed to be an urban phenomenon, rather than a rural one, and there is no evidence of any American county ever being given or exercising the authority to enact county-wide censorship laws.

Cities organized censorship activities in three patterns, usually instituting only one, but sometimes a combination of two or all three, of these regulatory practices:

(1) In the great majority of cases the inspection duties were left to the police department. The police usually acted only upon complaint, and seldom upon their own initiative; and police standards seldom meant

rigid censorship. In some cities the mechanism for police control required the securing of a permit which necessitated showing every film meant for public exhibition to police officers. Chicago used this method very successfully for several years. In other cities policewomen did the previewing inspections, but there were few cities willing to allocate full-time police staff for these duties.

(2) A variation on this form of regulation was the appointment of censorship boards within police departments or other inspection bureaus specifically to examine motion pictures. Los Angeles in 1917 created the Office of Commissioner of Films; Quincy, Illinois, in 1913 created a board of five inspectors known as Motion Picture Theater Inspectors; while the City of Birmingham, Alabama, passed an ordinance in 1921 regulating amusements, including motion pictures, and creating the office of City Amusement Inspector.[22]

(3) The third form was the formal creation of a board of city censors, sometimes acting under the police department, and consisting of regularly appointed officers assigned to this special duty and responsible to the mayor for their work. The Kansas City Office of Censor of Films and Pictures, established in 1913, was one of the first of this type of municipal office. Seattle passed an ordinance in 1915 creating an advisory committee of nine members to enforce its censorship regulations. While other large cities all across America followed, the "local censorship" movement was by no means a universally accepted one.

The creation of suitable legislation to control motion picture houses was a difficult problem which tested all the skills of the new class of professional city administrators. These early theaters were a motley assortment and ranged widely in quality. Existing local regulations were unsuitable for handling these new phenomena and more specific ordinances had to be passed, mostly in the face of strong opposition from the exhibitors and landlords, who resented any interference. On the other side were the vociferous critics of the medium's current "freedom," anxious to see it brought under stricter local control and subject to local standards of morality.

New York City's problems were typical of those faced by other urban centers in America, except that there were far more theaters to bring under regulation. Between 1909 and 1913 the city had struggled to enact effective motion picture regulations without success. John Collier, the secretary of the National Board of Censorship, noted in 1913 that "no American city has yet regulated its motion picture shows in a scientific way, and any attempt to do so runs counter both to thoughtless prejudice and powerful special interests."[23] He pointed out that at this time there were over 800 motion picture theaters in New York City alone, and approximately 16,000 in the entire United States. The total daily audience was estimated to be over 400,000 in New York City, and 7,000,000 in the whole country.[24]

The New York City Council finally enacted the first comprehensive municipal law in the United States for the regulation of motion picture theaters on August 12, 1913. The history behind these regulations is indicative of the difficulties encountered in the integration of a new mass medium or mass entertainment into the existing social and legal structure. Following Mayor McClellan's failure to control the movies in 1909, very little was accomplished officially until Mayor Gaynor in 1911 instructed his commissioner of accounts, Raymond Fosdick, to make an examination of the whole theater scene. (Ironically, Gaynor had been the judge who issued the injunction against Mayor McClellan's censorship order.) Fosdick's report to the mayor indicated that several major problem areas existed: (1) the lack of definite laws and uniform regulations to control the new "business"; (2) the presence in the building code of a section virtually restricting the moving picture industry to small, store-front shows (this was the infamous "299 seat" capacity ruling for "common shows"); and (3) the lack of centralized control by the existing municipal authorities.

Following the report, a special commission was appointed by the mayor to draft a law based on Fosdick's findings and recommendations. It took three years, however, for the passage of an ordinance through the city council.[25] The opposition came from the vaudeville interests, from the theaters, from the small exhibitors, and also from those who favored a stricter form of prior censorship — a group with decidedly mixed interests, having in common only their opposition to this particular piece of legislation. Tammany Hall agreed with the special interests and insisted on attaching a prior-censorship clause. As a result the mayor argued that the proposed legislation was unconstitutional and vetoed the whole ordinance. In stating his opposition to prior censorship, Gaynor observed that "the criminal law is ample to prevent the exhibition of such pictures," and he insisted upon the retention of the original ordinance.[26] Finally, with some compromises, the ordinance was passed late in 1913, and covered such items as lighting, ventilation, heating, standing room, fire regulations, unobstructed exits, and so forth. An important provision was the elimination of vaudeville in movie houses "because of the fire hazard of the scenery." The law also provided for regular inspection of movie houses and centered all responsibilities within the licensing bureau.[27]

The local censorship of motion pictures was viewed as both the best and the worst form of censorship. In 1916, one writer commented that the chief criticism against city censors was that "their standards are provincial, narrow, and lack uniformity."[28] A second objection came from the film producers, who for obvious reasons did not want any sort of interference with their finished product. They were particularly incensed at the large number of local variations in regulations, which made it impossible to foretell what changes should be made during production to comply with the accepted community standards. Because of this, the film industry was forced to engage in costly reediting to conform to every local variation in censorship criteria.

It was often rumored that some film makers, in hopes of avoiding the large number of costly changes, actually favored the introduction of standardized and thus national federal regulation. However, the only real evidence for this is contained in Ellis P. Oberholtzer's book *The Morals of the Movie* (1922). Oberholtzer, a noted historian and also a prominent member of the Pennsylvania Board of Censors, claimed that the agents of the Famous Players and Lasky companies had indicated their support for a proposed federal motion picture regulation bill in 1916. He provided a quote from their statement:

While the idea of censorship of motion pictures is distasteful to our clients as well as to others in the business, our support of the principle of regulations embodied in the bill before you is due to our realization of unfavorable conditions in the industry, which cannot be corrected by ordinary means, or by sporadic and occasional criminal prosecutions. . . . The motion picture business, now of vast financial importance, has had a mushroom growth and is not yet homogeneous and standardized.

. . . Unfortunately the public is not yet discriminating, and goes to see both bad and good. . . . This state of affairs constitutes a temptation hard to resist, and, in fact, the production of vicious pictures is constantly increasing. . . . If the industry is to endure, if decent people are to stay in the business, this cancer must be cut out. *A Federal regulatory commission should prove a fearless surgeon and we, therefore, favor such a commission.*[29]

There is every indication that local censorship boards, once established, were generally ineffective or otherwise failed to carry out their duties. Oberholtzer in his examination of American censorship boards commented that "only in Chicago and in two or three smaller cities is the control sincere and effective."[30] Certainly the conditions under which films were changed almost daily, and schedules were altered to take advantage of current events, did not lend itself to effective surveillance on such a small territorial unit. The Smith-Hughes bill to establish a federal motion picture commission, presented to Congress in 1916, made this failure of local censorship a major argument in support of federal control. Also in 1916, the Congressional Committee on Education noted:

The character of the motion picture industry renders state and municipal regulation inadequate. Motion picture films are essentially articles of interstate commerce. They are not manufactured for use in any one state or municipality, but practically every picture is exhibited in all of the states of the Union. Innumerable inspections by local boards work great hardships on the industry. . . . The only adequate method of regulating motion pictures is to be had in a Federal commission . . .[31]

There is almost no evidence or testimony in favor of local attempts at censorship, except for the support given to local efforts by the National Board of Review (see pages 130–132); but even here the N.B.R. was not in favor of official censorship boards and concentrated its activities in helping local "voluntary" citizen's groups. Donald R. Young in his examination of municipal regulation noted this failure and claimed: "However valuable local censorship is today, it cannot be regarded as anything final in motion picture legislation, but only as a stepping stone on the way to some better plan."[32] City censorship ultimately failed to provide the control demanded by most reform groups, and the industry had a legitimate case against the high costs incurred in trying to meet the numerous and often arbitrary local variations in standards. Even if the majority of city censorship boards did not function effectively, the continual threat which they implied, and occasionally exercised on specific films, was sufficient to cause the industry a great deal of discomfort.

State Censorship

It was at the state level that official censorship was the most effectively enforced, and therefore it was here that the industry chose to counterattack in the courts. The first state to legislate official censorship of motion pictures was Pennsylvania, which created a state board of censors in 1911.[33] No film could be sold, leased, lent or exhibited in the state until it had been submitted to and approved by this board of censors. The work of this pioneering board was closely watched and studied by other states, and its decisions served as paradigms for other state censorship boards. However, in their attack upon censorship in 1930, Morris J. Ernst and Pare Lorentz were less than enthusiastic about the work of the Pennsylvania board: "They accept no standards created by art, literature, drama, or even other censor boards. They work with a fury and an inconsistency that offer no clue as to what cause they purport to serve."[34]

The second of the state censorship boards was created in Ohio in 1913, and under the authority and supervision of the Industrial Commission this three-member panel existed until 1921. In that year the reorganization law transferred its powers and duties to the Division of Censorship of the Department of Education. The Ohio statute provided that "only such films as are, in the judgement and discretion of the board of censors, of a moral, educational, or amusing and harmless character shall be passed and approved by such board."[35] This particular board worked closely with industry interests, and was, in fact, created at the insistence of a number of motion picture men in the state.[36] The board set other precedents by cooperating with parent-teacher organizations, women's clubs, and other community organizations. MacGregor reported: "It emphasized the matter of the protection of children, which undoubtedly was one of the purposes in transferring the board to the Department of Education."[37]

Other states created similar boards with similar powers: Kansas in 1914; Maryland in 1916; New York and Virginia in 1922. Two states devised indirect forms of censorship: Massachusetts in 1921 passed a state censorship law which was defeated in a referendum (see pages 166–168), but in 1932 finally accomplished effective control in another way. This 1932 law forbade entertainments on Sunday unless a license was obtained from the mayor or the town council, and these were given only if the film had been approved by the commissioner of public safety of the commonwealth, which effectively prevented the showing of any undesirable films. (According to most reports this law was never strictly enforced by the state.)

Florida passed a unique law in 1921, which authorized the governor of the state to appoint three citizens of the state to be members of the National Board of Review. The law prohibited the exhibition in the state of any film for commercial purposes not approved by this board. State censorship bills were at one time introduced in many other states, including Iowa, Maine, Nebraska, South Dakota and Wisconsin, but all were defeated. (The Nebraska bill was approved, but vetoed by the governor.) The significance of state censorship lay in the extension of control over a viable territorial unit; one within which the industry could ostensibly alter its product without too much complaint. This distribution of state-censored films was facilitated by the operation of many movie theater chains on a statewide basis. However, the institution of official censorship legislation at this higher level of government did not augur well for the film makers, and almost immediately after state censorship first appeared they decided to challenge the concept of prior censorship in the courts.

The Supreme Court Decision of 1915

In the case of *Mutual Film Corporation v. Ohio*,[38] the United States Supreme Court handed down a decision that was to have far-reaching consequences for the young industry. In a unanimous decision, speaking through Justice McKenna, the Court dismissed the Detroit-based company's complaint against the Ohio prior-censorship law. The distributing company contended "that it was an invalid delegation of legislative power to the board of censors because it failed to set up precise standards, and that it violated the free speech guarantees of the Ohio Constitution and the First Amendment."[39] The Court considered the company's charges unsound and they were dismissed, while the First Amendment claim was ignored. The most important aspect of the decision was the Court's refusal to construe the Constitution of Ohio to include the motion picture medium. (Section 2 of Article 1 of the Ohio Constitution stipulated: "Every citizen may freely speak, write, and publish his sentiments on all subjects, being responsible for the abuse of the right; and no law shall be passed to restrain or abridge the liberty of speech, or of the press.")[40]

The Court therefore effectively relegated motion pictures to the same entertainment category as carnival sideshows. Their decision stated in part:

It cannot be put out of view that the exhibition of moving pictures is a business pure and simple, originated and conducted for profit, like other spectacles, not to be regarded, nor intended to be regarded as part of the press of the country or as organs of public opinion. They are mere representations of events, of ideas and sentiments published or known; vivid, useful, and entertaining, no doubt, but . . . capable of evil, having power for it, the greater because of their attractiveness and manner of exhibition.[41]

Professor Richard S. Randall has made the point that "once the Court found movies not to be speech, it was unnecessary to take up the claim of federal protection."[42] In fact the question of First Amendment protection was premature, for it was not then regarded as binding upon the states. It was only in 1925 that the decision handed down in *Gitlow v. New York* established the principle that the states must be mindful of the guarantees of free speech and press as set forth in the Constitution of the United States.

In searching for the underlying premises believed to be the most influential in the minds of the justices as they rendered their judgment, we can see three fundamental suppositions upon which the Court's verdict was based. All three are highly dubious and would not stand up today, but given the lack of maturity of the film industry and the critical attitude toward the motion picture evident in 1915, the justices' decision is understandable. First, the Court's view of the motion picture was as "a business pure and simple," which was conducted solely for the financial rewards to the industry. In fact, the test of whether speech was free or at a price had never previously been a measure of its censorability, yet it was precisely the commercial nature of the motion picture which was held against it.

The second dubious premise was the judgment that the motion picture was merely a spectacle such as carnival sideshows or circuses, and therefore was not subject to the protection of the free speech clauses in state constitutions. The basis for this judgment lies in the traditional judicial suspicion of the arts. The legitimate theater, especially in England, had suffered from similar arbitrary judicial decisions. Apparently the justices saw definite differences between the dissemination of ideas and the provision of entertainment. While it was obvious to the Court that the motion picture could be a medium for spreading ideas or education, in this judgment only its entertainment role was considered. The numerous expressions of the movies as the "salvation of democracy," or "the poor man's art" were never taken into account, although by 1915 this was a common sentiment. Professor Ira Carmen has also made the point that by this time the motion picture had in fact aptly demonstrated its ability to produce intellectually and aesthetically significant movies such as *The Birth of a Nation, Hamlet, The Life of Abraham Lincoln,* and *Quo Vadis* — a fact which the Court conveniently ignored.[43]

The third of the dubious suppositions is the most difficult to substantiate, but was potentially the most far-reaching in its implications. Much of the Court's hostility shown in the final verdict was predicated on the belief that this powerful new medium, if misused by unscrupulous, commercially minded men, possessed a "capacity for evil" against which every community should be given the right to legitimately shield itself. The decision therefore had a profound effect upon the industry and its relationship to the local community, for it was construed to mean that motion picture censorship was permissible under the Constitution, and many state courts would uphold similar censorship laws on these grounds. Thus the whole issue of prior censorship was given an aura of judicial approval. Obviously the Supreme Court of the United States was not yet sure of how to deal with a mass medium which manifested the appealing characteristics of the motion picture, and it therefore gave the most conservative decision possible under the circumstances. In all fairness to the justices it must be pointed out that very little was known at this time about the effect of the mass media in general, and the motion picture in particular, and the strong opposition to the entertainment medium already obvious in certain quarters must have had some residual influence on the Court. Certainly, the Supreme Court was not prepared to give free license to such an unknown factor. Unfortunately this decision, and the premises upon which it was based, would result in much abuse of the privilege of prior censorship, and eventually shift the focus from a concern for the public's morals to a concern for its social and political thought as well.

Federal Censorship and Regulation

Surprisingly enough the United States is one of the few countries that has never had any major form of internal national motion picture censorship. Nonetheless, the threat of federal censorship engaged the industry's constant attention and was the main reason for the appointment of the postmaster general of the Harding administration, Will Hays, to head up a unified industry organization in 1922. In fact, however, these threats, while seriously intended by individual legislators and groups, were seldom very close to implementation.

There were several federal statutes covering aspects of motion picture exhibition, such as those regulating obscene or pornographic films; prize-fight films (repealed in 1940); films depicting the wearing of a military uniform in such a way as to bring "discredit" to the armed forces; and the taxation of imported films. A proviso of the 1909 tariff schedule, after fixing the duty on imported films, noted: "All photographic films imported under this section shall be subject to such censorship as may be imposed by the Secretary of the Treasury."[44] However, this power was never really spelled out, and not until the passage of the Tariff Act of 1930, which authorized the Bureau of Customs to examine imported films, did the federal government become really active in this area.

It was to the federal government, however, that most reform groups eventually turned in their search for an effective means of controlling the motion picture industry. As early as 1915, a sufficient number of complaints had filtered through to Congress on the problem of motion picture control to cause Congressman D. M. Hughes of Georgia to introduce a bill to provide for the creation of a federal motion picture commission as a division of the Bureau of Education in the Department of the Interior. This commission was to be composed of five members appointed by the President for terms of six years, and was to be charged with examining, censoring and licensing all films before they could be admitted to interstate commerce.[45] No standards for judgment were set, except for the provision that the committee should license every film presented, unless it was shown that the film was ". . . obscene, indecent, immoral, inhuman, or depicts a bull fight, or prize fight, or is of such character that its exhibition would tend to impair the health or corrupt the morals of children or adults, or incite to crime."[46]

This Hughes bill, coming so soon after the furor caused by the release of D. W. Griffith's *The Birth of a Nation,* and the Supreme Court's important decisions on censorship, caught the attention of the industry and the concerned public. There were extensive hearings before the House Committee on Education, and after exhaustive briefs from both sides, the bill was defeated. The evidence offered at these hearings was based almost entirely upon personal opinion, and failed to substantiate the charges of "insidious influence" made against the medium. Between 1915 and 1921 several other bills embodying the same or similar provisions were introduced, all meeting with the same fate — but the pressure for federal intervention was obvious and continuous.

In 1920, a bill was presented to the House to prohibit "shipment, exhibition of moving picture films, purporting to show or stimulate the acts of ex-convicts, desperadoes, bandits, train robbers, bank robbers, or outlaws, and to prohibit the use of mails in carrying the same," and providing punishment for these offenses. Senator Gore of Tennessee also introduced a bill dealing principally with the importation and transportation of films purporting to show crime and criminals. Although these bills also failed to pass, the industry was forced to mount a strong countercampaign to avoid these threats of indirect censorship by federal control of the interstate shipments of films.

In 1921, the Federal Trade Commission issued a formal complaint against the Famous Players–Lasky Corporation and five other organizations, charging that "block-booking" as practiced by these organizations was a restraint on trade.[47] The significance of this charge was the connection made between "block-booking" and the "suspect content" of films, in that it was alleged that local exhibitors were being forced by this practice to accept all films listed on the contract, and were therefore unable to allow for variations in local tastes or standards. It was this contractual obligation, together with the rapidly developing producer-distributor-exhibitor integration, that was held to be largely responsible for the continued presentation of poor films in the face of growing public opposition. (The whole issue of antitrust legislation is examined in several other chapters.)

The Seabury Proposal

On occasion forms of federal control other than censorship were advocated as a means of forcing the industry to become more aware of its "responsibilities," and such was the "Seabury Proposal." William Marston Seabury, a man who had been the general counsel to the National Association of the Motion Picture Industry, and who therefore had an opportunity to closely observe the innermost workings of the film industry, wrote an important critical attack on its operations in 1926. Entitled *The Public and the Motion Picture Industry*, this book offered a stinging condemnation of the industry and its failure to make a more substantial contribution to American and international society. Seabury's work with the League of Nations had led him to conclude that "in reality the motion picture has become and is today the greatest force and instrument in the world for the cultivation and preservation of the world's peace and for the moral, intellectual and cultural development of all people."[48] It was this realization, and Seabury was not alone in publicly voicing such overzealous pronouncements, that led him to conclude that the industry was failing dismally to fulfill its duties and responsibilities under the existing Hollywood regime, and that only a "complete commercial renaissance" could revitalize the industry.

After a clear but detailed examination and summary of the current operations of the American film industry, Seabury put forward his proposal for making the motion picture more socially responsible:

Specifically the remedy in America must include an Act of Congress *which will declare the motion picture to be a new public utility* and the business of producing, distributing and exhibiting pictures to be charged with the obligation and duty to eliminate any debasing influences, and to articulate friendly relations with the people of another nation and to promote the moral, educational and cultural development of the people.[49]

Seabury, leaving nothing to chance, included a complete outline of his proposed act of Congress as an appendix in the book. In simple terms this act would involve both Congress and each of the states declaring the motion picture to be a "public utility," and then passing uniform laws to encourage the production of better films and for the protection of the public's morals. It is interesting to note that Seabury did not favor legal prior censorship; instead he felt that his plan would enable "existing local authorities to suppress the exhibition of pictures which clearly ought to be suppressed." He also recognized clearly the wide variation in accepted community standards and practices when he claimed that the local judicial authority was quite capable of reflecting "a sound and decent local opinion." He noted that although censorship currently existed in six states, and that there were many local censorship boards, they had failed to achieve the desired result, and that "years of study and experience have demonstrated that motion pictures cannot be bettered culturally or intellectually by law of any kind."[50]

The final phase of the Seabury Plan was to ensure the separation of three basic industry practices of production-distribution-exhibition to bring about the "commercial renaissance" of the entire industry, which he felt was the key to the whole plan. His analysis of block-booking practices was the most thorough then available, and clearly indicated that the motion picture industry was by no means a "free trade" commercial enterprise, but was tightly controlled by a small number of large studios which virtually dictated what the American public was allowed to see.

Seabury's plans went beyond the reformation of just the American film industry, for his outlook was decidedly internationalist and he showed great concern about the excessive influence of the American film in the world market. Through the League of Nations, Seabury proposed to set up an official agency to encourage international cooperation which would eventually revitalize the world film market. Each country would be induced to recognize the international importance of the motion picture, at which point the medium would at last be allowed to realize the latent potential it had been forced to hide because of "commercial exploitation." Seabury expressed the vain hope that "with the awakening of each nation to the truth that the business of producing and exhibiting pictures had become more than a mere commercial pursuit, each nation would become conscious of its new duties towards the industry within its borders, towards its own people, and towards other nations."[51] In some mysterious way, this process would lead to the subordination of "the efforts to obtain sordid profits" to that of promotion of the public's welfare, and the industry would then "be brought to serve the needs of the world to the extent of its limitless capacity."[52]

For all his good and somewhat optimistic intentions, Seabury's ideas were never taken seriously by anyone in the United States — in fact, the industry itself completely ignored him, and no official reply of any kind was ever made to his suggestion that the industry be made into a "public utility." Internationally, however, and especially in the League of Nations he was taken much more seriously, and he subsequently helped to raise the prestige of the motion picture division of the world body. During its brief existence the League did in fact do a great deal to foster the international use and exchange of films, forming an international institute specifically for that purpose in the late 1920s.

In the period prior to 1922, the threat of some form of federal censorship or control reared its head almost annually. There was, however, no evidence to indicate widespread public support of the legalized previewing of films on such a national scale. This form of social control was repugnant to most Americans, and such functions as the regulation of public morals and social standards had traditionally been left to the individual states, which in turn had delegated their authority to the local communities. Certainly, as long as local communities, cities and states could not agree among themselves on the criteria for suitable social standards for the motion picture, such far-reaching federal censorship was both undesirable and nonviable.

The National Board of Review

The most significant result of Mayor McClellan's attempt in 1907 to close the motion picture houses in New York City was the establishment of the National Board of Censorship (later to become the National Board of Review). The exhibitors had been made acutely aware of their vulnerability and were particularly sensitive to the criticisms aimed at the "quality" of their product. To alleviate the pressures from social and religious groups, Dr. Charles Sprague Smith, the founder and director of the People's Institute of New York, a citizen bureau of social research, was asked by representatives of the industry to organize a citizen's committee which would preview all motion pictures before they were shown in New York theaters. In March, 1909, this committee was formed in cooperation with the newly created Motion Picture Patents Company, and called itself the National Board of Censorship of Motion Pictures. The aim of the organization was not that of true "censorship," but, as Ramsaye indicated, " 'censorship' became a necessary word, because to satisfy the public and official mind of the day the naughty, naughty motion picture had to be spanked on the wrist."[53] The situation, however, was much more serious than Ramsaye seemed to feel, because opposition to the motion picture was growing and now came from all segments of society. Fortunately, it would be many years before these forces would combine in such a way as to force the producers to comply with their concept of what a "pure" motion picture industry should be, and in the meantime the National Board of Censorship began its task of creating a public voice in that industry.

The basic philosophy of the National Board was based on the principal that the motion picture screen had a right to the same First Amendment freedom accorded to all the other media. Because it was difficult to establish precisely what was "moral" or "immoral" the board relied on the concept that "where questions of taste and morals overlap that public opinion, which is the compound of all tastes and all ideas of morals is the only competent judge of the screen, and that there can be no popular functioning of public opinion unless freedom of the screen exists in order that the public may judge what shall be presented to it. . . ."[54] The mechanism established by the board to carry out its vast task was to engage a large number of volunteers, and a limited staff of paid workers for the routine duties. The original aim of the board was to "censor" all the films before they were shown in New York City, but in June, 1909, apparently at the request of the industry, the scope of its activities was broadened to include the entire continental United States. This mammoth undertaking could be accomplished only through the use of voluntary representatives in various sections of the country. The financing of this venture was recovered by requiring a "fee" from each film maker for "examining" his film, and "suggesting" possible changes. The board had no legal powers to demand such changes, but there was very little indication that the producers deliberately ignored these "suggestions," as many critics later claimed. The method of requiring a fee for examination, which meant that the film producers became, in fact, the main financial support of the board, never satisfied the critics of the film industry, who quite justifiably doubted the board's independence under these arrangements. For six years the word "censorship" in the board's title caused much confusion as to its actual function. Finally, in 1915, the official title was altered to the National Board of Review of Motion Pictures (N.B.R.) — a title which it retains to this day.

It is important to note that although the board depended indirectly upon the film makers for the bulk of its support, it was *never* an official arm of the motion picture industry. However, it was this financial connection, no matter how innocent, that formed the basis of most attacks on the board, and was largely instrumental in the ultimate failure of this organization to become the "public's voice" to the film industry.[55]

The board was, however, a prominent organization in the motion picture world before 1922, and was the subject of numerous periodical and newspaper articles, characterized by a very definite "for" or "against" polarization. Generally those in favor saw in its function a constitutionally safe, but potentially effective, form of social control which had acquired a strong base in the community because of its local committee structure. It also met with approval because the "voluntary" submission of films by the industry removed the stigma of formal censorship. The board itself saw its prime function as being "the improvement of motion pictures, morally, educationally and artistically, through the gradual awakening of the consciences of motion picture patrons, producers and users to the finer elements to be found in the screen. . . ."[56]

Throughout its existence there has been widespread dissatisfaction with, and opposition to, the N.B.R. At first the board was welcomed by most critics of the medium as a valuable means of controlling the industry without having to resort to the rather drastic and "un-American" measure of official political censorship. However, the board's eventual failure to stem the tide of objectionable films was seen by many of its detractors as positive proof of the industry's control of the organization. Indeed, the board's reliance on the fees charged to the producers was admitted to be an unsatisfactory funding arrangement, but its critics seldom offered feasible alternative solutions.

Criticism of the board and its work became more unrestrained when the medium's critics saw no tangible signs of improvement in the "moral" quality of motion pictures after several years of "voluntary previewing." An editorial in the June 20, 1914, issue of *Outlook* discussed the continued difficulty in obtaining suitable films, and then posed this question:

In some way the motion-picture business must be put under restraint by the public. At present such restraint is exercised by the National Board of Censorship. . . . Is the control exercised by this Board of Censorship, to which principal moving-picture concerns voluntarily submit their products, and to whom they give considerable financial support, adequate for the protection of the public and for keeping the moving-picture in the place it belongs?[57]

This writer obviously felt that the board was not adequate for the task, and he suggested that the industry took pains to avoid submitting the worst of its films for board review. The editorial did note, however, that there was a great divergence of opinion on the whole question of "voluntary" censorship, "and that it was by no means universally desired by the American public."[58]

By the time the board legally altered its name to the National Board of Review, it had already changed its focus from solely "reviewing" or censoring to include the additional constructive function of cooperating with all the interests seeking the artistic, moral and social improvement of the movies. The board always considered itself to be a "public institution," which must "substantially satisfy the public, else its usefulness to the film business is gone and its power vanishes."[59] Among the activities it considered constructive were: serving as a bureau of information in all matters pertaining to the regulation of motion picture theaters; preparing lists of "better" films for public distribution; and waging a methodical campaign which was, in the board's own words, "frank, aggressive and on the whole successful" against legal censorship.[60]

After 1916 the board adopted as its basic philosophy the credo "Selection not Censorship," and to further this aim created the National Committee for Better Films. One official of the N.B.R. explained that "its function is to both liberate and formulate thought regarding motion pictures, their uses and possibilities, and the best way to achieve a free screen of the most desirable kind."[61] This committee published lists of approved motion pictures for various purposes, such as: *Best Motion Pictures for Church and Semi-Religious Entertainments; Pictures Boys Want and Grown-Ups Endorse; Industrial Motion Pictures; A Partial List of Film Subjects on Health, Disease, Nursing and Allied Topics; Motion*

Picture Aids to Sermons; Forty Best Photo-plays of 1920; and *Monthly List of Selected Pictures.*

In later years this committee (renamed the Better Film National Council) would issue weekly bulletins and lists to its members on the local committees. It was hoped that these groups, organizations and individuals would help to build up patronage at the box office, and by the creation of special programs and community interests emphasize the existence and availability of the board's services to the community. It is important in understanding the N.B.R. to note that its whole philosophy was based on agreement with the industry's credo that content was shaped by public demand and not by the deliberate design of the suppliers (the studios). Therefore, the board adopted as one of its prime aims the improvement of the public's taste in motion pictures. In order to obtain the type of film which the reformers seemed to want, the N.B.R. attempted to create a popular demand for the best in screen entertainment, and by so doing to encourage, through widespread exhibition and financial success, the production of such "better" films.

To achieve its objective of creating a demand for the "better" film, the board prepared a plan showing how local communities could take full advantage of the opportunities offered for the improvement of film standards in their locality. The first principle was cooperation, in which all interested people, including the exhibitors, would be brought together to discuss the good and bad of motion pictures. At this time the group would collectively make known its felt needs for special programs, such as "family nights," or "children's matinees." In the creation of the special programs the board envisaged that the community would be prepared to financially subsidize the exhibitor by patronage above the normal level for these "better" films. The creation of special children's programs and family shows was advocated because a "well considered system of education of parents to develop a public sentiment both for finer family pictures and for selected pictures for young people must be carried on." Further, the board emphasized that "there must be supervision and *there must also be recognition of the fact that most film dramas are made for the entertainment of adults.*"[62] While it was claimed that this ambitious program had the support of most of the industry, it nevertheless failed to generate any real enthusiasm among the general public.

Those interested in the history of the American film industry have yet to answer a puzzling question — how successful was the board both in its censorial or review duties, and in its role as the "public conscience" of the film industry? The difficulty in assessing the board's effectiveness lies in the fact that individual tastes will always prevail in any discussion concerning the morality of the motion picture. Thus, while the board and its supporters were enthusiastic about its ability to operate as a controlling mechanism for the industry, its detractors continued to find that many of the films "passed" by the review committees still contained "morally offensive" scenes or themes. At best the board represented a compromise between complete freedom from legal censorship, and the various forms of local, state or possible federal censorship by politically appointed boards. It was precisely this compromise status which disturbed those who doubted the board's ability to effect any real changes without the benefit of legal authority, and there was no denying that the board's reviewers were less strict than any of the state or local censorship boards. Whether this was due to any fear of damaging reprisal by the industry or was merely a result of the philosophic outlook that "films are generally made for adult entertainment" is impossible to know. In a study which compared 228 films examined by both the Pennsylvania State Board of Censors and the National Board of Review in 1920, the state board made 1,464 eliminations in accordance with their standards, while the National Board made only 47 eliminations in these same films. This difference of opinion is all the more remarkable when it is considered that the evaluation standards of the two organizations, as stated in the official publications of each, were practically identical.[63]

The Uniform Standards Problem

One obvious difficulty faced by the board, the censors and the industry was in the definition of standards — exactly what did "better films," or "immoral," or "family fare" mean? The wide variations in the accepted definitions of these terms led to much confusion and caused the industry a great deal of trouble. The N.B.R. was equally unsure how to solve this problem, and nowhere in its early literature are these definitions fully explicated. Instead the board established descriptive "standards" which were changed from time to time. In 1915, John Collier noted the board's difficulty in establishing criteria of evaluation:

Details of the board's theories and formulae in judging films would require a long article. The latest printed copy of its standards . . . fills twenty-three pages and is still far from exhaustive. These formal standards are designed primarily for the guidance of film makers and incidentally for the enlightenment of the public.

. . . practically all the rules of the published "Standards" are wisely general and serve well their proper aim — namely, to suggest the temper of the board and its probable action and reasons for action in any given case.[64]

Collier also indicated that a recent tendency to "over-specialize" its rules had the effect of limiting the board's freedom of action, and discouraged "the creative producer of films." By all means the "standards" should be kept flexible to accommodate new ideas or shifts in public tastes, for "consistency is the original sin of intellect."[65] He cited some typical standards of the board:

Section 39. As a general rule it is preferable to have retribution come through the hands of authorized officers of the law, rather than through revenge or other unlawful or extra-legal means.

Section 41. An adequate motive for committing a crime is always necessary to warrant picturing it. . . . It is desirable that the criminal be punished in some way, but the board does not always insist on this . . . the results of the crime should be in the long run disastrous to the criminal so that the impression is that crime will eventually find one out. The result (punishment) should always take a reasonable proportion of the film.[66]

The board created a standards committee in 1915 which examined certain contentious cases in detail in an attempt to formulate more precise rules or "standards," but without much success.

The problem of establishing uniform standards was universal, and much of the blame for this failure can be attributed to the composition of the various state and local censorship boards. As Randall observed, these boards were simply not designed to reflect the diverse elements and the broad range of tastes in the community, and "under these circumstances, extreme decisions on emotionally charged questions of public morality were not surprising."[67] The situation became really intolerable when on occasion a censorship board would become completely dominated by a few idiosyncratic members. Writing in 1923, Tamar Lane said of the censors:

There is no real reason for censors. Neither is there for cockroaches. But we have them just the same. . . . These self-appointed guardians have the dirtiest minds of anybody we know. They can find suggestion and obscenity in things that folks have been doing for years in all innocence and with good intentions. . . .[68]

The censors set themselves up as authorities with the ability to decide just what is fit for the public consumption and what is not. If there were any truth in this proposition then it would be reasonable to assume that the different State Boards would come very nearly agreeing [sic] on that which is proper and that which should be eliminated from films. The only thing they can be found agreeing upon is that larger appropriations should be made for censors' salaries.[69]

The censors and their supporters were hard-pressed to provide any rationale for censorship other than by their frequent use of the words "crime," "violence," "sex," "immorality," "antisocial behavior," "irreligious," "erotic," "bad taste," and "sordidness." These terms were also

never adequately defined and were subject to wide variations of interpretation. However, it was the word "immoral" which had the most
emotional aura, and Robert Davis in his study of mass media innovation
in America has noted the frequency of its use in this context:

Seeking the strongest available category for attack, opponents named the new
mass media moral problems. Thus the movies, radio and television could be
denigrated either by associating them with the contact of evil surrounding the
term *immoral* or by contrasting them to the good term *morality*. In each new
attack, and for each new generation of readers, arguers made certain that the
audience was aware that in dealing with the mass media they were involved in
a moral controversy.[70]

Obviously, one way to curb these excesses and to provide clarification
was to have the Supreme Court offer some guidelines on the whole issue
of censorship standards, but this was not to be. This was unfortunate, for
as Randall indicated, "censors abused their discretion on the questions
of what was 'indecent' or 'sexually immoral' on the screen; but it was far
worse in the thirties, when they turned their attention increasingly to
political and social ideas."[71] Because of the difficulties encountered with
such imprecise definitions, it was no surprise that the N.B.R. was unable
to create a set of universal standards for judging "better" films which
was acceptable to all groups.

The Fight Against Censorship

The failure to establish a universally acceptable set of standards for
films was responsible for the frequent misinterpretation of the actual
censorial or review function performed by the board. Most of this criticism indicated that too much was expected from this body in the way of
dramatic censure of films and in controlling the activities of the film industry. In actual practice the board's reviewers were instructed to keep
an open mind, and thus they were loath to tamper with what was after
all the "artistic creation of one man's mind." In commenting on the
nature of the board's review function in 1926, the executive secretary of
the board made this clear:

Regarding the passage of pictures, "passed by the National Board of Review,"
does not necessarily mean the Board approves or recommends the picture upon
which the legend appears. In all cases it means that in the opinion of the reviewing committee the picture will not have a morally subversive effect upon
large numbers of persons in different sections of the country.[72]

The members of the board, because of their wide organizational base, were uniquely aware of the great regional differences that could arise in preferences and standards in entertainment. The secretary noted this in his explanation of the board's philosophy:

In passing pictures to be exhibited throughout the whole country, it is essentially careful . . . to keep in mind the established, ascertained difference of opinion between individuals, groups, communities and whole sections of the country, with regard to screen entertainment . . . which differences of opinion . . . would seem, to render censorship totally unequal to deal fairly both with the motion picture and with the tastes, wishes and rightful freedom of expressing their opinions of the American people.[73]

In retrospect, perhaps more than to any other single factor the failure of the board can be attributed to its lack of wide financial support. Because of this it found itself unable to meet all the requests for cooperative assistance; particularly disappointing was the failure to organize more local community groups. This lack of support both financial and moral led to a serious curtailment of intended functions and a subsequent loss of confidence in the board's ability to effect changes in the film industry. As an example of these strained finances, in 1920, the running expenses of the board were $17,224 spent on reviewing films, and $20,717 spent on the "constructive" part of the program. During this same period $30,290 was taken in as revenue derived from reviewing films.[74] Again the questions linger: how much voluntary support would the board have received from the industry if it had made more cuts or rejections? And why were private groups reluctant to support the board's activities? The answers to these questions can only be surmised.

One reason for the lack of support from those groups interested in greater control of the medium was that the National Board never attempted to disguise the fact that it was strongly opposed to any form of legal censorship, and in fact actively campaigned against censorship wherever and whenever it was threatened. In its earliest years the board represented a relatively stable island in the troubled waters created by the use of widely divergent censorship standards. Therefore, it is not in the least surprising that several local communities and one state — Florida — utilized the board's decisions as the basis of their own censorship rulings. The Florida "Act to Regulate the Exhibition of Motion Pictures" was passed in June, 1921, and was an attempt to encourage a centralized system of censorship in the era before the Hays Office had been formed. While the act did provide for the setting up of a Florida board of censors, it also made it "unlawful for any person, film or corporation to display, exhibit, or promulgate any Motion Picture film or films in the State of

Florida, that has not been approved by the National Board of Review, its appointees or successors or by the State Censorship Board of the State of New York."[75]

The National Board was particularly anxious to make its "review" services available to all interested communities. These community services even became institutionalized when, in 1920, the New York State Conference of Mayors approved a legal alternative to film censorship devised by the N.B.R. This model ordinance, or state law, provided that films rejected by the board were not to be exhibited in the city or state in question, and it was this very model which was adopted by the state of Florida one year later. The city of Boston also made this practice official, and several smaller cities with police censorship boards used the N.B.R.'s ratings as an informal guide to those films considered contentious and therefore worthy of further examination.[76] The board offered these services on the basis that its "voluntary" censorship was more consistent (if not as strict) than official political censorship — a sound assumption by all accounts.

The National Board of Review did not stop at mere assistance but also actively campaigned against legal censorship bills in several states when these were introduced, and several pamphlets were prepared and used for this purpose. Among the more important and contentious of these were *Objections to State Censorship of Motion Pictures; Repudiation of Motion Picture Censorship in New York City;* and *The Case Against Federal Censorship of Motion Pictures.* The board also attempted to examine the moral effects of motion pictures, and one pamphlet in particular, *Motion Pictures Not Guilty* (1920), caused considerable argument among reform groups.

The anticensorship activity of the board was the direct cause of the withdrawal of support by the General Federation of Women's Clubs in 1919, at which time Mrs. Blanchard, chairman of the federation's committee on motion pictures, said of the N.B.R.:

Their stream of literature and bulletins pouring into every corner of our land, at enormous expense, is the motion picture industry's attempt to furnish well-intentioned, reform-bent ladies with "harmless busy work." ... By devious and misleading proportions, they have befogged the thinking, befuddled, delayed, diverted, emasculated and perverted the activities of many club women honestly interested in a crusade for better motion pictures.[77]

The vehemence of the board's fight against legal restrictions of the movies only added to the belief that the industry and the board were indeed one and the same.

Any final evaluation of the worth of the National Board of Review to the development of motion pictures must remain ambiguous. On the positive side it played an important part in preventing the imposition of major censorship legislation, and also made a significant contribution to the development of a "movie consciousness" in the American public. On the negative side, however, the board ultimately failed in its efforts to become the official "public voice" to the film industry; while the attempt to establish an alternative control mechanism which would satisfy all the pressure groups working for legal censorship was also unsuccessful. The board did, however, provide a service to the public which was available nowhere else until the industry established its own centralized office (the Hays Office) in 1922. Also, although the board was never free from suspicion, there is no recorded evidence of deliberate collusion between the industry and its "conscience." It presented constructive programs for the integration of the motion picture into the community, and prepared useful lists of motion pictures suitable for any occasion. These were widely distributed and used, and did much toward encouraging the use of motion pictures by educational and social groups. The board also tried to direct the public's attention to what its members considered the "better" type of film, in the rather vain hope that the public's taste could be improved, and that film makers would be financially encouraged to produce more such films. On the negative side, the board's inability to legally enforce any of its recommendations meant that the studios were still free to continue along their own, more profitable paths. When finally the board was no longer able to still the clamoring for more stringent censorship regulations, it became apparent to the industry that it must begin to look elsewhere for protection from restrictive legislation.

NOTES TO CHAPTER V

1. This chapter will examine the issue of film censorship only in the sense that censorship has played an important role in shaping the history of the motion picture; it will not attempt to give a detailed treatment on the subject. There are several excellent books and articles which do cover this topic, the best of which are: Ira H. Carmen, *Movies, Censorship and the Law* (Ann Arbor: University of Michigan Press, 1966); Richard S. Randall, *Censorship of the Movies* (Madison: University of Wisconsin Press, 1968); Neville March Hunnings, *Film Censors and the Law* (London: George Allen and Unwin, 1967); and Ruth Inglis, *Freedom of the Movies* (Chicago: University of Chicago Press, 1947). Another work which attempts to relate movie censorship to social and cultural development is Kathryn B. Linden, "The Film Censorship Struggle in the United States from 1926 to 1957, and the Social Values Involved" (Ph.D. dissertation, New York University, 1972).

2. A detailed explanation of this incident is found in Hendricks, *Kinetoscope*, pp. 77–79. Ramsaye, *A Million and One Nights*, describes a similar incident featuring a dancer called "Dolorita." It is not known whether this is the same film. See p. 256.

3. 14 App. Div. 117, 43 N.Y.S. 571 (1st Dept. 1897).

4. For more examples of early censorship of the motion picture industry see Randall, pp. 11–12; also Ramsaye, pp. 473–476.

5. Ramsaye, p. 478.

6. *New York Times,* May 26, 1897.

7. Ramsaye, p. 478.

8. *Ibid.,* p. 474.

9. Carmen, p. 186.

10. Ramsaye, p. 475.

11. *New York Times,* December 21, 1908.

12. *Ibid.,* December 24, 1908.

13. *Ibid.,* December 25, 1908.

14. *Ibid.*

15. *Ibid.,* December 26, 1908.

16. There is really no way to verify Fox's estimates, but the size of this investment, as early as 1908, is staggering, if true! For a more "colorful" account of this incident see Ramsaye, pp. 476–485.

17. *New York Times,* December 27, 1908.

18. For a full description of these important legal proceedings see Carmen, pp. 186–188; and Randall, pp. 11–12.

19. Randall, p. 12.

20. Ford H. MacGregor, "Official Censorship Legislation," *Annals of the American Academy of Political and Social Science,* no. 128 (November, 1926), p. 164. This is an extremely useful article which outlines the various types of censorship activity and their histories.

21. *Ibid.,* p. 170.

22. *Ibid.,* p. 171.

23. John Collier, in the *Survey,* February 8, 1913, pp. 643–644.

24. *Ibid.,* p. 644.

25. Sonya Levien, "New York's Motion Picture Law," *American City,* October, 1913, pp. 319–321.

26. Collier, in the *Survey,* February 8, 1913, p. 644.

27. It can safely be assumed that the "fire hazard" reasoning was secondary to the moral considerations. Levien, p. 321.

28. Short, "A Social Study of the Motion Picture," p. 34.

29. Ellis P. Oberholtzer, *The Morals of the Movie* (Philadelphia: Penn Publishing Company, 1922), pp. 151–152. (Italics added.)

30. *Ibid.,* p. 117. It was quite obvious that other "moral" considerations were taken into account when vaudeville was eliminated from movie houses.

31. Quoted in Oberholtzer, p. 150.

32. Young, *Motion Pictures,* p. 63.

33. Although the legislation for the creation of this board was passed in 1911, the board itself did not begin operation until 1913. This board was composed of three members, two men and one woman, appointed by the governor for terms of three years. The board members had to be "residents and citizens" of the state, "well qualified by education and experience to act as censors under this act." Oberholtzer, p. 205.

34. Morris Ernst and Pare Lorentz, *Censored: The Private Life of the Movie* (New York: Jonathan Cape and Harrison Smith, 1930), p. 64.

35. MacGregor, p. 166.

36. Young, p. 65.

37. MacGregor, p. 167.

38. 236 U.S. 230 (1915).

39. Randall, p. 18.

40. Quoted in Carmen, p. 12.

41. Carmen, p. 12; and Randall, p. 19.

42. Randall, p. 19.

43. Carmen, p. 15.

44. MacGregor, p. 164.

45. Randall, p. 13.

46. MacGregor, p. 164.

47. *Ibid.*, p. 172.

48. Seabury, *The Public and the Motion Picture Industry*, p. ix.

49. *Ibid.*, p. 187. (Italics added.)

50. *Ibid.*, pp. 182–192.

51. *Ibid.*, p. 178.

52. *Ibid.*

53. Ramsaye, pp. 480–481.

54. Young, p. 42.

55. The best sources for material on the National Board of Review are contained in *Annals of the American Academy of Political and Social Science*, no. 128 (November, 1926), in a series of articles on the motion picture industry; and in Donald R. Young. There are many articles on the subject, the best of which in the early period is a series written by John Collier, the secretary of the board, and published in the *Survey* from July to October, 1915. A useful analysis of the board's accomplishments, and its relationship with the industry, is found in Ruth Inglis, *Freedom of the Movies*, chapter 3.

56. Wilton A. Barrett, "The Work of the National Board of Review," *Annals of the American Academy of Political and Social Science*, no. 128 (November, 1926), p. 178.

57. Editorial in the *Outlook*, June 20, 1914, p. 598.

58. *Ibid.*, p. 598.

59. John Collier, "Censorship; and the National Board," *Survey*, October 2, 1915, p. 11.

60. *Ibid.*, p. 14.

61. Barrett, p. 179.

62. Young, p. 45. (Italics added.)

63. *Ibid.*, p. 47.

64. Collier, "Censorship; and the National Board," p. 13.

65. *Ibid.*, p. 13.

66. *Ibid.*

67. Randall, p. 21; Ernst and Lorentz also discuss this problem in some detail.

68. Tamar Lane, *What's Wrong with the Movies* (Los Angeles: Waverly Company, 1923), p. 175.

69. *Ibid.*, pp. 181–182.

70. Robert E. Davis, *Response to Innovation: A Study of Popular Argument About New Mass Media* (New York: Arno Press, 1975).

71. Randall, p. 21.

72. Barrett, p. 181.

73. *Ibid.*, p. 181.

74. Young, p. 49.

75. Hunnings, p. 189. This law was declared unconstitutional in 1937 as an unwarranted delegation of legislative power to a foreign board.

76. Inglis, p. 77.

77. *Ibid.*, p. 78.

VI

The Social Setting for Control, 1918–1930

BY 1922, THE MOTION PICTURE INDUSTRY had become the largest and most widespread commercial entertainment form the world had ever seen. On every continent, in the largest cities and smallest villages, the screen's magic enthralled hundreds of millions of people who had quickly learned that "movies" were synonymous with "entertainment."[1] In some countries even the dreariest religious, educational or travelogue films delighted audiences with their ability to capture and project visually the movements of everyday life. In America, and in other more industrially advanced nations, the motion picture was now accepted as a normal feature of modern civilization, as much a part of life in the twentieth century as taking the bus to work or making a telephone call. (The extent of the motion picture industry's growth by 1923 can be seen from the table on page 140.) Every segment of society now went to the movies, where they were not only entertained but were also profoundly influenced by what they saw. This influence had become obvious not only to critics but also to businessmen, and the motion picture's ability to cause changes in dress, fashion, home decoration, and even some aspects of social conduct such as courtship was beginning to be documented.[2] American industry lost no time in using this power for its own advantage, and the movies were soon turned into a potent medium for the "mass" merchandising of clothing, furniture, soft drinks and even new hairstyles. While these manifestations of movie influence were obvious, the overall influence of the medium on American social and cultural life was much more difficult to determine. One thing was certain — it was during the 1920s that the "movie craze" really became a national phenomenon.

While the twenties is an era that historians have a great deal of trouble categorizing, it is generally accepted that this was a period "of amazing vitality, of social invention and change . . . the Twenties were really the

TABLE 6
DETAILS OF THE SIZE OF THE MOTION PICTURE INDUSTRY, 1923

The Film Daily, *of January 23, 1923, printed the following concise state-ment of miscellaneous information on the industry:*

Motion picture theaters in the United States	15,000
Seating capacity (one show)	7,605,000
Average weekly attendance at picture theaters	50,000,000
Admissions paid annually	$520,000,000
Average number of reels used for one performance	8
Average number of seats in picture theaters	507
Number of persons employed in picture theaters	105,000
Persons permanently employed in picture production	50,000
Permanent employees in all branches of picture industry	300,000
Investment in motion picture industry	$1,250,000,000
Approximate cost of pictures produced annually	$200,000,000
Salaries and wages paid annually at studios in production	$75,000,000
Cost of costumes, scenery, and other materials and sup-plies used in production annually	$50,000,000
Average cost of one feature film production	$150,000
Average number of feature films produced annually	700
Average number of short reel subjects, excluding newsreels, annually	1,500
Taxable motion picture property in the United States	$720,000,000
Percentage of pictures made in California (1922)	84%
Percentage of pictures made in New York (1922)	12%
Percentage of pictures made elsewhere in United States (1922)	4%
Foreign made pictures sent here for sale (1922)	425
Foreign made pictures sold and released for exhibition	6
Theaters running six to seven days per week	9,000
Theaters running four to five days per week	1,500
Theaters running one to three days per week	4,500
Lineal feet of film exported in 1921	140,000,000
Lineal feet of film exported in 1913	32,000,000
Percentage of American film used in foreign countries	90%
Film footage used each week by newsreels	1,400,000
Combined circulation of newsreels weekly	40,000,000
Number of theaters using newsreels weekly	11,000
Amount spent annually by producers and exhibitors in newspaper and magazine advertising	$5,000,000
Amount spent annually by producers in photos, cuts, slides and other accessories	$2,000,000
Amount spent annually by producers in lithographs	$2,000,000
Amount spent annually by producers in printing and engraving	$3,000,000

Source: **William Marston Seabury,** *The Public and the Motion Picture Industry,* pp. 278–279.

formative years of modern American society."[3] America admitted its urban cast during this period, and prompted by the tremendous technological development and the rise of mass production, a new economic age of "consumerism" dawned. The historian George Mowry has suggested that this new economy was highly dependent upon the tastes and acceptance of the crowd, and had an "incredibly important influence upon such widely separated areas as religion, political philosophy, folkways, dress, moral precepts, and the use of leisure time."[4]

It was this revolution in morals, whether it was called the "Jazz Age," or "Flaming Youth," or the "Lost Generation," which created the bitter conflicts between the representatives of the traditional culture and those who favored the new order. The historian John D. Hicks has noted that "most Americans accepted with satisfaction the way of life that emerged in the United States during the 1920's."[5] Nonetheless, the fundamental changes in American society caused by the automobile, the motion picture and the radio were a source of great consternation to many who saw only the destruction of traditional values and norms in the wake of their acceptance. Religious beliefs in particular underwent dramatic transformations, and historian William E. Leuchtenburg has pointed out that "the growing secularization of the country greatly weakened religious sanctions. People lost their fear of Hell and at the same time had less interest in Heaven; they made more demands for material fulfillment on Earth."[6]

The defenders of the traditional culture were not prepared to let these radical alterations to American institutions go unchallenged and the result was a flurry of activity aimed at banning or censoring, not only movies, but also books and women's fashions. They were particularly incessant in demanding a more vigorous enforcement of the Prohibition law. John D. Hicks observed that "it was easy for hostile critics to make a case that American morality had in some fatal way broken down. The standards of right and wrong that earlier generations had accepted no longer commanded respect."[7] However, the task of preserving the values and beliefs of an earlier time was impossible. Many young adults now talked about "sex" in an open and somewhat carefree manner which shocked their elders; how much of this was due to the doctrines of Jung or Freud is difficult to say, but phrases such as "sexual inhibitions" suddenly crept into everyday discussions. Novelists and playwrights also took this opportunity to write with a "new bluntness," and women who had once prided themselves on being shocked by everything were suddenly immune to all sensation.[8]

A social revolution of major significance to the development of the motion picture was the movement aimed at achieving feminine equality. The First World War had much to do with bringing about the long-demanded change in the status of American women, and the large-scale movement of women into business in the twenties consolidated this position. However, William L. O'Neill in his study of feminism in America, *Everyone Was Brave,* has indicated that while women did achieve many of their objectives — the right to vote, access to important occupational categories — in the end the movement failed. This failure was due to the unwillingness of the movement to come to grips with the fact that marriage and the family were the chief obstacles to woman's emancipation.[9] Nevertheless, American women did emerge into the foreground of American life to a more significant degree than in the past. O'Neill also noted that "the 1920's, not the 1960's was the time of the greatest movement toward permissive sexual behavior."[10]

This then was the era of the movies' greatest expansion — a setting of economic prosperity, new values and norms, alterations in personal interrelationships, and the emergence of women. Each one of these changes encountered a strain of strong conservative reaction. While it remains difficult to accurately assess the role and influence of the motion picture in promoting or assisting these changes, John D. Hicks has suggested, "that the effect was considerable few would care to deny."[11]

The problem of the influence of the movies continued to be a major social issue throughout the twenties, in spite of the establishment of many local and state censorship boards. The attacks on the industry and its product had varied little since the movies were first exhibited, and criticism increased against the medium's ability to vividly communicate "immoral" ideas on "sex" and "crime" to children.

The Child, Movies and Crime

The growing influence of the motion picture on American life did not escape the notice of those who were busy examining the fabric of American society. Robert S. Lynd, in his study of Muncie, Indiana, published as *Middletown,* noted the controversy that the arrival of the medium had caused in the community:

Some high school teachers are convinced that the movies are a powerful factor in bringing about the "early sophistication" of the young and the relaxing of social taboos. One working-class mother frankly welcomes the movies as an aid in child-rearing, saying, "I send my daughter because a girl has to learn the ways of the world some how and the movies are a good safe way." The judge of the juvenile court lists the movies as one of the "big four" causes of local juvenile delinquency, believing that the disregard of group mores by the young is definitely related to witnessing week after week of fictitious behavior sequences that habitually link the taking of long chances and the happy ending.[12]

Lynd's research gave him an accurate perception of the nature of the motion picture's role in the social fabric of Middletown. His analysis of the infrastructure of the community and its lines of control allowed him to see this new medium as a definite intrusion into Middletown's established social pattern. (In the same way he saw the automobile and the radio doing much the same thing.) However, the motion picture with its conspicuous local exhibition sites suggested a much more manageable problem than the other intrusive factors. He was particularly concerned with the "commercial" nature of the entertainment, and the background and motivation of the movie-house owners: "While the community attempts to safeguard its schools from commercially intent private hands, this powerful new educational instrument, which has taken Middletown unawares, remains in the hands of a group of men — an ex-peanut stand proprietor, an ex-bicycle racer and race promotor, and so on — whose primary concern is making money."[13] Lynd dismissed the efforts of pressure groups in Middletown who wanted to clean up the motion picture, and doubted their sincerity. He commented: "Middletown appears content in the main to take the movies at their face value — 'a darned good show' — and largely disregard their educational or habitforming aspects."[14]

Lynd was not alone in his assessment of the motion picture as a powerful, but out of control, social force in American life. In 1919, in Chicago, a commission of "twenty representative citizens after two years of examination and the taking of testimony from all interested parties" voted unanimously for the censorship of all motion pictures in that city. The commission's decision was based upon their assessment of the influence that the medium seemed to have on the children of their city. The report contained their rationale for this action.

Heretofore, throughout all ages, the best thought, the most learned minds have been devoted to educating the youth along lines of betterment, and protecting the weak and thoughtless from the inroads of designing exploiters. It cannot be that in this progressive age we should silently consent or concur in having our wives and children, our homes, our schools and our churches turned over to the entertainer in order that he may make a profit regardless of the consequences to the individual. . . . It seems absolutely essential that the exhibitions should be publicly controlled in the interest of the education and good morals of the children.[15]

"Incitement to crime" was certainly the major issue when motion picture influence was discussed. The depiction of "sex" ran a very close second. Those who were anxious to place the movies under more stringent control argued that the child could be persuaded to engage in criminal activities by imitation of what he saw on the screen. During this period the psychological concept of "direct influence," which has been variously called the "stimulus-response theory," or the "hypodermic needle theory," was a prevalent notion of how the media acted to influence their audiences. Sociologist Melvin De Fleur has correctly indicated that this theory did not really assume that there were no intervening variables between the medium and the individual, but, in fact, "there were very definite assumptions about what was going on in-between." While these assumptions "may not have been explicitly formulated at the time, . . . they were drawn from fairly elaborate theories of human nature, as well as the nature of the social order."[16] It was, however, this perception of the nature of the communications process which provided the basis of this attack on the motion picture. (See Chapter IX for details on the development of social science research in this field.)

Not only the motion picture but all the mass media were attacked for what the *Christian Century* described as "the manner in which . . . [they] . . . have directly stimulated juvenile delinquency and crime, both in the United States and abroad . . . [which] . . . is too well known to require evidence."[17] Robert Davis in his catalogue of responses to the introduction of the motion picture has suggested that while the basic assumption that depiction of crime and violence on the screen caused crime and violence in real life, there was, after 1915, a change in the type of evidence offered to support these charges. The earlier attacks had been made on the basis of specific and infrequent examples of crimes which seemed to be inspired by films; however, it soon became apparent that this connection was tenuous. Gradually more substantial support for the connection between movies and incitement to crime was sought and obtained, mainly in the form of "testimony" from criminals, juvenile delinquents or even ordinary schoolchildren.[18]

In 1921, Dr. A. T. Poffenberger of Columbia University examined the question of "Motion Pictures and Crime" in a widely quoted article. While this was not a "scientific" study in any sense, Poffenberger, who was a psychologist, did examine the connection between the "wave of crime sweeping the country" and the influence of motion pictures. He attempted to present both sides of the influence question and noted the possibilities the new medium offered:

As an agent of publicity, with its immense daily audience of young people, it has great possibilities for creating and developing in them a spirit of true Americanism, a respect for law and social order. . . . Rightly used, the motion picture is indeed one of the most powerful educational forces of the twentieth century.... But wrongly used and not carefully guarded, it might easily become a training school for anti-Americanism, immorality and disregard for law.[19]

Poffenberger outlined the "mental characteristics" of the two groups "most subject to influence" — children and mentally deficient adults. These were listed as: suggestability; inability to judge the consequences of actions; lack of self-restraint; and uncontrolled imaginations — all factors which made these two groups more susceptible to motion picture influence. While he was particularly concerned with the influence of motion picture advertising, and the constant depiction of crime on the screen, he also took the time to attack the other "evil influences" in modern civilization. Regarding the film, he concluded that "prevention, not cure" was the answer, because "such organs of publicity as moving pictures, newspapers, magazines, advertising posters and the like, should not be allowed to contribute to the necessary burden of evil suggestion by the character of their productions. The purely commercial spirit should be tempered by a spirit of social welfare and education."[20]

Poffenberger believed that the motion picture could uplift the tastes of its audience by providing the "right" kind of content. This, however, was a rather naïve viewpoint that failed to take into account the existing producer-exhibitor-viewer relationship, which encouraged the production only of films that ensured a suitable financial return. There was no room for "art" in Hollywood.[21]

In 1926, the county judges of Brooklyn issued a joint statement on their views of the motion picture as a cause of criminal behavior. This statement noted in part that

most of the motion pictures glorify crime, or depict the rotten trail of sensuality. It is sought to justify their exhibition by the explanation that they print a moral. As sensible would it be to drag a child through flames so that later he might feel the soothing effect of salve! Sear the mind of a child with rottenness, and no moral will ever produce relief, much less a cure.[22]

Even the criminologists made their views known. At a meeting of the Ninth International Prison Conference in London, in August, 1926, several of the discussions were devoted to methods of protecting youth from the corrupting influences of the motion picture, "which admittedly incite to crime or immorality." A summary of these discussions, made for the Prison Association of New York, contained criticisms of "scenes which represent the worst criminal exploits and other sensational and immoral representations of all kinds" and which are often portrayed in the movies "under guise of romantic stories."[23]

145

Not everyone accepted the idea that the motion picture was a school for crime. In 1927, Ruth Millard, a reporter for the *New York World*, interviewed nearly one hundred inmates of Welfare Island in order to discover "one man, woman or child, fallen in the ways of lawlessness, who would attribute his fall in some way to the influence of off-color books, movies or plays." Try as she would the reporter was unable to find one inmate "who felt that his life had been influenced in any injurious way by such forms of art." One old woman said, "It's all applesauce, this being influenced stuff . . . nobody ever sees anything off-color in the movies that they didn't know before anyhow. . . . If a movie producer actually set out to influence people for the worse he'd have a hard time digging up hot stuff that boys and girls didn't know about already."[24]

All these investigations of the connection between the motion picture and crime were based upon personal observation and not on extensive research, and as a result had very little "scientific" validity. The epitome of this type of subjective evaluation, and the far-reaching effects it could achieve, was the previously mentioned Chicago Motion Picture Commission study of 1920. The study was undertaken by an "impartial" group in order to determine the need for control of the medium in that city, and the results of their findings were subsequently implemented into law.[25] Chicago had introduced a police censorship board operation in 1907, but its function had become less effective in the intervening years, and new industry distribution practices had made it almost obsolete. Even with this imperfect method, during the year from November 1, 1917, to December 1, 1918, the Chicago censors had deleted 55,604 feet of film, or a total of 974 subjects from the movies submitted to them.[26]

The study was supervised by Professor Ernest W. Burgess of the University of Chicago. Extensive questionnaires were sent to the teachers and principals of the Chicago schools, and the tabulations were made from 223 returns containing the views of the faculty from these different schools. While the survey contained only opinions, these were accepted as valid because they came from "those who are sincerely interested in the children's progress and who are in a position to observe and interpret the facts."[27] No attempt was made to measure the influence of motion pictures by any empirical means. The findings were not dramatic, but tended to confirm the suspicions of the reform groups; namely, that children attended movies on the average of twice a week; that there was a great divergence of opinion on the good or bad influence of the medium, with a very large majority of the educationists believing they were harmful and the general moral effect undesirable; that a board of censors was at least a partial remedy for this situation; and that absolutely no support could be found in favor of allowing "public opinion" to be the only social control placed on the motion picture. (The findings on this last issue were obviously a direct attempt to embarrass the National Board of Review and its basic philosophy that public opinion was the only "true guide" to control of movie content.) The survey proved to be a clear indication of the strong emotions in play when the subject of motion picture influence and social control was raised, and while there were a few dissenting voices in favor of a more tolerant attitude, these were swept aside in the avalanche of unfavorable comment.

The arguments surrounding the influence of the motion picture on criminal activity continue until this day, but like so many other aspects of the "motion picture problem" the bulk of these attacks have now been transferred to television. Nevertheless, with the development of more sophisticated measurement techniques, and the use of acceptable research designs, the nature and extent of the medium's ability to encourage criminal tendencies was later clarified, and modified.

Education and the Motion Picture Problem

Of all the social institutions which were most concerned with or affected by the introduction of the motion picture, none was more personally involved than American education. Educators were obviously the most perturbed by the influence of the movies because teachers were forced to deal with it daily in the classroom where children's fantasies became much more obvious. At the same time educational authorities were continually searching for ways in which the medium could be utilized as a controlled educational tool. In 1922, the National Education Association formed a committee to make a report on visual education in all its aspects — commercial and educational. When this report was tabled in 1923, the chairman of the N.E.A., Mr. L. N. Hines, warned his audience that

the daily work of the schools in all village and urban communities is affected by what goes on at the movie house. Over much seeing [*sic*] of the inanities and absurdities of the movie seems to be developing the so-called "movie-mind." School is a rather slow place to millions of our youngsters. The whole situation affects the work of the school, creates a demand for visual education, and at the same time tends to make that demand one for the vulgarities of the commercial film.[28]

Chairman Hines then attacked the "characteristics of the movie interests" with a rather acerbic summary of the industry's public posture. Among the more dangerous characteristics he noted were:

Opposed to censorship of any type;

In favor of Sunday desecration and the unlimited showing of films;

Shot through and through with the basest motives in devising plots and putting them on the screen;

Constant perverters of the morals of youth, through the pictures. Many movies are nothing less than lessons in crime.[29]

While Hines's position may appear extreme he was by no means the most extreme, but his status in the educational hierarchy in the United States carried much weight and his speech was of special concern to the motion picture industry.

While the N.E.A.'s public attitude toward the commercial motion picture industry was cautious and even cool on occasion, nevertheless in the 1920s the educational use of motion pictures increased dramatically, spurred on by the N.E.A.'s subcommittees, and other special interest groups. However, this effort was marred by several impediments to the proper utilization of the medium for educational purposes. The first problem centered on the failure to realistically evaluate the motion picture's potential as an educational device. Instead, in the period before 1920 this potential was exaggerated to an extravagant degree, and when the promised results were not forthcoming the medium itself was blamed. The second problem was the failure of educators and the industry to agree on what types of film materials were most needed for school use. Thus the industry tried to convince the schools to use commercial films which had already been paid for on theatrical circuits, while the teachers were unable to agree among themselves on what was really required. The inability to translate educational needs into concrete proposals meant that it was extremely difficult to produce high quality educational films at a profit. Instead, educational film-making generally became a sloppy, semiamateur industry, while vast sums of money were wasted in futile attempts to adapt commercial films for educational purposes.

Another major obstacle was that the early equipment for film projection was bulky, expensive and difficult to operate, and the film itself was an extreme fire hazard. This meant that motion pictures were out of the question for small schools, and most of America's schools were still small at this time. In the larger schools film showings required the construction of special projection booths, and the costly rental of films, while all showings had to be held in the central auditorium. Therefore each film rented was shown indiscriminantly to as many children as possible to keep the cost down, making motion pictures more an extracurricular activity than an integral part of the educational process. Under these circumstances it was impossible for the children to adopt an attitude toward the film that was favorable to its educational use. Until the motion picture was transferred to the classroom and more systematic use made of the medium as an aid to education there was little major progress. The introduction of films specifically with the classroom's needs in mind had to await the development of 16 mm equipment in the late 1920s, and to this significant innovation were added the developments of safety film and finally sound.[30]

The introduction of more clearly defined and integrated educational films resulted in several important studies on the effects of motion pictures as a teaching aid. The most prominent of these was the experiment conducted by the Eastman Kodak Company in cooperation with the National Education Association in 1927–1928. The results of this experiment indicated clearly that a group of children using reading material and films could learn more than a group using just normal reading materials, although the actual contributions of the films themselves could not be measured.[31] Certainly by the mid-thirties the motion picture had begun to make a valuable contribution to American education, but still without much support from the commercial film industry.

Educators were always prominent among those interested in improving the social contribution of the motion picture, by seeking more stringent control mechanisms, or suggesting further examinations of the impact of the medium. Educational publications contained many articles on the subject, ranging all the way from the most vitriolic criticisms of the commercial film industry to "how to use it properly." Even popular periodicals constantly quoted the opinions of educators as if they were experts on the subject of motion picture influence. Occasionally little gems of information were made available, as in the case of a letter published in *Outlook* in 1923, and signed by a teacher calling herself "Home Economist": "In a recent intelligence and current knowledge test given to them [schoolchildren in her class] one hundred percent of these children could name ten or more moving-picture actors and actresses, while [only] five percent could name ten names to be selected from President, Vice-President, Cabinet Member, Supreme Court Justice . . . [etc., etc.]"[32]

There was a very serious side to this letter — a sincere plea from an apprehensive teacher, who like many of her colleagues felt that she had to face the day-to-day "competition" from the movies for the child's attention. In 1926, Nelson L. Greene, the editor of *Educational Screen,* a journal established specifically to provide professional assistance to teachers, also noted the "competitive" aspects between teacher and movie house:

For the school children themselves it has an influence largely adverse, which carries over into the classroom to a degree little realized as yet by the rank and file of the teaching profession. It is of vital importance today that teachers should reckon with the theatrical movie as a definite competitor and frequently a dangerous opponent, of what they are trying to accomplish in the classroom.[33]

Greene suggested that pressure from teachers could force the industry to develop a commercial product that would prove to be an ally of formal education, but he too failed to articulate exactly what type of content he had in mind that would accomplish this dual purpose.

In the long run American education failed to make the most effective use of the new medium, and Cline M. Koon, the senior specialist in radio and visual education with the United States government, pointed out these failures in a detailed study published by an office of the League of Nations in 1935. Koon noted:

...the fact remains that the film has not been given its proper place as part of school equipment. This failure can be charged to an inexcusable indifference on the part of both administrative officers and school teachers. . . .

A first essential in the systematic introduction of the motion picture in the schools of our country is the necessary preparation on the part of our teachers. ...A second essential is the adaptation of films to the various instructional units. ... A third and very important essential is the matter of appropriating money in the annual budget for the purchase of films for use of school districts.[34]

Koon saw the problem essentially as lack of "cooperative effort," which could be overcome by "concerted action." He also noted that at this time only 10 percent of the public schools in the United States made systematic use of motion pictures for instruction.[35] It was this limited and ineffective educational use in comparison to the high attendance of children at commercial motion picture theaters which caused educators to become concerned about the amount of misinformation acquired at the movies.

The arrival of sound in 1926 added further complications. While this innovation obviously made the educational film more useful, its widespread commercial adoption was seen to be an additional "intrusion" into American educational aims. American teachers had always fought a losing battle to establish some sort of standard language usage, and the use of slang was widely discouraged. With the introduction of sound movies a new question was raised: "What is going to happen to the language once every movie house in the country starts to reproduce the dialogue conjured up by the mind of some Hollywood screenwriter?" One educator, discussing this subject in *School and Society* magazine in 1929, feared the worst, because the past performance of the motion picture industry gave little indication that it would "be actuated by any principles of social responsibility which extend beyond tangible results in the box-office."[36] He further observed that, before 1927, the influence of the movies on speech had been small, especially when placed alongside the comic strip!

However, now "movie speech" too was destined to have its impact on the minds of impressionable young people, and it was sure to be speech of the worst kind, for "inherent in the situation is the plain demand of the mass mind for something easy and for something broadly humorous. Slang, profanity, even obscenity have always satisfied that demand and probably always will."[37] In actual fact the problem of motion picture dialogue was never really identified as a separate issue by reform groups, but was considered to be just another facet of the misused influence of the commercial motion picture.

Educators often attacked the motion picture for presenting a distorted picture of the world, and for offering simplified solutions to complex problems, and thus presenting an unrealistic picture of life. However, the medium was also defended as "a magic telescope ... [which] ... has opened minds, and with them opened, people are forced to keep ahead of the intelligence thus awakened, and the imagination thus aroused."[38] In an important article entitled "The Motion Picture as Informal Education," published in 1934, the psychologist Paul G. Cressey offered a unique defense for the motion picture's educational influence by suggesting:

The cinema is almost unique among the agencies in a community in that it presents what are interpreted as unified segments of life.... In contrast to the traditional school, where motivation in learning arises extraneously, primarily through the teacher's special efforts and skill, the cinema provides for many children a means, vicariously at least, by which learning may really be a natural result of interest and activity.[39]

Thus the child could in fact "associate himself more intimately with the life situations and characters portrayed upon the screen" than was possible through more formal agencies such as the school.[40] Unfortunately for the commercial film industry, Cressey's positive concept of "education by the movies" was not widely accepted by the American educational community.

The Community and the Motion Picture

In an address before the nation's social workers in 1919, Mr. Orrin G. Cocks, the secretary of the National Committee for Better Films, observed: "In most communities of the United States there is one motion picture theater for every 5,000 to 10,000 of the population ... while it reaches more of the population than any other amusement agency, social workers have allowed it to develop almost entirely along commercial lines."[41] Cocks, as an officer of the National Board of Review, was obviously not in favor of censorship and his emphasis on the positive benefits to be derived from the motion picture was carefully enunciated. Nevertheless, he made a valid point that many social agencies had not utilized the medium in ways which could have been beneficial to them. This was why films were being made almost exclusively by professional organizations and corporations providing commercial entertainment, and the social groups, the educators, the churchmen, the "ethical leaders of the world," had only themselves to thank for this condition. Cocks continued:

At any time during the twenty-five years of the history of the motion picture they could have modified this art by putting aside their inertia and devoting as much real thought to utilizing this agency as have the motion picture manufacturers who have been dominated by the commercial motive. Nothing is gained now by destructive criticism or by demands for some form of legal censorship. The results do not justify the effort and simply hand to a small group of less or more intelligent state servants the work which must be performed by all of the population.[42]

Although Cocks can be faulted in his analysis for being an "interested" party, his points did have the ring of truth, for other than the U.S. government, no major non-film-industry group had ever attempted to produce films on a large scale. Of course, even by 1919 film-making was expensive and this was a handicap, but despite all the criticism aimed at the motion picture industry, no alternative had emerged which was able to attract and entertain large audiences the way the commercial product did.[43] Cocks ended his talk by suggesting, in much the same way Vachel Lindsay had, that the local theater manager was "an unused social factor in almost every community," and that surprisingly good results could be obtained "by treating this citizen in a friendly manner, as a potential social servant and discussing with him the problems of the finer forms of community recreation."[44]

In 1921, Cocks was once again invited to speak to the social workers of America on the vital issue of the problems associated with community control of the motion picture. This time Cocks made an all-out plea for the use of the Better Films Committee of the National Board of Review, basing this suggestion on the results of an extensive questionnaire which had been submitted to 18,000 boys and 21,000 girls in seventy-five high schools. The thrust of his argument was that:

Some plan needs to be adopted generally throughout the United States which will clearly express to the theater owner and to those who furnish regularly motion picture programs to him, a well-defined outline of community wishes. This plan must be of such character as will bring to his theater a sufficient attendance to make it commercially possible for him to continue his business.[45]

The "Better Film Movement" was the only such plan then available, and it was only natural that the committee's secretary suggest that social workers utilize the services of this existing program. There was no doubt that his plea was sincere, for the National Board of Review and its committee clearly recognized that the "movie problem" was largely one of divergent community standards and tastes. At the same time Cocks also hinted at the industry's frustration when he said: "Current irritation of individuals must give way to clearly expressed and cooperative community demand." The question was, how should the community voice this demand? Who was to speak for the community on this important question of local control, for after all, "every community and neighborhood has the right to have exhibited those motion pictures which they want." Cocks again suggested that only by using the services of the National Board could local communities make a "permanent modification in the present system."[46] Cocks's two addresses clearly presented some of the alternatives which were available to disgruntled critics of the medium. It was ironic that the much-maligned National Board was the only agency to ever offer a concrete plan whereby the responsibility for maintaining the standards of motion pictures and control of the industry would be placed squarely in the hands of the local community. Unfortunately, we can only speculate on the plan's ultimate viability because these suggestions were seldom adopted by the reform groups.

With the formation of a centralized office representing the industry in 1922, social workers became even more important as the industry attempted to elicit their support in creating a dialogue between the public and itself. (For a detailed discussion of the public relations activities of the motion picture industry see Chapter VII.) The industry also considered the social workers a major pressure group in their own right, and in 1927 they were addressed by the former governor of Maine, Carl E. Milliken, who had become the secretary of the Motion Picture Producers and Distributors of America, Inc. (MPPDA). The subject of Milliken's talk was "The Movie: Has It a Social Obligation?" Much of the speech was pure rhetoric of the kind that would only too often appear out of the offices of the MPPDA, but he was most anxious to give the details of an extensive motion picture attendance study conducted by the Department of Psychology at Columbia University. Among the more interesting and contentious findings was that the percentage of children (under sixteen years of age) in attendance varied greatly depending on the locale of the theater. In the downtown Manhattan theater district the average was 3.4 percent; in local theater districts, 7.4 percent; in residential urban districts, 8.0 percent; and in the suburban village the proportion was 31.8 percent. These figures were much lower than expected, and were subsequently attacked in another major study.[47]

After 1922, with the establishment of the centralized industry organization and the greater internal stabilization of the industry, social workers began to lose interest in the motion picture as a potential threat to urban social life. There is no evidence to indicate that social workers as a group ever supported the demand for federal control or censorship, for they were sensitive to the need for local control mechanisms as a means of creating changes in the motion picture industry. Also, their professional training and personal observations led many of them to conclude that the "myth of the movie monster" was being overblown and was the cause of needless concern. After twenty years of availability of motion pictures definite use patterns had been established, and the movies were now an accepted and welcomed part of community life.

Throughout the twenties religious groups continued to show concern about the quality of the entertainment their congregations attended with such frequency. Although they never solidified into one cohesive pressure group, these mainly Protestant organizations collectively represented a formidable foe to the film industry. In 1919, the General Conference of the Protestant Episcopal Church adopted a resolution endorsing the principles of regulation of motion pictures. A similar resolution was then passed by the Methodist Episcopal General Conference, while the Presbyterian church, working through its reorganized Board of Temperance and Moral Welfare, planned a "white list" of motion pictures.[48] In May, 1921, the General Assembly of the Presbyterian Church passed a resolution which deplored the "menace of the moving picture shows to young people," and particularly singled out films which "make light of the marriage relation." The assembly also urged "a nationwide commission for legal censorship by the federal government."[49]

The decade of the twenties was to see the motion picture industry under constant attack from those who desired to place it under greater restraint to control its growing influence in the community. This battle over censorship would continue unabated until the mid-1930s.

The Industry Retreats

The failure of the National Board of Review to stem the tide of criticism had left the industry virtually unprotected just at a time when the whole issue of the motion picture's influence on American morals and ideals was thrown into the public spotlight by a series of dramatic events. It was also evident by late 1918 that the industry's growth had slowed down and that some sort of stabilization period had been reached.[50] This serious financial consideration, combined with the unfortunate series of "incidents," created a situation where the industry was forced to stand back and examine its structure, its product, and its relationship with and responsibility to the audience.

The emergence of the sex film was an important factor in fanning the flames of censorship pressure. Spurred on by the popularity of the movies, the use of "sex appeal" became a popular theme in advertising and all forms of merchandising, but the central focus of this liberating drift remained the commercial motion picture. These films, dealing openly with sexual topics, were so well received by audiences that studios, anxious to overcome their losses sustained during the disastrous influenza outbreak and by the sudden lack of interest in war films, started to outdo each other in offering "frank and adult" entertainment. These films promised far more than they actually gave, and Benjamin Hampton pointed out:

Not one in fifty of these offerings contained more than a few "sexy" situations, but photographs of such scenes could be displayed in lobbies, and seductive sentences and drawings could appear in newspaper advertisements. Ticket buyers, led by occasional spicy advertisements to believe that the screen would present situations and dialogue as "naughty" as the spoken stage, were usually disappointed; movie sex appeal was reduced to a faint whisper of the lusty frankness of the theater.[51]

The emergence of these films and the glorification of their stars in the popular press increased the intensive pressure from reform-minded groups. Although many of the more blatant of these "sex" films were made by small "fly-by-night" producers, the whole industry was placed under a cloud of suspicion. The result was that the large studios, with the biggest investments, began a frantic search for a method to make the motion picture more "respectable." Certainly this was an inappropriate time for the industry to face the buffeting from reform movements, for the vision of the immediate profits to be made from "sensational" pictures was too attractive to outweigh the long-range effect on the industry as a whole. The industry had unfortunately developed an unwarranted confidence that it would emerge unscathed from any attack, and that the audience would continue to grow in spite of all these criticisms. Thus it was unprepared for the vehemence of the public's reaction to the events of 1920–1922.

A major obstacle to meeting reformist demands was that there was no solidarity in the industry which would have allowed a unified approach to these problems. The producers blamed the exhibitors for not pushing good films when these were offered; the exhibitors blamed block-booking for forcing them to show bad films; while "stupid" studio advertising and public relations "stunts" only added further fuel to the reformist's fires. Finally, major studios spent so much time being suspicious of each other that they paid very little attention to the growing demands for reform.

Prior to 1922, the motion picture industry had made two attempts to form a central organization to represent the film makers as a cohesive group. The first was in 1915 with the formation of the Motion Picture Board of Trade, which had a very short, uneventful life. In 1916, threatened by the first of a series of congressional bills and hearings, the industry formed the National Association of the Motion Picture Industry (NAMPI) for the prime purpose of sponsoring two changes in the federal statutes which it was hoped would legally place motion pictures under the rights guaranteed by the First Amendment. The first change sought by the industry was an amendment to the Constitution providing for freedom of the screen; this made absolutely no progress in Congress at all. The second, a revision of Section 245 of the United States Penal Code to include motion pictures as a form of matter subject to the obscenity regulations, was passed by Congress in June, 1920. Of this last change Ruth Inglis has pointed out that it made no difference whatsoever — it brought no tangible improvement in film content, and the demand for more specific federal control of the medium continued unabated.[52]

In February, 1921, the first of a series of articles by Benjamin Hampton was published in *Pictorial Review,* in which he declared that "unless producers and exhibitors cleaned their own house and cleaned it thoroughly, there might not be much house left." Hampton also called on the club women of America to work with decent producers and to agitate for the use of police power in sending indecent manufacturers, distributors and exhibitors to jail. The unexpected response to these articles was overwhelmingly favorable and this indicated to Hampton, and to the industry, that interest in the declining moral standards of the movies was not limited to just the special pressure groups. Hampton described his reaction:

For several years I had been learning something of the grip acquired by movies on American life, but when thousands of letters and newspaper clippings poured into my study I began to realize that neither I nor anyone else had an adequate conception of their deep hold on the classes as well as the masses. There were many letters from university and college presidents and professors, school teachers, lawyers, ministers, club women, bankers and members of other groups to prove convincingly that influence of the movies had permeated every section of American society.[53]

The industry's counterresponse was just as dramatic. Hampton was loudly condemned as a traitor, and even threatened with "blackballing." However, he was also praised for his stand by the trade press. Hampton noted that some of the most vigorous condemnations came from the "professional reformers," who had objected to his comment that censorship was "un-American and unworkable."[54]

After the indignation and anger had subsided, the leaders of the industry realized that an immediate, and impressive, move toward "cleaning house" had to be made. Thus, in March, 1921, a conference of top motion picture directors adopted a code known as *The Thirteen Points or Standards.* (See Appendix I.) Basically, this series of resolutions condemned the production and exhibition of certain types of film or film content known to be most frequently censored by the existing censorship boards. These subjects included sex, white slavery, illicit love, nakedness, prolonged "passionate love," crime, gambling and drunkenness, depreciation of public officials or religion, and "vulgar and salacious" films and advertising. The NAMPI passed a further resolution that called for all members of the association to cooperate fully in carrying out the implementation of the *Thirteen Points,* and threatened expulsion for those blatantly disobeying them.

The president of the NAMPI, William A. Brady, tried his best to publicize this unique industrial agreement in an attempt to stem the mounting tide of criticism. Unfortunately, no machinery was ever established whereby the *Thirteen Points* could be enforced with any real authority. Brady attempted to convince one of the leading proponents of federal censorship, the Reverend Wilbur C. Crafts, superintendent of the International Reform Federation, that implementation of this moral code would have the desired result.[55] The outcome of this meeting was rather confused, for Crafts, in an about-face, apparently utilized the *Thirteen Points* as the basis for a plan for official federal censorship, which he claimed the industry had agreed upon.[56] Hampton suggested that Crafts had in fact become convinced of the industry's ability to police itself, but that he had put forward the federal plan to "redeem himself" in the eyes of his disillusioned fellow workers on the federation, who had questioned his cooperation with the industry.[57] In any case, Brady repudiated Crafts's statement, and then to regain some of the lost prestige for the NAMPI he attempted to avert the passage of censorship legislation currently pending in the New York State legislature. This intrusion into state politics, although justified to some extent, was bungled so badly that it spelled the death of the NAMPI as the official industry organization.

The Producer's Association concentrated their attack directly on New York's Governor Miller and the legislature in this desperate attempt to stop the imposition of statewide censorship regulations in what was then the most important state to the film industry. It was easy to understand the industry's very real fear that if New York imposed censorship, many other states might follow this example. However, there was an even more important consideration: censorship in New York City, where most films received their initial first runs at the prestige movie houses, meant that, in effect, films would have to be made with the New York censor in mind.

Thus New York "versions" would become the industry standard, and in effect would mean a form of nationwide censorship at the behest of the New York State censors.

Desperate, the industry waved the *Thirteen Points* in front of the New York legislature and Brady promised:

...I stand ready to go before Governor Miller and the legislative leaders and enter into an iron-bound agreement that we will have this entire situation disposed of within a year. We will do it by pledging ourselves not to allow our pictures to be shown in theaters where objectionable pictures are being shown. We can close these theaters if necessary, and if by any chance this plan should not work out, I will be here next year and talk against the producers in stronger language than anyone did here today.[58]

The supporters of the bill in turn claimed that the industry had received sufficient warning and time to "clean itself up," and that obviously "one more year" was not going to change things appreciably. (It was obvious that New York was an important trump card for the reform groups as well.) The bill, however, was passed, and the motion picture industry then attempted to dissuade Governor Miller from approving the legislation, something which they had successfully accomplished in other states. It was in pressuring the governor that some incredible blunders were made. Presenting the producer's point of view, Mr. Paul D. Cravath of the NAMPI admitted that past mistakes had been made. He then presented a proposal for the establishment of an independent commission to investigate the motion picture industry, and to recommend means for protecting both the industry and the public from objectionable films and advertisements, with all expenses to be paid by the industry. This written proposal was signed by the presidents or principal executive officers of twenty motion picture concerns.

In the course of the discussion with Governor Miller, Cravath told the governor that "four men" could reform the movies if they had a mind to, and that the industry was now prepared to do "what had to be done." (Presumably he was referring to the heads of Famous Players, Metro-Goldwyn, and Fox.) This was an incredible admission of the powers then available to the top "movie moguls," and only confirmed the suspicions of many reform groups. The written proposal was even more damaging in its admissions, and showed that much of the criticism in the past had been justified. It stated in part: "We recognize that a certain number of films and advertisements of films have been so objectionable as to bring discredit on the entire moving picture industry. We recognize that the motion picture industry has not thus far wholly succeeded in working out fair measures to prevent the exhibiting of objectionable films and advertisements."[59]

The industry's public contrition did little good, and Governor Miller signed the bill, although he expressed his disapproval of censorship, except as a remedy for something worse. The governor acknowledged that in America the word "censorship" did not really have a democratic sound, but he explained that it was already being practiced in many ways, and referred to laws against obscene literature, the mailing of lewd objects, and other less obvious social controls. His main argument was that "liberty did not mean license," and that above all "decency had to be maintained." He concluded with the statement: "The moving picture people say now that they will be good, but you have heard that old story before."[60]

This bitter defeat in New York was a powerful blow to the motion picture industry and to the National Board of Review as well. Brady's and Cravath's statements made in the heat of battle came back to haunt them later when United States Senator Myers, in August, 1921, requested the Senate Judiciary Committee to conduct an investigation into the political activities of the motion picture industry. He cited as the basis of this investigation the statements made by the two industry representatives, and especially a comment made by Brady to the effect that the industry intended to become a factor in "the election of every candidate from alderman to President, from assemblyman to United States Senator." Myers also prepared to investigate the possible improper relationships between the industry and state boards of censorship. Although nothing officially ever came of this resolution,' it had the effect of reducing the effectiveness and prestige of both the NAMPI and the National Board of Review. During 1921, nearly one hundred measures relative to motion pictures were introduced in the legislatures of thirty-seven states.[61] The industry had every reason to be concerned.

There were other reasons for fearing federal intrusion into the affairs of the studios. For several years the federal government had kept a close watch on the trade practices of the motion picture industry. In 1915, the contracts issued by the General Film Company were declared void, and the film trust was ordered to desist from its methods of conducting business. The defendants were found to have "engaged in unreasonable restraint of trade and to have monopolized commerce in films, cameras, projectors, and accessories."[62] The government did not rest its efforts, however, and in 1918 the Federal Trade Commission issued an order against the Stanley Booking Corporation of Philadelphia, one of the largest and most successful combinations in the country. This order declared the company to be guilty of a wide variety of unfair trade practices.[63]

The most significant legislation in this early period was that aimed at the formidable Famous Players–Lasky Corporation in 1921. The evidence that the FTC had collected against Adolph Zukor and his corporation was overwhelming.[64] Zukor had established a carefully worked out plan to gain control, not only of the most popular stars of the day, but also of as many of the first-run theaters as possible. He soon had about 75 percent of the most popular stars in the industry, including Douglas Fairbanks, William S. Hart, "Fatty" Arbuckle, Blanche Sweet, and directors D. W. Griffith, Thomas Ince and Cecil B. De Mille. By 1918 Famous Players was distributing some 220 features a year, more than any one company before or since.[65] In 1917, as a defense against Zukor's increasing control of the film industry, First National Exhibitors Circuit was created to act as purchasing agent for twenty-six of the largest first-run exhibitors in the country. Eventually First National would work backward from exhibition to distribution and then to production itself.[66]

The growth of First National threatened Zukor's hegemony from several sides, for not only did it diminish his power over distribution, but it removed his control over the top stars as well. Both Chaplin and Mary Pickford were signed by the new combine to lucrative, profit-sharing contracts. Zukor decided to counterattack by going into the exhibition business for himself.[67] By August 31, 1921, Famous Players–Lasky had acquired 303 theaters. This immediately led to other production companies' attempting to acquire their own theater chains. It was at this point that the FTC filed its complaint against Zukor, charging unfair restraint of trade through monopoly control of the first-run theaters in the country.[68] The government's actions were but another prod in the direction of reform of the entire motion picture industry, and one which had direct financial implications for the disorganized producers.

The final, and in many ways the most devastating, blow against the movie industry came with a series of "incidents" involving several of the top stars in Hollywood.[69] Particularly unsavory was the scandal surrounding the popular comedian Roscoe "Fatty" Arbuckle. This story caused a sensation, and the popular press had a field day describing the death of a Hollywood "starlet" supposedly as the result of an incident in Arbuckle's San Francisco hotel room. This was followed by the still unsolved murder of director William Deane Taylor involving some top Hollywood personalities, and the divorce and quick remarriage of "America's Sweetheart," Mary Pickford. All these and other sensational stories captured the headlines as the public began to realize that many of their idols were but human after all. Benjamin Hampton claimed that the tremendous salaries paid to stars had much to do with this widespread public outcry of disapproval. "Admiration and adoration of movie celebrities had developed without any sound basis, and now many people who had formed the habit of idolizing their favorites as superior beings were shocked to discover that their divinities were money-grabbers of the most ordinary variety."[70] Obviously 1921 was not a very good year for the motion picture industry as all the resentments, failings and indifferences came to the fore. Terry Ramsaye, who had an intimate knowledge of the circumstances, dramatically described the dilemma faced by the producers:

The motion picture men had to be driven by the most desperate necessity before they could unite for a common cause. They now knew they must unite and that the only effective aid must come from outside the industry. None of those who had participated in letting the motion picture fall into the Slough of Despond could be of use in pulling it out.

They remembered what baseball had done in a similar if not quite so desperate a plight. . . .

The time was very ripe — over-ripe in fact.[71]

NOTES TO CHAPTER VI

1. The use of the term "movies" has persisted in America. It is interesting to note that this term is by no means universal. The European public remained faithful to the original "cinematograph," shortened to "cinema" in Britain and "kino" in continental Europe. In South Africa the term "bioscope" has remained the standard usage.

2. The issue of movie influence is discussed in detail in chapter XI.

3. George Mowry, ed., *The Twenties: Fords, Flappers and Fanatics* (Englewood Cliffs: Prentice-Hall, 1963), p. 1.

4. *Ibid.*

5. John D. Hicks, *Republican Ascendancy* (New York: Harper and Row, 1960), p. 167.

6. William E. Leuchtenburg, *The Perils of Prosperity* (Chicago: University of Chicago Press, 1958), p. 158.

7. Hicks, p. 181.

8. Leuchtenburg, p. 170.

9. William L. O'Neill, *Everyone Was Brave* (Chicago: Quadrangle Books, 1969), p. 262.

10. *Ibid.*, p. 300.

11. Hicks, p. 171.

12. Lynd and Lynd, *Middletown*, pp. 267–268.

13. *Ibid.*, p. 268.

14. *Ibid.*, p. 269.

15. Chicago Motion Picture Commission, *Report of the Commission*, September, 1920, p. 27.

16. De Fleur, *Theories of Mass Communication*, p. 115.

17. *Christian Century*, August 13, 1930, p. 987.

18. Robert E. Davis, *Response to Innovation*, p. 262.

19. A. T. Poffenberger, "Motion Pictures and Crime," *Scientific Monthly*, April, 1921, pp. 336–339.

20. *Ibid.*, pp. 336–337.

21. He noted: "It is the function of an educational medium and an entertaining medium also, to give the public what they should have in order that they may learn to want it." Poffenberger, p. 339.

22. *Christian Advocate*, July 16, 1925, p. 15.

23. *Christian Century,* January 22, 1930, p. 110.

24. *New York World,* October 30, 1927, p. 1.

25. *Report of the Chicago Motion Picture Commission.*

26. Young, *Motion Pictures,* p. 21.

27. *Ibid.,* p. 39.

28. *Proceedings of the National Education Association Annual Meeting,* 1923, p. 532.

29. *Ibid.,* p. 533.

30. The best review of this subject is William F. Kruse, "The Motion Picture and the American School," *International Review of Educational Cinematography,* vol. 4 (1933), pp. 645–654. For a comprehensive examination of the use of film as a teaching tool see Stuart A. Selby, "The Study of Film as an Art Form in American Secondary Schools" (Ed.D. dissertation, Columbia University, 1963).

31. Thomas E. Finegan, "The Results of the Experiments with Eastman Classroom Films," *International Review of Educational Cinematography,* vol. 1 (1929), pp. 131–147.

32. Letter in *The Outlook,* May 16, 1923, pp. 882–883.

33. Nelson L. Greene, "Motion Pictures in the Classroom," *The Annals of the American Academy of Political and Social Science,* no. 128 (November, 1926), p. 122.

34. Cline M. Koon, "Motion Pictures in Education in the United States," *International Review of Educational Cinematography,* vol. 6 (1935), pp. 476–477.

35. *Ibid.,* p. 483.

36. Ralph L. Henry, "The Cultural Influence of the Talkies," *School and Society,* February 2, 1929, p. 149.

37. *Ibid.,* p. 150.

38. *Collier's,* February 28, 1920, p. 16.

39. Paul G. Cressey, "The Motion Picture as Informal Education," *Journal of Educational Psychology,* vol. 7 (1934), pp. 508–509.

40. *Ibid.,* p. 508.

41. Orrin G. Cocks, "The Motion Picture and the Upbuilding of Community Life," the National Conference of Social Work, *Proceedings,* 1919, p. 311.

42. *Ibid.,* pp. 311–312.

43. The problem of the independent producer was that even if he could find the fairly large sum of money required to make worthwhile feature films, or even shorts, he then had to find a distributor. Obtaining distribution in first-run motion picture theaters was almost impossible in the face of the continuous product being turned out by the large studios; thus independent producers were seldom able to survive. Those that did were soon absorbed into the large studios. For a complete analysis of this problem see Heuttig, *Economic Control of the Motion Picture Industry,* pp. 94–95; and Lewis, *Motion Picture Industry,* pp. 81–141.

44. Cocks, "The Motion Picture," p. 313.

45. Orrin G. Cocks, "How a Neighborhood Can Improve Its Motion Picture Exhibitions," the National Conference of Social Work, *Proceedings,* 1921, pp. 340–343.

46. *Ibid.,* p. 342.

47. Carl E. Milliken, "The Movie: Has It a Social Obligation?," address before the National Conference of Social Work, *Proceedings,* 1927, pp. 352–360. The figures presented by Milliken were attacked by Edgar Dale in *Children's Attendance at Motion Pictures* (New York: Macmillan Company, 1935), pp. 64–66. Dale claimed that the data did not represent a true sample of the movie houses in New York, and were not representative of the country at large because at the time of the study New York had a law

which prohibited the attendance of children under sixteen without adult accompaniment. Also, the study had left out the figures on one theater where the children represented over 21 percent of the audience because it had showings only "three times a week." Milliken's presentation of these figures was an obvious attempt to refute the claims that children represented a significant segment of the audience for essentially adult films.

48. Claude A. Schull, "The Suitability of the Commercial Entertainment Motion Picture to the Age of the Child" (Ph.D. dissertation, Stanford University, 1939), p. 110.

49. *New York Times,* May 25, 1921.

50. Because industry figures are so difficult to obtain, and even then are not very reliable before 1922, one must rely upon reporters who were on the scene for a "textural analysis." For confirmation that the motion picture audience had indeed reached some sort of plateau in the period of late 1918 to early 1920 see Hampton, *History of the Movies,* pp. 200–202; and Jobes, *Motion Picture Empire,* pp. 176–196. Jacobs, *Rise of the American Film,* mentions the influenza outbreak as an important factor on p. 287.

51. Hampton, p. 282. Of course, this situation exists even today.

52. Inglis, *Freedom of the Movies,* p. 86.

53. Hampton, p. 291.

54. *Ibid.,* pp. 290–293.

55. For two slightly different accounts of this incident see Ramsaye, *A Million and One Nights,* pp. 482–483; and Hampton, p. 293.

56. Inglis, p. 86.

57. Hampton, p. 294.

58. *New York Times,* April 6, 1921.

59. *Ibid.,* April 27, 1921.

60. *Ibid.,* May 1, 1921. For a somewhat different version of this incident see Seabury, *The Public and the Motion Picture Industry,* pp. 149–150.

61. Inglis, p. 70.

62. Conant, *Antitrust in the Motion Picture Industry,* p. 20.

63. For a complete list of the specific complaints see Inglis, p. 23.

64. For more detailed examination of the Famous Players case see Inglis, pp. 31–39; Conant, pp. 23–27; and Seabury, pp. 21–23. H. T. Lewis, *The Motion Picture Industry,* has an excellent chapter on block-booking which centers on the Famous Players case on pp. 142–180.

65. Inglis, p. 32.

66. For a detailed examination of the methods of operation of First National see Inglis, pp. 33–34.

67. Zukor apparently based his desire for theaters on advice given to him by the financial firm of Kuhn, Loeb and Company in 1919. This report stated in part, ". . . the largest returns of the industry result from exhibiting pictures to the public, not from manufacturing them." Based upon this report Kuhn, Loeb and Company provided the capital with which Zukor entered the exhibition field. See Inglis, pp. 34–36; Conant, pp. 24–25.

68. *Federal Trade Commission v. Famous Players–Lasky et al.* Complaint no. 835.

69. The series of Hollywood scandals are described in several works, including Ramsaye; Hampton; and also in greater detail in Murray Schumach, *The Face on the Cutting Room Floor* (New York: William Morrow and Co., 1964).

70. Hampton, pp. 283–284.

71. Ramsaye, pp. 815–816.

VII

The Hays Office, 1922–1933

IN 1922 WHEN WILL H. HAYS, then the postmaster general of the Harding administration, decided to accept the position of president of the newly created Motion Picture Producers and Distributors of America (MPPDA), he faced this new challenge in his life with some trepidation and many doubts. He felt, however, that he could perform the task required of him. In his autobiography he commented on his thoughts at this moment:

I had been raised in a Christian home, and while I am not a reformer I hope that I have always been public spirited. It required no great insight to see that the young movie giant might well grow up to be a Frankenstein. And precisely because I was not a reformer, I dreaded the blunders the reformers would make in dealing with this new and vital force.[1]

Hays's concern for the motion picture industry in the hands of critics and reformers was largely based upon his belief that the official imposition of Prohibition had failed to produce the era of national sobriety that its proponents had contemplated. He wrestled with his decision whether or not to leave his government position for Hollywood for several weeks, and the reasons for his final decision are worthy of recall. Hays, spending Christmas with his family, overheard his son and two nephews arguing about who was to assume which star's identity in a game of cowboys:

"I want to be William S. Hart!" cried my boy. "No, I'm going to be him!" contradicted one of my nephews. "No, I am! You can be Doug [Fairbanks], and Bill can be the bad guy," yelled the other.

The text from the Scripture "out of the mouth of babes and sucklings Thou has perfected praise" flashed through my mind. They wanted to be Bill Hart. Not Buffalo Bill — Not Daniel Boone. But William S. Hart! To these little boys and to thousands of others throughout our land, William S. Hart and

Mary [Pickford] and Doug were real and important personages and at least in their screen characters, models of character and behavior.[2]

Hays may have exaggerated the drama of the moment that fateful Christmas morning when he recalled it some thirty years later, but he emphasized the sense of destiny and purpose he saw in the position of "czar" of the motion picture industry when he claimed: "I realized on that Christmas morning that motion pictures had become as strong an influence on our children and on countless adults, too, as the daily press, [and] . . . the great motion picture industry might easily become a corrupting as a beneficial influence on our future generations."[3] Hays accepted the challenge, and for over twenty-five years the "Hays Office" (as the MPPDA organization became known) played a major role in shaping the destiny of the motion picture industry.

Hays's selection as the man to "clean up Hollywood" caused a great deal of criticism. Hays himself surmised that the criticism "seemed to be that I was hiring myself out to the motion picture interests as a sort of a 'fixer,' to shield them from public and possibly legislative wrath."[4] The critics of the film industry were particularly upset when they discovered that Hays was vehemently opposed to legal censorship in favor of self-regulation. It was ironic that many exhibitors also attacked his selection on the grounds that he symbolized a threat of "blue-nosed regulation and political pressure." The general public was curious as to how effective he would be in his new position, and the newspapers gave the story of Hays's appointment a great deal of attention, for it represented a predictable conclusion to the series of scandal stories that had come out of Hollywood in the previous two years.

Hays's background was admirably suited to the task at hand. A lawyer, he had become a popular politician in his home state of Indiana, and had risen to the position of chairman of the Republican National Committee for the presidential campaign of 1920. His interest in motion pictures had been stirred by Woodrow Wilson's judicious use of peace propaganda films in the 1916 election, and during the Harding campaign he went out of his way to cultivate the newsreel men. He claimed that he was impressed by the potential of the motion picture based upon his experiences during and after the war, and he was more than likely one of the first major political figures to notice the social and political significance of the new medium.[5] His administrative abilities had been proven in his job as postmaster general, where he made several substantial improvements in the operation of the mail service, and his "moral credentials" as an elder in the Presbyterian church were impeccable. The motion picture industry could not have found a more prestigious figure to head up the MPPDA at a time when the industry was in danger of destroying itself.

The MPPDA was formally incorporated on March 14, 1922, when all industry support was withdrawn from the National Association of the Motion Picture Industry, and it was allowed to die an ignoble death. Ruth Inglis has indicated that the National Board of Review continued to receive the support of the industry, but that the Hays Office never really took any official notice of it. The creation of the MPPDA was a last-gasp effort by the motion picture industry to save itself from government regulation and to restore public confidence after the 1921 scandals. However, this new organization played both an external and an internal industry role. Although the external problems were acute and immediate, the resolution of internal squabbles was just as great a challenge. While very few of these intraindustry conflicts were ever made public, they caused a great deal of tension in Hollywood and especially in New York, where the industry had turned for financing. (Hays made the point that at the time of his appointment only one banker in New York — Otto H. Kahn — would do business with the industry at all.) Thus Hays's mandate was not only to improve the public image of the industry, but he was also charged with the complete reorganization of its internal cooperative structure. In the certificate of incorporation for the MPPDA one reason for incorporation was given as:

... to foster the common interests of those engaged in the motion picture industry in the United States, by establishing and maintaining the highest possible moral and artistic standards in motion picture production, by developing the educational as well as the entertainment value and the general usefulness of the motion picture, by diffusing accurate and reliable information with reference to the industry, by reforming abuses relative to the industry, by securing freedom from unjust or unlawful exactions, and by other lawful and proper means.[6]

To attain the goals the industry desired, Hays quickly surmised that he would have to achieve success in four major areas: (1) the motion picture had to be freed from the fear of any possible federal censorship, and also from any further incursions of political censorship in any form; (2) self-regulation had to become a viable and enforceable process; (3) public confidence had to be raised, and this could be done only by involving the public more directly in industry affairs; (4) relations had to be improved among various sectors that made up the industry and industry practices had to become more standardized. These goals absorbed the energies of the Hays Office for the next quarter of a century.[7]

The Hays Office and Censorship

While the threat of federal censorship aroused the film industry to hire Hays, it was the threat of further impositions of state censorship which commanded his immediate attention. In 1922 censorship bills were introduced into thirty-two states. The biggest test was in Massachusetts, where for the first time public opinion on censorship was to be tested by referendum. The outcome of this referendum was a good example of Hays's fine organizational capabilities combined with the motion picture industry's ability to bring its financial and other resources to bear on a particularly disturbing problem. The final results showed a resounding refutation of censorship by a vote of 563,173 to 208,252. Hays was elated, and so was the industry; in fact, it proved to be a turning point in the battle against censorship, as no major state censorship laws were enacted after that date.[8] Hays himself saw the result as a public vote of confidence and a willingness to allow the industry time to put its own house in order.[9]

Immediately after the defeat of the referendum bill, Hays's opponents charged that he had used his political connections and high-pressure methods to propagandize against it. The *Official Information to Voters,* in the argument against the bill, had quoted federal Secretary of State Charles E. Hughes as saying that such censorship was "un-American and intolerable." Hughes was later forced to send a telegram denying the accuracy of this statement.[10] The attitude of the Federal Council of Churches was also misrepresented, and their Massachusetts office disclaimed all responsibility 'for the distorted claims made on the council's behalf.[11] Hays destroyed all the pamphlets containing the misrepresentations.

At the hearings on the proposed federal motion picture commission in 1926, evidence was offered that Hays had in fact been visited by a representative of the Massachusetts State Committee on Motion Pictures, who informed him that the united churches of Massachusetts, the Roman Catholic and the Protestant, and 413 organizations were in favor of the law. Canon Chase noted with some chagrin that "Mr. Hays, however, increased his energies in applying his wonderful talents in influencing voters to vote contrary to the leadership of the churches." Chase also estimated that the MPPDA had spent well over $150,000 to finance their Massachusetts campaign, and that the distributors and exhibitors had probably spent a like sum.[12]

There was no doubt that Hays's methods were successful, and the MPPDA claimed that it had secured the support of over 90 percent of the daily and weekly newspapers in the state. The *Exhibitors Trade Review* of November 25, 1922, noted that "it was the first time in the history of the motion picture that the press threw its almost unanimous strength into a battle for freedom of expression. The influence exerted by the newspapers of Massachusetts was one of the biggest factors in the victory."[13]

Hays certainly left nothing to chance, and when the strategy he employed was spelled out in detail in the *Exhibitors Trade Review,* it showed the experienced hand of a first-class political organizer. The strategy provided for volunteer field men in many cities, furnished by MPPDA headquarters, who assisted the local secretary in coordinating the work of the citizens' committee and the theater owners and employees. The use of the telephone for canvassing was a major part of the anti-censorship campaign, and this technique was described as follows:

(a) Arrange to have wives of employees of theaters and their friends call up neighbors and friends urging a vote "No."

(b) In some instances theater owners could get telephone girls to mention it to their friends on their line. This requires a special arrangement.

(c) This is subject to big development, depending upon energy and resourcefulness of local committee.[14]

On election day Hays urged his workers to resort to an even more blatant piece of electioneering strategy:

1. Have one or more persons at each voting place urging voters to vote "No." There are 1,000 precincts in the State; 10 votes to the precinct gained by this work would be 10,000 voters, more than enough to assure victory in most any event.

2. Cards will be furnished workers to pass at point 150 feet from polls.

3. Badges may also be furnished by headquarters.

4. Let each worker know or learn the estimated total of his precinct, then proceed to get 51 per cent or more to vote "No." Each precinct worker to make his quota and go over the top in his sector.

5. Have our workers get on friendly terms with workers for candidates and get their help. At least keep them from combining against our referendum.

6. Get automobiles carrying voters to carry our placards.[15]

An analysis of the vote itself revealed very little other than the widespread anticensorship feeling in the state. Not one single county voted in favor of the bill, and only 36 of the 368 polling stations showed a "yes" vote. Most of these were very small constituencies in comparison to the overwhelming "no" vote in the larger centers.[16] There was not much difference between rural and urban sections, and the overall state vote ran at a 2.7:1 ratio against censorship. In Boston the vote was 38,240 in favor, and 104,824 against — a 2.8:1 ratio.[17]

The difficulty in making any final assessment of the Massachusetts referendum as an honest expression of public feeling was caused by the testimony of Canon Chase at the 1926 hearings. In discussing the vote Chase made this interesting observation: "This referendum . . . cannot be claimed to be a vote against Federal regulation but against State censorship. Many who voted against the bill did so because they favored Federal regulation and some of the speakers who were sent out by the Hays Office gave that as a reason for voting against State regulation or State censorship."[18] Chase also suggested that it was a "good-natured" vote designed to give Hays a chance to "prove his ability to improve the morality of the movies" without the use of outside laws. However, it is doubtful that the public's desire for federal regulation of the medium was as universal as Chase suggested.

There was also some suggestion that the public had deliberately been fed a distorted and terrifying picture of federal censorship. Canon Chase quoted a letter from the Reverend E. T. Root, secretary of the Massachusetts Federation of Churches, to this effect:

The newspapers were so hostile that advocates of the law could not get sufficient publicity to correct misrepresentations. I believe, therefore, that the vote reflects, not a reasonable opinion, but instinctive resentment against a censorship which nobody had proposed.

If this centralized industry can thus override the deliberate judgement of the legislature and churches of a State like Massachusetts, it possesses a most dangerous power to affect public opinion. *Might it not be used to sweep us into war?*[19]

Hays had drawn upon his vast political experience to overwhelm the opposition, because he realized the important psychological victory to be gained from this public defeat of censorship.

Even before the Massachusetts vote Hays had begun to lay the foundations for a constant opposition to censorship in any form. The offices of the MPPDA generated a flood of speeches, newspaper releases and magazine articles calculated to convince the public that censorship was un-American, autocratic, unconstitutional and would lead eventually to the curtailment of individual liberties. In a speech before a group of business-men in Los Angeles, Hays proclaimed: "Statewide or nation-wide censorship will fail in everything it undertakes. It has not been done successfully and never will be. Too many people who know nothing about the business are named to censorship boards."[20]

Certainly the industry had every reason to fear censorship, but there was never any indication that public opinion was solidly behind this drastic form of social control, even during the dark years of 1919–1922. Even the federal government was reluctant to consider this move, and there was no attempt made by the administration itself to introduce any legislation to control or censor the content of motion pictures. The only government action concerning motion pictures during this period was in the field of antitrust investigations. While there is no evidence of other than normal relations between the industry and the administration, the presence and prestige of Will Hays must have had some ameliorating influence. Besides, the American public as a whole seemed to agree with the philosophy of noninterference, and the word "censorship" did indeed have disagreeable connotations in that it suggested political suppression akin to the very unpopular Volstead Act.[21]

Public apathy did not deter those zealous reformers who continued their agitation for censorship regulations. In 1923 Congressman Upshaw introduced a bill to create a federal motion picture commission in the Department of the Interior. This bill also described standards of morality to govern the production of films and provided for the licensing of all films entering interstate or foreign commerce. Although this bill failed at this time, it was reintroduced in 1926, at which point it gained substantial support, and became the source of considerable industry trepidation. The hearings before the House Committee on Education on this 1926 bill, and a similar one introduced by Congressman Swoope, were significant, for they congregated in one place, and at one time, all the various arguments for and against federal legislation which had been offered in the previous twenty-five years. Those in favor of the bill, headed by Canon William Sheafe Chase, then general secretary of the Federal Motion Picture Council, testified for several days as to why federal legislation was so urgently needed. Dr. Chase summed up many of the frustrations that these reformers felt about the motion picture in his testimony:

The lamentable thing is that the motion picture in the history of the world has not yet been used educationally, scientifically, in our public schools. . . . The remarkable thing is that the motion picture has been seized upon by the amusement agencies of civilization, and the great problem now is how to change that situation.[22]

Now, then, this bill provides the only way of effectively and promptly meeting a great new and national evil. The producers have centralized their business and fortified it by engaging a political manipulator of wide experience and influence to whom it has entrusted czarlike power. To expect to meet this incorporated, highly financed, national evil by local or State laws or by the vague and academic process of education is puerile . . . whenever any business is so great and so intricate in its control and influence over the life and morals of the people, that business should be regulated by the United States Government or it should be regulated by some power big enough to regulate it — big enough to control it.[23]

Thus the social control problem had come full circle. Dr. Chase had been an opponent of the commercial motion picture ever since its early years and he had started his career as one of the chief supporters of Mayor McClellan's attempt to close the New York movie houses in 1908! For over twenty years he had fought the growing importance and influence of the motion picture as a commercial entertainment, and these 1926 hearings were to be his last major effort to bring about greater legislative control of the medium. Now he was advocating centralized federal control as the only means of combating the evils spread from a centralized source, for twenty years of experience had convinced him that local and state censorship had done very little to improve the overall moral quality of the movies. Chase's change toward favoring centralized control was typical of many others who advocated motion picture censorship. The reason for this change in emphasis from local to federal legislation is rather interesting, indicating not only that the censors had become thoroughly disillusioned by the failure of existing community controls to force the industry to improve its product but, significantly, that the nature of the reformers had also largely been altered. The appended list of proponents of the Upshaw bill showed a large number of Protestant clergymen, presidents of women's clubs and representatives of the WCTU. There were relatively few educators, and almost no professional social workers, psychologists or medical doctors. (The list of opponents of the bill is much shorter and was evenly divided among women's clubs, the industry and affiliated groups, and representatives of the N.B.R.'s Better Films Committee.)[24] Thus by the 1920s the battle standards were being carried high by two important, but somewhat elitist, groups — the reformers associated with the Protestant church, and the amalgam of various women's organizations. (Educators were more concerned with finding uses for the medium in the schools.) It was this mixed pressure group which formed the bulk of the opposition to the Hays Office's efforts to secure for the industry the right to regulate itself in the period between 1922 and 1933.

The Hays Office and Public Relations

Hays upon his appointment assumed immediate responsibility for establishing public confidence in the MPPDA and its avowed purpose to bring about changes in the industry. He lost no time in addressing a variety of social organizations in an attempt to "beg for time" to do the job. As an example, on July 6, 1922, he spoke to the National Education Association, where he made one of his many speeches indicating the industry's willingness to have its sincerity toward the public judged by its product:

Everyday there is an opportunity in the studios to take that action at the place and at the only place where effective action can be taken. Responsibility for these pictures now being made by members of our association can not be avoided. They will be proof either of our honesty of purpose or of our failure. They will be proof either of our ability to correct our evils ourselves or of our inability to run our own business. . . . While asking for your aid and cooperation I would like to ask, too, that you judge us by our actual performances rather than by any promises we may make.[25]

Twelve years later Hays would realize that the concerned groups had indeed taken him at his word, and, after judging the effectiveness of the self-regulatory process by the resultant product, they still found it unsatisfactory.

The Hays Office ultimately failed to still public criticism of the film industry. Although a large number of people and numerous organizations were enlisted in support of the MPPDA in the first years of its operation, by the end of the twenties the critics were as vociferous as ever, and pro-censorship groups were better organized. The Hays Office provided a convenient and prominent target for reform groups, for now the industry had a centralized decision-making authority which could be forced to shoulder the blame and accept the responsibility for the industry's product. The industry by its incorporation of the MPPDA had signaled that it was prepared to make a commitment to respond to public pressures. Unfortunately, many producers were under the impression that the mere creation of the Hays Office was sufficient to cope with this pressure. They were wrong; instead, the operations of the Hays Office were criticized as much as the films themselves, but this criticism was now directed at a supposedly responsible (and tangible) body.

The failure to appease these concerned groups lay in the inability of the Hays Office to implement any of the reforms they suggested, and which were sometimes publicly agreed to by the producers. It was only in the early thirties, some twelve years after he had assumed office, that Hays would indirectly secure the enforcement machinery necessary to fulfill many of the public promises he had made. Nevertheless, the attempts by the MPPDA to channel and control the criticism of the industry were not entirely unsuccessful, and many special groups were quasi-sponsored by the Hays Office to "advise" the film makers on what they were doing wrong. Before 1930 these advisory groups played an important role in maintaining an illusion of industry-public cooperation, but the arrival of sound and the attendant problems of a depressed industry soon destroyed even this sham.

After the fiascoes of 1921, the first major step in cementing public relations within the newly created Hays Office was to bring together as many interested social organizations as possible to explain the industry's new attitude of cooperation. Raymond Moley claimed that Hays's political experience had made him aware that "the public" was not a single entity, but "a complex mass of groups of people organized in societies, clubs, associations, fraternities, parties and other forms of group activity having economic, social, cultural, religious and many other purposes," and that all these groups had leaders who could be reached.[26] Many of these groups in their official capacities had already voiced their opposition to the current state of the movies, so Hays decided to meet his opposition halfway and to enlist their advice and support in improving the content of the medium to their satisfaction. By working through the film industry instead of against it, Hays hoped to convince the critics that the industry was willing to listen to rational suggestions. Sincere though he may have been, the welfare of the industry was, of course, uppermost in his plan.

On June 22, 1922, a conference of all interested parties was held at the Waldorf-Astoria Hotel, and was attended by more than two thousand delegates representing a wide variety of viewpoints. (The cost was borne by the MPPDA.) At this meeting Hays put forward the industry's position that it "stands at attention" to do the will of groups representing public opinion.[27] The immediate result of this conference was the appointment of a committee (consisting of Lee F. Hanmer, director, Division of Recreation, Russell Sage Foundation; Mrs. Oliver Harriman, president, Camp Fire Girls of America; and James E. West, chief scout executive, Boy Scouts of America) which was charged with the duty of nominating a board of national scope to develop a program for the improvement of motion pictures. After a few months a "committee of twenty" was formed which eventually became the official Committee on Public Relations, a body composed of official and unofficial representatives of more than seventy national organizations. Mr. Hanmer became chairman, and Colonel Jason S. Joy, who was unknown to Hays at this time, was appointed executive secretary.

For a period of over two and a half years this committee was the major point of contact between the industry and those groups wishing to "improve" motion pictures. The committee was subjected to many of the same criticisms directed at the National Board of Review because it too received financial support from the MPPDA. Raymond Moley defended this financial arrangement by pointing out that the industry had far more to gain through the undirected and uncontrolled action of such a committee than it could gain through attempts to dictate its policies — attempts which would inevitably have become publicly known. The expenses were paid because the committee was, in fact, "performing a service not only for the public, but for the industry."[28]

Some of America's most prestigious social organizations were represented on the Committee for Public Relations, including the Daughters of the American Revolution, the Boy Scouts of America, the General

Federation of Women's Clubs, the International Federation of Catholic Alumnae, the Russell Sage Foundation, the American Library Association, the YMCA, and the National Recreation Association. Organized religious bodies (especially Protestants) played a minor role in the work of this committee because their objectives still lay in the direction of censorship, and they saw this type of cooperation with the industry as a distraction created to draw attention away from their efforts.

This attitude of the church was exemplified in a statement made by Archbishop Curley, Bishop of Maryland, in 1926 at the hearings on bill H.R. 4094. He stated:

The moving picture might be a very practical vehicle of education and amusement, but as a matter of fact (and we are dealing with facts not theories), the major impression made by the movies of today is that they are more destructive than constructive. They tend to dissipate the mind, to cripple its power of concentration on serious work by our young people, and worst of all, they have little, if any, moral-uplifting effect. They treat of illegitimate love affairs, of triangular situations, of marital infidelity, and of sex problems, ad nauseam.[29]

At the same hearings a statement by Rabbi Rosenau of Baltimore was placed before the committee, in which he said: "Unless our tactics are changed, the movies must become the destroyers of all that humanity has valued as its greatest asset. . . . I do not wish to pose as a so-called 'uplifter.' I desire to help merely in the preservation and promotion of morals. It is for this reason that I point to the movie now fast becoming a menace to society."[30] These were but two of many such attacks on the Hays Office for failing to meet the criticisms of the moral content of films. Many organized religious groups would continue their fight for some form of national control or censorship while shunning the industry's offer of cooperation.

The primary function of the Committee for Public Relations was to influence the content of films by expressing to the industry, through the Hays Office, its specific objections to certain themes. The committee never attempted to function as a censorial body, but hoped to improve viewing tastes among the general public so that producers would find it financially advantageous to make better films. (This was, of course, exactly the philosophy which the National Board of Review had adopted ten years before without much visible success.) The committee itself never released a list of approved films, but encouraged many of its affiliated organizations to do so. The work of the committee dramatically illustrated once again the extremely wide divergence of opinion on suitable standards for motion pictures.

Dissension within the committee began as early as December, 1922, when Hays's attempt to reinstate "Fatty" Arbuckle within the film community was met with violent reactions from committee members. Hays in a well-intentioned attempt at fair play had obviously misread the mood of the public on this issue, and the storm of protest at his decision was one of the most vociferous and spontaneous outcries of public opinion ever aimed at the motion picture industry. Mayors, clergymen, educators, and women's club leaders all condemned this proposed action. The N.E.A. sent a telegram of protest, which said in part: "The actor is a teacher whose influence on public ideals is direct and powerful. Especially are motion picture actors idolized by tens of thousands of American youth."[31] Hays's actions were interpreted as a betrayal of the confidence the public had placed in the MPPDA. Feelings in the industry were just as strong and exhibitor groups pledged not to show Arbuckle films. The *New York Times* in an editorial commented that, while "Hays was employed to deodorize the movies," he now seemed to be reversing his policy.[32] The Committee on Public Relations immediately adopted a resolution asking Hays to advise the industry to "refrain from exhibiting pictures in which Mr. Arbuckle appears." The matter thankfully came to a close when Arbuckle, obviously distressed at the public's venomous reaction to his impending return as an actor, signed to direct films instead.

This incident was the first of several which destroyed the effectiveness of the Public Relations Committee, and between 1923 and 1925 the attrition rate of the groups constituting it was of great concern to Hays and his associates. Some of the representatives felt that they were engaged in "inconsequential work," while others referred to the work of the committee as a "smoke screen, an obvious camouflage, an approval stamp for salacious films and for the questionable, if not criminal conduct of the industry and its employees."[33] Among the most influential groups which defected were the National Congress of Parents and Teachers in October, 1924, and the General Federation of Women's Clubs in February, 1925. Their defection was a blow to the committee's prestige, and Hays attempted to induce both groups to renew their affiliation. However, his initial efforts were rebuffed.

The MPPDA was much more successful in improving intraindustry relations than in improving public relations, first by creating uniform contracts for most phases of the business, and then by establishing arbitration procedures for most disputes. It was not an easy task, and Hays met with recalcitrant producers at every turn. As we have previously seen, the Federal Trade Commission also became interested in the film industry, issuing the famous "cease and desist" order against Famous Players–Lasky for block-booking and other practices. The FTC entered into this "new spirit" of cooperation and subsequently called a trade-practice conference in 1927 "to encourage the industry to rectify abuses." Two other important industry groups were formed by the Hays Office — the

Copyright Protection Bureau in 1927, and the Studio Labor Relations Committee in 1928.[34]

The Open Door

The Public Relations Committee was finally absorbed officially into the MPPDA structure when Hays established a department of public relations in March, 1925. The creation of this department was based upon the theory that it would provide more direct contact between the public and the industry, and therefore negate the growing criticism from groups which felt that they had been denied a voice in the industry when they were excluded from the original committee. More important, the failure of the Hays Office after three years to tangibly improve the quality of motion pictures meant unabated public agitation, and Hays realized that the public's views were not yet fully integrated into the operational machinery of the MPPDA. He therefore developed what was known as the "open door" policy, which he outlined in this announcement:

Here in our Department of Public Relations is the Open Door of the industry. The public individually or through organization is invited to come in, bring complaints, suggestions, plans and ideas. Inside the open door is a table. On the table are motion picture problems. The solution of the problems challenges the help of every well-wisher for better things ... the organized industry sits in one chair. There is another chair right here for the organized moral forces of the country to occupy. Together, we can continue the solution of the problems. Everyone is invited who has a constructive suggestion. The door will always be open.[35]

Every organization in the country of any consequence was invited to send an authorized delegate, who would be in direct contact with the Hays Office to suggest improvements which could be adopted to make the medium more responsive to the public. The Public Relations Department was not only to be a service department for the industry, but Hays envisaged that it would also convey reports on public opinion systematically and directly to the industry. The Hays Office would thus be able to very quickly gauge which way the public mood was shifting, so that the industry would not be caught unprepared as it had been in 1918 and again in 1921. Colonel Jason Joy was appointed the head of this new department, a position that he was to retain until 1927, at which time he moved to Hollywood to take over the Studio Relations Department. After 1927 the department was headed by Carl E. Milliken, the former governor of Maine, who had always been a welcome spokesman on the industry's behalf.

The most obvious immediate benefit of this reorganization was a marked increase in the number of social and cultural organizations which established "friendly" relations with the Hays Office. Better arrangements were made for women's groups to preview pictures and to issue lists of approved films to their members. Even the two recalcitrant groups, the National Congress of Parents and Teachers and the General Federation of Women's Clubs, renewed cooperation with the Public Relations Department and utilized the improved previewing facilities. Within three years of starting operations, over three hundred national, state and local organizations had asked for information, made criticisms, complaints or suggestions, or had sought some form of cooperation from the MPPDA. Individuals too had utilized the "open door" so intensively that by 1932 the Public Relations Department's card index contained the names of more than 100,000 individual "friends of the movies."[36]

The department now prepared news releases, magazine articles and pamphlets. It also published the *Motion Picture,* a monthly magazine which described recent progress within the industry, and outlined the policies of the Hays Office. This publication also described the activities of public groups interested in motion pictures, and gave statistics on industry development. The public relations staff also compiled lists of favorable statements made by prominent persons regarding motion pictures, and wrote thousands of letters to correct misstatements, in addition to providing information on specific motion picture problems. The scheduling of public addresses was also an important activity; the department estimated that in 1926 more than 200 speeches were made by members of the staff, or by professional speakers whose cooperation had been enlisted by the department. In 1927 a special speakers' bureau was established to meet the demand for public addresses. In 1928 the department estimated that 102 formal addresses were made by members of the staff, and 453 were made by 77 other persons in over 20 states. By 1929 it was estimated that over 1,000 addresses were made by persons outside the industry, including approximately 750 radio addresses. The department also conducted personal interviews, and records of these indicated that in 1926, 3,650 were granted; in 1927 the number rose to 13,226; while in 1928 the beleaguered staff had to cope with over 15,000.[37]

The outgoing Committee on Public Relations had suggested in 1925 that annual meetings be held to maintain public interest and confidence. It was not until September, 1929, however, that the next major public conference was held under the auspices of the Hays Office. Even then, this meeting was attended only by specially invited guests who were present as private individuals, and not as designated representatives of their respective organizations. They were also mainly people who in the past had been "friendly" toward the industry, and the topics for discussion were selected beforehand. At this meeting of over two hundred "guests," four definite suggestions were made for immediate action: (1) a request for a direct representative of organized women in the motion picture industry to "interpret to the makers of motion pictures the feelings and wishes of womanhood in regard to the medium's development to its usefulness" (Mrs. Thomas G. Winter, former president of the General Federation, was nominated, and accepted the position); (2) the suggestion that a textbook or community handbook on the use of motion pictures be produced for widespread distribution; (3) the suggestion that a list of special children's films be made generally available; (4) the appointment of a committee to study the use of films in religious education.[38]

The Federal Motion Picture Council

The Federal Motion Picture Council (FMPC) was one of the very few nonindustry organizations which managed to organize national meetings to discuss the subject of moral reform for the movies. This organization was formed as a direct result of three conferences called by the Presbyterian church and other interested Protestant groups in 1922, 1924 and 1925. The council, more imposing and national in title than in reality, advocated the enactment of federal legislation to regulate the industry's trade practices and the quality of its product. This group actively lobbied in Washington in support of federal legislation, and distributed leaflets and offered its services for public addresses on the topic of control of the motion picture industry. However, it had no local chapters, but relied on the support of other local social organizations (such as the Women's Christian Temperance Union) in favor of its program.

The FMPC did succeed in arousing the interest, if not the ire, of the industry, and eventually it became the victim of one of the Hays Office's more unscrupulous public relations ploys. When the FMPC called its 1928 conference in Washington, the Hays Office "persuaded" some of its "friends of the movies" to attend this meeting, which included paying the expenses of several of these "delegates." A total of about fifteen people attended at the behest of the industry, and during the sessions of the conference, which attracted only about a hundred people in all, this group "obtained the floor and expressed their opinions regarding their own experiences in cooperation with the industry as evidence that such regulation as was proposed was unnecessary."[39] This industry-sponsored coterie also held a press conference and staged a "walkout," all of which was reported at great length in the press, while the official opinions of the FMPC were virtually ignored. Hays justified this action on the grounds that the FMPC's name implied a larger following than it had (which was quite true), and that the council "ignored the opinions of many individuals and organizations outside the industry whose membership and adherents far outnumber those of the F.M.P.C."[40]

Women's Organizations and the Motion Picture Industry

Mrs. Winter's appointment at the 1929 conference was significant, but almost backfired when a number of member groups of the General Federation of Women's Clubs made an official protest that this was merely another ploy by the Hays Office to "hoodwink the public."[41] The opposition to the appointment stemmed from the misunderstanding regarding her designation as "organized women's representative." This title left the impression that she had officially been selected by the various women's organizations, but the misconception was hastily corrected by the Hays Office. Nevertheless, there were suggestions that Hays, by this move, was attempting to regain the full cooperation of the prestigious General Federation. This speculation was later discounted after an extensive investigation of the public relations activities of the motion picture industry sponsored and published by the Federal Council of the Churches of Christ in America. The author of the study, Professor Herbert H. Shenton, of Syracuse University, pointed out that the General Federation had already reestablished official contact with the Hays Office in 1927 with the appointment of Mrs. A. A. Diehl as the federation's national motion picture chairman.[42] After weathering this initial criticism, Mrs. Winter proved to be a long-time and valuable employee of the MPPDA, and commanded a great deal of respect from the many women's organizations interested in films.

This interest of women's groups in the moral standards of the movies was a natural extension of their concern for the effects the medium was having upon their children. However, as their children grew up their viewpoint seemed to shift more toward an interest in the cultural and entertainment aspects of the movies. This meant that many women adopted the more realistic attitude that "audience suitability" was a more desirable goal to work toward, and recognized what the Hays Office had been saying for a long time — that there was a legitimate function for movies which went beyond the entertainment of children. (Interestingly enough, there was some suggestion by the industry that the coming of sound had caused a dramatic drop-off in attendance by children, presumably due to the fact that the substitution of spoken drama for pantomime made the film less attractive to children — a fact which was difficult to substantiate.)

Mrs. Diehl in her capacity as the official women's organization representative published several articles and made many speeches which put forward the "woman's point of view." Most of these were concerned with the "moral effects" of movies on individuals, especially the young. She reserved the right for women to be in the forefront of this fight for cleaner films because "it is our right to make our influence felt on all those phases of life which concern the happiness of our homes and children." She did, however, recognize the need for rational investigation of the problem, and stated in an article that "we must view clearly and set forth the harm that has been done by the screen and its potentialities for further harm. Then only will we be in a position to work intelligently to minimize the further evil possibilities of this gift of science and to capitalize on its inherent possibilities for service to the race."[43]

The three national women's organizations, the International Federation of Catholic Alumnae, the National Society of Daughters of the American Revolution, and the General Federation of Women's Clubs, each developed complete local, state and national motion picture programs in cooperation with the film industry. These national organizations undertook to distribute printed matter, chiefly lists of recommended films and pamphlets urging members to patronize the "better" films. They also previewed films at the facilities set up by the Hays Office, and functioned in much the same manner as the National Board of Review.[44] The real importance of the women's groups in Hollywood was little known or understood by the general public. In an article examining "Our Lady Censors" in 1929, theater critic Creighton Peet noted that "these Committees have no legal right to alter a film but their suggestions were almost invariably followed to the letter by the producers. The fact is that the women's clubs, by mere suggestion, probably achieve more changes in the films which you and I see in our theaters than all the state boards together." Peet also quoted Mrs. Winter as having said that "banality, not immorality, is the chief peril of the movies."[45]

Historian William O'Neill, in his study of the women's movement, has pointed out that the General Federation "never wavered on Prohibition and consistently endorsed all forms of moral censorship, especially the movies. Film censorship was almost an obsession with many social feminists in this period. The League of Women Voters supported it, and clubwomen ceaselessly investigated and inveighed against the movie industry."[46] Women did indeed play a major role in shaping the content of American films, both by favoring certain themes in their role as individual customers at the box office, and through the official influence of women's organizations as guardians of the public morality.

The Hays Office — Success or Failure?

Professor Shenton, in his important study of the public relations activity of the Hays Office, concluded that in the long run it would have been better if Hays had kept the public more fully informed about the internal difficulties he was experiencing in attempting to enforce self-regulation. This would have gained him public understanding and support, and provided him with a greater lever for insisting on more stringent controls. While the MPPDA did achieve remarkable progress in areas such as intraindustry relations, the establishment of special labor practices, and the development of preview facilities for interested groups, nevertheless by 1933 it had not yet satisfied the demands of those clamoring for "cleaner" films.[47]

It is difficult to accurately assess the achievements of the Hays Office in the first ten years of its operation because much of the work it accomplished was not reflected on the screen. The publicity surrounding the office's public performance tended to obscure its intraindustry successes. Thus while such important developments as the Central Casting Office, standardized contracts, improved international relations, the moral welfare of aspiring young actresses, and public services were all part of the overall achievements of the MPPDA, the important issues surrounding the "moral tone" of the movies were still unresolved. It was, nevertheless, in these external achievements that the "czar" was considered to have failed. Hays's title of "czar" was in fact a misnomer, for in the years before 1934 he had nowhere near the kind of authority and power necessary to force the producers to make any major shifts in content.

In all fairness, it should be pointed out that Hays was able to use the considerable power of the MPPDA to draw public attention to the "better films." As early as 1924, Hays went out of his way to call attention to the merits of the film *Abraham Lincoln,* which was then playing to small audiences in a first-run theater on Broadway. The film was ultimately a financial success. Later on Hays apparently applied the same "quick hypodermic" to the films *Nanook of the North* and *Grass* with "gratifying effect."[48] Writing in 1938, Sam Berman made the point that many "better" movies such as *A Midsummer Night's Dream* (1935) would most definitely not have been made had it not been for the existence of the Hays Office.[49]

Although it was a minority view, to many others Hays had in fact achieved what he had set out to do, a position which was offered in an article in the *Review of Reviews* in 1932. After approving of Hays's actions as head of the industry, the article continued:

Yet it would be impossible to make an appraisal of our manners, customs and social assets today without giving a top-line place to the motion pictures . . . [and] our greatest agency for public entertainment must be counted a positive means of welfare, with its abuses merely incidental to the conditions of American life that are steadily improving. . . . The Churches might borrow something — not of mechanism, but of energy and fascination — from this new form of entertainment and instruction.[50]

After 1930, the detractors and reformers became more vocal in their frustrated efforts to bring about greater social control, especially when it became obvious that the much discussed new self-regulatory code was not going to work. Hays's time was beginning to run out; for ten years he had managed to channel public opinion into fairly innocuous, but constructive, projects; eventually, however, the failure of the self-regulatory concept to bring about tangible results weakened many of the public relations connections that had been so carefully cultivated.

By the end of 1932 nearly forty national religious organizations and educational groups had adopted resolutions calling for some form of federal regulation of the motion picture industry.[51] Many felt that the industry had been using the Hays Office merely as a "straw man" and in fact had no real intention of ever changing its product away from the highly successful, but contentious, formulae it had developed. In February, 1932, United States Senator Brookhart introduced a resolution in the Senate to investigate the motion picture industry. Part of Brookhart's statement read: "Mr. Hays has done nothing toward improving the moral tone of the movies. . . . The truth is that Hays was employed primarily as a 'fixer' to protect the industry against any sort of reform or regulation through public action."[52]

Hays had tried his best, but unfortunately he could not withstand the internal social and economic forces which were then shaping the industry. The motion picture industry, unlike the United States Post Office, was not a stabilized, smoothly run organization. During his first twelve years in office, Hays presided over some of the most dramatic economic and technological changes in the industry's brief history. These institutional and technical alterations made it extremely difficult to implement any feasible plans for "reforming the movies."

NOTES TO CHAPTER VII

1. Will H. Hays, *The Memoirs of Will H. Hays* (Garden City: Doubleday and Co., 1955), p. 324. It should also be noted that Hays makes the all too common mistake of calling the creature "Frankenstein" instead of the doctor who created it.

2. *Ibid.*, p. 325.

3. *Ibid.*, p. 326.

4. *Ibid.*

5. Inglis, *Freedom of the Movies*, p. 88. Hays himself gives the details of his experiences with motion pictures during the war in W. H. Hays, pp. 135–136.

6. Cited in Raymond Moley, *The Hays Office* (New York: Bobbs-Merrill Company, 1945), p. 225, appendix A.

7. Moley, *The Hays Office*, p. 53. Hays himself worked out a "ten point" program for attention, five of which he thought were "emergency." See W. H. Hays, pp. 329–330.

8. For the best account of the Massachusetts referendum see U.S., Congress, House, Committee of Education, *Hearings, Proposed Federal Motion Picture Commission*, 69th Congress, 1st session, 1926, pp. 398–404. This is a much more balanced assessment of the role of the Hays Office, and the various methods used to bring about the defeat of the censorship bill.

9. W. H. Hays, p. 333.

10. *Hearings, Proposed Federal Motion Picture Commission*, 1926, p. 200.

11. *Ibid.*, p. 202.

12. *Ibid.*

13. Quoted in *Ibid.*, p. 200.

14. *Ibid.*, p. 200.

15. *Ibid.*, p. 201.

16. Commonwealth of Massachusetts, *Number of Assessed Polls, Registered Voters*, Public Document No. 43 (1922), pp. 428–431.

17. *Ibid.*, p. 431.

18. *Hearings, Proposed Federal Motion Picture Commission*, 1926, p. 203.

19. *Ibid.*, p. 202. (Italics added.)

20. *New York Times,* July 25, 1922, p. 12.

21. Leuchtenberg, *Perils of Prosperity*, p. 103.

22. *Hearings, Proposed Federal Motion Picture Commission*, 1926, p. 135.

23. *Ibid.*, p. 139.

24. *Ibid.*, pp. 458–464.

25. National Education Association, *Proceedings*, vol. 60 (1922), p. 254.

26. Moley, *The Hays Office*, p. 133.

27. Herbert Shenton, *The Public Relations of the Motion Picture Industry*, p. 66. This study was conducted by Professor Shenton for the Federal Council of Churches in 1931 (reprinted, New York: Jerome S. Ozer, 1971).

28. Moley, *The Hays Office*, p. 135.

29. *Hearings, Proposed Federal Motion Picture Commission*, 1926, p. 84.

30. *Ibid.*, p. 139.

31. *New York Times,* December 22, 1922, p. 1.

32. *Ibid.*, December 26, 1922, p. 12.

33. Quoted in Lewis, *Motion Picture Industry*, pp. 372–373.

34. The best sources for details on these achievements of the Hays Office to be found in Moley, *The Hays Office*, chapters 16 and 17; and Lewis, *passim.*

35. Quoted in Moley, *The Hays Office*, p. 138.

36. Shenton, p. 75.

37. *Ibid.*, p. 77.

38. Motion Picture Producers and Distributors of America, Inc., *The Community and the Motion Picture* (New York, 1929; reprinted, New York: Jerome S. Ozer, 1971), p. 13.

39. Shenton, p. 92.

40. *Ibid.*, p. 93.

41. *Christian Century*, March 5, 1930, p. 293.

42. Shenton, p. 85.

43. Mrs. Ambrose A. Diehl, "The Moral Effect of the Cinema on Individuals," *International Review of Educational Cinematography*, vol. 3 (1931), pp. 1123–1124.

44. The best single document for details of the total public relations activities of the Hays Office is found in Shenton.

45. Creighton Peet, "Our Lady Censors," *Outlook*, December 25, 1929, pp. 645–647.

46. O'Neill, *Everyone Was Brave*, p. 261.

47. Shenton, pp. 144–151, contains the conclusions of this study.

48. Sam Berman, "Will Hays," *Fortune*, December, 1938, p. 142.

49. *Ibid.*

50. Albert Shaw, "Will Hays: A Ten Year Record," *American Review of Reviews*, March, 1932, pp. 30–31.

51. Schull, "Suitability of Commercial Entertainment," p. 176.

52. *Harrison's Reports*, February 27, 1932. Quoted in Inglis, p. 119.

VIII

The Industrial Setting for Control, 1920–1933

AFTER THE SHORT PERIOD OF UNCERTAINTY at the end of the First World War, the motion picture industry continued to grow and spread throughout the world in an unprecedented manner. The development of the motion picture as an entertainment and art form had been inextricably enmeshed in the continuing improvement of the mechanical apparatus so necessary for filming or projection, and in most instances dramatic developments in the aesthetic aspects were the result of the introduction of more sophisticated equipment and techniques. In this improvement process, as film production became more technically sophisticated it also became more expensive, and the larger the required investment the more determined the studios became to ensure a profitable financial return on each item produced. It was this simple economic fact that caused the content of Hollywood films to adhere so rigidly to certain formulae, all proven successes at the box office. This economic requirement also accounted for the industry's insistence that producers needed to control exhibition sites in order to have a ready market for all their produce.

The motion picture industry's financial and marketing structure was not conducive to a great deal of aesthetic experimentation. Nevertheless, in the fifteen-year period before the Second World War the American film achieved a high level of artistic excellence. The studio became the focal point of all production, for here were concentrated a combination of talents — actors, producers, directors and technicians — called from all parts of the world. The result of these combined talents was the creation of a real entertainment "industry," and as one film scholar has noted, "In its [the studio's] hot house atmosphere were bred the worst excesses of Hollywood and its greatest glories."[1] The studios became smoothly functioning machines, turning out films with a regularity and sense of purpose that rivaled Henry Ford's assembly-line operations. It is indeed remarkable that so many memorable examples of the cinematic art did emerge from these "film factories" during this period.

Once Hollywood had readjusted itself to the series of disasters leading up to the appointment of Will Hays, the American film industry settled down to a long period of consolidation and growth which lasted even into the first years of the Depression. It is difficult to establish whether the medium during the decade of the twenties was truly the innovator of social or cultural changes, as its critics (and admirers) claimed, or whether the movies merely picked up the "least hint" of the latest trends and helped to spread these to a wider, but less sophisticated, audience. What is certain, however, is that after the war the motion picture quickly caught up with the mood of the twentieth century, and while some remnants of the earlier moralizing remained, the movies became, without doubt, the most popular entertainment of the "Jazz Age."

The Content of American Films, 1922–1933

In the period just before the coming of sound films in 1927, American motion pictures were undergoing severe criticism for their constant depiction of an "unreal" concept of life. Whereas the pre-1914 film was clearly aimed at the working class, by 1922 the industry's product almost exclusively reflected the lives of a somewhat imaginary leisure class, a genre which seemed to have broad appeal and acceptance that cut across all class lines. One film historian has remarked that the people in these films all had "lovely homes and lovely clothes and lovely cars and lovely lives. This was the desired, distorted mirror image of American 'normalcy.' "[2]

Much of this shift in emphasis can be attributed to a reaction to the harsh realities of World War I, but other factors, such as the seeming prosperity of the country evident in the growth of the stock market, the increasing "consumerism" as a way of life, and even the influence of Freud's ideas, contributed to the "new morality" so evident on the American screen. America in the 1920s was a paradox, for while there was an obvious change in the moral outlook of the younger generation, there also existed a strong reactionary attitude in political and economic life. Perhaps the two ideologies were not so incompatible as would be imagined, for faced with the undermining of the traditional values and beliefs, reactionary feelings became manifest in those institutions which had the most to lose.

Lewis Jacobs has noted that the motion picture industry, "like the Supreme Court, followed the election returns. They took up the cause of business, grew cynical, and participated in the repudiation of a pre-war conventionality."[3] The public in fact had grown tired of moralizing, and the popular directors of the earlier period, such as Porter, Blackton and even Griffith, had a great deal of difficulty in retaining the public's interest. While the old values and sentiments were not entirely swept away they nevertheless took on a more materialistic viewpoint that was also decidedly feminine in character, and which seemed to "be in equal part due to the effect of female emancipation and of defensive male reaction to it."[4] John Baxter has pointed out that "throughout practically every film of the class ["sophisticated" melodramas] it is the woman who is adoring, devoted, faithful, sacrificing; the man who philanders and allows himself to be distracted and seduced by the Wrong Girl."[5] There is no doubt that Hollywood had discovered the box-office appeal of sophisticated "sex" and film makers throughout these years were in intense competition to find new ways of presenting old sexual themes to an overeager audience. It was the continued prevalence of these themes and their success with audiences that most dismayed those who had hoped that the industry would accede to a workable form of self-regulation.

The motion picture industry for a short while even adopted the guise of a political propaganda machine, when it marshaled its forces to counter the threat of Bolshevism in America. The Bolshevik success of 1917 had alarmed many Americans who were concerned about the spread of revolutionary socialist principles to other countries. After a number of incidents in 1919 involving supposed revolutionaries, Attorney General Mitchell A. Palmer organized a series of raids to counter this "threat to the nation." Hollywood's assistance was elicited, and a string of films resulted, the most influential being an adaptation of a novel by Thomas A. Dixon (of *Birth of a Nation* fame) entitled *Bolshevism on Trial*. While this film was claimed to be an impartial representation of all sides of the question, it was in fact a polemic against socialist doctrine. The "power of the movies" was even harnessed by the federal government against socialism, and a report in the *New York Times* for January 1, 1920, claimed:

The movies will be used to combat Bolshevik propaganda as the result of the conference held yesterday. . . . Mr. Lane [secretary of the interior] emphasized in his address the necessity of showing films depicting the great opportunities which industrious immigrants may find in this country, and of stories of poor men who have risen high. He suggested that the industry organize immediately to spread throughout the country the story of America as exemplified in the story of Lincoln.[6]

However, the rising tide of prosperity did more to deemphasize the threat of Bolshevism than either the Palmer Raids or film propoganda, and the content of the medium quickly began to reflect a much less serious tone. Hollywood soon sensed the shifting mood of the country and, using every publicity ploy available, produced thousands of films with the new social and moral standards as their central theme. John Baxter has written of this period that "social comedies and domestic dramas found their motives in the new, post-Freud fascination with sex, the emancipation of American women, the working girl, the discarding of old codes of manners as of ethics, the slackening of marital ties."[7]

More than any other director, Cecil B. De Mille, in his numerous films, paid homage to this new morality and its superficiality. De Mille's success lay in his uncanny ability to gauge which way the public's interest seemed to be shifting, and to pattern his productions accordingly by extending these shifting moods to almost illogical conclusions. The audience loved it. It was De Mille who started the long cycle of modern "sophisticated" comedies and melodramas, and "dwelling on both the fashions and the foibles of the fabulously rich, he opened up a whole new world for the films, a world that middle-class audiences, newly won to the movies by the luxurious theaters then springing up, very much wanted to see."[8] De Mille's films were so popular that they became the paradigm for the successful commercial motion picture, and were slavishly copied by producers at other studios. Two French film historians, after a close examination of De Mille's work, gave this assessment:

With Cecil B. De Mille we encountered a man with other preoccupations [other than Griffith's aesthetic sense], more nearly related to commerce than to art. In this figure, who for five or six years, enjoyed a fame as great as that of most illustrious stars, can be detected the origins of much that was to orientate the cinema towards a brilliant mediocrity. He discovered and adapted formulas which were so successful commercially that they discouraged research by independent workers.[9]

It was De Mille who brought to perfection the art of "sex appeal," and he practically invented the "bathroom scene." Describing his brother's films, William de Mille noted: "The bath became a mystic shrine dedicated to Venus, or sometimes Apollo, and the art of bathing was shown as a lovely ceremony rather than a merely sanitary duty. Undressing was not just the taking off of clothes; it was a progressive revelation of entrancing beauty; a study in diminishing draperies."[10] After several highly successful films in this vein, De Mille sensed a new mood, and reversing his trend produced *The Ten Commandments* in 1923, just a few months after the formation of the Hays Office. His ability to give the public what it seemed to desire and yet to cloak it with religious respectability led to an even greater success than had his earlier, more blatant efforts. Analyzing De Mille's work, film historian Arthur Knight has noted: "Better than any other director of the era, he seems to have apprehended a basic duality in his audience — on the one hand their tremendous eagerness to see what they considered sinful and taboo, and on the other, the fact that they could enjoy sin only if they were able to preserve their own sense of righteous respectability in the process."[11]

While the sophisticated sex drama-comedy was a staple item in American cinemas, there were other genres which were equally popular. The Western continued to be the single most popular form among all ages and classes, and by the mid-twenties it had passed into its "classic period" with assembly-line production methods and formula plots, while the Western star remained the great American hero.[12] Costume melodramas came into vogue with Rudolph Valentino — *The Sheik* (1921) — and Douglas Fairbanks — *The Mark of Zorro* (1921), *The Thief of Bagdad* (1924), *Robin Hood* (1922), and others. Comedies remained popular, and besides the continued popularity of Chaplin, new comedy stars now appeared, notably Harold Lloyd and Buster Keaton.

Spurred on by the scenes of actual footage from the war, newsreels became very popular. In the twenties each of the major movie studios had its own newsreels; Zukor had Paramount News; Universal, International, and Loew's used Hearst Metrotone News at various times during the decade. John Baxter has pointed out that these were of great importance in cementing the industry's political connections, and Louis B. Mayer bound Hoover's affections to himself by the crucial support the Hearst newsreels gave to Hoover's election campaign. The public's interest in these more "educational" aspects of the medium was further evidenced by the success of the pseudo-anthropological documentary, such as Robert Flaherty's *Nanook of the North* (1920), which proved to be the surprise film of the decade. Upon the stength of this film Paramount hired Flaherty to film a documentary of life in the South Seas. Entitled *Moana of the South Seas* (1926), it was a beautifully filmed record of life among the Samoan tribes but without the usual South Sea sex story. Paramount subsequently became disenchanted and let Flaherty go.[13]

The animated cartoon also made its first appearance as a regular feature of the motion picture screen in the early twenties, and Felix the Cat, Oswald the Rabbit and Mortimer (later Mickey) Mouse became better known and loved than many human stars.[14]

While most of these new developments were welcomed by audiences and critics, it was, however, the sensational "sex" and, after 1925, "gangster" films which met the greatest opposition from reform groups. The Hays Office, as we have noted, was powerless to prevent these thematic explorations which proved to be so popular with the general public, and the accompanying high-powered Hollywood publicity campaigns only added to Hays's problems. In a competitive market the studios aggressively vied with each other to see who could promise the most in publicity while actually delivering the least on the screen. An examination of titles during the period gives some idea of why the motion picture was considered to be such a serious "moral" problem by many groups. *Why Change Your Wife?; Forbidden Fruit; The Married Virgin; Why Women Sin;* and *At the Mercy of Men* were just a very few of the many lurid titles used by the major film studios.

The advertising blurbs for these films were themselves a major point of contention, and the daily newspapers in the twenties and thirties continually featured enticements such as these:

She lured men. Her red lips and warm eyes enslaved a man of the world . . . and taught life to an innocent boy! Hot tropic nights fanning the flames of desire. She lived for love alone.

The scarlet truth about a reign of terror broken by a night of love! The smart set sought her secretly and compromised her privately.

Honor abandoned to crimson lips. Beauty incarnate, red-lipped, alluring. She tried men's souls in the fires of infatuation. For her kisses they shattered friendship, and faced dishonor.

She stopped at nothing. She wanted happiness, fun, romance, but the things she sought were denied, so she stopped at nothing to get what was forbidden. The shockingly real drama of a modern girl.[15]

It should be remembered that these publicity blurbs were all prepared at a time when the MPPDA supposedly had control over the advertising as well as the content of films. Hays and his assistants were embarrassingly aware of this situation, but as usual they seemed powerless to act effectively. C. C. Pettijohn, the general counsel of the MPPDA, made this quite clear in an address to the Indiana Board of Endorsers of Photoplays on April 23, 1930, when he stated:

Our advertising at times impresses me as being appropriate only for burlesque shows or honky-tonk performances of some other kind. Some of our advertising needs a "sitz bath." It is not all bad. Some of it is very good. But too much of it displays rotten taste and lack of business judgement. There is room, plenty of room, for improvement in our advertising.[16]

The Coming of Sound

Film producers had been striving to achieve "sound" films ever since the motion picture had become a viable commercial enterprise. However, it was not until 1927 that Warner Brothers achieved a complete technical and commercial success in this respect with the release of *The Jazz Singer,* starring the popular entertainer Al Jolson. For this important extension of the film medium Warners had adopted the Vitaphone process which utilized sixteen-inch, one-sided phonograph records that played at 33⅓ revolutions per minute, each record lasting for one reel. This unwieldy process was later improved by the use of a sound track recorded directly on the film — the method which is still in use today.

While the arrival of sound was viewed by most film makers and critics as merely another novelty, like tinted films, others were more convinced of its permanence. Warner Brothers Studios in fact had invested so heavily in the future of sound that had the innovation failed to garner public support the studio would have become instantly bankrupt.[17] Benjamin Hampton, who was intimately acquainted with the industry's complex economic structure, made a strong case that the coming of sound films in fact proved to be the financial "shot in the arm" that the industry so urgently needed in 1928–1930. He suggested that a combination of several factors had created a very difficult situation for the studios, who were desperately looking around for some new novelty to "overcome the lukewarmness and the silent antagonism" which were becoming obvious. Hampton's experience led him to believe that three factors were responsible for the slowdown in the rate of growth which had occurred in the years after 1924: first, prices of admittance had become too high; second, good pictures had educated audiences, and the appearance of mediocre films injured the industry; third, all pictures were made for the large patronage of first-run houses, and, as audiences now included the entire public, there was definite need of differentiation in both production and distribution.[18]

Hampton further suggested that the industry had been unable to find a method of satisfying the needs of the "more intelligent classes" which were "now represented in the democracy of movie patrons." This was because "the industry had no methods of differentiation; its machinery was set to make pictures pleasing to all individuals in the huge first-run audiences, constituting a cross section of society, in which all ranges of intelligence and taste and mood are represented."[19] The answer to this problem was to differentiate the types of movie houses and to make more minority-interest films, but the large studios which controlled exhibition were reluctant to risk this; the result was that toward the end of the decade many large movie houses were playing half empty much of the time.

How much of this apparent slowdown in growth was due to the rising popularity of radio is uncertain, but there is no doubt that by 1927 the American public was beginning to take commercial radio as much to their hearts as they had earlier done with the moving picture.[20] There is some evidence to suggest that radio did initially affect attendance at motion pictures, but the public soon returned to its regular movie-going patterns, except when a particularly thrilling event (such as a heavyweight title fight) was being broadcast — at which time the movie houses would be noticeably empty.

TABLE 7

COMPARISON OF RADIO SETS AND MOTION PICTURE
ATTENDANCE IN THE U.S., 1922–1936

YEAR	TOTAL NUMBER[a] RADIO SETS	SETS PER[a] HOUSEHOLD	AVERAGE WEEKLY[b] MOVIE ATTENDANCE (millions)	WEEKLY[b] ATTENDANCE PER HOUSEHOLD
1922	400,000	.016	40	1.56
1924	n.a.	n.a.	46	1.71
1925	4,000,000	.145	n.a.	n.a.
1926	n.a.	n.a.	50	1.78
1928	n.a.	n.a.	65	2.23
1930	13,000,000	.433	90	3.00
1932	n.a.	n.a.	60	1.97
1934	n.a.	n.a.	70	2.24
1935	30,500,000	.956	n.a.	n.a.
1936	n.a.	n.a.	88	2.7

[a] *Source:* Melvin De Fleur, *Theories of Mass Communication*, p. 66.
[b] *Source: Ibid.*, p. 40.

Bosley Crowther, the film historian and critic, has suggested that radio also created a dissatisfaction with the silent film:

The illustrations of soundless movies had prevailed as entertainment and as art so long as the public was unaccustomed to being stimulated by mechanical music and voice. But as soon as the public's ears were opened by the device of the radio, as they were, during the mid-1920's . . . and people's minds were stimulated to create images to match what they heard, a vague sense of the lack of aural content in motion pictures began to be felt. A subtle psychological rejection of the incongruity of the silent screen occurred.[21]

The automobile was also a major factor in the changing leisure patterns of the American people, and as historian John Rae has indicated, "1929 was a watershed in the history of the automobile. Production of motor vehicles in that year reached 5,337,087, a million more than in the previous year and a record that would not be surpassed or even matched for another twenty years."[22] The increase in family "joy riding" in the years before the Depression was a contributing factor in the slowdown in growth of the movie audience, although here, too, adjustments were made and soon families were using the automobile to transport them to the "talkies."

The motion picture industry was overextended due to its phenomenal growth in the early 1920s and the "battle for theaters" was beginning to take its toll. "In Southern California in 1926," Benjamin Hampton noted, "there was a great overabundance of neighborhood and downtown houses; experts estimated that five years must pass before increased population would absorb all their seating capacity. . . . Similar conditions existed in many sections, and when the growth in theater attendance failed to maintain its former speed, competition among theaters for the patronage of the public became very expensive."[23]

The movie theaters resorted to many tricks to lure patrons, including costly orchestras and vaudeville acts in the large, first-run houses, and sometimes even in the local neighborhood theaters. Eventually different types of "novelty nights" were tried, including lotteries, talent contests, giveaways and other special features. All of these succeeded in maintaining the audience in one way or another, but it was obvious that the original dynamic growth of the motion picture industry had disappeared. It was at this point that the cherished dream of fully synchronized "talking" pictures began to be realized. Its coming could not have been more propitious; it brought back the growth the industry had sought, but, more important, the novelty of sound helped sustain the industry through the first harsh years of the Depression and was largely responsible for its survival as one of America's more important commercial enterprises.

Prohibition and the Motion Picture Audience, 1919–1936

An interesting question is how much the motion picture industry owed to the imposition of Prohibition for the tremendous increase in audiences during the period 1920 to 1931.

It was noted earlier that one of the most-often-voiced sentiments in favor of motion pictures was that if this entertainment were handled judiciously, it would replace the saloon as the prime recreational diversion for a large section of the population. With the passing of the Eighteenth Amendment and the Volstead Act in 1919, the opportunity arose to see to what extent the motion picture could in fact replace the saloon as a form of recreation for the masses. Andrew Sinclair in his social history of the Prohibition movement noted that, by 1919, "there was a growing movement among the drys to regulate and censor the motion pictures, although not to prohibit them. For the drys realized that they [movie houses] had done much to fill the gap of the closed saloons."[24]

While the consumption of alcohol and motion picture attendance were not exactly "functional alternatives," they did have one thing in common — they provided cheap entertainment.[25] Laurie and Green in their history of show business observed that, during 1919, "retired liquor dealers were buying up movie theaters, rivalling their investments in other forms of show biz by war profiteers. Both knew that, deprived of places to drink, John Doe would seek relaxation at shows instead." These displaced liquor men also noted that when states went dry, the amusement revenues rose 50 to 100 percent following prohibition. It was obvious that the less money the public drank away, the more it would have to spend on movie-house tickets. Laurie and Green pointed out that "even the most blue-nosed theater managers in the country recognized the black-ink virtues of Prohibition."[26]

As shown in the table on page 195, the statistical evidence to support the contention that Prohibition contributed to the increase of motion picture audiences is inconclusive. From this comparison of expenditures it is impossible to make any significant correlations, other than to point out that while official reports of expenditures on alcoholic beverages indicated a slight decline in the yearly average between 1919 and 1932, the expenditure on motion pictures rose dramatically. Nevertheless, there is much to be said for the theory that lack of opportunity for recreation in the saloon did force many people to attend motion pictures more frequently. Further, it is interesting to note that while the decline of audiences in 1932–1933 has traditionally been attributed to the "depression catching up with the movie industry," 1933 was also the year in which Prohibition was repealed. Table 8 indicates that while alcoholic consumption quite expectedly went up in 1933, the movie audience continued to decline. By 1934, however, the audience began to increase once again. Whatever the cause of this fluctuation there is no denying that it was during the 1920s that most Americans caught the "movie-going" habit.

Andrew Sinclair has also noted the fact that motion pictures were considered by those in favor of Prohibition to be one of the prime anti-Prohibition forces at work in America during this era.[27] The WCTU was always a prominent advocate of federal censorship for motion pictures. Edgar Dale in his important study *The Content of Motion Pictures* (1933) indicated that over two-thirds of the 115 films his group examined contained "liquor situations," and intoxication was shown in 43 percent of these cases. Dale concluded: "It is evident that the prohibition law received scant support from the producers of motion-picture drama. Further, the conviction that drinking is universal in the United States must inevitably have received a tremendous impetus from the nature and extent of the drinking shown in motion picture films."[28] Certainly the millions who

TABLE 8
CONSUMPTION OF LIQUOR AND
EXPENDITURE ON MOTION PICTURES,
1919–1936

YEAR	LIQUOR CONSUMPTION $ MILLION	EXPENDITURES ON MOVIES $ MILLION
1919	2,000	265 (est.)
1921	1,400	301
1923	1,500	336
1925	1,700	367
1927	1,800	526
1929	2,000	720
1930	1,900 (est.)	732
1931	1,700 (est.)	719
1932	1,400 (est.)	527
1933	1,600 (est.)	482
1934	1,600 (est.)	518
1935	1,800 (est.)	556
1936	2,000 (est.)	626

Source: Historical Statistics. For liquor consumption see
Series G. 221, p. 179, and G. 193, p. 178. For motion pictures see Series H. 506, p. 224.

enjoyed such films were not the millions who voted against repeal of
Prohibition.

The Criticism of Sound Films

Adverse critical reactions to the first sound films were quite understandable, in that current technology did not facilitate the smooth integration
of the audio dimension into the existing state of the motion picture art.
Thus the early sound films seemed to be a retrogressive step; action was
static, the sound was atrocious and all extraneous noise was picked up by
the microphones, while the number of sets in a film were reduced to the
minimum to avoid moving the heavy sound equipment. Lewis Jacobs has
pointed out that these difficulties were very quickly corrected, and "once
sound was permanently accepted the progress made in perfecting its instruments and in learning its artistic functions and principles was amaz-
ingly swift."[29] It was, however, the professional critics who found the
most fault with the medium's added element, and "sophisticated screen
critics and professional commentators on the movies, who had spent years
in perfecting themselves in the art of sneering and jibing at current offer-

ings of the silent drama, suddenly reversed their positions and poured out paeans of praise to the beautiful art that was disappearing before the onward march of the unspeakable talkies."[30]

Gilbert Seldes, who would later become one of the most erudite supporters of the "popular arts" in America, was initially skeptical of the sound film. In a November, 1928, article in *Harper's* entitled "The Movies Commit Suicide," Seldes suggested that the addition of sound actually brought about the creation of an entirely new art form.[31] He visualized the formation of a dual system with "the film with full dialogue [becoming] a separate form of entertainment, drawing to itself nearly everything tawdry and vulgar in the silent film and leaving the silent film in the hands of the people, mostly foreigners and amateurs, able to appreciate its values."[32] Seldes claimed that while the movies were "committing suicide" they were also "achieving salvation" because with the sound film catering to the mass audience, "the silent film . . . may be relieved of all obligation to record the actual and give itself up to fantasy and imagination."[33] While Seldes's dream for the independent art of the silent film has never been fully realized, it is interesting to note that much experimentation has been done with the silent film — the high cost of adding sound being an important consideration, but the emphasis placed on the visual rather than the aural sensation also being a major aesthetic factor.[34]

The American public, however, left no doubt about where it stood on the subject of "talking pictures," and the "novelty" became an immediate overnight sensation. This wholehearted acceptance actually presented several new problems for the industry. Many studios were not equipped to produce sound films, and only a few theaters were equipped to show them. The conversion of both studios and theaters required a great deal of new capital, which could not be found within the already overextended industry. (Many independent film producers voiced the fear that the large studios had introduced sound films specifically to reduce yet further their number and influence. This was precisely what did occur, but more by accident than design.) It was at this point that New York bankers again entered the motion picture business, this time to stay.

The introduction of sound also precipitated a bitter battle between the two most powerful financial groups in America at the time — the Morgan group (telephone interests) and the Rockefeller group (radio interests). This was eventually settled in favor of the radio group. The financial possibilities of the film industry were becoming obvious to investors eager to make up for the dramatic losses incurred in the stock market collapse of 1929, and the advent of sound had proved to be an unexpected stimulation at the box office. The result was that the motion picture industry was one of the few major American business enterprises which was not adversely affected by the first stages of the Depression. So intent was Wall Street to move into the movie business that by 1929 all the pioneer film executives, with the notable exceptions of the trouble-laden William Fox and Carl Laemmle, had relinquished financial control of their enterprises to the anonymous financiers from New York.[35] In their important study of the financial structure of the international film industry, Klingender and Legg observed that "the adoption of sound led to the emergence — after violent struggles . . . of a new patents monopoly very nearly as complete in fact, if not in form, as the old patents trust of the pre-war years."[36]

The final effect of this need for capital was to concentrate the production and exhibition of films in even fewer corporations than before, as many theater owners, unable to install the expensive equipment, or disillusioned with the growing complexity of the industry, sold out to the large studios. At the close of 1930, Paramount-Publix, Fox-Loew, Warner Brothers, and RKO owned a total of 2,500 to 3,000 theaters in the United States and Canada. These were nearly all of the first-run theaters then in existence, and many of the best second-runs. The U.S. government quickly saw the dangers in this situation, and the Federal Trade Commission in November, 1929, brought antitrust suits under the Clayton Act against Fox for having acquired Loew's and against Warners for having bought Stanley–First National.[37] The attempt by the federal government to force the studios to divest themselves of theater ownership would continue until the late 1940s.

While the coming of sound did manage to stave off economic disaster for several years, by 1931 it was evident that not even "talking" films could postpone the inevitable, and audiences began to decline dramatically as the great Depression took hold. Although audiences would start to come back after 1934, never again would the American film achieve the absolute popularity it claimed in 1930, when there was an average of three attendances per week for each American household.

Industry Developments and the Critics

Once the actors were given the gift of speech the style of film acting underwent a complete change; no longer was elaborate pantomime necessary, and development of specific film acting techniques for use with sound brought to Hollywood many more legitimate stage personalities. This, in turn, caused a major problem, because many of these stage personalities were from the worlds of burlesque and vaudeville and their vocal jokes were soon part of the everyday content of films, thereby adding to the wrath of reformers. The Hays Office actually admitted that this was one of the major reasons the motion picture was so difficult to control in the years between 1929 and 1933.

Many reform groups did not miss the opportunity to link the obvious economic ills of the movie industry to the declining moral quality of the product. An article in the *Christian Century* in late 1931 entitled "Movies Are Brought to Judgement" epitomized this viewpoint. The article pointed out that for years the industry had asked to be "judged at the box office," where true public opinion on the quality of the medium could be more accurately assessed. The writer then gave the details of the internal financial struggles which were convulsing Hollywood, and accused all the major studios of overextension in real estate, slipshod business methods, "fantastic nepotism," and overpaying stars. The main cause for their desperate condition, however, was the dramatic decline in box-office receipts:

It is at the box office that movies have gone down to defeat. Hundreds of thousands of Americans, forced by conditions to consider their expenditures with some care, are awakening to the fact that they are tired of the movies. They are tired of stereo-typed plots. They are tired of the cheap allurements of synthetic film-sin. They are tired of the everlasting sameness of the programs. . . . So they stay away. . . . Unless the industry can find "new stuff" of a sounder nature, the crash will come.[38]

While some reformers gloated at the motion picture industry's long awaited fall from power, and hoped that it would remain in trouble as long as it failed to regulate itself, there were others who saw more ominous economic and social dangers in the decline of the film industry. In 1933 the novelist Rupert Hughes, noting the economic difficulties in which the industry now found itself, suggested that this should not be cause for rejoicing, for, "in spite of their Waterloo, the motion pictures continued to be a necessity through the Depression. The helpful diversion they have given to a despondent populace has had incalculable effect upon public morals."[39] Hughes quoted some figures to back up his contention that it was not in the public's best interests to have a dead movie industry. In 1931 there were 21,284 moving picture theaters in the United States, about 14,000 of them equipped for sound, and with a total seating capacity of more than 12 million. Weekly attendance sometimes exceeded 100 million, and a disaster to the movies would have been a shock to the entire populace. Hughes continued: "It would be hard to think of any other interest that affects so many people. Church attendance and even attendance on sports do not approach such figures."[40]

The motion picture industry in 1931 carried a capital investment of two billion dollars, and employed 30,000 people in production, 10,000 in distribution and 250,000 in theaters. Hughes pointed out that other industries benefited from a healthy movie industry — "in 1931 about 15,000 advertisements were published daily and the industry expended for advertising and exploitation about a hundred million dollars." Thus the continued financial good health of the movies was necessary to ensure "more than the salvation of the group of actors, managers, and theater-owners. It has an indirect bearing on the financial prosperity of nearly everybody, including many of its enemies, including even the censors, and not forgetting the tax collectors. . . ."[41] Hughes concluded by thanking the "movie giants" who had brought diversion to hundreds of millions of people, while noting that the movies "have taught the world not one sin that it did not practice before. . . ."[42]

Block-Booking

The subject of block-booking was an important issue in the motion picture industry, and it was the source of vigorous attack and defense on both sides of the "problem with the movies" question. In simple terms block-booking, or "blind-booking," as it was sometimes called, was the "simultaneous leasing of groups of films at an aggregate price fixed upon the condition that all films in the block be taken."[43] What this meant was that the unaffiliated exhibitor was forced to take the entire "block" offered by the studio or distributor because the cost of a single rental was prohibitive. The main impact of this marketing practice was felt by the local, independent exhibitor running the neighborhood movie house, and not the downtown first-run theater, which was already owned by the large studios, and used as an exclusive exhibition site.

This industry practice was considered by many of the reform groups, women's and other social organizations, and even the federal government, to be in large part responsible for many of the moral problems associated with motion picture content, in that it stymied attempts at local control. Neighborhood exhibitors continually defended themselves against customers' complaints by claiming that they were forced to take whatever films were being offered in order to receive the more "acceptable" (meaning profitable) films at a reasonable cost.[44]

Was all this furor about block-booking justified? The answer must be in the affirmative, for only in this manner were the studios able to force local exhibitors to take and exhibit films of inferior quality, or those which might not otherwise meet local standards. On the other hand, there is much evidence to show that this practice did result in lower marketing costs to the distributor and hence to the exhibitor.[45] Block-booking was the cornerstone in the production-distribution-exhibition triad, for it ensured the studios of an automatic outlet for all of their productions, thus accommodating the studio "factory" system.

In 1927, Dora H. Stecker of Cincinnati addressed the National Conference on Social Work on the subject of "Some Desirable Goals for Motion Pictures." Her speech turned out to be an incisive attack on the film industry's marketing practices as they affected thousands of smaller communities and neighborhoods all across America. She pointed out that it was in the smaller urban or rural centers where the problem of socialization by the motion picture was more acutely manifested, because it was here that traditional social norms were affected to a much greater degree. While the larger cities constituted only one-fifth of the U.S. population, the influence of this urban sector on the motion picture industry was overpowering. This was evidenced by the disproportionate influence of the first-run, downtown movie house on the films shown at suburban theaters. Of the 17,836 movie houses in the United States in 1927, only 1,720 were first-run, approximately 3,140 were downtown, while 12,700 were neighborhood theaters. But, the major downtown theaters contributed over 25 percent of all rental fees. The problem was that the type of film catering to a fairly transient inner-city population did not always fit into the needs of a neighborhood theater. Also, block-booking often prevented local movie houses from putting on suitable weekend programs for younger audiences. Unfortunately, little notice was taken of Miss Stecker's contribution to the problem of how to make movies more sensitive to community demands.[46]

The failure to react to Miss Stecker's suggestions vividly illustrated the point that such calm, rational criticism never seemed to disturb the motion picture industry. Earlier "scholarly" and rational works on the motion picture by Donald R. Young, Hugo Munsterberg and others, which examined the problems caused by the lack of social control, had also been ignored, and had in fact received very little publicity even in the other media. The industry did, however, respond promptly to criticism in newspapers and periodicals; an indication perhaps that the film makers felt that diehard "movie fans" seldom bothered to read books, but might be susceptible to the arguments of popular publications. The fact that newspapers relied upon movie advertising for a large part of their revenue was also a factor in the failure to make these "suggestions to the industry" more widely known.

Certainly there was no reason for the industry to give the Seabury Plan any credence by publicly replying to it, but it was even more disappointing that more organized social groups did not take up many of the ideas put forward by people such as Young, Stecker, Seabury, Poffenberger, and even those of the National Board of Review. Each reform group was so concerned with its own specific attack on the industry that it had little time to consider the plans of others, even though they all voiced basically the same concerns. Ironically, these groups had to rely upon the film industry to bring them together, and almost every major national conference on motion pictures was organized by the industry through the Hays Office or the National Board of Review. At these meetings the same industry rhetoric would be heard about the need for public cooperation, but after agreeing and returning home, the reform groups would soon begin to talk once again about the industry's "lack of faith."

One suggestion which was favored by many of the medium's critics was that the industry should be removed from "commercial interests." Nobody, however, including Seabury with his "commercial renaissance," had ever put forward a feasible plan whereby this could be achieved. It is doubtful that this suggestion would have been taken seriously by an administration which was as definitely on the side of "big business" as the Republicans were in the 1920s.

Other than the very meaningful move made by Will Hays from postmaster general to the head of the MPPDA, the exact relationship between the motion picture industry and the Republican party during these important years has been little analyzed. It was known that Calvin Coolidge did not favor legal censorship, and in 1926 he had spoken out against yet another bid to create a federal motion picture commission. Earlier, when he was still the governor of Massachusetts, he had vetoed a film censorship act passed by the state legislature on constitutional grounds (which was somewhat inconsistent, considering the Supreme Court ruling in 1915). One newspaper noted, however, that "the Motion Picture Industry is recognized by President Coolidge as one of the leading businesses in the United States, and as such he feels the Government should encourage it in every legitimate way."[47]

Block-Booking: An Evaluation

There was no single answer to the problem created by block-booking. Facing a group of students at the Harvard Business School in 1927, Sidney R. Kent, the general manager of Paramount-Famous-Lasky Corporation, engaged in this dialogue with a student:

Question. I have heard that in selling motion pictures you try to sell a whole series of pictures so that the exhibitor to get one picture may have to take others that perhaps he does not want?
Mr. Kent. We have a term in this business known as block booking and it is a very much misunderstood term. As a matter of fact, the government is now litigating the question of what block booking really is.

. . . Let me show you where there is advantage to the exhibitor. . . . What exhibitor is in a position to put his individual judgement against that of all these men who contribute everything they know to the making of the motion picture? Therefore the exhibitor who has stayed with a well known brand of motion pictures has invariably done better than the fellow who went out and sought to put his own judgement against that of all the best showmen in the country.[48]

Kent's lecture was illustrated by several organizational charts indicating the complex marketing operations of his company. There is little doubt that his use of phrases such as "brand of motion pictures" was deliberate, to convey to the business school graduates that the production, distribution and exhibition of films were industries like any other.

William Seabury condemned block-booking as "plainly an unfair method of competition which should be prohibited."[49] However, Martin Quigley, the influential editor of *Motion Picture Herald* who was in the forefront of the motion picture reform movement after 1930, saw little harm in the practice as it affected the content of films, saying: "Block-booking as a practical matter may be and should be viewed as something unassociated with the best arrangements in theory and in practice for the right regulation of the moral character of motion pictures."[50]

However, it was the success of this practice which discouraged the motion picture industry from experimenting with less popular themes aimed at smaller, more specific audiences. We have seen earlier that Benjamin Hampton had suggested that the preferences of a large minority were being ignored, and there is ample evidence that this was indeed the case. The movies by now appealed to all segments of American society, but the constant product emanating from Hollywood did not take into account the possibility that there existed a potential audience for more "highbrow" fare. In an article in *Outlook* in December, 1930, Creighton Peet suggested that one of the reasons for the slowdown in growth was that people no longer went to movies because they had nothing else to do, but they wanted to be entertained as well, and thus the audience went to see a *particular* film, not just *any* film. Furthermore, Hollywood was also ignoring the potential of the older audience, neglected since the death of the live theatrical road show caused by the advent of the movies. This group could be enticed to visit the movie house much more frequently with more intelligent films. Unfortunately, Peet's prophecy that "it is highly probable that in a few years there will be a regular supply of films aimed at the now despised 'highbrow' " was never really fulfilled.[51]

In the final analysis, while it was obvious that block-booking was a major contributing factor to the "local standards" problem, it was nevertheless the equivalent of normal wholesaling practices in other commercial fields. The real issue, therefore, was the continued conception of the motion picture as the end product of a large mass production industry; a concept which was difficult to reconcile with the individual psychological impact of the medium and its demonstrated ability to influence the social and cultural life of the nation. The motion picture was the first of the vast "national" media to face this problem; radio would suffer less; while the most massive of all the public media — network television — has still not found the answer to catering to America's regional-cultural variations.

The American Film Abroad

In the 1920s the influence of Hollywood was not confined to North America, and the industry estimated that "an average of about seventy-five per cent of the motion pictures shown day in and day out the world over are of American origin."[52] The gross revenues for 1925 accruing from this foreign trade were approximately $50,000,000. The most important aspect of foreign trade in movies, however, was the fact that about 30 percent of the gross revenues to the industry from all sources were obtained from overseas trade, and this meant that there was a vital need to maintain this source of revenue.

It was because of this heavy financial dependence on foreign distribution that the industry was particularly sensitive to criticism from foreign sources. Furthermore, while the American federal authorities might be reluctant to implement any national controls or restraints on the medium, many foreign governments with greater powers of centralized control did not hesitate to act in protection of their domestic film industries, or to protect their people from an "assault on national life." The normal method of controlling the financial dominance of the American product was to impose some sort of quota, as was the case in Britain in 1927 and France in 1929, but this did not entirely solve the problem of the overwhelming influence of the ubiquitous American product. While the indigenous film industries had a legitimate request for economic protection, it was the threat created by the dissemination of "foreign ideas" which was uppermost in the minds of most groups and governments concerned with preserving national cultures and identities. So dominant was the Hollywood film that the spread of American fads and fashions by the medium became an international *cause célèbre*. As early as 1921 this influence was being seriously questioned, and Arthur Weigall, an English writer, noted:

To the remotest towns of England, as to those of America and other countries, these films penetrate, carrying with them this mild but ultimately dangerous poison; and gradually the world, from end to end, is being trained to see life as it is seen by a certain group of kinema producers and writers congregated in a corner of the United States. The world is being Americanised by the photoplay; but the trouble is that this Americanisation does not represent the best element of that nation, or even the most popular. . . .[53]

203

Weigall then echoed a sentiment familiar to reform groups in the United States — namely, that Hollywood films were a dangerous socializing influence because, "good or bad, they are altering the code of the Englishman; and . . . they are lowering our standards and those of the United States, by casually hinting at, or frankly representing as worthy of emulation, an attitude of mind that is not English and not American."[54] He went on to make the valid objection that all too often "an Englishman is the recognized buffoon of the American photoplay," and that the solution would be to have a much wider distribution of British films in the United States, for, "properly handled, the Kinema could be made to endear the two races to one another by the bonds of mutual admiration and fellow-feeling."[55]

This problem of a "cultural imperialism" imposed by the ubiquitous American motion picture was universally recognized but was not always considered to be a "dangerous" social condition. Earlier we saw the pleas of William Seabury for a greater exchange of ideas through the medium of an international cinema, and similar sentiments were also expressed by others, especially in the halcyon days of the twenties. In 1927, the noted French man of letters André Maurois stated upon a visit to New York: "This is the day of universal culture. The people of the world dress alike more or less, and it is from motion pictures that they get their idea of being alike." He went on to predict that cinema art would become one of the great arts of the future, and compared it to the building of the thirteenth-century cathedrals in its universal appeal to the masses. (This analogy must surely have been lost on the Hollywood moguls!)[56] The American film industry was obviously anxious to encourage any point of view which saw in the motion picture a means of providing greater international understanding, as long as it did not also entail governmental control, as Seabury had earlier advocated.

Addressing the Better Films Conference in 1927, Carl Milliken announced, "There is an ambitious plan well on the way to fulfillment for circulating around the world in the next few years films of the life, history and customs of each of the different nations of the world so that gradually they will be brought into close contact with each other."[57] Needless to say, nothing else was ever heard of this ambitious project, but Hollywood had paid lip service to the concept of an "international cinema."

Far more immediate problems faced the American film industry in the shape of the quotas and rigorous censorship imposed in foreign markets. France in particular threatened action after the Herriot Commission recommended that a quota be placed on American films, and that the United States be forced to accept French films in a four to one ratio. (It should be noted that after the initial flurry of interest before 1920, American audiences showed a definite distaste for "foreign" films, including those from Britain; thus talk of any sort of legislated exchange was anathema to film exhibitors.) The idea of a French quota becoming the forerunner of massive European action against the American industry was so threatening that Will Hays went to France in 1928 to try and prevent this action, which he claimed "would practically have kept American motion pictures out of France."[58] Even the League of Nations became embroiled in this controversy, and the international body made plain its objections to any sort of quota system. The reasons for the league's interest were ostensibly based upon a growing desire to abolish restrictions on all imports and exports, but they also went out of their way to endorse the motion picture as a means of international understanding, a dream which was unfortunately never realized.[59]

The "Great American Art"

By the end of the 1920s the American motion picture industry had already gone through several economic cycles in its short history, but with the addition of sound it entered the period of its greatest influence and, many felt, it greatest creativity. Writing in 1928, Thomas Craven called the motion picture the "Great American Art," and suggested that "as a reflection of life it has no parallel, nor has the creative labour of any past period . . . approached it in ability to reach the hearts of the people. It is an art that actually works; it travels to the four corners of the earth bearing a message within the scope of housemaids and children . . . it symbolizes the hopes and aspirations of the unfortunate."[60]

While it might have been the "Great American Art," by 1933 the motion picture industry was once again faced with the choice of reforming or being subjected to external controls in the form of either federal legislation or more severe public criticism which could lead to further financial losses. Eleven years earlier the industry had temporary solved a similar crisis by employing Will Hays, but it was becoming obvious that the concerned public would not tolerate another move designed to "buy time." In any case there was no one, short of the President of the United States, who had sufficient public stature to succeed where Hays had apparently failed. Hays was fully aware of the position in which he found himself, and he anxiously sought a solution, but unfortunately he was up against an industry which was itself struggling with an economic depression and taking desperate measures to maintain profits. The early 1930s saw an unprecedented number of films with "sex" or "gangsterism" as their central themes, and their immense popularity with film goers only alarmed reform groups more than ever. Raymond Moley examined the gloom that pervaded the Hays Office at this time: "... there was the deepening discouragement among those who had proudly hailed the adoption of the Code in 1930. It became clearer and clearer that the best of laws fail without adequate enforcement. Bad pictures continued to appear and public resentment and criticism steadily mounted."[61]

Added to these intensifying public pressures, the Depression began to make itself felt in Hollywood, and box-office receipts were declining. It was obvious that some important break would have to occur — and it did, in the form of the Catholic Legion of Decency. However, before the Legion of Decency came into being the public and the critics were finally given some tangible and scientifically respectable evidence that motion pictures could be, and in fact were, a major social influence. Armed with this evidence (in most cases grossly distorted), reform-minded groups lost little time in renewing the pressure for greater control of the medium.

While the general public still evinced an apathetic attitude toward the "menace of the movies," more and more people were becoming aware of the controversy, and there was some indication of a ground swell of genuine public resentment against many films released after 1930, especially those which glorified the life of the "gangster."[62] Movies such as *Little Caesar* (1930), *The Public Enemy* (1931), and *Scarface* (1932) proved to be extremely popular with film audiences, and this began an avalanche of similar films. Mention should also be made of the films of Mae West, such as *Diamond Lil* (1928), *She Done Him Wrong* (1933) and *I'm No Angel* (1933), which have been credited with precipitating the formation of the Catholic Legion of Decency. Alexander Walker has noted that "in word and gesture Mae West was the living mockery of all the Code's [the Production Code of the MPPDA] pieties. But Hollywood made her welcome for one excellent reason: her early films were enormous moneymakers."[63] In the end her career was seriously curtailed by the imposition of such "voluntary censorship."

In an address delivered in October, 1933, Mary G. Hawks, the retiring president of the National Council of Catholic Women, evaluated the current motion picture situation in these terms:

Public consciousness is now aroused to the fact that the movies as they are produced and distributed today, are a menace to the physical, mental and moral welfare of the nation.... These injurious effects are greatly enhanced by the shameless sex appeal of the advertising.... We must face the unpleasant fact that constant exposure to screen stories of successful gangsters and "slick" racketeers, of flaming passion and high power emotionalism, may easily nullify every standard of life and conduct set up at home and at school and will almost inevitably effect a moral decline at the very outset of life's venture....[64]

Harrison's Reports, which reviewed the films produced during 1933–1934, found that 66 percent were classified as for adults only.[65] The New

York censors rejected fifteen films outright in 1934, making 2,195 eliminations of which 838 were classified as "indecent," 752 as "immoral or tending to corrupt morals," and 511 as "tending to incite to crime."[66] The extent of public dissatisfaction over the poor "moral" quality of motion pictures in 1933 was attested to by the fact that "9,000 letters protesting the vulgarity and coarseness of current productions were received at the White House."[67] (How many of these were due to organized letter-writing campaigns is unknown.) While the situation was reminiscent of 1921, the mood was much more strident for tangible reform, only now there was the added factor of eleven years of disillusionment with the efforts of the Hays Office.

How much the pervading gloom of the Depression had to do with this change in public attitude is difficult to assess. Olga G. Martin in her book *Hollywood's Movie Commandments* suggested that it was the uncertainty of the times, coupled with hunger and terror, which turned many people back to religion for solace, and that this had brought about a much more serious attitude toward life in general. The time seemed ripe for a moral revolution and the motion picture was as ever a ready target, only this time the industry itself, caught up in a desperate financial struggle for survival, was much more vulnerable to attack, and therefore more amenable to change.[68]

NOTES TO CHAPTER VIII

1. John Baxter, *Hollywood in the Thirties* (New York: A. S. Barnes and Co., 1968), p. 10.

2. *Ibid.*, p. 35.

3. Lewis Jacobs, *Rise of the American Film*, p. 397.

4. Baxter, p. 36.

5. *Ibid.*

6. As reported in Lewis Jacobs, p. 398.

7. Baxter, p. 37.

8. Arthur Knight, *The Liveliest Art* (New York: Macmillan Company, 1957), p. 118. For an excellent biography of De Mille see Charles Higham, *Cecil B. De Mille* (New York: Charles Scribner's Sons, 1973).

9. Maurice Bardeche and Robert Brasillach, *The History of Motion Pictures*, translated by Iris Barry (New York: W. W. Norton and Co., 1938), p. 203.

10. Quoted in Knight, p. 118.

11. *Ibid.*, p. 119.

12. The importance of the "Western Hero" in American mythology has been the subject of much critical analysis. An authoritative treatment of the Western movie is contained in George N. Fenin and William K. Everson, *The Western* (New York: Orion Press, 1962).

13. An excellent historical treatment of the development of the newsreel is Raymond Fielding, *The American Newsreel 1911–1967*. For a detailed account of Robert Flaherty's

life the best source is Arthur Calder-Marshall, *The Innocent Eye* (Baltimore: Penguin Books, 1970). The Paramount incident is found on pp. 119–120.

14. For the history of the animated cartoon see Ralph Stephenson, *Animation in the Cinema* (New York: A. S. Barnes and Co., 2nd edition, 1973).

15. Clifford G. Twombly, untitled article in *Christian Century*, April 13, 1932, p. 480.

16. Quoted in Schull, "Suitability of Commercial Entertainment," p. 160.

17. This fact is mentioned in almost all the histories of the motion picture. Among the best treatments are those found in James L. Limbacher, *Four Faces of the Film* (New York: Brussel and Brussel, 1968), pp. 207–208; and Gertude Jobes, *Motion Picture Empire*, pp. 263–265. For a more romantic account see Fitzhugh Green, *The Film Finds Its Tongue* (New York: Private edition, 1929; reprinted New York: Benjamin Blom, 1971).

18. Hampton, *History of the Movies*, p. 370.

19. *Ibid.*, pp. 372–373.

20. The best history of radio in this period is contained in the two volumes written by Erik Barnouw, *A Tower in Babel* and *The Golden Web* (New York: Oxford University Press, 1966, 1968).

21. Bosley Crowther, *The Lion's Share: The Story of an Entertainment Empire* (New York: E. P. Dutton, 1957), pp. 142–143.

22. John B. Rae, *The American Automobile* (Chicago: University of Chicago Press, 1965), p. 105.

23. Hampton, p. 373.

24. Andrew Sinclair, *Era of Excess*, p. 320.

25. For the use of this concept of "functional alternatives" in mass communication see De Fleur, *Theories of Mass Communication*, especially p. 19.

26. Green and Laurie, *Show Biz*, p. 220.

27. Andrew Sinclair, p. 321.

28. Edgar Dale, *The Content of Motion Pictures* (New York: Macmillan Company, 1933), pp. 169–170.

29. Lewis Jacobs, p. 438.

30. Hampton, p. 384.

31. Gilbert Seldes, "The Movies Commit Suicide," *Harper's*, November, 1928, pp. 706–712.

32. *Ibid.*, p. 711.

33. *Ibid.*, p. 712.

34. For a more detailed explanation of this thesis see Lewis Jacobs, "Experimental Cinema in America 1921–1947," a supplement in Jacobs, *Rise of the American Film.*

35. The financial structure of the motion picture industry is a highly complex subject. The best sources for an understanding of this subject are Lewis, *Motion Picture Industry;* Huettig, *Economic Control of the Motion Picture Industry;* and the undocumented claims of Gertrude Jobes.

36. F. D. Klingender and Stuart Legg, *Money Behind the Screen* (London: Lawrence and Wishart, 1937), pp. 71–72.

37. Hampton, p. 393.

38. "Movies Are Brought to Judgement," *Christian Century*, December 30, 1931, pp. 1647–1648.

39. Rupert Hughes, "Calamity with Sound Effects," *New Outlook*, September, 1933, p. 22.

40. *Ibid.*, p. 25.

41. *Ibid.*

42. *Ibid.*, p. 26.

43. Huettig, p. 116.

44. The Federal Trade Commission carried out an intensive investigation of block-booking between 1921 and 1922, during which time it collected some 17,000 pages of testimony and 15,000 pages of exhibits, and concluded in 1927 that it was indeed "an unfair trade practice." After a cease and desist order was reversed by the United States Circuit Court of Appeals in 1932, the entire matter was temporarily shelved. (The practice was finally modified in 1940 after a series of antitrust suits against the eight major studios.)

45. F. L. Herron, "Block-Booking," *International Review of Educational Cinematography*, vol. 4 (1932), p. 600.

46. Dora H. Stecker, "Some Desirable Goals for Motion Pictures," the National Conference of Social Work, *Proceedings*, 1927, pp. 360–370.

47. *United States Daily*, April 21, 1926. Quoted in Lewis, p. 379.

48. Joseph P. Kennedy, ed., *The Story of the Films* (Chicago: A. W. Shaw Company, 1927), pp. 226–228.

49. Seabury, *The Public and the Motion Picture Industry*, p. 60.

50. Martin Quigley, *Decency in Motion Pictures* (New York: Macmillan Company, 1937), p. 90.

51. Creighton Peet, "Letter to Hollywood," *Outlook*, December 17, 1930, pp. 612–613.

52. C. J. North, "Our Foreign Trade in Motion Pictures," *Annals of the American Academy of Political and Social Science*, no. 128 (November, 1926), p. 100.

53. Arthur Weigall, "The Influence of the Kinematograph upon National Life," *Nineteenth Century*, April, 1921, p. 668.

54. *Ibid.*, p. 670.

55. *Ibid.*, p. 672.

56. *New York Times*, December 21, 1927.

57. *New York Herald Tribune*, January 29, 1927.

58. W. H. Hays, *Memoirs*, p. 403.

59. *New York Post*, June 3, 1929.

60. Thomas Craven, "The Great American Art," the *Dial*, December, 1926, pp. 483–492.

61. Moley, *Hays Office*, p. 77.

62. A good examination of the gangster film is found in Stephen Karpf, *The Gangster Film: Emergence, Variation and Decay of a Genre, 1930–1940* (New York: Arno Press, 1973). Another very interesting study of the whole role of the motion picture during the Depression is Andrew Bergman, *We're In the Money: Depression America and Its Films* (New York: New York University Press, 1971).

63. Walker, *The Celluloid Sacrifice*, p. 76.

64. Quoted in Schull, p. 178.

65. *Harrison's Reports*, December 29, 1934.

66. *Motion Picture Herald*, November 3, 1934, p. 24.

67. Quoted in Inglis, *Freedom of the Movies*, p. 120.

68. Olga G. Martin, *Hollywood's Movie Commandments* (New York: H. W. Wilson Company, 1937), pp. 30–31.

IX

Social Science and the Motion Picture

VERY SOON AFTER ITS INTRODUCTION the motion picture and its influence on the American people became the subject of investigation and study. In the years prior to the Second World War, hundreds of such studies were undertaken by many divergent groups using a wide variety of investigative techniques. The findings they produced were used to substantiate practically every point of view then held on the impact and influence of the medium. While the research techniques and sponsoring agencies may have differed, each of these studies had one overriding consideration — a concern for the power and influence of a medium which, because of its tremendous popularity with the American public and especially the young, had become an important focal point in the social and cultural life of the nation.

The discussion of the influence of the movies in the period before 1920 had been colored by charge and countercharge, by reformist attack and industry defense, but these discussions lacked substantive empirical evidence gained through dispassionate scientific inquiry. One problem was that the social sciences at this stage were ill equipped to cope with the task of mass survey analysis, and the techniques of survey research, sampling procedures and multivariate analysis had not yet reached an adequate level of sophistication. However, the development of fields such as sociology, psychology and economics during these years laid the groundwork for the emergence of a true "science of man." Spurred on by the need to understand the nature and extent of the enormous changes then occurring in American society, the social sciences were first brought into contact with government and became an important part of the bureaucratic decision-making process. At first these techniques were used on the local level by the social workers employed by municipalities and state governments, but later the federal government also began to adopt more empirically based methods of analysis.[1]

Certainly the social tensions caused by the rapid alterations to the American social structure placed a demand upon the social scientists to provide answers to some of these problems. This had the effect of giving the social scientists the incentive they needed to develop their techniques, while at the same time the American public began to take their work much more seriously. Louis Wirth has noted that

the character of the developing social science at the turn of the century was significantly shaped by the dominant philosophy of the period with its empirical and pragmatic temper, its consequent emphasis upon the actual problems of the developing American society, its revulsion from doctrinaire metaphysics and armchair speculation, and its accent upon observation and experimentation. . . .[2]

The growing importance of social science departments in major American universities added considerably to the public's acceptance of these disciplines.

Initially, many of the efforts of the emerging social scientists were taken up with the struggle for reform and were linked with social settlement work, and it was in this context that the motion picture was first subjected to close scrutiny by empirical or survey methods. It was only natural that the burning questions surrounding motion picture influence should occupy the attention of social scientists such as Hugo Munsterberg, William Healy, Donald R. Young, and others. They were anxious to dispel the myths clouding the issue, and gradually employed more sophisticated investigatory techniques for this purpose. Gene Lyons suggested of these pioneers that "by the time the war had broken out they had created a social science that was based on empirical methods of investigation and that rejected folklore and maxims as explanations of human behavior and social institutions."[3]

When this desire for objective evaluation of social issues came up against the problem of motion picture influence the investigators found themselves contending with an emotion-tinged situation. The historical antecedents for this confrontation lay in the development of the then prevalent notions of the relationship between the mass media and "mass society." In the early twentieth century the concept of a form of social organization known as a "mass society" was commonly expressed. Many men noted that society seemed to be moving toward a social system where the individual would play a minor role. In this type of social order the major institutions would be organized to deal with people in the aggregate, and the life of individuals would be governed by mass relations, particularly through the mass media.[4] The influential nineteenth-century sociologists, including Comte, Spencer, Tönnies, Durkheim and Weber, had all dealt with this theme in their analyses of social development, and sociologists have noted that these prevailing theories of "mass society" had an important influence on the development of the social sciences.[5] This view of the emerging social order, coupled with the then current psychological theory that man's conduct was largely a product of his genetic endowment, had serious implications for the initial interpretation of the motion picture's influence, for the medium was considered to be a prime disseminator of such "mass" images and messages.

There is no doubt that much of the criticism of the medium in the early years was based upon this theoretical and emotional combination of "mass society" and "direct influence." Elihu Katz and Paul Lazarsfeld in their important study *Personal Influence* observed that these early views of the mass media's capabilities were erroneously based on theories which postulated "first of all . . . an atomistic mass of millions of readers, listeners and movie-goers prepared to receive the Message; and secondly, they [the critics] pictured every Message as a direct and powerful stimulus to action which would elicit immediate response."[6] These theories were widely held, and De Fleur and McQuail have both indicated the important influence which propaganda efforts in World War I had in fostering these fears and in hastening the development of research into persuasive communication. The revelations by George Creel on the effectiveness of the Committee for Public Information, and the acknowledged success of motion pictures as propaganda tools, only served to increase the demands of reformers who sought greater social control of the visual entertainment medium.[7]

The pervasive acceptance of the stimulus-response theory (as the concept of direct influence is known) was a major factor encouraging studies of motion picture impact and influence. Certainly, the theory seemed entirely valid given the currently held psychological theories which suggested a uniform basic nature for all men. Essentially the stimulus-response theory stated that ". . . powerful stimuli were uniformly brought to the attention of the individual members of the mass. These stimuli tapped inner urges, emotions, or other processes over which the individual had little voluntary control. Because of the inherited nature of these mechanisms, each person responded more or less uniformly."[8] Only after 1920 was the nature of human individuality made clearer with the increasing use of mental and aptitude tests, and the growing influence of Freudian and Jungian psychiatric theories. These new ideas would lead to a gradual modification of the stimulus-response theory with the emphasis being placed on the concept of individual differences. Between 1919 and 1933, encouraged by these modifications and the rising level of sophistication in measurement techniques, several studies on motion picture influence and intent were carried out. Many of these investigations were conducted by professional social scientists, while others were the product of curious minds eager to gauge the impact of the movies on their own communities. Most of these studies were naturally concerned with the influence of the motion picture on children. While the evaluations differed greatly in the highly subjective area of "moral influence," the studies seldom varied widely in their statistical findings on attendance, frequency of viewing, age of viewers, time of day or week, and so on.

There were three basic problems facing potential investigators: First, they had to define the exact nature of their investigation — which of the many questions posed by the introduction of this new medium were they hoping to answer? Second, in many cases they had to devise new techniques to acquire their data. Third, once the data were acquired and analyzed, how could the findings be translated into relevant action? Most of these studies succeeded in coming to terms with the first two problems, but seldom with the third.[9]

Louis Wirth has noted that after World War I social scientists began to move away from their earlier preoccupation with reform movements, and the emphasis shifted toward a "more detached program of scientific inquiry, characterized by the development of scientific method and more long-range empirical research."[10] Nevertheless, as scientifically objective as most social scientists tried to be, those who studied the influence of motion pictures almost always found themselves embroiled in heated arguments between the reformers and the industry. Both sides at times even resorted to employing their own "scientists" to produce competing studies or to refute previously published evidence. There were very few impartial and objective voices where this issue was concerned. The industry was, after all, fighting for its survival, while the reformers clearly saw their mandate to prevent the insidious influence of an uncontrolled mass medium. It was little wonder, therefore, that the issues were so volatile.

The Toledo Study

The Reverend John Phelan, while still a graduate student at Toledo University, began one of the most comprehensive surveys ever conducted of the "exact physical, financial, and 'moral' state of motion pictures" in one community. His analysis of the motion picture in Toledo, Ohio, published in 1919, stood alone at the time in its concentrated treatment of the medium as an urban amusement phenomenon. Phelan's primary reason for conducting this survey was "to gather all available social data and allow the reader to make his own interpretation." The community seldom "knows" itself, claimed Phelan, and he was utilizing this survey method because "it is the only reliable one by which we can ascertain the educational significance of those social factors and forces which make or mar our fellow-citizens."[11] The result of Phelan's desire to "inform the community" was a painstaking survey of the entire motion picture business and its impact on the life-style of this urban community.

One of his more significant findings was that the total number of movie houses in Toledo had recently decreased, while the population had increased. In 1914 there were sixty-six movie theaters, while in 1919 there were only forty-nine active exhibition sites. Phelan noted, however, that three giant new movie palaces were already being built in the center city area. Further, the decrease in the total number of exhibition sites was an indication of the declining number of old neighborhood theaters situated in the residential sections, while there was a corresponding increase in the larger, first-run houses in the downtown section. Twenty of these newer theaters were located in the Sixth Ward, "where property and land value are very high."[12]

The attendance figures in Phelan's study indicated the tremendous attraction of the motion picture as an urban entertainment and recreational activity. In 1919 the City of Toledo's population was slightly over 260,000. Phelan's estimated attendance figures were:

Average daily attendance	45,000
Average weekly attendance	316,000
Average yearly attendance	16,380,000

Six of the downtown houses alone accounted for 12,500 daily, or 75,000 a week. It was not unusual for these houses to each have 5,000 to 9,000 patrons every day! The admission price varied from seven to fifty-five cents, with fifteen cents being the average, and the total box-office receipts were $2,457,000 for 1918, almost $10 annually for every man, woman and child in the community.[13]

The study examined every facet of the physical condition of the movie houses, the attendance of children, and the nature and availability of alternative recreational activities in the city. Phelan could not resist the temptation and voiced some grave doubts about the "moral tone" of many films, noting that this "tone" endangered the large number of children attending these shows. He recognized the need for diversion, for "proper recreation and amusement are as necessary as food and raiment," but in evaluating the arguments for and against the film he could find only eight "advantages." On the negative side he noted five "physical dangers," five "social dangers," and twelve "moral dangers."[14]

Phelan commented, "The whole question in a nutshell is one of control."[15] He visualized this control taking place on the local level, with "a civic awakening on the part of the public that only the best pictures be allowed to be exhibited and the determination to patronize only the best show-houses."[16] (Again, the philosophy of the National Board of Review.)

The Toledo study is valuable because it was the first large-scale investigation of the pervasiveness of the motion picture as a recreational activity in an urban area. Its main finding was that the motion picture was now the preferred entertainment for most city people, especially the young, even when a large number of alternative organized recreational opportunities were available. It was, of course, precisely this point which disturbed the medium's critics.

Social Science, Delinquency and the Movies

It was only natural that social scientists, particularly psychologists, should turn their attention toward the problem of motion picture influence on crime, especially juvenile crime. The possible connection between delinquency and the movies had always been a favorite complaint of reformers, educators, criminologists and even some early psychologists. Certainly, it was to be expected that a medium which the highest court in the country had noted had "a capacity for evil" would be labeled as a major contributing factor in the increase in juvenile and other crime. (Whether in fact there was such an increase is another question, and the subject of some historical controversy.)[17]

Prior to the appearance of these specialized studies on "children and the movies" the connection between crime and motion pictures had depended largely on the pioneering work of William Healy and those social workers who had found children to be "unduly influenced by movies." While there was much conjecture about the role of the movies in "educating" children into a life of crime, in fact very little valid research on this specific topic was conducted until the late 1920s and early 1930s.

The development of sophisticated investigatory techniques in psychology and social psychology allowed more precise measurements of influence to be determined. Noting the central position occupied by psychology in the social sciences, Louis Wirth claimed that the "most significant" development in this discipline in this century was "the emergence of social psychology as a more or less autonomous discipline."[18] This development was due to the recognition by social scientists of the importance of treating and examining mental phenomena in their social and cultural milieu. No longer were generalizations concerning human behavior acceptable unless they referred to the specific societal context and considered interaction between individuals or groups.

Social scientists lost no time in using some of these new techniques of "rigorous observation, experimentation, and systematic theorizing" to investigate the whole issue of "movies and crime." In 1928, the well-known child psychologist Dr. Phyllis Blanchard, of the Philadelphia Child Guidance Clinc, made the most significant contribution to this discussion since Healy, when she devoted an entire chapter in her influential book *Child and Society* to an analysis of "The Child and the Motion Picture." After summarizing many of the previous studies on children's attendance at motion pictures, Dr. Blanchard suggested that movies, even more than reading, satisfied the "wish-fulfilment motive," in that "they transport the child into another world, geographically, economically and emotionally."[19] While condemning "the stimulation of useless fear and undue emphasis on sex in distorted ways," she praised the medium's ability to give the child, especially those from the slums, an opportunity to escape from unhappy home conditions. On the subject of juvenile delinquency and the movies she quoted from a new, more valid study undertaken by Healy and Brommer in 1925, which showed that only 1 percent of 4,000 cases examined was motivated to misconduct through the influence of motion pictures. She also claimed that her own research corroborated this low incidence of influence and added, "In comparison to the intimate relationships between delinquency and unfavorable conditions of family life, recreation and other social institutions, the role of the motion picture in the production of youthful misdemeanors is a very minor one."[20] She did, however, acknowledge that indirectly the motion picture was the cause of crimes such as petty theft to gain the necessary admission price, or occasionally truancy.

If valid research did not indicate the guilt of the motion picture, as many reformers had suggested, why then was the medium still regarded with such scorn and fear? Dr. Blanchard had a suggestion: "Mankind is always glad to find a scapegoat upon which it can project its sins. It is much less painful to accept the opinion that the motion pictures together with other new economic and social forces, are the causes of unruly conduct in children than to face the fact that the failure of family life is in large measure the most responsible agent."[21] What she suggested here was that the community, feeling itself threatened by forces which eschewed the traditional values and beliefs, had lashed out at the visible symbols of this transformation, and the motion picture was extremely open to this type of criticism because of its wide availability to all social groups, and because of the central position it then occupied in American life. Seldom, as a contrast, did the live theater receive the harsh treatment accorded the screen, mainly because the elite audience attending stage productions was more sophisticated and the medium had historically defined itself as "adult entertainment," and was therefore accepted as such. The motion picture industry on the other hand had never been able to convince the public that many of its offerings, too, were basically "adult." Much of the misunderstanding was due to the industry's failure to provide alternative attractions for children in sufficient quantity or quality to make a two-tiered market economically viable. Thus children were forced to watch what the industry itself admitted was largely adult fare, while all the schemes to prevent adolescent entrance to "adult" attractions had proved difficult to enforce at the exhibitor's level. Other than the outright banning of children from the theaters (which actually occurred in some small American communities and in the Province of Quebec), there seemed to be very little that the local community could do to regulate and control child attendance without the complete cooperation of the industry. On the other side, the industry appeared unwilling to alter its successful content formulae as long as the majority of the public appeared willing to accept them.

One year later, in 1929, Dr. Blanchard lectured to the Congress on Psychology held in New York on the subject of "Crime and the Motion Picture." At this time she reiterated that no valid scientific views had ever been advanced to prove that movies unduly influenced crime, and that, in fact, the motion picture may actually have rendered a socially useful service in improving notions of morality and good behavior of the young. She cited as an example how children cheered the capture of the villain (which almost always happened at the end of American films).[22]

The Pitkin "Formula," 1931

Even the sound, empirically based research of social scientists such as Dr. Blanchard did not deter others from making idiosyncratic observations under the guise of "scientific" research. An outstanding, if not outrageous, example of the misuse of the stimulus-response theory is found in the work of Walter Pitkin, the well-known innovator of improved reading techniques. In an article entitled "Screen Crime vs. Press Crime," appearing in Outlook in 1931, Pitkin responded to movie producer Carl Laemmle's earlier suggestion that the press should clean itself up before asking the motion picture industry to do the same. He pointed out that there were enormous differences between the effects of the same story in the press and on the screen, and that this created a dangerous situation, for while the illiterates in the population cannot read, they do attend the movies. Children, he continued, seldom read newspapers, but they too attend the movies in very large numbers. Pitkin then estimated the semiilliterate population to be in the area of fifteen million, "many of whom must have poor minds . . . [and] . . . this is the sort who turn joyfully to the pictures." He also voiced his concern over the fact that it was "the abnormal mental class" which was most affected, for "the printed work inflames them less readily than does a picture, and a silent picture unbalances them far less readily than does a sound picture, and a sound picture unbalances them far less easily than does a talking picture."[23]

What was most worthy of attention, however, was Pitkin's attempt to construct a formula to measure the "psychic intensity" of the various forms of mass media. "Psychic intensity" he defined as "the quantity of stimulus-response per unit of time," which was measured in "kinetic energy." Based upon this formula Pitkin noted that "the talking picture has the highest intensity than any other known medium of communication," and in fact approached the intensity of real life situations. This was because "during its performance, it hurls at eye and ear far more units of sight and sound, of gesture and language, of action and reaction than any weaker medium. . . . One minute before the screen excites them [the "hypersuggestibles"] more than a week of reading crime stories . . . it also thrills infinitely more than any formal lesson conveyed through talk or reading."[24]

Pitkin continued his attack by estimating that there were 37,000,000 people in America under the "influence of the movies" who never read newspapers. He continued: "These same people constitute the bulk of the movie fans; they attend the pictures more frequently than *our superior classes*. From the screen they derive nearly all of the joy, the excitement, the sexual thrill, and the underworldly wisdom which they ever acquire."[25]

While Pitkin's bias in favor of reading and readers was understandable, one can safely argue with his generalization that "those who gain something from reading are markedly more intelligent . . . for . . . reading requires far more brains than eyeing a flicker of light."[26] Although Pitkin's views must obviously be considered to represent one of the extreme ends of the "movie problem" spectrum, they were in fact merely a more articulated and "pseudo-scientific" version of what many reform groups actually felt to be the case.

The Mitchell Study, 1929

In 1929, the first major investigation devoted entirely to an analysis of the problem of children and the influence of motion pictures was published. Alice Miller Mitchell's *Children and the Movies* was a pioneering study based upon an extensive survey questionnaire. This was administered to 10,052 Chicago schoolchildren representing three groups: average public-school children; juvenile delinquents; and a specific group of children who had a certain degree of organized leadership in their lives, such as the Boy Scouts or the Camp Fire Girls.[27] While many arguments could be and were made that eliciting responses from children by means of written answers was not the most reliable method for this type of research, the completed study nevertheless made a major contribution to the understanding of the important role played by the motion picture as an integral part of the American child's everyday world.

Some of the findings made by Mrs. Mitchell were very similar to those made earlier by Phelan, and confirmed the very large part played by the motion picture in the overall recreational activity of the average urban child. She found that 90.6 percent, or 9,014, of the 10,052 children attended the movies at regular intervals ranging from once a month to seven times a week, the average being between once and twice a week. A higher frequency rate was found among the juvenile offenders.[28] Interestingly, there seemed to be only a very slight relationship between the proximity of the movie theaters to the homes of the children and the rate of juvenile attendance at these theaters, indicating that children sought movie shows regardless of distance from home.[29] The most outstanding factor which apparently influenced the frequency of juvenile attendance at the movies was the degree to which alternative organized recreational interest entered into the life of the child. While home environment and parental supervision played important parts in determining the extent of film-going, the study indicated that some guidance toward outside interests such as the Boy Scouts would lower the rate of attendance.

The Mitchell study comprehensively examined "going to the movies" as a social institution, including: the hours of most frequent attendance; who took or accompanied the moviegoer; the price of admission; the most favored content forms; the differences in attendance at the neighborhood movie house and the first-run theaters; the relationship between the child's preference for movies and participation in other recreational activities; how movies affected reading habits; and delinquency and the movies. Even after examining the relationship between delinquency and attendance at motion pictures the author was forced to admit that the results were inconclusive and proved only that "the delinquent does have a wider movie experience than do the other children studied."[30] Mrs. Mitchell's analysis of the medium's influence led her to believe that the youthful movie experience could be harmful, in that children were exposed to adult problems at too tender an age, noting, "these children . . . perhaps are robbed of some of their preciousness of childhood."[31]

The Mitchell study was something of a landmark in social research, for it was one of the first large-scale examinations of the influence of a mass medium on a specific segment of the population and the resulting patterns of usage. While many questions still remained to be answered, especially in the area of the long-term socializing influence, the basic raw data gave an accurate picture of the pervasiveness of the motion picture and its importance as a recreational activity for all Americans, especially the urban child.

Unfortunately, the Mitchell study seems to have suffered the same fate that those of Munsterberg and Young had earlier, and it was seldom referred to or used by the industry, or, even more surprisingly, by the reform groups. This was a great pity because it certainly was among the more valid and useful research studies undertaken on the subject, and its judicious use could have provided a common meeting ground for opposing factions.

The Payne Fund Studies, 1933

It was not entirely coincidence that in 1933, when the Hays Office found itself besieged from all sides, the first really comprehensive examination of motion picture effects on American society appeared in the form of a series of studies sponsored by the Payne Fund. These studies, originally intended to examine motion picture influence in a rational scientific atmosphere, instead provided much of the ammunition needed by reform groups to pressure the industry to abide by its own self-regulatory rules. More important, these studies gave graphic credence to the view that the motion picture *was* a major influence in American life. While the studies by Mitchell and others had indicated that the movies were indeed a social and cultural influence of significance, they had only further emphasized the need for a more thorough, objective evaluation of the medium and its effects. Therefore, in 1928, the Reverend William H. Short, the executive director of the Motion Picture Research Council, a group organized for the express purpose of doing research in this field, secured a grant of $200,000 from the Payne Fund to carry out a nationwide study to determine the degrees of influence and effect of films upon children and adolescents. The task of actual investigation was given to a group of social scientists — psychologists, sociologists and educators — who were under the direction of Dr. W. W. Charters, the director of the Bureau of Educational Research, Ohio State University. The actual field research was conducted over the four-year period from 1929 to 1933, and the first volume appeared in 1933.

The initial purpose of such a unique and immense undertaking was "the development of a national policy concerning motion pictures." Later this aim was amended to "providing a broader understanding of the total effect at home and abroad of motion pictures." However, the foreign investigations were dropped because the investigators felt that they were not equipped to handle this aspect, and the studies were then redesigned "to provide data for answering completely or in part a wide range of separate queries" relating to the effects of motion pictures on the youth of America.[32] The result was a series of twelve studies published under the generic title of "Motion Pictures and Youth," which was the most comprehensive investigation of the motion picture ever undertaken in the United States.[33]

While each study was a self-contained research work, the significant findings were conveniently summarized in the volume entitled *Motion Pictures and Youth*, by Professor Charters. In discussing the overall design of the studies, Charters developed a formula, which in simplified form stated:

GENERAL INFLUENCE $\times$ CONTENT $\times$ ATTENDANCE = TOTAL INFLUENCE

To arrive at this formula, Charters reasoned that "if, in short, the general influence of motion pictures is ascertained, if the content is known and the number of visits of children has been computed, the total influence of the pictures will be in general a product of these three factors."[34] The formula as thus computed was open to criticism, but it was never applied in the final assessment in any meaningful manner. Charters's formula did, however, influence the design of the individual studies, which focused on such areas as attendance, content of motion pictures, the mores depicted on the screen relative to accepted social standards, the retention of information, the ability to change attitudes, the effects upon sleep and health, the emotional effects, the relationship between motion pictures and juvenile delinquency, and even how children could be taught to discriminate between "good" and "bad" cinema.

The studies utilized four general research methods to obtain their results: (1) the strictly physiological experimental procedure, used in the studies on emotions and the effects of movies on sleep; (2) the "paper and pencil" testing technique; (3) the use of rating scales; and (4) the questionnaire, life story, and interview methods. In order to meet the objectives set for this pioneering inquiry many novel research techniques had to be devised. As examples, Dysinger and Ruckmick measured the immediate effects of exciting movie scenes by the use of the psychogalvanic reflex, while Renshaw and his colleagues devised a method of studying the after-effects of the motion picture by measuring divergences from the normal motility of children during sleep.

Peterson and Thurstone used specifically devised scales to test changes caused by motion pictures in the beliefs and attitudes of nearly four thousand elementary and high school pupils upon various public questions such as war and peace, racial and nationalistic prejudices, Prohibition and the treatment of criminals. Holaday and Stoddard examined the extent to which children and adults retained the ideas and concepts taken from the movies, while Shuttleworth and May made a special analysis of the relation of personal character and interests to the frequency of attendance at the movies. Peters had the difficult task of comparing the content of motion pictures with the accepted standards of morality in America and used specially devised rating scales for this purpose.

Blumer and Hauser used the questionnaire method in an attempt to study the effects of motion pictures upon conduct, both normal and delinquent, and upon ideas and emotions. They studied several hundred young men and women in correctional institutions, a small group of fifty-five ex-convicts and a rather large group of boys and girls of school age living in sections of Chicago marked by high delinquency rates. In another study, which attempted to relate the motion picture to conduct and emotional attitudes and "schemes of life," Blumer employed autobiographical interviews and formal questionnaires to secure his data.

The final studies were done by Edgar Dale. The first was the most comprehensive content analysis ever made of American motion pictures up to that time. Dale and his associates analyzed the themes of five hundred feature films shown in each of the years 1920, 1925, and 1930, and classified them into ten basic categories. Dale also investigated the attendance of children, both the frequency and the total number of admissions, and who accompanied the child to the movies. It was Dale who was entrusted with writing the volume on film appreciation for children.

The Payne Fund studies revealed the extent of the medium's use as a commercial entertainment in the United States by conservatively estimating that the average weekly attendance in 1929 was 77 million. Of these 77 million, about 28 million were under twenty-one; 11 million were fourteen years old or younger; and 6 million were seven years old or less.[35] These were average figures, and in some congested urban areas the percentage of children's attendance was calculated to be much higher.

Taken as a whole, the most striking feature of the conclusions reached was the wide range of "individual differences" evidenced in the subjects examined. Factors such as age, sex and experience, and cultural backgrounds such as home and family, neighborhood, community standards, social and economic status — all these contributed to the individual's response to the motion picture. Thus in the study on children's sleep, Renshaw and his associates pointed out that they did not believe that any sweeping generalization could be made about the "type" of film, or "type" of child most likely to be influenced (excepting, of course, the "abnormals"). On a similar note of caution, Dysinger and Ruckmick pointed out that "individuals differed widely in response to the emotional stimulation of the motion picture as measured by the psychologalvanic technique,"[36] and that "in the last analysis attendance at the motion picture theater is a matter of individual mental lives and must be regulated or at least judged according to the individual psychophysiological organism."[37]

In the studies on attitudes and beliefs, the retention of information, and the effects on interests and ideas, the results were more specific and demonstrable. Peterson and Thurstone showed quite clearly that prejudices for or against war, on race issues, and toward criminals, were significantly affected by viewing motion pictures on these subjects. The permanence of these changes was also demonstrated by repeated tests given weeks and months after the original viewings, although without reinforcement there was a gradual shift back to the original position. Holaday and Stoddard's research into the problem of information retention indicated that information, correct or incorrect, was easily assimilated from motion pictures and that retention was relatively permanent.

Shuttleworth and May examined the "social conduct of the movie fan" and concluded that the ardent moviegoers among children "have lower deportment records, poorer school records, are rated lower in reputation by their teachers, are less cooperative and less self-controlled, and slightly more deceptive in matters of school behavior." They were also "slightly less emotionally stable." Surprisingly (or perhaps not so), the movie fans were more frequently named by their classmates as "best friends." This study too was tempered by the wide variations which were evident, and the authors were forced to conclude with this statement:

That the movies exert an influence there can be no doubt. But it is our opinion that this influence is specific for a given child and a given movie. The same picture may influence different children in distinctly different opposite directions. . . . We are also convinced that among the most frequent attendants the movies are drawing children who are in some way maladjusted and whose difficulties are relieved only in the most temporary manner and are, in fact, much aggravated. In other words, the movies tend to fix and further establish the behavior patterns and types of attitudes which already exist among those who attend most frequently.[38]

Peters's study on motion pictures and standards of morality showed definitely that movies were depicting scenes in stark contrast to the accepted mores, as measured on his scales. Thus, in regard to the aggressiveness of women in lovemaking, the motion picture's depiction was completely contrary to the accepted norm. However, in other areas such as democratic action or racial tolerance, "the motion pictures are setting patterns of democratic conduct that are somewhat better than those to which people are accustomed in their daily lives, and are making these patterns attractive by associating them with persons whom observers would be disposed to emulate [e.g., the hero]."[39]

The studies conducted by the questionnaire or autobiographical methods were the most contentious, for they attempted to examine the difficult problem of the effects of the motion picture upon conduct and ideas. Blumer and Hauser in their study on movies, delinquency and crime approached their subject with extreme caution, but nevertheless they did conclude that movies could have a decidedly negative influence, and were a factor of importance in the delinquent or criminal careers of about 10 percent of the male and 25 percent of the female offenders studied.[40] Even discounting the methodological dangers of the autobiographical technique in causing rationalization or subjective interpretation, it appeared that, coupled with other environmental and cultural factors, the motion picture could furnish a powerful incentive for antisocial conduct. The authors suggested that the motion picture indirectly influenced criminal behavior, "through the display of crime techniques and criminal patterns of behavior; by arousing desires for easy money and luxury, and by suggesting questionable methods for their achievement; by inducing a spirit of bravado, toughness, and adventurousness; by arousing intense sexual desires; and by invoking daydreaming of criminal roles."[41] And yet there was no consistently negative influence because "movies may direct the behavior of delinquents and criminals along socially acceptable lines and make them hesitant about, and sometimes deter them from, the commission of offenses."[42] Blumer and Hauser explained these conflicting influences by concurring with the other researchers that the individual's background determined in large part the type of influence the medium had:

Motion pictures play an especially important part in the lives of children reared in socially disorganized areas. The influence of motion pictures seems to be proportionate to the weakness of the family, school, church, and neighborhood. Where the institutions which traditionally have transmitted social attitudes and forms of conduct have broken down, as is usually the case in high-rate delinquency areas, motion pictures assume a greater importance as a source of ideas and schemes of life.[43]

In Blumer's study on motion pictures and conduct the question of the movies' general influence was brought into focus. This particular study was possibly the most important of all; but it was also the most "suspect" in its findings, because it was based entirely on motion-picture "biographies" from college students, office workers and factory workers. After ensuring that several checks and balances were placed into the research procedure, Blumer concluded that the motion pictures did indeed have a deep and permanent psychological effect on many people — both adults and youths. The motion picture provided the source for rich fantasy and imitation, especially among adolescents, and it offered a means of "emotional possession" during the actual performance, and even afterward, which could profoundly influence an individual's conduct and philosophy of life. This constant exposure to a wide variety of emotional experiences was bound to have a disintegrating effect on many persons, especially those who had not yet developed a sufficient emotional detachment or an "adult discount" which permitted them to place these vicarious experiences in proper perspective.

Blumer's findings tended to confirm many of the suspicions which had been voiced by the medium's critics for nearly twenty-five years. He suggested that the content of films was more than just entertainment to many adolescents, but "authentic portrayals of life, from which they draw patterns of behavior, stimulation to overt conduct, content for a vigorous life of imagination, and ideas of reality."[44] The motion picture biographies revealed facts which caused educators to take notice, and Blumer's analysis also confirmed their worst fears:

Because motion pictures are educational . . . they may conflict with other educational institutions. They challenge what other institutions take for granted. The schemes of conduct which they present may not only fill gaps left by the school, by the home, and by the church, but they may also cut athwart the standards and values which these latter institutions seek to inculcate.[45]

Throughout the studies there was a note of cautious interpretation in an attempt to present the material as objectively as possible.

Unfortunately, the intentions of the original researchers were thwarted by the early publication of *Our Movie Made Children,* a popularization of the studies written by journalist Henry James Forman with the full cooperation of Dr. Charters and the Motion Picture Research Council. While there is no denying that the studies showed an underlying but subtle hostility toward the immense socializing influence of the movies, Forman's book was a blatant attack on the industry, and its thrust was in the direction of outside control of the motion picture industry.[46] Forman had a decided flair for selecting those findings of the studies (and even of earlier studies) which indicated the harmful effects to be derived from attending movies, and continually played on the fact that love, sex, and crime, or any combination thereof, were the central themes of most American films.

Sociologist Kimball Young in his review of the Payne Fund studies pointed out that Forman had deliberately overemphasized certain aspects of the findings, and thereby "done . . . the fields of psychology, education and sociology a genuine disservice," and he predicted that this would result in an unwarranted "wave of sentiment against the movies."[47]

The Forman book caused a mild sensation, was reprinted at least four times and was widely reviewed and discussed. Its acceptance on a popular level unfortunately obscured the importance of the findings in the studies themselves.[48]

The publication of Forman's volume signaled only that the battle had begun. On the academic level the rebuttal to the findings of the Payne Fund studies came from a rather unexpected source in one of the works of Professor Mortimer Adler. The noted neo-Aristotelian philosopher in his book *Art and Prudence* used the studies to illustrate his argument that "scientists" should not, and cannot, really judge the moral or political consequences of an art form such as motion pictures. Adler's lengthy critique was ponderous, and yet in its rather stolid fashion contained glimmers of the truth. Unfortunately, the critique was marred by Adler's obsessive desire to inflict upon all scientists the philosophic teachings of St. Thomas Aquinas. Also, his unmistakable bias against all social scientists and what they represented made him an eminently unfair judge of this type of research.[49]

Adler's arguments were difficult for most readers to follow; however, the industry was so impressed with the "massiveness" and prestige of Adler's response that Raymond Moley, formerly assistant secretary of state in FDR's cabinet and a definite "friend" of the movies, was asked by industry representatives to write a brief, easily comprehensible book outlining Adler's philosophical attack. This slim, sixty-four-page volume appeared in 1938 under the title *Are We Movie Made?* — an obvious attempt to cash in on the publicity garnered by Forman's well-received work. Moley's summary proved to be a faithful distillation of the main thrust of Adler's argument with much of the philosophic discourse removed, but it received nowhere near the publicity accorded Foman's book.[50]

The motion picture industry was obviously disturbed by the published findings of the Payne Fund studies, and particularly by the public reception of Forman's book. Unfortunately, much of the industry's response took place behind closed doors and the information has never been made public. We do know that the Hays Office was greatly concerned, because Raymond Moley's book on the MPPDA had a brief account of the consternation caused by Forman's summary, which Moley referred to as "a minor manifestation of public resentment." He noted that

Hays accurately foresaw the uncritical reviews, the denunciatory speeches and the clicking of tongues that would follow its publication. He knew that in the long run only the analyses of experts could dispel the myth of the book's scientific basis.

But the imminence of the uproar, combined with the fact that letters complaining of particular movies were coming into the Hays Office by the hundreds, provided the immediate excuse for the summoning of the M.P.P.D.A. Board of Directors in extraordinary session.[51]

What then transpired was an all-night meeting after which, on March 7, 1933, in the middle of the "bank holiday" decreed by FDR, the heads of the industry signed a reaffirmation of their responsibility to the patrons of their business. Three weeks later, on March 27, the full board of directors agreed to a complete renewal of their original 1922 dedication to "establish and maintain the highest possible moral and artistic standards," and gave an oral promise that the producers would start work immediately on a number of better films. While the latter promise seems to have been kept, the observance of self-regulatory procedures still left a great deal to be desired.

Exactly how much influence the Payne Fund studies had in bringing about the stricter enforcement of self-regulation is very difficult to estimate, although their publication must have had a catalytic significance. Certainly their major findings, mainly in the form of digests of Forman's book, were widely published and in many cases formed the background data for strong attacks on the motion picture industry. The *Christian Century* had often called attention to Hollywood's refusal to improve its product and the Payne Fund studies supplied the confirmatory ammunition. Through editorials and articles the publication now became a major thorn in the side of the producers. No sooner was Forman's book announced than Dr. Fred Eastman, the *Christian Century*'s chief Hollywood critic, used the findings as the basis of a series of seven major articles on the subject, "Your Child and the Movies."[52] In the *Survey Graphic*, the publication read by most social workers, Arthur Kellogg used this same material when he wrote an important article entitled "Minds Made by the Movies."[53] Later, in July, 1934, a series of articles appeared in the Scripps-Howard newspapers, entitled "What's Wrong with Hollywood?"[54] Organizations concerned with children acknowledged this research, and *Parent's Magazine* awarded the Payne Fund studies its annual medal as the most important study of the year in the field of the child, while the American Educational Research Association voted it the most important research report of the year.

One major response to the findings of the Payne Fund studies came from organized women's groups, when they banded together to form the Film Estimate Board of National Organizations. This board was especially created to review films which carried the seal of approval from the Production Code Administration, and included such organizations as the Parents and Teachers Associations, the General Federation of Women's Clubs, the Daughters of the American Revolution, the National

Council of Jewish Women, and the United Church Brotherhood. The board provided information on a film's content and treatment, allowing parents to make up their own minds in exercising responsibility for their children's movie-going habits. This information was made available in a monthly publication titled originally *Joint Estimates of Preview Committees on Motion Pictures,* and was available free of charge. This ponderous title was later changed to simply the *Green Sheet.*[55]

While the motion picture industry tried to ignore the Payne Fund studies as much as this was possible, the Hays Office did in fact circulate a document entitled "Authoritative Statements Concerning the Screen and Behavior," which was a twenty-six-page compilation of opinions and research which refuted all claims linking motion pictures with socially deviant behavior. The introduction to this document contained an attack upon the Motion Picture Research Council for sponsoring research detrimental to the movies. The council was particularly criticized for so vigorously promoting Forman's book, because "it is . . . an indefensible policy to publicize real or alleged 'scientific findings' through popular interpretations, addresses, and statements months before such findings are published or discussed by scientific authority."[56]

The Payne Fund studies, while they can be criticized on purely methodological grounds, nevertheless were important documents, not only for what they described, but also for what they represented.[57] In many ways their publication symbolized the culmination of the long struggle to make the motion picture industry more responsive to certain public attitudes. More important, their findings tended to confirm some of the suspicions of reformers who for years had counseled that uncontrolled influence of the medium had created an undesirable and dangerous socializing force.

After 1936, the whole subject of motion picture influence underwent a change away from proving or disproving "harmful" influences on the child, and moved toward a more rational examination of the medium's ability to induce attitude change, or its effectiveness in education. The development of more sophisticated social science research techniques enabled researchers to make valuable suggestions for improved educational use of motion pictures — suggestions which carried over into the medium's use in wartime propaganda activities.

Empirical research of the mass media was a recognized subfield of sociology and social psychology by the mid-thirties. The importance of such research was later made clear by Paul Lazarsfeld:

. . . what people can now read, see, and hear is provided in the main by a number of large-scale, fairly centralized communications industries. What, then, are the effects of this general development on the spiritual and social life of our times? . . .

No one believes that there are any ready answers to this vast array of problems. But everyone realizes that a necessary, although not a sufficient condition for such answers is the accumulation and interpretation of facts from every corner of the communications field. *Thus communication research becomes an important element in the formulation of both policy and social philosophy.*[58]

Lazarsfeld was careful to point out the dangers of rushing into such research without giving the problem careful thought, for "nothing could be more detrimental than to sacrifice the careful development of appropriate research methods on the altar of quick findings."[59]

It had taken over thirty-five years for social science to come to grips with the motion picture, and the publication of the Payne Fund studies was as much a minor triumph in the development of social science research as it was for those who wanted to know the depth of influence of the medium. However, the application of the results of this intensive research was disappointing, and they were seldom used to "formulate policy and social philosophy" as Lazarsfeld suggested. Instead, the arguments ranging around the motion picture continued on the far more subjective subject of "moral influence," and it was ultimately the decision of the Catholic church to combat this "immorality" in the medium that led to a viable form of social control.

NOTES TO CHAPTER IX

1. For the history of government use of the social sciences see Gene M. Lyons, *The Uneasy Partnership* (New York: Russell Sage Foundation, 1969), pp. 3–10.

2. Louis Wirth, "The Social Sciences," in Merle E. Curti, ed., *American Scholarship in the Twentieth Century* (Cambridge: Harvard University Press, 1953), p. 40.

3. Lyons, p. 26.

4. The best examinations of the concept of "mass society" are found in Daniel Bell, *The End of Ideology* (New York: Collier Books, 1961), especially in chapter 1; Leon Bramson, *The Political Context of Sociology* (Princeton: Princeton University Press, 1960); and William Kornhauser, "The Theory of Mass Society," in *International Encyclopedia of Social Sciences* (New York: Macmillan and Free Press, 1968), vol. 10, pp. 58–64.

5. See De Fleur, *Theories of Mass Communication,* pp. 110–111.

6. Elihu Katz and Paul F. Lazarsfeld, *Personal Influence* (New York: Free Press, 1955), p. 16.

7. De Fleur, pp. 112–117; and McQuail, *Towards a Sociology of Mass Communications,* p. 52.

8. De Fleur, p. 116. For a detailed history of shifts in psychological theorizing see Edwin G. Boring, *A History of Experimental Psychology* (New York: Appleton-Century-Crofts, 1950).

9. The one exception to this has already been noted in chapter 6. The totally subjective study undertaken by the Chicago Motion Picture Commission was immediately translated into legislative action in the form of a new city censorship ordinance. See *Chicago Code,* 1922, Sections 2785 to 2794.

10. Wirth, p. 56.

11. Rev. J. J. Phelan, *Motion Pictures as a Phase of Commercialized Amusement in Toledo, Ohio* (Toledo: Little Book Press, 1919), p. 12.

12. *Ibid.*, p. 29. The decline of movie houses, as indicated in Phelan's study, confirmed Benjamin Hampton's contention that larger theaters had replaced smaller ones.

13. Phelan, pp. 37–39.

14. *Ibid.*, pp. 107–112.

15. *Ibid.*, p. 112.

16. *Ibid.*, p. 122.

17. For a further exposition of the problem of historically assessing crime rates see Daniel Bell, "The Myth of the Crime Wave," in *The End of Ideology*, pp. 137–158. For an excellent account of the international dimensions of the problem of motion picture influence and criminal behavior see "Immorality, Crime and the Cinema," *International Review of Educational Cinematography*, vol. 2 (1930), pp. 319–334.

18. Wirth, p. 62.

19. Phyllis Blanchard, *Child and Society* (New York: Longmans, Green and Co., 1928), pp. 191–195.

20. *Ibid.*, p. 204.

21. *Ibid.*

22. *New York Times,* September 4, 1929.

23. Walter B. Pitkin, "Screen Crime vs. Press Crime," *Outlook and Independent,* July 29, 1931, pp. 398–399, 414.

24. *Ibid.*, p. 399.

25. *Ibid.*, p. 414. (Italics added.)

26. *Ibid.*

27. Alice Miller Mitchell, *Children and the Movies* (Chicago: University of Chicago Press, 1929; reprinted New York: Jerome S. Ozer, 1971), p. 6.

28. *Ibid.*, pp. 21–22.

29. *Ibid.*, p. 23.

30. *Ibid.*, p. 143.

31. *Ibid.*, p. 148.

32. Henry James Forman, *Our Movie Made Children* (New York: Macmillan Company, 1933).

33. The Payne Fund studies are listed below. All have been reprinted by Arno Press, New York, 1971.
Herbert Blumer, *Movies and Conduct* (New York: Macmillan Company, 1933).
Herbert Blumer and Philip M. Hauser, *Movies, Delinquency and Crime* (New York: Macmillan Company, 1933).
W. W. Charters, *Motion Pictures and Youth* (New York: Macmillan Company, 1933).
Edgar Dale, *Children's Attendance at Motion Pictures* (New York: Macmillan Company, 1935).
Edgar Dale, *The Content of Motion Pictures* (New York: Macmillan Company, 1935).
Edgar Dale, *How to Appreciate Motion Pictures* (New York: Macmillan Company, 1937).
Wendell S. Dysinger and Christian A. Ruckmick, *The Emotional Responses of Children to the Motion Picture Situation* (New York: Macmillan Company, 1935).
Perry W. Holaday and George D. Stoddard, *Getting Ideas from the Movies* (New York: Macmillan Company, 1933).
Charles C. Peters, *Motion Pictures and Standards of Morality* (New York: Macmillan Company, 1933).

Ruth Peterson and L. I. Thurstone, *Motion Pictures and the Social Attitudes of Children* (New York: Macmillan Company, 1933).

Samuel Renshaw, Vernon L. Miller, and Dorothy P. Marquis, *Children's Sleep* (New York: Macmillan Company, 1933).

Frank K. Shuttleworth and Mark A. May, *The Social Conduct and Attitudes of Movie Fans* (New York: Macmillan Company, 1933).

34. Charters, p. 5; Holaday and Stoddard, *passim;* Shuttleworth and May, *passim;* Peters, *passim.*

35. Dale, *Attendance,* p. 73.

36. Dysinger and Ruckmick, p. 110.

37. *Ibid.,* p. 115.

38. Shuttleworth and May, p. 93.

39. Peters, p. 117.

40. Blumer and Hauser, p. 198.

41. *Ibid.*

42. *Ibid.,* p. 199.

43. *Ibid.,* p. 202.

44. Blumer, p. 196.

45. *Ibid.,* p. 197.

46. Forman, *Our Movie Made Children.*

47. Kimball Young, "Review of the Payne Fund Studies," *American Journal of Sociology,* September, 1935, p. 255. See also *Variety,* November 13, 1934, pp. 2, 51, in which Young denounced Forman's book and noted that the movies were being unfairly accused of an influence which could "not be separated from the influences of comic strips, the newspapers and magazines, the radio, vaudeville and all other modern devices of communication."

48. There is some unsubstantiated evidence that the Reverend William H. Short did in fact intend the studies to form the bulwark of an attack upon the industry that would result in some form of organized control, and he thus encouraged and supported Forman's "popular" account. In a personal letter to this author, Professor Mark A. May, one of the original researchers involved, and the author together with Frank K. Shuttleworth of *The Social Conduct and Attitudes of Movie Fans,* stated: "There was [a] time . . . when Mr. Short . . . threatened to withhold my study from publication." (The study was not strongly enough against the industry.) May continued, "That man . . . was really out to damn the movies straight away to hell!" (Letter dated November 5, 1970.)

49. Mortimer J. Adler, *Art and Prudence* (New York: Longmans, Green and Co., 1937).

50. Raymond Moley, *Are We Movie Made?* (New York: Macy-Masius, 1938).

51. Moley, *Hays Office,* p. 78.

52. Fred Eastman, "Your Child and the Movies," *Christian Century,* May 3, 10, 17, 24, 31, June 7, 14, 1933.

53. Arthur Kellogg, "Minds Made by the Movies," *Survey Graphic,* May, 1933, pp. 245–250.

54. Schull, "Suitability of Commercial Entertainment," p. 182.

55. The only detailed account of this organization is contained in John A. Sargent, "Self-Regulation: The Motion Picture Production Code, 1930–1961" (Ph.D. dissertation, University of Michigan, 1963), p. 60.

56. Motion Picture Producers and Distributors of America, Inc., "Authoritative State-

ments Concerning the Screen and Behavior," in the files of the Museum of Modern Art Film Library (no date).

57. On November 24, 1933, the motion picture industry appeared before a U.S. Senate subcommittee on crime control, and claimed that the Payne Fund studies "had used improper techniques in gathering their findings." *New York Times,* November 25, 1933, p. 32.

58. Paul F. Lazarsfeld and Frank N. Stanton, *Communications Research: 1948–1949* (New York: Harper and Brothers, 1949), p. xiv. (Italics added.)

59. *Ibid.*

X

The Motion Picture Controlled

EVER SINCE THE MEETING in Mayor McClellan's office in New York in December, 1908, the motion picture industry had asked for an opportunity to regulate itself, free from external social or political pressures. When Will Hays assumed the presidency of the MPPDA fifteen years later, the industry intensified this plea, because Hays himself was committed to reform by internal regulation.[1] However, in the fifteen years prior to the formation of the MPPDA every attempt to bring about a viable system of self-regulation had failed. There were many reasons for this failure, but they all stemmed from the industry's inability to form a central independent body with sufficient power and authority to oversee its total operation. This was particularly difficult to do while individual companies were jockeying for premier positions and the vertical integration of the production and exhibition functions was under way. However, after the First World War when the industry settled into a comfortable pattern of tolerant cooperation, the establishment of the MPPDA seemed at long last to offer the promise of such a strong centralized control agency.

The Attempt at Self-Regulation

With the creation of the MPPDA in 1922 the producers had indicated their commitment to the concept of self-regulation as the only alternative to more official forms of control; therefore in the ensuing years Hays would overlook no opportunity in an attempt to establish a workable system. This was not an easy task, for many producers were afraid that the results of such strict internal control would dilute their product to

233

such a "wishy-washy" level that audiences attracted to more adult fare would turn away from the movies. There was also the very real problem of how to control the highly idiosyncratic talents of the men who ran the studios and those who created the films. The important Hollywood "moguls" were all self-made men who had seldom tolerated outside interference while building their empires, and Hays, the ultimate Protestant politician, would find his task made more difficult by what could best be termed a "cultural gap."[2]

Raymond Moley in his paean to Will Hays, *The Hays Office* (published in 1946), discussed these differences between Hays and his employers and suggested that the ethnic and entrepreneurial backgrounds of the men who had built the movie industry had much to do with the manner in which the medium had become associated with vulgarity, and that their own standards were based on a morality which was out of touch with that of the vast majority of Americans.[3] Moley further suggested that in their drive for success they had become "curiously unfamiliar with that public of which their customers were only a part, however large a part." Starting in the penny arcades, they had never really come face to face with the vast audiences which they had created across the nation — "diversified, complex, with its manifold prejudices and ideals, its innumerable traditions, its capacity to feel and act — an industry with a national market."[4] It was only when that vague and mysterious phenomenon "public opinion" began to manifest itself in the threatening forms it took in 1921, and after, that the industry was forced into a realization that no longer was it operating on a purely local basis. Moley was right, for the needs of the movie audience had indeed outgrown the taste of the producers.

In the years after 1922, the movie industry, through the auspices of the Hays Office, showed an amazing transformation in its relationship with the viewing public. Considering the size and importance of the industry it was remarkable that before 1922 the only continuous public relations activity for motion pictures was that engendered by the National Board of Review, a supposedly independent body. The industry itself was mainly content to build up its stars and its productions, but seldom found time for institutional self-promotion. The NAMPI did not have sufficient time, money or authority to successfully combat the adverse publicity resulting from the 1921 scandals, and thus the MPPDA inherited an industry image requiring drastic face-lifting and renewed public confidence.

Hays insisted that self-regulation be made the cornerstone of the industry's new public image, and he lost no time in starting to forge a plan acceptable to both the industry and the public. It would be more than ten years before he ultimately achieved this goal. Nevertheless, his total dedication to this concept was unyielding, and while commercial expediency obviously played some part, his basic motivation was a sincere desire to prevent by all means possible the further imposition of political censorship damaging for the industry. In an important article published in 1927, entitled "Motion Pictures and Their Censors," Hays spelled out his philosophy on the problems of censorship:

It is fully as necessary to protect this great agency the movies from undue political aggression as to guard against the misuse from within. There must be the same guarantee of freedom for artistic and inspirational development as has been accorded other methods of expression.

Motion pictures are not dead things, to be regulated like commodities such as freight and food ... they contain a potency of life in them to be as active as the soul whose progeny they are.... They are evidences of human thought; and human thought, on which all progress depends, can not be tampered with safely.[5]

Hays made a strong plea that the public be allowed to judge for themselves whether or not films should be officially censored; and he noted that the only time the public was given the chance to voice its opinions, in the Massachusetts referendum, it had voted against censorship. The film producers, Hays claimed, should be given the right to exercise their "moral responsibilities" and not be made to justify their product before a politically created board. This would leave the audience as the ultimate judge of whether the film industry was fulfilling its social obligations, and if not, then the extant punitive statutes in criminal law could be invoked. The public in turn could and should become more directly involved by patronizing the "good" films then available, for this would ensure a continued supply of "vital and wholesome pictures." But Hays was not content to let self-regulation continue merely as a public posture with little substantive meaning, and he therefore initiated a series of steps which eventually, with the aid of much outside pressure, led to an enforceable system.

The *Formula:* A major problem faced by the Hays Office in its early years was the adoption for the screen of books and plays with "mature" themes. While plays had limited and mainly adult audiences, and books had small circulations, these same stories on the screen were available to all, young and old. The historian Merle Curti noted that the arts in America in the 1920s were undergoing a rather drastic change from the "genteel tradition" to a greater desire for "self expression and pleasure, especially in the realm of sex, and the corresponding reaction against so-called Puritanism and Victorianism constituted one of the most obvious patterns amongst both intellectuals and the 'flaming youth' of the period."[6] It was the era of Dreiser, D. H. Lawrence, Dos Passos, Fitzgerald, Hemingway and Sinclair Lewis. Curti noted further, "In plays and books alike the whole American emphasis on standardization, conformity, moral idealism, utilitarianism, service, 'keeping-up-with-the-Joneses,' and 'bigger-and-betterism' was satirized."[7] While the appeal of these works of art in their original forms was substantial, their appearance on the screen was immediately condemned by those groups who saw the possible dangers in the mass dissemination of these "new ideas" to millions of movie goers.

In 1923 an incident caused by a film based upon the book *West of the Water Tower* resulted in the introduction of the *Formula*. (See Appendix II.) The story presented difficulties for screen adaptation because of its subject matter, the portrayal of a situation involving illegitimacy, a robbery, a dissolute clergyman, and the pettiness of the story's small-town characters. The book had been reviewed by members of the Public Relations Committee of the Hays Office and rejected for screen presentation, but it was nevertheless subsequently produced and released under the original title.[8] Moley observed that Hays had used this occasion "to shape a method of dealing with those plays and books of the Jazz Era which were making the house-wives shudder and the clergymen storm."[9]

On February 26, 1924, the MPPDA passed a resolution which called upon each member studio to instruct its reading department to forward to the MPPDA office a copy of its synopsis of each play, book or story read, together with any appended comments regarding questionable themes, or treatments. The Hays Office in turn was to "advise" the studios of any objectionable play, story or themes which might not be suitable for screen treatment. This so-called *Formula* was amplified and reaffirmed on June 19, 1924, and was in fact the first practical attempt at centralized self-regulation. Unfortunately this too was destined to fail, for the MPPDA had no vested authority with which to reject objectionable material, or to impose penalties for nonobservance; and the instructions were vague on the specific situations or elements that could be considered undesirable for screen treatment.[10]

Although the *Formula* was just the first step and had no legal weight, Hays took the position that the members of the MPPDA would be violating their articles of incorporation and pledges to the public if they did not comply. While the *Formula* was under consideration at least one company notified Hays that it had decided to "shelve" a film already in production. The Shenton study on industry public relations noted that "within a week after the adoption of the resolution communications were received from four other companies naming specific books or plays which they had decided, in conformity with the new policy to reject."[11] An ironic problem with the *Formula* was that the censorial decisions made by the studios were not made public in order to prevent any possible antitrust violations; therefore, its publicity value was quite limited and most pro-censorship groups were unaware of its existence or function until much later.

Further complications arose when member companies, having invested sizable amounts of money in these properties, insisted that certain objectionable materials could be given suitable screen "treatments" which would eliminate the undesirable elements. The Hays Office steadfastly refused to allow this to happen in spite of numerous objections from authors who felt that they being deprived of a chance to make a living. In 1927, however, an agreement was worked out with the Authors League of America which allowed the rewriting of books and plays for screen presentation; these works had to be given new titles, and the fact of their previous rejection was not to be advertised in any way. Ruth Inglis indicated that this solution failed to meet the basic objections to these books and plays, because the film critics "usually pointed out the connection between the original story and the revised screen version."[12] Also, the *Formula* did not apply to original film scripts, which in many cases contained the most objectionable material. Hays, nonetheless, saw the *Formula* as a major breakthrough in the battle for self-regulation and he vigorously promoted it. As a result, between 1924 and 1930, there were 125 rejections of objectionable material.

The Studio Relations Department: The establishment of a studio relations department in 1926 was an important step in centralizing decision-making within the MPPDA, and Colonel Jason S. Joy, the director of the Public Relations Department, was dispatched to Hollywood to work with the producers. Joy's experiences in dealing with the public's and special interest groups' reactions to films gave him a unique insight into the problems that producers could expect from certain types of content, and he held continuous conferences with studio officials to acquaint them with the most frequent objections voiced by censors. He also visited various state and municipal censorship boards in an attempt to clarify some of their criteria for objection or approval — a task which Raymond Moley suggested would have "reduced a Daniel Boone to fingernail-biting."[13] Gradually producers began to show films to Joy before they were released, and they even let him argue with them about certain necessary deletions; but this was a purely informal arrangement. Then producers began submitting scripts for prerelease examination and elimination of possible problems. All this informal help by Joy bore fruit because the producers soon became aware that censorship boards made fewer cuts in films that had been previewed and adjusted to the MPPDA's standards.

237

Joy's activities proved to be an important intermediate stage in the evolution of self-regulation.

The *Don'ts and Be Carefuls:* The next major step was to formalize the activities of the Studio Relations Department and to codify the rejections and deletions of the state censorship boards, together with the various objections that had been raised by social groups over the years. After a study of the problem was completed in 1927, the MPPDA unanimously adopted a report prepared by Joy's staff after consultation with studio officials. The resolutions agreed to list eleven things which "shall not appear in pictures produced by members of this association, irrespective of the manner in which they are treated," and twenty-six other subjects with respect to which the producers agreed to exercise special care "to the end that vulgarity and suggestiveness may be eliminated and that good taste may be emphasized."[14] These regulations became known as the *Don'ts and Be Carefuls,* and were included as Rule 21 of the Code of the Motion Picture Industry adopted at a trade practice conference conducted by the Federal Trade Commission in New York in 1927. (See Appendix III.)

Hays's success in promoting these measures was greatly assisted by the advent of sound pictures in 1926, for producers soon became aware that alteration of these films was a much costlier process than that incurred with silent films. The cutting of dialogue often destroyed the entire sequence and sense of scenes and sometimes required expensive retakes. Joy used this as a selling feature of the *Don'ts and Be Carefuls* and his argument was a strong one, because he could point out that on films in which the Studio Relations Department had been involved before 1929, the censors had averaged 1.9 cuts, while the average on other films was 5.9 deletions. Joy's experience in public relations had also made him aware of the important role that public pressure could play, and he stressed that trends in public taste rather than the idiosyncrasies of various censorship boards should be the guiding factor in establishing industry standards.[15]

The formalization of various self-regulatory measures was, however, not the entire answer, for even these internal operational changes and controls instituted by the MPPDA did very little to stem the tide of criticism then being aimed at the content of the films. While the *Formula* and the *Don'ts and Be Carefuls* were heralded as an indication of the industry's awareness of its social obligations, the criticisms not only continued, but increased in intensity with the arrival of the ex–vaudeville and burlesque personalities following the introduction of sound in 1926–1927. Raymond Moley described the changes that this influx brought to Hollywood:

Execrable girl-and-music shows, heretofore seen only by the out-of-towner on an occasional trip to New York, were being brought by the talkies to every hamlet.

The frenzied filming of Broadway plays without regard for the fact that a motion picture, whether talking or silent, is certainly not a play from the point of view of either art or prudence, brought the clink of highball glasses, the squeal of bedsprings, the crackle of fast conversation to a thousand Main Streets.[16]

While the industry was still searching for the elusive solution to the problem of making its product fit the tastes of the individual American community, the reform groups continued their clamoring for greater control at the federal level. Unlike the suggestions made by the National Board of Review, which was fully cognizant of localized differences in preferences, the major pro-censorship groups active at this time were more concerned with making the industry responsible to a national authority because they themselves were national organizations with a matching outlook.

Indicative of the industry's failure to alter its content was the fact that state censorship boards continued to be as active as ever. In 1928 the New York censors made over 4,000 eliminations in 661 films, with over 1,300 listed as "indecent or inhuman," while over half were made on the grounds that the films or scenes were "tending to incite to crime."[17] The Chicago censorship board during the same year made 6,470 deletions, while a review of films released between November, 1927, and April, 1928, made by a joint national committee of the General Federation of Women's Clubs, the National Congress of Parents and Teachers, and the American Farm Bureau was highly critical of the industry. Of the 216 films closely examined, the joint committee reported that 177, or 82 percent, were unfit to be shown to children under fifteen, and in fact only 40 percent were suitable at all for "young people."[18] This was also the first year of operations under the *Don'ts and Be Carefuls;* an indication that a wide gap still existed between the industry's standards and those of the community at large.

An analysis of the *Don'ts and Be Carefuls* showed a great similarity to the old *Thirteen Points* of the NAMPI.[19] In many ways it proved to be just as ineffective because of the familiar reason that its implementation was impossible without any authoritative legislation for enforcement. Martin Quigley, the influential Catholic publisher of the important trade magazine *Motion Picture Herald,* remarked that "the list was of such broad general character that the application of its injunction and demands was difficult or impossible . . . its generalized and vague character encouraged them [the producers] either to circumvent its injunctions or to ignore them."[20] Quigley understood the film industry's plight, being both an insider in the trade and a prominent agitator for motion picture reform. He suggested that the lack of communication between the producers and the public was due to: "(1) Lack of interest and pressure on the part of public opinion; (2) The practical and technical difficulties involved; [and] (3) The lack of pertinent information and guidance on the subject of the morality of public entertainment."[21] Quigley's first point is interesting because it indicated that he considered the pressure groups (which at that time were mainly Protestant) to be ineffectual, and without strong public support. This was significant because Quigley later became one of the major figures in the formation of the Catholic Legion of Decency, which coalesced Catholic public opinion into a highly effective pressure group.

The Hays Office tried to convince the producers that strict observance of the moral code could only benefit the public image of the movies. Nevertheless, only a small portion of the industry seemed willing to voluntarily adhere to the various regulatory resolutions. The introduction of sound with its attendant large financial investment, and the booming economic prosperity, created in the America of 1927–1929 a climate that was not propitious for moral reform, and few studios were willing to attempt "purification" at the risk of losing audiences to the risqué films of their competitors. John Haynes Holmes, the head of the Community Church in New York City, reviewed those years in an article written in 1936. He pointed out that "the indecent era of the movies came along with the national era of prosperity," and that "hungry for money, the movie producers suddenly descended to levels of vulgarity and sheer obscenity which did much to make the movie theaters a pornographic institution."[22] While Holmes's comments greatly overexaggerated the morals of the film industry, it was soon obvious that the 1927 resolution was as useless as all the other previous attempts at self-regulation, and in his *Memoirs* Hays wistfully noted, ". . . it is a commentary on human nature that while the studio heads and directors hung on Joy's words when he was merely the advance scout for possible censorship hurdles, many of them began ignoring his admonitions when he was backed by a body of rules."[23]

The Motion Picture Production Code

In 1930 the *Don'ts and Be Carefuls* were superseded by the *Motion Picture Production Code,* which differed from the previous codes of self-regulation, all of which had been purely negative, in that it was considered to be more a "philosophy" of producing films, and as such was designed to force the producers into a greater awareness of their responsibility and commitment to the public. (See Appendix IV.) The origins of the *Code* have always been disputed.[24] The authorship seems to have been a joint effort between Martin Quigley and Father Daniel A.

Lord, S.J., a Catholic priest who had often acted as a technical adviser for Hollywood films.[25] There was no doubt, however, that this new *Code* was the direct outcome of the intense and continuous public pressure being exerted on the industry by a small but dedicated group determined to make the medium more responsive to what they felt were acceptable social standards.

It was also now obvious that the interest in motion picture reform was widening beyond those groups who had maintained the pressure all through the twenties. The reasons for this expansion were unclear, but it appeared that time had finally run out for the Hays Office and its unkept promises. No longer was the mere presence of Will Hays sufficient to forestall the criticism, and after eight years in office there had been no noticeable improvement in the moral standards of the movies. The introduction of sound and the onset of the Depression had in fact made many films even more "morally objectionable" as the studios fought each other for the diminishing entertainment dollar. The early thirties was a period that did not auger well for the introduction of yet another regulatory code, but the industry realized that massive public appeasement was inevitable.

Father Lord and Martin Quigley polished their canon of ethics for the industry, and after several meetings with Hays, and presentations to the producers, the *Production Code* was formally adopted by the directors of the MPPDA on March 31, 1930. The *Code* itself had two parts: the first was called simply "The Code," while the second was called "The Reasons." The explanation for the *Code*'s division in this manner was somewhat obscure, but it appears highly likely that Hays was deliberately attempting to play down its Catholic origins. In a comparison of the *Code* and the *Don'ts and Be Carefuls,* Ruth Inglis noted that while the *Code* itself stemmed directly from the earlier list, "The Reasons" were the new element which represented the work of Father Lord and Martin Quigley. She suggested, "Many of the specific rules of 1927 [the *Don'ts and Be Carefuls*] had nothing to do with Christian morality, and their union with the philosophical rationale for morality in motion pictures resulted in a document [the *Production Code*] which is somewhat divided in nature."[26]

The *Code* without "The Reasons" was made public in 1930 as the *complete Code,* and even Quigley's own publication adopted this position by observing: "This Code . . . was formulated after intensive study by members of the industry and, according to Will H. Hays, by church leaders, leaders in the field of education, representatives of women's clubs, educators, psychologists, dramatists 'and other students of our moral, social and family problems.' "[27] It was not until after the Catholic Legion of Decency campaign in 1934 that the Hays Office allowed full disclosure of the philosophical sections. The only possible motivation for obscuring the *Code*'s origins was to stop the growing criticism that the Hays Office was dominated by Catholic influence. Raymond Moley went to great lengths to make the point that the *Code,* while originally drafted by members of the Catholic church, was based on the "Ten Commandments," which "are universally acceptable by the members of all Western religions . . . so the Code suggests the basic moral unity of Western civilization."[28]

In substance the *Code* tried to encompass all the problems previously encountered, but, even more important, it gave public reaffirmation of the MPPDA's desire to implement the original resolutions outlined in the incorporation document of 1922. The *Code* was based on the premise that motion pictures as entertainment and art affected the moral life of a people, and that therefore the medium was charged with special moral responsibilities because of its wide appeal and availability. (It is interesting to note the similarity between this position and that of the majority opinion in the Supreme Court decision of 1915. See Chapter V.) Therefore it followed that "the latitude given to film material cannot, in consequence, be as wide as the latitude given to book material." The "Preamble" section also compared the motion picture to newspapers and plays in this context, and even noted the crucial problem of community differences in one section: "Small communities: remote from sophistication and from the hardening process which often takes place in the ethical and moral standards of groups in larger cities, are easily and readily reached by any sort of film."[29]

For all its good intentions the *Production Code* of 1930 was not the immediate success Hays had hoped it would be, and as usual the initial enforcement regulations were not tight enough to effect those changes which Hays had so long desired. At first the *Code* provided that "each production manager may submit in confidence a copy of each or any script to the Association of Motion Picture Producers, Inc." Later, on October 8, 1931, the submission of scripts to the Studio Relations Committee was made compulsory. Despite all these efforts and the approval and tacit acceptance of the *Code* by the entire industry, the years 1930–1933 "passed without a noticeable improvement in the quality of pictures and without the eliminations of those objectionable themes and treatments which had brought about the creation and adoption of the Code."[30] Howard T. Lewis, of the Harvard Graduate School of Business, in his excellent study of the motion picture industry stated in 1933 that

it is not likely that anybody, whether within the industry or outside, has any idea that this code would be sufficiently effective to cause those responsible for the production to rid pictures of the characteristics which render them unsatisfactory to many diverse groups of interest ... a substantial number of producers never would take the code seriously.... It is difficult to believe that directors have always even attempted to comply with its provisions.[31]

Attempts at Local Control

In 1929, two states — New York and New Jersey — had statutes which prohibited the admission of children under sixteen years of age to motion pictures at any time, unless accompanied by parent, guardian or authorized adult. Six other states, New Hampshire, Massachusetts, Connecticut, Rhode Island, Michigan and Mississippi prohibited the admission of children during school hours and after certain hours in the early evening. The remaining forty states had no regulations except for very minor restrictions, such as Oregon, where a curfew law forbade unescorted children to attend motion picture shows after nine in the winter and ten in summer.[32] The fact that children were forbidden to attend the movies in certain states did not solve the problem; on the contrary, for the open flaunting of these laws only created disrespect for this type of regulation. Even the so-called special children's matinees were often misnomers, and merely meant that a cowboy or a serial picture had been added to the regular adult feature.

Some communities, particularly where strong pressure groups existed, became frustrated by the Hays Office's failure to provide adequate control of the medium, and attempted to establish their own extralegal forms of control. More often than not such occurrences were precipitated by "incidents" in the community itself, and which were directly linked to supposed motion picture influence. One such incident occurred in the communities of Orange and Maplewood in New Jersey in 1931, and received national headlines. At the very moment that the local Better Films Committee and the Women's Division of the Chamber of Commerce were putting pressure on the local theater managers to stop the cycle of gangster films then making the rounds, a young boy was accidently shot and killed by a friend "while demonstrating a scene from an underworld picture." The outcry in the communities was so great that Mayor Simon H. Rollinson of West Orange "ordered all managers to remove gangster films from their programs." This order was repeated in his own community by Mayor Charles H. Martens of East Orange. The local movie-house managers refused to comply, claiming that block-booking practices forced them to accept this type of film. The managers also made a strong case that the audiences seemed to enjoy these films immensely. (A very accurate observation.) At this time in the Depression the competition for the entertainment dollar was particularly keen and the industry was unwilling to comply with this selective action for fear that it would spread elsewhere. When the Hays Office rejected a direct plea from Mayor Martens to stop such showings, this dramatic attempt to assert local control failed. The industry took great pleasure in the fact that in spite of all the unfavorable publicity there was no appreciable drop-off in audience in the community.[33]

Despite the best efforts of Will Hays to set standards for the industry, and those of many reformers, religious and educational authorities, and politicians to bring about an agreeable method of control that would satisfy the industry, the motion picture, by 1930, was still considered an uncontrolled problem. The industry resisted real reform until a unique combination of circumstances and ingredients — the arrival of sound, the Depression, the Hays Office and the Catholic Legion of Decency — finally caused the industry to adjust its position to accommodate many of the reforms so long sought.

The NRA Code, 1933–1935

On June 16, 1933, President Roosevelt signed the National Industrial Recovery Act. What this act did was to set aside the antitrust laws, and to permit businessmen to devise and codify their own rules of competition, production and marketing. These were called "codes of fair competition." The NRA was a major step in the break with the tradition of laissez-faire, but was still far short of the completely controlled economy sought by many of the radical economic planners offering solutions to the Depression.[34] In the end over six hundred various industry codes were drawn up, and the NRA *Motion Picture Code* had the distinction of being the longest. This was because all the elements of the industry — production, distribution and exhibition — were deemed to be "entirely inter-related with and dependent upon each other."[35] Louis Nizer noted that the NRA *Code* "reduced to unified statement the violent differences amongst the various elements in the Industry which had existed for thirty years. Furthermore, it provided for judicial self-determination within the Industry on a scale never before attempted in Industry."[36] Under the NRA *Motion Picture Code* sixty-two intraindustry courts were set up with local jurisdiction in thirty-one zones in the United States, and the Code Authority was given power to act as the Supreme Court of the industry. While the economic investment in the motion picture industry (two billion dollars) was sufficient to warrant the establishment of an NRA code, there were other factors at stake. The NRA administration noted the social significance of the motion picture industry in its report to the President: "The Industry assumes a position of unusual importance because of its far-reaching influence upon social and economic standards and conduct throughout the world."[37]

It is significant to note that the NRA *Code* covered not only the internal workings of the motion picture industry, but in Article VII it dealt with the moral standards of films:

ARTICLE VII
GENERAL TRADE PROVISIONS

PART 1. Moral Standards of Motion Pictures

(a) Pledge of Industry

The industry pledges its combined strength to maintain right moral standards in the production of motion pictures as a form of entertainment.

(b) Self-Regulation

·The industry pledges itself to adhere to the regulations made within the industry to attain this purpose.

PART 2. Standards of Advertising and Publicity

(a) Pledge

The industry pledges its combined strength to maintain the best standards of advertising and publicity procedure.

(b) Self-Regulation

The industry pledges itself to adhere to the regulations made within the industry to attain this purpose.[38]

Raymond Moley observed that Will Hays had the "keen satisfaction of seeing the film code take over much of the fruits of more than ten years of the industry's experiments in self-government such as labor standards, industry ethics. . . . The NRA code specifically delegated to the M.P.P.D.A. the question of self-regulation under its existing Production and Advertising Codes."[39]

It was only natural for the studios to see the NRA *Code* as the dangerous first step in establishing full federal control over the industry, and many reform groups also saw this as an opportunity to gain what they had sought for so long. Advisers close to Roosevelt even went so far as to devise a plan for the establishment of a "superorganization" to oversee the whole movie industry. Will Hays noted that the President was able to deal with this threat quite easily:

When the scheme reached the President he said that "any plan will have to be okayed by Hays, he will have to favor it," and he sent for me. Before the end of our conversation he assured me that neither this plan nor any similar one would be contemplated further, in view of my representations concerning the industry's self-regulation and the fact that our plan was working as well as any plan could work. No more was heard of a federal coordinator.[40]

On May 27, 1935, the Supreme Court unanimously ruled that the NRA was unconstitutional and an improper abdication by Congress of its law-making powers. With this decision the Blue Eagle symbol of the NRA died, but few, including Roosevelt, really mourned its demise. During its short life the NRA had given industry the needed "shot in the arm."[41] However, for the film industry the removal of the NRA *Code* was much more serious, for the studios had learned through many years of bitter experience that unregulated competition was extremely wasteful. By 1933, the work of the Hays Office had established a reasonably viable system, but even this had grown rusty with disuse during the life of the NRA. The result was absolute chaos, with no clear leadership emerging to pick up the pieces of the self-regulatory trade practices which were still useful. Even the continuous pressure from the Federal Trade Commission and the threat of further antitrust prosecutions failed to bring order. Hays himself was powerless to act in the face of recalcitrant exhibitors and distributors, and Moley pointed out that "1938 found the trade-practice structure of the industry in the United States without arbitration, without conciliation, without a uniform system of clearance, without a standard contract — in short, without any of the benefits, actual or potential, of self-regulation and with all the problems of anarchy."[42] The industry was, once again, inviting federal interference, and the FTC was only too happy to oblige in 1938.

The Catholic Legion of Decency

The Catholic church's official attitude toward the recreational revolution in general and the motion picture in particular had always been a rather ambiguous one. In many respects the Catholic church held a far looser rein on its adherents than did Protestant churches; in observance of Sundays, as an example, the Catholics had placed the emphasis on regular attendance, with far fewer restrictions upon conduct and recreation during the rest of the day. Also, while the Catholic church had urged temperence, it had not officially favored Prohibition. The Catholic church, largely because of its strong European background, seemed to understand the need for the recuperative powers of recreation and kept such restrictions to a minimum, provided only that the individual's "faith" remained strong. However, when the church officially decided that there were morally objectionable and dangerous influences at work on the lives and beliefs of its members, it made every effort and sacrifice necessary to eradicate or control this influence. Thus, when at long last the church decided that much of movie content ran counter to Catholic doctrine it was able to mount an impressive campaign in an attempt to force the industry to fulfill the promises made over the years. The unanswered question is why, after all the years of comparative silence, did the Catholic church suddenly decide to bring its massive influence to bear on the problem of motion picture morality. Even Father Paul W. Facey, the single best source on the subject, has failed to offer any definite answer to this puzzle.[43]

There is no doubt that Martin Quigley's efforts played a major role in getting the Catholic church officially involved in its institutional capacity; but this occurred only after it had become obvious that pressure from Catholics as individuals was as ineffective as that from the Protestant pressure groups. Quigley, together with several other prominent Catholics, including Joseph I. Breen (who later became Hays's assistant), Father Daniel Lord (the coauthor of the *Code*), Father Wilfred Parsons, S.J. (the editor of the influential Jesuit weekly *America*), Father F. G. Dineen, S.J. (a Chicago priest interested in communications), and Monsignor Joseph M. Corrigan (rector of Catholic University, Washington, D.C.), had for several years discussed the problems of the movies and the appropriate role for the Catholic church. After the introduction of the *Production Code* at the behest of this group, the groundwork was laid for a greater Catholic involvement in Hollywood's internal affairs. Initially the group had attempted to establish Catholic church pressure by what was termed "individual ethical leadership," in which "public opinion . . . was to be represented by ethical leaders who would exert pressure on the industry for conformity to the Code." Father Wilfred Parsons wrote to Cardinal Hayes in describing this plan that "what we must do . . . is to create in the industry's minds an impression that influential people expect the Code to be obeyed; if that happens it will be obeyed."[44]

While this plan was endorsed by the Pope and other prominent Catholics, the attempt to exert pressure on the industry by simple "moral persuasion" was ineffective. Father Parsons, through the vehicle of *America*, tried to sustain public interest but he too was unsuccessful. In November, 1930, he noted this apathy: "It is a curious commentary on our civilization that the Code [the *Production Code* of the MPPDA] passed almost unnoticed by the public at large. . . . With certain exceptions Catholic leaders have been conspicuously silent and ineffective."[45] Quigley himself was greatly disappointed at the failure of this plan to take hold, saying later that "despite the recent worldwide recognition of the moral potency of the screen the problem was one that only dawned tardily on the consciousness of important moral leadership."[46] Out of this failure to interest Catholics as individuals emerged a more ambitious and far-reaching plan to involve the Catholic church as an institution committed to the control of the American motion picture.

The first important move was to rally all Catholics to the cause. Thus in October, 1933, the newly appointed Apostolic Delegate, Monsignor Cicognani, delivered an address to a Catholic Charities Convention in New York — a speech which bore the unmistakable stamp of a rallying cry: "What a massacre of innocence of youth is taking place hour by hour! How shall the crimes that have their direct source in immoral motion pictures be measured? Catholics are called by God, the Pope, the Bishops, and the priests to a united and vigorous campaign for the purification of the cinema, which has become a deadly menace to morals."[47] Father Parsons followed up this speech with an editorial in *America* on October 28, in which he observed that "it is perfectly clear that letters and other written protests to Will Hays or anybody else will do little good. . . . Since they have made it perfectly clear that they have no intention whatever of heeding these protests, something else will have to be thought up."[48]

The next step was taken at the annual American Bishop's Convention, when Bishop Cantwell of Los Angeles, who had earlier campaigned for "cleaner motion pictures," described the problem to the assembled churchmen. Cantwell's preparation for this hour had been thorough, and having become convinced that nothing but direct action would suffice, he had corresponded with all the bishops before the meeting, and arranged that the film issue would be one of the principle items on the agenda. The outcome of this meeting was that the bishops condemned the immorality in films, demanded that the industry reform, and appointed an Episcopal Committee on Motion Pictures to plan, control and conduct a national campaign to improve the "moral quality" of films. After studying the situation this committee made three major organizational decisions: (1) to recruit a pressure group; (2) to propose a buyer's strike as a sanction; and (3) to direct the pressure toward more efficient operation of industry self-regulation.[49] (It is interesting to note that unlike the Protestants, the Catholics made no mention of the need for federal control agencies — they had *full* confidence in their ability to enforce adherence to established self-regulatory mechanisms.)

The committee's first step was to initiate a publicity campaign through the 310 Catholic news organs in America. These local newspapers and news sheets had a combined circulation of over seven million. The over thirty thousand Catholic priests were urged to use their influence with local congregations in order to create public pressure for "better films."

Catholic conventions, which averaged two or three a week, were exhorted to join the effort; with the result that many resolutions in favor of organized Catholic pressure on the movie industry were passed. Even Catholic college and high school students were organized into local units. Finally, after six months of preparation, on April 11, 1934, the Episcopal Committee announced the details for launching a crusade against immorality in motion pictures. This announcement was not made public, but was communicated directly and separately to the bishops of each of the 104 dioceses of the Catholic church of the United States.[50]

The primary function of the local bishops was to recruit followers, and each bishop was encouraged to conduct his own decentralized recruitment program. Paul Facey pointed out that no new local organization was needed to carry out this campaign and the ordinary channels of communication of the church were sufficient for the purpose. The local priests read pastoral letters from the bishops; there were also letters to the clergy instructing them to preach "on the moral ills of the movies, [and] urging the signing of the pledge."[51] These local campaigns were backed by radio addresses, newspaper editorials and articles, and even a few mass gatherings, but each diocese ran its own program, choosing when to start recruiting and adopting its own recruitment techniques.

The bishops also put pressure on the local exhibitors, mostly by writing letters, but there were many instances of organized demonstrations and "visits" to the exhibitors by protesting delegations. Only in Philadelphia was there an actual boycott of all motion picture theaters by Catholics, and this was a direct result of a pastoral letter written by Cardinal Dougherty. The cardinal's attack on the film industry was a vehement call to arms: "Nothing is left for us except the boycott, and this we must put in force if we are to achieve success. The Catholic people of this diocese are, therefore urged to register their united protest against immoral and indecent films by remaining away entirely from all motion picture theaters."[52]

This action in Philadelphia achieved national prominence for the Legion of Decency, and the *New York Times* report of this boycott on June 9, 1934, was the first mention of the Legion in that paper. From then on the Legion and its efforts to "purify Hollywood" received almost daily attention. The success of this strong action in Philadelphia resulted in decreased audiences and supposedly caused severe economic loss to local exhibitors. The manager of the Warner chain in the Philadelphia area reported that unless the boycott was discontinued he would be forced to close his theaters.[53]

The Success of the Legion of Decency

The Catholic church, with its intensive campaign against what it considered to be essentially immoral doctrines prevalent in American motion pictures, had succeeded in focusing public attention on this social problem to an extent never before accomplished by any pressure group. Whereas the Protestant groups had for twenty-five years taken the initiative in the fight against the encroaching social influence of the motion picture, they had failed to make any real or permanent gains; however, the Catholic church was able to accomplish its appointed task within one year. The industry itself, although always very defensive, had never taken these Protestant reform groups seriously as a long-term threat. As late as 1932, an article in the *Christian Century* reported that a film trade publication had stated that Carl Milliken, of the Hays Office, was developing a new channel of communications with a national association of Protestant churchmen in order to "line them up!" The trade magazine was quoted as indicating to its interested readers that "since nine-tenths of the criticism of motion pictures from religious denominations are estimated to come from Protestant sects this move is expected to avert many complaints." The *Christian Century* strongly attacked this attitude of the industry on the basis that "the Protestant Churches have provided enough victims for the Hays-Milliken type of cooperation."[54] While the Hays Office concerned itself with placating the Protestants by creating even more preview committees, it was just not able to cope with the intensity and solid organizational structure of the Catholic campaign. Once again the film industry had been caught unprepared.

The Catholic church was in an ideal position to carry the fight to Hollywood, and once they began to organize, the industry was forced to take notice. The *Survey* pointed out in an assessment of the Legion that the movie makers might "get a real headache" when they saw the figures quoted in the *Christian Herald* on the registered membership of churches in America. The 1933 total was over sixty million, with the Catholic membership placed at over twenty million.[55] Moreover, the internal organizational structure of the Catholic church was such that it was able to carry its battle plan directly to every member of the church in every community. Catholic men and women of all ages were asked to sign a pledge that read in part:

I wish to join the Legion of Decency, which condemns vile and unwholesome moving pictures. I unite with all who protest against them as a grave menace to youth, to home life, to country and to religion....

Considering these evils, I hereby promise to remain away from all motion pictures except those which do not offend decency and Christian morality. I promise further to secure as many members as possible for the Legion of Decency. I make this protest in a spirit of self-respect, and with the conviction that the American public does not demand filthy pictures, but clean entertainment and educational features.[56]

Taking the oath was completely voluntary, but the weight of the church's influence cannot be overlooked or overstressed. All members of the Catholic church recognized the authority of the head of the church as represented by the Pope. As one scholar of religion has noted, the church "is not a collection of individuals; it has a character and a life of its own . . . the member of the Catholic Church is made conscious of the great organization, of its supreme authority within its peculiar sphere."[57] Thus the church's request that its members sign the pledge was answered by anywhere from nine to eleven million devoted followers.[58]

The Catholic Legion of Decency was so successful in capturing the imagination of the general public that soon after its emergence it was welcomed and joined by many non-Catholic groups. The Federal Council of Churches, in response to demands from all parts of the country, began to prepare a similar pledge for Protestants. In Philadelphia, the Methodist ministers invited their congregations to support the boycott, while the Protestant *Christian Century* backed the crusade in almost every respect. Father Facey claimed that the Episcopal Committee compiled a list of fifty-four organizations of Protestant or Jewish churches, ministers and rabbis, who cooperated in securing pledges or publicly announced their support of the Legion's campaign.[59]

There were, however, quite a few who did not view the emergence of the Legion with such elation. Margaret Thorp in her book *America at the Movies* articulated this position;[60] while Rabbi Sidney E. Goldstein, writing on "The Motion Picture and Social Control," questioned the Legion's power to impose Catholic standards on the whole of the American public: "No group, whether it be selected by an official of the Government or by a Catholic, Protestant or Jewish body, has the right to make mandatory upon the city or State or country standards that the group itself believes at the time to be correct."[61] He questioned whether the Catholic disapproval of divorce, birth control or suicide should mean that the entire country should be forbidden to see films dealing with these topics.

However, attacks on the Legion were not often reported in the period before 1940, and there is no real evidence of any organized opposition. Instead, educational and fraternal organizations rallied to join the Catholic crusade. The National Education Association sent a message of congratulation and cooperation, while representatives of five of the most important fraternal organizations — the Knights of Columbus, B'nai Brith, Elks, Masons, and Odd Fellows — formed an Emergency Council of Fraternal Organizations specifically for the purpose of assisting the Legion to gather pledges.

Paul Facey suggested that the "silence" in the press and the other media regarding any negative aspects of the Legion's activities was not due to Catholic intimidation, but rather because "the bulk of the members of these groups support essentially the same values as those upheld by the Legion of Decency." He also indicated that while other religious groups were not generally opposed to divorce and suicide in the same manner as the Catholic church, nevertheless they did not support them as positive values to be flaunted on the screen. To substantiate his argument Facey pointed out that the major criticism of the Legion came from "unreligious" sources, and that this opposition did not "vocalize its hostile attitude toward particular moral standards supported by the Legion; its opposition is usually predicated upon aesthetic or social considerations."[62] These two areas were, of course, the special concerns of the film critics. Facey pointed particularly to the *Nation* and its strong campaign against the imposition of the Legion's doctrine and aesthetic standards on all American films, as the extreme sample of this type of "elitist" attack. Nevertheless, it appeared that even the film critics were placated in their earlier harsh judgment of the Legion when later they saw the "improved" Hollywood product which resulted.

The Machinery of the Legion

The Legion functioned essentially by publishing lists of films which had been "morally rated" and making them available to anyone or any group that was interested. Because of its long experience in the preview rooms of Hollywood, the International Federation of Catholic Alumnae was chosen to be the "core of the Legion's rating staff."[63] In preparation for their task the reviewing staff went through a six-month training and indoctrination program, which included reading Martin Quigley's *Decency in Motion Pictures;* Richard and Dana Skinner's *The Morals of the Screen;* an eight-page booklet entitled *How to Judge the Morality of Motion Pictures;* and, most important, Pope Pius XI's encyclical on films, *Vigilanti Cura.*[64] The reviewers were asked to examine the films submitted from only the moral point of view: Is the theme moral? Is the treatment moral? Are there any voices of morality to articulate the moral principles involved? Is sin treated as a mistake or as a shameful transgression? Is the film contrary to Christian and traditional standards of morality? Each report was weighed with the others, and these in turn with judgments made by specially chosen priests and laymen. In this manner the decision was made on whether a film should be condemned, or assigned to a "lower" rating.[65]

By February, 1936, the Legion had evolved a system of ratings for all commercial films: "Class A-1," morally unobjectionable for general patronage; "Class A-2," morally unobjectionable for adults; "Class B," morally objectionable in part for all; "Class C — Condemned," "positively bad." The "Class B" category was ill defined, and was used as a residual classification for films which did not belong in either the "condemned" or "unobjectionable" categories. The Legion did, however, urge its members to stay away from "B" films, although they were not compelled to do so.

The lists, prepared weekly, were made available to the diocesan presses and carried by most of them; or were posted in the vestibules of churches and on bulletin boards of parochial schools. Some dioceses chose to organize councils of the Legion of Decency to carry on promotional and publicity work in the local community. In this way almost every parishioner was reached by the Legion, enabling the Catholic church to communicate its motion picture preferences directly to almost twenty million Americans. Thus it was able to combat the problem of variations in local standards by imposing one "national" standard for all Catholics. Nevertheless, local pressure was still the key to the operation of the Legion — pressure on the Catholic congregation and pressure on the individual exhibitors. This meant that the Catholic church was able to accomplish by "institutional force" what other groups such as the National Board of Review had been unable to achieve, even though the board's attempts to involve local communities through the Better Film Committees were very similar to the goals of the Legion.

The Response of the Industry

The motion picture industry initially responded to the Legion of Decency in several ways, but the ultimate and most important response was one of compliance with the wishes of the Catholic church. At first the industry assumed that this was just another attempt by a religious group to bring about "moral reform" of the movies, and would eventually fail as the others had done. Hays, however, claimed that he was always aware that the Catholic church was a force to be reckoned with.[66] When the bishops' committee met in Cincinnati in June, 1934, Hays shrewdly asked

Martin Quigley and Joseph I. Breen, both "friends of the movies," to appear before it as official representatives of the Hays Office. The bishops explained their position; they were not telling the industry what kind of films it should produce, but they were very interested in protecting the members of their church from contamination by films they thought improper and immoral. The bishops also reaffirmed their support of the motion picture as an entertainment form, but they wanted to see it grow and develop "under conditions they thought right and proper."[67]

The outcome of this meeting was an important one in the history of the film industry in America. In July, 1934, less than three months after the formation of the Legion of Decency, the MPPDA agreed to the establishment of the Production Code Administration Office (PCA). Joseph Breen, who had been made chairman of the Studio Relations Committee in February, was placed at the head of this new regulatory department. It was agreed that no company belonging to the MPPDA would distribute or release or exhibit any film unless it received a certificate of approval signed by the PCA. These regulations were strengthened by a resolution providing a $25,000 penalty for failure to comply: the first time that such a "punishment clause" had ever been agreed upon by the members of the industry association.

Did the Legion of Decency campaign so adversely affect the motion picture industry at the box office that at long last the producers were willing to acquiesce to reformist pressure? There is no certain answer concerning the financial impact of the Legion's crusade, and there are conflicting versions of how successful this aspect of the campaign really was. Raymond Moley claimed that while the industry was deeply impressed with the Legion's ability to marshal its forces, much of the "improvement" in film content immediately evident after 1934 was the result of preparations "made long before the storm of 1934," and the constant efforts of Will Hays to improve the situation. Moley did, however, concede that Hays had been unable to force the industry leaders to mend their ways and that "only the appearance of some spectacular guarantor of mass support as the Legion of Decency . . . and . . . only when support was mobilized for all to see, could Hays bring to swift fruition the work of the previous twelve years."[68]

In a special study made of the impact of the Legion's campaign in the city of Chicago, the researcher, Robert Janes, indicated definite declines in attendance in heavily Catholic sections of the city when "Class C — Condemned" films were shown. This was also evident to the managers of these local theaters, because they soon stopped showing "condemned" movies. Janes also indicated that the local exhibitors were personally placed under a great deal of pressure by the Legion, and that this, in fact, was where the campaign was most successful. Janes could find very little evidence of any dramatic box-office declines in the Chicago area as a whole.[69]

Paul Facey's history of the Legion detailed the difficulty in trying to assess the exact effect the campaign had on the industry's financial situation, and he quoted several newspaper and trade publication articles with opposing views. He was forced to conclude that there was no substantial evidence that Legion pressure had created a box-office slump. More important, Facey correctly noted that "the best indication of the intensity of the pressure of the Legion is given, not by figures, but by the reaction of the film industry to the pressure."[70]

The Legion achieved success in two important areas: it forced the industry to strengthen its commitment to the *Production Code* by the creation of the Production Code Administration; and it did bring about a marked change in the content of the Hollywood product in the years immediately after its organization. The bishops themselves were so pleased with the achievements in finally making the industry more responsive to its public that they formally resolved in November, 1934, to make the Legion of Decency a permanent institution. This move was indicative of the Catholic church's concern that the film industry would return to its previous pattern once the Legion pressure was removed.

It is important to note that the Legion did not see itself as a "censor." The official position was that the rating activity provided "effective guidance" to the church's followers by telling them which films were more or less apt to be "occasions of sin." The Legion saw its function primarily as that of a pressure group, whose aim was to represent Catholic opinion and thereby assist in maintaining the effectiveness of the industry's self-regulatory bodies. The Hays Office and the PCA continued to be the only source of direct authoritative control over the industry's product, although of course the many state and local censorship boards still continued to function, as did the National Board of Review.

Will Hays begrudgingly acknowledged the Legion's role in the successful establishment of the PCA and the creation of enforceable self-regulatory machinery. He had finally achieved his goal with the help of the Catholic church, and for this he was grateful. Looking back on this moment Hays recorded in his autobiography:

We had finally reached our goal; a reasonable code that could be enforced by the will of the majority. . . . Is there an honest man or woman alive who has failed to experience the endless problems of self-discipline? The motion picture industry has had the same experience — always will. At least it has acknowledged the fact, defined the difficulties, and drawn up a clear set of moral principles to guide it — with a real seal as the reward, public obloquy and a fine as a penalty. This it has done of its own free will. Is that a bad record?[71]

Hays, in his eagerness to praise the concept of self-regulation, certainly underestimated the role of the Catholic church in this process, for by 1935 the motion picture industry was essentially under the control of a Catholic hegemony. The Catholic church had achieved in a few short months what others had sought for nearly forty years. Protestants could debate control, and social scientists could measure, but only organized power and authoritative morality could achieve effective control. The result was not the smooth integration into American society which the industry and its supporters had hoped for, but instead it placed a superficial Catholic veneer on the medium which remained in effect until after the end of the Second World War. While the industry was never entirely comfortable under these restraints, except for isolated incidents it complied with this form of control. This state of affairs lasted until the advent of television in the early fifties, when the pressures of survival once again forced the industry to break away from the confining restrictions imposed by the Catholic church and the *Production Code*.

NOTES TO CHAPTER X

1. Hays explained his position in his autobiography: ". . . I have always believed that the principle of self-regulation as contrasted with regulation from without, will take firm root if given a chance; that, if watered by patience and optimism . . . the principle will at length flourish and prove lasting. This is because *self-regulation educates and strengthens those who practice it.*" W. H. Hays, *Memoirs*, p. 327. (Italics added.)

2. The backgrounds of the men who made Hollywood the "film capital" of the world are examined in two studies: Philip French, *The Movie Moguls* (Baltimore: Penguin Books, 1971), and Norman Zierold, *The Moguls* (New York: Avon Books, 1972). Both authors make a point of the largely immigrant backgrounds of these men and their early careers in "tough" businesses such as junk dealerships or clothing manufacturing. French also notes that "of the eight major companies six can be said to be substantially or entirely of Jewish foundation and Jews played an important role at most stages in the development of the other two" (pp. 36–37).

3. Ben B. Seligman, *The Potentates: Business and Businessmen in American History* (New York: Dial Press, 1971), contains an excellent section on the motion picture industry. Seligman gives a concise description of how the "financial" men wrested control from the "adventurous" men who had built the industry. See pp. 259–267.

4. Moley, *Hays Office*, p. 24.

5. Will H. Hays, "Motion Pictures and Their Censors," *American Review of Reviews*, April, 1927, pp. 393–394.

6. Merle Curti, *The Growth of American Thought* (New York: Harper and Brothers, 1951), p. 710.

7. *Ibid.*, p. 714.

8. For details of this incident see Moley, *Hays Office*, p. 48.

9. *Ibid.*, p. 58.

10. *Ibid.*, pp. 55–59.

11. Shenton, *Public Relations of the Motion Picture Industry*, p. 117.

12. Inglis, *Freedom of the Movies*, p. 113.

13. Moley, *Hays Office*, p. 63.

14. Shenton, p. 125.

15. Moley, *Hays Office*, p. 64; and Shenton, pp. 126–127.

16. Moley, *Hays Office*, p. 65.

17. Quoted in Schull, "Suitability of Commercial Entertainment," p. 157.

18. *Christian Century*, January 22, 1930, p. 110.

19. Ruth Inglis has an excellent analysis and comparison of the various moral codes adopted by the industry. This shows the great similarity among all of them, and their continuity (pp. 131–138).

20. Quigley, *Decency in Motion Pictures*, p. 45.

21. *Ibid.*, p. 47.

22. John Haynes Holmes, "The Movies and the Community," in William J. Perlman, ed., *The Movies on Trial* (New York: Macmillan Company, 1936; reprinted New York: Jerome S. Ozer, 1971), p. 200.

23. W. H. Hays, *Memoirs*, p. 434.

24. For a detailed examination of the history of the *Motion Picture Production Code* see Sargent, "Self-Regulation." The dispute over the origins of the *Code* are discussed in Sargent, pp. 31–34; Inglis, p. 116; and Moley, *Hays Office*, p. 58.

25. W. H. Hays, *Memoirs*, pp. 439–441.

26. Inglis, p. 127.

27. Quoted in *ibid.*

28. Moley, *Hays Office*, p. 71.

29. The Motion Picture Producers of America, Inc., *The Motion Picture Production Code: Reasons Supporting the Preamble* (appendix 4).

30. Moley, *Hays Office*, p. 75. For a detailed examination of the failure of the *Code* in this period see Sargent, pp. 43–69. The events described show that the establishment of the Legion of Decency was inevitable.

31. Lewis, *Motion Picture Industry*, p. 388.

32. Roy F. Woodbury, "Children and Movies," *Survey*, May 15, 1929, pp. 253–254.

33. *Christian Century*, August 12, 1931, p. 1015.

34. For details of the NRA see Cabell Phillips, *From the Crash to the Blitz, 1929–1939* (New York: Macmillan Company, 1969), pp. 212–232. A major examination of the NRA *Motion Picture Code* is Louis Nizer, *New Courts of Industry: Self-Regulation Under the Motion Picture Code* (New York: Longacre Press, 1935; reprinted New York: Jerome S. Ozer, 1971). This book was written before the NRA was declared unconstitutional, but Nizer gives the impression that the NRA *Code* provided the motion picture industry with much-needed stability in its trade practices.

35. Nizer, p. xvii. It is interesting to note that although the NRA *Code* provided for the establishment of wage guidelines, Moley claimed that actors, actresses, directors and producers "protested vehemently" against code provisions which related to "excessive salaries" (*Hays Office*, p. 204).

36. Nizer, p. xvii.

37. *Ibid.*

38. *Ibid.*, p. 236. The Code Authority noted that "all schemes in which something is given away other than motion picture entertainment are inherently evil." Furthermore, "once these schemes are introduced into a competitive community, the exhibition of

motion pictures falls into the background and the race becomes one in which exhibitors see which can give the most prizes of the greatest value and still stay in business." Moved by this principle, the Code Authority held "Bank Nights," "Race Nights," "Screeno," and other similar schemes illegal. This was an extremely unpopular ruling, and many of the ensuing issues were never resolved before the demise of the NRA. For details see Nizer, pp. 61–73.

39. Moley, *Hays Office*, p. 203.

40. W. H. Hays, *Memoirs*, p. 448. To balance off Hays's views of his relationship with the Democratic administration of Roosevelt, Charles Higham in his book *Hollywood at Sunset* (New York: Saturday Review Press, 1972) suggests that the president did not like Hays at all. Higham also suggests that in the president's "whole New Deal philosophy and in the policies that sprang from it, [he] was utterly opposed to strength of the kind Hollywood exercised" (p. 24).

41. Cabell Phillips noted that the "NRA did more for the nation's morale than for its pocketbook . . . it made people aware, in a way they had never known before, that through their government they could strike directly and tellingly at flaring social evils. . . ." (p. 232).

42. Moley, *Hays Office*, p. 207. He noted that New York City did have its own arbitration system.

43. Paul W. Facey, *The Legion of Decency: A Sociological Analysis of the Emergence and Development of a Pressure Group* (New York: Arno Press, 1974). This is the most authoritative source on the origins of the Catholic Legion of Decency available. For a detailed history of the Legion see also John M. Phelan, S.J., "The National Catholic Office for Motion Pictures: An Investigation of the Policy and Practice of Film Classification" (Ph.D. dissertation, New York University, 1968).

44. Facey, pp. 41–42.

45. "Motion Picture Morality," *America*, November 15, 1930, p. 131.

46. Quigley, *Decency*, p. 24.

47. Quoted in Schull, p. 187.

48. Editorial in *America*, October 28, 1933.

49. Facey, pp. 45–46.

50. *Ibid.*, p. 54.

51. *Ibid.*

52. *Ibid.*, p. 151. Sargent noted that boycotts were also threatened in St. Louis and Boston. See p. 71.

53. *New York Times*, July 8, 1934.

54. *Christian Century*, October 26, 1932, p. 1292.

55. The *Survey*, August, 1934, p. 254.

56. Quoted in Sargent, pp. 31–32.

57. James Hayden Tufts, *America's Social Morality: Dilemma of the Changing Mores* (New York: Henry Holt and Co., 1933), p. 18.

58. Richard Corliss, "The Legion of Decency," *Film Comment*, vol. 4, no. 4 (Summer, 1969), p. 26.

59. Noting this large non-Catholic participation, the *Christian Century* editorialized:

It is heartening to see the Protestant reaction to the launching of this Catholic Crusade. Seldom has there been as clear an illustration of the essential unity of purpose of the religious bodies in the realm of social and moral action. . . . Thousands of Protestant ministers and laity . . . say: "Thank God that the Catholics are at last opening up on this foul thing as it deserves! What can we do to help?"

Christian Century, June 26, 1934, p. 822. See also Facey, p. 61.

60. She noted:

Since there are twenty million Catholics in the United States the industry, with its guiding principle of the greatest happiness of the greatest number, finds it well worth while to regard their wishes, very clearly defined in terms of box-office. Though the Catholics are a minority group as compared to Protestants and Jews they are able by expert organization to make their peculiar prejudices prevail. . . . The warning to producers is clear. The Catholic Church is the chief guardian of the American Screen. The Church will tolerate on the screen other religions but, not, despite the freedom of thought permitted by the American Constitution, any point of view which runs counter to "traditional morality" as defined by the Catholic Church.

Margaret Thorp, *America at the Movies* (New Haven: Yale University Press, 1939), pp. 208, 214.

61. Sidney E. Goldstein, "The Motion Picture and Social Control," in Perlman, pp. 214–215.

62. Facey, p. 173.

63. Corliss, p. 30.

64. For a detailed examination of the moral philosophy of these documents see Phelan, pp. 45–47.

65. *Ibid.*, p. 31. Although the submission of films to the Legion was voluntary, no film producer could hope to receive wide distribution of his film without a Legion rating.

66. In his autobiography he noted: "Apparently Hollywood was not greatly alarmed at the action indicated by the Church leaders. . . . The sentiment seemed to be that this threat, like so many others, would blow over. But I sensed that it was something different." W. H. Hays, *Memoirs*, p. 451.

67. Moley, *Hays Office*, p. 87.

68. *Ibid.*, p. 85.

69. Robert William Janes, "The Legion of Decency and the Motion Picture Industry" (M.A. thesis, University of Chicago, 1939), *passim.*

70. Facey, pp. 151–153.

71. W. H. Hays, *Memoirs*, p. 454.

XI

America at the Movies, 1930–1941

LOOKING BACK FROM THE 1960s, the writer Harvey Swados noted that "despite the historic fact of recurring crisis, the American people were as absolutely unprepared for the Great Depression as if it had been a volcanic eruption in Kansas or Nebraska, pouring red-hot lava from coast to coast and border to border."[1] Certainly, the motion picture industry was as unprepared as everyone else for the financial collapse of the American economic system, and the shock was especially unwelcome after the costly introduction of sound systems in movie theaters throughout the country. In 1928, close to $162 million was spent on new movie houses, and the possible dangers feared from the introduction of radio had been successfully countered by the attraction of sound movies.[2] The average weekly attendance rose from 57 million in 1927, to an estimated 80 million in 1929, and then to 90 million in 1930.[3] This growth in attendance in the face of increases in the price of admission was all the more significant as the cost of producing feature films rose alarmingly. In 1920, the average cost of a feature film had been between $40,000 and $80,000, but, with the introduction of sound films, the cost in 1929 rose to between $200,000 and $400,000.[4]

This growth during the most traumatic period in American economic history due to the audience-attracting novelty of reliable sound films created an instant myth that the movies were immune to the effects of the Depression. Alas, the movie industry found that films, like every other consumer commodity, were subject to the same relentless economic pressures, and in 1931 the weekly attendance declined suddenly to 75 million, and fell further to 60 million in both 1932 and 1933. It was not until 1934 that there were signs of recovery, and attendance rose to 70 million.[5] The economic damage of the Depression was permanent, however, and the combination of the cost of conversion to sound and declining audiences resulted in the closing down of nearly 5,000 movie houses. It was a perverse stroke of economic planning that in 1932 that epitome of "picture palace" ostentation, the Radio City Music Hall, was opened.

The Movies as Recreation

It was during the disastrous years of the Depression that many millions of Americans were made aware of how the mass media now played an indispensable part in their lives, as the nation turned to the media, not only for news and information, but also for entertaining relief from the oppressive economic situation. The media responded accordingly, and conscious of the need for such relief they did their best to provide it. Newspapers ran contests, sponsored numerous "events," and gave extra coverage to sports and entertainment. It was also during these years that commercial radio assumed a new importance in the lives of all Americans. Erik Barnouw has pointed out that, "according to social workers, destitute families that had to give up an icebox or furniture or bedding still clung to the radio as to a last link with humanity."[6] The development of the large radio networks helped to ensure the nationwide popularity of this medium and its stars — many of whom were also popular screen personalities.

The movies, however, were still the premier entertainment attraction in America, and their role in Depression America was a vital one. Writing in *Forum* in 1935, James Rorty noted somewhat sarcastically that, while the movie industry had suffered economic losses, proportionately these were less than those of any other industry except food products. He continued: "The industry is more necessary, hence more stable, than steel or housing or power. . . . Indeed, the suffering and bewilderment of the depression augmented the demand for dreams, in so far as it became less and less possible for the average person to master or adjust to the intolerable realities of disemployment and destitution."[7]

Rorty's comments were based upon the economic facts, and the public expenditure on movie attendance as a percentage of total recreational expenditures actually increased during the period 1929–1935. As appendix five shows, the public's allegiance to the movies was particularly strong all during the thirties, claiming on the average one-fifth of the entertainment dollar. In a detailed study of motion picture economics, Anthony Dawson has demonstrated that, in fact, the motion picture industry as a whole was much more stable than the economy. This stability, Dawson noted, was due to "the attitude of the consumer, who revealed in his expenditure pattern, that motion picture attendance is a comparative necessity, or at least more necessary than most other forms of recreation."[8]

The sudden thrust of American society into a deep economic and then moral depression resulted in numerous official and unofficial attempts to provide answers to what exactly had happened and how it had come about. Much of this took the form of introspective examination to discover what was unique about America, what internal strengths should be hung on to, and which weaknesses in the system should be discarded. The historian Warren Susman, in his perceptive essay on the thirties, observed that "it was during the thirties that the idea of culture was domesticated, with important consequences. Americans then began thinking in terms of patterns of behavior and belief, values and life-styles, symbols and meanings. It was during this period that we find, for the first time, frequent reference to 'an American Way of Life.' "[9]

It was also during the thirties that we find the emergence of what William Stott has called "Documentary Expression" — the use of photographic and journalistic techniques to present actual fact "in a way that makes it credible and vivid to people at the time. . . . The heart of documentary is not form or style of medium, but always content."[10] The intellectual legacy of this movement has left us with an invaluable record of life in thirties America. And it was only natural that as an integral part of American life the movies would receive their share of examination. However, while there still remained a strong residual interest in movie "effects," a much greater emphasis was now placed on describing the nature of the "movie-going experience" and on analyzing the role and function of the motion picture as part of the total social and cultural infrastructure.

In 1935, the Lynds went back to *Middletown* (Muncie, Indiana) to study the effects of the Depression on that city. They found that the number of movie theaters had declined from nine in 1925 to seven, "but one of them, a resplendent new house with a decidedly 'big city' air, has the, for Middletown, entirely unprecedented seating capacity of 1,800." Three of these movie houses were "first run," one of which catered primarily to the working class and farmers. While attendance figures could not be obtained, there was a suggestion from the manager of the largest house that "movies have been hit just like jewelry and other luxury trades." Lynd himself discounted such a drastic decline, and noted that 1933 census figures indicated that total movie house receipts for that year in Middletown were $244,000. This constituted an amount equal to 2.1 percent of the total area retail sales, and 4.15 percent of the total factory and retail payroll.[11]

The evidence gathered on this second trip to Middletown indicated that the Depression had, in fact, made some changes in movie-going habits. One theater owner suggested that patrons were more discriminating, selecting "the good, worthwhile pictures, the four-star hits," while other exhibitors commented that audiences wanted more pictures "on the happy side." The Lynds quote one exhibitor as saying of the audience: "They have wanted the movies more than ever to supply the lacks in their existence. The 'fairyland' type of picture has been more popular than ever — the type of picture that lifts people into a happy world of gaiety and evening clothes; and both our business people and working class have shied off serious and sad pictures — they have too much of that at home."[12]

Insofar as "movie influence" was concerned, the Lynds noted that "adolescent Middletown goes to school to, as well as enjoying the movies," and they cited examples of high-school girls imitating Joan Crawford to the bewilderment of their tongue-tied young male companions.[13] A more ominous example is noted in connection with the alteration in family role expectations as a result of large-scale male unemployment. No longer were men so sure of their traditional roles as breadwinners, fathers, and heads of households. The motion picture added to this male confusion by promoting new female roles in business, and contributed to male feelings of inadequacy as husbands and lovers, by nightly parading "grand passions" before Middletown movie audiences.[14] Finally, this return visit confirmed for the Lynds something that they had observed earlier; that there was a marked trend among Middletowners to become more cosmopolitan in outlook due to the "heavily democratic character of the movies, radio, periodicals, and other mass media which import the outside world."[15]

In their study of *Yankee City* (Newburyport, Massachusetts), the sociologists Lloyd Warner and Paul Lunt examined the motion picture as a significant part of the leisure infrastructure in that community. The motion picture data was relatively easy to compile because at the time of the fieldwork there was only one movie house in operation in Yankee City, and this was owned by one of the large national chains with central offices in New York City.[16] Warner and his associates were able to gain almost full cooperation from the management to conduct the research and this even included access to box-office records.

The attendance patterns of movie audiences in Yankee City showed very little variation from those already indicated in the earlier studies by Mitchell and Dale. There was one significant contribution, however, in that Warner and Lunt were able to break down their subject-population into social classes, and were therefore able to provide attendance data by socioeconomic group. This data (see Table 9) indicated the rather unexpected low attendance rate of the lowest class, for with this exception, attendance decreased as the status of the class increased. Nevertheless, those confirmed patrons from the lowest group attended with greater frequency. Another interesting point was that patrons from the upper-upper class were predominantly female (indicating a greater amount of available leisure time), while those of the lower-lower class "had more than double the number of male than female admissions."[17] It is perhaps a mark of the objective investigator, but Warner and Lunt made no attempt at qualitative judgments about the role of the movies in the lives of the people of Yankee City.

TABLE 9

MOVIE ATTENDANCE BY CLASS GROUP IN YANKEE CITY
(SURVEY TAKEN OVER 25-DAY PERIOD IN 1935)

CLASS GROUP	PERCENTAGE OF TOTAL POPULATION	PERCENTAGE OF PAID ADMISSIONS	AVERAGE ATTENDANCE FREQUENCY FOR INDIVIDUAL PATRON	PREDOMINANT SEX ATTENDING
Upper-upper	1.45	1.83	2.0	female
Lower-upper	1.57	2.90	1.92	male-female
Upper-middle	10.30	12.53	1.95	male-female
Lower-middle	28.36	34.16	2.30	male-female
Upper-lower	32.88	34.47	2.43	male-female
Lower-lower	25.44	14.11	2.65	male

Table compiled from *The Social Life of a Modern Community,* pp. 412–419.

The question of sex composition of cinema audiences was extremely important in that it was usually assumed that the content of films was largely determined by the female segment, even though the numerical predominance of this group had never been clearly demonstrated.[18] In Herbert Blumer's study, *Movies and Conduct,* twice as many girls as men admitted that they had daydreamed of playing opposite the actor or actress in love pictures.[19] The males seemed to secure a greater vicarious satisfaction in having witnessed someone being brave, dashing or amorous. While a case could be made that this difference is not inherent but due to social conditioning, this did not disprove the actual existence of such differing sexual approaches and appeals in motion pictures. Certainly, such differences were taken into account by the producers of motion pictures, who tended to embellish and define the concept of "the women's picture" even further. Women liked to see themselves (in female roles), and men liked to see women — this became the foundation upon which the majority of films were constructed.[20] As Catherine de la Roche noted, "backers pay extraordinary attention to this thing called 'feminine interest,' perhaps even more than to the things that are supposed to attract men, and one of the reasons for this is the widely held belief that it is the citizen's wife who sets the tone for the average film."[21]

Which social group or groups were most attracted to the movies? The Yankee City statistics suggest that the lower classes attended more often, although all strata of society did go to the movies. A confirmation of this comes from a study done in San Francisco in the early thirties which found that while for a member of the professional class earning $6,085 a year, $11 was a sufficient average allocation for movie-going, twice as much ($23) had been allocated for the same purpose in the budget of a worker, who earned only $1,632. The same study showed that a clerk earning $2,175 also spent $23 a year on movie admissions.[22] If we make the reasonable assumption that on the average the worker pays much less for a seat than does the professional, it is clear that he not only spent much more in total, but that he attended far more frequently.

The ubiquity of the motion picture as the major form of commercial leisure was widely recognized, even if it was not clearly understood, and in many important studies of American society this fact was simply taken for granted. The best example of this attitude is found in the 1934 study of leisure activities in Westchester County, N.Y., by George Lundberg et al. This famous study simply noted that there were fifty-four movie houses in the area, and that "in Westchester, as elsewhere the movies constitute the most common form of commercial amusement. With the exception of a stock company in Mt. Vernon . . . the movie has the field to itself."[23] After this acknowledgment of the importance of the movies, there is almost no further examination of its role within the leisure infrastructure of the community.

Margaret Thorp's "America at the Movies"

During the thirties, and the period of Hollywood's greatest influence on American life, there were literally hundreds of books written about the movies. These covered a wide range of topics, from all facets of film production and exhibition to biographies of film stars, and not forgetting the inevitable number of "attacks" on and "defenses" of the industry. Surprisingly, there was an almost total absence of any systematic examinations of the motion picture as an important social and cultural institution, except where mentioned in community studies and the Payne Fund studies. It is for this reason that two books stand out from all the others

FILM

in providing such information. The first is Margaret Thorp's *America at the Movies* (1939), and the second is Leo Rosten's in-depth examination of *Hollywood: The Movie Colony and the Movie Makers* (1941).

Margaret Thorp set out to write a book which, while sociological in tone and methodology, could be read by the nonprofessional with ease.[24] The result of her efforts was an absorbing and accurate examination of the relationship between the audience and the industry and a revelation of how important the movies were as an influence in American life. She clearly recognized that film producers had to appeal to as wide an audience as possible, and her examination of the medium was not made under any pretext or illusions of finding "art" in the movies. Instead, the book is a wealth of information on the manner in which the studios "marketed" films as commodities; the influence of the motion picture on material culture, especially fashions and reading matter; and its importance as a source of "common knowledge" in America. She also examined in some detail the effects of the Legion of Decency campaign, and the growing "academic" interest in motion picture studies.[25]

Margaret Thorp's contribution to motion picture history has been sadly underrated, and her book deserves much wider recognition than it has received. She achieved in this one volume the admirable mixture of unique insight with a realistic appraisal of the motion picture's role and function as an integral part of American life. Her view of the movies as a new form of collective symbolism is particularly worthy of note:

The movies are furnishing the nation with a common body of knowledge. What the classics once were in that respect, what the Bible once was, the cinema has become for the average man. Here are stories, names, phrases, points of view which are common national property. The man in Cedar Creek, Maine, and the man in Cedar Creek, Oregon, see the same movie in the same week.... The movies span geographic frontiers; they give the old something to talk about with the young; they crumble the barriers between people of different educations and different economic backgrounds.[26]

The creation of such a new "mass" public was an important factor in American society. While the motion picture was the first medium to achieve this on such a vast national scale, radio and later television would bring about the creation of even greater "publics." Communications scholar George Gerbner has observed that "communication is *public* when the messages form the basis for open interaction among groups of generally anonymous individuals. . . . Public communication provides the *common* currencies of social interaction and defines public perspectives. It cultivates the most broadly shared notions of what *is*, what is *important*, what is *right* and what is *related to what else*."[27]

266

Leo Rosten's "Hollywood"

An article entitled "Fever Chart for Hollywood" appeared in *American Magazine* in October, 1939, and announced that Dr. Leo Calvin Rosten (who, as "Leonard Ross," had written the hilarious *Education of H*Y*-M*A*N K*A*P*L*A*N*) was currently completing a major study of Hollywood, with the help of a grant from the Carnegie Foundation.[28] The article was really an excuse to provide a pictorial layout of some of Hollywood's personalities, with a few words of pertinent copy added for credibility. When it finally appeared in 1941, Rosten's book, *Hollywood: The Movie Colony and the Movie Makers,* proved to be an important examination of the style of life, the practices and values of the Hollywood community. Using his training as a social scientist, Rosten gathered statistics, did in-depth interviews with a large cross section of the Hollywood population, and attempted an analysis of why the mythology which surrounded the film capital played such an important role in American popular culture. In doing this, Rosten, in fact, completely destroyed many of these same myths. As an example, his detailed analyses of the birthplace of directors, salaries of actors, and immorality (divorce) in the movie community all provided results contrary to accepted public images and beliefs.

Rosten decided to examine the Hollywood community and the practice of movie-making "as one might study the people and practices of Tahiti." The result was that

when seen as a social complex; when viewed with insight, when studied with patience and analyzed with detachment, Hollywood loses many of its bizarreries. The fallacy of our stereotypes about Hollywood is strikingly illustrated by the fact that whereas uneducated captains of industry are praised as "self-made men," uneducated movie executives are dismissed as "illiterates." . . . And where the private indiscretions of Park Avenue are winked at as all too-human peccadillos, those of Beverly Hills are paraded forth as proof of movie licentiousness.[29]

Hollywood had become a place that was so ballyhooed that it was preposterous, and subject to so much lampooning that "the ridicule ceases to carry any credence."

Rosten had previously done a similar "field study" on *The Washington Correspondents* (1937) and he was familiar with the power of the press, and how important continuous publicity was to the movie industry. However, Hollywood, in turn, was also of importance to the world's press corps as a source of highly marketable news stories. Both Margaret Thorp and Rosten pointed out that there were nearly four hundred newspapermen, columnists, and feature writers (including a correspondent for the Vatican) assigned to full-time duty in Hollywood. The movie city was in fact the third largest news source in the United States, exceeded only by Washington and New York, and "no other community in America is reported upon each day so intensely, so insistently, and with such a deplorable premium on triviality."[30]

Leo Rosten saw Hollywood and its people as the equivalent of "the American Royalty," and thought that this aristocratic role encouraged much of the philandering associated with movie people.[31] It was for this reason that Hollywood marriages were frequently endogamous, and the romantic ideal of all movie fans. However, in his detailed (and difficult to perform) analysis of marriage patterns, Rosten did not find the Hollywood divorce rate to be much higher than the American average. The somewhat unstable and mobile life of the actor did provide cause for a higher rate, but here, as in other things, the intense public scrutiny was the major factor, for "Hollywood does what is 'done,' does more of it, does it less discreetly, and gets it into all the papers."[32]

This study of the movie colony was an important document in American film and social history, and provided much-needed data on the extent and nature of the movies as an influence in American society which went far beyond the empirical findings of the Payne Fund. While Rosten did not attempt to measure effects on individuals, his evaluation of the motion picture as an important "goal-image" for millions of young and old Americans helps to explain the continued attraction of this entertainment all through the Depression.

Men have always loved the Cinderella story and have always dreamed of magical success. Hollywood is the very embodiment of these. One reason for Hollywood's stars becoming national idols is that they represent a new type of hero in American experience. . . . They represent a new type of folk-hero in a society whose ethos rests upon hard work and virtuous deportment. Furthermore, the public *sees* the actors at their trade; it sees *how* they earn their living. . . . The visual evidence of the films offers the waitress a chance to compare herself to the movie queen; it gives the shoe clerk a chance to match himself against the matinée idols. It provokes the thought, "Say, *I* could do that. . . ." No other industry presents so simple an invitation to the ego.[33]

The movies were indeed one of the few fields of enterprise in Depression America where youth was promised high rewards, and where youthfulness was, in fact, an advantage over age. Also, a career in the films required very little training, and therefore a small capital investment. All that was required was a certain amount of physical "presence," the intelligence to receive minimal training and direction, and an enormous slice of luck. In an age where intelligence, skill and ability seemed to count for so little and guaranteed nothing, luck became all-important, and more desperately sought. Hollywood was seen as the "last frontier" by those who still believed in the American concept of unbounded personal achievement. The influence of Hollywood on the fantasies of American youth was immense and Rosten noted that "in the movie colony, as in the content of the movies themselves, romantic individualism, the most compelling idea in American history, has reached the apogee of its glory."[34]

The Movies as Influence

Writing in 1965, John Clellon Holmes suggested that it was not so much the Second World War which had shaped the mind of his generation; instead,

...everyone who is now between the ages of thirty-odd and forty-odd had already shared a common experience by the time they entered the armed services. It was the experience of moviegoing in the 1930's and early 1940's, and it gave us all a fantasy life in common, from which we are still dragging up the images that obsess us.[35]

...for the movies of the 1930's constitute, for my generation, nothing less than a kind of Jungian collective unconsciousness, a decade of coming attractions out of which some of the truths of our maturity have been formed.[36]

Holmes's observations were not only eloquent but steeped in reality, for there was ample evidence of the depth to which "movie influence" had penetrated in the American "collective unconsciousness." Certainly, as an informal educational force the motion picture was unsurpassed, not only for children but for adults as well. In 1934, in a perceptive examination of "The Motion Picture as Informal Education," the sociologist Paul G. Cressey observed, "Though organized commercially to 'sell' entertainment, the motion-picture industry dispenses a great deal of informal education — general information, patterns and not a little in the way of standards and personal ideals. That such is true cannot now be disputed."[37] He specifically pointed out that movies were a prime source of information on realms of life of which the individual did not have any other knowledge; they demonstrated "countless techniques" for gaining special favors and for interesting the opposite sex; and also provided "the

269

schemes of life, the aesthetic standards, and the personal ideals and values" which can become a significant part of the life patterns of the movie viewer.[38]

Cressey was one of the foremost researchers in the field of movie "influence" and his work has stood the test of time extremely well. Taking as his inspirational starting point the findings of the Payne Fund studies, he concentrated on analyzing the nature of "individual differences" as they modified the response to movie content. In an important summary of his theories, published in 1938, he carefully pointed out that no one could deny "the simple facts that boys and young men, when suitably predisposed, sometimes have utilized techniques of crime seen in the movies. . . ."[39] The key phrase here was "suitably predisposed," for, as Cressey noted, this did not indicate that movies were a "cause" of crime, merely that someone already "predisposed" to crime could use ideas and techniques seen at the movies. He attacked those critics of the Payne Fund (and other) studies who claimed that the available data did not "prove" that movies "caused" crimes and personality changes, and suggested that "we must make clear the methodological distinctions between a study of the cinema as *a source* for patterns of thought, feeling and behavior and a study of its *net contribution* in terms of the total social situation, or 'configuration,' in which it is experienced."[40]

What Cressey desired was a recognition of the motion picture as part of the total "unified" experience of the individual moviegoer, which always involved a specific film, a specific personality, a specific social situation and a specific time and mood. The consideration of all these variables would prevent the grossly distorted generalizations which were frequently heard regarding movie influence. Essentially this would involve the creation of a methodological framework which would recognize the cinema's function as an instrument of communication and informal education and from which quantitative and experimental research could provide more precise data on this function. In Cressey's own words, "It should provide a conceptualization of the whole motion picture experience by which we may be able to study the cinema's 'contribution' under various circumstances and social situations and to perceive more fundamentally its role in the growth of attitudes and personality."[41]

This particular article is perhaps the most cogent examination of this highly complex topic, and could have been written only by someone who had done several years of practical research on motion picture influence. Summarizing his own findings, Cressey noted:

In a society in which there are many factors making both for disorganization and social amelioration, the cinema is an important social and educational force contributing directly and incidentally to both. Under certain circumstances, it has been found to influence greatly the shaping of attitudes and the acquisition of information, and even to affect overt behavior in certain situations. The *nature* of these "effects" is determined by many forces external to the motion picture but the fact of its educational and social role cannot be denied for that reason. . . . In fields of vital interests not adequately met through other community institutions and agencies, in fields where prestige is attached to the acquisition of the "latest thing," as in fashion, popular songs, and slang, and in fields where the movie facilitates trends in standards or public opinion which are already under way, the motion picture makes some of its most distinct "contributions."[42]

Unfortunately, not everyone was willing to adhere to Cressey's advice to avoid "particularistic" studies, which he felt contributed to the gross overgeneralizations about movie influence, and these continued at an alarming rate. In a *Forum* article in 1935, Clemence Dane asked, "What Is Love? Is It What We See in the Movies?" The writer attacked the notion of love on the screen as "a synthetic emotion which is rapidly debauching popular taste,"[43] which "would have you believe that love is a pleasant and easy sentimental adventure."[44] Such fictional conventions, accepted by the young "impressionable" audience, not only led to disastrous marriages, but ultimately to a total misconception of "true love." In 1935, Ruth Suskow examined the influence of the "Hollywood Gods and Goddesses" and suggested that the only value of these stars was their ability to show the American people "what they want." She commented sadly that Hollywood's commercial orientation only permitted themes which scraped "the gaudy and tawdry surface of American life and legend," and therefore "the image of its gods and goddesses are now magnified out of all proportion to their genuine value and significance."[45] E. B. White attacked Hollywood's conception of the "normal" standard of living, noting that "by its adherence, over so long a period of years, to a standard of living well in excess of anything known in the lives of its audiences, it has at last communicated to its audiences a feeling of actually living in this dream world and a conviction that the standards of this world are the norm."[46]

The defenders of the movies were no less eloquent or vociferous in their explanations of the "need" for the motion picture as an integral part of American social and cultural life. With the arrival of the Depression, and the totally unexpected elevation of the movies to such a prominent morale-building role, they could now claim, with some justification, that the movies were, indeed, "the Art of the People." Thus Frances Taylor Patterson, in an article entitled "Bread and Cinemas," examined "fundamental human hungers," and observed that "These needs persist in our own day, the only difference being that circuses have now given way to cinemas. The movies satisfy a deep hunger of the peo-

ple. They are not an accident of our times; they are a result of our times.
. . . The cinema is a folk art. To a large extent it has grown out of our
ways of thought, our patterns of behavior."[47] This explanation allowed
the author to claim that unreality on the screen was not to be condemned
because it was created to meet the audience's desire for such escapist material. The audience wanted "to be free from the cares of life, from the
press of economic necessity, to be beautiful, to be loved."[48] And Hollywood could satisfy these "elemental longings" precisely because they were
so elemental.

Frances Patterson's article could have been written only during the
latter stages of the Depression, after the American public had indicated
its continued allegiance to this form of entertainment in the face of economic adversity. It was quite obvious that by the mid-thirties there were
many basic societal needs which the movies did satisfy, and these were
quite different from those experienced by the first movie audiences thirty
years earlier. Patterson suggested that

in last analysis the strength of the screen lies in kinship. It springs from the
recognition on the part of audiences that the moving picture is inherently our
own. We invented it. Its life is bound up in our life. It is our contribution to
our day and age. Together with air flights and skyscrapers and jazz, it is the
index to our temperament. . . . Our whole kaleidoscopic culture is caught on the
screen.[49]

That the American public was so influenced by the movies created a
problem for the Hays Office. On the one hand, Hays always made a point
of saying that the industry was aware of its power and therefore its responsibilities; on the other, it meant dealing with a wide variety of organizations, individuals and even foreign governments who felt that they
had been slighted by one movie or another. While these incidents can be
seen as quite amusing, and an overreaction, in fact they indicate the perceived power of the medium, especially by the aggrieved. Raymond
Moley detailed several such incidents in his study of the Hays Office:

A comedy showing the troubles of a householder with his coal furnace and ending with his decision to buy an oil burner infuriated anthracite coal producers
and countless coal distributors — not to mention furnace makers and dealers. . . .

From a number of hotel men and businessmen in Atlantic City there came the
complaint "that recent motion pictures seem to stress the fact that Atlantic City
is the place to take one's secretary for a week-end." They added that they "would
appreciate it if the wives could be brought to Atlantic City once in a while . . ."

The portrayal of one brutal brakeman brought the immediate protest from
the Brotherhood of Railroad Trainmen that "it strongly suggests the idea that
railroad men are brutal and immoral."[50]

These and other similar incidents kept the Hays Office constantly alert to the dangers of "unfavorable portrayals" on the screen. This danger was particularly great when it came to depicting people or customs of foreign countries, and the *Code* specifically provided that "the history, institutions, prominent people and citizens of other nations shall be presented fairly."

Both Margaret Thorp and Leo Rosten have entire chapters devoted to what Rosten called "The Long Arm of Hollywood," in which are recounted incident after incident dealing with movie influences, specifically as they affected material culture such as fashion or speech.[51] The most famous of these incidents involved Clark Gable's undressing in the movie *It Happened One Night* (1934) to reveal a torso *sans* undershirt. This apparently was sufficient to send the men's underwear business into a decline which, Rosten noted, "glassy-eyed manufacturers estimated, cut their business from forty to fifty percent within a year."[52] Such incidents were obviously unintended, but on the other hand Hollywood quickly developed the art of "merchandising" products associated with its films. Nobody has ever done this more systematically, and with greater effect, than Walt Disney, who set up a specific division within his company to handle such activities.[53] Whether Hollywood wanted to admit it or not, whether the movie makers were reluctant to consciously utilize their powers of manipulation, the motion picture was capable of exerting an influence which was vast and significant.

The movies reached their period of greatest influence in the thirties, for in this pretelevision era, enhanced by the demands made upon it by a public eager to be transported away from everyday reality, the motion picture became a true social and cultural phenomenon, which closely reflected, and was conditioned by, the events, whims and vagaries of everyday living. If Hollywood films were often criticized for being simpleminded; if their content was found lacking in profundity; if they seemed to concentrate on the sensational, lurid or ephemeral, then American society as a whole was to blame. It is impossible to discuss the American popular film outside of that context. Judging by the success of the movie industry, and the manner in which the public accepted its product, the motion picture must have ministered to some basic needs, and like all basic commodities, it was subject to the pressures of the marketplace. Thus movies were supplied by enormous manufacturing establishments, which constantly sought improvements that would make their product more desirable than those of their competitors, and yet they seldom ventured out of the well-worn groves of public tolerance and recognition. Each picture had to be acceptable and attractive to millions of people throughout the world, never too difficult or obscure, and providing, if possible, the full range of vicarious gratification. But primarily, the product must always yield a profit.

The Movies as Educator

Thanks to the research work of Blanchard, Healy, Blumer, Cressey, Thrasher and many others, the importance of informal educational influences within the societal context was now understood. Educators were being made aware that children learned as much, if not more, through informal means, and that the social influences on the child outside school were even more important than those in the classroom.[54]

In 1935, a report was made to the National Education Association which indicated the extent to which motion pictures were being studied in schools and colleges. According to this report, over two thousand high schools were teaching courses in motion picture appreciation, and film producers were beginning to recognize the value of such courses "and the relation of this movement to the future of the screen."[55] In 1937, a special committee was formed through the MPPDA to select from the Hollywood vaults films for use in schools. Dr. Mark A. May, director of the Institute of Human Relations at Yale (and author of one of the Payne Fund studies) was made chairman. May's group spent the summer in New York City, analyzing thirty films a day, and suggesting changes in these pictures which would make them suitable for educational use. Their target was to create a pool of some fifteen hundred films. The report of the creation of this committee went on to say, "This is the first large scale attempt to effect a union between education and the motion picture industry. Several member companies of the Hayes [sic] organization are prepared to produce new educational films as soon as the committee is ready with its recommendations."[56] Needless to say, very little to effect a viable union between Hollywood and American education was ever achieved, but this was not through lack of effort on the part of the educators.

In 1938, Ralph Jester, a producer of educational and religious films with Selznick-International, and formerly with Paramount Pictures, made a remarkably candid revelation: "There are to be heard in numerous places these days more or less recurrent discussions of the social obligation of the motion picture industry. Hollywood is not one of these places. . . . Sociological concepts are not a part of the equipment of film producers, whose felt obligations are more closely allied to balance sheets." Further, he noted, "the men who *make* the motion pictures, are singularly disinterested in the social implications of the motion picture."[57] It was quite clear that Hollywood was not prepared to divert any of its finances to the production of educational films per se, until such time as the schools of America represented an already developed market.

The ubiquitous Fred Eastman, writing in *Christian Century* in 1937, noted that while the American motion picture industry controlled one of the "most powerful social forces in modern times," it was still not making full use of this potential. His suggestion was that the movie industry enter the "nontheatrical" field in a much more systematic way, making films for schools, churches and various community organizations. Eastman pointed out that in 1937, the weekly attendance at the movies (88 million) was more than three times the enrollment in public schools and colleges, and more than three times the combined attendance of all churches — Catholic, Protestant and Jewish. The essential problem, Eastman noted, was that Hollywood had a virtual monopoly on all production and exhibition facilities, and against this monopoly small independent producers of nontheatrical films could not compete. Thus the public was deprived of high-quality educational and other nontheatrical films because the movie industry concentrated all its facilities and efforts on entertainment films for theaters.[58]

The various "scientific" and other studies all confirmed that the movies were a profound influence on the behavior, the ideals, and the social outlook of most Americans. While the depth to which these influences were felt differed from individual to individual, the motion picture was now widely recognized and accepted as the most important informal educational force in American society. (While it is doubtful that this could ever be clearly proved, it was nonetheless accepted by educators, clergymen and the general public. Even the movie industry was moved to admit their "power" on occasion.) As far as educators were concerned, the depth of "movie influence" had increased since the introduction of sound films, and in reality there now existed two educational systems in America — the public school and the movies. The problem was that these two systems more often than not upheld different standards of life, different values and different goals.[59] The common basis for cultural patterns was no longer the Bible or Shakespeare. Instead, motion pictures starring James Cagney, Clark Gable, Myrna Loy or Jean Harlow now provided a common cultural foundation. While these stars might be ephemeral and forgotten by tomorrow, there were always others waiting to step into the public's heart and mind.

The Consent Decree (1940)

All through the thirties, despite the attempts by Will Hays and others to make the "big eight" studios adhere to a more acceptable policy of marketing their product, the practices of block-booking, "blind-selling" and "zoning" continued unabated.[60] All these practices gave an undue advantage to movie theaters associated with large "circuits" especially organized to create buying power. The market for films was divided into three segments: the independent theaters, the unaffiliated chain theaters, and the affiliated chains. While the first group was by far the largest numerically, it was the least important source of film rentals. More and more, these tended to consist of the smallest houses in the less lucrative locations. It was the unaffiliated chains which were the most important revenue source for the major distributors, and they formed the largest buying circuits.

As a result of the preferential treatment given to the circuits, the relative importance of the individually operated independent theater was in a rapid decline. In the years between 1933 and 1938, the total number of movie theaters in America increased from 13,416 to 16,251, or by 21.1 percent. Of this increase, 65 percent came from growth in the chain theaters, which grew from 1,968 to 3,829, while the number of studio-owned affiliates remained almost the same. The small independents had constituted 68 percent of the total number of theaters in 1933, but by 1938 their proportion had declined to 62 percent. Likewise, the number of independent chains (as distinct from the number of theaters) had increased during this period from 233 to 379.[61] However, the most important fact of all was that throughout the thirties, the five major companies retained the first-run theaters in most of the key cities. In a 1940 survey of 35 cities made for the Justice Department, it was shown that Paramount owned 63 first-run movie houses, Warner Brothers 35, Twentieth Century–Fox 30, RKO 29, and Loew's 24.

Public agitation against industry marketing practices (particularly block-booking) had never been really widespread. However, relentless pressure was kept on the industry from certain quarters, notably the *Christian Century,* and later in the thirties by *Business Week.* Both these publications took an editorial stance which focused on these unfair trade practices as being the cause of all industry problems — financial and moral.

In 1935, Representative Francis D. Culkin of New York introduced a bill into Congress which sought to establish a federal motion picture commission. This bill was different from previous such bills because, first, it sought to have the movie industry declared a "public utility" (as William Seabury had suggested nine years earlier), and second, it specifically prohibited the trade practices of block-booking and blind-selling.[62] This precipitated a series of similar bills, all of which gained great publicity in the trade publications, but none of which left committee. In the period 1936–1940, several more attempts were made to legislate these practices out of existence, but only the Neely bill (S. 280) in 1939–1940 caused any real fears. However, each of these bills received the enthusiastic support of the *Christian Century,* with articles and editorials entitled, "Give the Exhibitor a Chance," "Free the Movies Now!," and "A Fateful Hour for the Movies."[63] The thrust of these was to urge readers and their friends to write to the politicians presenting these bills, expressing total support, for "until their [the politicians] main purpose is accomplished, neither the public nor the real artists of the theater will be free to make motion pictures a permanent and constructive force in American Culture."[64]

The PTA came out in favor of an earlier Neely bill in 1936, and the *Christian Century* noted: "Their action is especially significant because they simultaneously rescinded earlier actions looking in other directions for steady improvement of the public's motion picture fare. They now concentrate on the abolition of block-booking as the *sine qua non* of cinema advance."[65] Having failed to obtain legislation for national censorship of the movies, many of these groups were now concentrating their efforts on eliminating what they thought to be the major cause of most of the problems. The removal of block-booking as a trade practice could then place responsibility for the choice of films entirely on the shoulders of the local exhibitor; and he was the most vulnerable to direct outside pressure.

In April, 1939, a subcommittee of the Interstate Commerce Committee of the Senate held two weeks of public hearings on the reintroduced Neely bill. At these hearings twenty-nine national civic and educational organizations presented facts and figures to show the effects of monopoly practices on local theaters. The independent theater owners also enthusiastically backed the bill, for obvious reasons. The opposition came from paid lobbyists of the industry; several writers, actors and others employed in the industry; a representative of the National Board of Review; and "a group of ladies . . . chanting the old slogan 'Endorse the best, ignore the rest.' "[66] The subcommittee and the exhibitors rejected an offer from the industry of "concessions," and the bill was reported to the Senate, where it was passed, and sent to the House.

To say that the movie industry was worried would be a gross understatement, for in the period 1938 to 1940, many legal issues which had long hung over the industry like an ominous cloud suddenly reached the precipitation point. On July 20, 1938, Thurman Arnold, chief of the Department of Justice's antitrust division, personally filed proceedings in equity, in the Federal District Court of Southern New York, which charged the eight largest motion picture producing companies, twenty-four of their subsidiaries and one hundred thirty-three film executives with violation of the Sherman Antitrust Act. (The MPPDA was not a defendant in this suit — a procedure almost unheard of in the case of an antitrust action against an industry which had a recognized trade association.) This suit was the result of five years of intensive investigation by federal agents who had gone into cities and towns all across America to check into the monopoly and restraining practices. Hays attempted to intervene with a personal plea to Roosevelt on July 25, 1938, but the President apparently was on the side of his Department of Justice and referred the entire matter back to his attorney general.[67] An amended and supplemental complaint was filed on November 14, 1940.

After more than two years of legal fencing, on November 20, 1940, the government and the five majors were parties to a consent decree.[68] The decree's main provisions were an agreement to refrain from further government pressure to separate exhibition and production activities for the duration of the decree's existence; an agreement to modify block-booking by restricting the size of blocks to a maximum of five; and the end to the expansion of theater holdings by the five majors.[69]

Surprisingly, the decree did not demand separation of producer and distributor interests from the exhibition of films. Instead, the government agreed to refrain from disturbing the status quo with respect to theater holdings for the life of the decree. This was the *quid pro quo* required from the Justice Department in exchange for the concessions offered by the film producers. The consent decree lasted for three years, and finally in August, 1944, the government reactivated the *Paramount* case by petitioning the district court for a modification to the decree. Essentially, this modification called for divorcement of the exhibition branches of the five majors from the production-distribution activities.[70]

However, while all these complex legal maneuvers were taking place in the courts, attempts were still being made to introduce special bills into Congress. As we have previously noted, the Neely bill, having passed the Senate, was due for House approval in 1940. Under the guise of public "education," the movie industry launched an all-out campaign to discredit this bill, and claimed that passage of this legislation would: (1) throw thousands of people out of work; (2) increase the cost of movies and movie admission prices; (3) decrease the number of outstanding films; and (4) set up a form of federal censorship.[71] In fact, the Neely bill dealt only with block-booking and blind-selling and was not in any way concerned with moral issues other than to allow "community choice" of films.

Once again the indefatigable Will Hays succeeded in getting the industry off the hook. After two weeks of House committee hearings in late May and early June, 1940, the congressmen discussing the Neely bill concluded that "the moral issue of films" was no longer an important consideration. Andrew Kelley reported in *Variety*: ". . . The House Committee in its exhaustive and painstaking hearings . . . brought out definitely and convincingly that the Breen organization . . . had done such a complete job of deodorizing, that Congressmen for the Neely Bill conceded that the moral issue, as such, no longer need occupy the attention of the committee."[72] As the consent decree appeared imminent Senator Neely indicated a willingness to drop his bill, and indeed it was dropped at the end of the hearings.[73] Hays's opposition to the Neely bill was no secret, and in his annual report as president of the MPPDA he had scorned the idea of "community selection" of film entertainment as imposing the worst form of censorship imaginable.[74] In the short run the movie industry was much happier with the consent decree than they would have been with the Neely bill. However, in the long run the results were virtually the same.

Certainly the exhibitors were not satisfied with the decree, and even government agencies divided on the issue. In March, 1941, the Temporary National Economic Committee (TNEC) issued a monograph on the motion picture industry, which attacked the consent decree and the method of its enforcement. The "block-of-five" regulation failed to halt block-booking, only this time distributors threatened to withhold entire "blocks"; and preview trade showings proved to be costly, and attendance was small. One Maine exhibitor bluntly grumbled that it cost him more to travel to Boston to see a trade showing than it cost him to rent the film he previewed there.[75] It was the arbitration system alone which seemed to find any champions, and the system was fast, cheap and unilateral. Only the exhibitors could request arbitration, not the defendant-distributors, and only independent exhibitors, operating five theaters or fewer, were eligible.[76] (The actual impact of the consent decree will be examined in Chapter XIII.)

While the public was seldom aroused by the issue of monopoly practices in the movie industry, there were odd instances where certain trade practices did precipitate some reaction. In late 1937, a group of movie fans in Nutley, New Jersey, banded together to form something called "The Anti-Movie Double Feature League of America," and told the world that they were fed up with Class B pictures. The article in *Newsweek* noted that while 1936 and 1937 had been boom years in the movie industry, nearly two-thirds of the productions seen by the 88,000,000 weekly customers were Class B — double feature — films. Now fans were beginning to recognize these for what they were — "a small budget film, thrown together as quickly as possible, with routine plot and treatment, and without important box-office names."[77] Later, in 1940, Samuel Goldwyn wrote a scathing attack on double features in the *Saturday Evening Post*. He had commissioned a study by Dr. George H. Gallup on the question of whether audiences preferred double bills to single bills, and the preliminary data indicated "that the general population in this country is opposed to double bills in the proportion of three to one. . . ."[78]

In this same article (entitled, somewhat prophetically, "Hollywood Is

Sick"), Goldwyn also attacked theaters which gave away prizes such as bake ovens or dishes, or held bingo nights. Such practices had crept back in after the NRA *Code* had banned them, but here the public sentiment seemed to be in favor of retention, especially in the smaller neighborhood movie houses. Of all these "giveaways," Bank Night was the most popular. Bank Night was a copyrighted scheme invented by a one-time Fox booking agent named Charles U. Yaeger, who leased it to theaters for from five to fifty dollars a week, depending upon their size. Essentially it amounted to a clever evasion of state and municipal lottery laws, whereby, by registering his name at a theater, a patron became eligible to win a substantial prize if he was present at the theater on Bank Night. The size of this operation was immense, and in 1936, in Chicago alone, the prize total exceeded $6,000,000.[79] Many attempts were made to ban Bank Nights, but the legal arguments were complex and the course of justice moved slowly. Eventually such schemes died out during the boom years of wartime movie attendance.

It was not only antitrust legislation which concerned Hollywood in the late thirties, for by now the specter of television had begun to haunt the dreams of the studio magnates. However, the growth and popularity of commercial radio represented a much more immediate threat. After an initial aloofness, when movie studios forbade their contract stars to appear before radio microphones, the promotional potential of radio was realized. In February, 1934, a radio program called *Forty-five Minutes in Hollywood* made its debut featuring interviews with stars. (The scripts were studio approved beforehand.) This program was soon followed by others such as *Hollywood Hotel* (1934), and *Lux Radio Theater* (1934). By 1938, a symbiotic relationship between commercial radio and the movie industry had been established. Hollywood recruited for the screen many popular radio stars, and radio increasingly used movie stars as featured performers.[80] The National Broadcasting Company built a lavish studio in Hollywood in 1937 to meet the demand for West Coast programs. In 1932, NBC had programed twelve radio hours from Hollywood; by 1937 this had grown to nearly seven hundred.[81] One studio — MGM — sold the talents of its stars, writers and producers to a single advertiser (Maxwell House) for $20,000 to $25,000 a week. In late 1937, over 90 percent of the personality programs on the NBC and CBS networks originated in the film capital.[82]

The first serious experiments on the possibilities of television as an entertainment medium had begun in the late 1920s. By the mid-thirties it had become obvious that television would have an effect on the movie industry, but the extent of this impact was grossly underestimated. Most of the concern about television was voiced by radio-station owners, who saw their medium bearing the brunt of the economic losses. However, a few farsighted individuals, such as Gilbert Seldes, foresaw the dangers from television, and suggested that this competition would completely alter the "habit of movie-going." Seldes's solution was to make more "memorable" films, so that people would want to return to them, like famous works of written fiction.[83] Even after the tremendous publicity surrounding the exhibition of television at the New York World's Fair in 1939, Hollywood was too concerned with its own immediate financial problems to worry about television.[84] The totally unexpected financial success of the movie industry during the Second World War created further illusions about the cinema's invulnerability; but all this would soon change. Between 1939 and 1946, seven thousand homes in the New York metropolitan area were beginning to get into the "television habit." They were the forerunners of the video tidal wave which would roll across the nation after 1947.

The Controlled Motion Picture

Since 1934, the combination of the influential power of the Catholic Legion of Decency and the quasi-legal authority of the *Production Code* had forced the motion picture industry to modify its content. Did these modifications in fact satisfy those groups who for over thirty years had demanded more control over the medium? The Catholic church was at first extremely wary of Hollywood's pronouncements, and in late 1934 vowed to intensify its campaign.[85] At their annual November meeting in 1934, the Catholic bishops issued a general statement which read in part: "The Legion of Decency will be maintained as a permanent protest against everything in the moving pictures which is subversive of morality."[86] However, some improvement in movie content was being noticed and in October, 1934, the Chicago censors, long acknowledged to be the most difficult in the country, praised the industry for showing its sincerity to "clean up the movies."[87]

An example of the "success" of the PCA in persuading producers to alter film content can be seen in Appendix VI, which provides a history of the New York censor's activities between 1925 and 1938. In 1933, the year before the combined pressure, 3,035 scenes were eliminated from 1,762 films reviewed, or an average of 1.7 eliminations per film. By 1938, with 772 cuts from 1,955 films, this average had been reduced to 0.4 eliminations per film. Many of these deletions or outright rejections were from films not produced by members of the MPPDA. In fact, between 1935 and 1941, no film with the PCA seal of approval was rejected by the New York board.

The Legion of Decency classifications (see Table 10) also reflected similar improvement, with the proportion of "Class C" (condemned) films being reduced from 14.6 percent to 1 percent. Here too not all the offending films were made by producers under the control of the Hays Office. Joe Breen, who was now firmly in charge of the PCA, was obviously doing his job with extreme efficiency.

TABLE 10
COMPARATIVE LEGION CLASSIFICATIONS

	TOTAL	CLASS A-1	CLASS A-2	CLASS B	CLASS C
1933–34 (2 years)	977	412 — 42.2%	—	422 — 43.2%	143 — 14.6%
1936–37 (2 years)	1,271	780 — 61.3%	380 — 29.9%	98 — 7.7%	13 — 1.1%
1938 (1 year)	535	332 — 62%	164 — 31%	32 — 6%	5 — 1%

Source: Claude A. Schull, "The Suitability of the Commercial Entertainment Motion Picture to the Age of the Child," p. 210.

By the middle of 1936, it seemed as if the years of pressure had finally brought about a quiescent and obliging movie industry. In June, 1936, the Hays Office received a double blessing. First, the Federal Council of Churches of Christ in America gave a vote of confidence to the PCA.[88] Later, Pope Pius XI issued an eighteen-page encyclical letter on the use and misuse of motion pictures in modern society. The Pope was obviously pleased at the success of the Legion of Decency's efforts, and he indicated this by stating:

Because of your [all Catholics] vigilance and because of the pressure which has been brought to bear by public opinion, the motion picture has shown improvement from the moral standpoint; crime and vice are portrayed less frequently; sin no longer is so openly approved or acclaimed; false ideals of life no longer are presented in so flagrant a manner to the impressionable minds of youth. . . .

In particular, you Venerable Brethren of the United States, will be able to insist with justice that the industry in your country has recognized and accepted its responsibility before society.[89]

In the fall of 1936, *Variety* proclaimed that movie censors all across the country were "jittery" over their futures because of the great improvement in film quality.[90]

During 1937, the only major problems the PCA was forced to handle concerned the depiction of foreigners and the "excessive drinking" in

American films. The problem of offending foreign nations was particularly touchy, because by 1937, Hollywood studios depended on foreign markets for about 45 percent of their gross revenues.[91] The industry was, however, well aware that the gathering war clouds over Europe would seriously curtail this vital source of earnings. As well, quota laws were being introduced throughout the world to restrict the number of American films being imported.

Of course, not everyone agreed with the Legion of Decency's efforts to force changes on Hollywood. In an article in 1936, the *Christian Century* advised Protestants and Jews to form their own organizations "embodying their own ideals, and bear their share of the responsibility for keeping America decent."[92] The problem was that while the Legion was doing an admirable job of moral censorship, this power "may as easily be applied to blacklist any film which arouses the displeasure of the Catholic Church."[93]

A more serious accusation was made by the *Christian Century* in 1940 when, seeking support for the Neely bill to outlaw block-booking, the periodical discovered evidence of official Catholic opposition to this bill. In reply to a Methodist minister's request for support, the Legion of Decency office in Minneapolis wrote a letter which said in part:

In reality block-booking as it exists in the country has been a protection to us because it has crowded out the bad pictures. If the Neely bill, which aims at destroying block-booking, goes through, our theaters will be flooded with cheap, independent pictures and we shall have a task on our hands which will exceed our powers. Hence, I am advising all Catholic organizations to write to their congressmen in Washington and oppose the Neely bill. The *Catholic Register* of St. Cloud took a similar stand last week.[94]

The reason for such a position was quite obvious, for not since 1936 had there been a "condemned" film from the "big eight" studios. The article continued:

The Big Eight, apparently, will produce nothing offensive to the Roman Catholic Church provided the Roman Catholic Church keep its hands off the Big Eight's monopoly and its strangle hold upon the independent exhibitors. What happens to the whole democratic principle of free enterprise and the right of community choice in the selection of its films seems of no consequence to the Legion. But it matters a lot to some of the rest of us.[95]

The whole matter was allowed to die with the Neely bill itself, but the reason for the accusation remained. While the evidence is purely circumstantial, there is much suspicion suggesting a strong connection between the PCA and the Legion of Decency. This connection was unofficial, but the similarity in philosophical outlook, and the obvious cooperation between the MPPDA and the Catholic church, was responsible for a change in American film content in the years after 1934.

In 1939–1940, the industry began to hear the familiar complaints, but once again these were judiciously handled by the Hays Office.[96] The problem was that the *Production Code* was by its nature a static document, and times and ideas are subject to change. In the late 1930s the entire world was going through a series of convulsions, and by the end of World War II, the motion picture industry would find itself facing a totally new series of problems.

Special Studies

• In 1926 a study of rural preferences in motion pictures, performed in four rural communities in Vermont and New Hampshire, indicated the following responses to the question, "What kind of pictures do you like best?":

Action Pictures	58%
"Westerns"	47
"Adventure"	11
Educational Pictures	
"Educational"	6
"Historical," "Scenic," "Travel," etc.	9
Comedy	10
"Artistic"	3.5
"Society Pictures"	1.5
"Love Stories"	2

When asked the question, "What picture do you like least?" the great majority answered (usually with underscoring) "Society Pictures." This study also asked the respondents to name their favorite screen actor or actress. Cowboy star Tom Mix received 25 percent of the votes, with another western hero — Hoot Gibson — a distant second with 13 percent.

The psychologist who performed the research noted: "In the rural groups studied, a strong Puritanical tradition is still flourishing, and . . . evil must be painted in murky colors, and the consequences of misdeeds must be clearly exposed."[97]

• In 1935, Paul F. Cressey conducted a study of the influence of foreign movies on students in India. The results were mixed, and out of 148 male respondents, 52 of them mentioned only good effects of American movies; 20 of them, only bad or demoralizing; 62 mentioned both good and bad; only 6 of them thought there had been no influence; and 8 of them did not answer. Cressey summarized his study by noting: "Foreign moving pictures are simply one factor in the general impact of Western Culture upon India . . . in the long run this greater intimacy of contact may be expected to produce a franker and more realistic comprehension of European and American life."[98]

• In April, 1936, *Fortune* magazine conducted a survey on movie attendance. The survey observed that besides the fact that there were some 70,000,000 paid admissions each week, little was known about U.S. moviegoing habits. The survey asked the question, "How often do you go to the movies?"

More than once a week	13.0%
Once a week	24.9
More than once a month	12.1
Once a month	13.2
Less than once a month	21.1
Never	15.7

Further, to the question, "Do you go to see any good film, or do you wait and go to see only certain pictures?" 46.7 percent replied that they went to see "any good" film. Examining the attendance by class, the survey found that of the "prosperous," 28.0 percent went once a week, 26.6 percent of the lower middle class, even 19.0 percent of the poor, "who are by definition . . . the unemployed and the partially employed." Negro attendance was much lower, with 45.7 percent "never going" — but this was "chiefly because he lives in scattered rural communities."[99]

• In a study in late 1937, one thousand British schoolchildren (ages thirteen to sixteen) were asked the question, "What is the main source of your information about the United States?" Second and third choices were also requested if possible. The movies came out far ahead of all other information channels:

TABLE 11
BRITISH SCHOOLCHILDREN'S
SOURCES OF INFORMATION
ABOUT THE U.S., 1937

SOURCES OF INFORMATION	CHOICE		
	1	*2*	*3*
The cinema	583	360	22
Newspapers	99	110	184
Schoolbooks	70	192	302
Teachers	46	119	236
Magazines	29	30	49
Imagination	20	24	26
Radio	7	12	2

285

When asked if American movies gave a "true picture of American life," 420 respondents "strongly agreed" with the statement; 285 "agreed"; 223 "disagreed"; and 32 "strongly disagreed."[100]

NOTES TO CHAPTER XI

1. Harvey Swados, *The American Writer and the Great Depression* (Indianapolis: Bobbs-Merrill Company, 1966), p. xv.

2. Conant, *Anti-Trust in the Motion Picture Industry*, p. 29.

3. These figures are taken from Richard E. Chapin, *Mass Communications: A Statistical Analysis* (East Lansing: Michigan State University Press, 1957), p. 125. Chapin also notes: "The *Film Daily Yearbook* issues a large amount of statistical data on the motion-picture industry, much of which is estimated. . . . The Yearbook gives no indication of how these estimates were made. For this reason one cannot state positively, from these estimates, that we know anything about the motion-picture audience" (pp. 125–126).

4. Conant, p. 29.

5. Chapin, p. 125. There is still some argument that the elasticity of demand for movies was lower than that for other commodities. One economist noted that between 1929 and 1933 consumer expenditure for shoes fell by 41 percent, and that for food for home consumption by 40 percent, while motion picture theater receipts dropped only 33 percent. See Floyd B. Odlum, "Financial Organization of the Motion Picture Industry," *Annals of the American Academy of Political and Social Science*, vol. 254 (November, 1947), p. 24.

6. Barnouw, *The Golden Web*, p. 6.

7. James Rorty, "Dream Factory," *Forum*, September, 1935, p. 162.

8. Anthony Dawson, "Motion Picture Economics," *Hollywood Quarterly*, vol. 3 (1948), p. 234. This is an excellent examination of the economics of the motion picture industry at a crucial period in its history.

9. Warren I. Susman, "The Thirties," in Stanley Coben and Lorman Ratner, eds., *The Development of an American Culture* (Englewood Cliffs: Prentice-Hall, 1970), p. 184. This is an important examination of the thirties, in which the author makes a strong case for a historical reevaluation of the cultural contribution of the Depression era.

10. William Stott, *Documentary Expression and Thirties America* (New York: Oxford University Press, 1973), p. 14.

11. Robert S. and Helen M. Lynd, *Middletown in Transition* (New York: Harcourt, Brace and World, 1937), p. 260, n. 23.

12. *Ibid.*, p. 261.

13. *Ibid.*, p. 262.

14. *Ibid.*, pp. 177–178.

15. *Ibid.*, pp. 177–178.

15. *Ibid.*, p. 467.

16. W. Lloyd Warner and Paul S. Lunt, *The Social Life of a Modern Community* (New Haven: Yale University Press, 1941), p. 412. All four volumes in this study make important contributions to understanding the process of community development. One major discovery made by Warner and his coresearchers was the importance of bureaucratization in addition to urbanization and industrialization as forces in the lives of the

workers. The fact that the movie house was controlled from New York was significant. Maurice R. Stein notes of Warner's findings that "the classes in Yankee City — once joint participants in a common communal system — now confront each other as embodiments of collectivities under the control of remote power centers which determine their relationships to each other far more than factors arising in local life." In Maurice R. Stein, *The Eclipse of Community* (New York: Harper and Row, 1960), p. 93.

17. Warner and Lunt, p. 418.

18. The question of the sex and class composition of the motion picture audience is an intriguing one. In his study of Ohio schoolchildren, Edgar Dale found a consistent pattern of slightly higher attendance of males, and this ranges over all age groups and in all "types" of movie houses. The following table is particularly interesting because it indicates a phenomenon which is true even today — that male audiences predominate in "poorer" movie houses.

TABLE 12
PERCENTAGE OF MALES AND FEMALES IN FIFTEEN
COLUMBUS THEATERS

| | | | AGE GROUPS | | | |
| | *7–13* | | *14–20* | | *21* OR MORE | |
THEATER	MALE	FEMALE	MALE	FEMALE	MALE	FEMALE
Good downtown						
1.	57.5	42.5	57.2	42.8	54.3	45.7
2.	50.0	50.0	37.1	62.9	59.1	40.9
Poor downtown						
3.	62.7	37.3	68.9	31.1	75.2	24.8
4.	70.0	30.0	85.5	14.5	88.8	11.2
All-Negro						
5.	64.1	35.9	55.0	45.0	55.6	44.4
Good neighborhood						
6.	61.2	38.8	56.0	44.0	50.0	50.0
7.	69.2	30.8	54.2	45.8	48.9	51.1
8.	67.7	32.3	53.0	47.0	50.6	49.4
9.	62.3	37.7	57.2	42.8	55.8	44.2
10.	58.7	41.3	55.1	44.9	52.7	47.3
11.	53.9	46.1	54.9	45.1	53.9	46.1
Poor neighborhood						
12.	76.8	23.2	68.3	31.7	56.0	44.0
13.	66.2	33.8	60.5	39.5	57.0	43.0
14.	71.7	28.3	65.5	34.5	64.3	35.7
15.	69.8	30.2	63.3	36.7	63.4	36.6
Total	64.4	35.6	57.2	42.8	59.3	40.7

Source: Edgar Dale, *Children's Attendance at Motion Pictures*, p. 64.

Dale noted: "Expressed in average attendances per year, the average girl (8 to 19) goes 46 times, and the average boy (of same ages) 57 times" (p. 37).

Alice Miller Mitchell in her earlier study had observed similar results in overall attendance, but she added the very interesting breakdown of audience types — Delinquents, Scouts, and Public School — and the days of the week of attendance.

TABLE 13
MOVIE ATTENDANCE OF CHILDREN BY DAYS OF WEEK, BY CLASS AND SEX

MOVIE ATTENDANCE BY DAYS OF WEEK

CLASS AND SEX	TOTAL	MONDAY		TUESDAY		WEDNESDAY		THURSDAY		FRIDAY		SATURDAY		SUNDAY		NO SPECIAL DAY		CHILDREN NOT ATTENDING		NOT REPORTED	
		No.	%	No.	%	No.	%	No.	%	No.	%	No.	%	No.	%	No.	%	No.	%	No.	%
Total children	10,052	447	4.5	287	2.8	501	4.9	198	1.9	999	9.9	3,253	32.3	2,825	28.1	1,171	11.6	168	1.7	203	2.3
Boys	6,015	274	4.6	158	2.6	229	3.8	93	1.5	461	7.7	2,009	33.4	1,935	32.2	661	11.0	76	1.3	119	1.9
Delinquent	1,046	82	7.8	43	4.1	63	6.0	21	2.1	25	2.4	294	28.1	309	29.5	165	15.8	7	0.7	37	3.5
Scout	3,114	125	4.0	65	2.1	95	3.1	34	1.0	226	7.3	1,185	38.1	1,078	34.6	217	7.0	43	1.4	46	1.4
High school	1,153	31	2.7	29	2.5	44	3.8	20	1.7	183	15.9	287	24.9	271	23.5	246	21.3	12	1.0	30	2.7
Grade school	702	36	5.1	21	3.0	27	3.8	18	2.6	27	3.8	243	34.6	277	39.5	33	4.7	14	2.0	6	0.9
Girls	4,037	173	4.3	129	3.2	272	6.7	105	2.6	538	13.3	1,244	30.8	890	22.0	510	12.7	92	2.3	84	2.1
Delinquent	373	44	11.8	25	6.7	62	16.6	14	3.7	8	2.1	139	37.3	27	7.2	42	11.3	2	0.5	10	2.8
Scout	719	19	2.6	8	1.1	23	3.2	11	1.5	117	16.3	302	42.0	166	23.2	54	7.5	5	0.7	14	1.9
High school	2,180	69	3.2	79	3.6	148	6.8	45	2.1	367	16.8	557	25.5	438	20.1	373	17.1	54	2.5	50	2.3
Grade school	765	41	5.4	17	2.2	39	5.1	35	4.6	46	6.0	246	32.2	259	33.9	41	5.4	31	4.1	10	1.1

Source: Ibid., p. 158.

TABLE 14
NUMBER OF TIMES A WEEK CHILDREN ATTEND MOVIES, BY CLASS AND SEX

CLASS AND SEX	TOTAL	LESS THAN 1 TIME A WEEK		1 AND 2 TIMES A WEEK		3 AND 4 TIMES A WEEK		5 TIMES AND MORE A WEEK		CHILDREN NOT ATTENDING MOVIES		ATTENDANCE NOT REPORTED	
		No.	%	No.	%	No.	%	No.	%	No.	%	No.	%
Total children	10,052	1,404	14.0	6,450	64.1	972	9.7	288	2.8	168	1.7	770	7.7
Boys	6,015	712	11.8	8,907	65.0	686	11.4	248	4.1	76	1.3	386	6.4
Delinquents	1,046	17	1.6	512	48.9	285	27.2	212	20.4	7	0.7	13	1.2
Scouts	3,114	438	14.2	2,162	69.4	216	6.9	14	0.4	43	1.4	241	7.7
Public school	1,855	257	13.9	1,233	66.5	185	10.0	22	1.2	26	1.4	132	7.0
Girls	4,037	692	17.1	2,543	63.0	286	7.1	40	1.0	92	2.3	384	9.5
Delinquents	373	19	5.1	193	51.7	107	28.7	36	9.7	2	0.5	16	4.3
Scouts	719	154	21.4	459	63.9	19	2.6	1	0.1	5	0.7	81	11.3
Public school	2,945	519	17.6	1,891	64.2	160	5.4	3	0.1	85	2.9	287	9.8

Source: Alice Miller Mitchell, *Children and Movies*, p. 154.

It is worth noting the increase in attendance by high school students on Fridays — this was traditionally date night!

19. Blumer, *Movies and Conduct*, p. 65.

20. The whole question of the role of women in American films is too complex for detailed discussion in this book. The subject is an important one, however, and has begun to receive some attention in the last few years. There is no doubt that the movies have for a period of over half a century played a major part in shaping and reflecting the changing image of women in America. There was a paradox in Hollywood's attitude toward women, and as Molly Haskell has noted, "Through the myths of subjection and sacrifice that were its fictional currency and the machinations of its moguls in the front offices, the film industry maneuvered to keep women in their place; and yet these very myths and this machinery catapulted women into spheres of power beyond the wildest dreams of most of their sex." In Molly Haskell, *From Reverence to Rape: The Treatment of Women in the Movies* (New York: Holt, Rinehart and Winston, 1973), p. 3. Other examinations of this topic are found in Marjorie Rosen, *Popcorn Venus* (New York: Coward, McCann and Geoghegan, 1973); and Joan Mellen, *Women and Their Sexuality in the New Film* (New York: Horizon Press, 1973).

21. Catherine de la Roche, "That 'Feminine Angle,'" *Penguin Film Review*, no. 8 (January, 1949), p. 26. Margaret Thorp also noted: "It is really that solid average citizen's wife who commands the respectful attention of the [movie] industry, just as, in a smaller group, she regulates the best-seller lists of novels." (Thorp, *America at the Movies*, p. 5. See pp. 4–8 for a full examination of the influence of women on the movies in the thirties.)

22. Quoted in *Recent Social Trends*, p. 895.

23. George A. Lundberg, Mirra Komarovsky, and Mary Alice McInerny, *Leisure: A Suburban Study* (New York: Columbia University Press, 1934), p. 76.

24. She noted: "The excuse one has for writing at all is that there are so many things that ought to be known . . . to assemble some of it . . . seems to be a kind of public service. For it is perfectly obvious that people want, and need, to know more about the movies, about what the movies are doing to them and what they can do to make the movies nearer to their hearts' desires. It is perfectly obvious that whether or not they are 'your best,' motion pictures are your most absorbing entertainment" (p. x).

25. Specific findings from the Thorp study are used throughout this volume where they are most relevant, rather than concentrated just in this section, which examines the *importance* of the work as a whole.

26. Thorp, pp. 271–272.

27. George Gerbner, "An Institutional Approach to Mass Communications Research," in Lee Thayer, ed., *Communication: Theory and Research* (Springfield: Charles C. Thomas, 1967), p. 430.

28. "Fever Chart for Hollywood," *American Magazine*, Vol. 128 (October, 1939), pp. 67–74. In the subsequent book Rosten made the point that the Rockefeller Foundation also contributed funds for this study.

29. Leo C. Rosten, *Hollywood: The Movie Colony and the Movie Makers* (New York: Harcourt, Brace and Co., 1941; reprinted New York: Arno Press, 1970), p. 6.

30. *Ibid.*, p. 9.

31. *Ibid.*, p. 124.

32. *Ibid.*, p. 132.

33. *Ibid.*, p. 13.

34. *Ibid.*, p. 16.

35. John Clellon Holmes, "15¢ Before 6:00 P.M.: The Wonderful Movies of 'The Thirties,'" *Harper's*, December, 1965, p. 51.

36. *Ibid.*, p. 55.

37. Paul G. Cressey, "Motion Picture as Informal Education," p. 505.

38. *Ibid.*, p. 506.

39. Paul G. Cressey, "The Motion Picture Experience as Modified by Social Background and Personality," *American Sociological Review*, vol. 3 (August, 1938), p. 517.

40. *Ibid.*

41. *Ibid.*, pp. 518–519.

42. *Ibid.*, pp. 524–525.

43. Clemence Dane, "What Is Love? Is It What We See in the Movies?," *Forum*, vol. 94 (December, 1935), p. 336.

44. *Ibid.*, p. 338.

45. Ruth Suskow, "Hollywood Gods and Goddesses," *Harper's*, vol. 173 (July, 1936), p. 200.

46. E. B. White, "One Man's Meat," *Harper's*, vol. 179 (July, 1939), p. 217.

47. Frances Taylor Patterson, "Bread and Cinemas," *North American Review*, vol. 246, no. 2 (December, 1938), p. 259.

48. *Ibid.*, p. 260.

49. *Ibid.*, p. 266.

50. Moley, *Hays Office*, pp. 114–115.

51. Thorp has an entire chapter (4) devoted to "Cinema Fashions," pp. 106–134. Rosten's chapter (16) is found on pp. 355–368.

52. Rosten, p. 362.

53. The best examination of the Disney empire is contained in Richard Schickel, *The Disney Version* (New York: Avon Books, 1968).

54. For a good summary of the whole issue of the movies as informal education, and the various research approaches to the question, see Frederic M. Thrasher, "The Sociological Approach to Motion Pictures in Relation to Education," *Education*, vol. 58 (April, 1938), pp. 467–473.

55. "Motion Pictures in the Schools," *School and Society*, vol. 42 (October 12, 1935), p. 498.

56. "Motion Picture Films for the Schools to Be Selected from Hollywood Vaults," *School and Society*, vol. 46 (July 24, 1937), pp. 107–108.

57. Ralph Jester, "Hollywood and Pedagogy," *Journal of Educational Sociology*, November, 1938, p. 137. In this same article Jester has a comment about the Hays Office which is too good to ignore: "The producers recognize this inherent lack and support a well-ordered organization to handle the situation. Mr. Hays and Mr. Breen are efficient zoo attendants, in charge of the monkey house, and fully realize that upon the slightest provocation their charges are ready to make indecent gestures for any who offer more abundant peanuts" (p. 137).

58. "Chances the Movies Are Missing," *Christian Century*, vol. 54 (May 12, 1937), pp. 617–618.

59. For a detailed examination of the differences in movie mores and those in general public acceptance see Charles C. Peters, *Motion Pictures and Standards of Morality*. This study raises the fundamental issue of whether the movies were leading or following society. Certainly the movies were ahead of changes in accepted mores in many areas.

60. For more explicit details on the marketing of motion pictures in this period see Huettig, *Economic Control*, pp. 113–142.

61. Huettig, pp. 132–134.

62. U.S., Congress, House, Subcommittee of the Committee on Interstate and Foreign Commerce, *Hearings, on H.R. 4757, H.R. 8877, and H.R. 6472, Motion Picture Films*. 74th Cong., 2nd session, 1936, pp. 83–84.

63. "Give the Exhibitor a Chance," vol. 52 (June 19, 1935), pp. 819–821; "Free the Movies Now!" vol. 53 (March 25, 1936), pp. 454–455; "A Fateful Hour for the Movies," vol. 53 (May 27, 1936), p. 757. All in the *Christian Century*.

64. "Free the Movies Now," p. 455.

65. "A Fateful Hour for the Movies," p. 757.

66. "Anti-Block-Booking Bill Reported to Senate," *Christian Century*, no. 56 (May 17, 1939), p. 630.

67. Charles Higham, *Hollywood at Sunset* (New York: Saturday Review Press, 1972), p. 24. For a detailed examination of the personalities involved in the antitrust legislation see pp. 22–32.

68. This decree was agreed to by the five majors only — Paramount, Loew's (MGM), RKO, Warner Brothers, and Twentieth Century-Fox. The three minor defendants — Columbia, Universal and United Artists — did not own any theaters, but had been charged with combining with the five majors to restrain trade unreasonably and to monopolize commerce in motion pictures. These three did not agree with the consent decree, and were not bound to it.

69. For more details about the decree and its effects see Huettig, pp. 139–142; and Conant, pp. 95–97.

70. Conant, p. 98.

71. "Pass the Neely Bill," *Christian Century*, no. 57 (February 21, 1940), p. 240.

72. *Variety*, September 25, 1940, p. 20.

73. *Ibid.*, June 19, 1940, p. 3.

74. "Why We Need a Neely Bill," *Christian Century*, April 10, 1940, p. 468.

75. "Anti-Trust Scenario," *Business Week*, September 6, 1941, p. 33.

76. This arbitration procedure had one novel aspect, in that it applied not only to contract disputes but also to complaints about "status" (the "run" to which the theater

was entitled). Thus an exhibitor could claim that the clearance before his designated run was unreasonably long and discriminatory. He could ask the board to force the defendants to contract to license him films with shorter clearance. Conant notes that most arbitration cases in fact concerned status problems, rather than contested contracts. Approximately 450 arbitration cases were filed between early 1941 and May, 1946. Of these more than 300 related to clearance, and about 100 to both run and clearance of the complaining exhibitor (p. 96).

77. "Fans Organize to Fight Double Bills," *Newsweek,* no. 10 (October 4, 1937), p. 25.

78. Samuel Goldwyn, "Hollywood Is Sick!" *Saturday Evening Post,* vol. 213 (July 13, 1940), p. 18.

79. "Bank Night Bans," *Time,* January 11, 1937, p. 55.

80. Barnouw, *Golden Web,* pp. 103–107.

81. "Hollywood and Radio," *Business Week,* November 6, 1937, p. 27.

82. "Hollywood Makes a Bid as New Broadcasting Center with 'Good News,' " *Newsweek,* no. 10 (November 15, 1937), p. 25.

83. Gilbert Seldes, "The Quicksands of the Movies," *Atlantic Monthly,* vol. 158, no. 4 (October, 1936), pp. 422–431.

84. Only one movie company foresaw the possibility of television as early as 1938. Paramount purchased 56,000 shares of DuMont Broadcasting stock for $1 a share. By 1949, this stock had soared in value to $7,650,000, and it later reached more than $10,000,000. The question, of course, is was this purchase the result of brilliant foresight, or a lucky investment? (See Higham, *Hollywood at Sunset,* p. 67.)

85. "Legion of Decency Campaign Intensified," *Literary Digest,* vol. 118 (December 22, 1934), p. 20.

86. *Report of the Episcopal Committee on Motion Pictures* (Washington, D.C.: National Catholic Welfare Conference, 1935), p. 378. Quoted in Phelan, "National Catholic Office," p. 35.

87. *Variety,* October 30, 1934, p. 23.

88. *New York Times,* March 31, 1936, p. 17.

89. Pius XI, *Motion Pictures,* encyclical letter (Washington, D.C.: National Catholic Welfare Conference, 1936), pp. 5–14. Quoted in Sargent, "Self-Regulation," p. 91.

90. *Variety,* September 30, 1936, p. 3.

91. "Film Exports Set Record," *Business Week,* June 26, 1937, p. 50.

92. "Decency and Censorship," *Christian Century,* vol. 53 (July 29, 1936), p. 1030.

93. *Ibid.,* pp. 1031–1032.

94. "The Legion of Decency and the Big Eight," *Christian Century,* vol. 57 (March 20, 1940), p. 373.

95. *Ibid.,* p. 373.

96. For an in-depth examination of these continued complaints, none of which were of major significance, see Sargent, pp. 104–108.

97. Harold E. Jones and Herbert S. Conrad, "Rural Preferences in Motion Pictures," *Journal of Social Psychology,* vol. 1 (1930), pp. 419–423.

98. Paul F. Cressey, "The Influence of Moving Pictures on Students in India," *American Journal of Sociology,* vol. 41, no. 3 (November, 1935), pp. 341–350.

99. *Fortune,* vol. 13 (April, 1936), p. 222.

100. Richard Heindel, "American Attitudes of British School Children," *School and Society,* vol. 46, no. 1200 (December 25, 1936), pp. 838–840.

XII

Hollywood Goes to War, 1939–1945

ON THE MORNING OF DECEMBER 7, 1941, the sun shone brightly in Hollywood. There were many pleasant ways to fill the Sunday in the warm southern California climate, and the movie people were already disporting themselves on the beach at Malibu, the desert at Palm Springs or the High Sierra mountains, all within motoring range. For those not interested in outdoor activities, *The Great Dictator, Sergeant York* and *Citizen Kane* were playing in downtown Hollywood movie houses.

At 11:26 A.M. the stunning news of the Japanese attack on Pearl Harbor flashed over the radio. Hollywood, like the rest of the country, was dazed. The Sunday golfers returned to their clubhouse; downtown, soldiers on leave and civilians gathered at street corners, while Los Angeles' Little Tokyo area resembled a deserted village. The next day Japanese employees at the studios were told not to report for work until their status had been clarified. They never returned.

One studio hastily decided to shelve a planned musical called *Pearl Harbor Pearl,* while another dropped the title *I'll Take Manila.* Twentieth Century was luckier in having *Secret Agent of Japan* ready to go in front of the cameras.[1] The studios moved swiftly to secure copyright to titles such as *Sunday in Hawaii, Wings Over the Pacific, Bombing of Honolulu, Remember Pearl Harbor, Yellow Peril, Yellow Menace,* and so on. Despite these titles, it was not until March, 1942, in *A Yank in Burma Road* that an actor denounced the Japanese attack, because in the immediate aftermath of public criticism over unpreparedness the studios felt sensitive to the use of the words "Pearl Harbor."[2] However, 1941 only signaled the official start of the war for America; Hollywood had, in fact, begun to fight the Second World War several years earlier.

The Movies Enter Politics

The American film industry had always made a conscientious effort to remain politically neutral. While much of this concern was based upon a genuine desire to avoid public controversy and charges of blatant propagandizing, Hollywood also took care to avoid arousing the wrath of the federal government. Thus in the First World War, when the United States officially entered the battle, the industry immediately turned its creative talents to making "morale-building" movies which appealed to the general public ethos. But once the war was over the film industry quickly returned to more innocuous material. During the 1930s, the only in-depth film examination of the Great War was *All Quiet on the Western Front* (1930), although the war was used as a plot device in other films to explain away social conditions (e.g., *I Am a Fugitive from a Chain Gang,* 1932; and *The Roaring Twenties,* 1939).[3]

The Depression years had changed many things in Hollywood, not the least of which was the creation of an increasing political awareness on the part of many who worked in the film industry. The failure of the world's economic system and the gradual awakening to the growing international fascist menace were two facts which not even Hollywood could ignore. With the introduction of sound, the film industry attracted many writers and other "intellectuals" who were not reticent in making their political views known. It was only natural that the movies, the most potent mass medium for persuasion in the world, would be seen as the ideal vehicle for dissemination of "new" ideas, and in the end it was less remarkable that the movies were utilized for propaganda than that they were so sparingly and belatedly used in this fashion. If the "Communist menace" in Hollywood had been only half as dangerous as was later claimed, there was precious little to indicate its presence in the content of American-made films in the period before 1939. Even during the Second World War, those films which can be identified as "pro-Russian" could not be labeled as being "pro-Communist," and almost all of them were made with the cooperation or at the behest of the U.S. government.

In 1934, the noted American writer and social critic Upton Sinclair decided to run for the seat of governor of California as the Democratic candidate. The author of many books such as *The Jungle* and *The Brass Check,* as well as a revealing biography of maverick film producer and studio owner William Fox, Sinclair was a self-proclaimed socialist, having spent a lifetime attacking the profit system. In Sinclair's own words he entered the gubernatorial campaign in order "to apply my rejected scenarios!" Asked by a New York reporter what he intended to do with all the unemployed motion picture actors, he answered: "Why should not the State of California rent one of the idle studios and let the unemployed actors make a few pictures of their own?" This statement sent a shudder through the entire film industry, and ultimately caused Sinclair's defeat.[4]

Sinclair ran a surprisingly strong campaign, adopting the slogan "End Poverty in California" (EPIC) with great success. Conservatives from both major parties became alarmed as they realized that Sinclair could not be stopped by "ordinary methods." And so the movies entered politics as Louis B. Mayer and William Randolph Hearst combined forces to defeat Sinclair's march to Sacramento. Richard Sheridan Ames noted that "surprised patrons of neighborhood movie houses [all over California] were suddenly treated to pictures of an indigent army disembarking from box cars on Los Angeles sidings. These repulsive looking bums appeared to have swarmed in from all corners of the United States, determined to enjoy the easy pickings of the promised Sinclair regime. Their appearance was enough to terrify any citizen who already had a job and a roof over his head."[5] These faked "newsreels" featured some interesting melodramas. One showed an interviewer approaching a demure old lady, sitting on her front porch and rocking away in her rocking chair:

"For whom are you voting, Mother?" asks the interviewer.
"I am voting for Governor Merriam," the old lady answers in a faltering voice.
"Why, Mother?"
"Because I want to have my little home. It is all I have left in the world."[6]

In another newsreel the interviewer approached an ominous-looking character, with shaggy hair, bristling Russian-type whiskers, and a rather menacing look in his eye:

"For whom are you voting?" asked the interviewer.
"Vy, I am foting for Seenclair."
"Why are you voting for Mr. Sinclair?"
"Vell, his system vorked vell in Russia, vy can't it vork here?"[7]

These "newsreel" scenes were, in fact, made in the Hollywood studios in a carefully orchestrated attempt to destroy the Sinclair threat to the film industry. In the end Sinclair was defeated, but many of his supporters were elected to seats in the California Assembly. The threat that the motion picture could be used as a propaganda weapon against any issue which irritated the heads of the studios was ominous, and Sinclair himself quoted an article from the *Hollywood Reporter* which gloated over his impending defeat:

And this activity [the movie industry's campaign against Sinclair] may reach much farther than the ultimate defeat of Mr. Sinclair. It will undoubtedly give the big wigs in Washington and politicians all over the country an idea of the real POWER that is in the hands of the picture industry. Maybe our business will be pampered a bit, instead of being pushed around as it has been since it became a big business.[8]

Writing in 1934, Richard Sheridan Ames attacked the movie industry's dishonest campaign against Sinclair, and wondered where it would all end:

...What if Hollywood decides to convert the nation to any of its principles? It has the money, the studios, and the talent. It controls the major theaters and can command the best advertising media. ... It knows how to arouse mass emotion. ... Is there anything then to prevent the motion picture industry from flooding the United States with adroit propaganda of its own choosing so long as it contains nothing seditious or of an immoral character? ... What it has done once it can do again if occasion arises, and there is no constitutional provision or Federal commission to interfere.[9]

However, it was not an attack on the left wing to which Hollywood turned its talents and attention, but to combating the growing fascist menace in Europe, as well as its disturbing manifestations in America itself.

As early as 1936, the Anti-Nazi League of Hollywood was founded as the first public indication of the movie industry's support for the fight against anti-Semitism. The Anti-Nazi League, realizing the potential publicity value of their work, held monster mass meetings to draw attention to conditions in Europe, and organized protests against pro-Nazi activities in America. The membership quickly grew to several thousand, including some of the most important stars, directors and producers in Hollywood. Later the Spanish civil war brought into existence a new group, the Motion Picture Artists' Committee, which was very successful in raising money for the Loyalist cause. There was, in fact, so much political activity in Hollywood during this period that some studios threatened to insert "political clauses" (which prohibited stars from public political involvement) in movie contracts.

The internal politicization of Hollywood was also a major point of contention in the late thirties, with some forty craft groups, notably the Screen Writers Guild, requesting recognition from the National Labor Relations Board as bargaining agents. Ella Winter, writing in the *New Republic,* noted the animosity with which these efforts were greeted by the producers, who claimed that Hollywood was traditionally unpolitical; however, she correctly observed that "it might be somewhat difficult to ban politics generally without citing which side specifically. It was just three years ago that Mr. Louis B. Mayer conscripted from every worker on his lot, from millionaire actor to prop boy, a day's pay to defeat Upton Sinclair for Democratic Governor of California."[10]

There were others who saw the "worker's revolution" in Hollywood in quite a different light. In a vicious review of how "revolution came to Hollywood," written in early 1940, William Bledsoe predicted the end of "the goofiest era in cinema legend — a compound of high ideals and low I.Q.'s," because of the shock to the activists of the Soviet-Nazi pact, and the Soviet invasion of Finland. Bledsoe claimed that

to understand how the Revolution overwhelmed Hollywood, you must know that nearly every high-priced actor, writer, and director detests his work. They hate to make pictures, considering it below their potentialities as creative artists — birds snared in gilded contracts dreaming of literature and real theaters beyond the horizons . . . on the whole Hollywood is a city of unhappy successful people. And that, it seemed to me, was the basis for communism with two butlers and a swimming pool.[11]

The Movies as Propaganda

By 1936, film makers found it more and more difficult to ignore developments in Europe as Hitler's forces began to spread their terror across the continent, and Mussolini attempted to recapture the glories of ancient Rome for his fascist state. The producers of newsreels were among the first to feel the conflicting pressures of reporting the dramatic European events, while at the same time recognizing the public posture of neutrality in the United States. The news from Europe and the Far East provided sensational fare for the audience, but far too often these important stories were surrounded by others featuring bathing beauties, fashion shows, or performing monkeys. The American newsreel has rightly been criticized for failing to inform the American public of the true danger of the fascist menace until it was far too late. Raymond Fielding quotes one critic as saying:

As history, as bottled samples of what is happening now, to be handed down to our great grandchildren, the newsreels are more often than not trivial, lazy, and misleading. As witnesses of great contemporary events, as impartial eyes and ears which wander over the world to record red-hot actuality, they have degenerated rather than improved with time. . . . They have largely abandoned the service of history and set up shop as entertainers. . . .[12]

When newsreels did attempt in-depth analyses, this often led to misinterpretation and criticism. In one case even *The March of Time* was considered to be pro-fascist and a propaganda tool for the J. P. Morgan interests.[13]

A much more serious issue was the censorship of commercial "entertainment" motion pictures for blatantly political reasons. An analysis of film censorship in the *Columbia Law Review* in 1939 noted that censorship was far worse in the field of political differences, and "although the instances are not so numerous, they are more significant. Here there often is actual curtailment of freedom of expression, whereas the other category at worst entrenches on art."[14] The ideological struggle between the Right and the Left, both abroad and in the United States, was beginning to be reflected in a small number of films in the late 1930s, and it was to these films that the censors increasingly turned their attention. Movies dealing favorably with Soviet Russia and the Spanish civil war met the greatest opposition; but this time the public outcry against political censorship was loud and constant. Too many prominent American intellectuals were personally involved in these causes to ignore what state and municipal censorship boards were doing.

In 1936, a documentary film of the Spanish civil war entitled *Spain in Flames* was banned in Pennsylvania, with the proviso that if all references to "Fascist," "Nazi," "German," and so on, were deleted wherever they appeared, the picture would be approved. This decision was reversed in the courts on the grounds that the film, being a documentary of current events, was exempt from censorship under the state statute.[15] This same censorship board had yet another decision reversed in the case of the ban on the Soviet film *Baltic Deputy* on the grounds of "immorality." The judge noted that only the existence of a local or national emergency would "permit the Censors to extend the definition of 'immoral' to include a controversial subject unrelated to a matter of public decency."[16]

The biggest furor over political censorship was reserved for Walter Wanger's film *Blockade* (1938), a fictional and reasonably well-disguised treatment of the Spanish conflict, which ventured to condemn the bombing and starvation of women and children. This film infuriated the adherents of General Franco, who considered it to be pro-Loyalist, and it was actively boycotted and picketed by the Knights of Columbus and by other Catholic groups throughout the United States. The screenplay for *Blockade* was written by John Howard Lawson, who later gained notoriety as one of the "Hollywood Ten," and the script had received the prior approval of the Hays Office. Nevertheless, the film proved to be something of an embarrassment to Hays, and surreptitious efforts were made to bring about its economic failure. Despite a good financial record, the film failed to receive a booking for a regular second-run chain release on the West Coast, and the Hollywood trade press, notably Martin Quigley's publications, launched a series of attacks on the motion picture.

Winchell Taylor, writing in the *Nation* in 1938, saw this as "fundamentally an attack not so much on an inferentially pro-Loyalist film, as on the whole idea of making films on serious social and political themes."[17]

The number of films of this type increased slowly but surely, as 1939 brought the world closer to war. The question which most disturbed the Hollywood studios was how to make films with such topical and relevant themes, without jeopardizing their important financial dependency on foreign markets. However, the loss of both the European and Asian markets was inevitable, and on August 17, 1940, the Nazi government in Germany announced the exclusion of all American films from Germany and all countries then occupied by German troops; Italy later introduced a similar measure. This loss of the European market cost the U.S. studios about 30 percent of their foreign profits, an estimated $2,500,000 annually.[18] Not only in Europe but in England and throughout the British Empire restrictions were placed on the transfers of profits out of these countries, while profits from Japan had been completely lost to Hollywood since 1938, even though American films were still being allowed into the country.[19]

The loss of those markets held in "enemy" hands (even though the United States was still neutral at this point) meant that Hollywood was now free to explore previously forbidden themes, although political opinion was still divided on the home front. In 1939, Warners produced *Confessions of a Nazi Spy*, based upon the real-life exposure of a German spy ring in New York in 1938. The thesis of this film was that the German-American Bund was a dangerous and disloyal organization, dedicated to the overthrow of the United States government. The film's patriotic message was unmistakable — Nazi Germany was an enemy of the United States — and this anti-isolationist viewpoint was severely criticized. Nineteen thirty-nine also saw the release of Chaplin's *The Great Dictator*, a satirical examination of fascism which made a strong plea on behalf of the mistreated Jews of Europe.

In 1940, MGM released *The Mortal Storm*, a film which made clear that not all Germans were Nazis; but Hitler was named and portrayed in a fictional film for the first time. These films were followed by others such as *Escape* (1940), and *Man Hunt* (1940), in which the hero (Walter Pidgeon) has a chance to assassinate Hitler, and fails to take it! In all, fifty such films were released between 1939 and Pearl Harbor.[20] Even the classic pacifist motion picture *All Quiet on the Western Front* (1930) was re-released in November, 1939, embellished by a commentary and a number of insertions of stock shots of prewar and postwar Germany, as a strongly anti-Nazi (but pro-German people) contribution to this trend.

John Grierson, one of the founders of the documentary film tradition, happened to be in Hollywood in 1939 when war broke out in Europe.

He noted the anxiety and confusion among the film makers, except on one issue. "Everyone in this particular modernist group was for going into propaganda of some kind," he recalled, "but everyone I noticed was for avoiding hatred."[21]

It was not only in such blatantly propagandistic films that Hollywood attempted to underline the danger of the fascist menace, but films such as John Ford's *The Grapes of Wrath* (1939), Frank Capra's *Meet John Doe* (1940) and the series of biographical studies on Zola, Curie, Juarez and Lincoln, popular in 1930s, all attempted to reinforce a belief in the democratic tradition. Frank Capra's "comedy" was especially effective as an exposé of the possibility of fascism in America, and was directed against the manipulators of public opinion who misused the slogans of democracy.[22]

While the rest of the world was at war, Hollywood began to glamourize the joys of military life. The film studios soon discovered that the military was only too anxious to cooperate with any project which promised to increase the recruitment rate. The War Department, in fact, brought pressure to bear on the studios to keep out all antiwar sentiment when making films with military backgrounds.[23] In line with this regulation films such as *Navy Blue and Gold, Submarine, D-1, Wings of the Navy, Submarine Patrol* and *Duke of West Point* were all made in 1938–1939 with the aid and cooperation of the federal government.[24] These films usually dealt with the training of the armed forces, rather than actual combat, and often served as a background for a musical or love story.

These so-called preparedness films did not do all that well at the box office, but in 1941, Universal Studios came up with an unexpected winner when they featured the comedy team of Abbott and Costello in a peacetime draft farce called *Buck Privates*. The American film audience was apparently still able to see the funny side of men caught up in such a dramatic shift in life-style, and later that same year the pair made *In the Navy*, another smash hit. In the midst of the tensions of 1941, this unlikely ex-vaudeville duo were the leading box-office attractions.

Far more important were the series of films designed to gain sympathy for the plight of the British in their struggle to prevent the German forces from crossing the Channel. Arthur Knight notes that during this "lend-lease" period, "the screen began a kind of orientation course, introducing the American people to their future allies, exposing the nature of their future enemies."[25] Thus *A Yank in the R.A.F.* (1941), *Mrs. Miniver* (1942), *This Above All* (1942), and *The White Cliffs of Dover* (1943) all tried to explain the British (and the British class system) to the American public.

The use of the movies as an agent in the fight against fascism was based upon a clear understanding of the importance of the motion picture as a worldwide social and cultural influence. The Hitler regime had been using "commercial" motion pictures for its own ideological purposes since 1933, although these were small in number, and with few exceptions much more innocuous than later American efforts.[26] Nevertheless, Propaganda Minister Josef Goebbels was particularly entranced by the possibilities of the documentary and the "long" newsreel, and every German theater was required to include such items on its program.

The role of the commercial motion picture in these crucial years cannot be underestimated. There is very little doubt that the movies were an important social influence, and their importance increased as the American public consciously sought "information" on which to base their reactions to world events. The motion picture industry was well aware of the responsibility that had been thrust upon it; however, philosophical conflicts within Hollywood were obvious and these conflicts were intensified by the obvious inconsistencies in the Roosevelt administration's policies of neutrality. While the United States was officially neutral in the European hostilities, the President's personal bias in favor of Britain was quite obvious, particularly after the German victories in the spring of 1940. Early in the conflict Roosevelt had genuinely wanted the United States to remain neutral; however, he gradually came to believe that an Axis victory (Japan had joined Germany and Italy with the Berlin Pact of September 27, 1940) was more dangerous than American entry into the war. At some time in mid-1941, he apparently became convinced that without American participation, the Allies could not win, and he created a new policy of nonbelligerence, which historian David Shannon describes as "not at war but actively supporting one belligerent side through loans, armament aid, and to a limited degree, military and naval cooperation."[27] Between 1939 and 1941, public opinion in the United States lagged behind the President's position, but gradually moved in the same direction. By the spring of 1941, a majority of the American public were in favor of risking war with Japan rather than allowing her to continue expansion in the Pacific.[28]

Roosevelt's policy of "nonbelligerence" created a great deal of domestic political dissension between the interventionists and the noninterventionists. These differences were heightened by the passing of a "peacetime" conscription bill — the Selective Service Act of 1940 — which called for the registration of all men between the ages of twenty-one and thirty-six, with draftees being chosen by lottery. The American public apparently favored Roosevelt's policies, for he easily won reelection in 1940, even though he had promised not to send American soldiers to "foreign wars."

Faced with such official policy vacillations, it was little wonder that the American film industry was confused about the content of its product, and the "position" it was required to present to its audience. The movies were carefully scrutinized by both sides; the War Department encouraging the glorification of the armed services, while the noninterventionists criticized any film which could harm the fragile façade of neutrality. Everyone was acutely aware of how important motion picture content was in this ideological battle. Albert Benham, of the National Council for Prevention of War, observed that "the far-reaching influence of the motion picture makes it a potent factor in any critical period of public opinion. It not only influences public opinion, but, in influencing it, goes far toward determining Government policy."[29]

Even in the late 1930s, there were still many optimists who saw the motion picture as an important source for the dissemination of international goodwill. (This notion would become even more popular after the war.) In mid-1937, the World Educational Congress, meeting in Tokyo, voted unanimously to support a plan to have motion pictures used "to interpret the facts about the world in the schools of the various countries of the world."[30] Nevertheless, by late 1937 the European conflict had already brought about the closing of the League of Nations–sponsored International Educational Cinematographic Institute in Rome, which had been a major force in promoting the educational use of motion pictures, and in encouraging research on movie influence.[31]

The intrepid independent producer Walter Wanger took advantage of the increasingly difficult international situation to make a plea for greater freedom of content in the American film. Writing in *Foreign Affairs* in October, 1939, Wanger noted that over 120,000 prints of American films were circulating in overseas markets, and "that these 120,000 travelling prints are America's most direct ambassadors to the masses of the world."[32] These films were important channels for informing the rest of the world about the American "way of life," with the stress on entertainment rather than overt proselytizing. Wanger presented an eloquent case on behalf of the American film as an agent of international goodwill:

The common people of other lands do not often hear our radio and never see our newspapers. They do not know, or care, what Mr. Kennedy says at Downing Street or Mr. Bullitt at the Quai d'Orsay. Only one reminder remains, for millions upon millions, that there still exists a way of life in which the individual counts, in which hatred and regimentation do' not comprise the sole motive and method of existence. The reminder is the American motion picture. Along with the gangster and the racketeer, the gun-toting westerner and the city-slicker, the American screen play presents a perpetual epic of the ordinary unregimented individual. This individual chooses a profession, travels at will, loves whom he pleases, outguesses the boss and wisecracks the government. In the evening he returns to his home without terror; when he is abed no knock at the door freezes his heart. Surely it is not flag-waving to believe that this simple miracle, the routine of freedom, which we accept as our simple right, may bring cheer and thought to peoples less fortunate. In no other way can they receive the message.[33]

Wanger's essential point was that the Hollywood leadership had "retreated too far before the winds, and imagined winds, of public opinion." He suggested that the time had come to stand up to minority pressure groups, and for the industry to say, "Go fuss at someone else. We are going to make strong pictures, and let the *public* judge them and us." Further, any attempts at international pressure to influence the content of American films shown on American screens should be resisted, and boycott should be fought with boycott, for despite the loss of some international markets, Hollywood seemed to be surviving. "We shall win respect by such a firm policy; films not nurtured in timidity will have fresh and added entertainment value; and in the long run the industry as well as the American public will profit."[34]

Unfortunately, Hollywood still had to contend with the powerful isolationist group in the U.S. Congress, and the increasing number of "antifascist" films which were released in the period after 1940 created a genuine cause for concern. Senator Gerald P. Nye of North Dakota, one of the leaders of the attack on the film industry, together with Senator Burton K. Wheeler of Montana, made a widely reported radio address in St. Louis on August 1, 1941, in which he severely criticized the Hollywood studios for their role in bringing America "to the verge of war." Nye noted:

To carry on propaganda you must have money. But you must also have the instruments of propaganda. And one of the most powerful, if not the most powerful, instrument of propaganda is the movies. . . . In this country the movies are owned by private individuals. But, it so happens that these movie companies have been operating as war propaganda machines almost as if they were being directed from a single central bureau.[35]

Nye went on to name the heads of the major studios, most of whom were Jewish, and he also pointed out that many producers and directors were "Europeans." Thus, he reasoned, "in this great era of world upset, when national and racial emotions run riot and reason is pushed from her throne, this mighty engine of propaganda [the motion picture industry] is in the hands of men who are naturally susceptible to these emotions . . . these men, with the motion-picture films in their hands, can address 80,000,000 people a week, cunningly and persistently inoculating them with the virus of war."[36] Nye noted that Hollywood "swarms with refugees . . . [and] . . . with British actors," all of whom were intent upon propagandizing America into the war. Also, the studios stood to lose a significant chunk of their British revenues if Britain was defeated.

Nye questioned the United States government's role in encouraging and cooperating with the studios to make pro-military films. This, he reasoned, meant that only one side of the issue was being presented, and in the most insidious manner — disguised as entertainment:

But when you go to the movies, you go there to be entertained. You are not figuring on listening to a debate about the war. You settle yourself in your seat with your mind wide open. And then the picture starts — goes to work on you, all done by trained actors, full of drama, cunningly devised, and soft passionate music underscoring it. Before you know where you are you have actually listened to a speech designed to make you believe that Hitler is going to get you if you don't watch out. . . . The truth is that in 20,000 theaters in the United States tonight they are holding war mass meetings, and the people lay down the money at the box office before they get in.[37]

In September, 1941, the motion picture industry was called upon to appear before a hearing of the Senate Interstate Commerce Committee to answer charges of war propagandizing. The hearing stemmed from a bill which had been introduced by Senators Nye and Bennett C. Clark of Missouri, both isolationists, charging that the film studios and the radio networks "have been extensively used for propaganda purposes designed to influence the public mind in the direction of participation in the European war." For once, the industry decided to fight back, and hired ex-presidential candidate Wendell Willkie to represent it at the hearings. One of Willkie's first actions was to question the legality of the investigation, and he declared that the motion picture industry's witnesses would appear under protest. Willkie stated that the film makers were, frankly, against the Hitler regime, and were anxious to cooperate with the government's defense program. At the same time, an organization known as Fight for Freedom, Inc., branded the Senate inquiry a "barefaced attempt at censorship and racial persecution."[38]

(These Senate hearings should not be confused with the 1938 House Un-American Activities Committee hearings into the Works Progress Administration's Federal Theater Project. These HUAC hearings, chaired by Representative Martin Dies, were called to examine the "Communist" influence in the theater, and did not directly affect the American film industry. In 1947, this same committee, now chaired by J. Parnell Thomas, began the infamous investigation of Communist influence in Hollywood.)

The issue of the motion picture as a propaganda vehicle aroused great interest in the press. An editorial in the *Nation* attacked the motion picture industry for being a "near monopoly" subject to "the censorship of private bigots operating without any authorization of law under a production code which enables the Catholic church to bully the movie magnates. . . ." This control had recently extended into politics, and "far from being too vigorously anti-Nazi, the movies, as long as they could, avoided making any films that might endanger their markets in Germany and Italy. Business was their first consideration." The editorial then launched an attack on the Senate committee, and claimed that "the inquiry was only one aspect of a campaign to soften up the American people, to make them believe that Nazism . . . holds no danger for this country. . . . The American people are expected to believe, after all that has happened in the past decade, that the Nazi menace is a figment of the Jewish imagination." The editorial pulled no punches and bluntly stated that "the purpose of the . . . inquiry is to spread the impression that the reason we have anti-Nazi movies is because many of the big motion-picture companies are owned by Jews, and conversely that the evils of Nazism depicted in the pictures are grossly and deliberately exaggerated."[39]

However, Margaret Frakes writing in the *Christian Century* was in total agreement with the reasons for the inquiry. The trouble, she noted, was that there were no "objective standards of what is meant by 'loyalty' and 'patriotism.'" She also accused the industry of deliberately siding with the administration because of the government's threatened anti-trust action.[40]

The Senate hearings were held from September 9 to 26, 1941, and several senators and movie industry people gave evidence. The important philosophical point around which the hearings revolved was the actual *intent* of the movie producers, no less than the effect of the films themselves. Wendell Willkie began the industry's defense by making a strong plea for "freedom of the screen":

The motion-picture screen is an instrument of entertainment, education and information. Having been pioneered and developed in our country, it is peculiarly American. . . . The motion picture industry has always been permitted freedom of expression. [This was not, of course, the whole truth.] The impression has now arisen, and very naturally, that one of the hoped-for results of the pressure of your investigation will be to influence the industry to alter its policies so that they may accord more directly with the views of its critics. The industry is prepared to resist such pressure with all of the strength at its command.[41]

All the industry witnesses supported this statement, and they maintained that the so-called propagandistic films were based upon indisputable facts, and that, furthermore, many of these plots were faithful executions of material taken from books and plays which had already won widespread public approval. Also, the customer was always free to choose his product in a "free market," and films were made with the prime intention of earning a profit. Finally, the industry witnesses continually asserted that the movies were entitled to the same considerations of freedom of expression as was granted under the Constitution to the press.[42]

Ultimately this strong defense, essentially an attack on the investigation itself, proved to be highly successful. Leo Rosten observed that "the failure of the Senate committee to demonstrate an avowed intention to produce 'Un-American' or war propaganda on the part of Hollywood represented a historic liberation of the movies as an instrument of mass communication."[43] Will Hays claimed that he was preparing to complete the testimony for the industry by providing a comprehensive summary statement covering the industry's "philosophy" and an analysis of recent films. The statement was in fact ready by September 22, but "more urgent" congressional business interrupted the work of the Senate subcommittee.[44] In October the hearings were temporarily discontinued, and on December 8, 1941, the day after the attack on Pearl Harbor, Senator Clark publicly announced their abandonment.

The hearings did have a small effect on the industry, as Norman Cousins, the editor of the *Saturday Review of Literature,* noticed. Cousins wondered why it had taken the movies so long to comment on "the natural drama of the Nazi regime," when novelists had been exploiting it all along. Also, why was the motion picture industry being singled out for propagandizing when almost every newspaper and many novelists were also guilty, if anti-Nazi sentiments in fact constituted guilt. Cousins's real point, however, was the apparent disappearance of many films dealing with these topical issues which had previously been scheduled for release, and he equated the compliance of the industry to an acceptance of an intrusion into freedom of the press.[45] In reality, the hearings were held so close to that fateful day in December that they had very little opportunity to affect the industry one way or the other, but the fact that the movies were once again under attack was indicative of their perceived ability to influence the American public. The industry was naturally alarmed, and it could conceivably have delayed the release of certain films pending the outcome of the hearings.

Whatever the feelings may have been about the movies' role in fostering anti-Nazi or anti-Japanese propaganda in the United States, after December 7, 1941, this problem no longer existed. Once America was thrown into a full-scale war, the motion picture industry immediately started to do that which it did best, provide entertainment for the public. Only this time it had an even greater mission — to provide strong moral support in a time of crisis.

The Movies at War, 1942–1945

Faced with the question, "What can Hollywood do to help win the war?", the industry's first reaction was offer its services to the government in an official capacity. Immediately after Pearl Harbor, a formal request was made by the Hollywood producers that the President designate one federal agency to which the industry could make its requests known and offer assistance in the war effort. As a result, Mr. Lowell Mellett, the former coordinator of government films, was named chief of the Motion Picture Bureau of the Office of War Information (O.W.I.) and served as the liaison between the industry and the government.

The Bureau of Motion Pictures (B.M.P.) was an arm of the domestic branch of the O.W.I., and the directive setting up the bureau stipulated that it ". . . will serve as the central point of contact between the motion picture industry, theatrical and nontheatrical, and . . . will produce motion pictures and will review and approve all proposals for the production and distribution of motion pictures by Federal departments and agencies." The overseas branch of the O.W.I. had its own Bureau of Overseas Motion Pictures, directed by Robert Riskin, the Hollywood writer and producer. This unit was charged with responsibility for all film materials destined for nations outside the western hemisphere.[46]

The Motion Picture Bureau had three main activities: (1) original creation and production of war films; (2) coordination of the motion picture activities of other government agencies; and (3) liaison with the motion picture industry in order to obtain the greatest possible distribution of government war films, and to assist the industry in making its own films significant to the prosecution of the war. It is this last function which is of most interest here.

The motion picture industry had not entirely ignored its possible importance in the event of war, and the week the British evacuated Dunkirk in mid-1940, the leaders of the industry "signaled their awareness of the situation" by forming the Motion Picture Committee Cooperating for National Defense, a group that was to distribute, transport and exhibit government-made films dealing with national defense.[47] Many of these films were dull and tedious, but with the expert advice and assistance of the Hollywood studios, the government did produce several highly successful recruiting shorts featuring many popular movie stars. After Pearl Harbor, the committee changed its name to War Activities Committee — Motion Picture Industry, but its function remained the same, only this time the production and release of government films was much more systematic. The War Activities Committee also expanded its membership to include exhibitors and theater owners, and over 16,000 movie houses were pledged for the exhibition of war information films.

As could have been foretold, the Motion Picture Bureau of the O.W.I. and the Hollywood producers did not always see eye to eye. The bureau chief, Lowell Mellett, a former newspaperman with no real film industry experience, had an unfortunate habit of attracting opposition to everything he did or said, while the film industry was naturally reluctant to accept any form of official government "censorship." While Mellett can never be accused of threatening censorship, many of his "suggestions" gave this implication. In December, 1942, Mellett requested that all motion picture scripts be sent to him before production started, and that all films be shown to him in long version, before cutting. The industry became extremely alarmed and protested vigorously. Mellett justified his action by denying any desire to censor, but insisted that he was merely trying to ensure that the commercial motion picture was being of maximum service in the war effort.[48]

In May, 1943, Mellett attempted to clarify this position by noting that the December letter was "completely in line with the voluntary cooperation between the motion picture industry and the Government in all matters affecting the war effort. . . . There is a clear understanding on the part of the producers that they are completely free to disregard any of our views or suggestions. . . . In effect our operation is largely one of keeping producers informed of wartime problems and conscious of possible implications of proposed pictures or details of pictures."[49]

By 1943, Walter Wanger had become president of the Academy of Motion Picture Arts and Sciences, and once again it was he who stepped forward to champion the industry's position on the O.W.I. issue. In an article in *Public Opinion Quarterly,* Wanger explained the industry's concern: "Hollywood is concerned about more than censorship. The O.W.I. shows a growing desire *to write things into* scripts. Indeed, there is a mounting urge to dominate production. The officials moving in this direction are not equipped by any past relation to the motion picture industry."[50] The Bureau of Motion Pictures, Wanger claimed, did not understand the nature of the commercial motion picture — that "entertainment films are successful because they interest audiences." Even during wartime, Hollywood was still concerned with maintaining its audience; all else was secondary. "Producers hold a logical conviction," claimed Wanger, "the film with a purpose must pass the same test that the escapist film more easily passes — theater-goers must want to see the picture."[51]

Wanger's criticism of the O.W.I.'s Hollywood operation was based on two irritations: the first, that the "amateur" Mellett was discounting the vast experience of the men in the industry as to what constitutes entertainment, and that therefore "an inevitable result is that producers are continually urged, under pressure, to make so-called propaganda pictures that can effect no purpose except to empty theaters."[52] The "second great fallacy" hindering the domestic work of the O.W.I. in the motion picture field was "the conviction that the American people are boobs." Wanger's defense of the sophistication of the American film audience and their resentment at being treated like unknowing children fell on very sympathetic ears. Americans knew why they were fighting, and most of them resented being told, especially pedantically, that they had to make sacrifices in order to win the war. On the other hand, audiences were still willing, more obviously so, to be moved by genuine storytelling — "anything that legitimately warms the heart and stirs the spirit." American audiences were especially resentful of blatant propaganda of the type seen in Europe, and clumsy and obviously amateurish efforts were the most irritating. While Americans were willing to make an all-out effort in the face of danger, they were simply not willing to tolerate boring movies, especially if they had to pay to see them. Wanger was quite right when he suggested, "Any 'truths' you wish to impart, with and in the drama, had better be skillfully integrated."[53]

The Motion Picture Bureau, not unexpectedly, ran into opposition from Congress as well as from the film industry, and during the O.W.I. budget hearings in the spring of 1943, Elmer Davis, the well-known journalist and director of O.W.I., was hard-pressed to defend the agency's domestic activities.[54] The film industry had asked for an opportunity to make an "unimpaired" contribution to the war effort so that the "entertainment power of the American motion picture, which constitutes its great strength," could be used to best effect.[55] Now it would get its chance, for a suspicious Congress slashed the budget for the domestic branch from $7,000,000 to just $2,750,000. The Bureau of Motion Pictures was allotted a mere $50,000, barely enough to maintain the office of the chief. Mellett, realizing that his role had come to an end, resigned immediately. The War Activities Committee for all intents and purposes now had things to itself, and continued to perform an admirable service, distributing both Hollywood- and government-made films to theaters throughout the United States.[56]

The Hollywood community adjusted surprisingly well to the strictures imposed upon it by wartime regulations, although newspapers and magazines took some delight in giving their readers details of how rich and famous movie stars were coping with shortages and the curtailment of their usual nighttime entertainments: "Claudette Colbert and Dorothy Lamour gave up their houses and took apartments. Robert Young deserted his ranch in San Fernando Valley and moved near the M.G.M. studios in Culver City. Linda Darnell closed her home and offered it for sale."[57] Studios, too, were facing the problem of critical shortages of materials, particularly lumber, metal and raw film stock, and Hollywood's ingenious technicians were hard pressed to meet the limitation of $5,000 in new materials per picture imposed by the War Production Board. The shortage of raw film required that directors be more selective in what they filmed, and long rehearsals were suddenly in vogue. Location shooting also proved to be a suitable alternative to the creation of expensive studio sets.

To everyone's surprise the business of making films continued, although the volume of films released decreased from 673 in 1940 to 533 in 1942. There were further decreases in the number of available films as the war went on, and in 1945, only 377 films were released by Hollywood studios. It can be seen from the table below that the independents suffered far more than the big studios. The reasons for this were obvious, in that the problems of wartime shortages favored those producers who had access to an already established plant and equipment. Also, the independents traditionally produced a large number of "B" features, which were more expendable with a shortage of raw film stock.

TABLE 15
FEATURE MOTION PICTURES RELEASED

DATE	MAJORS	% MAJORS	INDEPENDENTS	% INDEPENDENTS	TOTAL
1937	408	52	370	48	778
1938	362	47	407	53	769
1939	388	51	373	49	761
1940	363	54	310	46	673
1941	379	63	219	37	598
1942	358	67	175	33	533
1943	289	68	138	32	427
1944	270	61	172	39	442
1945	234	62	143	38	377
1946	252	54	215	46	467
1947	249	51	237	49	486

Source: Various issues of *Film Daily Yearbook*.

Ironically, one of Hollywood's greatest difficulties was in finding suitable leading men. With most of the established male performers and even the rising young stars in the service, parts had to be rewritten for much older or younger actors. In many cases, actors long since past their prime as box-office attractions were given a new lease on life, and where possible stories featuring children or even animals were eagerly sought by production heads. (Among the stars to emerge during this period were a dog, Lassie; a horse, Flicka; and an aging actor, Charles Coburn, who won an Academy Award in 1943.) Then there was the story of the Hollywood agent who whispered to a producer: "I got a great prospect for you — a young guy with a double hernia."[58] But there was a much more serious question which the American film industry had to face — what was the best role for the movies to play in maintaining the morale of the American people?

The Movies and Morale

When President Roosevelt appointed Lowell Mellett as the chief of the Motion Picture Bureau of the O.W.I. in December, 1941, he sent shivers of pleasure through the Hollywood community at the same time when he stated: "The American motion picture is one of our most effective mediums in informing and entertaining our citizens. The motion picture must remain free in so far as national security will permit. I want no censorship of the motion picture. . . ."[59] Roosevelt's evaluation of the motion picture was an accurate one, and his eventual refusal to back Mellett against the film industry was largely due to the administration's awareness of the importance of the movies in the social life of Americans, whether civilians on the home front or GI's on a beachhead. This lesson had been learned from the British experience, when in September, 1939, the government closed all movie theaters. The public outcry was such that after two weeks they were allowed to open again in the interests of civilian morale. Lord Halifax, the British foreign secretary, noted at this time that "motion pictures are a vital element in maintenance of the high morale of both our civilian and fighting forces, and our appreciation is indeed deep and genuine."[60]

It was quite obvious, as we have seen, that American audiences would not tolerate blatant propaganda in their motion pictures, and it was therefore necessary to define a role for the movies which contributed to the war effort without deliberately alienating the large potential audience by overstating the obvious. The administration wisely decided to let Hollywood do what it did best — entertain the American people, and audiences all over the world. It was for this reason that there were no irritating interjections of patriotic declamations and bond-sales appeals into bedroom farces; and many films ignored the war altogether. Nobody, least of all the increasing number of wartime movie patrons, seemed to mind.

On February 8, 1942, the selective-service director, General Hershey, declared the motion picture industry to be "essential," and that employers could apply for deferment of "irreplaceable" workers. Unfortunately, this announcement was made in a press release by the War Activities Committee Office in New York, instead of coming directly from Washington. This left the mistaken impression that the producers themselves had appealed for special treatment, and the Screen Actors Guild immediately repudiated the idea and demanded that actors be accorded no favored status. They reasoned that anything else would inevitably throw the entire acting community open to the charge of draft-dodging. While the guild's concern was sincere, it failed to take into account the importance of the movie star as a "necessary" war commodity.

During the early years of the war there was a continuous debate on the issue of whether or not film actors and actresses should enter the armed services. Of course, the choice was really up to the individual, but the loss of a James Stewart and a Clark Gable to the air force, or a Robert Montgomery and a Henry Fonda to the navy, was the subject of serious discussion. From a recruiting point of view the enlistment of a major star was a boon, as such action was always accompanied by a press barrage, while ushers, studio guards, prop men, and others in the industry enlisted without any fanfare whatever, Nevertheless, the question of the best wartime role for such stars indicated the urgent need to maintain national morale.

Journalist Kyle Crichton examined the problem of the enlistment of Hollywood stars in an article in *Collier's* in early 1943, and suggested that fear of public resentment was the major reason for this misuse of movie talent. He made a strong argument that while such enlistments were patriotic, they were also foolish in the long run, for almost all of the Allied nations depended upon American motion pictures.[61] Crichton's sentiments were echoed in other quarters, but somehow Hollywood not only survived but thrived during the war years. In the end actors were treated like other draftable males, and so were the thousands of other men in the film industry's studios, offices and theaters. By the end of 1944, more than 1,500 guild members — including 49 stars and leading men — had enlisted or been drafted. In all, nearly 40,000 of the 240,000 persons manufacturing, distributing and exhibiting motion pictures entered the services.[62]

But how best could the motion picture industry serve the cause of morale-building? In 1942, through the Motion Picture Bureau of the O.W.I., the government suggested six basic categories of "war information" which the movie makers could keep in mind as they went about their primary business of entertaining people: (1) the Issues of the War: what we are fighting for, the American way of life; (2) the Nature of the Enemy: his ideology, his objectives, his methods; (3) the United Nations and United Peoples: our allies in arms; (4) the Production Front: supplying the materials for victory; (5) the Home Front: sacrifice and civilian responsibility; and (6) the Fighting Forces: our armed services, our allies and our associates; and the job of the fighting man at the front.[63] The B.M.P. also suggested that film makers evaluate their productions by asking themselves seven questions before beginning a film. The basic question was, "Will this picture help win the war?" Other criteria were whether or not the film clarified, dramatized or interpreted a "war information problem," how much of a contribution it made to a better understanding of the world conflict; was the war being used solely as a basis for profit; would changing conditions make the film outdated even before release; did a nonwar "escapist" film "create a false picture of America, her allies or the world we live in"; and would the film stand up to the test of time: "Does the picture tell the truth or will the young people of today scorn it a few years hence, when they are running the world, and say they were misled by propaganda?"[64]

Those whose job it was to maintain and foster morale in the United States were well aware of the moral bankruptcy which now existed in those countries which had been overrun by the Nazi forces, and they were determined that it would not happen here. The Depression, as we have seen, precipitated a reevaluation of the basis of American life, and this mood was carried over into the war years, but with a more precise purpose. In a world convulsed by new ideologies and false issues it was necessary to reaffirm a faith in democracy, only now it needed more than ever before to be imbued with positive virtues and with a virile and aggressive mass spirit. The American people, and those of other countries, needed to be "emotionalized" about the necessity to defend what they had so long taken for granted.

Hollywood was best able to accomplish its task by providing entertainment for the millions; for entertainment was not a luxury, but a necessity upon which the people of the "free" world came to depend. This entertainment was not exclusively escapist, for it could also be inspiring and enlightening at the same time, and thus provide the necessary emotional ingredient while continuing to attract the large audiences upon which the industry depended. Left to its own devices, the American film industry on the whole did a satisfactory job, especially if we consider that there was no overall master plan guiding the film makers. While recognizing the military imperative, the movies made a vital contribution to the transformation of the social, political and military attitudes of the American public, and proved to be a potent source of national inspiration.

Even before the United States officially entered the war, the ubiquitous and articulate Walter Wanger had analyzed the role of the movies in morale building and concluded that the motion picture as a medium of communication could be used to clarify, to inspire and to entertain; but in order to make maximum use of the medium's abilities, Wanger suggested: "Our political thinkers must formulate basic purposes, ideals, and concepts around which Americans can orient themselves. . . . The determination of what ought to be said is a problem for our national leaders and our social scientists. The movies will make significant contributions to national morale only when the people have reached some degree of agreement about the central and irrefutable ideas of a nation caught in the riptide of ideological warfare."[65]

Wanger was essentially correct, for the motion picture in the final analysis was really nothing more than a means of communication, but with certain inherent characteristics which made it both popular and powerful. The question then was, what ideological concepts should the movies disseminate in order to boost and strengthen national morale? Once America entered the war this problem was solved, for these issues were clarified by the nation's leaders, and the motion picture industry went on to play an indispensable part in "clarification, inspiration and entertainment."

The "Beachhead Bijou"

Because of the need to protect the immense investment in the existing domestic market base, the film industry's primary concern was in building morale on the home front. However, the use of commercial motion pictures as entertainment for troops in theaters of war, and the visits of Hollywood performers to front lines, was of major significance to the total war effort. With the West Coast an important staging area for the Pacific front, the film capital was called upon to provide entertainment services, and the Hollywood Canteen became justly famous for its hospitality. This building was designed by studio art directors, and built after hours by donated studio labor. A "name" dance band was available every night, and servicemen were able to fulfill all their fantasies by dancing with stars such as Hedy Lamarr, Betty Grable, Olivia de Havilland, and sometimes with the canteen's president, Bette Davis. Between dances, stars appeared on the stage in impromptu acts, while the busboys and waiters were often actors such as Walter Pidgeon, Spencer Tracy and Humphrey Bogart. On weekends servicemen outnumbered civilians ten to one on the streets of downtown Hollywood, while studios opened their gates to conduct special tours for servicemen. By the end of 1944, it seemed as if every serviceman in southern California with a forty-eight-hour pass descended on this little suburb of Los Angeles — the place where American dreams and fantasies were manufactured.

Even before America entered the war, it was recognized that entertainment for troops in camp was vital to morale. Movies were an obvious answer, but the use of live entertainment was also encouraged as being more "personal," and under the United Service Organization (USO) four special camp "circuits" were set up. These dwarfed the old vaudeville circuits in size and scope. The Victory Circuit played 600-odd installations with adequate theaters, where they put on full-sized revues, plays and concerts. Smaller troupes played the Blue Circuit, the 1,150-plus installations lacking first-rate facilities, while the Hospital Circuit provided entertainment in wards and auditoriums of military hospitals. Perhaps the best known and most beloved was the Foxhole Circuit, which toured war fronts and other overseas installations. By the end of 1944, over two thousand performers (about one in six was a "big name" working without compensation) had gone on USO tours outside the United States.[66]

The point was often made that movies were second only to mail as a means of maintaining a link with home. These "two-hour furloughs" also had the advantage of being compact and easy to ship, but most of all, an absorbing movie took the soldier's mind off the war, or the discomfort of the place in which he was serving. In many cases films were being shown overseas before audiences at home had a chance to see them, and the therapeutic value of these links with home were recognized by medical personnel as important weapons. As an example, at Bougainville, battle-shock was counteracted by a tent theater that showed movies day and night, providing weary soldiers an opportunity to regain balance.[67]

There was some controversy about the content of films which were shown to the fighting forces, with the general conclusion being that whatever they saw, it should not be about war. The army made fairly detailed surveys of soldiers' tastes in films, and concluded that servicemen preferred musicals, comedies, mysteries, romantic drama, documentaries and newsreels showing authentic war action. "Best of all are movies whose components — street scenes, normal people on the streets, women who look like mothers, wives, sweethearts — bring them near home."[68] Film critic Bosley Crowther claimed that the generalization that servicemen did not like serious films was not entirely accurate, but that "it is true that our soldiers are resistant to blatantly heroic war films and to the more incredible Westerns. They are also professionally critical of Hollywood's military techniques, which are usually altered to suit the convenience of plot."[69]

These overseas showings of movies also assisted troops in their relationships with friendly neighbors around their posts, although this led to many stories of natives pitching coconuts at Hollywood "heavies."[70] In recognition of Hollywood's wartime service, the United States government issued a special postage stamp honoring the fiftieth anniversary of the industry. The design showed GIs and WACs looking at an open-air screen on a South Pacific island.

Perhaps one of the most important morale-building contributions of the movies was in providing "pin-up" photographs for millions of servicemen. Stars like Betty Grable and Rita Hayworth built their reputations during the war as a result of the wide publicity they received as the "favorites" of the armed services, and studios were only too willing to underwrite the costs of distributing these "autographed" publicity stills.

Movies on the Home Front

The war proved to be an unexpected economic bonanza for the motion picture industry as millions of workers with enlarged paychecks to spend went to the movies more often than ever before. Other factors favoring movie attendance were the rationing of gasoline, which reduced motoring, and the closing down of competing sources of amusement such as nightclubs and racetracks. In truth, there was little else to do to relieve the tedium of long working hours in busy defense plants, and with the increasing number of women now earning their own money, movie audiences averaged eighty-five million a week during the war years, while the total expenditure on motion pictures increased quite sharply. (See Appendices V and VII.) It should be noted that the average weekly attendance figures were notoriously inaccurate.[71] There are other indications that audiences were in fact much larger than the industry was willing to admit. In early 1943, *Business Week* magazine noted that, because of the war, 1942 had been a "stupendous-colossal" year for the film industry, and the weekly average attendance was estimated to be 100,000,000. The total box-office was $2,300,000,000, or more than $200,000,000 above the 1941 level.[72] Statistics compiled by Anthony Dawson show clearly how much the war contributed to a revitalization of the motion picture industry:

TABLE 16
PROFITS BEFORE TAXES, 1938–1946
(dollar figures in millions)

DATE	MOTION PICTURES	ALL PRIVATE INDUSTRY	RATIO
1938	40	3,329	1.20
1939	42	6,467	0.65
1940	52	9,325	0.56
1941	79	17,232	0.46
1942	156	21,098	0.74
1943	255	24,516	1.04
1944	261	23,841	1.09
1945	239	20,222	1.18
1946	316	21,140	1.49

Source: Anthony H. Dawson, "Motion Picture Economics," in
Hollywood Quarterly, vol. 3 (1948), p. 219.

At the end of the war, the motion picture industry had the greatest year in its history in 1946, with the combination of returning ex-servicemen, greater available leisure time, and the return of the profitable foreign markets. Then, too, earnings were not subject to the wartime excess-profits tax, and improvement in financing reduced the interest burden on the industry.[73] So outstanding was the movie industry's performance in the 1945–1946 period that motion picture stocks were eagerly sought, and the 1946 Standard and Poor index for such stocks was 140 percent above the 1945 level, and double that of 1937.[74]

During the course of the war itself the tastes and requirements of the American public changed, and Hollywood was sensitive to these changes. Initially, there was a need to "emotionalize" the public, and to "inform and inspire" as Wanger suggested, but after 1943, the American public demanded less emotionalizing and more entertainment. The demand for information was still paramount, but newsreels, radio and newspapers filled this need, leaving the movies free to provide "escapist" entertainment. Nevertheless, Hollywood continued to make films about the war, and nearly 30 percent of the total production output between 1942 and 1944 were films directly concerned with some aspect of the war.[75]

The Movies' Contribution: An Evaluation

In 1945, Dorothy Jones, who had been head of the Film Reviewing and Analysis Section of the Hollywood office of the O.W.I., published a detailed analysis of Hollywood's performance in meeting its responsibilities "to . . . [the] . . . nation and to the United Nations during wartime."[76] She examined the content of Hollywood feature films for the years 1942 to 1944, in an attempt to evaluate how the film industry had performed within the six categories which the O.W.I. had suggested would be most useful in providing a wartime information service. (Table 17 indicates the trends within the various categories for these years.)

Most notable is the decline in the number of films which dealt with the enemy — his nature, ideology and aims — as the war progressed. This was particularly significant because of the sixty-four films in this category released in 1942, all but two dealt with sabotage and espionage activities, following the timeworn spy formula. For several reasons, particularly at the outset of war, such screen treatment of the enemy was dysfunctional. For one thing it tended to focus attention on and arouse suspicion toward many innocent aliens in the United States, and it contributed to a sense of danger at home which was totally out of proportion to the actual situation. This in turn detracted from the real danger overseas, and as Dorothy Jones suggested, "the overemphasis on an unseen enemy at work within this country was poor diet for a nation striving to become fully united in order to fight the most important war in its history . . . danger from spies and saboteurs was greatly exaggerated on the screen."[77] In fact, statements

TABLE 17
HOLLYWOOD WAR FILMS, 1942–1944

CATEGORY OF INFORMATION	1942	%	1943	%	1944	%
Films telling why we fought — films dealing with the issues of the war	10	7.9	20	15.0	13	11.3
Films about the enemy, including examinations of ideology	64	50.8	27	20.3	16	13.9
Films about the Allies— the "United Nations" theme	14	11.1	30	22.6	24	20.9
Films on American production — the war effort and production front	5	4.0	9	6.8	7	6.1
Films about the home front — problems at home	4	3.2	15	11.3	21	18.3
Films about the fighting forces — the fighting man, his training, combat and adventures on leave	29	23.0	32	24.1	34	25.4
Total number of war films	126		133		115	
Percent of total releases	25.9%		33.2%		28.5%	

Source: Dorothy Jones, "Hollywood War Films, 1942–1944," in *Hollywood Quarterly,* vol. 1 (1945), pp. 1–19.

issued by the Department of Justice in late 1943 indicated that no major acts of sabotage or espionage had been uncovered that were definitely traceable to recognized enemy sources. Films about the enemy were, on the whole, disappointing, and "this subject . . . received a distorted and inadequate portrayal on the screen."[78]

Films dealing with the reasons for the war, or examining the "American way of life," were generally successful, and contributed to an understanding of America overseas. It is significant that by 1944, Hollywood had already begun to turn its attention to the forthcoming peace, and the film *Wilson* (1944), a biography of Woodrow Wilson, dealt with the domestic issues involved in forming a world organization, while *Tomorrow the World* (1944) examined the question of what to do with the Nazi youths whose minds had been poisoned by the teachings of fascism. Movies which dealt with the Allies were "some of the best war pictures produced by Hollywood," even though the usual screen stereotypes were often portrayed. These caricatures were usually overlooked or accepted in good humor "because of the underlying spirit of admiration and friendliness implicitly expressed."[79]

Production-front films were not only few in number, they were also poor in quality. Dorothy Jones noted: "The story of the American worker has always been one which Hollywood has dodged, and the heightened interest in production due to the war did not counteract this tendency. . . . It is beyond question that Hollywood failed deplorably in its responsibility to portray and interpret the role of management and labor in the winning of this war."[80]

Films about the home front were equally chastised, and the motion picture industry's contribution toward civilian mobilization was lacking in sincerity. Particularly dangerous was the series of films about juvenile delinquency in wartime America which was released in 1944. Conditions on the home front had contributed to an alarming increase in juvenile crime, and Hollywood's contribution was a cycle of films entitled *Where Are Your Children?*, *Are These Our Parents?*, *Youth Runs Wild*, *I Accuse My Parents*, and so on. The subject was treated in the usual sensational manner, but no solutions were offered. Instead, these films contributed to the hysteria and, in fact, may have prevented some women from entering the work force because they were fearful of leaving their children.[81]

In the period 1942–1944, nearly a hundred films about the armed services were released to American movie theaters, but here too, the O.W.I. analysis found that the portrayal given the fighting forces was far from satisfactory. The musical and comedy treatment accorded many of these films tended to underestimate the seriousness of the war, while the melodramatic exploits of swashbuckling American heroes who conquered the enemy single-handed caused much criticism abroad. This emphasis on individual heroes in a war which relied upon teamwork was particularly unfortunate. Hollywood did, however, produce some fine and honest films which dramatized the difficult job facing the American soldier. Films such as *Air Force, Bataan, Guadalcanal Diary,* and *Action in the North Atlantic* contributed much toward a better understanding, not only of the fighting services, but the whole meaning of the war.[82]

In the final analysis, Dorothy Jones estimated that of the 1,313 motion pictures released during the first three important war years, only 45 or 50 "aided significantly, both at home and abroad, in increasing understanding of the conflict," and that only one out of ten war films made such a contribution.[83] Mrs. Jones, obviously taking the movie industry to task for refusing to accept the O.W.I.'s suggestions or advice, noted that Hollywood's past reliance upon formula musicals, domestic comedies, Westerns, and murder mysteries did not prepare it for a role in a war emergency. She commented:

For years producers had been adamant in their opinion that what the American public wants, above all else, is to be entertained. It is small wonder, then, that faced with the task of making films which would educate the public about the war, most Hollywood movie makers did not know where to begin. They lacked experience in making films dealing with actual social problems. And, like the rest of America, they themselves lacked real understanding of the war.[84]

While Dorothy Jones had every right to be critical of the movie industry's wartime performance, these views were not shared by the majority of the film-going public, who, as we have noted, made the movies the primary wartime entertainment outside the home. It was also quite obvious by 1943 that movie audiences were tiring of war films, and now sensitive to such trends, Hollywood was only too happy to oblige with a spate of musicals, comedies and escapist romances. Harry M. Warner, the president of Warner Brothers Pictures, Inc., denounced this move away from war films, and attacked his fellow film makers in commenting that "a small group of entertainment appeasers are trying to keep the truth from audiences."[85] Bosley Crowther suggested that this move was a misinterpretation of the public mood, for "the public is not tired of war's realities, but of woefully cheap make-believe. What we want in our war films is honest expression of national resolve and a clear indication of realities unadorned with Hollywood hoopla."[86] The film industry did not completely abrogate its responsibilities, however, and by 1944, those movies which dealt with the war, and especially battle conditions, were much more realistic.

The "Why We Fight" Films

One of the more interesting phenomena to emerge from the United States government's attempts to use the motion picture as a propaganda weapon was the series known as the "Why We Fight" films.[87] These documentary films were produced by Frank Capra, who eventually became a lieutenant colonel in the U.S. Signal Corps, and were originally intended to be used as orientation films to inform soldiers about their enemy, their allies and the reasons they were being asked to go into battle. According to most sources the idea for the series came from the chief of staff, General George C. Marshall himself, who felt that the usual orientation lectures given to new service personnel were so ineffective that something much more dramatic was needed. It was he who selected Capra, a man with a demonstrated talent for entertainment, and a long string of successful Hollywood films (*It Happened One Night, Mr. Deeds Goes to Town, Lost Horizon, Mr. Smith Goes to Washington,* and his latest "antifascist" comedy, *Meet John Doe*), to produce a series of films which would "win the battle for men's minds . . . that will explain to our boys in the Army why we are fighting, and the *principles* for which we are fighting."[88]

Capra claims to have been "practically paralyzed" after seeing Leni Riefenstahl's *Triumph of the Will,* and seriously wondered if there was sufficient creative talent in America to counter such a powerful propaganda weapon; but in the end, and after a series of bureaucratic wrangles, he succeeded in making the seven "Why We Fight" films. The first of these, *Prelude to War,* was shown to civilian audiences in movie theaters throughout the United States in 1943, while all seven were shown to civilian audiences in Allied countries. According to Capra, Roosevelt himself suggested that *Prelude to War* be shown to all the American people, and the War Activities Committee somewhat reluctantly cooperated in making the film available to a wider audience. It was precisely this type of "suggestion" which caused concern in Hollywood that the government would utilize more and more screen time for propaganda purposes. The film itself was criticized in the Senate by Senator Rufus Holman, an Oregon Republican who saw it as a vehicle for Roosevelt's attempt at a fourth term as president. Nevertheless, the film was widely shown, and proved to be generally useful in giving military and civilian personnel a background to the war itself.[89]

The entire "Why We Fight" series was required viewing for all new recruits, and a notation of this was made on service records. Several of the films were used extensively in a series of studies by the Experimental Section of the Research Branch in the War Department's Information and Education Division, as part of a large-scale attempt to utilize modern sociopsychological research techniques in the evaluation of educational and "indoctrination" films. Significantly, these wartime experiments heralded a new age of research into the uses of instructional media, and involved several prominent experimental and educational psychologists. Not only did this group make extensive evaluations of the orientation value of the "Why We Fight" series, but they also reported on an important group of studies which investigated short- and long-term effects of indoctrination films, the effects of presenting one or both sides of a controversial subject, and the effects of audience participation upon learning. These studies encouraged some of the most sophisticated theoretical discussions of the factors involved in film communication effectiveness then known, and formed the basis of more detailed work in later years. In summary, the work of the Research Branch tended to discount the "mass" impact of such propaganda films, but once again indicated that there were many factors to be considered before "effects" could be measured.[90]

The Movies and "World Understanding"

The use of the motion picture in the war effort, and the growing awareness on the part of some movie makers of the vital role the medium could play as a constructive social and cultural force, contributed to a revival of the theme that "movies could be an agent for good." When the American people were able to turn their thoughts toward peace, the motion picture was once again subjected to intensive critical examination, this time with a view to finding a proper role for the medium in the "new world" which would emerge from the conflict.

The United States government had become acutely aware of the importance of the movies as a "subtle and powerful weapon to spread the story of democracy and make friends for this country."[91] By the end of 1945, five major federal departments (the State Department, the Department of Commerce, O.W.I., the Office of Coordinator of Inter-American Affairs, and the Justice Department) were working with the film industry in order to ensure the maximum development of overseas markets. The war had taught the government that movies could be used to good effect to stimulate both trade and friendly relations, and the Office of Coordinator of Inter-American Affairs (CIAA) had made particular use of specially produced films to cement relations with South American countries. At the request of the CIAA and under a financial guarantee, Walt Disney made the film *Saludos Amigos,* which was a sensation wherever it was shown. Several other films of a similar nature were produced, and all of them made money for the studios. Based upon this kind of success, one writer observed that "the lines are being drawn for a postwar Washington-Hollywood cooperation that will rival the teamwork of the present war years."[92]

In 1945, John Grierson, now the innovative head of the National Film Board of Canada, also noted the new "international" role of the motion picture and the need for the movies to be far more sensitive in its approach to these markets. He suggested that Hollywood become more conscious of the international implications of its market domination, and that the American (and British) film industries be more willing to accept the necessity to develop an indigenous film production capability in other countries:

It seems clear that the American film industry has come to the most difficult period in its long international career. Its problems reflect the foreign problems of statesmen and demand a new and high degree of international knowledge and goodwill. . . . International success in a sphere of influence so extensive as that of films will demand finally, as in the political sphere, considered and creative cooperation in the pursuit of common values and common ideas.[93]

Grierson went on to suggest that Hollywood create an institute of international affairs through which producers, directors, and writers could "study the relationship of their films to the wider and more difficult world in which they will operate after the war."[94]

Because of the war, and the semimobilization of the motion picture industry, many Hollywood producers became aware that even "escapist" films were capable of becoming an influential social document. The traditional portrayal of minority groups, especially the Negro, had come in for particular criticism and it was evident that such stereotyping would have to end. Also, the experience of studio personnel who had actively participated in the war would have a profound influence in postwar Hollywood. Dorothy Jones suggested that "certainly men who for the past several years have been making the film a dynamic weapon of war will not be content to produce exclusively escapist films which recognize no social or political responsibility."[95] Unfortunately, her judgment did not take into account the fact that Hollywood would be too busy fighting for its own existence to concern itself with "assuming the progressive leadership of the nation." Nevertheless, the content of Hollywood films in the immediate postwar period did indicate an increased social and political awareness on the part of a few film makers, but the combination of a declining movie market and increasing political pressure destroyed even this short-lived movement.

Social critic John A. Kouwenhoven, then an editor of *Harper's,* examined the forthcoming role of the movies in May, 1945, and concluded that increased government control, direct or indirect (through cooperative efforts), would be dangerous, not only for the film industry, but also for the whole structure of "a free screen."[96] He suggested that while there was no valid basis for objecting to wartime restrictions on movies, there was evidence "of a desire among some people in authority to perpetuate government influence or control over the subject matter of the movies. . . ."[97] While the film industry would certainly need the government's help, especially in international markets after the war, this should not be obtained in return for control or supervision of content. Kouwenhoven made an eloquent plea for an unrestricted screen in the international marketplace:

Furthermore, the movies are not a mere commodity. They are, as the government is well aware, a powerful instrument for molding public opinion at home and abroad. But it must be emphasized — and never forgotten — that . . . [the movies] . . . in spite of their gangsters and incredibly swank offices and voluptuous females in satin-quilted boudoirs — have been among the most appealing representatives of our civilization because of the very fact that they were so blatantly uninterested in putting our best foot forward. They were movies made to please American movie fans, and it turned out that everybody else liked them too. . . .

It is worth remembering too, that when — as sometimes happens — official propaganda makes a misstep it kicks back harder on the nation's good name than any conceivable blunder which a commercial film company might commit.[98]

An entirely different approach was taken by Harry L. Hansen in the *Harvard Business Review* in 1946. Hansen suggested that a study should be conducted to ascertain what impressions about the United States the movies have created in foreigners, and that the industry establish close liaison with the State Department in order to gain a "better understanding of each other's problems." However, he too stopped short of advocating "direct guidance" by the State Department, as this would have invited criticism that Hollywood films were instruments for government propaganda. In the long run, the solution, he suggested, lay in an increasing awareness by the industry of its public responsibilities; and this could be assisted by an expanded Production Code Administration staff specifically to deal with this problem. Hansen's closing comment typified the "new enthusiasm" for the motion picture in the immediate postwar period: "World attention is directed at achieving better understanding among nations, and the motion picture industry's new and refreshed leadership should help it to make a significant contribution."[99]

The Movies in the Postwar Period

Before the war had officially ended American films were being shown in occupied countries, and a reporter for *Look* magazine noted: "In every country liberated by Allied arms the first civilian demand was for food; the second was usually for American movies."[100] The overseas branch of the O.W.I. saw as one of its primary duties the distribution of American films in occupied areas, and in Sicily, as an example, native audiences were watching American movies in Palermo before the island was entirely clear of Germans. To many liberated peoples, the return of Hollywood movies meant escape from war weariness. In Italy, after a few months of Allied occupation, more people were going to the movies than before the war, while in France, audiences first demanded newsreels of the war, to learn what was going on, and how they were affected, and then turned their attention to entertainment films.

The use of films in occupied Germany was entirely a different matter, and the choice of which movies were allowed to be shown to the defeated enemy was the responsibility of the Information Control Division (ICD) of the War and State Departments. Once it became obvious that the United States and Russia were deadlocked in a grim struggle for ideological supremacy in Europe, the motion picture became an important propaganda weapon. However, the ICD's choice of films for the first year of occupation was immediately criticized, and a report in *Variety* claimed that "American film companies are being left at the post in Germany with Russia racing down a straightaway field in utilizing pictures as a propaganda medium for their political philosophy." It was further claimed that nothing but old American films were being shown, and "the content had no relation whatsoever to the problem of reviving the beaten and desolated German people with a democratic spirit."[101] Another *Variety* report noted that "selection of films by State Department people has been singularly erratic and unintelligent. Not only do they present Americans in a bad light, but they are not particularly good entertainment to begin with. They perpetuate the already rife impression that Americans are a race of gangsters and jitterbugs."[102]

Both of these reports were refuted by Robert Joseph, who pointed out in an article in *Hollywood Quarterly* that severe bureaucratic restrictions had been responsible for the final list of selected films, but that these showings had not had an adverse effect on German audiences, or on German attitudes toward the United States. Joseph suggested that the criticism stemmed from the motion picture industry's own "natural aversion . . . to government intrusion into [its] business."[103]

However, Gladwin Hill, a noted foreign correspondent, in a companion article to Joseph's chronicled a long list of mistakes made by the O.W.I. in the use of motion pictures for propaganda purposes. He quoted from a military government report which said that the film program had served little in the reeducation of the Germans, had held Americans up to public ridicule, and had hurt the reputation of the American film industry in Germany.[104] Hill suggested that movies could be much more judiciously used to fill the "factual vacuum" in which the German people had lived for nearly twelve years as a sound foundation for any future political indoctrination. This was a task which could not be met by "a film crop designed, not to re-educate the Germans or anyone else, but to ring the bell at the box office in Wilkes-Barre and Omaha."[105] Hill concluded by putting the challenge directly to the American film industry: "It seems high time to call upon Hollywood to justify its pretensions to educational powers, in the face of a historic opportunity."[106] Here again, the American film industry was much more concerned with its own domestic problems to accept the challenge; but the United States government could also be blamed for not utilizing the potential of the medium to greater advantage.

On the home front, psychologist Franklin Fearing pointed out that returning soldiers presented the nation with a serious problem of adjustment and mass education for which the traditional methods of formal education were inadequate. Fearing suggested that radio and motion pictures offered the best, if not the only, solution, but that those who were professionally concerned with the utilization of the media needed "new insights into types of human relationships which are peculiarly complex."[107] In a survey of motion pictures which he had conducted, Fearing found that, "with certain notable exceptions, the attempts to state the problem and clarify the meaning of the impact of war on civilian life have not only been superficial, but in some instances dangerous." However, while motion pictures, radio dramas and novels could not by themselves solve many of the adjustment problems for returning servicemen, they could be used to "offer positive and creative solutions."[108] Here again Hollywood proved itself unwilling to allow its product to be consciously used for a worthy social cause, and the few films which did address the problems of the ex-serviceman were made within the context of proven box-office formulae.

Hollywood and World War II: An Assessment

In the preface to *Look* magazine's paean to the movies *Movie Lot to Beachhead,* war correspondent Robert St. John suggested that "when Hollywood went to war, Hollywood became mature and began to win the respect of those who had been the most cynical toward it. . . . Now that Hollywood has grown up, it knows that it must play its role in creating the world of tomorrow, just as it helped to destroy the kind of world desired by the enemy."[109] Unfortunately this was not to be the case, for as the war drew to a close in 1945, Hollywood was already beginning to prepare for the return to "normalcy" in American domestic life. Despite all the rhetoric and self-praise, the motion picture industry was not prepared to alter its guiding philosophies to allow its product to be used as an educational tool for "world understanding." This was the way it had been prior to the war, and this was the way it would remain.

However, while the movies' wartime role had not been what their fondest admirers had hoped for, they had still made an absolutely vital contribution to the total war effort. To the fighting man they brought entertainment, diversion and a link to home; while to the millions on the home front who relied upon the movies as their major source of entertainment, they helped to bring the vividness of war itself, even if these portrayals were not always authentic or realistic. It is also impossible to really assess the therapeutic value of those films which were almost total diversions from the tensions of wartime conditions, although we can gauge the obvious level of audience satisfaction by the increased attendances. Even the worst movies can prove to be welcome distractions at some times.

More specifically, in the years 1942–1945, the Hollywood film industry demonstrated a conscious effort to bring about greater understanding between the various racial and ethnic groups in America, and among the many nationalities and races allied with the United States.[110]

In the final analysis, the American motion picture essentially did what was asked of it during World War II. It furthered the military effort by disseminating information about the war to the public; it helped to explain the enemy and his ideology; it emotionalized the American public as no other medium was capable of doing; it told Americans about their allies and what they were fighting for; and last, and most important, it continued to entertain millions of people. To this very day Hollywood has continued to use World War II as a major thematic source for action films (or even those dealing with "morality" problems), while subsequent conflicts in Korea and especially Vietnam have been virtually ignored.[111] As historian Peter A. Soderbergh has noted, "There is an inescapable irony in this. The only vestige of Hollywood's halcyon days (1942–1946) remaining is the war film of that dazzling, glory-filled, high-spirited interlude. Every other aspect of movie-making has adjusted, or been forced to adopt, to the realities of the 1960's."[112]

NOTES TO CHAPTER XII

1. *Movie Lot to Beachhead* (New York: Doubleday, Doran and Co., 1945). This volume, by the editors of *Look* magazine, was a paean to the movie industry's wartime contribution, but contains a great deal of useful information, and excellent photographs.

2. Richard R. Lingeman, *Don't You Know There's a War On?* (New York: G. P. Putnam's Sons, 1970), p. 168. This interesting study of social life on the American home front includes a detailed examination of the movies as a major source of wartime entertainment.

3. For more details of the Hollywood war film see the articles by Peter A. Soderbergh: "'Aux Armes!': The Rise of the Hollywood War Film, 1916–1930," *South Atlantic Quarterly*, vol. 65 (1966), pp. 509–522; and "The Grand Illusion: Hollywood and World War II, 1930–1945," *University of Dayton Review*, vol. 5 (1968), pp. 13–22.

4. Upton Sinclair, "The Movies and Political Propaganda," in William J. Perlman, ed., *The Movies on Trial*, p. 190.

5. R. S. Ames, "The Screen Enters Politics," *Harper's*, vol. 171 (May, 1935), p. 473.

6. Sinclair, "The Movies and Political Propaganda," p. 193.

7. *Ibid.*, p. 193. Apparently many of these newsreels used clips from commercial films made on the MGM lot. See Raymond Fielding, *American Newsreel*, p. 268.

8. Sinclair, "The Movies and Political Propaganda," p. 195.

9. Ames, p. 480.

10. Ella Winter, "Hollywood Wakes Up," *New Republic*, no. 93 (January 12, 1938), p. 278.

11. William Bledsoe, "Revolution Came to Hollywood," *American Mercury*, vol. 49 (February, 1940), p. 153. For more details of the unionization of the American motion picture industry see Murray Ross, "Labor Relations in Hollywood," *Annals of the American Academy of Political and Social Science*, vol. 254 (November, 1947), pp. 58–64.

12. Fielding, *American Newsreel*, p. 235. For further criticism of the newsreel's failure to inform the American public see Gilbert Seldes, "Screen and Radio," *Scribner's*, vol. 102, no. 1 (July, 1937), pp. 56–58.

13. For more details of this accusation see George Dangerfield, "Time Muddles On," *New Republic,* no. 88 (August 19, 1936), pp. 43–45.

14. "Film Censorship: An Administrative Analysis," *Columbia Law Review,* vol. 39 (December, 1939), p. 1403. This is an excellent review article.

15. "Censorship of Motion Pictures," *Yale Law Review Journal,* vol. 49 (November, 1939), p. 95.

16. "Film Censorship," *Columbia Law Review,* p. 1399.

17. Winchell Taylor, "Secret Movie Censors," *Nation,* vol. 147 (July 9, 1938), p. 38.

18. For a detailed look at the whole topic of the motion picture as an international influence, and the various measures taken by foreign countries to restrict this form of "cultural imperialism," see John E. Harley, *World-Wide Influences of the Cinema* (Los Angeles: University of Southern California Press, 1940; reprinted New York: Jerome S. Ozer, 1971). The discussion of the financial aspects is found on p. 266.

19. "War Hits Hollywood," *Business Week,* no. 544 (February 3, 1940), pp. 49–50.

20. Soderbergh, "The Grand Illusion," p. 14.

21. Quote from *ibid.,* pp. 14–15.

22. Knight, *Liveliest Art,* pp. 261–262.

23. For more details on these cooperative ventures see Albert Benham, "The Movie as an Agency for Peace or War," *Journal of Educational Sociology,* vol. 12 (March, 1939), pp. 410–417.

24. Further background is contained in "Liberty Bells in Hollywood," *Christian Century,* vol. 56 (March 8, 1939), p. 310.

25. Knight, *Liveliest Art,* p. 262.

26. An excellent account of the Nazi's use of films is found in David Stewart Hull, *Film in the Third Reich* (Berkeley: University of California Press, 1969). One German film, *Jud Süss* (1940), was widely used as a propaganda vehicle, and under an order issued by Heinrich Himmler the whole of the SS and the police corps were forced to see this film. See Furhammar and Isaksson, *Politics and Film,* p. 44.

27. David Shannon, *Twentieth Century America* (Chicago: Rand McNally and Co., 1969), p. 440.

28. *Ibid.,* p. 441.

29. Benham, p. 410.

30. Herbert S. Houston, "A Plan to Develop International Understanding Through Motion Pictures," *Education,* vol. 58 (May, 1938), p. 560.

31. Hilla Wehberg, "Fate of an International Film Institute," *Public Opinion Quarterly,* July, 1938, pp. 483–485. This raises a very interesting question for film scholars — where are the institute's files now located? Their recovery could add a great deal to current film history.

32. Walter Wanger, "120,000 American Ambassadors," *Foreign Affairs,* vol. 18 (October, 1939), p. 45.

33. *Ibid.,* pp. 45–46.

34. *Ibid.,* p. 59. Walter Wanger was one of the more interesting Hollywood producers. At one time he was an attaché to President Wilson's American Peace Mission, and after an illustrious career became president of the Academy of Motion Picture Arts and Sciences in the early 1940s. In 1951 he was convicted of shooting his wife's agent, and served three months in jail. This did not diminish his career, and in 1963 he was the first of several producers who tried to make *Cleopatra* for Twentieth Century–Fox.

35. Gerald P. Nye, "Our Madness Increases as Our Emergency Shrinks," *Vital Speeches,* vol. 7 (September 15, 1941), pp. 720–721.

36. *Ibid.*, p. 721.

37. *Ibid.*, p. 722.

38. Moviemakers Bank on Willkie to Foil Propaganda Inquiry," *Newsweek*, no. 18 (September 15, 1941), pp. 51–52.

39. "Propaganda or History?," *Nation*, vol. 153 (September 20, 1941), pp. 241–242.

40. Margaret Frakes, "Why the Movie Investigation?," *Christian Century*, vol. 58 (September 24, 1941), pp. 1172–1174.

41. Quoted by Bosley Crowther in *Sunday New York Times* Drama Section, July 6, 1947, p. 1.

42. Leo C. Rosten, "Movies and Propaganda," *Annals of the American Academy of Political and Social Science*, vol. 254 (November, 1947), p. 121, n. 7.

43. *Ibid.*, p. 121.

44. W. H. Hays, *Memoirs*, p. 540.

45. Norman Cousins, "Our Heroes," *Saturday Review of Literature*, vol. 24, no. 27 (October 25, 1941), p. 10.

46. Cedric Larson, "The Domestic Motion Picture Work of the Office of War Information," *Hollywood Quarterly*, vol. 3 (1948), p. 436.

47. *Movie Lot to Beachhead*, p. 188.

48. For more details of the O.W.I. and Lowell Mellett see MacCann, *The People's Films*, pp. 129–137.

49. Larson, p. 441. For another view of this issue see "Tempest in a Hollywood Teapot," *Theater Arts*, vol. 27 (February, 1943), pp. 71–72.

50. Walter Wanger, "O.W.I. and Motion Pictures," *Public Opinion Quarterly*, vol. 7, no. 1 (Spring, 1943), p. 100.

51. *Ibid.*, p. 103.

52. *Ibid.*

53. *Ibid.*, p. 104.

54. For details of the overseas branch of the O.W.I. see MacCann, *People's Films*, pp. 133–135.

55. Wanger, "O.W.I. and Motion Pictures," p. 102.

56. For a different view of O.W.I.'s role in making films more responsive to domestic wartime requirements see Harold Putnam, "The War Against War Movies," *Educational Screen*, vol. 22 (May, 1943).

57. Kyle Crichton, "Hollywood Holocaust," *Collier's*, February 13, 1943, pp. 16, 23. This article examines many other "difficulties" which beset the film community.

58. Kyle Crichton, "Hollywood Gets Its Teeth Kicked In," *Collier's*, January 9, 1943, p. 34. For further details on the problem of finding suitable "stars" see Lingeman, pp. 179–180.

59. "Hollywood in Uniform," *Fortune*, vol. 25, no. 4 (April, 1942), p. 94.

60. *Ibid.*, p. 94.

61. Crichton noted: "The movies are one of our lines of defense. It is as stupid to throw away a Mickey Rooney or a Henry Fonda as it would be to draft an airplane designer to make him a grease monkey." "Hollywood Gets Its Teeth Kicked In," p. 37.

62. *Movie Lot to Beachhead*, pp. 58–59.

63. *General Information Manual for the Motion Picture Industry*, quoted in Lingeman, p. 184.

64. *Ibid.*

65. Walter Wanger, "The Role of the Movies in Morale," *American Journal of Sociology*, vol. 47 (November, 1941), p. 381.

66. For more details see *Movie Lot to Beachhead*, pp. 82–111.

67. *Ibid.*, p. 105.

68. *Ibid.*

69. Bosley Crowther, "The Movies Follow the Flag," *New York Times Magazine*, August 13, 1944, p. 18.

70. For a vivid description of the movie show at the warfront see Pete Martin, "Tonight at Beachhead Bijou," *Saturday Evening Post*, vol. 217 (August 12, 1944), pp. 20, 81–82.

71. The director of research for the Motion Picture Association of America observed in 1947: "It is amusing to note that some sources have not adjusted the weekly attendance figure for several years. This fact has caused one person to remark facetiously that this must be a truly unique industry — a business which, in spite of fluctuations in economic conditions, changes in product, variations in sales campaigns, and other equally notable factors, has managed to maintain exactly the same number of customers throughout the period." See Robert W. Chambers, "Need for Statistical Research," *Annals of the American Academy of Political and Social Science*, vol. 254 (November, 1947), pp. 169–172.

72. "Big Movie Year," *Business Week*, no. 702 (February 13, 1943), pp. 37–38.

73. "Hollywood — A Postwar Record Breaker," *Business Week*, December 7, 1946, p. 96.

74. "Hollywood Wows Wall Street," *Business Week*, May 11, 1946, p. 60.

75. Dorothy B. Jones, "Hollywood War Films," *Hollywood Quarterly*, vol. 1 (1945), p. 2. Dorothy Jones had been a member of the Hollywood office of the O.W.I. and was a recognized authority on the analysis of motion picture content. This is an important article, although Mrs. Jones's bias against the film industry is quite obvious.

76. *Ibid.*, p. 1.

77. *Ibid.*

78. *Ibid.*, p. 6.

79. *Ibid.*, p. 8.

80. *Ibid.*, p. 9.

81. For further details about the delinquency problem see Lingeman, pp. 85–89. An interesting method of solving this problem was outlined by Mr. W. H. M. Watson, the manager of the Mission Theater in El Paso, Texas. He walked up and down the aisles wearing a Sam Browne belt, a .38 automatic (with three extra clips of cartridges), an iron claw in a scabbard, a blackjack, a pair of handcuffs, a "very shiny" gold badge, and on busy nights a twenty-four-inch police club. The result was that the kids "have learned who is boss." See "How to Run a Theater," *Time*, no. 42 (November 22, 1943), pp. 94–95.

82. When the Marines set up recruiting stations near theaters showing the film *Guadalcanal Diary*, they secured nearly 12,000 extra recruits. See *Movie Lot to Beachhead*, p. 113.

83. Dorothy B. Jones, "Hollywood War Films," p. 12.

84. *Ibid.*, p. 13.

85. *New York Times*, May 23, 1943. Quoted in Lewis Jacobs, "World War II and the American Film," in Arthur F. McClure, ed., *The Movies: An American Idiom* (Rutherford: Farleigh Dickinson University Press, 1971), p. 167.

86. *New York Times*, May 23, 1943. Quoted in Jacobs, "World War II and the American Film," p. 167.

87. For more detailed information of the "Why We Fight" films, see MacCann, *People's Films,* pp. 155–159; Frank Capra, *The Name Above the Title* (New York: Macmillan Company, 1971), pp. 325–367; and Thomas Bohn, "An Historical and Descriptive Analysis of the 'Why We Fight' Series" (Ph.D. dissertation, University of Wisconsin, 1968).

88. General Marshall quoted in Capra, p. 327.

89. Lingeman quotes an incident which indicates that many audiences were restless during these films; see p. 190. Capra, however, claims quite the reverse on pp. 349–350.

90. C. I. Hovland, A. A. Lumsdaine, and F. D. Sheffield, *Experiments in Mass Communication* (New York: John Wiley and Sons, 1965). This volume is one of four in the series "Studies in Social Psychology in World War II," prepared under the auspices of a special committee of the Social Science Research Council.

91. Herman A. Lowe, "Washington Discovers Hollywood," *American Mercury,* vol. 60 (April, 1945), p. 407.

92. *Ibid.,* p. 414. For a detailed examination of this issue, see Allen L. Woll, "Hollywood's Good Neighbor Policy: The Latin American Film, 1939–1946," *Journal of Popular Film,* vol. 3, no. 4 (1974), pp. 278–293.

93. John Grierson, "Tomorrow the Movies I: Hollywood International," *Nation,* vol. 160, no. 2 (January 6, 1945), p. 13.

94. *Ibid.,* p. 14.

95. Dorothy B. Jones, "Tomorrow the Movies IV: Is Hollywood Growing Up?," *Nation,* vol. 160, no. 5 (February 3, 1945), p. 125.

96. John A. Kouwenhoven, "The Movies Better Be Good!," *Harper's,* vol. 190 (May, 1945), p. 534.

97. *Ibid.,* pp. 537–538.

98. *Ibid.,* p. 540.

99. Harry L. Hansen, "Hollywood and International Understanding," *Harvard Business Review,* vol. 25, no. 1 (Autumn, 1946), p. 45.

100. *From Movie Lot to Beachhead,* p. 216.

101. Quoted in Robert Joseph, "Our Film Program in Germany I: How Far Was It a Success?," *Hollywood Quarterly,* vol. 2 (1947), p. 122. This article is recommended reading for anyone interested in the total inability of government to comprehend the educational nature of the commercial motion picture.

102. Among the thirty-odd films originally selected for showing in Germany were *The Maltese Falcon* (1941); *Seven Sweethearts* (1942); *Pride and Prejudice* (1940); *All That Money Can Buy* (1941); *Thirty Seconds Over Tokyo* (1945) — this film was supposed to emphasize that America "was a mighty nation, capable of fighting a two-front war"; *It Started With Eve* (1941); and *Going My Way* (1944). Fine films such as *The Grapes of Wrath* (1939) were avoided because of "the background it shows and the story it tells." Joseph, pp. 122–125.

103. *Ibid.,* p. 130.

104. Gladwin Hill, "Our Film Program in Germany II: How Far Was It a Failure?," *Hollywood Quarterly,* vol. 2 (1947), p. 135.

105. *Ibid.,* p. 136.

106. *Ibid.,* p. 137.

107. Franklin Fearing, "Warriors Return: Normal or Neurotic?," *Hollywood Quarterly,* vol. 1 (1945), p. 98.

108. *Ibid.,* p. 102.

109. Robert St. John in the preface to *Movie Lot to Beachhead.*

110. For more specific details on the social changes reflected in the movies during the years 1942–1945, see John T. McManus and Louis Kronenberger, "Motion Pictures, the Theater, and Race Relations," *Annals of the American Academy of Political and Social Science*, vol. 244 (March, 1946), pp. 152–159.

111. An important contribution to our understanding of the war film is Russell E. Shain, *An Analysis of Motion Pictures About War Released by the American Film Industry, 1939–1970* (New York: Arno Press, 1975). Shain clearly indicates that war films cannot be completely understood outside of the historical environment in which they are created, and without examining the various forces impinging upon the institutions that produced them. He also indicates that war movies have moved through three stages since 1939: the first (1939–1947) dealing sympathetically with America at war; the second (1948–1952) examining the problems of the Cold War and the professional soldier; and the third (1963–1970) concerned with the legitimacy of war. Also, he points out, because of the increasing importance of the international film market, Hollywood has had to tone down its nationalistic tendencies. Two other excellent examinations of the continued use of the war theme are Peter A. Soderbergh, "On War and the Movies: A Reappraisal," in *Centennial Review*, vol. 11, no. 3 (Summer, 1967), pp. 405–418; and by the same author, "The War Films," *Discourse: A Review of the Liberal Arts*, vol. 11, no. 1 (Winter, 1968), pp. 87–91.

112. Soderbergh, "The War Films," p. 90.

XIII

The Decline of an Institution

WHEN THE FIGHTING ENDED IN 1945, there was widespread anxiety that the cessation of war spending would bring about the economic hardships of the Depression all over again. Fortunately, this was not the case, and in the immediate postwar period, the United States experienced the greatest and most sustained economic growth in its history. Not that the domestic scene was untroubled, for labor difficulties, inflation and shortages, a housing crisis, and increasing social unrest were all features of "peaceful" America. In particular, the inconsistencies in the outdated segregationist policies which pervaded all aspects of American life became conspicuous, and a source of irritation for many — both black and white — who had risked their lives for "democracy."

The war had ended with the explosion of the atomic bomb, and coupled with the increasing political polarization between the Communists and the "free world," the knowledge that man now had weapons capable of destroying the world created a mood of fear and suspicion which would manifest itself in many facets of social as well as political life. In particular, those powerful agencies capable of molding public opinion — the mass media — would themselves be under attack from all sides, as the ideological battle among left, right and center dominated the period 1946–1960. The motion picture industry was especially hard hit and affected by this troubled domestic scene, for it had to contend not only with an irreversible decline in audience due to shifting leisure patterns, but also with an unprecedented political attack, this time aimed more at the people who made the movies, and less at the actual films they produced.

The Broken Promise

The war had once again brought into sharper focus the issue of the "proper social and cultural role" for the motion picture. All through the Depression, and especially during the war, the motion picture had proved its worth, if not as an "information medium," then certainly as an indispensable form of recreation and diversionary entertainment. The surprising loyalty which the American public had demonstrated for this medium only served to make both the movies' devotees and its critics wish that its tremendous powers were being put to use for some higher purpose than mere entertainment. This view had persisted for fifty years, and the motion picture was no nearer defining its role in 1946 than it had been in 1896.

In 1944, James T. Farrell, the author of the *Studs Lonigan* trilogy and a noted social critic, examined "The Language of Hollywood" in the *Saturday Review of Literature,* and attacked the "tremendous commercial culture [which] has developed as a kind of substitute for a genuinely popular, a genuinely democratic culture, which would recreate and communicate how the mass of the people live, how they feel about working, loving, enjoying, suffering, and dying."[1] What Farrell really objected to was the fact that the tremendous influence of all the mass media, and the motion picture in particular, was determined by "business considerations." This fact of economic necessity denied the writer the opportunity to work free of restrictions, and those who wrote for the screen "reveal a retrogression in consciousness."[2] According to Farrell, the Hollywood "commodity" failed to "fulfill the real cultural needs of the masses of the people," because the movies as a cultural influence did not "help to create those states of consciousness, of awareness of oneself, of others, and of the world, which aid in making people better, and in preparing them to make the world better. Hollywood films usually have the precisely opposite effect; most of them make people less aware, or else falsely aware."[3]

Farrell's attack on commercialization of culture was merciless, and although overstated, his basic premise was sound. However, he did acknowledge that the movies were more the end product of long-noticed tendencies in American society than the cause, although the medium was now so powerful an influence that Hollywood's demands threatened all forms of creative writing.[4]

As was noted in the previous chapter, the motion picture industry had the biggest year in its history in 1946. (See Appendices V and VII.) However, after this blaze of glory, the industry went into a fairly steady economic decline from which it has never recovered. This was not what the industry or its devotees had envisaged in late 1945, when, buoyed by the public's response to the movies' contribution to the war effort, they foresaw a new "golden age" for the medium. It was especially hoped that the war experience would revitalize Hollywood, and that, having learned something about making documentary films, it would infuse the commercial product with a "greater realism." Philip Dunne, who had been chief of production with the O.W.I. overseas branch, suggested that documentary film makers and Hollywood producers had much to offer each other, but this would not be a fruitful exchange "as long as some in Hollywood persist in looking on the documentary as a poor relation of 'The Industry'; as long as so many in that 'Industry' continue to consider the typical documentarian a long-haired crank, his mind cluttered with impracticalities."[5] Dunne noted that many of Hollywood's finest films had dealt with material usually considered purely documentary, movies such as *Fury* (1936), *The Grapes of Wrath* (1940), and the very recent masterpiece *Citizen Kane* (1941). He hoped that more producers would "grasp the enormous responsibility" facing the movie industry "in the critical years ahead," which could best be achieved if their preparation "be not only spiritual but technical . . . by closely observing the methods, and sometimes absorbing the personnel, of the documentary field."[6]

Producer and critic Kenneth MacGowan also noted a trend toward "new techniques" as evidence of the documentary influence in the films released in late 1945. He singled out *The House on 92nd Street, The Story of G.I. Joe, The Pride of the Marines* and the Academy Award–winning *The Lost Weekend* as examples of this trend. MacGowan, however, observed with regret Hollywood's continued reliance on books and plays as the source of its best material, indicating a fear within the film industry not to attempt anything the least bit controversial, unless it had proved publicly acceptable in another medium.[7]

Unfortunately, this hoped-for amalgam between documentary and entertainment was seldom achieved, although the late 1940s was a particularly rich period for creativity in the American film.[8] The problem really stemmed from the inability of the movies' critics (even those who wished to be constructive in their criticism) to understand the power of entertainment to "influence" as much as any documentary. It was precisely this failure to equate entertainment with ideas which had led to the acceptance of control over the movies (and in some cases the same philosophy had affected radio). Nevertheless, the long history of the motion picture had demonstrated over and over again that "entertainment" was capable of exerting a powerful influence on its audience.[9]

Still, the movies were continually criticized for failing to make the most of their potential as an educational influence. As an example, in January,

1947, an editorial in the *Christian Century* complained that, "as one of the three principal media of mass information and education, the motion picture is notably failing to do its share in instructing the American people concerning their responsibilities as citizens of the atomic age . . . the millions who attend the movies each week find there little or nothing to awake them to the possibilities for good or evil of this new dimension of power." The problem, the editorial suggested, lay in the "provincialism" of those who controlled the movie industry, and whose dictum was, "Let others instruct. Our job is entertainment." Thus the movies were abrogating their responsibility and "drugging the national consciousness into slumber." The editorial concluded by noting that nothing would be done about this misused potential "until it is recognized that under its present owners the motion picture industry is supplying the opiate which keeps the people lethargic when they should be aroused as never before."[10]

The movies had achieved some recognition in the hierarchy of American arts in 1935, when the Museum of Modern Art Film Library was opened in New York. Between 1935 and 1945, the museum had done a creditable job of collecting prints and negatives, and now owned the best collection in the United States. Nevertheless, cooperation from Hollywood in this venture had been inconsistent, and Iris Barry, one of the founders of the film library and the current curator, suggested that "now was the time for Hollywood and its technicians to join with the Film Library in a collaboration that would once and for all give precise information to students about . . . the achievements that have carried the motion picture from its celebrated infancy to near maturity and made it indeed an art (as well as an industry) with which one can truly be proud to be connected."[11] Unfortunately, this cooperation was slow in developing, and the film industry continued along its commercial path oblivious to its wider responsibilities. Clara Beranger, a screenwriter and instructor in film, noted that in order to develop new technical talent for the screen, students needed greater practical experience because "the art was so closely tied to its technology." Here too, Hollywood did not seem anxious to encourage such cooperative training ventures.[12]

By 1947, the American film industry was still struggling to come to terms with its potential in the educational field, but here the educators were still partly to blame, because they had not yet discovered the key to the successful utilization of in-the-classroom film instruction. Charles Palmer, writing in *Hollywood Quarterly,* called for a greater effort of cooperation on the part of educators and the film industry to make films which would be integrated into the current curriculum. Such films would be "bought, rather than rented, and bought in large enough numbers to justify the use of top talents and facilities of the motion picture industry."[13] Edgar Dale disagreed with Palmer's call for more "entertainment" in educational films, and suggested in turn that the remedy was "to have more teachers understand what a good film is, and to have producers of these films understand what teaching is." It was obvious that Dale was suspicious of the "entertainment" film which had no obligation to "start a train of thinking."[14] However, Palmer got in the last word in reply to Dale, and reiterated Hollywood's enormous potential, and suggested further that "this potential contribution should not be barred through unjustified prejudice, not be resented as an intrusion on a private reserve."[15] Palmer had made his point — the movies were too important to leave to well-meaning amateurs.

In 1948, the MPAA (the MPPDA had altered its name to the Motion Picture Association of America in 1945) set up a project known as the Children's Film Library, consisting of twenty-eight feature films which were reissues of favorites with juvenile audiences in the past. According to reports in the trade press, the exhibitors, the studios and distributors stood to make very little money from this venture. Sondra Gorney, examining the nature of children's cinema in the United States, commented on the selected films that "one thing is certain: they were never produced with the young audience in mind."[16] She also noted the recent revival of censorship activity aimed directly at movies for children, and which threatened the industry with the loss of almost 20 percent of its audience.[17] The development of special children's films was always an unfulfilled dream for concerned educators, parents, teachers, psychologists and social workers. The eternal question was, "If the MPAA could see some merit in selecting reissues for children's viewing, why could it see no value in making new films exclusively for this audience?" The children of 1948 were to be the adult audiences of 1958; but then Hollywood had never been able to think of the future.

It remained for film director Irving Pichel to sum up the unkept promise of the movies in the postwar period. The war had been an exhilarating experience for those in the film industry who "were able to put the medium . . . to the most effective use it had ever, in their experience, served."[18] By 1948, however, the industry had been "caponized." While Americans had fought for the survival of democracy, he noted, in reality many of the "great issues were left unresolved and their residue constitutes the most derisive factor in our social, economic and political life today." Pichel attacked the film industry for turning its back on the important domestic issues facing America in the late 1940s. He suggested that it was clearly the function of "the art of fiction," including "the dramatic film," to examine and depict the "antagonisms, the aggressions, the strains," in society. However, the movies were being limited in their ability to contribute to an understanding "of those sources of strain which have the greatest contemporary interest for us." Pichel's anger was directed at those politicians who continued to attack "message" films, and also at the "industrial organization" of the film industry which prevented anything "sensitive" from reaching the screen. Thus, Pichel reasoned, "the screen remains a medium but is not a voice. . . . The screen is asked to ignore the antagonisms most current among us, most productive of disruption in the contemporary scene, most dramatic in their threat to our social and political present and future. . . ."[19]

He was making an important point. Because the film industry depended upon such large audiences, it could not afford to antagonize any section of it, and therefore movie content was largely limited to examining problems about which the studios, and the censors, believed that the American public had reached something close to unanimity. Thus the screenplay was seldom able to give the audience wholly new viewpoints. As long as Hollywood was constrained by a rigid form of ideological and political censorship, dependent upon the mentality of "big business," and threatened with extinction by a small box in the living room, this philosophy would prevail.

The Audience Examined

After the glorious year in 1946 when close to 1.7 billion dollars was paid by movie patrons to see their favorite entertainment, the fortunes of the American motion picture went steadily downhill, with only the odd year in which this decline has been momentarily halted. In the fourteen-year period between 1946 and 1960, the average weekly attendance dropped from ninety million to forty million. More important, the expenditures declined even more sharply, from one-fifth to less than one-tenth of the available recreational dollars. (See Appendix V.) It was quite obvious to those inside and outside the motion picture industry that for a variety of reasons, the intense love affair between the mass of the American public and their movies was coming to an end. While the movies would continue as a major entertainment medium, by the early 1950s it could no longer claim to be the *major* source of commercial recreation.

At precisely the time that the audience started to decline, Hollywood started to show some curiosity about the nature and taste preferences of its patrons. Earlier, in 1933, Howard T. Lewis had commented on the industry's inability to predict success or to produce films to meet the requirements of "particular classes of audiences," and he pointed out that no satisfactory methods of prediction had been developed, and that "experiment, reliance upon hunches, or blind guess seems to be the usual practice."[20] In 1947, Ernest Borneman, writing in *Harper's* about "The Public Opinion Myth," examined the increasing use of public opinion polls, and suggested that such research went far beyond merely statistical or psychological investigation, but was "essentially tied to the economic structure of the entertainment industry."[21] Borneman questioned whether such "market research" practices were adaptable to the "cultural field," and suggested that the danger lay in the industry's placing far too much reliance on the pollster's findings. So far, according to Borneman, this trend toward "scientific" analysis of the market for movies had been disastrous, for

. . . the closer they came to a definition of today's demand, the further they found themselves moving away from the creation of an active and continuing market for tomorrow. The perpetual application of consumer analyses to the cultural market had turned that market into a sterile, glutted, and intractable thing. . . . Surrendering the job of firing the public mind to new horizons of adventure, the showmen followed the pollsters so deeply into the morass of the lowest common denominator that their birthright as entertainers and artists got stuck somewhere along the road.[22]

Of course, not everyone agreed with Borneman, and earlier, in 1945, Bosley Crowther had looked at the same phenomenon, and while he made no qualitative judgment, the tone of his article suggests approval for any method which would assist the movie industry in developing a product to meet the wide variety of tastes exhibited by the movie-going public. To demonstrate this "general predisposition of preference," Crowther included a table which had been compiled by the Audience Research Institute (A.R.I.), a subsidiary of the Gallup Poll organization. This table of preference proportions was calculated against an index of 100; the total exceeds 100 because respondents were allowed to make more than one choice:

TABLE 18
FILM CONTENT PREFERENCES, 1945

TYPE	MALES	FEMALES
Musicals	35	49
Light comedy	35	42
Serious drama	23	42
Excitement, adventure	39	25
Slapstick comedy	43	18
Army, navy, aviation	40	23
Detective, mystery	36	24
Romance, mystery	9	32
Westerns	16	7

Source: Bosley Crowther, "It's the Fans Who Make the Films," in the New York Times Magazine, June 24, 1945, p. 14.

A.R.I. was busy developing new methods of audience research which included the calculation of the "want to see" or "expectancy level" of a film, which was determined by asking people their opinion of a verbally outlined plot. (Borneman had quoted the famed British film maker Sir Alexander Korda, producer of *The Private Life of Henry VIII*, as saying, "How would you react if someone stopped you on the street, or rang your doorbell, and asked, 'Would you like to see a picture about a sixteenth century English king and his several wives?' ")[23] The tests on completed films were more sophisticated, and utilized specially devised electronic equipment which charted the "enjoyment" level throughout a film by averaging out individual responses. If the "enjoyment level" was lower than the "expectancy level" the trick was to exhibit such films as fast as possible to take advantage of the "want to see" impulse. However, if the reverse was true, then the film had to be carefully "marketed" while the "want to see" was increased by advertising and other forms of exploitation, especially "word of mouth."[24]

The development of these new techniques was part of a desperate bid by Hollywood to minimize any losses. There were two big reasons for such action. One was the rapidly increasing production costs — up 70 percent since 1941. The second was the continued threat of the antitrust action which was bound to cause drastic alterations in movie distribution. If distributors were forced to deal with single films, and not blocks, then each film would have to be sold on its own merits. Naturally, producers wanted each production to be potentially profitable, and were therefore willing to use any technique they could to ensure this.

In a series of articles which culminated in an important book, Dr. Leo A. Handel, the man responsible for MGM's audience research, examined these new techniques in some detail, and concluded that, in fact, such research was far behind audience research for the other mass media. Handel noted that "Hollywood, by and large, resisted the development of high-level audience research. In the race between intuition and the IBM machine the latter came in a poor second."[25] One example of the myths which such haphazard methods had perpetuated was that regarding the sexual composition of the film audience, which supposedly was heavily weighted toward women. Handel pointed out that several independent studies in the 1940s had shown that the audience was, in fact, evenly split between men and women.[26] (This of course, does not take into account the possibility of a historical shift in audience composition between the 1920s and the 1940s — but why this would have happened is uncertain.) Handel also noted after the initial flurry, there was a decrease in the use of general audience research in the late 1940s, and that A.R.I. lost many of its clients in spite of the valuable service the organization had rendered. He suggested that A.R.I.'s own psychological approach to the traditionally reticent film industry was partly to blame, for, "instead of advising what decisions might be taken as a result of the audience studies, they often told the industry executives what to do."[27] This surely would have been the "kiss of death" in Hollywood!

The main thrust of all Handel's writings was that the motion picture industry was "the only major business in the United States which has never made a serious attempt to study its potential market."[28] The reliance on intuition was dangerous, and in any case, different industry luminaries had different intuitions. Thus, at a crucial period in its history, the film industry ignored all the warning signs and continued to use outdated business methods from a previous, and more predictable, period in its past. Not that the industry was alone in its ignorance; even an "expert" like Leo Handel was unable to predict the disastrous effects of television in his 1950 book, *Hollywood Looks At Its Audience*.[29]

Eric Johnston, who had taken over from Will Hays as president of the Motion Picture Association of America (MPAA) in 1945, was a fact-minded man who almost immediately established a research department for the industry. This ambitious research program was to be governed by a committee of audience research consisting of key members of the industry, but in spite of Johnston's urging them to procure sound statistical data about America's moviegoers, the member companies of the MPAA were never happy with the project. After sponsoring some minor inter-industry statistical studies, the research committee discontinued its activities.[30]

Because of the heavy reliance on intuition, and the very haphazard attempts made to understand its audience, the motion picture industry placed a great deal of faith in the persuasive ability of its advertising campaigns to attract patrons into movie theaters. The advertising associated with the movies had always been severely criticized, and had proved to be beyond the control of the Hays Office. Toned down somewhat during the happier days of booming wartime attendance, movie advertising returned to "normal" after 1946. John Elliot Williams, an advertising executive with wide experience in the field of movie publicity, noted that "no form of advertising is more extravagant, more misleading, more mendacious, and sometimes more vicious than the printed matter which exploits the motion picture." Williams continued his devastating, and well-chronicled, attack on movie advertising, pointing out that most campaigns totally and consciously misled the public as to the true nature of the film's content. The independent theaters were particularly guilty of such questionable tactics, although the chains were not without blame. He concluded by suggesting that "film advertising today seems a typical product of those forces which have made the motion picture not only the most timorous of industries . . . but also the most inconstant, slothful and supine."[31]

Movie critic Jay E. Gordon also examined the "dishonest" advertising methods of the film industry and suggested that instead of relying on the studio publicity department, the industry use "specialists" to promote its products, that is, advertising agencies. This practice, Gordon felt, would mean greater honesty, more precise campaigns aimed at specific audiences, and greater benefits for the studios and the public. "Every motion picture produced is a thing apart, a separate and distinguishable entity, an isolated artistic creation . . . [and] . . . should be sold as a separate article of commerce, advertised in accordance with its own merits . . ."[32]

Among the many suggestions made by Jay Gordon was one to "discourage movie gossip columns both in public prints [sic] and on radio and television."[33] This was not an easy, or, for the studios, a desirable thing to do, for the Hollywood gossip columnist had become an indispensable cog in studio publicity machinery. All through the forties and fifties Hollywood continued to be a prime source for news which was dispatched to media outlets all over the globe. In 1954, there were still 411 men and women accredited to the studios by the Johnston office as Hollywood reporters.[34] This group comprised one of the world's largest permanent congregations of journalistic talent and effort, and no other industry came close to achieving this intensity of coverage.

The top Hollywood reporter was, without doubt, Louella Parsons, who had started as a syndicated gossip columnist in 1925. By 1954, she was featured in 625 newspapers throughout the world, with close to 40 million readers. A close second was Hedda Hopper, featured in 70 newspapers, with a circulation of 32 million, and she and Louella had conducted a long-lasting, and publicity garnering, feud, which had finally been settled in 1948.[35] Behind these front-line columnists were the hundreds of independent press agents watching for every opportunity to "plant" an "item" about a client, and the studio publicity men paid to provide the insatiable public with information about their favorite stars, which might eventually lead to another sale at the box office. All of this was necessary for an industry which could only survive by creating illusion to feed the public's fantasies.

The State of the Industry, 1946–1950

In 1949, a screenwriter named Herbert Clyde Lewis was quoted as saying, "The swimming pools are drying up all over Hollywood. I do not think I shall see them filled in my generation."[36] Lewis's witticism was supported by the current state of the film industry, for by 1949, it was obvious that making movies was no longer the profitable business it had once been. While the economics of the movie industry have always been complex, the sudden shift from wartime boom to postwar recession, even before the introduction of television, can clearly be attributed to a combination of several factors. The first was the decline in audience which has already been noted, and although Hollywood attempted to reverse this trend, the task proved too difficult. Essentially, the difficulty lay in capturing the "Lost Audience" — that group between the ages of thirty-one and sixty who comprised only 35 percent of movie patrons. A.R.I. estimated that if all the people in this age group went to the movies only once a week, the box-office receipts after taxes would rise by $800 million a year.[37] While the number of paid admissions had exceeded four billion, according to industry statistics, this fact was broken down into a probable thirty million separate moviegoers, mainly under thirty, and who went several times a week. A further refinement revealed that a mere thirteen to fifteen million individuals actually saw the basic Hollywood staple — the "A" feature film.[38]

The real problem was how to attract the older adults without alienating the under-nineteen group. The movies could not really compete with radio when it came to providing fare for fragmented audiences, and the cost structure was quite different. Therefore, the film industry should have made a more conscientious effort to find out why this large potential group shunned the industry's offerings, but this was never done. Gilbert Seldes began his important book *The Great Audience* (1950) by noting:

Except for the makers of baby foods, no industry in the United States has been so indifferent to the steady falling away of its customers as the movies have been. . . . The parallel with strained foods breaks down in one detail: the foods would be worthless if the consumer didn't outgrow them, and the manufacturer virtually guarantees that they will become unnecessary in time and give way to other, more varied nourishment; the makers of movies pretend that what they offer is a balanced ration for adults also. But the reason the customers stop buying the product is the same: in each case the formula no longer satisfies.[39]

What were the reasons for this youthful concentration in the film audience? Certainly content was a major factor, but there were other reasons, as Paul Lazarsfeld pointed out:

The decline of frequent movie attendance with increasing age is very sharp. No other mass medium shows a comparable trend. This is probably due to a variety of factors. Movie-going is essentially a social activity . . . and young people are more likely to band together for the purpose of entertainment. Then, for the movies one has to leave the house, which probably becomes more distasteful as one grows older. Finally, radio programs and reading material offer a variety of choices, and each age group can select from these media items that interest them.

The supply of movies, however, is much smaller and the variety more limited, and they are patterned to the tastes of younger people.[40]

343

Whatever the reasons, the fact remained that movie audiences were declining long before television became a major competitor on the American entertainment scene. This was particularly obvious in the face of the rise in gross national product and disposable income, and the increase in expenditures on recreation. Also, the population of the United States had increased by 8 percent between 1940 and 1950. An examination of all these statistics together could point to only one thing — the movie industry was in trouble. (See Appendices V and VII.)

One reason may have been the public's reaction to the postwar Hollywood product. A survey conducted by *Fortune* magazine in late 1948 found that movie audiences were not overenthusiastic about the quality of the films of that period. When asked, "How do 1948 movies compare to those of two or three years ago?," 23 percent thought that there were "more good ones"; 30 percent felt that they were "the same"; 38 percent thought that there were "fewer good ones"; and 9 percent had no opinion. This particular *Fortune* survey was most revealing in that the results indicated that audiences were beginning to find alternatives to moviegoing, and 50 percent of the moviegoers who "are going less often" indicated that they were "too busy, or have other things to do"; 33 percent "did not like any of the current selections"; 16 percent "could not afford them"; and 14 percent gave "other reasons."[41]

The other important reasons for the audience decline can be attributed to the increasing growth of alternative spectator amusements, including professional sports, theater and even opera. Automobiles also enjoyed a healthy postwar sales boom; while the expected rise in the birthrate kept many young couples home. There was a shift in expenditure patterns away from amusement toward more materialistic acquisitions, and movies were unfortunately caught in the squeeze. The motion picture was shown to be not as indispensable a part of American social life as many had thought; all that was now required to diminish the power of the entertainment monolith was to provide a "functional alternative." This is precisely what television was able to do.

The other major problem faced by the movie industry in the period 1946–1950 was that of sharply declining profits, caused by a combination of financial factors over which the industry had very little control. The first was the dramatic rise in production costs, which threatened to destroy profits altogether.[42] The second was the continued difficulty in extracting profits earned out of foreign markets, as most governments were not anxious to submit to continued Hollywood domination of the international motion picture market.[43] Third, and in the long run the most damaging, was the final divorcement of exhibition from the production and distribution functions.[44]

The final victory by the Justice Department, and the enforcement of the divestiture decree, while perfectly legal and philosophically in keeping with Rooseveltian liberal thinking, had a disastrous effect on the film industry, and ultimately on the whole structure of movie-going in America. Charles Higham examined these effects and suggested:

For confidence in a product, the feeling that it could flow out along guaranteed lines of distribution, was what gave Hollywood films before 1948 their superb attack and vigor. Also, the block-booking custom, evil though it may have been, ensured that many obscure, personal, and fascinating movies could be made and released, feather-bedded by the system and underwritten by more conventional ventures.[45]

The exhibition segment had always been the most profitable part of the motion picture business, and in the postwar period this was even more obvious. Theater operating costs did not rise as fast as production costs, and the box-office split gave a decided advantage to the exhibitor in the initial weeks of a run. Finally, the independent sources of revenue, such as screen advertising and the sale of candy, were quite considerable and highly profitable. For these reasons, once the theaters were separated from the studios, it became extremely difficult for the film industry to show continuous profits; and it would take several years to transfer some of the exhibitor's profits back into production and distribution. In the meantime Hollywood's financial and political woes indicated that there was indeed "panic in Paradise" as studios desperately began to cut back on salaries and production budgets.[46]

Economist Simon N. Whitney noted that the final decree, known as the "*Paramount* decision," represented the most important experiment in vertical "disintegration" ever achieved under the Sherman Antitrust Act.[47] However, the decision was by no means universally popular, and the Department of Justice received more complaints against this decree than any other in history, and the Senate Small Business Committee held extensive and inconclusive hearings on the decision in 1953.

As a result of the 1948 decision by the Supreme Court, Loew's Paramount, RKO, Twentieth Century–Fox, and Warners were ordered to dispose of their theaters, and these five plus Columbia, Universal, and United Artists were forbidden to engage in certain monopolistic practices, including rental to theaters on a circuit-wide basis and block-booking. As a consequence, each of the integrated companies between 1948 and 1954 split into two, with a successor production-distribution company and a divorced theater circuit.

The divorcement, coming as it did during a period of economic hardship for the motion picture industry, was blamed for many of the ills besetting the movies in the early fifties. The decree was seen as the cause of the reduced number of productions released by member studios of the MPAA, but this was, in fact, a trend which had been predicted in 1954, when domestic releases declined by more than 20 percent. This drop was the result of a general cutback in major studio output, but in that year many of the smaller studios turned permanently to manufacturing shorter films (the old "Grade B's") for television. Movie theaters compensated by filling their screen time with independent and foreign films and reissues, and by giving some of the top features a longer playing time.

TABLE 19
FEATURES RELEASED IN
THE U.S. MARKET

DATE	U.S. PRODUCED	IMPORTED	TOTAL
1946	378	89	467
1947	369	118	487
1948	366	93	459
1949	356	123	479
1950	383	239	622
1951	391	263	654
1952	324	139	463
1953	344	190	534
1954	253	174	427
1955	254	138	392
1956	272	207	479

Source: Various issues of *Film Daily Yearbook.*

The decree's effects were mixed, and it did not take the exhibitors very long to see that many of the hoped-for benefits were not going to materialize. Rental costs for films increased, while some of the big producers, now no longer owning their own theaters, demanded exorbitant fees for "blockbusters" such as *The Robe* and *The Caine Mutiny.* Independent theaters were forced to outbid each other for "first runs" and this helped to drive the price for films up even further. (At one point an exhibitors' chain, the Allied States Association, after vainly demanding that rentals be made subject to arbitration, turned to a proposal that the movie industry be declared a *public utility* and its wholesale, not retail, prices be regulated by the Federal Trade Commission.)[48] Also, many exhibitors now belatedly realized the virtues of block-booking, and the time and cost which this practice had saved the independent operator.

In the long run the divorcement decree was but one of several social and economic factors which together caused a total shift in the pattern of motion picture attendance in the postwar period. However, it is worthy of note that the requirement that the motion picture industry disintegrate was against the trends then apparent in the American economy. While Hollywood was being asked to finally comply with a legal decision which had its antecedents in a period nearly forty years earlier, other industries were busy participating in one of the most remarkable merger movements in U.S. economic history.[49] It would not be until the mid-sixties that film companies themselves became prime properties for mergers with such unrelated industries as shoe manufacturing, hotel chains, distilleries and parking lots.[50]

Television and the Motion Picture Industry

It was in 1948 that television became a true mass medium in the United States, when for the first time the television industry was able to expand with a solid technological base. During this year the number of stations on the air increased from seventeen to forty-one, and the number of cities with television transmission from eight to twenty-three. The number of sets sold exceeded the 1947 total by 500 percent, and by 1951 even exceeded the sales of radio sets for that year. Also in 1948, the first attempts at network service started, and immediately attracted important, large national advertisers.[51]

However, by late 1948, the FCC became concerned over the nature of channel allocation and the technical arguments which surrounded the problem of color transmission, and therefore stopped processing new license applications on September 29. This was the famous television "freeze" which allowed existing stations to continue operation, but deferred all other applications pending further study of the technical problems. The number of stations allowed to operate was frozen at 108, but even then the number of sets in use continued to rise from 250,000 to over 15 million between 1948 and 1952.

After the expected initial losses, the television industry began to show enormous profit potential as early as 1951. In that same year, by use of coaxial cable and microwave links, the East Coast and West Coast were joined by a national network service which soon reached 40 percent of all American homes. After the freeze was lifted in 1952, the FCC was flooded with applications for station licenses; this further stimulated the sales of television sets. There was no holding the medium back after this artificial slowdown, and by the mid-1960s television had almost reached total saturation in American homes. A new entertainment favorite had emerged and the motion picture industry would never be the same again!

TABLE 20
THE GROWTH OF TELEVISION, 1946–1956

DATE	FAMILIES WITH TELEVISION SETS[a] (thousands)	NO. OF COMMERCIAL TV STATIONS[b]	AVERAGE WEEKLY MOTION PICTURE ATTENDANCE[c] (millions)
1946	8	6	90
1947	14	7	90
1948	172	17	90
1949	940	50	70
1950	3,875	97	60
1951	10,320	107	54
1952	15,300	108	51
1953	20,400	125	46
1954	26,000	349	49
1955	30,700	411	46
1956	34,900	442	47

[a] Source: *Historical Statistics of the United States,* Series R.98, p. 491.
[b] Source: *Ibid.,* Series R.93, p. 491.
[c] Source: *Ibid.,* Series H.522, p. 225.

It was noted in an earlier chapter that one of the reasons the motion picture industry was so unprepared for the introduction of television was that the experience with radio had left the studios complacent. This attitude was understandable, for although radio had acquired vastly greater audiences, there had been no visible influence on attendance at the movies. Television was seen by the film industry as a form of "visual radio" and not "movies in the home"; and while this was true from a technical and regulatory point of view, operationally the medium utilized the techniques and dramatic effects of motion pictures.

There were a few farsighted individuals who were able to see that television posed a serious threat to the motion picture industry, but even as late as the mid-fifties, most industry executives were still claiming that the movies would "make a comeback." In 1946, Harry P. Warner, a well-known specialist in communications law, warned Hollywood that "television constitutes a long-range threat to the motion picture business." But even he felt that "the day-by-day television product would not compete with the grade 'A' Hollywood production."[52] Once again, the radio experience was used as the criterion, as Warner doubted "whether the interest of the television audience in the home can be maintained for an hour and a half or two hours."[53]

There were several other reasons advanced by movie executives for not taking the television threat too seriously. The immediate decline in movie attendance in those areas where television was available was attributed to the desire on the part of the new viewer to realize the full value from his expensive purchase. Many in the movie industry hoped that once the television set had been paid for, then audiences would begin to return to the movies. This rationalization was coupled with a whole series of subrationalizations related to mankind's supposed gregariousness, which would eventually lead to a desire to return to the social interaction of the movie house. Thus people would tire of "individualized" and "commercial" entertainment in the home; women who were home all day would demand to be taken out at night; and television would not be able to satisfy the basic human demand to "get out and be entertained." Finally, and perhaps the most-often-voiced of all the rationalizations, was that television could never hope to achieve the same "quality" of production as the movies. This last point was the most accurate, but unfortunately quality did not appear to make much difference to the growing television audience, who seemed prepared to watch any- and everything. By 1956, the average daily viewing time per television household in the United States was over five hours![54]

One of the very few movie industry executives who grasped the potential impact of television was Samuel Goldwyn, who in 1950 suggested that after the silent period, and the sound era, Hollywood was now about to enter the third stage of its development — the "Television Age." He further predicted that "within just a few years a great many Hollywood producers, directors, writers and actors who are still coasting on reputations built up in the past are going to wonder what hit them." Goldwyn's solution was to get rid of the "deadwood of the present . . . [and] . . . the faded glories of the past," so that once again it would "take brains instead of just money to make pictures."[55] He also accurately foresaw that full-length feature films would become staple programming fare for television screens, and that Hollywood would eventually become the prime production center for television.

What really separated Goldwyn's evaluation from those of most other movie executives was his clear insight into the intrinsic nature of television — "a form of entertainment in which all the best features of radio, the theater, and motion pictures may be combined."[56] He was also able to identify the solution — movies had to be substantially superior to anything available on the home screen to bring the public out of their homes:

A factor on our side is that people will always go out to be entertained because human beings are naturally gregarious. But before the movie-goer of the future arranges for a baby sitter, hurries through dinner, drives several miles, and has to find a place to park, just for the pleasure of stepping up to the box office to *buy* a pair of tickets, he will want to be certain that what he pays for is worth that much more than what he could be seeing at home without any inconvenience at all.[57]

Goldwyn's point about the "organization" required to get out of the house and go to a movie was a valid one. With the "baby boom" just after the war, many of the movies' best customers in the under-thirty-five group were also parents of young children. One father described what going to the movies required of his household:

There was a movie my wife and I wanted to see. Then we began to add up the price. Two tickets at 60¢ each — that's not so bad. But then there was the babysitter. Three hours at 50¢ an hour plus car fare is $1.70. Parking the car — that would be another 50¢. Figuring gas and oil would be another 50¢. Add a coke or something afterward, say another 25¢. That's over $4.00. So we stayed home.[58]

With the introduction of television, the motion picture industry now found itself in the same position that the live theater had been in at the turn of the century. Only now it was movie-going that was seen as requiring more formal preparation, whereas watching television made few, if any, social demands of its audience.

The Impact of Television: A Statistical Analysis

What was the actual effect on the motion picture industry of the introduction of television? In a remarkable examination of the economic and social impact of television on movie-going, Fredric Stuart provided precise data to substantiate the theory that the introduction of the new medium was the *principal* reason for the decline in movie audiences in the period 1948–1956.[59] Stuart began by examining and comparing the introduction of television in specific geographic areas. From this comparison he established a strong statistical correlation ($r = 0.91$) between television's introduction and the drop in movie attendance. In fact, Stuart concluded, "The evidence suggests that in the absence of television competition there might have been a substantial increase in motion picture revenues between 1948 and 1954."[60]

Before 1948, per capita expenditures on motion pictures were predictable on the basis of per capita income. After the introduction of television, however, this correlation was no longer valid. If the additional independent variable of percent of households with television sets was also considered, then the equation, once again, provided a strong correlation. Thus Stuart clearly demonstrated that density of television penetration in any region was the *major* cause of loss of motion picture revenues.[61]

As part of his analysis Stuart also examined the closing of motion picture theaters. Between 1948 and 1954, the number of movie houses operating in the United States had declined from 18,631 to 18,491. While this does not appear to be a large drop, during this same period the population increased from 146 million to 161 million. Also, this net decrease of 140 theaters was actually made up of a net decrease of 3,095 conventional indoor movie houses, and a net increase of 2,955 drive-in theaters. Stuart's statistical analysis revealed an obvious relationship between dwindling receipts and the closing of movie houses. Surprisingly, and significantly, he found that there was *little* relationship between the opening up of drive-ins and the decline of the conventional four-walled theater. The choice between drive-ins and indoor theaters depended upon other factors, principally weather and the degree of population concentration. He noted: "This [evidence] indicates that Drive-In theaters have *not* appeared as direct replacements for closed indoor theaters."[62]

One of the many interesting points raised by Stuart's work was the seasonal shift in movie attendance patterns. He calculated the quarterly seasonal indices for the two five-year periods, 1943–1948, and 1952–1957, for a comparison of the pre- and post-television patterns. The results were as follows:

TABLE 21

QUARTERLY SEASONAL INDICES FOR
MOTION PICTURE ATTENDANCE

	I WINTER	II SPRING	III SUMMER	IV FALL
Seasonal index				
1943–1948	102	95	102	101
1952–1957	99	92	107	102

Source: Fredric Stuart, "The Effects of Television on the Motion Picture and Radio Industries," p. 45.

Quarterly variation in attendance had become much more pronounced, and Stuart concluded that these data supported his hypothesis that television was the major cause of changes in motion picture attendance. These seasonal shifts were significant because the movies' largest increase came in the summer quarter, when television viewing was at its weakest, while television had in turn kept audiences at home during the colder months.[63] The increase in summer attendance was, of course, also a reflection of the growing importance of the drive-in movie theater as a permanent fixture on the American landscape.

The Drive-In Theater

The introduction of the open-air drive-in theater was a significant post-war phenomenon, which was by far the most promising development for the movie industry during this difficult period. Numbering only 100 at the end of the war, by 1956 there were more than 5,000 operating drive-ins in the United States. The drive-in was the invention of Richard M. Hollingshead, Jr., who began in 1933 by combining the two luxuries which he felt that people in a depression would give up last — automobiles and movies.[64]

Hollingshead had once held a patent on the ramp idea used at drive-ins, but after a series of court battles it was finally ruled that ramps were just landscape architecture and not patentable. After this court decision there was a dramatic increase in drive-in construction all over the United States and Canada. By 1951, the drive-in represented 15 percent of the total number of movie houses, but, more important, they accounted for nearly 20 percent of total theater receipts.

In the early years, when the industry could afford to be more selective, outdoor theater operators had great difficulty in renting anything more than old "A" films, "B's" and Westerns. However, in the early fifties when the importance of drive-ins became obvious, and after the *Paramount* decree forbade such practices, the better first-run features began to find their way into drive-in exhibition. Still, many studios were reluctant to rent their top features for first-runs at these "ozone theaters."

The drive-in represented an attempt to simplify those problems which young couples with families encountered by providing an opportunity for the whole family to go out together, with a minimum of fuss and formality. But they also attracted other groups — "young people with aged parents, people with dogs they won't leave at home, teen-agers, and college kids." Owners of these theaters cooperated with family clientele by offering free admission for children, entertainment parks, and even free laundry service for harried housewives who wanted a night out at the movies but were reluctant to leave their housework. In the early days before in-car heaters allowed year-round attendance in the colder regions, some operators offered a free gallon of gasoline so that patrons could keep their engines idling![65]

During its formative stage the drive-in theater had quite justifiably acquired the reputation as a "passion-pit," where young couples could steal a few private moments in the darkened confines of an automobile. It was for this reason that the Province of Quebec banned the construction of outdoor theaters until sometime in the sixties, but Quebec was not alone in its objections. In the early years of their growth, drive-in theaters faced a variety of problems such as municipal zoning regulations, charges of being traffic hazards, and convictions under antinoise bylaws. However, their biggest difficult by far was gaining acceptance and recognition by the motion picture industry itself. Once this was achieved, the drive-in became an important weapon in the industry's vain attempt to regain its former glories.

The Industry Fights Back

The years between 1948 and 1957 were possibly the most important years in the history of the motion picture industry, for it was during this period that the full impact of television was felt, and in the end it was the movies which had to make the adjustment to the acknowledged supremacy of the newer medium. While Hollywood tried many different approaches to entice audiences back into theaters, this was not the most important issue in the battle between the movies and television. The large audiences of the previous thirty years were gone forever; there was nothing that the movie industry could do to bring them back. However, television was permanent and all-pervasive; the issue was how best to integrate the existing framework of film production into the emerging superstructure of television production. Thus, while the public's attention was kept focused on the new technical innovations which the movie industry introduced from time to time, Hollywood was busy behind the scenes transforming itself from a film town into the major television production center. This was, of course, a totally natural transition, but it took a long time for many movie industry executives to accept the necessity of this move. Many have not yet accepted it.

By 1949, the industry was beginning to feel the economic effects of the introduction of television, in combination with the other social reasons which had led to the decline of audiences. In that year only 370 stars were under regular contract to studios, compared with over 750 in 1946. Writers under contract had fallen from 600 in 1946 to below 450. While the big-name performers still received enormous salaries, studios could no longer afford to carry a large stable of contract artists or writers.[66] Even at this early stage, it was quite obvious to many in the industry that salvation for Hollywood lay in cooperation and integration with the television industry, and not in futile, and financially dangerous, all-out competition.

One method of bringing about an amalgamation of movies and television which was widely discussed in the early fifties was the development

353

of a viable form of "theater television." This would have involved offering special features to patrons in color on large screens; thus a technically superior product, surrounded by the atmosphere of the theater and accompanied by "regular" motion pictures. While several such experiments were tried, there was little evidence of long-range economic viability. At one point the movie industry even discussed with the FCC the possibility of reserving certain television frequencies for future exclusive use by theaters.[67] In the long run the only programs which seemed to successfully lend themselves to this form of exhibition were sporting events, especially prizefights; but even such minor triumphs were enough to encourage movie executives to seriously consider large-scale use of theater television.

It was also obvious that the closing of a vast number of smaller movie houses did not really concern the studios, because traditionally 65 to 70 percent of the film rental income came from about 20 percent of the movie houses — from the large downtown theaters in the big cities. The growth of drive-ins more than made up for the rental loss from the smaller suburban theaters. Of the existing older theaters, many were in the run-down sections of cities, and marginal even at the best of times, so Hollywood was not sorry to see them go. Many producers suggested the elimination of all but the modern, well-run houses, where "the new, better movies could be appreciated in worthy surroundings."[68]

In the rush to cut costs, Hollywood studios drastically reduced the number of their productions, with the "B" film — the old second-feature staple — almost entirely eliminated. Particularly hard hit were those studios such as Republic and Monogram, which specialized in producing such films. It was therefore only natural that these hard-pressed studios would open their film vaults to feed the voracious appetite of television programming. However, the members of the MPAA (except Republic) continued to fight the sale of their films to television on the theory that the two media were directly competitive, and if TV wanted the best talent and stories, it could go into the marketplace and bid for them. In the long run such an attitude was counterproductive, and it was inevitable that sooner or later the studios would be forced to sell their libraries to television. In the meantime some studios began to set up separate television production units, which were kept carefully segregated from the movie production facilities. Some studios even contractually forbade their stars to appear on television.

Eventually, antitrust action again forced the studios to make their products available for television use, and the sale or lease of pre-1949 features was a primary source of income for distributors and producers. By 1958, an estimated 3,700 feature films had been sold or leased for television for an estimated $220 million.[69] The use of motion pictures on television proved to be an unexpected boom for many small distributors who held the rights to long-forgotten movies. One aging cowboy star — Hopalong Cassidy (William Boyd was his real name) — had wisely secured the television rights to sixty-six of his old films, and this made him a millionaire overnight. Other cowboy stars such as Roy Rogers and Gene Autry also successfully made the jump from "B" films to television stardom.

Whether it can be attributed to "novelty effect" is difficult to say, but in the period 1948–1952, the American public was obviously more content to stay home and watch old movies for free, than pay to see newer ones. This fact surprised the television industry as much as it did Hollywood.

Once the studios realized that there was money to be made by releasing older films for television distribution, there was a sudden flood of these on the home screen. A special report prepared by Sindlinger and Company for the Theater Owners of America indicated how important old movies were to television stations. The report noted that in the last quarter of 1957, old movies constituted almost one-quarter of the total television viewing time.[70] It was also no coincidence that 1957 was a year in which the movie audience declined quite sharply.

By 1957, Hollywood had already become a "TV town," and *Time* noted that "a single Hollywood TV show, NBC's daily *Matinee Theater,* hires 2,400 actors a year for speaking parts — 50% more than the players used by Warner and Paramount combined in all their 1956 movies. The show uses as many scripts — 250 a year — as all the studios put together."[71] Television was now by far the biggest money-maker and earner for the Hollywood community, with production companies such as Desilu turning out more footage than the combined output of the five major studios.

The pecking order in the community itself was being gradually altered to take into account the newfound status of television stars, but not without some reluctance on the part of the old guard. Social arbiter Mike Romanoff, the owner of one of Hollywood's most famous and prestigious restaurants, scoffed at the "dirty shirt" school which was becoming prevalent in Hollywood in the mid-fifties, and said: "The TV actors can afford to eat here, but they haven't progressed beyond the drugstore counter. They think differently, behave differently, live differently. The dirty shirt is a form of snobbery."[72] From all reports the television crowd in Hollywood took themselves too seriously — "too many men in empty grey flannel suits and expressions" — but what they lacked in glamour they made up in the youth and vitality they brought to the dying film capital, and this attitude was somewhat reminiscent of the early days of Hollywood. Where the old-time film director sported jodhpurs and riding crop, this new breed sported blue jeans and sneakers; but they got impressive results working to production schedules which would have terrified veteran movie makers. Eventually many of these younger men, who received their starts in television, would be at the forefront of the creative renaissance in the American film industry.

There were other indications of the movie industry's acceptance of the power of television with the increasing use of the home medium to advertise new feature films at local theaters, and the trend in the mid-fifties to turn TV plays into movies, using the TV shows as publicity buildups. Some of these were very successful, including Academy Award–winners *Marty* (1954), and *On the Waterfront* (1954), while popular programs such as *Dragnet* (1954) also made a successful transition to the motion picture screen. The success of these films, and others, indicated that the public would still pay for superior entertainment if it was available only in the movie theater. With the closing of many small-profit theaters, and the cutback in production, Hollywood now very deliberately began to turn its attention to providing entertainment which could not be found on the home screen.

Epics, Wide-Screen and 3-D

In order to present the public with a form of entertainment which would drag them away from their TV sets, the motion picture industry invested a great deal of money and effort in technological innovation designed to improve the visual and auditory (and even the olfactory) quality of realism associated with the movies. In many ways this could be seen as the logical extension of the move toward "realism" which had originally helped spawn the motion picture at the turn of the century. Only now the motion picture was being asked to provide an "experience" which was superior to that available, at no cost, in the privacy and comfort of the home.

Many film historians have pointed out that there was nothing new about the use of wide screens or three-dimensional movies; in 1900, 20,000 to 25,000 people at a time were able to view Lumiere's giant 70-by-53-foot screen in Paris;[73] and William Friese-Green had patented a three-dimensional movie process before 1900.[74] Nevertheless, such processes had always remained in the novelty category until, in a desperate bid to provide something different in answer to the television threat, Hollywood rediscovered them, gave them new names, and risked a great deal of money in promoting them to a curious public.

It was, in fact, two groups of independent producers who gave Hollywood the idea of making the movie screen look different from the television screen. In September, 1952, the newscaster Lowell Thomas, his friend Merian C. Cooper, a Hollywood veteran who had made the immortal *King Kong,* and the inventor of the process, Fred Waller, presented *This Is Cinerama* to astonished New York audiences.[75] The showing at the Broadway Theater was an enormous success as audiences screamed in masochistic delight as they were sent plunging down a Coney Island roller coaster, or flying through the Grand Canyon. The critics were almost unanimous in their praise for the new process that used three projectors and a curved screen, which in the original New York engagement was twenty-five feet high and fifty-one feet wide. Stereophonic sound was an additional refinement which greatly enhanced the illusion of depth. Cinerama gave the viewer the feeling of actually being involved "inside" the screen image, rather than being just an observer of a flat screen.

The technical requirements for Cinerama were such that few theaters could be converted to show these films. The result was that Cinerama spawned a whole new concept of marketing Hollywood motion pictures, which saw the invention of the "road show" movie designed to run in the larger urban centers for long periods of time, sometimes exceeding a year or more. (*This Is Cinerama* had a remarkable run of 122 weeks in New York, played to 2,471,538 people, and took in $4,707,688 at the box office. It subsequently played in eleven other cities in the United States, and five major cities abroad. On February 7, 1955, a new show replaced it for another series of long runs — *Cinerama Holiday.*)[76] While the Cinerama process still had quite annoying technical problems, such as obvious lines where the three images joined, the enthusiasm of the crowds convinced the motion picture industry that such innovations could lure patrons back into movie houses. Whatever the technical difficulties, and the eventual content deficiencies of future Cinerama productions (almost no dramatic productions have been made using the full process), the importance of this innovation should not be overlooked.[77]

While Cinerama was the first, and technically the most "realistic," of the wide-screen processes, the most widely used and promoted was Twentieth Century–Fox's Cinemascope. This utilized an anamorphic lens which spread out the image to give it more width than the ordinary motion picture image ratio of 1.33:1. The new ratio was now 2.55:1 (eventually settling down at 2.35:1), almost doubling the width of the screen, and with a slight curve it appeared as a smaller version of the Cinerama process. The important difference, however, was that conversion to accommodate the Cinemascope screen was less costly and therefore more acceptable to operators of movie theaters. After the initial success of the first Cinemascope production, *The Robe* in 1953, by the middle of 1954 production plans had been announced for seventy-five films using the new process. Fox had leased the process to other major studios, and by the middle of 1955, over twenty thousand theaters throughout the world could show Cinemascope films.

Several wide-screen anamorphic processes, such as Warnerscope, Vista-rama, Superscope, Naturama and others, were tried and eventually dis-carded in favor of the Fox system. Other wide-screen techniques involving larger film stock than the standard 35 mm met with more success. The first of these was Todd-AO, which used 65 mm film; the second was Paramount Studios' VistaVision, which ran the film through the camera sideways to produce the "golden ratio" of 1.85:1. Technically VistaVision was the best of all the wide-screen processes, winning an Academy Award for its developers in 1956.[78]

Perhaps the most publicity sensitive, and at the same time the most insignificant technical innovation, was the use of three-dimensional or stereoscopic optical techniques to make "3-D" motion pictures for theatri-cal presentation.[79] This process had, in fact, already had a long and un-successful history as a movie "gimmick." However, the success of Cinerama prompted a new look at the possibilities of the stereoscopic phenomenon. In the late 1940s a young man named Milton Gunzberg obtained the rights to a three-dimensional process which he called Natural Vision.[80] In order for the viewer to actually see the film on the screen in three dimensions, he had to use special Polaroid glasses. Gunzberg had some difficulty in selling his patented process to the large studios, but eventually an absolutely dreadful film, *Bwana Devil,* was released in "3-D" in late 1952. To everyone's surprise, including Gunzberg, the film broke box-office records all over the country although it had virtually nothing to offer but the illusion of depth. The public was annoyed at having to wear the special glasses, and yet they were still willing to leave the comfort of their homes to sit and stare at lions jumping out of the screen, or spears flying over their heads.

Immediately after this unexpected development, almost all the major studios announced their intention to make some films in 3-D, and in the next three years the movie-going public was periodically treated to such films as *The Charge at Feather River* (which symbolically saw a character spit into the patron's face), *Hondo,* and the best of all, *House of Wax.* Alfred Hitchcock shot one of his best thrillers, *Dial M for Murder,* in 3-D, but eventually decided to release it in a "flat" version. However, by 1955, it was quite obvious that this was not the permanent answer to the movie industry's difficulties, and the added success of the various wide-screen processes meant the death of 3-D. The really important point about all of these technical innovations or "gimmicks" was that Hollywood was revitalized for a short period between 1953 and 1956, as the increased publicity activity succeeded in attracting more people into movie thea-ters.[81] While there were many who were optimistic about the movies' future, others in the industry were more skeptical, and there is no evi-dence that any movie executive ever saw a permanent place for 3-D in feature films. Actress Gloria Swanson said bluntly: "Three-D will be a flash in the pan. . . . The only real future for films is in developing some kind of box to collect money for movies on TV." Producer Jerry Wald was more realistic: "I'm enthusiastic about anything that calls attention to Hollywood — 3-D, three colors, two legs or Marilyn Monroe."[82] London movie critic Dilys Powell had perhaps the best comment about the use of three-dimensional techniques: "If I must be placed in the position of a firing-squad victim . . . I want my eyes bandaged."[83]

No examination of the technical innovations used to combat television would be complete without mention of the two films which utilized smells to increase the audience's sense of realism. The film *Behind the Great Wall* opened in New York in December, 1959, and featured a process called AromaRama which released heavy oriental smells to coincide with scenes on the screen. By all accounts the film itself was an excellent documentary, but the scent-yielding process was considered to be "a good commercial one-shot gimmick."[84] Another film, *Scent of Mystery*, used the Smell-O-Vision process which pumped odors to each individual patron by means of a small tube on the back of the seat. Again the film was fairly well accepted, and the smells formed an essential plot element, but the process was considered to be nothing more than a passing novelty.

Besides wide-screen, three-dimensional projection and "smellies," Hollywood developed another plan of attack in the battle with television. Ever since the earliest days of the motion picture industry certain films had been designated "blockbusters" — movies which were singled out because of their production cost, their length, or even their theme, and subjected to special promotional treatment. In the thirties, and forties, with a guaranteed audience of avid movie goers willing to consume most of the studios' output, the production of such films and their costly promotional campaigns had fallen out of favor. One notable exception was the incomparable promotion of David O. Selznick's *Gone With the Wind* in 1939, and this film went on to become one of the greatest money-makers of all time.[85] Only producer-director Cecil B. De Mille was able to continuously turn out such "epic" films. Now, given the opportunity to work with a much larger screen, Hollywood began to turn out these special films with monotonous regularity. De Mille himself started the postwar trend with *Samson and Delilah* (1949), which was still shot in the regular 35 mm format, but all during the fifties studios invested vast sums of money in these spectaculars. After the success of *The Robe* biblical epics were very much in vogue, culminating in the $15 million remake of *Ben Hur* by MGM in 1959. This cycle of "toga epics" came to a sudden end with the fiasco surrounding the failure of Twentieth Century–Fox's *Cleopatra* in the early sixties. This film was reported to have cost more than $40 million, and almost totally wrecked the studio.[86] Nevertheless, forced into

providing an obvious alternative to television, the motion picture industry has had to resort to these "road shows" to attract audiences. Sometimes this ploy succeeded, often it failed. But in spite of the inroads made
by television in the fifties, at the end of the decade the motion picture
industry still survived, although it was a different industry from that of
the halcyon days of the thirties and forties, and it would have to change
even more if it was going to survive into the seventies.

NOTES TO CHAPTER XIII

1. James T. Farrell, "The Language of Hollywood," *Saturday Review of Literature,*
August 5, 1944, p. 29.

2. *Ibid.*, p. 30.

3. *Ibid.*, p. 31.

4. Farrell noted: "This entire structure can be metaphorically described as a gran-
diose Luna Park of capitalism. And if the serious artist enters it, he well may quote
these words from Dante: 'All hope abandon, ye who enter here' " (p. 32).

5. Philip Dunne, "The Documentary and Hollywood," *Hollywood Quarterly,* vol. 1
(1946), p. 166.

6. *Ibid.*, p. 171.

7. Kenneth MacGowan, "A Change of Pattern," *Hollywood Quarterly,* vol. 1 (1946),
pp. 148–153.

8. For a detailed examination of films in this period see Charles Higham and Joel
Greenberg, *Hollywood in the Forties* (New York: A. S. Barnes and Co., 1968). A refresh-
ing "revisionist" viewpoint is offered in Mark Bergman, "Hollywood in the Forties
Revisited," *Velvet Light Trap,* no. 5 (Summer, 1972), pp. 2–5.

9. Gilbert Seldes, astute as ever, understood this fact, and he called for a closer examination of such entertainment "propaganda" in the mass media. This would make
the public aware of "the prejudices which dominate radio and the movies," and under-
score the fact that entertainment was not "pure." Gilbert Seldes, "Law, Pressure and
Public Opinion," *Hollywood Quarterly,* vol. 1 (1946), p. 426.

10. "Are Movies the Opium of the People?," *Christian Century,* no. 64 (January 8,
1947), p. 36.

11. Iris Barry, "Why Wait for Posterity?," *Hollywood Quarterly,* vol. 1 (1946), p. 136.

12. Clara Beranger, "The Cinema is Ready for College," *Theater Arts,* vol. 31, no. 1
(January, 1947), pp. 61–63.

13. Charles Palmer, "Miracles Come C.O.D.," *Hollywood Quarterly,* vol. 2 (1948), p.
387.

14. Edgar Dale, "On Miracles Come C.O.D.," *Hollywood Quarterly,* vol. 3 (1948), p. 84.

15. Charles Palmer, "Reply to a Critic," *Hollywood Quarterly,* vol. 3 (1948), p. 87.

16. Sondra Gorney, "On Children's Cinema: America and Britain," *Hollywood Quarterly,* vol. 3 (1948), p. 57.

17. Miss Gorney noted that in Connecticut a bill was introduced which would have
created a special board to approve movies for children under the age of fourteen, while
Maryland introduced a bill especially to approve Saturday matinee films (p. 58).

18. Irving Pichel, "Areas of Silence," *Hollywood Quarterly,* vol. 3 (1948), p. 51.

19. *Ibid.*, pp. 52–53.

20. Lewis, *Motion Picture Industry,* p. 83.

21. Ernest Borneman, "The Public Opinion Myth," *Harper's,* vol. 195 (May, 1945), p. 33. This is an extremely useful examination of a "state of mind" in the motion picture industry in the immediate postwar period.

22. *Ibid.*, p. 40.

23. *Ibid.*, p. 31.

24. Bosley Crowther, "It's the Fans Who Make the Films," *New York Times Magazine,* June 24, 1945, p. 29.

25. Leo A. Handel, "Hollywood Market Research," *Quarterly of Film, Radio and Television,* vol. 7 (1953), p. 304. Other useful articles which discuss the nature of motion picture market research are: Marjorie Fiske and Leo A. Handel, "Motion Picture Research: Content and Audience Analysis," *Journal of Marketing,* vol. 11, no. 2 (October, 1946), pp. 129–134; "Motion Picture Research: Response Analysis," in *ibid.*, vol. 11, no. 3 (January, 1947), pp. 273–280; "New Techniques for Studying the Effectiveness of Films," in *ibid.*, vol. 11, no. 4 (April, 1947), pp. 390–393. The final product of Handel's written work was *Hollywood Looks At Its Audience* (Urbana: University of Illinois Press, 1950).

26. Handel, "Hollywood Market Research," p. 305.

27. *Ibid.*, p. 309.

28. *Ibid.*, p. 308. For one of the most detailed examinations of the motion picture audience see Paul F. Lazarsfeld, "Audience Research in the Movie Field," *Annals of the American Academy of Political and Social Science,* vol. 254 (November, 1947), pp. 160–168.

29. Handel, *Hollywood Looks At Its Audience,* p. 98. Handel quotes from a 20th Century Fund study conducted in 1948, which "indicated an enlargement of the domestic market for films because of the growth of population, continued reduction of the work week, wider distribution of national income, and changes in the spending pattern of the average family, with a greater proportion of expenditures going into recreation." Motion pictures were considered to be one of the "insensitive industries."

30. *Ibid.*, p. 308. For details of this MPAA committee see Chambers, "Need For Statistical Research."

31. John Elliot Williams, "They Stopped at Nothing," *Hollywood Quarterly,* vol. 1 (1946), p. 270.

32. Jay E. Gordon, "There's Really No Business Like Show Business," *Quarterly of Film, Radio and Television,* vol. 6 (1951), p. 181.

33. *Ibid.*, p. 183.

34. Of the 411, 32 represented the industry trade press; 13 covered the wire services; 66 worked for magazines (23 for "fan" magazines); 82 were classed as foreign correspondents; and 49 were photographers. The remainder were those who wrote occasional articles or books on the movies. "Hollywood's Press: Why the Stars Are in Your Eyes," *Newsweek,* no. 43 (February 22, 1954), p. 62.

35. For details of the famous feud between Louella Parsons and her arch rival Hedda Hopper, see George Eells, *Hedda and Louella* (New York: G. P. Putman's Sons, 1972).

36. Quoted in Thomas A. Brady, "This Is Where the Money Went," *New Republic,* January 31, 1949, p. 12.

37. Kenneth MacGowan, "And So Into the Sunset . . ." *New Republic,* January 31, 1949, p. 23.

38. Gilbert Seldes, *The Great Audience* (New York: Viking Press, 1950), p. 13.

39. *Ibid.*, pp. 9–10.

40. Lazarsfeld, "Audience Research," pp. 162–163.

41. "The Fortune Survey," *Fortune*, vol. 39, no. 3 (March, 1949), pp. 39–40.

42. For more details of the increasing cost of production see Brady, pp. 12–15.

43. Paul Jarrico, "They Are Not So Innocent Abroad," *New Republic*, January 31, 1949, pp. 17–19. This particular issue of the *New Republic* contains a wealth of information on the current state of the film industry.

44. The "divorcement issue" was extremely complex, and has been subject to varying interpretations. The best discussions are found in Conant, pp. 107–153, and Higham, *Hollywood at Sunset*, 18–32.

45. Higham, *Hollywood at Sunset*, p. 31.

46. "Panic in Paradise," *Time*, no. 50 (September 22, 1947), p. 97.

47. Simon N. Whitney, "The Impact of Anti-Trust Laws: Vertical Disintegration in the Motion Picture Industry," *American Economic Review*, May, 1955, p. 492.

48. *Ibid.*, p. 495.

49. For an embittered attack on the decree see Irving Bernstein, "Hollywood at the Crossroads: An Economic Study of the Motion Picture Industry," study prepared for the Hollywood A.F.L. Film Council, December, 1957.

50. For more information on the motion picture industry's absorption into conglomerates see Domenico Meccoli, "Conglomerates Gobble Up Movies," *Successo*, vol. 12 (March, 1970), pp. 90–95.

51. A sound introduction to this topic is Sydney W. Head, *Broadcasting in America* (Boston: Houghton Mifflin Company, 1972), p. 194.

52. Harry P. Warner, "Television and the Motion Picture Industry," *Hollywood Quarterly*, vol. 2 (1946), p. 16.

53. *Ibid.*, p. 14.

54. Fredric Stuart, *The Effects of Television on the Motion Picture and Radio Industries* (New York: Arno Press, 1975), p. 6.

55. Samuel Goldwyn, "Hollywood in the Television Age," *Hollywood Quarterly*, vol. 4 (1950), p. 145.

56. *Ibid.*, p. 146.

57. *Ibid.*, p. 147.

58. Robert Coughlan, "Now It Is Trouble that Is Supercolossal in Hollywood," *Life*, vol. 31 (August 13, 1951), p. 102. This is an excellent examination of the topic.

59. Stuart, *The Effects of Television*.

60. *Ibid.*, p. 28.

61. *Ibid.*, p. 31. The 1948 relationship between per capita motion picture receipts and per capita personal income indicated a correlation coefficient of 0.77. The interference of television with this relationship was evident with the decline of this coefficient to 0.38, when the same two-variable analysis was applied to 1954 data. When percent of households with television sets was added in a multiple correlation, the correlation coefficient was brought up to the 1948 level (0.78).

62. Stuart, p. 37. The coefficient of partial correlation between the net changes in both theater types by state was 0.14 when the influence of population was removed.

63. Stuart had not included drive-in attendance in his data, taken from *Variety* magazine. This tended to accentuate the change in seasonal attendance brought about just by television. Stuart, p. 47.

64. For details on early drive-ins see *Time*, no. 38 (July 14, 1941), p. 66.

65. Frank J. Taylor, "Big Boom in Outdoor Movies," *Saturday Evening Post*, vol. 229 (September 15, 1956), p. 101. This article contains very useful information on the various services which were being offered by drive-ins during the fifties.

66. These statistics are taken from "Television: Movies' Friend or Foe?," *U.S. News and World Report,* no. 26 (January 7, 1949), p. 24.

67. For further details on the early attempts to counter the threat of television see Rodney Luther, "Television and the Future of Motion Picture Exhibition," *Quarterly of Film, Radio and Television,* vol. 5 (1951), pp. 164–177. Another useful three-part series is Milton MacKaye, "The Big Brawl: Hollywood vs. Television," in *Saturday Evening Post,* vol. 224 (January 19, pp. 17–19; January 26, p. 30; February 2, 1952, p. 30).

68. Coughlan, p. 108.

69. *Wall Street Journal,* February 10, 1958, p. 3.

70. *New York Times,* January 27, 1958, pp. 1, 23.

71. "The New Hollywood," *Time,* no. 69 (May 13, 1957), p. 43.

72. *Ibid.,* p. 44.

73. Kenneth MacGowan, "The Screen's New Look — Wider and Deeper," *Film Quarterly,* vol. 11 (1956), p. 109.

74. Limbacher, *Four Faces of the Film,* p. 104.

75. For more details on the Cinerama process see Limbacher, pp. 91–134; and Higham, *Hollywood at Sunset,* pp. 90–103.

76. MacGowan, "Screen's New Look," p. 111.

77. Film historian James L. Limbacher, in his detailed history of technical developments in the movies, has noted: "Whatever Cinerama's future might be, its past cannot be overlooked. It was Cinerama which started the widescreen revolution and re-interested the public in going to the movies again. It made stereophonic sound something which captured the public's fancy. It caused groups of people to drive as far as 300 miles to see Cinerama. It caused a boom in the tourist business, especially the places where Cinerama had filmed its productions" (p. 98).

78. The permanent move to wide-screen created problems for television projection which still plagues viewers, because the shape of the television screen is quite different from those of the various wide-screen processes.

79. For details on 3-D see Limbacher, pp. 139–192.

80. The story of Gunzberg is dramatically retold in Higham, *Hollywood at Sunset,* pp. 82–89.

81. One enthusiastic screenwriter noted: "Hollywood is hopeful again. After four years of indecisive competition with television . . . the industry has emerged with new courage and confidence . . ." Richard C. Hawkins, "Perspective on 3-D," *Quarterly of Film, Radio and Television,* vol. 7 (1952), p. 325.

82. "Flash in the Pan?," *Time,* no. 61 (March 2, 1953), p. 90.

83. "The New Industry," *Time,* no. 61 (May 4, 1953), p. 102.

84. *Variety,* vol. 217 (December 16, 1959), p. 6.

85. For details on the fascinating story behind this film see Gavin Lambert, *The Making of "Gone With the Wind"* (Boston: Atlantic–Little, Brown, 1973).

86. For more details on the problems of making this film see Walter Wanger and Joe Hyams, *My Life with Cleopatra* (New York: Bantam Books, 1963). The authors aptly describe how a pampered star and lax studio control can combine to cause such immense economic chaos.

XIV

The Meaning of Hollywood

THE MOTION PICTURE INDUSTRY EMERGED from the war with a renewed sense of self-importance, and found itself in the rather unusual position of actually having surplus funds at its disposal. This happy financial situation proved to be short-lived, however, and by the early fifties, profits had dropped to one-quarter of their 1947 high.[1] The problems which beset the industry had a definite effect on the development of the content of Hollywood-produced films, as the availability of funds (and audience) dictated the amount of leeway studios were willing to allow their writers and directors to indulge in experimentation. As long as the studio system was the foundation of the American film industry, this experimentation was kept to a minimum.

The economic crunch caused by the rising costs of wages and production, and the decline in audience, had increased the number of independent producers in Hollywood. Men like Samuel Goldwyn and David Selznick, and the group called United Artists, had always functioned by producing one film at a time; preparing the entire package, from purchase of story through final editing. Such independent producers were, however, still reliant upon the large studios for wide distribution of their final product.

The major studios reluctantly began to cooperate with the independents after the war, seeing this as one way of softening the inevitable blow of antitrust action. At the same time, the studios were being drained of their top talents, as writers, actors, producers and directors all indicated a desire to become "independents." Because of their need to utilize extensive studio facilities to produce their films, it was only natural that the independent producing companies would eventually become affiliated with the majors. Thus, Paramount housed the companies of Hal B. Wallis, Cecil B. De Mille and Buddy DeSylva, making all its technical facilities

364

and stars available, and distributing the final film through its vast network of theaters, but collecting only 50 percent of the profits.[2] The independent producers were of increasing importance, for they brought a certain vitality to Hollywood, setting the pattern for the future structure of the American film industry.

The Content of Films, 1946–1960

It is impossible to specifically label a "forties" or a "fifties" film, for during the period of the decline of Hollywood as a movie production center, the content and quality of motion pictures varied greatly as the studios relinquished more and more control. Nevertheless, certain trends do become obvious, and these were as much a function of the necessity to attract a greater audience as an indication of the desire to explore new themes. Critics disagree about the quality of the postwar movies, but there is little doubt that, thematically, the fifteen-year period after the war witnessed important new directions in the American motion picture.[3] While the concept of "Hollywood" still dominated the movie industry, the studio system was disintegrating, and together with it, the *Production Code* and the reliance upon the old box-office "formulae." This presented an ideal opportunity for the more adventurous film makers to use the medium to explore new ideas and current problems on the American scene. As we saw in the last chapter, the "promise of the movies" was not always kept, but despite the necessity to fight the inroads of television with even more blatant commercialism, the American motion picture indicated a definite move toward maturity during these years.

It was already evident by the end of the war that Hollywood was fascinated by psychiatry and psychology. During the war years, films such as *The Lodger* (1943), *Hangover Square* (1944), *Love Letters* (1944), and Hitchcock's *Spellbound* (1944) had explored the "psychology" of their principal characters. Hitchcock's film in particular attempted to explore the subconscious mind of his hero (Gregory Peck), including a dream sequence conceived by Salvador Dali, and was loaded with Freudian symbolism. Franklin Fearing, the noted psychologist, examined this trend and suggested that depiction of the techniques and theories of psychiatry, without a clear description of the backgrounds of the "patients," could lead to a simplistic and overoptimistic view on the part of the audience.[4] Psychoanalyst Lawrence S. Kubie, writing in *Hollywood Quarterly,* also attacked the portrayal of psychiatrists in movies, and used the opportunity to suggest that the film industry establish a "permanent endowment" to study the use of films in psychiatric work. This research foundation would also examine the impact of films on the population as a whole, and "this could not fail to help the film industry . . . achieve maturity and to realize its extraordinary, undeveloped potentialities . . . [and] . . . it would open up vast new empires of expanding markets and save large sums of money annually lost on unsuccessful films."[5] Hollywood, as usual, ignored both these suggestions.

In the period 1946–1950, a series of "message" films were produced in Hollywood, largely as a continuation of the type of thematic exploration begun during the Depression, and perfected during the war. Thus movies like *The Best Years of Our Lives* (1946), *Boomerang* (1947), *Crossfire* (1947), *Gentleman's Agreement* (1948), *Pinky* (1949), and *Knock on Any Door* (1949) explored the darker side of American life — unemployment, corruption, anti-Semitism, racial prejudice and crime. Dr. Siegfried Kracauer, the author of a major psychological history of the German film, examined some of these message films, and concluded that they were a direct result of the "dreams of American democracy" which had arisen out of the nightmare of the war. Thus, "all of the films in question confronted the hopes of the war years with the reality of the postwar. All of them went as far as Hollywood could go in encouraging these same hopes."[6] And yet, Kracauer noted, each of these films also indicated that liberal thought was receding rather than advancing. They tended to be verbose in explanation, but short on real solutions to the problems they examined. The unfavorable political climate caused by the increasing anti-Communist crusade was already beginning to show its influence, and he continued, "On the domestic scene, chill expediency threatens to stifle public concern with any issues beyond the merely practical. The whole climate is unfavorable to searching minds, and so the search subsides."[7]

Hollywood's message films were but a small segment of the total and the studios continued to turn out the usual numbers of comedies, mysteries, musicals and Westerns. Musicals, in particular, emerged into their second "golden age" in the late 1940s and 1950s, with MGM producing a series of memorable contributions to the genre — *The Pirate* (1947), *Easter Parade* (1948), *On the Town* (1949), *An American in Paris* (1951), *Bandwagon* (1953), and *Singin' in the Rain* (1952). After *Seven Brides for Seven Brothers* (1954) the original movie musical almost disappeared to be replaced by films of proven stage musical successes like *Oklahoma* (1955), *The King and I* (1956), and *Guys and Dolls* (1955).[8]

Westerns declined in quantity with the demise of the "B" film production, but this resulted in an improvement in quality. *High Noon* (1952) gave the "psychological" Western a new popularity, and an Academy Award for its star Gary Cooper. But earlier Westerns such as *Duel in the Sun* (1945) and *The Gunfighter* (1950) had already begun this genre. William K. Everson and George Fenin in their history of the Western note of postwar Westerns that

. . . three new elements made their bow in the genre as a result of the postwar gloom and "psychology" that settled on American films. They were, in order of their appearance, sex, neuroses, and a racial conscience. All had been *used* as plot elements in Westerns before, but they had never succeeded in establishing themselves as *integral* parts of the simple and uncomplicated Western tradition. At first the three new elements went their separate ways, but it was not long before they came together to produce an entirely new kind of Western.[9]

The whole genre of films, now called *film noir,* which came, somewhat surprisingly, out of the American studio system in the early forties, gave promise of a break with the confining formula which had hindered the creative development of the motion picture since the introduction of the *Production Code.* Orson Welles's *Citizen Kane* (1941) and John Huston's *The Maltese Falcon* (1941) had demonstrated what American films could accomplish if given the opportunity.[10] Immediately after the war, a series of films such as *The Killers* (1946), *Criss Cross* (1949), *Cry of the City* (1949), *Nightmare Alley* (1947) and many others continued this tradition, but by 1948, the political pressures on Hollywood forced the industry to become more cautious about what themes it allowed its directors to explore. Still, in the late forties, film audiences were treated to films which looked at politics *(All the King's Men* — 1948), the medical treatment of insanity *(The Snake Pit* — 1948) and alcoholism *(The Lost Weekend* — 1945). The growing Communist menace was also explored in such films as *The Iron Curtain* (1948), *The Red Menace* (1949), and *The Red Danube* (1949).

The movies at long last began to explore the plight of the black man in America, but here the approach was more cautious and somewhat restrained. Much of the motion picture industry's thinking on producing films on this topic had been conditioned by a fear of the "southern box office," but in reality, in 1947 the southern belt contributed only 8 percent of gross film profits. (New York State alone contributed 14 percent.)[11] In fact, anti-Negro prejudice was universal throughout the United States, and most white Americans did not associate the racial conflicts which had underscored the war against Hitler with similar problems on the home front. Thus it took several years before the movies could consider race relations a suitable topic for film audiences and even then movie themes were ahead of domestic practices. Stanley Kramer's *Home of the Brave* (1949), directed by Mark Robson, started the cycle, and was followed by *Intruder in the Dust* (1949), and Louis de Rochemont's *Lost Boundaries* (1949), which was based on a true incident of a black doctor who had "passed" for white in New Hampshire. Elia Kazan also brought *Pinky* to the screen in 1949, and this became the subject of an important censorship legal battle (see Chapter XV). The examinations of the plight of the black man continued with even more explicitness and courage well into the fifties and sixties.[12]

It was, however, the influence of the 1947–1951 Hearings of the House Un-American Activities Committee which had the greatest effect on the development of the "problem" film. John Cogley, after an extensive examination of the influence of the hearings, suggested that Hollywood producers deliberately made unprofitable anti-Communist films to appease the committee. Even though this genre had attracted few patrons in its 1948–1949 cycle, the committee's 1951 hearings brought forth no fewer than thirteen anti-Communist films in 1952. Cogley notes: "Probably never before in the history of Hollywood had such a number of films been produced which the industry itself doubted would prove really profitable at the box-office."[13] A more important issue was the fact that most of these films did very little to improve the average American's understanding of the true nature of communism.

The fear of government reprisals, and the fate of the "Hollywood Ten," had a definite effect on the decline of the "social and psychological problem" genre (see Chapter XV). Table 22 indicates that while social-problem movies represented 28.0 percent of the industry's output in 1947, they had dropped to 9.2 percent by 1954. In the same period escapist material showed increases, and the Academy Awards in 1950, 1951 and 1952 went to *All About Eve, An American in Paris,* and *The Greatest Show on Earth,* all "pure entertainment" films.

By the mid-fifties, after the exposure of Senator McCarthy, there was a reaction by the film community, and a small revival of the social interest movie. It was heartening that in 1953 *From Here to Eternity* and in 1954 *On the Waterfront* received the Academy Award for the best productions. These films were followed by *Rebel Without a Cause* (1955), which dealt with juvenile delinquency, *The Man with the Golden Arm* (1955) which looked realistically at drug addiction, while *Twelve Angry Men* (1957) examined ingrained prejudice in normal American citizens, and *The Defiant Ones* (1958) dealt with race relationships, but on a more intense plane than before.

While these few outstanding films have been noted because they represented milestones, by far the majority of movies produced during this period were of the normal "escapist" variety. But even here, there were many outstanding examples of fine motion pictures. In particular science fiction emerged as an important new genre for expression, but here again very few of these films really took the opportunity, through the medium of fantasy, to explore the important issues in American society. Thus the nagging fears of the possibility of atomic conflict which plagued Americans were examined in *Five* (1951), which looked at survival after the holocaust (and also at race relations); *The Day the Earth Stood Still* (1951) prophesied doom if the world did not cease its atomic arms race; while the enigmatic *Invasion of the Body Snatchers* (1956) was seen as an allegory of the Communist invasion, by posing a similar threat from outer

TABLE 22
PREDOMINANT CLASSIFICATIONS OF FEATURE-LENGTH
MOTION PICTURES APPROVED BY
THE PRODUCTION CODE ADMINISTRATION OF THE MPAA*
(shown in percentages)
1947†–1954

	1947†	1948	1949	1950	1951	1952	1953	1954
Western	25.2	23.7	26.3	27.1	18.0	20.3	17.7	22.1
Social problems and psychological	28.0	20.2	17.7	11.7	12.5	12.7	9.2	9.2
Crime and crime investigations	12.6	15.3	16.3	20.3	16.2	12.1	13.2	16.3
Romantic	10.4	13.6	8.8	11.0	14.6	17.6	15.7	7.3
Musical	5.0	3.7	4.9	4.2	4.9	5.2	3.9	5.9
Adventure	5.0	5.7	5.6	4.0	4.4	4.6	7.6	10.0
Mystery, spy and espionage	4.4	6.7	2.2	2.6	3.0	1.5	4.2	3.0
Historical, biographical and autobiographical, and historical fiction	2.2	2.2	2.9	4.4	3.3	4.3	5.3	6.2
War and military	1.7	1.7	1.5	3.7	7.6	7.0	7.1	6.3
Total	94.5	92.8	86.2	89.0	84.5	85.3	83.9	86.3
All other classifications	5.5	7.2	13.8	11.0	15.5	14.7	16.1	13.7
Grand total	100.0	100.0	100.0	100.0	100.0	100.0	100.0	100.0

Source: John Cogley, Report on Blacklisting I: Movies, p. 282.
* Includes all films having major release in this country, and many which are released by smaller distributors. Productions of foreign companies comprise an average of about 10 percent for the period shown.
† Includes the last half of 1947 only.

space. Stanley Kramer's *On the Beach* (1959) was a big-budget production which in a low-key, highly believable fashion looked at the end of the world after a series of atomic explosions. A similar theme, including the racial issue again, was examined in *The World, the Flesh and the Devil* (1959). Unfortunately, while science fiction proved to be popular with the younger audience, these films were seldom given the quality of production they deserved, and it would not be until the sixties that the genre received wider recognition.[14]

The Problem Film and Movie Influence

The development in Hollywood of films specifically aimed at stimulating discussion, or drawing the attention of the audience to controversial issues, provided social scientists with interesting material with which to examine movie influence. These studies were in a direct line of descent from the Payne Fund studies, and the research involving the "Why we Fight" films.

In 1946, Wiese and Cole published the results of their investigation of the influence of *Tomorrow The World,* a film which examined the difficulties in reeducating a young boy (Emil), brought up as a member of the Hitler youth movement, who comes to live in America.[15] The researchers showed the film to about fifteen hundred high school students from a wide variety of backgrounds and socioeconomic groups, and attempted to elicit responses to such questions as "What would you do with Emil?" "Do you think that Emil should be punished?" There were striking differences in response from the various social groups, with children from depressed areas, or black or Mexican backgrounds, being more punitive and realistic in their attitude toward Emil. On the other hand, the middle-class students tended to take a more philosophical and detached attitude, accepting without question the existence in America of "liberty, justice and equality" for all. The Mexican, Negro and Jewish students showed the greatest sensitivity to discrimination, while the group from Salt Lake City were least aware of "the problem of squaring ideal and practice in community life." Essentially, the study confirmed what Blumer had indicated in his *Movies and Conduct* in 1933, that is, what the students got from the film was largely conditioned by their social and cultural backgrounds.

The release of both *Gentleman's Agreement* and *Crossfire* in 1947 was considered something of a breakthrough for Hollywood. While both films examined the problem of anti-Semitism in American life, they differed in their approach to the subject. *Crossfire* was the adaptation of a story which had originally dealt with homosexuality, and the film was therefore more an examination of the nature of prejudice per se. *Gentleman's Agreement,* however, was adapted from a successful novel of the same name, and looked specifically at ingrained anti-Semitism in American society. (It won the Academy Award for best film that year.) Social scientists were anxious to see what effect these two films would have on the audience, in view of their somewhat controversial subject matter.

In 1948, Raths and Trager published the findings of their study of the movie *Crossfire*. In the preamble they noted that while the problem of anti-Semitism had been examined on the air, in the press, in speeches, and had been commonly accepted as appropriate for discussion, objections had been raised to its portrayal on the screen. The question really seemed to be one of taste; would movie producers treat the problem intelligently and seriously? Conversely, would reviewers condemn Hollywood for trying to be serious as well as entertaining? And finally, would audiences condemn Hollywood for the same reason and stay away from the film? Raths and Trager were also interested in the "boomerang" effect; that is, would a segment of the audience identify with the villain because of the issue of anti-Semitism? (It is interesting to note that this study was done under the auspices of the Anti-Defamation League of B'nai B'rith, and received the full cooperation of the studio, RKO, and the producer, Dore Schary.)

The tests were conducted using high school students in Ohio, and average adult audiences in Boston and Denver. The results were quite heartening, for while the changes in attitude in the audience were small, they were uniformly in a favorable direction.[16] The one thing which surprised the researchers was the enthusiastic response to the film itself. They observed:

It is said that motion pictures do not challenge beliefs. They are instead simple, banal, propaganda devices. Where young high-school people, both boys and girls, say frequently that the motion picture was the cause for reflection, we have some hope that Hollywood films directed toward other and equally serious social problems may have the same effect of stimulating a reappraisal of values.[17]

The reviews carried in the metropolitan New York press on July 23 were on the whole "rave" reviews. But their "raving" was far less important than the obvious learning process which had started within them and which they, in effect gave voice to as they wrote their reviews. This is the salient characteristic of *Crossfire:* it initiates a learning process. It does not change anyone's basic attitudes; but it is one more instrument — many are needed — which can help in that learning process which ultimately will make of America a richer and fuller democratic society.[18]

Irwin Rosen's examination of the effect of *Gentleman's Agreement* on the audience, especially their attitudes toward Jews, was also published in late 1948.[19] The subjects were university students who saw the film under normal circumstances in a local theater. Again, the results revealed that 73 percent of the subjects in the experiment group indicated a more favorable attitude after seeing the film, but 26 percent became more prejudiced. (The control group showed a 47 percent favorable and a 52 percent less favorable attitude change.) One question asked of the subjects was, "Do you favor the production of more pictures dealing with the treatment of minority groups?" Of the experimental group, 81 percent answered yes.[20] Finally, the results confirmed what social scientists had known from previous studies; that the subjects whose attitudes were originally more favorable toward Jews tended to receive the film more favorably.

A less dramatic study, but one of considerable significance, was that conducted by J. E. Hulett, Jr., on the effect of the movie *Sister Kenny* on the trend of local public opinion.[21] Hulett set out to find the influence of a film on the whole community, not just on those who had seen the film. The community he selected was Champaign-Urbana, the site of the University of Illinois, and over two hundred subjects were interviewed in depth. The movie selected, *Sister Kenny,* was concerned with the rather controversial methods of physical therapy for polio victims which were advocated by Miss Kenny, and starred Rosalind Russell in the title role. The film was an oversimplified treatment of what was, in fact, an emotionally charged battle between Sister Kenny and the medical profession. The study went further than trying to assess the effect of the film, but also attempted to discover the natural trend of public opinion without the film's influence. Hulett's findings led him to conclude that the movie had had almost no influence at all, and was "an unexpectedly ineffectual propaganda instrument." The reasons, he suggested, were:

First, because it appealed only to a very small group in the local community; second, because its arguments, though dramatically and skilfully presented, in most cases were not intrinsically convincing; and third, because members of the community do not attribute accuracy and seriousness of purpose to films shown commercially. There seems to exist among the local audience a kind of "propaganda sophistication," and an expectation only of entertainment from commercial motion pictures, both of which militate against the effectiveness of a "one-shot" exposure to propaganda such as this film provided.[22]

Similar minimal effects on attitude change were reported in other studies which clearly indicated that the impact of mass communications cannot be conceived in simple cause-and-effect terms.[23] Several researchers were careful to point out that movies were only one of several secondary community influences on people's attitudes.[24] One researcher reiterated the necessity for parental guidance in supervising the media exposure of their children, even though psychiatrists and psychologists showed wide variations in opinion regarding media influence.[25]

The inconclusive results of these and other studies led Franklin Fearing to question the "impact" of the motion picture as a worldwide influence. Addressing the Consumer's Union Conference in 1951, he suggested that "other factors," as well as movies, may be operating in bringing about a degree of homogeneity in cultures throughout the world. Thus, before advocating any change in the content of films or other mass media, it would be wise to know what to expect from the media. Fearing also suggested that the demand for "good" films really meant films which were "not disturbing." However, this problem could be solved if the film's theme was placed in some sort of meaningful context. He recommended to this influential group that ". . . if motion pictures are to achieve their full potential, they will be more rather than less disturbing because they

will deal with disturbing problems. This will be achieved not by emas-
culating films through hampering restrictions, but by demanding that
they deal honestly with every kind of human problem."[26]

The Movies Psychoanalyzed

The interest in psychology evidenced in American films was mirrored
by the interest shown in the "psychology of the movies" by a new breed
of film analysts and critics. The best, and most thorough, of these analyses
was *Movies: A Psychological Study*, by Martha Wolfenstein and Nathan
Leites, published in 1950. The authors' premise for this study was based
upon the hypothesis that "where a group of people share a common culture, they are likely to have certain day-dreams in common. . . . The
common day-dreams of a culture are in part the sources, in part the
products of its popular myths, stories, plays and films."[27] Thus they examined all the American-produced "A" films with a contemporary urban
setting released in New York City for the year following September 1,
1945, and all the "A" melodramas between September 1, 1946, and
January 1, 1948. They also included some films from late 1948 and 1949.

The result of this research was a remarkable study which attempted to
match cultural patterns in America with themes in Hollywood movies.
Among their more publicized discoveries was the "good-bad girl," a female
character who appears to be bad, but who is, in actual fact, as virginal
as the girl next door. Thus the hero "has a girl who has attracted him
by an appearance of wickedness, and whom in the end he can take home
and introduce to Mother."[28] This study is rich in content, and provides
a provocative guide to the "subconscious" development of the dominant
themes of American films. As the authors noted, "Where these productions gain the sympathetic response of a wide audience, it is likely that
their producers have tapped within themselves a reservoir of common
day-dreams. The corresponding day-dreams, imperfectly formed and only
partially conscious, are evoked in the audience and given more definite
shape."[29]

While the Wolfenstein and Leites book was concerned with a wide
range of films, other studies examined the psychological appeal of the
Hollywood Western;[30] the stereotypes of nationalities as portrayed in
American movies;[31] and the image of the United States which was obtained by foreign audiences from American films.[32] This last problem was
a particularly serious one, which, as we have previously noted, was a
constant source of complaint and annoyance to the MPAA. (This issue
will be examined in detail later in this chapter.)

In dealing with the "psychology" of the movies, we cannot ignore the pioneering work by film critic Parker Tyler, who analyzed the latent (hidden) content of films according to Freudian interpretations. In two classic studies, *The Hollywood Hallucination* (1944) and *Magic and Myth of the Movies* (1947), he examined the iconography of movies, with what he himself called a "psychoanalytic-mythological" method. In the preface to *Magic and Myth of the Movies,* he noted: "I hope to have revealed a deeper sort of truth than that to be found on surfaces and at the same time to have assembled here a little mythology, a kind of concordance, showing the frequently unconscious magic employed by Hollywood — a magic of dream creation that far transcends its literal messages."[33] Tyler's analyses were complex mixtures of Freudian psychology and the theories of myth taken from Sir James George Frazer's *The Golden Bough,* and proved to be extremely provocative, although sometimes esoteric and subject to overintellectualization.

The question of the "function" of the movies in American society was an interesting and perplexing one, which had long intrigued both the serious researcher and the merely curious.[34] Some saw the movies primarily as "entertainment,"[35] while others were more concerned with their latent effects, and as a reflector of the stress patterns and the emotional needs of their audience.[36] Another theory suggested that people went to movies primarily to "get away from their problems." In 1952, sociologist Jay Haley examined this last theory in some detail, and suggested that "people attend movies more often, and in larger numbers, during economic crises and wars. . . . This anxiety must be relieved by some interpretation or form of reassurance."[37] He pointed out that movie attendance had increased following the stock-market collapse in 1929, and again during the war, and that the unexpected increase in 1951 could be due to the outbreak of hostilities in Korea. Thus movie attendance could act as "a thermometer of tensions in society." Haley further suggested that as the traditional family structure disintegrated, there would be a greater reliance by young people on all the mass media, to "provide an interpretation [of life] which was once the province of family and cultural traditions."[38]

It was consistent with the declining power of the motion picture as a form of entertainment that interest in the examination of the medium's influence declined dramatically in the fifties, and has never really been revived. The growing importance of television, and the unexpected speed of its acceptance by the American public, now captured the interest of social scientists, and "movie influence" was almost totally forgotten. This was quite understandable, for the number of hours spent viewing the television screen far exceeded those expended on the movies. The first studies of television were naturally concerned with the new medium's impact on the existing leisure patterns, while research into the effects of television were not far behind, and continue even today.[39]

The American Movie Audience, 1957

In 1957, alarmed at the loss of more than half of its customers, the MPAA commissioned the Opinion Research Corporation to conduct a major survey of the movie audience and its preferences.[40] This study consisted of over five thousand personal interviews, conducted with a representative cross-section of the population of the United States, fifteen years of age and over, and completed between June 13 and July 15, 1957. The results of this mammoth survey provide movie historians, and others, with one of the most comprehensive analyses of the American film audience currently available. The results were mostly predictable, and contained few surprises; nevertheless, the value of this study is in the verification of previous hypotheses, or the destruction of persistent myths about the movie audience.

Age of Audience: The survey estimated the audience for the "survey week" to be 54.2 million; but over half (28.1 million) of these were under the age of twenty, and another 11 million were between twenty and thirty years of age. Thus, 72 percent of the movie audience were under thirty, while this group constituted only 50 percent of the population. (See Appendix VIII.)

Sex of Audience: The age patterns for movie attendance were approximately the same for both sexes, but men accounted for a slightly higher percentage of the total admissions than the proportion they represented in the total population (51 percent of admissions to 49 percent of civilian population). Also, the number of admissions contributed by men in the thirty to thirty-nine age group was significantly higher than the number of female admissions in the same age group (4.1 million versus 3.0 million). (See Appendix IX.)

Audience Composition: The composition of the audience in terms of population characteristics other than age and sex indicated that single people accounted for more than half of all movie attendances, while constituting only 27 percent of the total population. The largest segment of the audience (27 percent) came from families earning between $3,000 and $4,999; while residents of large cities contributed a relatively larger proportion of admissions than those in smaller cities.

375

The one surprising fact was that the southern region contributed far more than its share of movie admissions than its population warranted, while the north-central region contributed far less. In 1947, one study had reported that the South contributed only 8 percent of gross film profits,[41] but in the intervening ten years there had been a considerable growth in the southern economy, and, more important, an increase in the number of drive-in movie theaters in this region. As an example, between 1948 and 1954, the net increase in theaters in selected southern states was as follows (number of new drive-ins in parentheses): North Carolina, 63 (140); South Carolina, 49 (63); Georgia, 89 (115); Florida, 98 (136); Kentucky 36, (89); Tennessee, 50 (92); Alabama, −2 (80); Mississippi, 3 (60); Arkansas, −58 (51); and Louisiana, −5 (58). This indicates a total net increase of 322 movie theaters.[42]

Movie attendance varied with education, with high school graduates representing more than their share of the population; while those with less than an eighth grade education contributed considerably less than expected. (See Appendix X.)

Frequency of Attendance: The frequent moviegoer was of great importance to the film industry, as can be seen from Appendix XI. While those who attended once a week or oftener constituted only 15 percent of the population fifteen years old and over, *they accounted for 62 percent of theater admissions.*

Movie-Going as a Group Activity: That movie-going was a group activity was clearly demonstrated by the fact that 81 percent of the week's admissions were accounted for by groups of two or more people. (See Appendix XII.)

The Attitudes of the Movie Audience: This survey went far beyond an analysis of the composition of the movie audience, and examined their attitudes toward movie advertising; the importance of stars (only 18 percent indicated that *who was in the movie* was important, while 45 percent stated that they were more interested in *what the movie was about*); and the reasons for the decreased frequency of attendance. Of the 54 percent who indicated that they went to the movies less frequently in 1957 than they had in 1954, 22 percent specifically mentioned television as being the reason. Only 4 percent mentioned cost, and 3 percent blamed the decline in the quality of movies themselves.[43] Interestingly, 41 percent of the television set owners indicated that they would have preferred to see current movies on television even if they had to pay for them, while 40 percent preferred to see them in the theater, even if they were available on television.[44] Also, 19 percent indicated that movies on television were "too old."[45]

Motivational Factors in Movie Attendance: By the use of "projective techniques," respondents were asked to describe why "other people" went to the movies, and thereby induced to reveal their own motivations. The results were stratified into three groups of reasons: Group I included the obvious "surface" reasons; Group II had to do with the desire to see a particular film or actor; while Group III centered on the idea of getting away from routine and doing something other than the usual daily activities. Of Group III, the researchers noted: "The frequency with which these reasons are mentioned suggests that this is a major appeal of the movies."[46] (See Appendix XIII.)

Theater Facilities and Exhibition Practices: Patrons of the movies cited comfortable seats, cleanliness, clear sound, and quiet and well-behaved audiences as their primary requirements of a movie theater. The interesting finding here was that frequent moviegoers cited a *double-feature* program considerably more often than a *single-feature* program as a reason for attending the theaters they went to.

While it was to be expected that 72 percent of the respondents indicated that they had attended a drive-in theater, it was a surprise that almost half of this group indicated that they would prefer to see a film at an outdoor theater if given the choice. The reasons cited were "greater comfort," "informal dress," and "better with children."[47] The drive-in was now quite obviously a permanent and accepted part of the motion picture industry. (See Appendix XIV.)

The results of this 1957 study have been quoted at some length because they provide one of the few comprehensive portraits of the motion picture audience in existence. Unfortunately, the data are isolated in time, as there are almost no other similar studies from an earlier period with which to judge any long-term changes in audience composition, attitudes and motivations.[48] To the motion picture industry's credit, it has continued to undertake periodic surveys of its audience and the data have provided a detailed view of the changing nature of the movie audience through the sixties and seventies. (See Chapter XVI.)

The Growth of the "Art" Movie

One postwar phenomenon which did much to influence both the production and distribution of American films was the growth and success of specialized movie theaters which exhibited "art" films. It was especially heartening to see this development at precisely the time that television was wreaking economic havoc in Hollywood, for it indicated the existence of a hard core of serious motion picture patrons who were prepared to pay to see films of good quality, or with provocative themes. By 1956, there were over 220 such specialized movie theaters in the United States, devoting their exhibition time to films from other countries, reissues of old-time Hollywood "classics," documentaries, and independently made American films with offbeat themes. (This did not include those theaters located in foreign-language neighborhoods which showed unsubtitled foreign films.) There were another 400 movie houses which exhibited specialty films on a part-time basis. Almost all of these art houses were located in the large metropolitan areas, and in college and university communities.[49]

The development of interest in art films can, in some measure, be attributed to the establishment of film libraries, and the increasing number of film appreciation courses given on U.S. campuses. While most of these courses were not yet part of recognized curricula, they provided the stimulus for the growth of university film clubs. Also, the interest in documentary films had increased since their use in the war, and improved distribution facilities had made these more widely available. Another important factor was the change in distribution practices brought about by the *Paramount* case, for now the importation and exhibition of foreign films was made much easier. The British, in particular, took advantage of the new situation, and by exerting reverse economic pressure on the American film industry, they were able to obtain wider distribution for their productions. It was, however, the Italian neorealist school which provided the aesthetic impetus, and the exhibition of Roberto Rossellini's *Open City* in New York in 1946 proved to be an unexpected catalyst. His next film, *Paisan,* did even better, grossing over one million dollars.[50] Another Italian director, Vittorio de Sica, scored great critical successes with his films *Shoe Shine* (1946) and *The Bicycle Thief* (1948). While the audience for these films was still very small, it was dedicated, and eventually this dedication would have some influence on American film makers.[51]

Who was the art film audience? In 1953, a study was made of the art-theater audience in the university community of Champaign-Urbana, Illinois, based upon extensive interviews with patrons of the only art theater in town.[52] While this sample was obviously biased because of the heavy weighting toward university students, the study does provide some interesting results. The researchers divided the audience into "gowns people" (university faculty and students) and "towns people" (citizens of the community not associated with the university). There was a further division into "casual" and "regulars" depending upon their attendance *at this one particular theater.*

The art-house audience, as a whole, was predominantly an avid movie-going group. As Table 23 indicates, 60.5 percent of them saw movies at least once a week. However, the heaviest attendance habits were dem-

TABLE 23
MOVIE ATTENDANCE OF THE ART-HOUSE AUDIENCE
(Percent)

FREQUENCY	TOTAL (N=728)	REGULARS 231	CASUALS 497	GOWN 478	TOWN 250
Twice a week or more	22.9	10.5	28.9	17.6	33.2
Once a week	37.6	38.6	38.3	40.2	32.8
Twice a month	21.4	26.0	19.2	25.3	14.0
Once a month	12.4	18.3	9.9	12.5	12.0
Less than once a month	5.7	6.6	3.7	4.4	8.0
	100.0	100.0	100.0	100.0	100.0

Source: Dallas W. Smythe et al., "Portrait of an Art-Theater Audience," *Quarterly of Film, Radio and Television,* vol. 9 (1955), p. 33.

onstrated by the casual moviegoer, while the regular art-house patron tended to go less often. The researchers noted: "The unique attraction of the art house for aesthetes presumably accounts for the substantially greater proportion of the seldom-go-to-movies group among the regulars; one fourth of whom go to a movie once a month or less often."[53]

The regular patrons showed a liking for foreign films, with almost one-third (30.5 percent) indicating a belief that they were "more realistic." An appreciable proportion (11 percent) indicated a liking for British films.[54] They also prefered "serious drama" (as opposed to the casual's preference for "comedy"); and the personalities of stars were considered unimportant, with acting and story being the main qualities sought in the art film.[55] In summing up, the researchers noted that the smaller group of regular patrons "may be thought of as self-dedicated to a thoughtful choice of their movie fare. In their movie-going behavior they act in a self-conscious inner-directed fashion, fitting their movies into a life style in which movies represent a relatively small portion of a fairly disciplined use of leisure time."[56] The larger group of more casual patrons were considered to be more imitative, and "peer-group oriented."[57]

The Meaning of Hollywood

Max Lerner, in his important study *America as a Civilization* (1957), observed:

Never in history has so great an industry as the movies been so nakedly and directly built out of the dreams of a people. Any hour of the day or the evening you can go into a darkened theater . . . and as the figures move across the wide screen you sail off on storm-tossed seas of sex, action, and violence, crime and death. . . . When you come home to sleep, your dreams are woven around the symbols which themselves have been woven out of your dreams, for the movies are the stuff American dreams are made of.[58]

In the fifty years of its somewhat troubled existence, Hollywood had become a major subculture, a little world unto itself, whose influence, consciously or unconsciously, was felt around the world. This small enclave of artists and technicians wielded an influence on Western culture far in excess of any popular culture form before or since.[59] But by the mid-fifties the American film industry was in an obvious state of industrial decline, and serious doubts were raised about its ability to survive the various pressures being placed upon it. The subject of the demise of Hollywood was treated very seriously in the world's press, with the majority viewpoint being one of genuine sorrow at the loss of an institution. Even though movie audiences had been cut in half, most people found it difficult to imagine a world without the movies. Television might provide some solace, but it lacked the glamour, technical perfection and emotional involvement which had become Hollywood's trademark. Even those people who no longer went to the movies still avidly followed the exploits of their favorite stars, and the decline at the box office was not paralleled by a dearth of journalistic interest. Hollywood was as alive as ever in the American imagination.

But what was Hollywood? What did it symbolize? Screenwriter and author Budd Schulberg, who had been brought up in close contact with the Hollywood community (his father had been general manager of Paramount Studios), suggested that Hollywood was all things to all people: "Is there any other medium or any other place about which you can say so many contradictory things and still have so good a chance of being right?"[60] He pointed out that "Hollywood is a massive embodiment of contradiction. It is a business that wants to be an art, and an art that is forever seeking the standardized efficiency of business."[61]

Leo Rosten returned to Hollywood in 1956, fifteen years after the publication of his earlier study, to examine the changes which had taken place in the interim. He noted "four great and glaring changes . . . Television, Wide-screen, Middle Age and Smog." The big change in the character of Hollywood, Rosten suggested, was that "the movie colony is more sensible, more sober, more restrained and more tired."[62] Moderation had replaced extravagance, not only in production but also on the social front, and actors no longer conspicuously lived like royalty. Rosten also noted that since television had ended the mass production of movies, each film was now "hand-tooled . . . [and] made with more care, more attention, more concern than ever before. . . ."[63] But it was the "movie people" who most fascinated Rosten, as they had done in 1939, and here he observed very little change in their life-styles.[64]

Rosten's was a positive, if not paternalistic, view of Hollywood; others had not been so kind. For many, especially those who could be classed as "intellectuals," the American film industry had never really warranted much attention, in the same way that General Motors did not warrant a close monitoring to see what impact its products would have on the patterns and rhythms of American culture. While there had always been a few farsighted men and women who tried to understand the nature and extent of the motion picture's influence on American society, they were an exotic minority. To most intellectuals, the products of Hollywood were the epitome of "commercialization" masquerading as art, and seldom worth examining in detail. Even if more attention was paid to commercial motion pictures, they reasoned, the Hollywood studios had never reacted positively to "intellectual" criticism; so why bother? There was an unfortunate ring of truth to this argument; however, Hollywood could claim, with justification, that the few attempts at experimentation within the context of the studio system (*Citizen Kane* was a good example) had not received much support from the intellectuals. Arthur Mayer noted: "All that is necessary is for the intellectuals to stop paying lip service to the better cinema and to start paying admission. When they do so the exciting thing about American movies will be, not how much wider they are, but how much better."[65]

"Hollywood: The Dream Factory"

In 1950, the noted social anthropologist Hortense Powdermaker published her important study of the film-making community, *Hollywood: The Dream Factory*.[66] This detailed examination of the social system in which the movies were made was based upon a full year of fieldwork done between July, 1946, and August, 1947. Using the techniques she developed in her studies of Melanesia, she set out to discover what function the social structure and mores of the movie colony had in determining the content and meaning of Hollywood motion pictures. When the study was completed, she had achieved much more than this, for following the tradition of Thorp and Rosten, she provided a detailed description of the nature of the Hollywood social infrastructure, and its importance as part of the total American social system. In outlining the reasons why a social anthropologist would want to look at Hollywood, she commented:

Movies meet, wisely or unwisely, man's need for escape from his anxieties; they help assuage his loneliness, they give him vicarious experiences beyond his own activities; they portray solutions to problems; they provide models for human relationships, a set of values and new folk heroes.

It would be difficult to underestimate the social and psychological significance of movies. Like all institutions, they both reflect and influence society.[67]

She examined, in great detail, the conflict between business and art which dominated the motion picture as an institution, and suggested that this was a reflection of the larger conflict in American culture, but here more sharply focused. Further, in America, business had always been more important than art. Hollywood, like any social system, had developed fairly rigid forms of social control, including such things as option contracts, salaries, the star system, and censorship. Also, the whole system operated in a constant atmosphere of crisis. It was only natural that such a society would leave its mark on the movies it produced, and was largely responsible for much of the frustration and anxiety associated with the film industry.

Miss Powdermaker displayed an uncustomary bias for a "detached scientist" in her assessment of the *Production Code,* which, she claimed, "simply does not belong to this world."[68] She suggested that it was presumptuous for one group to attempt to speak for the values of all, and that the *Code* was in fact "unChristian," because it did not recognize redemption, but insisted upon revenge. Also, the *Code* prevented presentation of the truth and therefore was itself a subversion of morality. The movies were not being allowed to "help man understand himself and his complicated world, and thereby reduce his confusion and fear . . . [for] . . . a system of morals which includes truthfulness, understanding and a concept of freedom cannot be achieved by men whose idea of morality is limited to a set of taboos imposed out of fear."[69]

Among the other aspects of the film-making process Hortense Powdermaker examined was the influence of the "front office." Here she felt that the system resembled that of a southern plantation or a feudal barony, but with a great deal more inefficiency and wastefulness. Of the "Men Who Play God" — the top executives — she noted that "it is only the men who have an understanding of drama who can integrate in any meaningful way the art of storytelling with mass production. . . . This cannot be done by men whose drive is for domination rather than creativity, who think in formulas and in cliches, and who have no realistic concept of the audience."[70] Her evaluations of the directors, writers and stars were equally incisive, but with greater sympathy for their frustrations at having to subvert their serious artistic expressions to commercial imperatives.

She developed an interesting (and somewhat devastating) analogy between Hollywood and primitive societies which depended on magic, myth and ritual to make the world intelligible to themselves, even down to equating the audience polling methods then in fashion to the use of chicken entrails for divining the future. She pointed out that in Hollywood there appeared to be a greater use of magical thinking on the conscious level, and as a tool for achieving success, than anywhere else in the modern world. Thus the film makers had evolved their own magical formulas: stars, gimmicks, traditional plots and the sacrifice of what is considered to be the most valuable commodity — money. Also, where the Melanesians placated hostile supernatural forces through a series of elaborate taboos, Hollywood attempted to appease its critics and enemies through the rationalizations of the *Production Code*.[71]

In the final chapter, "Hollywood and the U.S.A.," she looked at the nature of the business ethic and the effect that this had on the making of films, and pointed out that "in Hollywood the concept of a business civilization has been carried to an extreme. Property is far more important than man and human values have to struggle hard to exist at all."[72] The problem, as Hortense Powdermaker saw it, lay in the irreconcilable differences in the goals of business and art, and undeniably, the motion picture industry *was* committed to making a profit. This meant that practically everything else became of secondary importance in the drive to achieve financial success. Thus "the movies are the first art form of any kind, popular, folk or fine, to become a [business] trust."[73]

Finally, she noted that the Hollywood social structure and controlling ideology could be considered to be totalitarian, for "in Hollywood, the concept of man as a passive creature to be manipulated extends to those who work for the studios, to personal and social relationships, to the audiences in the theaters and to the characters in the movies. The basic freedom of being able to choose between alternatives is absent."[74] Thus even the movie plots tended to portray success or misfortune as the result of luck or accident, and only rarely did a movie show the actual process of becoming successful or of disintegration. The audience, too, were often regarded as "suckers," whose emotional needs and anxieties could be exploited for profit.

The question on Hortense Powdermaker's mind as she concluded her study was, "Can Hollywood change its ways of thinking and its values, so that the democratic concept of man becomes more important than a totalitarian one?"[75] She indicated that increased competition from independent film makers and foreign films was beginning to make a wider range of choices available, for artists and audience alike. What was required was a new concept of "democracy" in the system of film production which would give greater dignity to the creative talents involved, and encourage a belief that man is more important than property. She noted that societies could and did change, even while maintaining links with the past, by contact with others, through technological innovations, and as a result of changes in values and goals. All these "agents of change" would, of course, have a profound effect on the traditional structure of Hollywood, and while, as in most traditional societies, there was a reluctance to surrender long-accepted practices for newer ones, the film industry was eventually forced to accept a more democratic method of operation.

Hortense Powdermaker's work is an invaluable study of an important American industry and subculture, which provides us with many of the answers to the perplexing problem of the motion picture's failure to fulfill its long-awaited promise as the true "democratic art." While the movies had satisfied the entertainment needs of millions of people for over fifty years, the full potential of the medium had seldom been reached, and with the introduction of television, many now doubted that it ever would be.

Hollywood and the American Image Abroad

The question regarding the extent of the influence of the American motion picture in shaping the American image in the minds of hundreds of millions of people in foreign countries had always been a difficult one to answer. We have seen that the MPPDA and its successor, the MPAA, were vitally (and for economic, as well as cultural, reasons) concerned with this problem, although many, especially those in the film industry itself, doubted that any real problem existed. Essentially, the question was, "Did the image of the United States, as portrayed on films, have a detrimental effect on foreign perceptions of this country?" Norman Cousins, the editor of *Saturday Review,* noted in 1950 that while the Hollywood movie "is the main source of information about America to most of the people of the world," regretfully this portrayed the country predominantly as a "nation of murderers, gangsters, idlers, deadbeats, dipsomaniacs, touts, tarts and swindlers." Eric Johnston replied to this editorial by arguing that Hollywood was doing a good job making films of "entertainment devoid of ideological lecturing or sermonizing." He described the Hollywood product as "light and frothy musicals. Comedies, yes, and some 'bang-bang' pictures, too, in which rustlers bite the dust when the brave cowboys take after them. Fun stuff. Escape stuff."[76] The ideological battle between Communism and Democracy helped to fan the flames of this argument, and Hollywood found itself in the center of a continuous controversy. At one point, in 1947, even the State Department entered the battle, by suggesting that American films were not giving the best image of this country to foreigners.[77]

In 1955, this controversy reached new heights when the ambassador to Italy, Clare Booth Luce, forced the Venice Film Festival to drop the showing of the American film *Blackboard Jungle,* which dealt in a very dramatic and realistic manner with juvenile delinquency in U.S. big-city schools. (German audiences had mistaken the film for a documentary!) MGM, the studio which produced the film, claimed that this represented political censorship, but *Time* magazine, which could hardly be called neutral in any *cause célèbre* involving Ambassador Luce, saw it in an entirely different light:

Probably the deepest trouble of the contemporary U.S. is its inability to produce a reasonably accurate image of itself. In plays, movies, novels, it cruelly carica-tures its life, parades its vices, mutes its excellences. This tendency, far more than Communist propaganda, is responsible for the repulsive picture of U.S. life in the minds of many Europeans and Asians. . . .

. . . All that had happened [in this incident] was that Europeans had been informed that not all Americans are content to receive their mail addressed to "Tobacco Road."[78]

The other side of this argument was presented by Eric Johnston. When speaking to a very sympathetic audience at the New York Sales Executives Club in 1957, he claimed that "from its beginning, Hollywood has served as America's master salesman despite itself . . . [it] . . . sold mightily and still does because of its indirection, because of its lack of selling intent."[79] He then outlined the prodigious selling power of the motion picture, both in America and abroad, claiming that "the American assembly line . . . received its momentum and reached full speed in very large degree from the selling power of the Hollywood film."[80] Now, Johnston sug-gested, the movies were playing an even more important role, as "an agent for democracy," by demonstrating the American Way of life to millions of people throughout the world.

While Johnston's views may seem exaggerated, there is little doubt that the movies had done much to familiarize the rest of the world with America's material culture. Even while they conveyed erroneous impres-sions about the extent of crime and violence; love and sex; and corruption and financial waste, for over fifty years the movies had become clearly identified with the United States' position as the world's most rapidly growing unit of political and economic power. As John Houseman noted: "For negative as well as positive reasons, the peoples of the world are concerned with us; our presence is pervasive. To satisfy this curiosity and to allay this preoccupation have become the main function of our films abroad."[81] What the movies contributed to an international image of the United States was no different from that of the other forms of American mass communication, except, as always, they attracted far more attention. There is also some evidence that despite the tawdry side of American life they often portrayed, the movies also conveyed something of the American dream. Why else would this product of the "Dream Factory" be so much in demand?

Special Studies

• In 1948, Leo A. Handel published the results of his study designed to determine the "drawing power" of male and female stars upon moviegoers of their own sex, based upon one hundred in-depth interviews recorded by a trained psychologist.[82] The tabulation revealed that 65 percent of the respondents showed a preference for stars of their own sex. This was more apparent with men than with women. Seventy-six percent of the men showed more interest in male stars, while 54 percent of the women showed more interest in female stars.

The reasons for the moviegoers' preference for players of their own sex was traced back to "self-identification," ranging from conscious and obvious self-identification to motivations related only remotely to this phenomenon. The following table indicates a classification of the answers.

TABLE 24
REASONS FOR PREFERENCE OF STARS
OF OWN SEX

	NUMBER OF MENTIONS*
Conscious self-identification	35
Emotional affinity	27
Own sex better acting ability	22
Idealization, idolization	10
Admiration of fashion, styles	4

Source: Leo A. Handel, "A Study to Determine the Drawing Power of Male and Female Stars Upon Movie-Goers of Their Own Sex," *International Journal of Opinion and Attitude Research,* vol. 2 (Summer, 1948), pp. 215–220.

* Some respondents mentioned more than one reason.

• Sociologist Marvin E. Olsen examined the hypothesis that to a large extent people went to movies because they cannot find other more personal forms of recreation; "in other words, movies act as a substitute form of recreation for people who lack close friends."[83] The study was conducted on a community rather than an individual level of analysis by use of gross receipts as the dependent variable, measured against the independent variable — social isolation in the community. (Olsen used three indicators to measure social isolation: intercity mobility, intracity mobility, and the degree of urbanism.)

Using sophisticated correlation techniques, Olsen demonstrated that social isolation in a community, as measured by a combination of the three variables, is highly correlated with motion picture receipts. Especially important were the rates of intercity and intracity spatial mobility, which together "explained" .423 of the total variation. Olsen noted: ". . . suggested in the data is the prediction that — barring unforeseen cultural changes — as our society becomes increasingly mobile and urban, the volume of movie attendance will steadily increase. More and more people will find themselves, at least sometimes, without close personal friends, and so will turn to the movies for recreation and amusement."[84]

• In 1953, Dallas Smythe and his group of researchers at the University of Illinois conducted a study on the "First-Run Audience."[85] This was based upon interviews conducted with 869 patrons of the local first-run theater in Champaign-Urbana. The results indicate that the first-run theater audience "has the movie habit." More than one-third attend some movie theater at least twice a week, and another two-fifths attend once a week. Those who regularly attended this theater were also heavier consumers of movies than the casual patrons of the theater. (Again, the audience was divided into "town" and "gown.")

TABLE 25
MOVIE ATTENDANCE OF THE FIRST-RUN AUDIENCE
(percent)

FREQUENCY	TOTAL (N=869)	REGULARS 460	CASUALS 409	TOWN 501	GOWN 368
Twice a week or more	34.2	38.2	29.7	37.9	29.0
Once a week	37.8	37.2	38.3	33.3	43.8
Twice or three times a month	13.8	13.3	14.4	11.4	17.1
Once a month	7.8	6.5	9.3	9.4	5.7
Less than once a month	6.4	4.8	8.3	8.0	4.4
	100.0	100.0	100.0	100.0	100.0

Source: Dallas W. Smythe et al., "Portrait of a First-Run Audience," *Quarterly of Film, Radio and Television,* vol. 9 (1955), p. 394.

The study indicated: "The taste profiles of major segments in the first-run audience appear more fuzzily than those for the art house audience. [See pages 377–379.] In choosing a picture to attend, the regulars are more influenced by the identity of the stars appearing in the picture, by the type of picture, and by advertising than are the casuals. . . . The profile seems to add up to one of predominantly middle-class taste, with other-directed behavior organized within the values fostered by the motion-picture industry — e.g. the star system, the formula picture, and persistent advertising."[86]

NOTES TO CHAPTER XIV

1. For more explicit details on the financial position of the motion picture industry in this period see Donald L. Perry, "An Analysis of the Financial Plans of the Motion Picture Industry for the Period 1929 to 1962" (Ph.D. dissertation, University of Illinois, 1966), p. 115.

2. On the importance of the independents in Hollywood see "Trouble in Paradise," *Time*, vol. 45 (January 29, 1945), pp. 38–39; and Donald M. Nelson, "The Independent Producer," *Annals of the American Academy of Political and Social Science*, vol. 254 (November, 1947), pp. 49–57.

3. There is a wide disagreement about the quality of American films in the period 1946–1960. Useful surveys are Higham and Greenberg, *Hollywood in the Forties;* and Gordon Gow, *Hollywood in the Fifties* (New York: A. S. Barnes and Co., 1971).

4. Franklin Fearing, "The Screen Discovers Psychiatry," *Hollywood Quarterly*, vol. 1 (1946), pp. 154–158; and "Psychology and the Films," *Hollywood Quarterly*, vol. 2 (1947), pp. 118–121. See also Gordon Kahn, "One Psychological Moment, Please," *Atlantic Monthly*, vol. 178, no. 4 (October, 1946), pp. 135–137, which examines the same issues.

5. Lawrence S. Kubie, "Psychiatry and the Films," *Hollywood Quarterly*, vol. 2 (1947), p. 117.

6. Siegfried Kracauer, "Those Movies with a Message," *Harper's*, vol. 196 (June, 1948), p. 568. Kracauer also looked at another facet of the postwar films; see "Hollywood's Terror Films: Do They Reflect an American State of Mind?," *Commentary*, vol. 2 (1946), p. 132–136. For a provocative examination of Hollywood's foray into "message films," see Herbert J. Gans, "The Rise of the Problem-Film: An Analysis of Changes in Hollywood Films and the American Audience," *Social Problems*, vol. 11 (1964), pp. 327–336. Gans argues that changes in film content are due to changes in the audience, and that such films can be of benefit.

7. Kracauer, "Those Movies with a Message," p. 571.

8. Useful surveys of musical films are: John Kobal, *Gotta Sing Gotta Dance* (London: Hamlyn, 1971); Douglas McVay, *The Musical Film* (New York: A. S. Barnes and Co., 1967); and John Springer, *All Talking! All Singing! All Dancing!* (New York: Citadel Press, 1966).

9. Fenin and Everson, *The Western*, pp. 265–266. The authors note: "For example, *Reprisal!*, a Columbia Western made in 1956 with Guy Madison as an Indian who passes for white, with little commotion incorporated all three" (p. 266).

10. For the difficulty in defining *film noir*, see Amir Massoud Karimi, "Toward a Definition of the American Film Noir, 1941–1949" (Ph.D. dissertation, University of Southern California, 1971). *Citizen Kane* is not usually grouped in the *film noir* category.

11. Herbert F. Margolies, "The Hollywood Scene: The American Minority Problem," *Penguin Film Review*, vol. 5 (January, 1948), p. 84.

12. For more details on the development of the black image in films see Peter Noble, *The Negro in Films* (1950; reprinted New York: Arno Press, 1970); and more recently Donald Bogle, *Toms, Coons, Mulattoes, Mammies, and Bucks* (New York: Viking Press, 1973).

13. John Cogley, *Report on Blacklisting I: Movies* (Fund for the Republic, 1956), p. 231. A useful account of the films which were made in response to the "Communist Menace" is Russell E. Shain, "Hollywood's Cold War," *Journal of Popular Film*, vol. 3, no. 4 (1974), pp. 334–350. Shain notes: "The movie industry's enlistment in the Cold War was prompted by political coercion, economic uncertainty, and a national fear of communism that bordered on paranoia" (p. 348).

14. A useful survey of science fiction films is John Baxter, *Science Fiction in the Cinema* (New York: A. S. Barnes and Co., 1970). See pp. 102–109 for the science fiction movies of the fifties.

15. Mildred J. Wiese and Stewart G. Cole, "A Study of Children's Attitudes and the Influence of the Commercial Motion Picture," *Journal of Psychology*, vol. 21 (1946), pp. 151–171.

16. Louis E. Raths and Frank N. Trager, "Public Opinion and 'Crossfire,' " *Journal of Educational Sociology*, vol. 21 (1948), pp. 345–368.

17. *Ibid.*, pp. 365–366.

18. *Ibid.*, p. 368.

19. Irwin C. Rosen, "The Effect of the Motion Picture 'Gentleman's Agreement' on Attitudes Toward Jews," *Journal of Psychology*, vol. 26 (1948), pp. 525–536.

20. *Ibid.*, p. 532.

21. J. E. Hulett, Jr., "Estimating the Net Effect of a Commercial Motion Picture upon the Trend of Local Public Opinion," *American Sociological Review*, vol. 14, no. 2 (1949), pp. 263–275.

22. *Ibid.*, p. 275. Hulett noted that because the film was not clearly set in the present this may have diminished the importance of the issues under discussion; also that approximately three-fifths of the subjects indicated that they found the presentation to be biased.

23. Eunice Cooper and Helen Dinerman, "Analysis of the Film 'Don't Be a Sucker,' " *Public Opinion Quarterly*, vol. 15, no. 2 (1951), pp. 243–264. Other important studies are listed in Carl I. Hovland, "Effects of the Mass Media of Communication," in Gardner Lindzey, ed., *Handbook of Social Psychology* (Reading: Addison-Wesley Publishing Company, 1954), pp. 1062–1103. See also Daniel Wilner, "Attitude as a Determinant of Perception in the Mass Media of Communications: Reactions to the Motion Picture *Home of the Brave*" (Ph.D. dissertation, University of California, Los Angeles, 1950).

24. See particularly Marshall B. Clinard, "Secondary Community Influences and Juvenile Delinquency," *Annals of the American Academy of Political and Social Science*, vol. 255 (1948), pp. 42–54.

25. Josette Frank, "Chills and Thrills in Radio, Movies, and Comics," *Child Study*, Spring, 1948, pp. 42–48.

26. Franklin Fearing, "A Word of Caution for the Intelligent Consumer of Motion Pictures," *Quarterly of Film, Radio and Television*, vol. 6 (1952), pp. 129–142.

27. Martha Wolfenstein and Nathan Leites, *Movies: A Psychological Study* (Glencoe: Free Press, 1950), p. 13.

28. *Ibid.*, p. 27.

29. *Ibid.*, p. 13.

30. Frederick Elkin, "The Psychological Appeal of the Hollywood Western," *Journal of Educational Sociology*, vol. 24, no. 2 (1950), pp. 72–86.

31. Siegfried Kracauer, "National Types as Hollywood Presents Them," *Public Opinion Quarterly*, vol. 13, no. 1 (1949), pp. 53–72.

32. Ralph H. Gundlach, "The Movies: Stereotypes or Realities?," *Journal of Social Issues*, vol. 3, no. 2 (1947), pp. 26–32.

33. Parker Tyler, *Magic and Myth of the Movies* (1947; reprinted New York: Simon and Schuster, 1970), p. xxix. See also *The Hollywood Hallucination* (1944; reprinted New York: Simon and Schuster, 1970). Tyler continued to develop his critical abilities well into the seventies, and was one of the most respected film writers in America until his death in mid-1974.

34. For a detailed overview of this topic see Franklin Fearing, "Influence of the Movies on Attitudes and Behavior," *Annals of the American Academy of Political and Social Science,* vol. 254 (November, 1947), pp. 70–79.

35. Martin Quigley, "Importance of the Entertainment Film," *Annals of the American Academy of Political and Social Science,* vol. 254 (November, 1947), pp. 65–69.

36. For an excellent example of this point of view, see John Houseman, "Today's Hero: A Review," *Hollywood Quarterly,* vol. 2 (1947), p. 161.

37. Jay Haley, "The Appeal of the Moving Picture," *Quarterly of Film, Radio and Television,* vol. 6 (1952), p. 373.

38. *Ibid.,* p. 374.

39. T. E. Coffin, "Television's Effects on Leisure-Time Activities," *Journal of Applied Psychology,* vol. 32 (1948), pp. 550–558. See also Hovland, pp. 1070–1071.

40. Opinion Research Corporation, "The Public Appraises Movies," a Survey for the MPAA, Princeton, December, 1957.

41. Margolies, p. 84.

42. Stuart, *Effects of Television,* p. 38.

43. "The Public Appraises Movies," p. 54.

44. *Ibid.,* p. 70.

45. *Ibid.,* p. 74.

46. *Ibid.,* p. 75.

47. *Ibid.,* p. 107.

48. A comparison of these findings and those of Edgar Dale in *Children's Attendance at Motion Pictures* (1929 data) shows very little variation (p. 60).

49. John E. Twomey, "Some Considerations on the Rise of the Art-Film Theater," *Quarterly of Film, Radio and Television,* vol. 10 (1956), p. 240.

50. For more details of the success of foreign films, and the difficulties encountered in marketing them, see Arthur Mayer, *Merely Colossal* (New York: Simon and Schuster, 1953), pp. 217–218.

51. Not everyone agreed that "art films" were all they were claimed to be. See Paddy Chayefsky, "Big Changes in Hollywood, Art Films — Dedicated Insanity," *Saturday Review of Literature,* vol. 40, no. 51 (December 21, 1957), pp. 9–17.

52. Dallas W. Smythe, Parker B. Lusk, and Charles A. Lewis, "Portrait of an Art-Theater Audience," *Quarterly of Film, Radio, and Television,* vol. 9 (1955), pp. 28–50.

53. *Ibid.,* p. 32.

54. *Ibid.,* p. 43.

55. *Ibid.,* p. 47.

56. *Ibid.,* p. 50.

57. This particular article shows a heavy influence of the theories of American society expounded in David Riesman, Reuel Denney, and Nathan Glazer, *The Lonely Crowd* (New Haven: Yale University Press, 1950). This book achieved national popularity in the fifties, and the terminology became part of the common language.

58. Max Lerner, *America as a Civilization* (New York: Simon and Schuster, 1957), p. 820.

59. While there may be some disagreement with this evaluation, it is suggested that while television has vastly greater audiences, its influence is still culturally confined, although in recent years there has been an increase in the international marketing of television programming, and a countermove by many governments to prevent this. See the symposium in *Journal of Communications*, vol. 24, no. 1 (Winter, 1974), on "Cultural Exchange — or Invasion?" Motion pictures tended to have a much more universal appeal across national boundaries.

60. Budd Schulberg, "Hollywood," *Holiday*, no. 5 (January, 1949), p. 44.

61. *Ibid.*, p. 48.

62. Leo Rosten, "Hollywood Revisited," *Look*, vol. 20 (January 10, 1956), p. 19.

63. *Ibid.*, p. 26.

64. Rosten noted:

To me, the people in Hollywood are bright, colorful, warmhearted, infinitely engaging. They talk like angels and suffer like poets. . . .
Artists have always been more unstable, psychologically, than say, grocers or accountants or manufacturers of paper towels. Movie making exploits the emotions of those who make movies; it feeds on feelings; it utilizes internal conflicts. And the instability of movie careers has generally been complemented by the instability of movie marriages.
For the kind of people who are *able* to make a movie or paint a picture, compose a concerto or write a play are precisely those who draw creativeness from a neurotic conflict and art from the deep and abiding wells of fantasy. Neuroses are the reservoir of art. Fantasy is the land in which the gifted and the infantile roam with ease.

"Hollywood Revisited," p. 28.

65. Arthur Mayer, "Hollywood Verdict: Gilt, but not Guilty," *Saturday Review*, October 31, 1953, p. 47.

66. Hortense Powdermaker, *Hollywood: The Dream Factory* (Boston: Little, Brown and Co., 1950). It is worth noting that Powdermaker's book was not well received at the time of publication, especially by the film magazines, which treated her as a naïve and gullible social scientist who accepted at face value everything she was told. See Penelope Houston, "Hollywood," *Sight and Sound*, vol. 21 (January–March, 1952), p. 137.

67. Powdermaker, p. 15.

68. *Ibid.*, p. 78.

69. *Ibid.*, p. 79.

70. *Ibid.*, p. 110.

71. *Ibid.*, pp. 281–286.

72. *Ibid.*, p. 313.

73. *Ibid.*, p. 316.

74. *Ibid.*, p. 327.

75. *Ibid.*, p. 332.

76. Quoted in John Howard Lawson, *Film in the Battle of Ideas* (New York: Masses and Mainstream, 1953), p. 7. This is an excellent, if somewhat Marxist, examination of the issue of movie influence by a member of the "Hollywood Ten." Of the argument between Cousins and Johnston he writes: "They agree that the film must be judged as an instrument of foreign policy, and that pictures sent to other countries must meet the publicity requirements of the government. Indeed, they both make such sweeping obeisance to governmental authority that they seem in danger of bumping their heads together. . . . Their articles are notably lacking in respect for aesthetic standards or human values. They dispute about methods of indoctrination. Art and life, truth and beauty, have no place in the argument" (p. 8).

77. For a convenient exposition of the pro and con issues see "Hollywood's America — Real or Unreal?," *Scholastic*, vol. 61 (January 21, 1953).

78. "The Image of the U.S.," *Time*, no. 66 (September 2, 1955), p. 22.

79. Eric Johnston, "Hollywood: America's Travelling Salesman," *Vital Speeches of the Day*, July 1, 1957, p. 572.

80. *Ibid.*, p. 573.

81. John Houseman, "How — And What — Does a Movie Communicate?," *Quarterly of Film, Radio and Television*, vol. 10 (1956), p. 237.

82. Leo A. Handel, "A Study to Determine the Drawing Power of Male and Female Stars Upon Movie-Goers of Their Own Sex," *International Journal of Opinion and Attitude Research*, vol. 2 (Summer, 1948), pp. 215–220.

83. Marvin E. Olsen, "Motion Picture Attendance and Social Isolation," *Sociological Quarterly*, vol. 1 (1960), pp. 107–116.

84. *Ibid.*, p. 116.

85. Dallas W. Smythe, John R. Gregory, Alvin Astrin, Oliver P. Colvin, and William Moroney, "Portrait of a First-Run Audience," *Quarterly of Film, Radio and Television*, vol. 9 (1955), pp. 390–409.

86. *Ibid.*, p. 408.

XV

The Decline of Control

IN THE PERIOD 1946–1960, much more than economic and competitive pressures were brought to bear on the motion picture industry. Adding to the industry's woes was an unprecedented political investigation of the film-making community in order to discover and purge any "Communist influence" in American films, and a renewed, vigorous attack by those groups which sought greater control of movie content. While the political investigation created enough pressure on the already nervous film industry to cause temporary changes in the content of motion pictures, the pro-control groups found their task made much more difficult by the shifts in the accepted standards of morality, and a series of Supreme Court decisions on movie censorship which gradually reflected these changes. Ultimately, the American motion picture industry would achieve a level of artistic freedom which many would have thought impossible in the prewar period; but by then the audience which was left to witness the product of this freedom had dwindled to one-third its former size.

The HUAC Hearings, 1947–1952

In the immediate postwar period, the emergence of Russia as a world power and the resultant ideological conflict ensured the return of the House Un-American Activities Committee to a prominent place in the American political hierarchy. Thwarted in his earlier investigations, Martin Dies, the intrepid chairman and originator of the HUAC, had watched with increasing anger the wartime cooperation between the motion picture industry and the Roosevelt administration. He was particularly upset because in 1940, he had attempted to uncover evidence of

Communist influence in Hollywood which could be behind the intense anti-Nazi activity then emerging in the film capital. Except for damaging a few reputations, Dies failed to substantiate any of his charges, and he was forced to retreat to Washington. All through the war the committee occupied itself by investigating fascism at home, and when Russia became an ally, communism was left unharassed. With the emergence of the "Cold War" in 1946, President Truman, inspired by one of Winston Churchill's speeches, demanded a loyalty oath from all government employees in the face of the sensational revelations about Russian espionage activities in America. This was the cue for the HUAC to recommence its communism investigations, and once again Hollywood was singled out as a major publicity-garnering target.

As we have seen, during the thirties and again during the war, there had been a heightened awareness of politics in Hollywood. Nevertheless, most of the film community had developed little more than a "rudimentary sophistication" in politics. The real reason for the HUAC's decision to come to Hollywood was obvious — publicity. Attacks on the film industry had always been guaranteed wide public exposure, and news about film stars, especially if they were in some sort of trouble, was even more certain of gaining public attention. Outside of the presidency itself, there was no more visible American institution for the HUAC to attack than Hollywood. Unfortunately, throughout the period of the investigations, the film industry, confused and reeling from the continued financial beating it was then taking, was unable to marshal its forces to successfully counterattack. As a result, the motion picture community bore the major brunt of the committee's all-out campaign to increase public awareness of the "insidious danger" communism posed for the American way of life.

The hearings themselves have been too well chronicled in other sources to make it necessary to recount them here, but the actual impact of the anti-Communist campaign on the nature of movie-going in America has never been fully examined.[1] In fact, we may never know how much these hearings contributed to the decline of the industry as an important aspect of American culture. When J. Parnell Thomas took charge of the HUAC in January, 1947, he announced that he would "expose and ferret out" Communist sympathizers in the film industry. For the next ten years, under a number of different chairmen, this committee would attempt to establish a connection between what was, or had been, seen on American motion picture screens and the Communist party's desire to "destroy the American way of life."

Hollywood had suffered a series of financially damaging strikes by various craft unions in 1945 and 1946, and beneath the surface these were as much ideological struggles as interunion disputes.[2] These strikes had left a bitter aftertaste, and it is against this background that the accusations and recriminations within the Hollywood community should be judged. Robert Ardrey, screenwriter and author, noted that whereas in the 1920s Hollywood had been attacked for its lack of moral conformity, now it was "the political waywardness of certain members of the Hollywood community that brought out the threats of various religious and veteran's groups." The key issue was the support that those under attack could expect from their colleagues, and Ardrey bitterly pointed out that "the industry responded as it had before, by siding with the pickets against its own members."[3]

The issues were complex, but it would not be unfair to say that the motion picture industry did not strenuously oppose the HUAC's attempt to uncover the "Communist conspiracy" which supposedly dominated Hollywood. Faced with strong economic pressure, and the growing and obvious threat from television, the heads of the studios were only too anxious to appear with "clean hands," so they could go about their business of making films, and money, with a minimum of interruption. It was for this reason that the heads of the studios issued the infamous "Waldorf Statement" condemning and dismissing the "Hollywood Ten" in November, 1947. This statement read in part:

In pursuing this policy, we are not going to be swayed by hysteria or intimidation from any source. We are frank to recognize that such a policy involves dangers and risks. There is the danger of hurting innocent people. There is the risk of creating an atmosphere of fear. Creative work at its best cannot be carried on in an atmosphere of fear. We will guard against this danger, this risk, this fear.[4]

In actual fact, the dismissal of the "Hollywood Ten" was a major retreat in the face of yet another public attack. Of course, this attempt to investigate, and indirectly control, the motion picture industry was made in the name of national security, but the end result was the same. A group of screenwriters using the pseudonym "X" pointed out in a 1952 article in the *Nation* that the firings had created "a monster" within the industry. "Since that day, the film industry has been in panicky retreat before every attack on civil liberties. It is now a hapless pushover for any witch-hunting outfit that seeks to collect blood or blackmail."[5] There was also a suggestion that, in some perverse fashion, the investigations were a "noxious blessing," as the movie executives used the threat of dismissal to prevent further wage demands, or to tear up existing contracts.

In the final analysis the Communist witch-hunt did have several important effects on the motion picture industry. First, all attempts to create a vital American "cinema of the Left" were destroyed; this was particularly unfortunate because of the promise shown in this direction in the years 1946–1949, when, inspired by their war experience, many of the creative talents in Hollywood exhibited a desire to move beyond the commercial dictates of the outdated box-office formulae. Second, the industry adopted an attitude of compliance precisely at the time when it should have shown greater courage. By the time the investigations had cooled off in the mid-fifties, television was already entrenched and all the movie industry could do to counter it was to introduce already outdated technological inducements. Third, and perhaps most important, the fear engendered by the Communist witch-hunt caused many of Hollywood's brightest talents to withdraw into a nonproductive cocoon which damaged the industry throughout the fifties and into the sixties. Also, the use of the "blacklist" effectively prevented many innocent people from making a contribution at the very time they were most needed. About the HUAC itself, the final word should be left to actor Robert Vaughn, whose book *Only Victims* is one of the most thorough examinations of this sorrowful incident: ". . . this author concludes that the committee, as constituted and procedurally operated since its inception, served . . . little benefit to the nation compared with its enormous injustices to individuals. . . ."[6]

The Code under Attack

Since 1933, the *Motion Picture Production Code* (with a great deal of assistance from the Catholic Legion of Decency) had in fact achieved what Will Hays had intended it to do — control the content of American films, and also the content of motion pictures imported from other countries and exhibited in American theaters. While the *Code* was considered by many of its critics, those both for and against censorship, to be a worthless façade, it nevertheless exerted an influence which in the long run was detrimental to the natural development of the American motion picture. In reality, the *Code* was able to survive only by virtue of the backup threat of the Legion of Decency, but it also provided the film industry with a legitimate administrative mechanism to offset the continuous threats of official political censorship. While no one in Hollywood liked the *Code*, producers and directors (but not writers) were willing to tolerate its restrictions as long as a guaranteed movie audience kept coming to see the resultant product. Once this guarantee was removed in the postwar period, neither the *Code* nor the Legion of Decency could do anything to prevent a dramatic shift in the content of American-produced films.

From the first, there had been an uneasy alliance between the Production Code Administration and the Legion of Decency, but this did not prevent the Legion from continuously complaining about many of the films which had received the PCA seal. With the entry into the war, these objections reached an all-time low, and interest in the morals of the movies declined. But not for long, for in 1943 the PCA was faced with the greatest challenge in its ten-year history, when producer Howard Hughes decided to exhibit his film *The Outlaw* without a *Code* seal. Hughes's film, loosely based on the story of Billy the Kid, starred the relatively unknown actress Jane Russell, and had received a heavy publicity buildup. Because of several "suggestive" scenes the *Code* seal was refused, and when Hughes persisted in exhibiting the film anyway, there was a strong reaction from reform groups.[7]

Almost every aspect of the production of *The Outlaw* had caused trouble for the PCA, from the first script submissions in 1940, to the advertising in 1943 and 1946. The advertising campaign was especially embarrassing for the Hays Office. After the brief exhibition in 1943, the film "vanished," but in 1946 Hughes began to exhibit it once again, this time with a *Code* seal but with an even more lurid advertising campaign. Infuriated by Hughes's use of such slogans as "How would you like to Tussle with Russell?" and "What are the Two Great Reasons for Jane Russell's Rise to Stardom?" the Code Authority revoked the seal of approval. Hughes in turn sued the MPAA, and charged the association with violation of the antitrust laws by conspiring in restraint of trade. He also demanded that the film be awarded a seal and that the MPAA stop interfering with his advertising campaign for the film.

The case went against Hughes in June, 1946, when Judge D. J. Bright issued his decision that held: "Experience has shown that the industry can suffer as much from indecent advertising as from indecent pictures. Once a picture has been approved the public may properly assume that the advertisement and promotional material is likewise approved."[8] Defiant, Hughes continued to show the film in those theaters willing to risk the wrath of the MPAA by exhibiting it. The film was heavily censored by all censorship boards, and in Maryland, where a ban on the film was fought in the courts, a Baltimore judge ruled in favor of the ban, and noted that Jane Russell's breasts "hung over the picture like a thunderstorm spread out over a landscape."[9]

It was not until 1949 that Hughes finally made all the changes and deletions required by the PCA, and it was once again awarded a seal, and the Legion of Decency changed its rating from "Condemned" to " 'B' — morally objectionable in part for all." But the damage had already been completed, and the crowds attracted to the film, even without the seal and with the added burden of a "condemned" rating, did not go unnoticed by other hard-pressed producers. An interesting historical note is that this film is credited with originating the "mammary madness" which has become a part of American popular culture, but, more important, Hughes's challenge to the *Code* created a precedent for a series of similar challenges in the next decade.

When Hughes challenged the PCA in 1946, it was obvious to many critics and film industry people alike that the *Code* had outlived its usefulness. Serious questions were raised about the necessity of maintaining even the Hays Office itself, especially after Warner Brothers temporarily pulled out of the MPPDA in 1945. Hays, having occupied his position as president of the association for twenty-three years, finally resigned, and his successor, who had been nominated almost a year earlier, was Eric Johnston, president of the Chamber of Commerce of the United States. Johnston, known as a champion of free enterprise and with strong White House connections, took office in September, 1945, and received a salary of $150,000 per year, plus $50,000 for expenses. During his first press interview, the new president of the MPPDA set the tone for the next decade by exclaiming, "I think the Hays' job has to be remodeled and changed."[10] Three months after he took office, Johnston authorized a name change in the industry organization, calling it simply the Motion Picture Association of America (MPAA). This was the first of several moves in an announced program to improve the administration of the movie industry.

In reality, the early years of Johnston's regime were very similar to that of Hays, and the MPAA found itself hard pressed to fight the pro-censorship forces which reemerged after the war. The increasing sensitivity of foreign nations to their depiction in American films was another important issue with which Johnston was forced to deal. However, his biggest task would be to reconcile the outmoded requirements of the Production Code Administration to the changing content of American movies necessitated by both economic and social imperatives. The MPAA under Johnston did exhibit a greater desire to do legal battle with the forces of censorship, but even here the way was led by independent producers, distributors and exhibitors.

By 1947, the question of movie censorship was once again in the news, and the increasing public discontent with the quality of postwar films had led to renewed attempts to create more state censorship boards. Ironically, the British film industry, which was then trying to establish a strong market for its product in the United States, experienced great difficulty in meeting the *Code*'s restrictions. *Life* magazine noted:

The thing that annoys British film-makers most about the Production Code is the highly legalistic way it works, especially regarding sex. To remove any symptom of sex from the traditional symbol of a happy marriage, a double bed is never shown on the screen except with only one person in it. "Indecent exposure" is prohibited, but any bathing suit passes as long as it has a high bodice. "Cleavage" is banned, but a tight sweater is permissible. . . . Brutality and drunkenness are prohibited except "when essential to the plot." Very often producers insist that such things are essential. Thus, though the Production Code is restrictive, movie companies have worked a nice compromise. They observe its letter and violate its spirit as much as possible.[11]

In order to explain the *Code* to British producers, Joe Breen went to London in late 1945, where he was promptly attacked by the British press as a bluenose. The major problem, as the *Life* article had indicated, was in the interpretation of the *Code*'s restrictions, and several of Britain's top postwar movies had run afoul of the PCA — *The Wicked Lady* (1945) and *Bedelia* (1946) with Margaret Lockwood; and *The Notorious Gentleman* (1946) with Rex Harrison. These films displayed either too much cleavage or unrepentant sin, such as adultery. The British, who were far more appalled by violence and brutality, were naturally suspicious that the MPAA was trying to keep British films off American screens. The *New Statesman* took to rhyme to complain:

> . . . America's *artistes* may strip
> The haunch, the paunch, the thigh, the hip,
> And never shake the censorship,
> While Britain, straining every nerve
> to amplify the export curve,
> Strict circumspection must observe. . . .
>
> And why should censors sourly gape
> At outworks of the lady's shape
> Which from her fichu may escape?
> *Our* censors keep our films as clean
> As any whistle ever seen.
> So what is biting Mr. Breen?[12]

Attitudes toward the *Code* were clearly polarized in the United States. On the one side were the groups traditionally concerned with control of motion picture content, while on the other were the "liberal" thinkers who opposed any form of prior restraint as being against the spirit of the Constitution. It is important to note that the Catholic church, through the Legion of Decency's strong ties to the PCA, openly supported the *Code,* although many of the authority's decisions were challenged on occasion.[13] The Protestant groups, however, tended to be more anti-*Code,* mainly because they saw it as a deliberate (and Catholic influenced) smoke screen which did very little to really control the content of motion pictures. Thus the *Christian Century* in 1947 protested the extensive use of liquor in American films, and countered Breen's defense that producers were "not establishing any new pattern but merely reflecting a condition that already exists" by commenting that

all who study the effect of movies on human behavior agree that portrayal of the casual use of liquor conditions the observor to accept such as desirable. Mr. Breen's new alibi should be considered in the light of the revelation last year by a Hollywood columnist that a distillers' association maintains a paid agent whose job it is to see that liquor is frequently and favorably used and mentioned in films. . . . The movie makers have done a good job in establishing the pattern they describe. Now they say they must continue that pattern because it already exists.[14]

Ruth Inglis's "Freedom of the Movies"

The liberal position on the *Code,* and the whole issue of social control of the motion picture, was succinctly stated in Ruth Inglis's book *Freedom of the Movies* (1947). This important study was one of a series undertaken by the Commission on Freedom of the Press, which operated under a grant of funds made by *Time* and *Encyclopaedia Britannica* and administered by the University of Chicago. The commission was created after the war "to consider the freedom, functions, and responsibilities of the major agencies of mass communication in our time."[15]

After an exhaustive study of the history of self-regulation and censorship in the American film industry, Miss Inglis gave qualified support to the concept of self-regulation. She was able to isolate four major problems in the current PCA operation, which she suggested were the cause of most of the criticism aimed at industry self-regulation. First was the belief that the PCA was dominated by Catholics, which she felt was "unfounded," although, in fact, the Catholic origins of the *Code* were obvious.[16] Second was the criticism that "self-regulation hampers free expression on the screen of social and political as well as moral issues." Here Miss Inglis placed much of the blame on the producers for lack of imagination, but nevertheless suggested that "the Breen Office has been one of the means by which the industry has avoided trouble with pressure groups and hence has contributed to the timidity of the movies."[17]

The third criticism was that "the Code itself promotes a kind of sophisticated immorality." The argument here was that the *Code* defeated its own purpose by making it impossible for films to treat sex naturally and honestly, and that this had led to a hypocritical game of double-entendre. Miss Inglis acknowledged that this was a valid criticism, and suggested that "the time has come to reconsider the basis, language, and

current interpretation of the codes," and to create a new agency to oversee motion pictures.[18] The final criticism was that "independent producers
do not receive the same treatment as members of the Motion Picture
Association." The problem here had become more obvious with the threat
of the antitrust legislation, for many independent producers saw the PCA
seal as a means of maintaining a monopoly for MPAA members. This had
been the reason for Howard Hughes's suit in the *Outlaw* case. The solution, she suggested, lay in removing the monopolistic practices and creating effective local community controls.[19]

Ruth Inglis had one major advantage in her analysis of the problem
of movie control — she had been allowed access to the files of the PCA.[20]
Therefore, she was able to assess the actual role of the PCA in the control
of motion picture content. As a result, she was sensitive to the very difficult
problem of walking the narrow line between total freedom (and probable
federal censorship), and the development of a vital and responsible screen.
The theme of her study was that "the movies are entering a new phase
in their development as a mature organ of mass communication,"[21] and
to foster this it would be necessary to provide "improved self-regulation
which is oriented to the needs of a mature screen purveying meaningful
entertainment to mass audiences and which is entered into freely by the
movie companies."[22]

Based upon the Inglis report, the Commission on Freedom of the Press
recommended the formation of a national advisory board to review and
propose changes from time to time in the production and advertising
codes. The commission noted that the current regulations "were devised
at an early stage of the movies, and, however useful they may be, they
do not encourage the screen in attaining its full stature as a civic and
artistic medium." The board was to consist of "diverse elements, including
creative talent from within the industry as well as educators, religious
leaders, and men of affairs."[23] Essentially this board would have been
much wider in representation than anything proposed by the National
Board of Review or the Public Relations Department of the Hays Office,
and would have had three major functions: first, to produce a "realistic"
code in which obscenity was prevented, but which at the same time allowed the screen to develop its full potentialities; second, to report annually on the number and kind of rejections and changes which were
made in films during the production process;[24] and third, to contest the
decisions of censorship boards which requested changes or deletions, and
which the advisory group believed were unwarranted.[25]

Leo A. Handel reviewed Miss Inglis's book very favorably, but he
observed that the commission's recommendation on the establishment
of a national advisory board was not really feasible, for the organization
and operation of such a large body sounded better in theory than in

practice. Handel suggested that it was far better to rely upon "the present streamlined and industry-integrated Production Code Administration."[26] Handel need not have worried; the motion picture industry paid very little attention to the commission's suggestions, and besides, the difficulty in persuading the studios to give up their powers of self-regulation would have been insurmountable.

One other important issue raised by the commission was the problem of "audience pressure." The report noted:

The motion picture industry offers the most elaborate example of accommodation to the pressure of the audience . . . pressure groups, because they have or are thought to have influence on attendance, have shaped the motion picture to their desires. Hollywood's efforts to develop the documentary film may be thwarted by its habit of yielding to this kind of intimidation.

. . . How can a medium of communication which almost by definition must strive to please everybody perform the function which it should perform today?[27]

Ruth Inglis had pointed out that a major reason for "stereotyped and empty films" was that they were made by the large studios "for the mass undifferentiated heterogeneous audience to see," while the possibility for serious films for "smaller, selected audiences has never been explored."[28] In truth, the level of audience appreciation for movies of a more specialized nature was very low, and despite the continuous efforts of the National Board of Review and other groups, there had been almost no discernible improvement in over thirty years. Those in the film industry who genuinely wished to see changes in film content in an attempt to interest and therefore upgrade public taste were hampered by existing distribution and promotional practices. In essence, "experimental" or "exceptionally fine" films (to use two current euphemisms for what were later called "art films") were seldom given sufficient play dates to return their production costs, and the "lost audience" who might have been attracted usually heard about them long after they were out of circulation. Still, the most important obstacle to the development of a mature American cinema was the cloistered atmosphere created by the requirements of the *Production Code*.

Changes in the Code

It was really only a matter of time before the economic plight of the film industry caught up with the *Code*, but it continued to survive as a vital force for much longer than anyone would have expected. This was due in part to Hollywood's constant fear of censorship and in part to the continued and surprising postwar strength of the Catholic Legion of Decency. Eventually, however, even the sacrosanct *Code,* sham though it had often been, could no longer justify its existence in the face of a massive shift in American beliefs and values.[29] The Legion of Decency would suffer much the same fate, but here the issue was even more fundamental — the declining power of clerical authority over the secular activities of its adherents.[30]

In late 1947, the PCA announced two *Code* changes to offset increasing criticisms from pro-censorship groups, and also as a result of pressure arising from the *Outlaw* incident. An amendment was added strengthening the section on crime, forbidding the depiction of real-life criminals "unless the characters shown in the film be punished for crimes shown in the film," and a revision was made of Section 11 dealing with the titles of films.[31] The *Code,* in effect, was becoming even more restrictive!

However, by 1949, the Code Authority found itself subjected to serious criticism from both within and outside the movie industry. *Life* magazine held a "Round Table on the Movies" in that year, at which time director Robert Rossen suggested that the *Code* be reexamined, "because we now accept certain words in the language which we did not when the code was drawn."[32] Even Eric Johnston suggested that the industry produce films which were "more adult."[33] But, as it had done nearly forty years earlier, it took the example of foreign-made films to force the industry to alter its product. When the Italian neorealist classic *The Bicycle Thief* was refused a seal in 1950, and subsequently won for its director, Vittorio de Sica, an Academy Award as the best foreign-language film, Bosley Crowther noted that "one cannot help but wonder whether the Code has not here been used to support some parochial resentment toward aliens and adult artistry."[34] Generally, foreign films were far less acceptable than domestic films, and the Legion of Decency pointed out that it had rated more than 50 percent of the nonseal foreign films as "objectionable," while only 20 percent of the PCA domestic product had fallen into this category.[35] There was yet another outcry when the PCA refused to grant a seal to the British film *Oliver Twist* in 1951, because it violated the *Code* by "characterizing a race unfairly" in its portrayal of Fagin, the Jewish leader of the young thieves. (In an uncharacteristic clash of standards, the Legion gave this film a satisfactory rating.)

Why did the movie industry continue to tolerate the *Code* when it was so obviously and embarrassingly out of tempo with the times? The answer is quite clear — the alternative was far more odious. Eric Hodgins, the man who organized *Life*'s "Round Table," noted the lack of criticism of the *Code,* and suggested:

There are times when the Code bears heavily on a script writer or director — but the experienced movie makers at the Table, regardless of other divergences of opinion, accept the Code as a haven of refuge — refuge from a censoriousness in the American public which might otherwise, long before this, have stifled them altogether — and was on its way to doing that when the Code was first drawn.[36]

What was really required was some legal reassurance that American film studios could produce more "mature" films without being subjected to costly censorship battles on the state and municipal level. As long as motion pictures were still legally considered to be in the same category as circus sideshows, then the PCA was the least political and most economical means of providing an acceptable product to the public. Many people concerned about the future of the movies suggested that if the Supreme Court could be persuaded to review its 1915 decision, then Hollywood would have only the Catholic church to contend with. It was for this reason that, in the late 1940s, a determined effort was initiated to fight movie censorship in the courts.[37]

The Fight Against Censorship: The "Miracle" Decision

In 1952, for the first time since 1915, the Supreme Court of the United States agreed to hear a case involving motion picture censorship. This was the celebrated *Miracle* decision *(Burstyn v. Wilson),* which on May 26, 1952, reversed the 1915 *Mutual Film* ruling.[38] After ignoring the issue for thirty-seven years, the Supreme Court had at long last recognized the motion picture as an important medium for the communication of ideas, and therefore entitled to the same protection under the First Amendment as speech and press. It is ironic, but the first intimation that the Court would entertain this idea came in 1948, in the *Paramount* case, when Justice Douglas asserted that the Court's focus on the issues would be regulated by the basic principle that "we have no doubt that moving pictures, like newspapers and radio, are included in the press whose freedom is guaranteed by the First Amendment."[39] Nevertheless, the Supreme Court waited four years before agreeing to listen to *Burstyn v. Wilson.*

The Miracle was a fairly obscure Italian film starring Anna Magnani, and directed by Roberto Rossellini. The story concerned a demented peasant woman who was seduced by a bearded stranger who she thinks is Saint Joseph. The woman becomes pregnant, and after being tormented by the people of her village, she is forced to flee into the hills, where she delivers her child in an isolated church as the film ends.[40] The film had been granted a license for exhibition in New York by the state censors, and opened at the Paris Theater on December 12, 1950, as part of a trilogy, *Ways of Love*. Critical response to *The Miracle* was mixed, and some of the newspaper critics found it "sacrilegious" and "distasteful," while others found it had compassion and "basic faith."

Eleven days after it opened, New York City's license commissioner, Edward T. McCaffrey, informed the management of the Paris Theater that he found *The Miracle* "officially and personally blasphemous," and ordered it removed from the screen on penalty of having the license of the theater revoked. The theater complied the next day, which was the day before Christmas. McCaffrey was a prominent Democrat, and a former state commander of the Catholic War Veterans, and he claimed that he had acted personally because he "felt that there were hundreds of thousands of citizens whose religious beliefs were assailed by the picture."[41] Joseph Burstyn, the film's distributor, took action to secure a temporary injunction against the commissioner, and on December 29 this was granted by Justice Henry Clay Greenberg of the Supreme Court of New York. On January 5, 1951, Justice Aaron Steuer of the Supreme Court of New York ruled that neither McCaffrey nor any other municipal official could interfere with the exhibition of a motion picture that had already received an official license from the New York State censors.

When the Paris Theater resumed its showings of *The Miracle*, large crowds turned out to see what the fuss was all about. The Legion of Decency had already condemned the film as "a sacrilegious and blasphemous mockery of Christian and religious truth," when, on January 7, a letter from Cardinal Spellman was read at all Masses in Saint Patrick's Cathedral calling upon Catholics throughout the United States to remember their pledges to stay away from indecent and immoral films. The cardinal specifically urged Catholics not to see *The Miracle*, and to avoid patronizing theaters where the film was scheduled to be shown. He further noted that the film tended to divide Americans; a technique used by "atheistic Communism."[42] On the same afternoon that Spellman called for the boycott, a delegation of over two hundred pickets representing the Catholic War Veterans and other organizations of Catholic men began to march in front of the Paris Theater; and they continued to do so every evening thereafter. According to Bosley Crowther, "An ugly and fanatic spirit was often apparent among the marching men as they shouted in the faces of people lined up to buy tickets, 'Don't enter that cesspool!' and 'Don't look at that filth!' A grim sort of jingoism was also confused in their cries. 'This is a Communist picture!' and 'Buy American!' "[43]

On January 20, a busy Saturday night, the theater received a bomb threat, which caused a temporary disruption. No sooner had the audience been reseated than the fire commissioner, Edward Coughlan, served a summons on the house manager for allowing thirty-five people to stand in the rear of the theater.[44] The following Saturday night the police emptied the theater again, because "two men were overheard talking in a bar" about throwing a bomb into the theater.

Perhaps the most reprehensible aspect of this affair was engineered by Martin Quigley, who was responsible for having the New York Film Critics' Awards ceremony switched out of Radio City Music Hall, because the critics had voted *Ways of Love* the best foreign film of 1950. Quigley suggested to the management of the Music Hall that their theater might be subject to boycott if they permitted their stage to be used for the presentation of an award to *Ways of Love*.[45] Quigley's warning was reiterated by Monsignor Walter Kellenberg, chancellor of the New York Archdiocese, in a letter to the Radio City management, in which he suggested that holding the ceremony there would offend Cardinal Spellman. As a result of this pressure, the critics voluntarily withdrew, and the awards were moved to the Rainbow Room of the RCA Building.

Despite the pickets and the pulpit, attendance at the Paris did not decline; instead the excitement seemed to draw crowds of customers who might otherwise never have seen a film of this type. After three weeks the picketing was voluntarily ended.

On the legal front, the New York Board of Regents made it known that they had received "hundreds" of complaints against the film, and on January 19, in an unprecedented move, Mr. Burstyn was called before the board to show cause why the film's license should not be revoked. In the meantime, a three-man team formed by the Board of Regents had found the film to be "sacrilegious." Burstyn's lawyers took the position that the board lacked jurisdiction to revoke a license once it had been granted. On February 15, the full board viewed *The Miracle* and unanimously agreed that it was "sacrilegious," and revoked its license. The film was subsequently withdrawn from exhibition at the Paris Theater. Burstyn immediately filed an appeal to the New York Supreme Court to review the board's decision.

On March 12, the Appellate Division of the New York Supreme Court heard the argument in the case known as *Burstyn v. Wilson* (Wilson was the commissioner of education for the State of New York who had actually rescinded the film's license). Burstyn's brief claimed that (1) the statute violated the First and Fourteenth Amendments because it was a prior restraint upon the rights of freedom of speech and press; (2) it impinged upon the right of a free exercise of religion guaranteed against state action by the same amendment; and (3) that the term "sacrilegious" violated due process because it was vague and provided no guidelines for the scope of administrative authority. In each instance the New York court found in favor of the board's ruling, voting 5 to 2 to uphold "sacrilegious" as a valid censorship standard.[46]

Burstyn's last chance lay with the United States Supreme Court, and he duly filed yet another appeal. Throughout this lengthy, and costly, process, Burstyn had received no real support from the American film industry. Instead, the industry threw its weight behind the *Gelling* case, a similar censorship appeal which involved a movie produced in Hollywood — *Pinky*. On May 26, 1952, the Supreme Court unanimously reversed the New York Court of Appeals and struck down the ban on *The Miracle*. Speaking for the Court, Justice Clark found that it was necessary to consider only the contention that the New York law was an unconstitutional abridgment of free speech and free press, and he declared that ". . . it cannot be doubted that motion pictures are a significant medium for the communication of ideas. They may affect public attitudes and behavior in a variety of ways, ranging from direct espousal of a political or social doctrine to the subtle shaping of thought which characterizes all artistic expression.[47]

Thus the motion picture was, at long last, brought within the free speech and free press guarantees of the Constitution. Justice Clark noted that it was of no consequence that many motion pictures were designed to entertain or to be exhibited for private profit, or that they might possess a greater capacity for evil than other forms of expression. The last "hypothesis," he noted, might be "relevent in determining the permissible scope of community control, but it does not authorize substantially unbridled censorship. . . ."[48] Clark was, however, careful to point out that movies were still not to be afforded the same full constitutional protection as books, newspapers and other forms of publication, which were subject to the restraints of subsequent punishment, rather than prior restraint. He observed: "It does not follow that the Constitution requires absolute freedom to exhibit every motion picture of every kind at all times and all places. Nor does it follow that motion pictures are necessarily subject to the precise rules governing any other particular method of expression. Each tends to present its own peculiar problems."[49]

Prior restraint would be recognized by the Court only in "exceptional cases," and even then the state would have a "heavy burden" to clearly demonstrate that the particular restraint in question was justified. In the case of *Burstyn v. Wilson* the state had clearly not demonstrated the necessity for prior restraint, and the standard of "sacrilegious" was unconstitutional.

Justice Clark went out of his way to issue a warning to those anxiously awaiting this landmark decision. The Court, he noted, was not deciding such questions as whether or not a city or a state could censor motion pictures under a "clearly drawn statute designed and applied to prevent the showing of obscene films."[50] Thus the Court chose not to deal with the issue of the constitutionality of the institution of prior restraint. What, in fact, was the legal position of the movies at this point? Richard Randall, in his history of movie censorship, pointed out that the *Miracle* decision

. . . left unanswered the question of how the theory of free speech — essentially elitist in terms of the tolerance it assumes and requires — would be reconciled with a mass medium which, except for a relatively brief period in its history, was neither distinguished for its self-restraint, nor subject to any collaborative restraint by advertisers. Would the theory of free speech undergo a kind of mutation that would allow the limited prior censorship of motion pictures? Or, on the other hand, would the *Miracle* decision be, in effect, only the first stage of a complete transition of status for motion pictures that eventually would see them entirely freed of official prior censorship?[51]

The decision had no immediate effect on the Catholic campaign against *The Miracle,* and the National Council of Catholic Men pointed out that now "the only effective bulwark against pictures which are immoral, short of being obscene, is public opinion manifested through such organizations as the Legion of Decency."[52] An editorial in the *Evangelist,* the weekly of the Albany diocese, claimed that the Court decision was a victory "for the forces of paganistic secularism," and "tragic in its implications."[53] Richard Corliss, in his study of the Legion of Decency, suggested that the *Miracle* decision was the first great defeat for Catholic motion picture pressure and was perhaps the beginning of a "new" Legion. He noted: "For once the Legion had realized that a simple massing of the laity in front of a theater might not be enough to force an independent-minded exhibitor or distributor to knuckle under to the kind of pressure that had succeeded in Hollywood."[54]

What was clear from this historic incident was that the achievement of free speech in the motion picture would take more than court decisions, and restrictions on censors; it would also require a desire on the part of the film industry to make the most of its newfound freedom to create the "mature and responsible" cinema it had promised for so long. It was not an accident that *The Miracle* was a foreign film, for the audience for such films had not yet developed in sufficient numbers to support domestic production of a similar genre of mature motion pictures. When the Supreme Court made its decision in 1952, there were slightly more than a hundred first-run art theaters in the United States, most of which were fairly small and in the New York area.[55]

Censorship Defeated

In the nine-year period after *Burstyn,* the Supreme Court heard six licensing cases, and in each one the powers of the censors were further reduced. In a series of *per curiam* decisions (usually one-sentence, anonymous opinions) the Court continued to strike down statutes authorizing censorship. Thus in *Gelling v. Texas* (1952), the Court reversed the conviction of a Texas exhibitor who had shown the film *Pinky* without censorial approval. Although the facts were not mentioned in the case, the film dealt with a story of a young nurse with white skin and Negro blood, who returns to her home in Mississippi after having been raised in the North. The Supreme Court merely cited *Burstyn v. Wilson* in its *per curiam* opinion.[56]

In its next censorship case, the Supreme Court reversed the decision in *Superior Films, Inc. v. Dept. of Education of Ohio,* which removed "harmful" as a standard for censorship,[57] and at the same time struck down "immoral" in *Commercial Pictures Corp. v. Board of Regents of New York*.[58] In 1955, the Court considered the important case involving the movie *The Moon Is Blue,* and in *Holmby Productions, Inc. v. Vaughn* reversed the Kansas Censor Board's decision that the film was ". . . obscene, indecent and immoral, and such as tend to debase or corrupt morals."[59] This marked the third time since 1952 that the Court had used *per curiam* opinions to reverse lower court rulings upholding the censors. As Ernest Giglio notes, "It is not surprising then, that the frustration of the lower courts becomes evident in future cases . . . [as] . . . judges were left to guess the meaning and scope of *per curiam* opinions."[60]

On the state level as well, courts were beginning to cite *Burstyn v. Wilson* as they reversed censorship ordinances. Thus in 1956, the Maryland Supreme Court reversed a state censorship board's ruling on the film *The Man with the Golden Arm,* but refused to pass on the constitutionality of the censorship statute.[61] After 1956, almost the only grounds for movie censorship that remained appeared to be "obscenity," and more and more the state and municipal censors used this as the reason for ordering deletions. In late 1957, the Supreme Court ruled that the film *The Game of Love* was not obscene,[62] based upon the definition of obscenity it had previously given in two cases involving printed material earlier in the year — *Roth v. United States* and *Alberts v. California*.[63] These two cases created the famous "utterly without redeeming social importance" test for obscenity, and the Court also made clear that "sex and obscenity are not synonymous." To determine the obscenity of an utterance, the test would be "whether to the average person, applying contemporary community standards, the dominant theme of the material taken as a whole appeals to the prurient interest."[64]

The march toward full constitutional rights for the motion picture moved forward another stage with the Supreme Court's consideration of *Kingsley Pictures v. Regents* in 1959.[65] This case involved the film *Lady Chatterley's Lover,* which had been denied a license in New York State because its basic theme was "immoral under law, for that theme is the presentation of adultery as a desirable, acceptable and proper pattern of behavior."[66] Mr. Justice Stewart, speaking for the Court as a whole (in the first non–*per curiam* motion picture ruling since *The Miracle*), noted that the film was clearly not obscene, nor would it incite to illegal action; the reason the film had been banned was that New York law required that no film could be granted a license if it approved of adultery. He also made the point that the Constitution guaranteed the freedom to advocate ideas even if these were not popular, or were held by only a minority: "It [the Constitution] protects advocacy of the opinion that adultery may sometimes be proper, no less than advocacy of socialism or the single tax. And in the realm of ideas it protects expression which is eloquent no less than that which is unconvincing."[67] However, the Court still refrained from ruling on the constitutionality of prior restraint regulations.

The Times Case

In 1961, the fundamental constitutional question of the permissability of local censorship of motion pictures finally reached the Supreme Court in the case of *Times Film Corp. v. Chicago.*[68] This involved the film *Don Juan,* a film version of Mozart's opera *Don Giovanni,* which was specially selected by the distributor to create a "test" case. After paying the permit fee, the distributor refused to submit the film to the police commissioner of Chicago for examination as required by the municipal code. The city refused to grant a license for exhibition, and the distributor sued on the grounds that the city's police power was limited to punishment after the fact, and that a movie licensing system was unconstitutional. Both the district court and the court of appeals dismissed the complaint on the grounds that the case presented merely an abstract question of law, since neither the film itself nor evidence of its content had been involved in the proceedings. In the court of appeals, Judge Schnackenberg dismissed the constitutional claims as a "theoretical remedy of prevention," and noted that the possible damage done by a film's exhibition could never be repaired. He continued: "A film which incites a riot produces that result almost immediately after it is shown publicly. Likewise, the effect upon the prurient mind of an obscene film may result harmfully to some third person within hours after the film has been shown."[69]

On January 23, 1961, the Supreme Court handed down a close 5 to 4 decision which upheld the city's power to license films. Justice Clark, speaking for the majority, saw the distributor's complaint as involving the claim that constitutional protection "includes complete and absolute freedom to exhibit, at least once, any and every kind of motion picture." This would automatically void the city ordinance requiring prior submission. Obscenity was clearly not protected by the Constitution, and to accept this argument against prior censorship would be to strip a state of "all constitutional power to prevent, in the most effective fashion, the utterance of this class of speech."[70] He also noted that the movies' "capacity for evil may be relevant in determining the permissible scope of community control," and that movies were not "necessarily subject to the precise rules governing any other particular method of expression."[71] However, the justice was careful to point out that the Court was not holding that censors should be granted the power to prevent exhibition of any film they found distasteful.

Chief Justice Warren submitted a long, rambling dissent on behalf of the minority opinion, in which he agreed that First Amendment protection did not include unlimited freedom from prior restraint, but he claimed that licensing or censorship was never considered to be within the concept of "exceptional cases" as defined earlier. The courts, in the majority opinion, had upheld prior restraint without any indication that the City of Chicago had sustained any "heavy burden" of proof that this was an "exceptional case." The Chicago ordinance also offered no procedural safeguards, and there was no trial on the issue before restraint became effective. Also, the act of censorship itself was considered to be wrong, in that the censor's decisions were insulated from the public and subject to no defense on the part of the film owner; and it was "a form of infringement upon freedom of expression to be especially condemned." Finally, Warren noted that the Court had not even attempted to justify why motion pictures should be treated any differently from other media, to the extent that they should be denied protection from prior restraint or censorship. Even if they had greater impact than other media, this was not a sufficient basis for subjecting them to greater suppression. Justice William O. Douglas filed a separate dissenting opinion, together with Justice Black, in which he reiterated his steadfast position that censorship of films by governmental licensing was unconstitutional, because it was a prior restraint on free speech.[72]

The immediate reaction to the Court's decision in the *Times* case was mostly critical. The *New York Times* favored the opinion of the minority judges, who "took the sounder view and the one that in the long run will prevail."[73] Bosley Crowther, long the champion of freedom for the movies, commented that "the effect is to continue the ancient stigma of motion pictures as a second-class, subordinate art."[74] Even the liberal Catholic publication *Commonweal* found the Court's ruling unacceptable, and reprinted an anticensorship editorial from the Catholic *Register* in Peoria, which said:

If a government, city or otherwise, can prevent the showing of "undesirable" movies, what is to stop them moving into the fields of magazines and newspapers, and deciding that certain publications are "undesirable" on political, or even personal grounds?

Obscenity is evil. But for a free society, there is something a whole lot more evil — giving a government the right to silence ideas that are "undesirable" before they even have a chance to reach the public.[75]

In spite of the *Times* ruling, the expected flood of new censorship regulation did not occur, with no new state or municipal regulations emerging. City censorship, in fact, went into rapid decline all through the fifties and sixties, to be replaced by some sort of classification system.[76] More important, the *Times* decision did not result in lower courts' upholding the censors. Richard Randall notes that in eleven appellate decisions between 1961 and 1965, not once were the censors upheld on the merits, and the highest courts of three states — Pennsylvania, Oregon and Georgia — all found that motion picture prior censorship violated the free speech provisions of their respective state constitutions.[77]

The next major movie censorship case, *Freedman v. Maryland* in 1965, while it did not elicit a definite ruling on the constitutionality of prior censorship, did find the middle ground between the two positions in the *Times* case. In this case the distributor, Freedman, challenged the licensing procedures of the Maryland Board of Censors, and no question of obscenity was involved in the "test" film *Revenge at Daybreak*. The right claimed by the distributor was freedom from criminal prosecution for showing a constitutionally protected film — one free from obsenity. The Supreme Court unanimously decided for Freedman, yet the Court did not find licensing procedures unconstitutional; rather, the justices were more concerned with the actual licensing procedure itself, and what it required. Speaking for the Court, Justice Brennan noted: ". . . we hold that a noncriminal process which requires the prior submission of a film to a censor avoids constitutional infirmity only if it takes place under procedural safeguards designed to obviate the dangers of a censorship system."[78] Essentially, the Court required the entire licensing procedure to be speeded up, and that judicial participation be built into it. However, the decision still recognized the exercise of licensing power, and noted that motion pictures "differ from other forms of expression."

The *Freedman* decision was immediately used to launch an attack upon licensing boards in all four states, and those cities, which still continued to censor films, and also to challenge the Bureau of Customs' inspection of imported films.[79] As a result there was a wholesale reformation of movie licensing procedures, or a complete collapse of censorial legislation where such reformation proved to be impossible. The *Freedman* case was most significant, because it forced censors to adhere to unusually high standards of procedural fairness, although the whole issue of the constitutionality of prior censorship was still not settled.

Thus, by the mid-1960s, the American motion picture industry had achieved a degree of judicial freedom that would allow it to move down many previously forbidden pathways. Now, at long last, the screen was free to explore, with relative impunity, adult subject matter in a mature fashion in the hopes of attracting "the lost audience." The way was open for greater specialization — movies for people of all ages — but, alas, the freedom of artistic expression had taken too long to arrive, for Hollywood's only use for it seemed to be a last-gasp flood of pseudo-pornography in a desperate bid to recover some of the tremendous financial losses the movie studios had sustained. It would take the American film community several years to learn how to handle with taste, dignity and maturity the trust which had been placed in their hands by the courts of the land. Many would say that this trust has not yet been earned, but there have been clear signs of an emerging "maturity" in American films since the Supreme Court began its assault on censorship in 1952.

The Demise of the Code

Once the Supreme Court decided to accept movie censorship cases, it was only a matter of time before the PCA was forced to make changes in the *Code* which would acknowledge the legal freedom then being accorded the motion picture. However, to the surprise of many film makers, the PCA proved to be a much more difficult body to deal with than the highest court in the land. In spite of the Supreme Court's rulings, the industry still feared massive political censorship, and the PCA was the industry's best defense. Further, almost all the films which were used to test censorship legislation were foreign-produced and imported into the country by independent distributors. Despite the antitrust decrees, the American motion picture market continued to be dominated by the "big eight" studios, and distributors and exhibitors were loath to handle movies that did not have the seal of approval from the MPAA. While there is no real proof that the MPAA was against the "freedom" granted by the Supreme Court, there are strong suggestions that the PCA found these rulings something of an embarrassment; especially because the *Code* was so obviously out of tempo with changing audience demands. Thus, in many ways the key battle for greater freedom of expression on the screen took place within the motion picture industry itself.

In March, 1951, the PCA showed how difficult it would be to force it to become more liberal, when new regulations dealing with narcotics, suicide, criminals and abortion were introduced. To offset the constant complaints that Catholic philosophy dominated the PCA, suicide was now allowed, but only under very specific conditions, and "should never be justified or glorified, or used to defeat the due process of law." Abortion and drug addiction were completely forbidden.[80]

The Legion of Decency continued to be an undeniable force on the American motion picture scene, even though its direct influence on the PCA was always vigorously denied. The main thrust of the growing number of complaints against Catholic censorship and pressure was that it went beyond the normal bounds of obscenity or accepted public standards into areas which were largely denominational. Thus, of the seventy films the Legion rated "objectionable in part" in 1947, only 40 percent were called "suggestive," while the objections to the rest were based upon differences with Catholic doctrine. About one-third of these were downgraded because of the "light treatment of marriage and divorce."[81] In actual terms, this meant objection to divorce; thus divorce could not be shown as being a practical way to terminate an unhappy marriage, nor could divorced people ever be shown happily remarried. The ridiculous extremes to which this particular doctrinaire approach was carried can be seen in the "Class B — objectionable in part" ratings given to films such as *Gentleman's Agreement* (1947); and, even more ludicrous, *Miracle on 34th St.* (1947). There were many examples of history having to be rewritten in order to meet Catholic objections, and films such as *The Three Musketeers* (1948), *Bride of Vengeance* (about Lucretia Borgia, 1949), and even *Blockade* (1939) suffered this fate. In order for the movies to mature, Catholic pressure would also have to be countered, for as Paul Blanchard noted in the *Nation:*

They [Catholic censors] have extended into the world of politics, medicine, and historical research, and have impaired the integrity of the media of information which serve non-Catholics as well as Catholics. Most serious of all, the hierarchy has stifled judgement among its own people . . . it seems inevitable that sooner or later they will recognize the censorship system of their priesthood for what it is, a survival of medieval coercion which has no place in the American environment.[82]

"The Moon Is Blue" versus the Code

In early 1953, the PCA faced its first real challenge since the *Outlaw* incident, when producer-director Otto Preminger decided to exhibit his film *The Moon Is Blue* without a seal. This rather innocuous comedy was refused the seal, and had also been condemned by the Legion of Decency because it dealt in a lighthearted way with seduction and adultery. United Artists announced their determination to release the film, and Preminger claimed that the *Code* was "antiquated," and that many other films with PCA seals were not as clean as his film.[83] The New York and Pennsylvania state censorship boards passed the film, and the MPAA, faced with this serious threat to its power, retired to study the situation. In August, Eric Johnston announced that "the Board has reaffirmed its firm and wholehearted support of the Code . . . the Code has nothing to do with 'styles' or changing customs. It is a document that deals with principles of morality and good taste. These are changeless."[84]

The Moon Is Blue was eventually banned in Maryland, Ohio and Kansas (where the state's censorship decision was later overturned by the Supreme Court in *Holmby Productions, Inc. v. Vaughn* in 1955), but nevertheless was rented to 4,200 theaters and earned over $3 million, and was a box-office success wherever it was exhibited. The publicity surrounding the film had been enough to guarantee large audiences curious to see for themselves what the fuss was all about. However, there were some places, mainly small towns, where police stood in front of theaters and put down the names of people who went in to see the film.[85] This predictable desire by audiences to see films which were in censorship difficulties is illustrated by a poll of Californians cited by Leo A. Handel in his book *Hollywood Looks at Its Audience:*

TABLE 26
QUESTION: WHEN A MOVIE DOES HAVE TROUBLE WITH THE CENSORS, DOES THAT MAKE YOU MORE LIKELY TO SEE IT, OR LESS LIKELY TO SEE IT?

	MEN	WOMEN	TOTAL
No difference	44%	37%	41%
More likely	37	35	36
Less likely	13	25	19
No opinion	6	3	4
TOTAL	100%	100%	100%

Source: Leo A. Handel, *Hollywood Looks at Its Audience,* p. 129.

In 1954, the *Code* amended its sections on miscegenation, liquor and profanity, and "Section XII, Repellent Subjects," was changed to "Special Subjects." However, this was not enough to satisfy the increasing demands by critics for wholesale changes. The question of violence in American films also became an important issue, and complaints were heard that while the PCA concentrated on stamping out sex, it ignored violence and sadism.[86]

Another Howard Hughes film, *The French Line*, caused trouble in 1954, when it too was refused the PCA seal and condemned by the Legion. After the film opened in St. Louis, the archbishop of that city warned Catholics not to see it under pain of mortal sin. About this same time, Samuel Goldwyn warned the film industry that unless the *Code* was drastically altered, more and more producers were going to bypass it, and this would result in total loss of control by the PCA.[87] William P. Clancy, writing in *Commonweal*, advised Catholics to go along with major revisions to the *Code* because "to set our power against even the possibility of revising the Hollywood Code is a mistake which will cost us in the end. For this Code will, either now or eventually, be revised. The question is: will we be absent when this happens?"[88] However, in spite of the entreaties of liberal Catholics, the church, through the Legion, fought *Code* changes every step of the way. While the economic influence of the Legion's ratings was difficult to assess, the continued threat of Catholic boycott hung ominously over the industry. This was particularly onerous during the difficult financial period in the mid-fifties, when any further loss of audience could cause disaster, and two major studios — MGM and United Artists — therefore included new clauses in the distribution contracts with independent producers which required them to deliver their films with no worse than a "B" rating from the Legion.[89]

In 1956, Senator Estes Kefauver, chairman of the Senate Juvenile Delinquency Committee, called two days of hearings into the motion picture industry as part of the committee's study of mass communications. Kefauver praised the industry's self-regulation as "the best example . . . I have seen" (after looking at the comic-book industry, this was no surprise), but still attacked the movies for their tendency to show "brutality, violence and sex." The committee suggested that most antisocial behavior "caused by movies" could be stopped if the *Code* was updated, the enforcing arm (the PCA) was staffed with more people from the behavioral sciences, and producers were forced to follow suggestions from this new agency.[90] Unfortunately, neither the industry nor private pressure groups paid much attention to the committee's suggestions.

Otto Preminger's decision in late 1955 to release *The Man with the Golden Arm* without a seal of approval created another crisis for the MPAA. The film, graphically depicting the problems of drug addiction, was both a critical and financial success, and even the Legion gave it a "B" rating. The film's distributor, United Artists, withdrew from the industry association as a result of the refusal to grant a PCA seal, and once again demands were made for an "updating" of the *Code*. Nevertheless, as 1956 began, the Catholic church was once again readying itself for a new national campaign for better quality films.[91]

Beset by pressure from both sides, Eric Johnston announced extensive revisions to the *Code* in late 1956. These included the removal of outright bans on depicting illegal drug traffic, abortion, white slavery and kidnapping. In fact, only two subjects were now forbidden: sex perversions and venereal disease. The depiction of crimes was limited, and the *Code* now prohibited any film that tended "to incite bigotry or hatred among people of different races, religions or national origins."[92] Reactions to the revisions were mixed; most of the movie industry personnel approved, but were a little disappointed that the PCA did not go further, while traditional *Code* critics, such as the ACLU, saw very little evidence of real changes.

No matter how much the industry or the liberal critics fussed about the *Code,* in the end it was the movie-going public which eventually forced changes by their acceptance or rejection of certain types of films, and this was why Otto Preminger had won his fights. However, the most vicious of the battles between the MPAA and the Legion of Decency was reserved for Elia Kazan's *Baby Doll,* released in 1955. *Time* magazine called *Baby Doll* ". . . the dirtiest American-made motion picture that has ever been legally exhibited."[93] Nevertheless, it received approval from the PCA, and opened to mixed critical reviews. The Legion of Decency attacked the film with a vehemence reserved only for special occasions, and pointed out that this particular film, unlike *The Miracle,* offended the moral standards of the entire community.[94] Cardinal Spellman this time personally mounted the pulpit in Saint Patrick's Cathedral on December 16, 1956, to condemn the film, and to warn Catholics to stay away "under pain of sin." The cardinal complained that films such as *Baby Doll* constituted a "definite corruptive moral influence" on American society, and he was shocked that the industry would approve such a film. Knowing the probable result of his opposition, the cardinal went to some pains to point out that "it has been suggested that this action on my part will induce many people to view this picture and thus make it a material success. If this be the case, it will be an indictment of those who defy God's law and contribute to corruption in America."[95]

As a result of the cardinal's words the film did indeed become the subject of a national controversy, with some Protestant leaders defending the "essential morality" of the movie. However, everybody agreed that the advertising for the film was particularly undesirable.[96] Catholics all over America were forbidden to attend the film, picket lines were set up at theaters showing the film, and the expected bomb scares also materialized.[97]

The worst aspect (for the film industry) was the threat of continued economic boycott of those theaters which exhibited *Baby Doll.* Archbishops and bishops placed six-month boycotts on attendance at some of these, and the ACLU noted that this action "is contrary to the spirit of free expression in the First Amendment. It can threaten a theater's existence, and may deny to other groups within the community a chance to see films of their choice."[98] Again, there was some disagreement as to whether the film had been damaged financially by the church's actions: *Variety* noted that the film received only 4,000 play dates, about one-quarter of its booking potential.[99]

This clash between the Catholic church and the movie industry in 1956 represents a symbolic turning point in the Legion of Decency's impact on the content of American-produced films. It was the last real attempt to dictate to the majority of the movie-going public what they would be allowed to see on the screen, although a similar series of incidents surrounded the Brigitte Bardot film *And God Created Woman* later in 1957.[100]

In January, 1958, the Legion of Decency revised its classification system, which now included a new rating — "A-2 — Morally Unobjectionable for Adults" became "A-3" This was to assist adolescents in selecting morally acceptable, but more mature, movie subjects than was possible under the old scheme. The "B — Morally Objectionable in Part for All" category was strengthened and Catholics were advised to avoid attendance at films placed in this category. Thus the Legion was beginning to break the mass audience up into more appropriate and refined age groups.[101]

Between 1957 and 1965, there was a gradual easing of the Catholic church's attitude toward motion picture content, which resulted in a more positive attitude toward encouraging attendance at approved films, and continued opposition to government censorship of motion pictures. Even the original pledge to the Legion was changed to reflect this positive tone: "I promise to promote by word and deed what is morally and artistically good in motion picture entertainment. I promise to discourage indecent, immoral and unwholesome motion pictures especially by my good example and always in a responsible and civic-minded manner. . . ."[102] Finally, in 1960, the Episcopal Committee for Motion Pictures came out with an important policy statement favoring classification of films by the PCA. This was the result of the increasing number of major Hollywood films which were oriented toward adults, but were, in reality, "sold to impressionable youth."[103] The church also sought to actively promote film study groups and film festivals and to devise constructive plans for the education of discriminating moviegoers. It would not be until 1965 that the Legion of Decency would again make a major controversial decision, this time concerning the "nudity" in the film *The Pawnbroker*. In 1966, the Legion of Decency became the National Catholic Office for Motion Pictures (NCOMP).

The Move to Classification

With the increasing "liberalization" of the Catholic church's attitude toward motion picture content, the MPAA found itself being pushed toward devising a classification scheme which would label adult films as such, in order to recognize the growing sophistication and specialization of audiences' tastes and preferences. Most film makers now considered the *Code* an anachronistic device which existed only as a buffer to outside censorship. In 1959, Stanley Kubrick, one of Hollywood's brightest talents, noted that "the Code has become the loose suspenders that hold up the baggy pants of the circus clown. It allows the pants to slip dangerously, but never to fall."[104] By 1959, movie audiences indicated a definite willingness, even desire, to accept controversial themes which would have created public outcries only ten years earlier; but as *Look* magazine pointed out, ". . . the Production Code remains a long-winded document of niggling technicalities."[105]

Geoffrey Shurlock, an English-born Episcopalian, had succeeded Joe Breen as head of the PCA in 1954, and he was apparently unsuccessful in an early bid to "get rid of the Code."[106] Again in 1960, the MPAA rejected classification because it had failed in other countries.[107] Controversies surrounding the films *Happy Anniversary* (1959), an innocuous comedy about a married couple who reveal that they had sexual relations before they were married, and *Suddenly Last Summer* (1959), a film dealing with homosexuality, cannibalism and mental illness, tended to point out the difficulties in trying to make "new" themes meet the *Code's* outdated requirements.

The movie industry itself began to realize the necessity for some form of industry-regulated classification system, and in 1961, United Artists took it upon themselves to label their production *Elmer Gantry* as being suitable for "adults only." For this reason the Legion gave the film a "B" rating; without the "adults only" warning, it would surely have been "condemned."

In late 1961, the PCA was given greater freedom to interpret the *Code* provision which forbade "sex perversion." Shurlock found himself faced with a deluge of films from the large Hollywood studios dealing with such themes, and wisely requested a ruling from the MPAA board.[108] There was nothing quite like the investment in a major production such as *The Children's Hour* (1961), which dealt with lesbianism, and Otto Preminger's *Advise and Consent* (1962), this time dealing with homosexuality, to make the MPAA change its mind. By 1962, the old *Code* was unrec-

TABLE 27
MOTION PICTURE PRODUCTION CODE CHANGES,
1930–1961*

YEAR	SUBJECT AREA INVOLVED	GREATER FREEDOM ALLOWED	LESS FREEDOM ALLOWED
1938	Crime		X
1939	Authentic scenes of native life in foreign lands	X	
	Objectionable words and phrases		X
1946	Narcotics	X	
1947	Treatment of crime and the use of titles		X
1951	Suicide	X†	
	Crime	X†	
	Abortion		X
	Drugs		X
1953	Smuggling	X	
	Branding of children and animals	X	
	Cruelty to children or animals	X	
1954	Miscegenation	X	
	Liquor	X	
	Profanity	X	
1956	Mercy killing	X	
	Brutality and physical violence		X
	Blasphemy		X
	Drugs	X	
	Profanity	X	
	Miscegenation	X	
	Childbirth	X	
	Crime	X†	
	Abortion	X	
	Vulgarity		X
	Obscenity	X	
	Costumes	X†	
	Religion	X	
	Special subjects	X	
	National feeling	X	
	Titles	X	
	Cruelty to animals	X†	
1961	Sexual perversion	X	

Source: John Sargent, "Self-Regulation: The Motion Picture Production Code, 1930–1961," pp. 222–223.
* Compiled from revised codes dated 1931, 1948, 1949, 1955, 1956, and 1961.
† Formerly part of special resolutions adopted earlier.

ognizable. John Sargent in his study of self-regulation devised a table to show the various changes which had taken place in the *Production Code* since its origin in 1930.

The United States, prior to 1968, was one of the few Western countries which did not practice a national form of film classification, although the MPAA did assist voluntary groups such as the Protestant Motion Picture Council, which began to classify films in 1945. The Protestant council was one of ten organizations which contributed to the *Green Sheet,* a monthly publication which reviewed and rated motion pictures, and was reportedly read by ten million Americans.[109] Other publications such as *Consumers' Reports, Parents' Magazine, Seventeen,* and the *Christian Science Monitor* also furnished their readers with lists of films classified as to their audience suitability.

The increasing success of many "adult" foreign films, like *Hiroshima Mon Amour* (1959), *La Dolce Vita* (1959), *The Virgin Spring* (1960), *Two Women* (1961) and *Blow-Up* (1966), served to stimulate American audiences to demand better films from Hollywood. In the case of *The Pawnbroker* (1965), *Who's Afraid of Virginia Woolf?* (1966) and *Alfie* (1966), the studios voluntarily restricted audiences, and it was clear that classification was becoming a *de facto,* if not a *de jure,* reality.

Eric Johnston died suddenly in 1963, Joe Breen and Martin Quigley in 1964, while Will Hays had died earlier in 1954. The old guard were now all gone and Hollywood was no longer the major social and cultural force it had once been. Nevertheless, motion pictures were still an important form of entertainment, and a whole new generation of young moviegoers had emerged. The American motion picture industry was faced with yet another challenge: how would it handle its new artistic freedom and still maintain its unique appeal across all socioeconomic groups? Could the motion picture, long a "mass medium," begin finally to develop a product to meet the specialized differentiation of audiences, which had often been proffered as its salvation?

Special Studies

• In 1967, psychologist Philip Anast tested the hypotheses that frequent moviegoers, compared to persons attending movies less, (1) rank higher in the erotic and interpersonal violence interests; (2) perceive greater similarity between movie life and reality; (3) are relatively more hero- or heroine-oriented than plot-oriented. Using answers obtained from 259 respondents, Anast found that persons with a high vicarious interest in love, luxury and violence find an outlet for these in movies, since movie content aims its appeals toward these motives. Unexpected was the negative correlation between adventure interest and movie attendance, because movies have made a determined attempt to appeal to this interest. He explained this by noting that ". . . strong vicarious interest in love, violence, mishaps and luxury can more easily be satisfied by substitution than adventure and achievement can, hence the greater movie attendance on the part of those with high interests in the former."[110]

• In an interesting study of audience preferences in film content following a series of murders on a college campus, the authors tested the hypothesis that "given safe conditions of exposure, individuals in a state of heightened fear will show preference for a stimulus situation containing an event or object representative of the real source of their fear."[111] By examining attendance patterns at two local theaters, one showing a film about psychopathic murders (In Cold Blood), the other about lesbian relationships (The Fox, based upon D. H. Lawrence's novel), and using a sophisticated statistical analysis of phone interviews offering a choice of a free ticket to either of the two shows, the authors concluded ". . . that attendance at the violent movie increased markedly following the murder, whereas attendance at the "control" movie [The Fox] showed a slight decrease from the previous week . . . this finding supports the general hypothesis . . ."[112]

• In 1974, Ryland A. Taylor examined the variation in television audience size for motion pictures which had won awards.[113] The results showed that Academy Awards, New York Film Critics' Awards and Film Daily's awards are significantly related to television audience size. Thus, the data suggest that "audience size can be increased substantially (one-fifth to nearly one-third) if an award-winning film is presented. Film producers can expect to continue to command premium prices for films of recognized quality and popularity."[114]

• In an important and detailed study of movie attendance in the southern California area by the marketing research department of the Los Angeles Times, the highlights of the findings were as follows:

1. As a favorite activity, movie-going ranked very low, with only 2 percent of the total sample mentioning it. It was slightly more popular among teenage girls than it was among all other groups.

2. Seventy-five percent of the teens, compared to only 32 percent of the adults, attended one or more movies a month. Another third of the adults never attend a movie, or attend less than once a year.

3. The kind of movies being made, lack of time and price of admission were given as the main reasons for not attending movies more often.

4. Frequent moviegoers were considerably younger and better educated than infrequent moviegoers. Nonmoviegoers spent considerably more time watching television than did moviegoers.

5. The subject of the movie was the most important factor in determining whether or not to see a particular picture, with the stars in the film being a secondary consideration.[115]

NOTES TO CHAPTER XV

1. The House Un-American Activities Committee Hearings on Communist influence in the American film industry have been examined in several useful studies. See Eric Bentley, *Thirty Years of Treason* (New York: Viking Press, 1971); Alvah Bessie, *Inquisition in Eden* (Berlin: Seven Seas Publishers, 1967); John Cogley, *Report on Blacklisting I: The Movies;* Gordon Kahn, *Hollywood on Trial* (New York: Boni and Gaer, 1948); Merle Miller, *The Judges and the Judged* (Garden City: Doubleday and Company, 1952); Howard Suber, "The Anti-Communist Blacklist in the Hollywood Motion Picture Industry" (Ph.D. dissertation, University of California at Los Angeles, 1968); Howard Suber, "The 1947 Hearings of the House Committee on Un-American Activities into Communism in the Hollywood Motion Picture Industry" (M.A. thesis, University of California at Los Angeles, 1966); and Robert Vaughn, *Only Victims* (New York: G. P. Putnam's Sons, 1972).

2. For more details of these strikes see Cogley, pp. 60–73; and Murray Ross, "Labor Relations in Hollywood," pp. 63–64.

3. Robert Ardrey, "Hollywood: The Toll of the Frenzied Forties," *Reporter*, vol. 16 (March 21, 1957), p. 30.

4. Cogley, p. 22.

5. "X," "Hollywood Meets Frankenstein," *Nation*, vol. 174 (June 28, 1952), p. 629. For a vitriolic and contrary view, see Oliver Carlson, "The Communist Record in Hollywood," *American Mercury*, vol. 66, no. 290 (February, 1948), pp. 135–143.

6. Vaughn, p. 272.

7. The best description of the *Outlaw* incident is found in Schumach, *Face on the Cutting Room Floor*, pp. 52–62.

8. *Hughes Tool v. Motion Picture Association of America*, 66 F. Supp. 1006 (S.D., N.Y., 1946).

9. Schumach, p. 59.

10. *New York Times,* October 7, 1945, sec. 2, p. 1.

11. "Movie Censorship," *Life*, vol. 21 (October 28, 1946), p. 80.

12. This poem is quoted in "Cleavage and the Code," *Time*, no. 48 (August 5, 1946), p. 50. The poem itself is entitled "The Offense Is Rank," and was written by a regular political poet, "Sagittarius," in the *New Statesman and Nation* (July 20, 1946), p. 42.

13. As one example, after claiming that there was an increase in the number of indecent films, members of the Church of Southern California ordered a boycott of all movies for the month of February, 1947. See Sargent, "Self-Regulation," p. 125.

14. "Hollywood Produces a New Alibi," *Christian Century*, no. 64 (February 5, 1947), p. 165.

15. Inglis, *Freedom of the Movies*, p. iv.

16. *Ibid.*, pp. 180–181. The evidence here is that Inglis was not correct in her underestimation of the Catholic influence on the Production Code Administration.

17. Inglis, p. 183.

18. *Ibid.*, pp. 183–186.

19. *Ibid.*, pp. 187–194.

20. *Ibid.,* pp. 220–221. However, the agreement was that all unprinted data were confidential, and not to be quoted. Miss Inglis is one of the very few people ever given access to the files of the PCA.

21. Inglis, p. 1.

22. *Ibid.,* p. 193.

23. *Ibid.,* p. viii.

24. The reason for this function was based upon the belief that without public review, "the work of any private regulatory agency is open to abuse." Inglis, p. 187.

25. *Ibid.,* pp. 186–187.

26. Leo A. Handel, "The Social Obligation of Motion Pictures," *International Journal of Opinion and Attitude Research* (December, 1947), pp. 97–98.

27. Commission on Freedom of the Press, *A Free and Responsible Press,* pp. 58–59.

28. Inglis, p. 201.

29. There is a great deal of intellectual controversy on the subject of changing values. For a detailed examination of this difficult issue see Clyde Kluckhohn, "Have There Been Discernible Shifts in American Values During the Past Generation?" in Elting E. Morison, ed., *The American Style* (New York: Harper and Brothers, 1958), pp. 145–217. There is also the fact that the movies' exploration of "adult" themes had never really caught up with either literature or the theater. This was especially true in the period 1946–1960. Eventually, facing economic ruin, the film industry pushed ahead of the theater, especially in the portrayal of sexual material.

30. It is difficult to determine exactly how much power the Legion of Decency really does have. Richard Corliss notes: ". . . the Office will continue to hold power with the industry as long as it has the ear of more than forty million Catholics." See Corliss, "The Legion of Decency," p. 59.

31. For more details see Sargent, pp. 128–129.

32. Eric Hodgins, "A Round Table on the Movies," *Life,* vol. 26 (June 27, 1949), p. 104.

33. *Variety,* March 9, 1949, p. 1.

34. *New York Times,* April 2, 1950, sec. 2, p. 1.

35. *Sargent,* p. 133.

36. Hodgins, p. 104.

37. For a useful review of the topic of film censorship in this period see Douglas Ayer, Roy E. Bates, and Peter J. Herman, "Self-Censorship in the Movie Industry: An Historical Perspective on Law and Social Change," *Wisconsin Law Review,* no. 3 (1970), pp. 791–838. The authors take the point of view that Hollywood had sound economic reasons for preferring self-censorship, and that, "moreover, our political heritage has conditioned us to feel a greater sense of alarm when a governmental agency orders the suppression of expression than we feel when a private institution does the same thing" (p. 806).

38. 343 U.S. 495 (1952). The best accounts of the importance of this case are found in Carmen, *Movies, Censorship and the Law;* Ernest David Giglio, "The Decade of the Miracle, 1952–1962: A Study in the Censorship of the American Motion Picture" (D.SS. dissertation, Syracuse University, 1964); and Randall, *Censorship of the Movies.* See also Alan F. Westin, *The Miracle Case: The Supreme Court and the Movies;* Inter-University Case Program No. 64 (Alabama: University of Alabama Press, 1961).

39. 334 U.S. 131 (1948). Quoted in Carmen, p. 45.

40. For a more detailed account of the motion picture see Bosley Crowther, "The Strange Case of 'The Miracle,' " *Atlantic,* vol. 187 (April, 1951), pp. 35–39.

41. *Ibid.,* p. 37.

42. *New York Times,* January 8, 1951, p. 14.

43. Crowther, " 'Miracle,' " p. 37.

44. *New York Times,* January 21, 1951, p. 53.

45. Crowther, " 'Miracle,' " p. 38.

46. 303 N.Y. 242 (1951).

47. 343 U.S. at 501.

48. Randall, p. 29.

49. 343 U.S. at 502–503.

50. *Ibid.,* at 506.

51. Randall, p. 31.

52. *Ibid.,* p. 32.

53. Giglio, p. 245.

54. Corliss, p. 44.

55. Ayer et al., p. 807.

56. *Gelling v. Texas,* 343 U.S. 960 (1952).

57. *Superior Films, Inc. v. Department of Education of Ohio,* 346 U.S. 587 (1954).

58. 305 N.Y. 336, 113 N.E.2d 502 (1953).

59. 350 U.S. 870 (1955).

60. Giglio, p. 72.

61. *United Artists Corp. v. Maryland State Board of Censors,* 210 Md. 586, 124 A.2d 292 (1956).

62. *Times Film Corp. v. Chicago,* 355 U.S. 35 (1957), rev'g 241 F.2d 432 (7th Cir. 1957).

63. 354 U.S. 476 (1957). These two cases were decided together.

64. Randall, p. 56. This is a very complex legal argument; for more details see Randall, pp. 55–57; and Carmen, pp. 66–89.

65. 360 U.S. 684 (1959).

66. Carmen, p. 97.

67. 360 U.S. 684 (1959) at 689.

68. 365 U.S. 43 (1961).

69. Giglio, p. 97.

70. Randall, p. 35.

71. Carmen, pp. 101–102.

72. For more details see Randall, pp. 36–39; and Carmen, pp. 102–105.

73. *New York Times,* January 25, 1961, p. 32.

74. *Ibid.,* January 29, 1961, sec. 4, p. 1.

75. "Censoring Movies," *Commonweal,* no. 74 (March 31, 1961), p. 17.

76. For more explicit details on censorship at the municipal level see Giglio, pp. 112–151. This is an excellent background treatment. For a more formal legal approach see Thomas B. Leary and J. Roger Noall, "Entertainment: Public Pressures and the Law," *Harvard Law Review,* vol. 71 (1957), pp. 344–353. One of the more interesting of the municipal censors was Lloyd T. Binford of Memphis, whose colorful career is covered in Linden, "The Film Censorship Struggle in the United States," especially on pp. 268, 322.

77. Randall, pp. 39–41.

78. 380 U.S. 51 (1965) at 57–58.

79. For more details on the decision as it affected the Bureau of Customs, see Randall, pp. 45–50.

80. *New York Times*, March 28, 1951, p. 33.

81. Paul Blanchard, "Roman Catholic Censorship II: The Church and the Movies," *Nation*, vol. 166 (May 8, 1948), pp. 499–500.

82. *Ibid.*, p. 502.

83. *Variety*, May 27, 1953, p. 5. (The interesting point here is that *The Moon Is Blue* had been shown on the Broadway stage without any complaint.)

84. *Variety*, August 19, 1953, p. 5. Quoted in Sargent, p. 143.

85. Interview with Preminger by Peter Bogdanovich in *On Film*, vol. 1, no. 0 (1970), p. 40. (Unfortunately, this was the only issue of what promised to be a very interesting publication.)

86. For a good description of the problems facing censors in dealing with the issues of crime and violence see Gordon Mirams, "Drop That Gun," *Quarterly of Film, Radio and Television*, vol. 6 (1951), pp. 1–19. This article by the New Zealand censor contains interesting statistical information on the content of violence in motion pictures.

87. "The Censors," *Time*, no. 63 (January 11, 1954), p. 80.

88. William P. Clancy, "Censorship and the Court: Freedom of the Screen," *Commonweal*, vol. 59, no. 20 (February 19, 1954), p. 501.

89. *Variety*, June 29, 1955, p. 1.

90. U.S. Congress, Senate Committee on the Judiciary, Subcommittee to Investigate Juvenile Delinquency, *Motion Pictures and Juvenile Delinquency*, S. Rep. 2055, 84th Congress, 2d Session, 1956, pp. 66–68, 70–71.

91. For more details on this new Catholic campaign see Sargent, p. 163.

92. *Variety*, December 12, 1956, p. 1.

93. "Cinema," *Time*, no. 68 (December 24, 1956), p. 61.

94. Giglio, p. 210.

95. *New York Times*, December 17, 1956, p. 28.

96. An editorial in *Commonweal* pointed out: "If, in the case of *Baby Doll*, its producers consider it a serious and artistic treatment of an adult theme, they have no business advertising it in the way they have. If Hollywood wants to make adult pictures and to be taken seriously as an artistic medium, movie advertising should not suggest that the industry is simply a highly organized scheme to merchandise French postcards that talk." "Baby Doll," *Commonweal*, vol. 65 (January 11, 1957), p. 372.

97. For more details of the crowds, and the various threats, see *Variety*, January 9, 1957, p. 13.

98. *New York Times*, December 30, 1956, p. 24.

99. *Variety*, May 1, 1957, p. 1. An interesting anecdote sprang up regarding the supposed "disappearance" of this film. Warner Brothers Studios were rumored to have destroyed all the prints, but the director, Elia Kazan, claims that this is not true. However, to the knowledge of this writer, the film has never been shown on national television. See Corliss, p. 47.

100. For more details on the incidents caused by this film see Giglio, pp. 220–223.

101. The best description of the philosophy behind these changes is found in Phelan, "The National Catholic Office for Motion Pictures," p. 98.

102. *Ibid.*, p. 74.

103. *Ibid.*, p. 86.

104. Jack Hamilton, "Hollywood Bypasses the Production Code," *Look*, September 23, 1959, p. 82.

105. *Ibid.*, p. 83.

106. Jack Vizzard, *See No Evil* (New York: Simon and Schuster, 1970), pp. 159–171.

107. *Variety*, December 9, 1959, p. 17.

108. Sargent, pp. 203–205.

109. For more information on the *Green Sheet*, see Giglio, pp. 243–245; and Sargent, pp. 197–198.

110. Philip Anast, "Differential Movie Appeals as Correlates of Attendance," *Journalism Quarterly*, vol. 44 (1967), p. 90.

111. Ehor O. Boyanowsky, Darren Newtson, and Elaine Walster, "Film Preferences Following a Murder," *Communication Research*, vol. 1, no. 1 (January, 1974), pp. 32–43.

112. *Ibid.*, p. 40.

113. Ryland A. Taylor, "Audiences and Movie Awards: A Statistical Study," *Journal of Broadcasting*, vol. 18, no. 2 (Spring, 1974), pp. 181–186.

114. *Ibid.*, p. 186.

115. *A Look at Southern California Movie-Going*, report prepared by the Marketing Research Department of the *Los Angeles Times*, 1972, pp. 2–3.

XVI

The Uncertain Future

THE MOTION PICTURE INDUSTRY entered the 1960s in a state of confusion, a condition which endured all through the decade, and well into the seventies. There were many reasons for this panic, but they all came together under one heading — "Uncertainty." With the gradual decline in the studio system, the loosening of the censorship restrictions, and the almost complete hold that television had on the American public, there was absolutely no way to gauge, or predict, what sort of motion pictures would entice audiences back into movie theaters. It was quite obvious that a fairly sizable movie audience still existed, but no longer was it entirely dependent upon the large screen for visual entertainment. As a result, the film makers were hard pressed to continually produce material which was capable of dragging people away from their television sets, or from the many other new ways to occupy leisure time which had sprung up since the end of World War II.

While the movies had always experienced competition from other forms of entertainment and leisure, the period after 1945 saw an unprecedented growth in alternative recreational activities. Besides the ubiquitous television set, Americans turned eagerly to more "elitist" cultural pursuits such as art, books, music and theater. Once the preserve of the wealthy and upper classes, millions of ordinary Americans now participated in all forms of cultural expression. Alvin Toffler, in his book *Culture Consumers* (1965), noted:

What this represents is not merely money, but a massive investment of time, energy, and emotion. Millions of Americans as consumers and participants, hundreds of thousands as members and volunteer workers, are putting a little bit of their lives not merely into a search for aesthetic satisfaction, but into building and leading the institutions needed to produce and distribute culture in America.[1]

428

It was not that America had suddenly been turned into a nation of aesthetes, but that the combined forces of automation, enormous economic growth and impressive increases in the levels of education had combined to produce a significant number of people who now had the time, money and education to pursue a wide range of alternative recreational and cultural pursuits.

Many other Americans turned their attention to more active forms of recreation, and outdoor activities such as camping and boating, participation in sports, and attendance at sporting events all showed significant increases. More and more people, especially the young college group, traveled overseas; while hobby shops and hardware stores increased their sales to the growing army of "do-it-yourselfers."

Thus the motion picture industry was faced with a formidable array of competitive enticements for the recreational dollar, while it also had to compete with television for what remained of leisure time. The only positive statistic for the movie industry in these boom years was the growth in the population base from 151 million in 1950, to 179 million in 1960, and well over 200 million by the early 1970s. Most of this population growth came from the cities, for by 1960, over two-thirds of all Americans lived in urban areas. Unfortunately, while an increased population base should have created a stabilization in the size of the motion picture audience, the physical characteristics of cities themselves were changing in such a way as to forever alter the pattern of movie attendance.

The growth of suburbia has been well chronicled, and this move away from the inner and outer ring of cities into the suburbs destroyed many of the traditional patterns of recreation.[2] The fact that the suburbs were usually long distances from the downtown sections, where most of the large, first-run movie houses were located, reduced even further the possibility of attendance by older, married couples (those thirty years of age and above). In the suburbs themselves, the new arrivals had too many other things to do (and less available money) to allow frequent moviegoing. Herbert Gans, in his fascinating study of *The Levittowners* (1967), has reported that 93 percent of those moving from city to suburb indicated a considerable change in leisure time and activity. He also noted that, "except among the children, going to the movies became an unusual occurrence, even though Levittown eventually had two movie theaters, for television offered a more easily accessible and cheaper substitute."[3] Thus, as the population shifted away from the inner city areas, this necessitated yet another marketing adjustment for the movie industry.

Besides competition and changing demographics, Hollywood was faced with still another problem — the amorphous, and rapid shifts in the lifestyles of American youth.[4] The sixties spawned an unprecedented alteration in the values and behavior of the young, which some sociologists and

429

historians have termed "the counterculture."[5] The movie industry simply
did not know how to cope with the frequent and facile shifts in their
young audience's life-style, and try as Hollywood could, one accidental
success which might capture the audience's imagination would be followed by a succession of failures exploiting the same theme.

The combined assault of changes in leisure pursuits, the move to the
suburbs, and the unpredictable shifts in norms and values proved to be
a formidable obstacle for the American film industry. With the demise of
the integrated studio system, producers were no longer guaranteed exhibition dates for their films, and film-making became an even more
precarious occupation.[6] And yet, while absolutely nothing was certain
in the movie business, there were enough enormous box-office and critical
"hits" to suggest the continued existence of a large potential audience
waiting for the "right" film. Despite all the difficulties encountered by
the movie industry, it was obvious that many Americans were still willing
to pay increasingly higher admission prices to go to the movies.[7]

The State of the Industry

Throughout the sixties, the number of motion pictures released in the
United States averaged approximately 450 per year (Appendix VI). The
total number of releases remained remarkably steady, but during the
period 1961–1965, imported productions accounted for more than two-
thirds of all films seen on American screens. However, toward the end of
the decade, the number of American productions began to show signs
of increasing once again. Film production in the United States is still
dominated by the major studios, but in recent years the percentage of
independent productions has almost doubled (Appendix XV). While
the independents may appear to be gaining control of the industry, this
is not really so, for the independents still work largely through the major
studios for financing, and sometimes distribution.

While the statistics indicate that in recent years the motion picture
industry has recouped some of its financial losses, in actual fact there
has been a gradual decline in the annual expenditure on movies as a
percentage of total recreational expenditures (Appendix V). Nevertheless, through steady increases in the price of admission, the industry has
been able to show an improvement at the box office (Appendix XVII).
While no accurate attendance figures are available, there is some indication that weekly movie audiences have stabilized at between fifteen and
twenty million.[8] Also, these box-office figures do not take inflation into
account, which would reduce the 1974 figures by approximately 70 percent when measured in 1958 dollars.

Despite the financial woes of the movie industry, there was a steady increase in construction of new and much smaller movie theaters (Appendix XVIII). This was the "third generation" of movie theaters, and the wheel had now come full cycle since the destruction of the small nickelodeons, and the construction of the picture palaces in the 1920s. Between 1971 and 1973, approximately 1,670 new theaters, both indoor and outdoor, were opened, announced, or placed under construction.[9] Like the film industry itself, these new theaters incorporated many changes, the most important of which was the "multiple-theater" — designed to cut overhead costs, while accommodating several audiences with different tastes. Such buildings housed two, three or even more separate theaters, with a shared lobby, rest rooms, and concession facilities. About 70 percent of these new theaters were being located in suburban shopping centers in order to take advantage of shift in residential areas. The shopping center was ideal — parking space was readily available, and the long trip downtown was eliminated. In pursuit of cost-cutting methods many theater owners began to install projection equipment so fully automated that only one operator was required. Once set, the equipment automatically dimmed the houselights, opened the curtains, started the projector, changed the reels, and, at the end of the show, brought the houselights back up again.[10] In some cases, where it was still convenient to be located downtown, the large picture palaces were converted into several smaller ones.[11]

Drive-ins too underwent a change, for by the mid-sixties, the continuing urban and suburban sprawl found many of them located on extremely valuable property. The result was a net decline in the number of drive-ins from the 1958 high of 4,063 to 3,800 in 1973 (Appendix XVIII). However, drive-ins still accounted for approximately 25 percent of the total box-office gross in 1973.[12]

Hollywood International

One important trend during the sixties was the increasing number of films produced outside the United States. This gradual move away from studio production in Hollywood itself was due to a variety of reasons. First, the development of new cinematographic technologies eliminated the need for expensive studio sets, where the director could exercise tight control over lighting and sound. These new cameras and other equipment were more portable, and location shooting lent authenticity which audiences now demanded. But there was another, and perhaps more important, reason for the proliferation of these "runaway" productions. The cost of production within Hollywood had risen steadily since 1945, and

431

the decade between 1960 and 1970 saw a further 50 percent increase.[13] These increases came from all segments of the industry: the cost of properties; the price of raw film stock; the costs of promotion; the payments to stars, producers and directors; but most onerous of all, the huge, and sometimes unnecessary, wage bill for the numerous union-protected craftsmen and technicians needed to mount a film. The unions were, unfortunately for them, the least willing to adjust to the realities of the problems of making profitable motion pictures in a highly competitive market. While actors, producers and directors all realized the need to modify their previously extravagant behavior, the unions continued to press their wage demands. Not that anyone could blame them for seeking a better standard of living, but it soon became obvious that it was far cheaper to make a film almost any place other than Hollywood.

The Hollywood craft unions criticized what they considered an irresponsible and unpatriotic tendency toward "runaway" productions, but producers were acutely aware of the cost savings which were possible outside the United States. Particularly if the film was a multimillion-dollar epic, requiring the hiring of armies, or thousands of extras, the producer and his Hollywood backers could probably scour the Mediterranean, Slavic and perhaps the Eastern European countries to obtain soldiers, horses and cannons in return, usually, for a modest amount of hard currency.[14] It was rumored that the Spanish Army was run as a profit-making enterprise because of its constant use by foreign film production companies.

The increased use of location filming was only one aspect of the growing internationalization of the motion picture industry, and the move toward totally international productions had started in the late fifties. Hollywood had always been sensitive to the importance of its overseas markets, and as the industry declined at home, the profits to be made elsewhere loomed even larger. By the early sixties, foreign markets were no longer the dumping ground for domestic films which had already recouped their profits, for overseas trade now accounted for more than 50 percent of the gross income from American films.[15] With the increasing emphasis on foreign distribution, producers were now free to seek financing anywhere in the world, as they were no longer entirely dependent upon pleasing the tastes of audiences in New York, Chicago or Peoria. Also, competition in the international film market was increasing and the United States was no longer the major producer of films in the world, having been surpassed by such countries as Japan, India, and even Hong Kong. Nevertheless, American films still occupy more than half of the world's screen time, although many of these films are "coproductions," with financing from several countries.

Professor Thomas H. Guback, in his excellent study of *The Inter-*

national Film Industry (1969), points out that such coproduction among several countries has many advantages: first, it broadens the base of financial investment; second, it assures a film two (or more) home markets where no import quotas can be applied to it; third, it allows the collection of subsidies in as many places where such production assistance is available; and last, and perhaps most important, it "permits the inclusion of a greater range of stars and other artistic and technical personnel without endangering the nationality of the film."[16] Another important aspect was that it allowed the film to be made in several versions, tailored to suit the idiosyncrasies of the various national censors, and with varying degrees of violence and sex to meet different American and European standards.[17]

With the increased use of location filming, the Hollywood studios found less and less use for their famous "backlots," that magic land wherein stood the hundreds of carefully constructed sets which had graced so many movies. The notorious spread of the City of Los Angeles had made these parcels of land worth far more to the housing developer than to the largely idle movie studios. In fact, one way in which the studios were replenishing their dwindling coffers was through the sale of this unneeded land. MGM, for example, sold 68 acres of its famous Culver City lot to a land developer for more than $7 million in 1971.[18] Other studios also "diversified" in order to maintain their income. Universal Studios, now largely into television production, offered conducted tours of its 420-acre lot, and charged $1.85 to $3.75 for a sightseeing trip in miniature buses. The studio also operated a $6 million visitor's center on the lot, which contained shops, restaurants and other entertainment attractions. More than 8 million visitors have paid admission to tour the studio since 1964, as the opportunity to see "how the movies are made" still holds a strong fascination.

Hollywood and Television

In deserting the movie theaters, Americans did not desert the movies, and, in fact, they are seeing more motion pictures today than ever before — but on television. Movies, both the regular feature film and the special made-for-television variety, now occupy a significant segment of total television viewing time. In the past year, television has even witnessed the production of special eight-hour "blockbusters" designed solely for network showing, and featuring big-name casts. The popularity of movies on television was well established in the early years of television, but in the mid-sixties the use of Hollywood's top films as special television attractions pointedly demonstrated that a well-made cinematic production could still attract large audiences, even if they were at home. For two showings of *The Bridge on the River Kwai,* which had earned the Academy Award for best film in 1960, ABC Television paid Columbia Studios $2,000,000. The first of these showings attracted an audience of over 60,000,000 viewers in 25,000,000 homes. Later, ABC agreed to pay Twentieth Century–Fox nearly $20,000,000 for television rights to seventeen films, including $5,000,000 to screen *Cleopatra* twice.[19] (This was still not enough to recoup the studio's incredible loss on this film.) It was recently announced that the last holdout — Selznick's *Gone With the Wind* — would be shown on NBC network television as part of the bicentenary celebrations in 1976; the cost was $5,000,000.

Television had helped to destroy the old film industry, but it had also helped to create a new one. (Today Hollywood is turning out the equivalent of six hundred feature films a year, and while employment in the craft unions is down, Hollywood is surviving largely as a result of the money it makes from television production.) But television production, too, could be a risky business, and studios were now at the mercy of the men who made the programming decisions at network headquarters in New York.

With the emergence of the special made-for-TV motion picture, Hollywood was witnessing the rebirth of the old "B" film — "long neither on imagination, nor cash, skirting budget limitations, using able and familiar if not top price names . . . and showcasing the studio's promising unknowns."[20] As with the "B" film, an occasional minor classic emerged, while directors and actors were given the opportunity to gain experience. Also, the studios usually marketed most of these television movies for exhibition in regular movie theaters overseas, adding to their much-needed income.

The "New" Hollywood

By the end of the sixties, the Hollywood revolution was almost completed; the old mass production studio system was gone forever (or into television production), and in its place there emerged a new philosophy of film-making which had its roots more in the boardrooms of the large New York corporations than on the sound stages of the studios. All through the sixties, Hollywood studios had experienced the occasional incredible success, only to have their profits dissipated by unpredictable losses. Thus the enormous profit Twentieth Century–Fox made from *The Sound of Music* (1966) was subsequently wasted in films like *Doctor Dolittle* (1967), which cost $17 million, and *Star!,* which cost over $15 million and starred Julie Andrews, who had been featured in both *The Sound of Music* and Walt Disney's hit *Mary Poppins* (1964). MGM's profits from *Dr. Zhivago* (1966) were lost on a series of disasters like *Zabriskie Point* (1969). In 1968, faced with an inexplicable shift in audience tastes in the late 1960s, the large studios found themselves holding inventories of unshown films which reached $1.8 billion, about three years' normal production. By 1969, five of eight major studios were awash in red ink, much of this difficulty being attributable to an attempt to gain "that one big smash hit film" which would put the studio back on its feet. David Melnick, the vice-president for production at MGM, recalled that "everybody acted as if there were some God of the movies who would periodically come down and save people from their follies by giving them a big hit. All they had to do was churn out movies and wait for the big smash that would make them well."[21] Unfortunately, not enough of these gifts were forthcoming.

While the studios gambled, and mainly lost, on the "blockbusters," a group of young independent producers were turning out low-budget hits such as *The Graduate* (1967) — $3 million; *Easy Rider* (1969) — $500,000; *Midnight Cowboy* (1969) — $3.1 million; *Alice's Restaurant* (1969) — $2.2 million; *Bonnie and Clyde* (1967) — $3 million; and *Medium Cool* (1969) — under $1 million. The success of these films resulted in a long series of newspaper and magazine articles which oversimplified the problems faced by the motion picture industry, and the suggestion was made that all Hollywood needed to survive was a hand-held camera, fast film and fast lenses, a succession of trendy young movie makers and undiscovered actors, and stories which dealt with, and therefore appealed to, the young. It was not that simple, as the studios found out when they attempted to appeal directly to the vacillating tastes of those under twenty. Once the audience sensed that they were being exploited, they stayed away. For every accidental success such as the insipid *Love Story* (1971), there were several failures like *The Strawberry Statement* (1970), or *Getting Straight* (1970); but then along would come a film like *Woodstock* (1970), and the industry would start on another cycle of hopeless imitations.

Part of the problem was a failure by the old guard in Hollywood to recognize that movie-making was no longer "show business" — the "business" of churning out "shows" for a mass audience. Television had clearly taken over this function, and kept its immense audience relatively happy, while the increasingly selective movie customers, willing to pay higher and higher prices for a seat in a theater showing a program of their own choice, began inexorably to alter film-making away from aimless mass production into a quasi-art or even a form of simplified social commentary. In the minds of their customers, the movies were now quite

435

clearly differentiated from television, and audiences expected something more than the old Hollywood formulae, and even more explicit visual thrills.

It was in the late sixties that the true significance of the *Paramount* decree became obvious; for with the gradual dissolution of the historic links between the studios and the theater chains (which exist, in part, even today), and the actual tearing down or conversion of the older movie houses, the way was now clear for the emergence of a form of proto-specialization for smaller, more select audiences in smaller movie theaters. While this specialization has yet to take definite shape, there are indications that this development holds the best hope for the future of the American film industry.

The continued promise of the motion picture industry, and its apparent unwillingness to lie down and play dead, is the major reason for the revitalized financial structure of the Hollywood studios. Why else would the knowledgeable "money men," who collect vast and unrelated undertakings because they are potential money-makers, have invested heavily in the film industry precisely at the time when none of the industry's indicators looked good? In 1969, MGM was taken over by Kirk Kerkorian, a hotel magnate; Warner Brothers was purchased from Seven Arts by Kinney National Service, Inc., which operated parking lots, construction companies, and a comic book empire; Embassy was controlled by the AVCO Corporation, which built aviation equipment; Paramount was in the hands of Gulf and Western, a multifaceted conglomerate; Universal Studios went from Decca Records to MCA, Inc., the monolithic talent agency, and large television production company; while United Artists was owned by TransAmerica Corporation, which also controlled banks, insurance companies and oil wells.[22] Of the three independent studios remaining, Walt Disney Productions, Inc., has been busily turning itself into an entertainment conglomerate for years, with its Disneyland and Disneyworld amusement parks, and television shows; while Twentieth Century–Fox and Columbia Pictures Industries (note the corporate name) have been frequent targets for takeover attempts. Not surprisingly, in a series of cost-cutting moves, almost all the studios closed their New York offices, and transferred their management to California to be closer to the base of operations — and also to dispose of their valuable New York real estate.

While Wall Street had long been an important factor in the financial structure of the American film industry, these new money men took a far greater interest in the actual operation and management of the studios. This new breed were different in other ways from the original movie moguls, in that they were highly educated, many holding advanced degrees in business, and they attacked business problems with management teams and dialogues, instead of the ruthless and raw power of the old studio bosses. They also cooperated with each other, sharing facilities and technological developments in order to cut costs. But most important, they are more interested in making profits than in making movies, and at this they have been most successful, for under new management the eight motion picture companies earned profits of $173 million in 1972, compared to losses that had totalled $41 million in 1969–1970 (Appendix XIX). One source put the actual loss at closer to $168 million.[23]

There is, of course, another way of looking at this takeover of Hollywood by the conglomerates. As one skeptical writer in the British publication the *Economist* noted:

. . . some of the conglomerates saw before the industry did that there would soon be an end to the day of big salaried staffs in the studios, of producers, directors and actors on retainer. The hope now is that financial killings can be made "simply" by spotting low cost box office winners and raising the money (as little as possible) to have them made. Meanwhile the glamour of escorting film stars and of first nights brings an added brightness to the far from dull lives of such conglomerators as Mr. Bludhorn of Gulf and Western.[24]

The technique of management which this group brought to Hollywood was fairly simple — cut unnecessary overheads, and try not to commit yourself too deeply. The man who most typified this approach was the hard-nosed president of MGM, James T. Aubrey, who also bore the brunt of the attacks on this philosophy of film-making launched by the writers, directors and stars, and even by those movie fans who deplored what Aubrey was doing to the once-great MGM studios. Nevertheless, he achieved positive financial results, but at what artistic cost we shall never know. After taking over in 1970, Aubrey (who was once president of CBS Television until fired for creating a "folksy image" for the network) removed over 5,000 people from MGM's payroll, sold the studio's famous property room, and unloaded the company's record business, its English studios, and its chain of theaters in South Africa. Much of the funds from these sales went into paying off the enormous $80 million debt incurred in 1969, and to raise front money for the 2,000-room MGM Grand Hotel which the company had built in Las Vegas. Aubrey also annunciated a policy of "minimizing risk," which meant that MGM could make only sixteen to twenty movies a year at a cost of under $2 million each. In 1972, MGM was able to make a profit of $9.2 million on revenues of $157 million.

However, with the fiftieth anniversary of MGM approaching in 1974, James T. Aubrey resigned as president of the studio in November, 1973. Hollis Alpert examined Aubrey's impact on MGM in *Saturday Review/*

World, and suggested that Aubrey did not know how to work with creative people, and that his experience in the "quick and dirty" television production business did not make him a fine judge of good cinema. One former MGM executive, with long experience in the movie world, observed of the new breed of financiers that "these people think that motion pictures would be a good business if approached on a businesslike basis, which means a cost-accounting kind of procedure. There's nothing wrong with this in theory, except in practice the manufacture of dreams is hardly likely to be responsive to that kind of procedure."[25] In late 1973, MGM announced that they would be minimizing their future film-making activities, and in November, the entire MGM film library was taken over by United Artists, who now distributed the once great studio's product in the United States. For all intents and purposes MGM no longer existed, except as a giant hotel in Las Vegas.

Each of the studios followed similar procedures, producing only sixteen to twenty films a year, but with the increase in independent productions there has been no dearth of films. A new kind of corporate producer is also now entering the motion picture production scene, as such companies as Quaker Oats *(Willie Wonka and the Chocolate Factory,* 1971), Bristol-Myers *(Sleuth,* 1973), and Mattel, Inc., the toy maker *(Sounder,* 1973), have indicated their faith in the future of motion pictures.[26]

What exactly is this magnetic attraction that big business feels for becoming involved in the movies? Certainly some of it is the glamour and the excitement of being associated with Hollywood; but of far greater importance is the potential windfall profits to be made. A movie like *The Godfather* (1971) can cost $6 million to produce, and gross over $200 million, while films based upon proven hits, such as *Hello, Dolly!* (1972) with top box-office stars, and costing over $15,000,000, fail to recoup their production costs.

It was obvious to all that there was still a vast potential movie audience, not only in the United States, but throughout the world. The question was how to attract them into the growing number of new, smaller theaters. Nobody had the answers, and reading through the Hollywood trade papers made it clear that the motion picture industry was floundering around for a solution. The studios, distributors and exhibitors tried a variety of new merchandising methods, with varying degrees of success.[27] The *Independent Film Journal* reported in mid-1974 that, angered at their declining share of the profits, many exhibitors were considering bypassing the regular distribution channels, and financing productions themselves. Meanwhile, the editor of *Boxoffice* proposed the careful development of new talent and a large reduction in production budgets as the best means of making the U.S. film industry healthy. He noted that the profit-making ability of small-budget films was well documented.[28] In May, 1974, the *Wall Street Journal* reported that the major film companies were adopting Broadway's usually successful financing techniques, and had begun to use outside investors, or "angels," to put up money for films. The reason was that, despite the emergence of new highly profitable films, movie-making was a more risky business than ever. The *Journal* quoted producer Joseph E. Levine as saying that the chances of success were now 1 in 20, as opposed to 1 in 10 in pre-TV days.[29] More than ever before in its seventy-year history, the American film industry found itself fighting for its life, while occasionally producing spectacularly successful films.

The Attempt to Classify

One aspect of American film production about which there was little disagreement was the increased freedom afforded film makers to explore any and every theme they chose. We have already seen in the previous chapter how the long struggle over movie censorship had been an almost total victory for the movie industry; the only question now was, with legal censorship all but removed, what would take its place? The fact that the Supreme Court of the United States had seen fit to grant freedom of expression to film makers did not mean overnight public acceptance of this philosophy. Both Catholic and Protestant groups continued their pressure on the MPAA to remember its responsibilities, and to adhere to its pledge to "police" the industry's products. The fact was, of course, that with the demise of strict legal censorship, and the continued need to find some form of content which would attract audiences, the MPAA was helpless to prevent the gradual increase in films which concentrated on previously forbidden themes, or which used sex and nudity as their main attractions.

As early as 1961, *Time* magazine had noted:

Few regret the passing of the phony Hays ethics in which morality was supposedly satisfied as long as movies stuck to a long list of artificial don'ts. . . . But Hollywood's new freedom, while making more room for honest art, has also made more room for calculated smut, drawing a barrage of protests from parents, pastors and assorted pressure groups. . . .

But the real trouble with movies today is not so much the choice of subject matter, since even the most sordid subject can be treated with dignity and art; the trouble is precisely their lack of art, their crass and speculative exploitation of sex.[30]

Inevitably, the subject of what would replace the anachronistic *Production Code* led to a debate on "classification." After the drastic stream-

439

lining of the *Code* in 1966, the PCA was empowered to divide approved films into two categories, and for the next two years, many of these new films found themselves with a label exclaiming, "Suggested for Mature Audiences." This label was purely advisory, and there were no legal restrictions involved. In 1968, the Supreme Court of the United States handed down two decisions on the same day which would have a profound effect on the MPAA's decision to devise its own classification system. In *Interstate Circuit v. Dallas,* the Court invalidated an age classification system in Dallas because of the vagueness of the classification standards, but left the path clear for future attempts by hinting that age classification systems with more tightly drawn standards might survive the application of constitutional tests.[31] On the same day, the Court ruled in *Ginsberg v. New York* that a New York statute which prohibited the sale to minors of material that young people would find obscene was legal, even though the same material could not be considered obscene if adults were to read it.[32] Thus the *Dallas* case, if examined in the context of the *Ginsberg* ruling, clearly allowed cities and states to attempt movie control through more tightly drawn classification laws.

The MPAA was at first elated by the *Dallas* decision, and president Jack Valenti, who had succeeded Eric Johnston in June, 1966, observed that now the question of offensiveness in films would be decided by the criminal statutes of the states, where he felt it should belong.[33] However, by mid-May, Valenti had changed his mind after having been counseled by Louis Nizer, who was legal adviser to the MPAA. Nizer apparently pointed out that the way was now open for every city or state in the country to devise its own classification system, and that "classification . . . by the industry would give public notice that it was doing everything possible to distinguish between adult entertainment and films suitable for all ages."[34] But it was not a simple matter of merely introducing a motion picture industry classification scheme, for Valenti had more than the producer members of the MPAA to contend with. As a result of the merger of the two largest exhibitor organizations, Allied States and Theater Owners of America, to form the National Association of Theater Owners (NATO), a new force had emerged in the film industry, and one which represented exhibitors who owned approximately 70 percent of all the movie theaters (including drive-ins) in the United States. A third organization, the International Film Importers and Distributors of America Inc. (IFIDA) would also have to be involved in any discussions of a national classification system.

The problem was that while Valenti may have sought comfort in now being able to battle censorship through criminal prosecutions for obcenity, the members of NATO and IFIDA were not anxious to spend their time and money on extensive legal battles. The target for legal action would no longer be the producer or distributor, but the exhibitor, and even the projectionist. Part of the difficulty lay in the fragmented nature of NATO itself, with members spread all across the country and with vastly different outlooks on the specific content of films. Valenti was obviously concerned that the federal government would step in with a classification system of its own, and after extensive discussions with both NATO and IFIDA, a specific system was devised, which included an "X" rating which proscribed the attendance of young people at certain movies, even if accompanied by their parents. The new code (or ratings system) was publicly unveiled on October 7, 1968, and was set to go into effect on November 1.[35]

The ratings system was designed to do away with the old *Code* and its prohibitive restrictions, and to allow the film maker "unprecedented creative freedom, while at the same time maintaining a system of 'self-regulation' that would ease the pressures for some form of government classification."[36] Under the plan, there were no restrictions on thematic content or treatment of any film, but the final result would be assigned one of four ratings: G (all ages admitted; general audiences); M (suggested for mature audiences — adults and mature young people); R (restricted; children under sixteen required an accompanying parent or adult); or X (no one under sixteen admitted). The MPAA was careful to point out that these were not qualitative ratings, but were meant only to inform the public as to the film's suitability for children. However, the industry retained an abbreviated version of the old *Code*, consisting of eleven "Standards for Production" in regard to violence, criminal behavior, illicit sex, profanity, sex aberrations, and cruelty to animals. Films which were rated X were denied a *Code* seal, but this act no longer had any meaning. Stephen Farber notes that the reason for withholding the seal from X-rated films was that the association was committed to legally defending any film carrying its seal, and it could not afford to defend every "skin-flick."[37] In early 1970, the M rating was changed to GP (all ages admitted; parental guidance suggested), as the M had tended to be confusing. At the same time the R and X age limits were upped to seventeen. (Some exhibitors took it upon themselves to make the age limit eighteen.)

With the introduction of the ratings system, the old PCA was replaced by the MPAA Code and Rating Administration (CARA). There are seven permanent members of the CARA based in Los Angeles, who examine both scripts and the final films, and who are supposed to classify films only with regard to their suitability for viewing by children. Stephen Farber's inside look at CARA in *The Movie Rating Game* (1972) provides ample evidence that the MPAA has still not freed itself from the "censorship" philosophy which maintained the *Production Code* for more than thirty years. Valenti's intention was to create a system which would inform the public of what the motion picture industry considered to be a film's nature or content, but the CARA used the ratings as a threat to force producers to make alterations and deletions in order to obtain a more acceptable rating. Also, the standards for assigning a rating were arbitrary and never clearly articulated.

It was a great personal disappointment to Valenti that the ratings system did not meet with overwhelming acceptance. While he was citing a study which indicated that 64 percent of movie-going adults felt that the system was either "very useful" or "fairly useful" in determining those movies which children should attend, there was, in fact, strong opposition from many segments of the public, who were distressed with the degree of explicitness currently displayed in films. Much of this opposition was due to the fact that the ratings were not constructed to be coercive (but which, Farber noted, they were in practice), and it soon became apparent that an X rating did not mean automatic disaster at the box office. Some producers even consciously strove for an X rating in order to take advantage of the publicity value, while being unconcerned about the loss of the under-eighteen audience. Also, the ratings themselves were not very informative, and the categories were quite broad and encompassed a wide range of criteria. Thus a GP-rated movie was not guaranteed to be free from violence. One extreme point of view was expressed by Charles H. Keating, Jr., in his minority report to the Commission on Obscenity and Pornography in 1970:

Motion picture theaters are to be found in every nook and cranny of the United States. These theaters today present explicit sexual conduct, more often abnormal than normal, as the principal bill of fare. Thanks to Jack Valenti, we have a condition in the motion picture industry today that literally constitutes a course of instruction in decadence, perversion and immorality. Honored companies as Twentieth Century–Fox retain pornographers such as Russ Meyer, and produce obscenities such as "Beyond the Valley of the Dolls." It is a sad and dangerous day in America when an industry with as much influence as the motion picture industry turns its back on responsibility and moral code [sic] and permits a man such as Russ Meyer access to their hallowed circles.[38]

Keating was not alone in his anger and disappointment, and there was a rash of legislation based upon the ratings system introduced into various state legislatures in the early seventies.[39] Also, on May 18, 1971, both the National Catholic Office for Motion Pictures and the National Council of Churches' Broadcasting and Film Commission withdrew their support from the MPAA because of "the growing number of films unsuitable for the young, coupled with the clearly unrealistic ratings handed out. . . ."[40] It was specifically the increasing number of films exploiting sex and violence that were given GP ratings which aroused these religious groups. Writing in the Catholic weekly *America*, Philip C. Rule noted that the MPAA and its ratings were no more equipped to handle the current movie content than the MPPDA was with the old *Code*. Rule prophesied ominously, "It all appears to be building up to something: either a change in film fare, a better and more effective rating system or some form of control from outside the industry [censorship]."[41]

The New Freedom

After the series of Supreme Court rulings had removed (in theory, at least) many of the restrictions on film-making and exhibition, it was not long before American movie theaters were being deluged with a series of films which quite blatantly used various kinds of sexual activity as their only selling feature. Starting innocuously in 1959, with producer-director Russ Meyer's *The Immoral Mr. Teas*, by 1974 neighborhood theaters in cities all across the country were casually exhibiting hard-core pornography in double-bill shows. *Mr. Teas* was the breakthrough film; costing $24,000 to make, it netted Meyer over $1,000,000. Meyer lead the way with further "sexploitation" epics such as *Lorna* (1964) and *Vixen* (1968), each one a step closer to the ultimate pornographic feature film, but he stopped short of actual sexual intercourse on the screen. As a result of his proven successes at the box office, Meyer was invited by Twentieth Century–Fox to direct *Beyond the Valley of the Dolls*, a milestone in that it was the first, and possibly the last, attempt by a big studio to enter the sexploitation market. The film failed to attract much of an audience.[42]

By far the majority of these sexploitation films were sleazy, cheap productions, but occasionally a producer like Alex de Renzy or Radley Metzger would make a movie which, while pornographic, still met normal exhibition quality, and would receive play dates in the best first-run theaters. However, most of these smaller productions were shown in "special" theaters which were euphemistically known as "art houses."

In 1972, a hard-core pornographic film called *Deep Throat*, featuring an unlikely actress with the improbable name of Linda Lovelace, created a national sensation. The film attracted publicity that had every big studio green with envy, and, more important, it was an enormous success at the box office. *Deep Throat* became part of the "new liberalism," and Nora Ephron commented in *Esquire* that "there was an overwhelming amount of conversation and column space concerning the film; not to have seen it seemed somehow . . . derelict."[43] For a $25,000 investment, the film had earned its producers over $1,500,000 within a year of its release. The film's "star," Linda Lovelace, was featured on the cover of *Esquire* and *Playboy* — pornography had become chic!

In August, 1972, *Deep Throat* was seized from the World Theater in New York City by the city police under a warrant issued by the New York County Criminal Court. The case eventually came to trial on December 19, and ran through until January 3, 1973. Although the theater owner had such expert witnesses as author and critic Professor Arthur Knight testify on behalf of the film, the final verdict, rendered by Judge Tyler, was a violent (and sometimes humorous) attack on pornographic films. The judge ruled that the film was "obscene."[44]

This one decision did not stop *Deep Throat* from being exhibited in places outside New York, and the film has continued to make money. More important, the movie had demonstrated what the Commission on Obscenity and Pornography had pointed out two years earlier — that there was no causal connection between the viewing of pornography and the decline in the morals of an individual. The commission suggested that pornography should be available to those adults who wished to avail themselves of it, for ". . . explicit sexual materials are sought as a source of entertainment and information by substantial numbers of American adults. . . . The most frequent purchaser of explicit sexual materials is a college-educated, married male, in his thirties or forties, who is of above average socio-economic status. . . . Society's attempts to legislate for adults in the area of obscenity have not been successful."[45]

The success of the sexploitation film encouraged the major studios to increase the amount of sexual frankness in their bigger-budgeted films, and the hard-won freedom of expression which American film producers had achieved was now being used to show total nudity whenever this could be worked into the plot. (More often than not, such displays destroyed the essential rhythm of the film!) Many were angered at this abuse of the right to artistic freedom. Social critic, and professor of urban values at New York University, Irving Kristol noted that whereas critics of censorship had "wanted a world in which 'Desire Under the Elms' would be produced, or 'Ulysses' published," without interference from the Philistine busybodies, "they have got that, but they have also got a world in which the public flocks during lunch hours to witness varieties of professional fornication."[46] Sociologist Robert Nisbet, author of several important books on the social bond and the quest for community in America, also noted: "I think it would be difficult to find a single decade in the history of Western Culture when as much barbarism, as much calculated onslaught against culture and convention in any form, as much sheer degradation of both culture, and the individual passed into print, into music, into art, and onto the American stage as the decade of the 1960's."[47]

It was not so much a Puritan revolt against artistic freedom that motivated these outbursts, but a genuine concern for the failure of art to exercise self-restraint. Without the restraints which were once artificially imposed, film makers thrashed about in a confused state, attempting to utilize this freedom in ways which would attract customers; but in the process they had lost sight of the real possibilities which had been offered to them. It was an old story in Hollywood, and as long as seemingly intelligent people found and justified "redeeming social values" in films like *Deep Throat,* the film industry was only too pleased to satisfy them. However, even Hollywood has some scruples, and wisely the big studios never really entered the hard-core pornography field — simulated intercourse being the accepted practice. Even the much-heralded *Last Tango in Paris* (1973), while extremely frank in language and nudity, did not show actual intercourse on the screen. It is ultimately only a matter of time before the strong strain of puritanism, which lurks just beneath the surface of American society, will rise up to once again impose artificial restraints on freedom of expression. "Pornotopia," as sociologist Daniel Bell calls it, will eventually cause its own downfall; it is hoped that, before there is a total rejection of the new freedom, all artists, and especially film makers, learn to use it for mankind's benefit, and not its degradation.

The fact that Hollywood could use artistic freedom to produce important landmarks in film history has been repeatedly demonstrated in the last ten years, and films like *Midnight Cowboy,* which won the Academy Award for best film in 1969, and smaller masterpieces such as *The Last Detail* (1973) indicate the heights to which Hollywood can rise. Even a film like *The Exorcist* (1973), which would never have been made with the same realism prior to 1968, showed what could be achieved within a more commercialized context.

It appeared that the use of blatant sex and violence in big-budget Hollywood films was on the decline in early 1974. In 1973, *Variety*'s annual survey of film earnings in key cities showed that two of the biggest box-office attractions were outright pornography. A Technicolor epic entitled *The Devil in Miss Jones* had placed fifth, earning $7.3 million, while the peripatetic *Deep Throat* was eleventh with $4.6 million. *Last Tango in Paris* had placed third, earning $8.9 million. Still, the top film and the surprise of the year was *The Poseidon Adventure,* which earned over $13 million for its jubilant producers.[48] This last film was a throwback to the old Hollywood adventure film, featuring lavish sets, an all-star cast, and a good story. Of course, this film was itself based upon the successful formula used a few years earlier in such star-studded epics as *Hotel* (1967) and *Airport* (1969). The film studios took note of the success of *The Poseidon Adventure,* and 1974 saw a veritable slew of movies being made about mass destruction, including the highly success-ful *Towering Inferno.*[49]

The Supreme Court's Indecision

In the mid-sixties there was a remarkable "revolution" in public ac-ceptance of explicit sexual content, most of which was allowed under the First Amendment. In fact, theatrical pornographic films were a rather late development, and followed the acceptance of the sale of pornographic books and magazines, the introduction of topless and then bottomless restaurants and bars, the showing of simulated sex acts on the stage, and the appearance of "specialty" magazines like *Screw.* While desultory attempts were made to suppress all of these, the courts continuously ruled in favor of "freedom of speech." It was the open manner in which this material was available which led to public outcries, and as a result, in 1968, a Presidential Commission on Obscenity and Pornography was ap-pointed. When this commission finally reported in 1970, and recom-mended that pornography be legalized, President Nixon disowned the findings, and continued to make his conservative appointments to the Supreme Court.

In June, 1973, the Supreme Court of the United States once again entered the picture with a series of rulings which served to create even more confusion in the movie industry. Since the last major censorship and obscenity cases in 1968, four new members had come to the bench by the personal choice of President Richard Nixon. This was supposed to swing the balance of the Court back to a more strict definition of ob-scenity, but the justices continued to show an independent spirit which must have angered their conservative mentor in the White House. Never-theless, the majority ruling on a redefinition of obscenity presented a possibly disastrous situation for the movie industry, and opened the way for a return to conditions resembling those of 1915.

"This is an area in which there are few eternal verities," wrote Chief Justice Warren E. Burger in announcing a new definition of obscenity on June 21, 1973. In a complex of five decisions, the Court's conservative majority, prevailing by a one-vote margin, opened the way for states and the federal government to limit further the distribution of sexually oriented material deemed to be offensive by local community standards. The majority held that:

To fall into the category of obscene material which states can suppress or regu-late without violating the First Amendment, material no longer has to be found utterly without redeeming social value, but only to lack serious literary, artistic, political or scientific value.

446

The question of the offensiveness of material can be judged against local, not national, community standards.

"Adult" books and films, exhibited and distributed in theaters and bookstores from which juveniles are excluded and from which persons offended by such material are warned, are not exempt from state regulation if found obscene.

Congress can constitutionally ban the importation or the carrying in interstate transportation of obscene material, even if the material is intended only for the personal use of the possessor.[50]

The Court, Burger noted, had agreed on "concrete guidelines to isolate 'hard core' pornography from expression protected by the First Amendment . . . to provide positive guidance to the federal and state courts alike." Thus states could regulate obscene works which depicted or described sexual conduct. The material would be judged as obscene or not under these guidelines:

Whether "the average person, applying contemporary community standards" would find that the work, taken as a whole, appeals to the prurient interest. This was almost the same as the first part of the 1966 test. But the court modified it by making clear that the community standards could be local, not national, ones: "It is neither realistic nor constitutionally sound to read the First Amendment as requiring that the people of Maine or Mississippi accept public depiction of conduct found tolerable in Las Vegas or New York City."

Whether the work depicts or describes, in a patently offensive way, sexual conduct specifically defined by the applicable state law. Offensiveness too would be measured against community standards.

Whether the work, taken as a whole, lacks serious literary, artistic, political or scientific value. This new test replaced the most-criticized third part of the 1966 test, the criteria that — for material to be obscene and subject to state regulation — it must also be utterly without redeeming social value. This criteria, wrote Burger, had required the prosecution to assume "a burden virtually impossible to discharge" — the responsibility of proving a negative. Even Brennan, its author, Burger noted, had now abandoned this test as unworkable. Brennan pointed out that the new test still required the prosecution to prove a negative.[51]

Burger did, however, concede that "the 'Sexual Revolution' of recent years may have had useful byproducts in striking layers of prudery from a subject long irrationally kept from needed ventilation." But he also observed that this did not mean that all regulation should be removed from "hard-core" materials, for "civilized people do not allow unregulated access to heroin because it is a derivative of medicinal morphine."

The result of the Supreme Court's rulings was predictable, and Jack Valenti lost no time in articulating the dangers which they presented. He pointed out on NBC's Today Show that "the great, artistic, serious filmmakers will be harassed and possibly convicted because of the lack of clear guidelines." Valenti also protected MPAA members by suggesting,

447

"The responsible motion picture industry is not the intended target of the Supreme Court's decisions . . . [it] . . . never intended for serious, well-intentioned films to be banned."[52] Valenti had every reason to be apprehensive, for while the Court's ruling was clearly aimed at destroying the commercial exploitation of hard-core pornographic films, many local and state authorities saw this as an opportunity to legally attack serious, well-intentioned films. An early indication of this came two weeks later, when the Georgia Supreme Court ruled that the critically acclaimed film *Carnal Knowledge* was obscene. Valenti declared that the MPAA would pursue to the highest court in the land the legal freedom for responsible film makers to tell their story without the harassment which was inevitable under these rulings.

The situation now was entirely reminiscent of the era before the introduction of the *Production Code* in 1933. Expressing their dismay over the Court's decision, the Screen Actors Guild (SAG) described it as "truly mind-boggling . . . a staggering blow to an industry already beset with numerous problems." An editorial in the *Screen Actor,* the official quarterly of the SAG, pointed out the absurdities the rulings had created:

Filmmakers will now have to prejudge what moral standards they may be offending in every town and hamlet in the U.S. before making a film. . . . The films we see will not be able to accommodate a general national standard, but rather must be made to accommodate the requirements of communities with the most restrictive standards. . . . These local standards will have the effect of curtailing creativity to the point where the view of our social life on the screen may have little, if any, relationship to reality.[53]

As a result of the Court's decision, agents of the Manhattan district attorney stepped up action against theaters showing pornographic films,[54] while the six New England states banded together to crack down on obscene films, and attempts were made to reinstitute the old film review boards of a decade ago.[55] The movie industry had every reason to be alarmed, and much of the blame was placed at the door of Valenti and the MPAA's ratings system, which many believed had outlived its usefulness.

The ratings system had, in fact, failed to reduce the pressure on the industry, or to provide the guidance which Valenti had hoped it would. Instead, exhibitors were discovering that R and X ratings were tantamount to waving a red flag in front of bluenoses. While the ratings were intended as a voluntary form of self-regulation, all too often they were being used against exhibitors by local law-enforcement officers, who threatened action against the showing of X-rated films. In some cases newspapers refused to run advertisements for X-rated films, and a virtual news blackout was imposed by television and radio stations.[56] Certain states and cities even attempted to impose "smut taxes" on admission tickets to all X-rated movies;[57] but, more important, a survey of NATO in 1969 indicated that almost half of the theater owners refused to show an X-rated film.[58] What had started out as a well-intentioned method of assisting personal choice had, in effect, become a means of suppression, and a more clearly marked target for bluenoses to aim at.

In late 1973, the Supreme Court gave some cause for hope by agreeing to review the *Carnal Knowledge* case, in which Albany, Georgia, theater manager Billy Jenkins had been convicted by the Georgia Supreme Court. Jenkins had the solid support of the Association of American Publishers, the Authors League of America and NATO, all of whom hoped that the Court would opt for statewide obscenity standards, rather than the local standards indicated in the June decision. In June, 1974, the Supreme Court ruled, in a unanimous decision, that *Carnal Knowledge* was not obscene. Justice Rehnquist, writing for the Court, noted: "Our own view of the film satisfies us that 'Carnal Knowledge' could not be found under the [Court's 1973] standards to depict sexual conduct in a patently offensive way."[59] The problem was that the justices still offered no clear guidelines to what *was* obscene, and Justice Brennan pointed out the ridiculous situation that "one cannot say with certainty that material is obscene until at least five members of this Court, applying inevitably obscure standards, have pronounced it so." (Justice Douglas stuck to his long-held view that the Constitution prohibits any ban on obscenity.) Jack Valenti claimed that he was "delighted" and that the decision upheld "the freedom of the film market to tell an honest story without hard-core pornography."[60]

After nearly sixty years the motion picture was no nearer achieving freedom from legal restraint than it had been in 1915. While the grounds for censorship had been gradually refined down to a test of "obscenity," the vagueness of the concept, and the fact that its application was to be left to local communities, each applying their own standards, could only encourage continued harassment. The current situation will mean a constant stream of censorship ("obscenity") cases before the Supreme Court, until such time as the justices issue firm and clear guidelines; or finally concur with Justice Douglas that the movies should be freed totally from the burden of censorship.

The Public and the Movies

What was the public reaction to the increasing frankness in American films? Earlier in this chapter it was noted that hard-core pornographic

449

films had achieved considerable financial success; but then so had traditional adventure, romance, comedy and mystery films. The majority of the public did not really seem to mind sexually oriented films, but that did not mean that they would necessarily attend them with any frequency.[61] Exactly what they would go and see at any given time remained a mystery, and was beyond the prediction of even the most experienced film makers. For this reason, every success precipitated a plethora of faded copies of the original; each worse than the first and achieving diminishing financial returns.

Early in the sixties, the success of the James Bond series in such films as *Dr. No* (1962), *To Russia with Love* (1963) and *Goldfinger* (1964) inspired a succession of dismal spy-thrillers, and even the Bond films eventually became parodies of themselves although they remained box-office successes. Similarly, in the early seventies, Warner Brothers accidently discovered that oriental martial arts films had a vast audience in the United States, and literally overnight kung fu swept the nation's movie houses. One such film, *Five Fingers of Death,* made in Hong Kong for $300,000, grossed $3,800,000 in only eleven weeks in the United States, and $4,100,000 in other countries.[62] These films also inspired the openings of a large number of kung fu schools, where Americans could learn oriental fighting techniques, and a successful television program which combined kung fu and the traditional Western idiom.

In between these two fads, Hollywood went through a variety of cycles, forever searching for the key to the audience's interest. However, there was no single and simple key for audiences, and their tastes had become so diversified that the appeal of any one film lay in an intangible combination of ingredients — plot, star, director and lucky timing. Sometimes they all came together to produce a film like *Mary Poppins* (1964) which attracted children and adults alike; or *The Devil in Miss Jones* (1973), a hard-core pornographic film which attracted curious adults; or one of the biggest films of the postwar period — *The Godfather* (1972), which attracted everybody, and grossed over $85 million in just nine months, and returned more than 1,000 percent on its investment for Paramount Studios. The sequel, *Godfather II,* was to be an even greater artistic, if not box-office, triumph.

There were other trends, some more successful than others, which saw a slew of motorcycle gang "cheapies," which attracted their own cult audience; a constant stream of horror films imported from the dungeons of Hammer Films in England, a few of which were classics of the genre; and an interesting series of "caper" films in which the entire story revolved around the attempt to engineer an improbable theft of some fabulous art treasure or mounds of gold bullion. Mysteries were popular, and they also became increasingly violent and frank as the decade wore on; the same happened to Westerns, culminating in director Sam Peckinpah's *The Wild Bunch* (1969), which was deliberately created to show the horror of violence.

While the courts battled with sexual issues, the public seemed to be far more concerned with the violence in movies, which became increasingly more gory and realistic. Films such as *Bonnie and Clyde, The Wild Bunch,* and *Straw Dogs* (1972) precipitated serious critical debates about the merits of depicting violence in such graphic terms on the screen. Much the same debate was taking place in the U.S. Senate about the influence of violence on television screens, and a special advisory committee was formed to investigate this issue. In 1972, the *Surgeon General's Report on Television and Social Behavior* was issued — the most comprehensive examination of visual mass media influence ever undertaken. While the results were cautiously interpreted, the report noted:

. . . there is a convergence of the fairly substantial experimental evidence for *short-run* causation of aggression among some children by viewing violence on the screen and the much less certain evidence from field studies that extensive violence viewing precedes some *long-run* manifestations of aggressive behavior. This convergence of the two types of evidence constitutes some preliminary indication of a causal relationship, but a good deal of research remains to be done before one can have confidence in these conclusions.[63]

The fact that motion pictures had not lost their power to influence an audience was dramatically illustrated by the release of *The Exorcist* in late 1973. This film, a mixture of sex, sadism and the occult, created more public furor than any motion picture since *The Birth of a Nation* in 1915. Everywhere the film was shown there were reports of fainting and vomiting in theaters, but of greater significance was the reported increase in belief in the devil, demonic possession, and serious psychological disorders manifested by people who had seen the film. The film was also accused by many knowledgeable people of fostering a false sense of fatalism, through which the audience was led to believe that they were not responsible for their actions. As was usual in such cases, the greater the publicity, the more audiences were willing to masochistically submit themselves to endure the admittedly well-made, but frightening, actions on the screen. In 1974, there was an unexpected swing back to the "personality" film, and the success of movies like *The Sting* and *The Way We Were* was due almost entirely to the audience attraction to the stars, Robert Redford, Paul Newman and Barbra Streisand.

In the early summer of 1975, Universal Studios released the movie *Jaws,* the story of a man-eating shark with Moby Dick-like pretensions, based upon the best-selling novel by Peter Benchley. For whatever unlikely psychological or cultural reason this film has shown every indication of becoming the biggest motion picture box-office attraction of all time. More importantly, the summer of 1975 proved to be one of "shark-mania" throughout the United States, all of which, *Variety* noted in its July 2, 1975 issue, "can't help but hype the b.o., but it's clear that in addition to being a business blockbuster, 'Jaws' is proving to be a cultural curiosity as well." What long-term effect this extremely well-made and terrifying film will have on the public's perception of the horrors of the deep is difficult to predict, but doubtless it may change ocean swimming habits for many. Once again, *Jaws* has demonstrated the power which an individual motion picture can exercise on the collective imagination of the mass public. The success of *Jaws* threatened to launch the movie industry into a series of similar films featuring killer bees, giant rampaging bears, crocodiles, dogs, and even piranha fish.

The Black Films

Only in recent years has the topic of blacks in films received any serious treatment. The work of historians Thomas R. Cripps and Daniel J. Leab has been important in uncovering the abortive attempts to establish an indigenous black movie industry in the American cinema.[64] Hollywood at last discovered the potential of the film aimed directly at the black audience in the late sixties, when the film makers noted two salient facts: first, whites had begun to flee the inner city areas, leaving a vacuum in many of the big downtown movie houses which the burgeoning number of black moviegoers could fill; and second, black audiences would turn out in far greater numbers for films which featured black heroes and heroines, and were liberally sprinkled with sex and violence, than they would for white adventure movies.[65] The result was a race by the big studios to see who could sign up the best black actors, writers and even directors to transform scripts originally intended for whites into films which would appeal to black audiences. In most cases what had been cheap white films were transformed into cheaper black films, and the black community was split into "those for whom the entire phenomenon is a violent blow to black dignity and social well-being,"[66] and those who saw it as a necessary step in the acceptance of the black in American society.

It was estimated that between 1970 and 1972, some fifty feature films were specifically aimed at the black audience, while blacks were estimated to spend $120 million annually at movie theater box offices.[67] Much to the surprise of Hollywood, many of these films appealed to white audiences as well, and films like *Shaft* (1971) earned over $12 million, while a black Western — *Buck and the Preacher* (1972) — earned $10 million. Forecasts suggested that nearly one-quarter of future American film productions would be made for primarily black audiences.[68]

The question was whether or not these films gave an accurate portrayal of American black life. One NAACP official angrily stated: "We must insist that our children are not constantly exposed to a diet of so-called black movies that glorify black males as pimps, dope pushers, gangsters and super males with vast physical prowess but no cognitive skills."[69]

Naturally those who were concerned with the production of these films defended their product as "serving . . . [a] . . . therapeutic function," or destroying "the myth that crime does not pay."[70] However, there were serious manifestations of a negative influence in films like *Super Fly* (1972), which glorified the exploits of a dope pusher, when ghetto youngsters began imitating the dress and mannerisms of the film's hero, Ron O'Neal. Was this in fact any different from the imitation of James Cagney or Edward G. Robinson by white youngsters in the thirties? The noted black psychiatrist Alvin F. Poussaint took a different view, suggesting that

these latest film-inspired events are having an insidious effect on young lives. They are far from being innocent indicators of another teen-age fad like the Davy Crockett or the Batman crazes of a few years ago.

. . . These movies glorify criminal life and encourage in black youth misguided feelings of machismo that are destructive to the community as a whole. . . .

Negative black stereotypes are more subtle and neatly camouflaged than they were in the films of yesteryear, but the same insidious message is there: blacks are violent, criminal, sexy savages who imitate the white man's ways as best they can from their disadvantaged sanctuary in the ghetto.[71]

While thoughtful members of the black community raised serious questions about the impact of these "blaxploitation" movies, the studios were only too happy to find a successful formula, no matter how temporary it might be. One top movie executive was actually quoted as saying, "*We give the public what it wants.* The market for black films is the inner-city market. They want action/adventure movies." He was convinced that the majority of blacks enjoyed movies like *Super Fly,* which had grossed over $12 million by 1974.[72] An attempt by a coalition group, Committee Against Blaxploitation (CAB), to obtain better jobs for blacks in the movie industry, as well as an improvement in the portrayal of blacks on the screen, was unsuccessful, mainly because black actors felt threatened by the group's goals. The production of blaxploitation movies continues, while black community leaders now ironically seek the protection of legal censorship as a means of stopping the exhibition of such films.

The Movies Today

In an important article in the *New Yorker* in late summer 1974, the noted movie critic Pauline Kael wrote an impassioned and eloquent attack on the movie industry, in which she pointed out that while "American movies . . . are probably the best in the world," the studios were strangling creativity by concentrating their efforts only on the "big hits."[73] The unexpected upturn of the movie business during 1973–1974 had created an unfortunate attitude on the part of the movie industry which resulted in many important, but minor, films being shunted aside, while only the potential "big grossers" received the much-needed promotional push. According to Mrs. Kael, "It's becoming tough for a movie that isn't a big media-created event to find an audience, no matter how good it is . . . the public no longer discovers movies. . . . If the advertising for a movie doesn't build up an overwhelming desire to be part of the event, people just don't go."[74]

The problem, she complained, stemmed directly from the control of the movie industry by businessmen, who, with the added advantage of saturating advertising techniques, were now able to control public reaction as well. Thus the content and quality of a film could be transcended by judicious promotional methods, and the result was triumph for "the businessmen's taste and the businessmen's ethic." Thus movies no longer strove to convey a "message," as many films in the early sixties had attempted to do with mixed success. Much of this change can be attributed to the fear of the uncertainty which had existed since the mid-fifties, for having once again found a formula that worked, the industry was determined to stay on firm ground. The result was aesthetic sterility, for as Mrs. Kael noted:

Traditionally, movies were thought linked to dreams and illusions, and to pleasures that went way beyond satisfaction. Now the big ones are stridently illusionless, for a public determined not to be taken in. Audiences have become "realists" in the manner of businessmen . . . they believe only in what gives immediate gratification. It's got to be right there — tangible, direct, basic, in their laps.[75]

The solution to the problem of "the hatred of the moneyman for the ungovernable artist" lay in devising new methods of producing and distributing films — to "abandon the whole crooked system of Hollywood bookkeeping, with its kited budgets and trick percentages." This would entail bypassing the business interests and having directors and actors finance their own productions, and arrange their own distribution and publicity. She ended rather pessimistically by suggesting that

there's no way of knowing whether a new audience can be found; it's a matter of picking up the pieces, and it may be too late. But if the directors started talking to each other, they'd realize that they're all in the same rapidly sinking boat, and there'd be a chance for them to reach out and try to connect with a new audience . . .

The artists have to break out of their own fearful, star-struck heads; the system that's destroying them is able to destroy them only as long as they believe in it and want to win within it — only as long as they're psychologically dependent on it.[76]

Pauline Kael's article did cause quite a stir in the industry, but coming as it did during a profitable period, it elicited mainly scorn, and she was accused of naïveté in her lack of understanding about the workings of the film industry.[77]

Many of the film industry's troubles of the sixties and early seventies were temporarily forgotten as *Variety* proclaimed on January 22, 1975: "U.S. '74 Film Rentals: $549-Mil. Annual Gross Best Since 1946 Peak."[78] The trade paper revealed that the 1974 box-office gross was $1,908,500,000, exceeding the 1946 total by more than $200,000,000. Of course, much of this increase was due to increased admission prices, but the MPAA reported that actual 1974 admissions were over one billion, exceeding the 1973 total by 17 percent, and 23 percent higher than the 1971 total. In fact, the 1974 attendance mark was the highest since 1966.[79] Once again, in the midst of an economic recession, the movie industry was holding its own. One source attributed much of the increased attendance to fuel shortages, which tended to keep people closer to home for entertainment, and *Variety* boldly predicted: " '74: Economic Gloom, Show Biz Boom."[80] However, one writer warned that the movie box office "seems to be immune to national economic turndowns — until the final months of the country's slump, at which time the [box office] softens."[81] With this historical cycle in mind, the 1975 industry performance would be closely watched. The industry had no reason to worry, for *Variety* reported in the August 13, 1975 issue that the "key city theatrical boxoffice in July soared more than 22% . . . for the period." The unprecedented success of *Jaws* made almost all the difference, again indicating the movie industry's dependence upon that one big "blockbuster." At the end of July the key city box office was running 12 percent above the first six months of 1974.

Was the 1970s movie audience any different from earlier audiences? In 1972, the MPAA conducted another of its comprehensive audience surveys, the results of which led Jack Valenti to note that the "industry has a solid and regular audience, not as large as we would like it, or as it should be, but one that appears unwavering in its devotion to motion pictures shown in theaters. *It is also increasing.*"[82] The backbone of this ardent following was found in the twelve to twenty-nine age group, which, although representing only 40 percent of the twelve-and-over population, accounted for 73 percent of total movie theater admissions. The average number of admissions per moviegoer in the twelve-and-over population rose from 11.7 in 1971 to 12.2 in 1972. Valenti also noted that the admissions for the forty to forty-nine age group had risen from 6 percent of total admissions in 1971 to 10 percent in 1972, but that the major attendance problems were still with the older population (Appendix XX).

The more frequent moviegoers, as expected, were found among teenagers, and the "frequent moviegoers" accounted for 86 percent of yearly admissions, while constituting only 23 percent of the twelve-and-over population. Education and family income were positive stimulants to movie attendance, while males still held a small lead in frequent moviegoing (Appendix XXI).

Ethnically, movie audience breakdowns offered some noteworthy comparisons. Of the white population twelve and over, 62 percent are moviegoers, while among the nonwhite, only 49 percent indicated that they went to the movies. However, whites accounted for 11.9 average yearly admissions per moviegoer, while the figure for nonwhites was 15.9. Significantly, the proportion of nonwhite frequent moviegoers rose from 37 percent in 1971 to 43 percent in 1972, while the proportion of whites remained the same.[83]

Valenti took the optimistic viewpoint that the "demographics of the American population are on our side," and noted that the fastest-growing segment of the population up to 1980 will be those in the late twenties and in the thirties, and that these were key groups in the makeup of the movie audience. For this reason he foresaw "opportunities for the growth of our business" well into the 1980s.[84]

The Discovery of the Movies

In 1975, Hollywood was by no means pessimistic about its future, but there was no real cause for unbounded optimism either. The problem was one of "creative chaos," as *Newsweek* observed, in which "the movie business is lost in the dark, and inevitably it scans the heavens for the lodestar of 'entertainment.' "[85] At the same time that American film makers were concerned with attracting audiences, the interest in motion pictures as art and as historical documents had reached an all-time high, not only on university campuses, but in film societies and clubs all across the country. Film magazines of both the popular and the academic variety are numerous, and the publication of film books has reached epidemic proportions in recent years. Much of this renewed interest can ironically be attributed to the continual showing of old movies on television, as this enables young audiences to see the "old classics"; but of greater significance is the ongoing enchantment with the visual medium, which cannot be suppressed.

More and more, academics, critics and everyday film "buffs" are beginning to realize the importance of the motion picture as an integral part of American social development in the twentieth century. The founding of the American Film Institute in 1967 was a belated admission that an important part of American culture was going to be lost forever unless it was given the recognition it deserved.[86] The movies have always been a business, yes, but at the same time they have provided entertainment for countless millions of Americans, and others throughout the world. The movies have also been a mirror, both absorbing and reflecting the society that created it; and while they do not necessarily provide us with an accurate historical portrait of their milieu, they can, with careful analysis, tell us a great deal. They have also often reached that level where they can be called an art. Perhaps they have not reached such heights often enough in their long history, but for many people, the movies have been the only really artistic "experience" in their lives. While the American film has been dominated by commercialism, and functioned primarily as an industry, it has also been a major socializing influence, and the true "democratic art" — the art of the people. It would be difficult to imagine the American landscape without the movies.

NOTES TO CHAPTER XVI

1. Alvin Toffler, *The Culture Consumers* (Baltimore: Penguin Books, 1965), p. 31.

2. From 1950 to 1960, when the population increased by 28 million, 84 percent of this growth took place in the nation's 212 metropolitan areas. The population of these areas increased by 26 percent. The largest growth took place in the suburban areas, which registered an increase of 49 percent compared to the 11 percent increase in central cities. Between 1960 and 1963, the growth rate of the suburbs was more than three times that of the central cities. See Wilfred Owen, "Problems of a Motor Age," in Allen M. Wakstein, ed., *The Urbanization of America: An Historical Anthology* (Boston: Houghton Mifflin Company, 1970), p. 419.

3. Herbert J. Gans, *The Levittowners* (New York: Alfred A. Knopf, 1967), p. 269. This is an excellent study of life in a suburban community, and destroys many of the myths which have developed about suburban life-styles.

4. For an extremely acute synthesis of the importance of the "counterculture" and the trends of the youth movement during the sixties see William L. O'Neill, *Coming*

Apart: An Informal History of America in the 1960's (Chicago: Quadrangle Books, 1971), pp. 233–271.

5. The evaluation of the full impact of the "counterculture" has yet to be determined; some have viewed it as mankind's hope for salvation, while others have seen it as a portent of Western civilization's ultimate ruin. An interesting attempt to deal with this issue of the "counterculture" is Theodore Roszak, *The Making of a Counter-Culture* (New York: Doubleday, 1969).

6. For more details on the extremely complex nature of the motion picture business in the sixties and seventies, see the collection of articles in A. William Bluem and Jason E. Squire, eds., *The Movie Business* (New York: Hastings House, 1972).

7. The difficulty in trying to ascertain trends in movie tastes is succinctly outlined in Aljean Harmerz, "How Do You Pick a Winner in Hollywood? You Don't," *New York Times,* April 29, 1973, sec. 2, p. 1.

8. This attendance figure is subject to some speculation, but it is realistic based upon dividing the total box office for the year by the average admission price. See Fletcher Knebel, "Hollywood: Broke, and Getting Rich," *Look,* vol. 34 (November 3, 1970), p. 52. However, one knowledgeable Hollywood journalist claims that the current weekly audience is forty million; see William Fadiman, "Hollywood, Shivering in the Sun," *New Republic,* vol. 162, no. 26 (June 27, 1970), p. 18.

9. As with all industry statistics, it is difficult to obtain an accurate estimate of the number of theaters in the U.S. The number of new theaters quoted here comes from figures supplied by the MPAA and originally obtained from *Boxoffice* magazine.

10. For more details of these automated theaters see "Hollywood: Fewer Stars, More Profits," *U.S. News and World Report,* January 18, 1971, pp. 48–50.

11. In Toronto, long known as a good "movie town," most of the large movie theaters have been converted into several smaller ones. See a detailed and interesting article on this subject in *Canadian Architect,* vol. 15 (August, 1970), pp. 26–30. Even though these theaters are "downtown," they attract large audiences, but then Toronto does not have many of the same problems as American cities.

12. Even 25 percent of the total box office is less than it should be, for drive-ins comprise approximately 35 percent of the number of theaters. Drive-in prices are usually, but not always, less than those of indoor theaters, and this could account for the discrepancy.

13. Fadiman, "Hollywood, Shivering in the Sun," p. 17.

14. John Quirt, "The Movies Go International," *Exchange,* vol. 30 (June, 1969), pp. 8–13. Overseas filming was also one way of freeing "frozen" currency.

15. *Film Daily Yearbook,* 1969, p. 96, contains figures for the largest markets for U.S. films.

16. Guback, *The International Film Industry,* p. 181. See also a very important discussion of American domination of the European film industry in Thomas H. Guback, "Cultural Identity and Film in the European Economic Community," *Cinema Journal.* vol. 14, no. 1 (Fall, 1974), pp. 2–17.

17. For more details on the shifting standards of sex and violence in the international movie market see Richard Dyer MacCann, "Hollywood Faces the World," *Yale Review,* vol. 51 (June, 1963), pp. 593–608. One economist has suggested that "the search for a product that has international appeal tends toward homogenization of the medium. . . . One formula that seems to possess a high probability of market success is the adventure story, often involving a disaster of enormous proportions. . . . This formula . . . calls for 'blockbuster' treatment involving investment of great lumps of capital, which of course, the major U.S. film companies are best able to provide. Thus the tendency toward concentration of the industry and homogenization of the product is reinforced." Joseph D. Phillips, "Film Conglomerate 'Blockbusters,'" *Journal of Communication,* vol. 25, no. 2 (Spring, 1975), p. 181.

18. "Hollywood: Fewer Stars," p. 50.

19. Charles Champlin, "Can TV Save the Films?" *Saturday Review*, December 24, 1966, p. 11.

20. *Ibid.*, p. 13.

21. "Making the Movies into a Business," *Business Week*, June 23, 1973, p. 116.

22. For more details on the complex history of the studios' involvement in new financial arrangements see "Making the Movies into a Business," p. 116, and Meccoli, "Conglomerates Gobble Up Movies," pp. 90–95.

23. "Making the Movies into a Business," p. 116.

24. "Is There Any Future in Hollywood?," *Economist*, February 28, 1970, pp. 52–53.

25. Hollis Alpert, "The Lion Meows," *Saturday Review/World*, January 26, 1974, p. 57. This is an excellent account of Aubrey's tenure at MGM, and gives an insight into the incompatability of the "money men" with the creative talent in studios.

26. For more details of this new financing arrangement see "Film-making Gets Some Tight-fisted Angels," *Business Week*, February 5, 1972, pp. 68–69.

27. One new marketing concept was known as "four-walling," in which entire theaters were rented, including the staff and concession stand, by companies making special "family" films, usually featuring wildlife stories. The film was then heavily advertised on television. While this concept was reported to be successful, it too began to run into difficulties in 1974.

28. *Independent Film Journal*, May 29, 1974, p. 1; and Ben Shlyen, in *Boxoffice*, November 5, 1973, p. 2.

29. *Wall Street Journal*, May 30, 1974, p. 1.

30. "The Big Leer," *Time*, vol. 77 (June 9, 1961), p. 55.

31. 390 U.S. 676 (1968).

32. 390 U.S. 629 (1968).

33. *Variety*, April 24, 1968, p. 3.

34. *Ibid.*, May 22, 1968, p. 4.

35. See Ayer et al., "Self-Censorship," pp. 820–836, for more details on the history of the delicate negotiations required before the ratings system was accepted by all parties.

36. Stephen Farber, *The Movie Rating Game* (Washington, D.C.: Public Affairs Press, 1972), p. 15. This is an excellent source for background information on the new ratings, and how they have been misapplied.

37. *Ibid.*, p. 17.

38. Charles H. Keating, Jr., in *The Report of the Commission on Obscenity and Pornography* (New York: Bantam Books, 1970), p. 612.

39. For more details of this misapplication of the ratings see "Private Ratings of Motion Pictures as a Basis for State Regulation," *Georgetown Law Review*, vol. 59 (May, 1971), pp. 1205–1236.

40. "Film-Rating Fiasco," *America*, vol. 124 (May 29, 1971), p. 557.

41. Philip C. Rule, "Film Ratings: 1934 Revisited," *America*, vol. 124 (May 29, 1971), p. 571.

42. There are several histories of erotic films, the most useful of which is Kenneth Turan and Stephen F. Zito, *Sinema* (New York: Praeger Publishers, 1974). See also William Rotsler, *Contemporary Erotic Cinema* (New York: Random House, Ballantine Books, 1973); and Martin A. Grove and William S. Ruben, *The Celluloid Love Feast* (New York: Lancer Books, 1971). A more incisive view is Fred Chappell, "Twenty-Six Propositions About Skin-Flicks," in W. R. Robinson, ed., *Man and the Movies* (Baltimore: Penguin Books, 1969), pp. 53–59. The lengthy series "Sex in the Cinema," pub-

lished in *Playboy* magazine in the last ten years, and written by Hollis Alpert and Arthur Knight, is the most comprehensive examination of the topic.

43. Nora Ephron, "Women," *Esquire,* vol. 89, no. 4 (February, 1973), p. 14. She further noted: "It may be a terrible mistake to take *Deep Throat* and its success seriously. These things may just happen . . . [it is] . . . one of the most unpleasant, disturbing films I have ever seen — it is not just anti-female but antisexual as well."

44. "The decision itself, running more than seven thousand words, was a tour de force of verbal fireworks. *Variety* called it 'the most colorful, readable, and explicit decision yet seen by the porno film trade,' and quoted one sexploitation publicist as saying that it was, 'the greatest money notice ever.' Judge Tyler could forge a new career in a porno promo, he suggested." See Richard Smith, *Getting into Deep Throat* (Chicago: Playboy Press, 1973), p. 281.

45. *Report of the Commission on Obscenity and Pornography,* p. 59.

46. Quote in Edwin McDowell, "The Critics Descend on Pornotopia," *Wall Street Journal,* May 15, 1973, p. 24.

47. *Ibid.,* p. 24.

48. Quoted in *Montreal Gazette,* January 19, 1974, p. 27.

49. For a note on the trends in disaster films see *New York Times,* June 8, 1974, p. 47.

50. "A Divided Court Rewrites the Definition of Obscenity," *Congressional Quarterly,* June 23, 1973, p. 1571.

51. *Ibid.*

52. "Jack Valenti Decries Confusion Caused by Supreme Court Ruling," *Boxoffice,* July 30, 1973, p. 4.

53. Quoted in "Supreme Court Ruling Was a Staggering Blow," *ibid.,* p. 4.

54. *New York Times,* July 25, 1973, sec. 1, p. 4.

55. "6 N.E. States Plan Concerted Action in Pornography," *Variety,* July 25, 1973, p. 1.

56. For a complete list of these kinds of restrictions see Ayer et al., pp. 832–833.

57. *Ibid.,* p. 832.

58. *Variety,* November 19, 1969, pp. 20, 22.

59. *New York Times,* June 25, 1974, p. 7.

60. *Ibid.*

61. The survey in Los Angeles by Research Associates indicated that 75.2 percent of the surveyed adults believe that an adult has the right to see a film depicting actual or pretended sex acts. *Boxoffice,* December 10, 1973, p. 8.

62. "The Men Behind Kung-Fooey," *Time,* June 11, 1973, p. 46.

63. *Television and Growing Up: The Impact of Televised Violence,* a report to the surgeon general from the Surgeon General's Scientific Advisory Committee on Television and Social Behavior, 1972, pp. 17–18.

64. For more details, and an excellent bibliographic source, see Thomas R. Cripps, "The Death of Rastus: Negroes in American Films Since 1945," *Phylon,* vol. 28, pp. 267–275. The most comprehensive examination of the black in the American film is a recent publication, Daniel J. Leab, *From "Sambo" to "Superspade": The Black Experience in Motion Pictures* (Boston: Houghton Mifflin Company, 1975).

65. For a useful overview of the topic of "blaxploitation" films see "Black Movies," *Newsweek,* October 23, 1972, pp. 74–81.

66. *Ibid.,* p. 74.

67. James P. Murray, "Black Movies/Black Theater," *Drama Review,* vol. 16 (December, 1972), p. 56.

68. "Black Movies," *Newsweek,* p. 77.

69. *Ibid.*

70. *Ibid.*

71. Alvin F. Poussaint, "Cheap Thrills that Degrade Blacks," *Psychology Today,* vol. 7, no. 9 (February, 1974), pp. 22, 26.

72. Barbara Morrow Williams, "Filth vs. Lucre: The Black Community's Tough Choice," *ibid.,* p. 102.

73. Pauline Kael, "On the Future of the Movies," *New Yorker,* August 5, 1974, pp. 43–58.

74. *Ibid.,* p. 44.

75. *Ibid.,* p. 45.

76. *Ibid.,* pp. 57–58.

77. For details on the reaction to Kael's article, see Stephen Farber, "L.A. Journal," *Film Comment,* vol. 10, no. 6 (November–December, 1974), pp. 2, 58.

78. *Variety,* January 22, 1975, p. 1.

79. *Ibid.,* p. 90.

80. *Ibid.,* January 8, 1975, p. 1.

81. *Ibid.,* January 22, 1975, p. 13.

82. *Ibid.,* January 3, 1974, p. 10. (Italics added.)

83. *Ibid.*

84. *Ibid.*

85. "Films: Creative Chaos," *Newsweek,* December 24, 1973, p. 40.

86. One of the finest achievements in film scholarship in recent years has been the development of the American Film Institute's comprehensive catalogue of all motion pictures released in the United States. This mammoth project will be of immense value to all film scholars and social historians.

Appendices

Appendix I
The Thirteen Points of the National Motion Picture Industry — 1921

These Thirteen Points were a series of resolutions specifically condemning the production and exhibition of certain kinds of pictures to which objection was taken and which were being most frequently cut by the existing censorship boards. They were pictures:

1. Which emphasize and exaggerate sex appeal or depict scenes therein exploiting interest in sex in an improper or suggestive form or manner

2. Based upon white slavery or commercialized vice or scenes showing the procurement of women or any of the activities attendant upon this traffic

3. Thematically making prominent an illicit love affair which tends to make virtue odious and vice attractive

4. With scenes which exhibit nakedness or persons scantily dressed, particularly suggestive bedroom and bathroom scenes and scenes of inciting dancing

5. With scenes which unnecessarily prolong expressions or demonstrations of passionate love

6. Predominantly concerned with the underworld or vice and crime, and like scenes, unless the scenes are part of an essential conflict between good and evil

7. Of stories which make gambling and drunkenness attractive, or of scenes which show the use of narcotics and other unnatural practices dangerous to social morality

8. Of stories and scenes which may instruct the morally feeble in methods of committing crimes, or, by cumulative processes, emphasize crime and the commission of crime

9. Of stories or scenes which ridicule or deprecate public officials, officers of the law, the United States Army, the United States Navy, or other governmental authority, or which tend to weaken the authority of the law

10. Of stories or scenes or incidents which offend religious belief or any person, creed or sect, or ridicule ministers, priests, rabbis, or recognized leaders of any religious sect, and also which are disrespectful to objects or symbols used in connection with any religion

11. Of stories or with scenes which unduly emphasize bloodshed and violence without justification in the structure of the story

12. Of stories or with scenes which are vulgar and portray improper gestures, posturing, and attitudes

13. With salacious titles and subtitles in connection with their presentation or exhibition, and the use of salacious advertising matter, photographs, and lithographs in connection therewith

The association further resolved:

That this association records its intention to aid and assist the properly constituted authorities in the prosecution of any producer, distributor, or exhibitor of motion pictures who shall produce, distribute, or exhibit any obscene, salacious, or immoral motion pictures in violation of the law, to the end that the recognized public good accomplished by the motion picture shall be preserved and advanced;

That any members of this association refusing to carry into effect these resolutions shall be subject to expulsion as a member of the association and further subject to such other penalties as the association may fix;

That all exhibitors, producers, and distributors of motion pictures, not members of this association, be urged to cooperate to carry into full effect these resolutions.

Appendix II
The Formula — 1924

"WHEREAS, The members of the Motion Picture Producers and Distributors of America, Inc., in their continuing effort 'to establish and maintain the highest possible moral and artistic standards of motion picture production' are engaged in a special effort to prevent the prevalent type of book and play from becoming the prevalent type of picture; to exercise every possible care that only books or plays which are of the right type are used for screen presentation; to avoid the picturization of books or plays which can be produced after such changes as to leave the producer subject to a charge of deception; to avoid using titles which are indicative of a kind of picture which should not be produced, or by their suggestiveness seek to obtain attendance by deception, a thing equally reprehensible; and to prevent misleading, salacious or dishonest advertising:

"Now, therefore, be it resolved by the board of directors of the Motion Picture Producers and Distributors of America, Inc., That said Association does hereby reaffirm its determination to carry out its purposes above set out; and does hereby repledge the best efforts of the members of the Association to that end; and does hereby further declare that they will not produce or promote the production, distribute or promote the distribution, exhibit or promote the exhibition, or aid in any way whatsoever in the production, distribution or exhibition by the members of this Association or by companies subsidiary to said members or by any other person, firm or corporation producing, distributing or exhibiting pictures, of any picture or pictures by whomsoever produced, distributed or exhibited, which because of the unfit character of title, story, exploitation or picture itself, do not meet the requirements of this preamble and resolution or hinder the fulfillment of the purposes of the Association set out herein."

Appendix III
The Dont's and Be Carefuls of Motion Picture Producers and Directors of America, Inc. — 1927

The Don'ts and Be Carefuls *were included as Rule 21 of the Code of the Motion Picture Industry adopted at a trade practice conference conducted by the Federal Trade Commission in New York City in October, 1927. The two resolutions which cover the subject read as follows:*

Resolved, That those things which are included in the following list shall not appear in pictures produced by the members of this Association, irrespective of the manner in which they are treated:

1. Pointed profanity — by either title or lip — this includes the words "God," "Lord," "Jesus," "Christ" (unless they be used reverently in connection with proper religious ceremonies), "hell," "damn," "Gawd," and every other profane and vulgar expression however it may be spelled;

2. Any licentious or suggestive nudity — in fact or in silhouette; and any lecherous or licentious notice thereof by other characters in the picture;

3. The illegal traffic in drugs;

4. Any inference of sex perversion;

466

5. White slavery;

6. Miscegenation (sex relationships between the white and black races);

7. Sex hygiene and veneral diseases;

8. Scenes of actual childbirth — in fact or in silhouette;

9. Children's sex organs;

10. Ridicule of the clergy;

11. Willful offense to any nation, race or creed;

And be it further resolved, That special care be exercised in the manner in which the following subjects are treated, to the end that vulgarity and suggestiveness may be eliminated and that good taste may be emphasized:

1. The use of the flag;

2. International relations (avoiding picturizing in an unfavorable light another country's religion, history, institutions, prominent people, and citizenry);

3. Arson;

4. The use of firearms;

5. Theft, robbery, safe-cracking, and dynamiting of trains, mines, building, etc. (having in mind the effect which a too-detailed description of these may have upon the moron);

6. Brutality and possible gruesomeness;

7. Technique of committing murder by whatever method;

8. Methods of smuggling;

9. Third-degree methods;

10. Actual hangings or electrocutions as legal punishment for crime;

11. Sympathy for criminals;

12. Attitude toward public characters and institutions;

13. Sedition;

14. Apparent cruelty to children and animals;

15. Branding of people or animals;

16. The sale of women, or of a woman selling her virtue;

17. Rape or attempted rape;

18. First-night scenes;

19. Man and woman in bed together;

20. Deliberate seduction of girls;

21. The institution of marriage;

22. Surgical operations;

23. The use of drugs;

24. Titles or scenes having to do with law enforcement or law-enforcing officers;

25. Excessive or lustful kissing, particularly when one character or the other is a "heavy."

Appendix IV
The Production Code of the Motion Picture Producers
and Directors of America, Inc. — 1930–1934

Preamble

Motion picture producers recognize the high trust and confidence which have been placed in them by the people of the world and which have made motion pictures a universal form of entertainment.

They recognize their responsibility to the public because of this trust and because entertainment and art are important influences in the life of a nation.

Hence, though regarding motion pictures primarily as entertainment without any explicit purpose of teaching or propaganda, they know that the motion picture within its own field of entertainment may be directly responsible for spiritual or moral progress, for higher types of social life, and for much correct thinking.

During the rapid transition from silent to talking pictures they realized the necessity and the opportunity of subscribing to a Code to govern the production of talking pictures and of reacknowledging this responsibility.

On their part, they ask from the public and from public leaders a sympathetic understanding of their purposes and problems and a spirit of cooperation that will allow them the freedom and opportunity necessary to bring the motion picture to a still higher level of wholesome entertainment for all the people.

General Principles

1. No picture shall be produced which will lower the moral standards of those who see it. Hence the sympathy of the audience shall never be thrown to the side of crime, wrong-doing, evil or sin.

2. Correct standards of life, subject only to the requirements of drama and entertainment, shall be presented.

3. Law, natural or human, shall not be ridiculed, nor shall sympathy be created for its violation.

I. Crimes Against the Law

These shall never be presented in such a way as to throw sympathy with the crime as against law and justice or to inspire others with a desire for imitation.

1. Murder
   a) The technique of murder must be presented in a way that will not inspire imitation.
   b) Brutal killings are not to be presented in detail.
   c) Revenge in modern times shall not be justified.

2. Methods of crime should not be explicitly presented.
   a) Theft, robbery, safe-cracking, and dynamiting of trains, mines, building, etc., should not be detailed in method.
   b) Arson must be subject to the same safeguards.
   c) The use of firearms should be restricted to essentials.
   d) Methods of smuggling should not be presented.

3. The illegal drug traffic must not be portrayed in such a way as to stimulate curiosity concerning the use of, or traffic in, such drugs; nor shall scenes be approved which show the use of illegal drugs, or their effects, in detail (as amended September 11, 1946).

4. The use of liquor in American life, when not required by the plot or for proper characterization, will not be shown.

II. Sex

The sanctity of the institution of marriage and the home shall be upheld. Pictures shall not infer that low forms of sex relationship are the accepted or common thing.

1. Adultery and illicit sex, sometimes necessary plot material, must not be explicitly treated or justified, or presented attractively.
2. Scenes of passion
   a) These should not be introduced except where they are definitely essential to the plot.
   b) Excessive and lustful kissing, lustful embraces, suggestive postures and gestures are not to be shown.
   c) In general, passion should be treated in such manner as not to stimulate the lower and baser emotions.
3. Seduction or rape
   a) These should never be more than suggested, and then only when essential for the plot. They must never be shown by explicit method.
   b) They are never the proper subject for comedy.
4. Sex perversion or any inference to it is forbidden.
5. White slavery shall not be treated.
6. Miscegenation (sex relationship between the white and black races) is forbidden.
7. Sex hygiene and venereal diseases are not proper subjects for theatrical motion pictures.
8. Scenes of actual childbirth, in fact or in silhouette, are never to be presented.
9. Children's sex organs are never to be exposed.

III. Vulgarity

The treatment of low, disgusting, unpleasant, though not necessarily evil, subjects should be guided always by the dictates of good taste and a proper regard for the sensibilities of the audience.

IV. Obscenity

Obscenity in word, gesture, reference, song, joke, or by suggestion (even when likely to be understood only by part of the audience) is forbidden.

V. Profanity

Pointed profanity and every other profane or vulgar expression, however used, is forbidden.

No approval by the Production Code Administration shall be given to the use of words and phrases in motion pictures including, but not limited to, the following:

Alley cat (applied to a woman); bat (applied to a woman); broad (applied to a woman); Bronx cheer (the sound); chippie; cocotte; God, Lord, Jesus, Christ (unless used reverently); cripes; fanny; fairy (in a vulgar sense); finger (the); fire, cries of; Gawd; goose (in a vulgar sense); "hold your hat" or "hats"; hot (applied to a woman); "in your hat"; louse; lousy; Madam (relating to prostitution); nance; nerts; nuts (except when meaning crazy); pansy; razzberry (the sound); slut (applied to a woman); S.O.B.; son-of-a; tart; toilet gags; tom cat (applied to a man); traveling salesman and farmer's daughter jokes; whore; damn, hell (excepting when the use of said last two words shall be essential and required for portrayal, in proper historical context, of any scene or dialogue based upon historical fact or folklore, or for the presentation in proper literary context of a Biblical, or other religious quotation, or a quotation from a literary work provided that no such use shall be permitted which is intrinsically objectionable or offends good taste).

In the administration of Section V of the Production Code, the Production Code Administration may take cognizance of the fact that the following words and phrases are obviously offensive to the patrons of motion pictures in the United States and more particularly to the patrons of motion pictures in foreign countries:

Chink, Dago, Frog, Greaser, Hunkie, Kike, Nigger, Spig, Wop, Yid.

VI. Costume

1. Complete nudity is never permitted. This includes nudity in fact or in silhouette, or any licentious notice thereof by other characters in the pictures.
2. Undressing scenes should be avoided, and never used save where essential to the plot.
3. Indecent or undue exposure is forbidden.
4. Dancing costumes intended to permit undue exposure or indecent movements in the dance are forbidden.

VII. Dances

1. Dances suggesting or representing sexual actions or indecent passion are forbidden.
2. Dances which emphasize indecent movements are to be regarded as obscene.

VIII. Religion

1. No film or episode may throw ridicule on any religious faith.
2. Ministers of religion in their character as ministers of religion should not be used as comic characters or as villains.
3. Ceremonies of any definite religion should be carefully and respectfully handled.

IX. Locations

The treatment of bedrooms must be governed by good taste and delicacy.

X. National Feelings

1. The use of the flag shall be consistently respectful.
2. The history, institutions, prominent people and citizenry of all nations shall be represented fairly.

XI. Titles

Salacious, indecent, or obscene titles shall not be used.

XII. Repellent Subjects

The following subjects must be treated within the careful limits of good taste:

1. Actual hangings or electrocutions as legal punishments for crime.
2. Third-degree methods.
3. Brutality and possible gruesomeness.
4. Branding of people or animals.
5. Apparent cruelty to children or animals.
6. The sale of women, or a woman selling her virtue.
7. Surgical operations.

Reasons Supporting Preamble of Code

1. Theatrical motion pictures, that is, pictures intended for the theatre as distinct from pictures intended for churches, schools, lecture halls, educational movements, social reform movements, etc., are primarily to be regarded as ENTERTAINMENT.

Mankind has always recognized the importance of entertainment and its value in rebuilding the bodies and souls of human beings.

But it has always recognized that entertainment can be of a character either HELP-FUL or HARMFUL to the human race, and in consequence has clearly distinguished between:

a) Entertainment which tends to improve the race, or at least to re-create and rebuild human beings exhausted with the realities of life; and

b) Entertainment which tends to degrade human beings, or to lower their standards of life and living.

Hence the MORAL IMPORTANCE of entertainment is something which has been universally recognized. It enters intimately into the lives of men and women and affects them closely; it occupies their minds and affections during leisure hours; and ultimately touches the whole of their lives. A man may be judged by his standard of entertainment as easily as by the standard of his work.

So correct entertainment raises the whole standard of a nation.

Wrong entertainment lowers the whole living conditions and moral ideals of a race.

Note, for example, the healthy reactions to healthful sports, like baseball, golf; the unhealthy reactions to sports like cockfighting, bullfighting, bear baiting, etc.

Note, too, the effect on ancient nations or gladiatorial combats, the obscene plays of Roman times, etc.

2. Motion pictures are very important as ART.

Though a new art, possibly a combination art, it has the same object as the other arts, the presentation of human thought, emotion, and experience, in terms of an appeal to the soul through the senses.

Here, as in entertainment,

Art enters intimately into the lives of human beings.

Art can be morally good, lifting men to higher levels. This has been done through good music, great painting, authentic fiction, poetry, drama.

Art can be morally evil in its effects. This is the case clearly enough with unclean art, indecent books, suggestive drama. The effect on the lives of men and women is obvious.

Note: It has often been argued that art in itself is unmoral, neither good nor bad. This is perhaps true of the THING PRODUCT of some person's mind, and the intention of that mind was either good or bad morally when it produced the thing. Besides, the thing has its EFFECT upon those who come into contact with it. In both these ways, that is, as a product of a mind and as the cause of definite effects, it has a deep moral significance and an unmistakable moral quality.

Hence: The motion pictures, which are the most popular of modern arts for the masses, have their moral quality from the intention of the minds which produce them and from their effects on the moral lives and reactions of their audiences. This gives them a most important morality.

1. They reproduce the morality of the men who use the pictures as a medium for the expression of their ideas and ideals.

2. They affect the moral standards of those who, through the screen, take in these ideas and ideals.

In the case of the motion pictures, this effect may be particularly emphasized because no art has so quick and so widespread an appeal to the masses. It has become in an incredibly short period the art of the multitudes.

3. The motion picture, because of its importance as entertainment and because of the trust placed in it by the peoples of the world, has special MORAL OBLIGATIONS:

A. Most arts appeal to the mature. This art appeals at once to every class, mature, immature, developed, undeveloped, law abiding, criminal. Music has its grades for different classes; so has literature and drama. This art of the motion picture, combining as it does the two fundamental appeals of looking at a picture and listening to a story, at once reached every class of society.

B. By reason of the mobility of a film and the ease of picture distribution, and because of the possibility of duplicating positives in large quantities, this art reaches places unpenetrated by other forms of art.

C. Because of these two facts, it is difficult to produce films intended for only certain classes of people. The exhibitor's theatres are built for the masses, for the cultivated and the rude, the mature and the immature, the self-respecting and the criminal. Films, unlike books and music, can with difficulty be confined to certain selected groups.

D. The latitude given to film material cannot, in consequence, be as wide as the latitude given to book material. In addition:
   a) A book describes; a film vividly presents. One presents on a cold page; the other by apparently living people.
   b) A book reaches the mind through words merely; a film reaches the eyes and ears through the reproduction of actual events.
   c) The reaction of a reader to a book depends largely on the keenness of the reader's imagination; the reaction to a film depends on the vividness of presentation.

   Hence many things which might be described or presented in a book could not possibly be presented in a film.

E. This is also true when comparing the film with the newspaper.
   a) Newspapers present by description, films by actual presentation.
   b) Newspapers are after the fact and present things as having taken place; the film gives the events in the process of enactment and with apparent reality of life.

F. Everything possible in a play is not possible in a film:
   a) Because of the larger audience of the film, and its consequential mixed character. Psychologically, the larger the audience, the lower the moral mass resistance to suggestion.
   b) Because through light, enlargement of character, presentation, scenic emphasis, etc., the screen story is brought closer to the audience than the play.
   c) The enthusiasm for and interest in the film actors and actresses, developed beyond anything of the sort in history, makes the audience largely sympathetic toward the characters they portray and the stories in which they figure. Hence the audience is more ready to confuse actor and actress and the characters they portray, and it is most receptive of the emotions and ideals presented by their favorite stars.

G. Small communities, remote from sophistication and from the hardening process which often takes place in the ethical and moral standards of groups in larger cities, are easily and readily reached by any sort of film.

H. The grandeur of mass settings, large action, spectacular features, etc., affects and arouses more intensely the emotional side of the audience.

In general, the mobility, popularity, accessibility, emotional appeal, vividness, straightforward presentation of fact in the film make for more intimate contact with a larger audience and for greater emotional appeal.

Hence the larger moral responsibilities of the motion pictures.

472

Appendix V
U.S. Motion Picture Box Office Receipts in Relation to Personal Consumption Expenditures

DATE	ADMISSIONS ($ MILLIONS)	PERCENTAGE TOTAL PERSONAL CONSUMPTION EXPENDITURES	PERCENTAGE TOTAL RECREATIONAL EXPENDITURES	PERCENTAGE TOTAL SPECTATOR AMUSEMENT EXPENDITURES
1929	720	0.93	16.62	78.86
1930	732	1.05	18.35	82.06
1931	719	1.19	21.77	84.19
1932	527	1.08	21.58	83.52
1933	482	1.05	21.89	84.12
1934	518	1.01	21.22	82.88
1935	556	1.00	21.14	82.74
1936	626	1.01	20.73	82.48
1937	676	1.02	19.99	82.64
1938	663	1.04	20.46	81.25
1939	659	0.99	19.09	80.27
1940	735	1.04	19.54	81.31
1941	809	1.00	19.08	81.31
1942	1,022	1.15	21.85	84.88
1943	1,275	1.28	25.70	87.63
1944	1,341	1.24	24.73	85.80
1945	1,450	1.21	23.62	84.60
1946	1,692	1.18	19.81	81.90
1947	1,594	0.99	17.23	79.58
1948	1,506	0.87	15.54	78.52
1949	1,451	0.82	14.50	77.51
1950	1,376	0.72	12.34	77.26
1951	1,310	0.64	11.33	76.34
1952	1,246	0.58	10.30	75.29
1953	1,187	0.52	9.33	73.96
1954	1,228	0.52	9.39	73.44
1955	1,326	0.52	9.42	73.63
1956	1,394	0.52	9.31	73.41
1957	1,126	0.40	7.34	68.04
1958	992	0.34	6.27	64.50
1959	958	0.31	5.51	60.98
1960	951	0.29	5.20	59.22
1961	921	0.27	4.72	56.58
1962	903	0.25	4.41	54.86
1963	904	0.24	4.07	53.43
1964	913	0.23	3.72	51.82
1965	927	0.21	3.52	51.19
1966	964	0.20	3.34	50.13
1967	989	0.20	3.22	48.72
1968	1,045	0.20	3.11	49.06
1969	1,099	0.19	2.98	48.59
1970	1,162	0.19	2.86	48.00
1971	1,198	0.18	2.79	47.33
1972	1,203	0.16	2.50	45.11
1973	1,292	0.16	2.47	44.58

Source: U.S. Department of Commerce, Social and Economic Statistics Administration, Bureau of Economic Analysis (Survey of Current Business).

Appendix VI
Comparison of New York Censors' Activities

YEAR	NO. OF FILMS REVIEWED (FEATURES & SHORTS)	NO. OF REELS REVIEWED	NO. OF FILMS REJECTED ENTIRELY	NO. OF FILMS FINALLY APPROVED AFTER LABOR REVISION	NO. OF APPEALS OVERRULED	NO. OF FILMS WITH ELIMINATIONS	NO. OF SCENES ELIMINATED (EITHER ACTION OR DIALOGUE)
1937–38	1,955	10,042	23		12	110	772
1936–37	1,924	9,734	24	8	2	162	1,291
1935–36	1,902	9,336	19	3	5	180	1,452
1934–35	1,737	8,745	12	3	5	225	1,883
1933–34	1,769	8,362	15	2	3	286	2,195
1932–33	1,762	8,916	10	2	1	328	3,035
1931–32	2,015	8,724	13			326	2,320
1930–31	2,149	8,966	14			366	3,031
1929–30	2,268	9,028	17			310	2,116
1928–29	2,543	8,496	16			448	2,710
1927–28	2,625	8,983	6			661	4,235
1925	3,310	8,949	12			712	4,296

	GROUNDS FOR ELIMINATIONS				
	INDECENT	IMMORAL	CRIMINAL	INHUMAN	SACRILEGIOUS
1937–38	364	265	80	28	55
1936–37	546	343	305	64	33
1935–36	522	275	496	101	58
1934–35	604	628	456	136	64
1933–34	838	752	511	79	15
1932–33	569	1,124	917	360	7 (58 obscene)
1931–32	315	811	1,116	266	72
1930–31	468	1,165	1,129	243	26
1929–30	308	612	931	251	9 (5 obscene)
1928–29	340	485	1,479	320	80 (6 obscene)
1927–28	607	643	2,101	764	121
1925	656	318	1,804	1,438	20

Source: Annual Reports of the Motion Picture Commission, State of New York, 1925, 1927–1938.

Appendix VII
The Growth of Motion Picture Attendance in the United States (1922–1965)

YEAR	AVERAGE WEEKLY MOVIE ATTENDANCE	TOTAL NUMBER OF HOUSEHOLDS	WEEKLY ATTENDANCE PER HOUSEHOLD
1922	40,000,000	25,687,000	1.56
1924	46,000,000	26,941,000	1.71
1926	50,000,000	28,101,000	1.78
1928	65,000,000	29,124,000	2.23
1930	90,000,000	29,997,000	3.00
1932	60,000,000	30,439,000	1.97
1934	70,000,000	31,306,000	2.24
1936	88,000,000	32,454,000	2.71
1938	85,000,000	33,683,000	2.52
1940	80,000,000	35,153,000	2.28
1942	85,000,000	36,445,000	2.33
1944	85,000,000	37,115,000	2.29
1946	90,000,000	38,370,000	2.35
1948	90,000,000	40,532,000	2.22
1950	60,000,000	43,554,000	1.38
1951	54,000,000	44,656,000	1.21
1952	51,000,000	45,504,000	1.12
1953	46,000,000	46,334,000	.99
1954	49,000,000	46,893,000	1.04
1955	46,000,000	47,788,000	.96
1956	47,000,000	48,902,000	.96
1957	45,000,000	49,673,000	.91
1958	40,000,000	50,474,000	.79
1959	42,000,000	51,435,000	.82
1960	40,000,000	52,772,000	.76
1961	42,000,000	53,197,000	.79
1962	43,000,000	54,369,000	.79
1963	44,000,000	55,705,000	.79
1965	44,000,000	56,956,000	.77

Sources: U.S. Bureau of Census, *Historical Statistics of the United States, Colonial Times to 1957* (Washington, D.C., 1960), Series H 522, p. 225 and Series A 242–244, p. 15.

U.S. Bureau of Census, *Historical Statistics of the United States, Continuation to 1962 and Revisions* (Washington, D.C., 1965), Series H 522, p. 35.

U.S. Bureau of Census, *Statistical Abstract of the United States* (Washington, D.C., 1968), Tables 11 and 302, pp. 12 and 208.

U.S. Bureau of Census, *Current Population Reports: Population Characteristics,* Series P-20, No. 166 (August 24, 1967), p. 1 and p. 4.

NOTE: Figures do not include Alaska and Hawaii. Data on attendance for 1964 not reliably reported in sources. Household data from 1951 to 1961 revised for consistency with contemporary estimates of total population.

Appendix VIII
Age of Motion Picture Audiences in 1957

Question asked of respondents: "How many times have you been to the movies in the last seven days?"

TOTAL PUBLIC (ALL AGES)	TOTAL ADMISSIONS (MILLIONS)	PERCENT OF TOTAL ADMISSIONS	PERCENT OF TOTAL POPULATION
	54.2	100%	100%
0–9 years of age	8.5 ⎤	16% ⎤	22% ⎤
10–14	8.4 ⎬ 28.1	15 ⎬ 52%	9 ⎬ 38%
15–19	11.2 ⎦	21 ⎦	7 ⎦
20—29	11.0	20	12
30–39	7.1	13	14
40–49	4.8	9	13
50–59	1.8	3	10
60 and over	1.4	3	13

Source: Opinion Research Corporation, *The Public Appraises Movies,* p. 3.

Appendix IX
Composition of the Survey Week's Audience by Sex and Age, 1957

	TOTAL ADMISSIONS* (MILLIONS)	PERCENT OF TOTAL ADMISSIONS	PERCENT OF TOTAL POPULATION
Male	27.9	51%	49%
0–9 years of age	4.4	8%	11%
10–14	4.4	8	5
15–19	5.5	10	3
20–29	5.4	10	6
30–39	4.1	8	7
40–49	2.5	5	6
50–59	.9	1	5
60 and over	.7	1	6
Female	26.3	49%	51%
0–9 years of age	4.1	8%	11%
10–14	4.0	7	4
15–19	5.7	11	4
20–29	5.6	10	6
30–39	3.0	5	7
40–49	2.3	4	7
50–59	.9	2	5
60 and over	.7	2	7

Source: *The Public Appraises Movies,* p. 5.

* Estimated admissions, based on projections of reported attendance during the "survey week" — the seven days preceding the interview.

Appendix X
Composition of the Survey Week's Audience, 1957

	TOTAL ADMISSIONS (MILLIONS)	PERCENT OF TOTAL ADMISSIONS	PERCENT OF TOTAL POPULATION
Public, 15 Years of Age and Older	37.4	100%	100%
Single	18.9	51	27
Married with children under 15	12.0	32	39
Married, no children under 15	6.5	17	34
Family income			
$7,000 or more	6.9	18	17
$5,000 to $6,999	7.5	20	21
$3,000 to $4,999	10.0	27	25
Under $3,000	5.6	15	19
Not reported	7.4	20	18
Cities 1,000,000 and over	11.0	30	26
Cities 100,000 to 999,999	8.3	22	22
Urban below 100,000	8.2	22	20
Rural	9.9	26	32
Northeast	9.8	26	27
North Central	9.5	25	30
South	13.0	35	30
West	5.1	14	13
Own television set	32.1	86	85
Do not	5.3	14	15
Own car	30.6	82	81
Do not or not reported	6.8	18	19
Public 20 Years of Age and Older	26.1	100%	100%
Educational attainment			
Less than 8th grade	2.0	8	14
8th grade	2.6	10	15
High school incomplete	6.0	23	22
High school complete	9.7	37	28
College	5.6	21	19
Not reported	.2	1	2
Men	13.6	52	48
Employed women	5.8	22	19
Other women	6.7	26	33

Source: The Public Appraises Movies, p. 7.

Appendix XI
Frequency of Attendance, 1957

Question asked of respondents:
"On the average about how many times do you go a month? Please include attendance at both regular theaters and drive-ins in your estimate."

If, "Less than once a month": "Well, about how many times do you go to the movies in a year?"

	TOTAL ADMISSIONS (MILLIONS)	PERCENT OF TOTAL ADMISSIONS	PERCENT OF TOTAL POPULATION
Public, 15 Years and Older	37.4	100%	100%
Average frequency of attendance			
Once a week or oftener	23.2	62%	15%
1–3 times a month	10.2	27	26
3–11 times a year	2.0	5	14
1–2 times a year	.9	3	17
Less than once a year	.1	0	22
Not reported	1.0	3	6

Source: The Public Appraises Movies, p. 9.

Appendix XII
Movies as a Group Activity, 1957

Question asked of respondents: "The last time you went to the movies, did you go by yourself or with someone else?"

	TOTAL ADMISSIONS	REGULAR THEATER ADMISSIONS	DRIVE-IN THEATER ADMISSIONS
Survey week's audience	100%	100%	100%
With someone else	87%	81%	98%
Alone	13	19	2

If "With someone else": "How many people went altogether, including yourself?"

	TOTAL ADMISSIONS	REGULAR THEATER ADMISSIONS	DRIVE-IN THEATER ADMISSIONS
Percent of admissions accounted for by groups of two or more persons	87%	81%	98%
Two	42%	47%	34%
Three	14	15	12
Four	17	10	29
Five or more	10	7	16
Don't recall	4	2	7

Source: The Public Appraises Movies, p. 11.

Appendix XIII
Motivational Factors in Movie Attendance, 1957

Question asked of respondents: "What do you think are the main reasons people go to the movies?"

	Public, 15 and over	100%
I.	Recreation, entertainment	57%
	Habit	2
	Just because they want to go	1
II.	To see a picture they're interested in; to see a certain show	9
	To see a certain actor or actress	7
	Educational or cultural purposes; to learn something	5
III.	To get away from everyday routine	39
	To pass the time, gives them something to do	23
	Tired of watching television, watch something different from television	2
	To cool off during summer	3
	Good place to go on dates	3
	Opportunity to be with other people	1
	Relatively inexpensive; less expensive than other forms of entertainment	1
	Other reasons	5
	Don't know	5

Percentages add to more than 100 because many people gave more than one reason for going to the movies.

Source: The Public Appraises Movies, p. 79.

Appendix XIV
Audience Preferences in
Theater Facilities and
Exhibition Practices, 1957

Respondents were handed a card containing the list of
theater characteristics shown below and asked: "Aside from
the picture that's playing, why do you like to go to the
theaters you attend most often. Please don't count drive-in
theaters. Name as many as apply."

	PUBLIC, 15 AND OVER	ATTEND MOVIES ONCE A WEEK OR OFTENER
Total	100%	100%
Comfortable seats	34%	44%
Clean theater	33	47
Clear sound throughout theater	31	44
Quiet and well-behaved audience	28	38
Reasonable admission price	25	36
Convenient parking nearby	20	25
Unobstructed vision	20	26
Convenient starting time	20	28
Attractive inside and outside	18	25
Desirable neighborhood	17	19
Convenient ending time	15	22
Single feature program	15	17
Double feature program	15	28
Courteous and helpful ushers	13	17
Good public transportation	7	9
Nearby shopping facilities	7	9
Smoking permitted	5	9
Other answers	8	6
None or no opinion	26	9

Percentages add to more than 100 because many respondents mentioned more than one characteristic.

Note: These characteristics are listed in order of frequency
of mention, not in the order in which they were presented
to respondents.

Source: The Public Appraises Moves, p. 91.

Appendix XV
Features Released in the
U.S. Market

DATE	U.S. PRODUCED	IMPORTED	PERCENTAGE IMPORTED	TOTAL
1957	300	233	43.7	533
1958	241	266	52.5	507
1959	187	252	57.4	439
1960	154	233	60.2	387
1961	131	331	71.6	462
1962	147	280	65.5	427
1963	121	299	71.2	420
1964	141	361	71.9	502
1965	153	299	66.2	452
1966	156	295	65.4	451
1967	178	284	61.4	462
1968	180	274	60.4	454

Source: Film Daily Yearbook, 1969, p. 98.

Appendix XVI
Major Studios vs. Independent
Productions

DATE	MAJORS	INDEPENDENTS	% INDEPENDENTS
1957	220	80	26.7
1958	174	67	27.8
1959	148	39	20.9
1960	119	35	22.7
1961	103	28	18.2
1962	102	45	30.6
1963	86	35	28.9
1964	86	55	39.0
1965	98	55	35.9
1966	93	63	40.3
1967	87	91	51.1
1968	98	82	45.5

Source: Film Daily Yearbook, 1969, p. 98.

Appendix XVII
Average U.S.
Movie Theater
Admission Price

DATE	ADMISSION PRICE
1933	23¢
1938	23¢
1943	29.4¢
1948	44.0¢
1953	50.9¢
1958	65.0¢
1963	84.6¢
1964	92.5¢
1965	$1.010
1966	$1.094
1967	$1.198
1968	$1.310
1969	$1.419
1970	$1.552
1971	$1.645
1972	$1.695
1973	$1.768
1974	$1.874

Source: MPAA Research Department.

Appendix XVIII
Estimated Number of
Movie Theaters in U.S.

DATE	INDOOR	DRIVE-INS	TOTAL
1939 (census)	n.a.	n.a.	15,115
1948 "	17,811	820	18,631
1954 "	14,716	3,775	18,491
1958 "	12,291	4,063	16,354
1963 "	9,150	3,502	12,652
1964 (est.)	9,200	3,540	12,740
1965 "	9,240	3,585	12,825
1966 "	9,290	3,640	12,930
1967 "	9,330	3,670	13,000
1968 "	9,500	3,690	13,190
1969 "	9,750	3,730	13,480
1970 "	10,000	3,750	13,750
1971 "	10,300	3,770	14,070
1972 "	10,580	3,790	14,370
1973 "	10,850	3,800	14,650

Source: MPAA Research Department.

Appendix XIX
Motion Picture Company Profits
(Figures in millions of dollars)

	1932	1933	1934	1935	1936	1937	1938	1939	1940	1941	1942	1943	1944	1945	1946	1947	1948	1949	1950	1951
Columbia	0.6	0.7	1.0	1.8	1.6	1.3	0.2	0.0	0.5	0.6	1.6	1.8	2.0	1.9	3.5	3.7	0.5	1.0	1.9	1.5
Loew's Inc./MGM	8.0	4.3	8.6	7.5	10.6	14.3	9.9	9.5	8.7	11.0	11.8	13.4	14.5	12.9	17.9	10.5	4.2c	6.0	7.6	7.8
Paramount	(In reorganization)				4.0	6.0	2.8	2.8	6.4	9.2	13.1	14.6	14.7	15.4	39.2	28.2	22.6	20.8a	6.6	5.5
20th Century-Fox		1.7	1.3	3.1	7.7	8.6	7.2	4.2	(0.5)	4.9	10.6	10.9	12.5	12.7	22.6	14.0	12.5	12.4	9.5	4.3b
United Artists	(Not a listed corporation until 1950)																			0.3
Universal		(1.0)	(0.2)	(0.7)	(1.8)	(1.1)	(0.5)	1.2	2.4	2.7	3.0	3.8	3.4	4.0	4.6	3.2	(3.2)	(1.1)	1.4	2.3
Warner Bros.	(14.1)	(6.3)	(2.5)	0.7	3.2	5.9	1.9	1.7	2.7	5.5	8.6	8.3	6.9	9.9	19.4	22.0	11.8	10.5	10.3	9.4
Walt Disney										(0.8)	(0.2)	0.4	0.5	0.4	0.2	0.3	(0.1)	(0.1)	0.7	0.4

Sources: Moody's Industrial Manual and annual reports.

Losses in brackets. Figures after taxes and write-offs, before special credits.

a Divorcement: United Paramount Theatres hived off, with profits of $16.7m in 1948 and $17.6m in 1949.
b Divorcement: National Theatres hived off.
c Divorcement: Loew's Theatres hived off.

Appendix XIX (continued)

	1952	1953	1954	1955	1956	1957	1958	1959	1960	1961	1962	1963	1964	1965	1966	1967	1968	1969	1970	1971	1972
Columbia	0.8	0.9	3.6	4.9	2.6	2.3	(5.0)	(2.4)	1.9	(1.4)	2.3	2.6	3.2	2.0	2.0	6.0	10.0	6.0	6.0	(29.0)	(4.0)
Loew's Inc./MGM	4.6	4.5	6.3	5.0	4.6	(0.5)	0.8	7.7	9.6	12.7	2.6	(17.5)	7.4	7.8	10.2	14.0	8.5	(35.0)	(8.2)	7.8	9.2
Paramount	5.9	6.7	8.1	9.4	4.3	5.4	4.6	4.4	7.0	5.9	3.4	5.9	6.6	6.3	na^e	na	na	na	(2.0*)	(22.0*)	31.2*
20th Century-Fox	4.7	4.8	8.0	6.0	6.2	6.5	7.6	2.3	(2.9)	(22.5)	(39.8)	9.1	10.6	11.7	12.5	15.4	13.7	(36.8)	(77.4)	6.5	6.7
United Artists	0.4	0.6	0.9	2.7	3.1	3.3	3.7	4.1	4.3	4.0	3.8	(0.8)	9.3	12.8	13.6	15.5	19.5^f	16.2	(45.0)	1.0	10.8
Universal	2.3	2.6	3.8	4.0	4.0	2.8	(2.0)	4.7	6.3	7.5	12.7	13.6	14.8	16.2	13.6	16.5	13.5	2.5	13.3	16.7	20.8
Warner Bros.	7.2	2.9^h	3.9	4.0	2.1	3.4	(1.0)	9.4	7.1	7.2	7.6	5.7	(3.9)	4.7	6.5	3.0	10.0	(52.0)^d	33.5	41.6	50.1^g
Walt Disney	0.5	0.5	0.7	1.4	2.6	3.6	3.9	3.4	(1.3)	4.5	6.6	7.0	7.0	11.0	12.4	11.3	13.1	15.8	22.0	26.7	40.3

^d Warner Bros. brought by Kinney Services, which changed its name to Warner Communications in 1971.
^e Bought by Gulf & Western: figures burned.
^f Bought by Transamerica Corporation.

* Operating loss profits.
^g Records & Music $23.8m. Films $15.8m, publishing $2m. Cable television $1.8m.
^h Divorcement. Stanley Warner hived off.

Source: The *Economist*, July 7, 1973, pp. 68–69.

Appendix XX
Age of Motion Picture
Audiences, 1972

	PERCENT OF TOTAL YEARLY ADMISSIONS	PERCENT OF POPULATION
Total public, age 12 and over	100%	100%
Age:		
12–15 years	13% ⎫ 43%	10% ⎫ 22%
16–20 years	30 ⎰	12 ⎰
21–24 years	16	8
25–29 years	14	9
30–39 years	11	15
40–49 years	10	15
50–59 years	4	13
60 years and over	2	18
12–16 years	21%	13%
17 years and over	79	87
12–17 years	25%	15%
18 years and over	75	85

Source: Opinion Research Corporation, *MPAA Study IV.*

Appendix XXI
Frequency of Movie-Going
by Education

AGE 18 AND OVER

	HIGHER EDUCATION (AT LEAST SOME COLLEGE)	HIGH SCHOOL COMPLETE	LESS THAN HIGH SCHOOL COMPLETE
Movie-Going:			
Frequent	35%	24%	10%
Occasional	29	25	11
Infrequent	16	18	13
Never	20	33	66

Frequency of Movie-Going
by Family Income
(current survey — 1972)

AGE 12 AND OVER
YEARLY FAMILY INCOME

Movie-Going:	$15,000 OR OVER	$7,000 TO $14,999	UNDER $7,000
Frequent	31%	27%	15%
Occasional	32	23	15
Infrequent	16	18	10
Never	21	32	60

Frequency of Movie-Going by Sex
(current survey — 1972)

	AGE 12 AND OVER		AGE 18 AND OVER	
Movie-Going:	Male	Female	Male	Female
Frequent	25%	22%	24%	18%
Occasional	22	22	21	21
Infrequent	13	16	13	17
Never	40	40	42	44

Source: Opinion Research Corporation, *MPAA Study IV*.

Bibliography

This bibliography contains only the books, articles and other materials of major significance; because of the complete notes at the end of the chapters, readers anxious to pursue references are directed to these. Two other bibliographies are recommended: the excellent annotated list in Ian C. Jarvie, *Movies and Society,* and the recent *New Film Index* by Richard Dyer MacCann and Edward S. Perry.

Books

Addams, Jane. *The Spirit of Youth and City Streets.* New York: Macmillan Company, 1909.

Adler, Mortimer J. *Art and Prudence.* New York: Longmans, Green and Co., 1937.

Barnett, Homer G. *Innovation: The Basis of Cultural Change.* New York: McGraw-Hill Book Company, 1953.

Barnouw, Erik. *A Tower in Babel.* A History of Broadcasting in the United States, vol. I. New York: Oxford University Press, 1966.

———. *The Golden Web.* A History of Broadcasting in the United States, vol. II. New York: Oxford University Press, 1968.

———. *The Image Empire.* A History of Broadcasting in the United States, vol. III. New York: Oxford University Press, 1970.

Baxter, John. *Hollywood in the Thirties.* New York: A. S. Barnes and Co., 1968.

———. *Science Fiction in the Cinema.* New York: A. S. Barnes and Co., 1970.

Bergman, Andrew. *We're In the Money: Depression America and Its Films.* New York: New York University Press, 1971.

Bessie, Alvah. *Inquisition in Eden.* Berlin: Seven Seas Publishers, 1967.

Blanchard, Phyllis. *Child and Society.* New York: Longmans, Green and Co., 1928.

Blumer, Herbert. *Movies and Conduct.* New York: Macmillan Company, 1933.

Blumer, Herbert, and Philip Hauser. *Movies, Delinquency and Crime.* New York: Macmillan Company, 1933.

Brown, Les. *Television: The Business Behind the Box.* New York: Harcourt Brace Jovanovich, 1971.

Brownlow, Kevin. *The Parade's Gone By.* New York: Alfred A. Knopf, 1968.

Butler, Elizabeth Beardsley. *Women and the Trades: Pittsburgh 1907–08.* New York: Charities Publication Committee, 1909.

Byington, Margaret F. *Homestead: The Households of a Mill Town.* New York: Charities Publication Committee, 1910.

Capra, Frank. *The Name Above the Title.* New York: Macmillan Company, 1971.

Carmen, Ira H. *Movies, Censorship and the Law.* Ann Arbor: University of Michigan Press, 1966.

Ceram, C. W. *Archaeology of the Cinema*. New York: Harcourt, Brace and World, 1965.

Chapin, Richard E. *Mass Communications: A Statistical Analysis*. East Lansing: Michigan State University Press, 1957.

Charters, W. W. *Motion Pictures and Youth*. New York: Macmillan Company, 1933.

Cogley, John. *Report on Blacklisting I: Movies*. Fund for the Republic, 1956.

Commission on Freedom of the Press. *A Free and Responsible Press*. Chicago: University of Chicago Press, 1947.

Conant, Michael. *Antitrust in the Motion Picture Industry*. Berkeley: University of California Press, 1960.

Creel, George. *How We Advertised America*. New York: Harper, 1920.

Cremin, Lawrence A. *The Transformation of the School*. New York: Random House, Vintage Books, 1964.

Crowther, Bosley. *The Lion's Share: The Story of an Entertainment Empire*. New York: E. P. Dutton, 1957.

Curti, Merle. *The Growth of American Thought*. New York: Harper and Brothers, 1951.

Dale, Edgar. *Children's Attendance at Motion Pictures*. New York: Macmillan Company, 1935.

———. *The Content of Motion Pictures*. New York: Macmillan Company, 1933.

———. *How to Appreciate Modern Pictures*. New York: Macmillan Company, 1937.

Davis, Allen F. *Spearheads for Reform*. New York: Oxford University Press, 1967.

De Fleur, Melvin. *Theories of Mass Communication*. New York: David McKay Company, 1970.

Dulles, Foster Rhea. *A History of Recreation: America Learns to Play*. New York: Appleton-Century-Crofts, 1965.

Dysinger, Wendell S., and Christian A. Ruckmick. *The Emotional Responses of Children to the Motion Picture Situation*. New York: Macmillan Company, 1935.

Emery, Edwin. *The Press in America*. Englewood Cliffs: Prentice-Hall, 1962.

Ernst, Morris, and Pare Lorentz. *Censored: The Private Life of the Movie*. New York: Jonathan Cape and Harrison Smith, 1930.

Facey, Paul W. *The Legion of Decency: A Sociological Analysis of the Emergence and Development of a Pressure Group*. New York: Arno Press, 1974.

Farber, Stephen. *The Movie Rating Game*. Washington, D.C.: Public Affairs Press, 1972.

Fenin, George N., and William K. Everson. *The Western*. New York: Orion Press, 1962.

Fielding, Raymond. *The American Newsreel, 1911–1967*. Norman: University of Oklahoma Press, 1973.

———, *A Technological History of Motion Pictures and Television*. Berkeley: University of California Press, 1967.

Forman, Henry James. *Our Movie Made Children*. New York: Macmillan Company, 1933.

French, Philip. *The Movie Moguls*. Baltimore: Penguin Books, 1971.

Furhammer, Lief, and Folke Isaksson. *Politics and Film*. New York: Praeger Publishers, 1971.

Gow, Gordon. *Hollywood in the Fifties*. New York: A. S. Barnes and Co., 1971.

Grau, Robert. *The Theatre of Science*. 1914. Reprint. New York: Benjamin Blom, 1969.

Green, Abel, and Joe Laurie, Jr. *Show Biz: From Vaudeville to Video*. New York: Henry Holt and Co., 1951.

Griffith, Richard. *The Movie Stars*. New York: Doubleday and Co., 1970.

Guback, Thomas H. *The International Film Industry*. Bloomington: Indiana University Press, 1969.

Hall, Ben M. *The Best Remaining Seats*. New York: Bramhall House, 1961.

Hampton, Benjamin. *A History of the Movies*. New York: Covici-Friede Publishers, 1931.

Handel, Leo A. *Hollywood Looks at Its Audience*. Urbana: University of Illinois Press, 1950.

Harley, John E. *World-Wide Influences of the Cinema*. Los Angeles: University of Southern California Press, 1940; reprint ed., New York: Jerome S. Ozer, 1971.

Haskell, Molly. *From Reverence to Rape: The Treatment of Women in the Movies.* New York: Holt, Rinehart and Winston, 1973.

Hays, Will H. *The Memoirs of Will H. Hays.* Garden City: Doubleday and Co., 1955.

Healy, William. *The Individual Delinquent.* Boston: Little, Brown and Co., 1915.

Henderson, Robert M. *D. W. Griffith: His Life and His Work.* New York: Oxford University Press, 1972.

Hendricks, Gordon. *Beginnings of the Biograph.* New York: Beginnings of the American Film, 1964.

————. *The Edison Motion Picture Myth.* Berkeley: University of California Press, 1961.

————. *The Kinetoscope.* New York: Beginnings of the American Film, 1966.

Higham, Charles. *Cecil B. De Mille.* New York: Charles Scribner's Sons, 1973.

————. *Hollywood at Sunset.* New York: Saturday Review Press, 1972.

Higham, Charles, and Joel Greenberg. *Hollywood in the Forties.* New York: A. S. Barnes and Co., 1968.

Holaday, Perry W., and George D. Stoddard. *Getting Ideas from the Movies.* New York: Macmillan Company, 1933.

Hovland, C. I., A. A. Lumsdaine, and F. D. Sheffield. *Experiments in Mass Communication.* New York: John Wiley and Sons, 1965.

Huettig, Mae D. *Economic Control of the Motion Picture Industry.* Philadelphia: University of Pennsylvania Press, 1944; reprint ed., New York: Jerome S. Ozer, 1971.

Hull, David Stewart. *Film in the Third Reich.* Berkeley: University of California Press, 1969.

Hunnings, Neville March. *Film Censors and the Law.* London: George Allen and Unwin, 1967.

Inglis, Ruth. *Freedom of the Movies.* Chicago: University of Chicago Press, 1947.

Jacobs, Lewis. *The Rise of the American Film.* New York: Teacher's College Press, 1939.

Jarvie, I. C. *Movies and Society.* New York: Basic Books, 1970.

Jobes, Gertrude. *Motion Picture Empire.* Hamden, Conn.: Archon Books, 1966.

Karpf, Stephen. *The Gangster Film: Emergence, Variation and Decay of a Genre, 1930–1940.* New York: Arno Press, 1973.

Katz, Elihu, and Paul F. Lazarsfeld. *Personal Influence: The Part Played by People in the Flow of Mass Communications.* New York: Free Press, 1955.

Kennedy, Joseph P., ed. *The Story of the Films.* Chicago: A. W. Shaw Company, 1927; reprint ed., New York: Jerome S. Ozer, 1971.

Klapp, Orrin F. *Heroes, Villains and Fools.* Englewood Cliffs: Prentice-Hall, 1962.

Klingender, F. D., and Stuart Legg. *Money Behind the Screen.* London: Lawrence and Wishart, 1937.

Knight, Arthur. *The Liveliest Art.* New York: Macmillan Company, 1957.

Kracauer, Siegfried. *From Caligari to Hitler.* Princeton: Princeton University Press, 1947.

Lane, Tamar. *What's Wrong with the Movies.* Los Angeles: Waverly Company, 1923; reprint ed., New York: Jerome S. Ozer, 1971.

Larrabee, Eric, and Rolf Meyersohn, eds. *Mass Leisure.* Glencoe: Free Press, 1958.

Lawson, John Howard. *Film in the Battle of Ideas.* New York: Masses and Mainstream, 1953.

Lazarsfeld, Paul F., and Frank N. Stanton. *Communications Research: 1948–1949.* New York: Harper and Brothers, 1949.

Leab, Daniel J. *From "Sambo" to "Superspade": The Black Experience in Motion Pictures.* Boston: Houghton Mifflin Company, 1975.

Lerner, Max. *America as a Civilization.* New York: Simon and Schuster, 1957.

Lewis, Howard T. *The Motion Picture Industry.* New York: D. Van Nostrand Company, 1933.

Limbacher, James L. *Four Faces of the Film.* New York: Brussel and Brussel, 1968.

Lindsay, Vachel. *The Art of the Moving Picture.* New York: Macmillan Company, 1915; reprint ed., New York: Liveright Publishing Company, 1970.

Lingeman, Richard R. *Don't You Know There's a War On?* New York: G. P. Putnam's Sons, 1970.

A Look at Southern California Movie-Going. Los Angeles: *Los Angeles Times,* 1972.

Lounsbury, Myron. *The Origins of American Film Criticism.* New York: Arno Press, 1973.

Lundberg, George A., Mirra Komarovsky, and Mary Alice McInerny. *Leisure: A Suburban Study.* New York: Columbia University Press, 1934.

Lynd, Robert S., and Helen Merrell Lynd. *Middletown.* New York: Harcourt, Brace and World, 1929.

———. *Middletown in Transition.* New York: Harcourt, Brace and World, 1937.

Lyons, Gene M. *The Uneasy Partnership.* New York: Russell Sage Foundation, 1969.

MacCann, Richard Dyer. *Hollywood in Transition.* Boston: Houghton Mifflin Company, 1962.

———. *The People's Films.* New York: Hastings House, 1973.

McClure, Arthur F., ed. *The Movies: An American Idiom.* Rutherford: Farleigh Dickinson University Press, 1971.

MacGowan, Kenneth. *Behind the Screen.* New York: Dell Publishing Company, 1965.

McLaughlin, R. G. *Broadway and Hollywood: A History of Economic Interaction.* New York: Arno Press, 1974.

McLean, Albert F. *American Vaudeville as Ritual.* Lexington: University of Kentucky Press, 1965.

McQuail, Denis. *Towards a Sociology of Mass Communications.* London: Collier-Macmillan, 1969.

Martin, Olga G. *Hollywood's Movie Commandments.* New York: H. W. Wilson Company, 1937.

Mayer, Arthur. *Merely Colossal.* New York: Simon and Schuster, 1953.

Mellen, Joan. *Women and Their Sexuality in the New Film.* New York: Horizon Press, 1973.

Miller, Merle. *The Judges and the Judged.* Garden City: Doubleday and Co., 1952.

Mitchell, Alice Miller. *Children and the Movies.* Chicago: University of Chicago Press, 1929; reprint ed., New York: Jerome S. Ozer, 1971.

Moley, Raymond. *Are We Movie Made?* New York: Macy-Masius, 1938.

———. *The Hays Office.* New York: Bobbs-Merrill Company, 1945; reprint ed., New York: Jerome S. Ozer, 1971.

Morin, Edgar. *The Stars.* New York: Grove Press, 1960.

Motion Picture Producers and Distributors of America, Inc. *The Community and the Motion Picture.* New York, 1929; reprint ed., New York: Jerome S. Ozer, 1971.

Mott, Frank Luther. *American Journalism.* New York: Macmillan Company, 1962.

Movie Lot to Beachhead. New York: Doubleday, Doran and Co., 1945.

Munsterberg, Hugo. *The Photoplay: A Psychological Study.* 1915. Reprint. New York: Dover Publications, 1970.

Nizer, Louis. *New Courts of Industry: Self-Regulation Under the Motion Picture Code.* New York: Longacre Press, 1935; reprint ed., New York: Jerome S. Ozer, 1971.

North, Joseph H. *The Early Development of the Motion Picture, 1887–1909.* New York: Arno Press, 1973.

Oberholtzer, Ellis P. *The Morals of the Movie.* Philadelphia: Penn Publishing Company, 1922; reprint ed., New York: Jerome S. Ozer, 1971.

O'Neill, William L. *Coming Apart: An Informal History of America in the 1960's.* Chicago: Quadrangle Books, 1971.

———. *Everyone Was Brave.* Chicago: Quadrangle Books, 1969.

Peters, Charles C. *Motion Pictures and Standards of Morality.* New York: Macmillan Company, 1933.

Peterson, Ruth, and L. I. Thurstone. *Motion Pictures and the Social Attitudes of Children.* New York: Macmillan Company, 1933.

Phelan, Rev. J. J. *Motion Pictures as a Phase of Commercialized Amusement in Toledo, Ohio.* Toledo: Little Book Press, 1919.

Phillips, Cabell. *From the Crash to the Blitz, 1929–1939.* New York: Macmillan Company, 1969.

Poggi, Jack. *Theater in America: The Impact of Economic Forces, 1870–1967.* Ithaca, N.Y.: Cornell University Press, 1968.

Powdermaker, Hortense. *Hollywood: the Dream Factory*. Boston: Little, Brown and Co., 1950.

Quigley, Martin. *Decency in Motion Pictures*. New York: Macmillan Company, 1937; reprint ed., New York: Jerome S. Ozer, 1971.

Quigley, Martin, Jr. *Magic Shadows: The Story of the Origin of Motion Pictures*. Washington, D.C.: Georgetown University Press, 1948.

Rahill, Frank. *The World of Melodrama*. University Park: Pennsylvania State University Press, 1967.

Ramsaye, Terry. *A Million and One Nights*. New York: Simon and Schuster, 1926.

Randall, Richard S. *Censorship of the Movies*. Madison: University of Wisconsin Press, 1968.

Recent Social Trends in the United States. Vol. I. New York: McGraw-Hill Book Company, 1933.

Renshaw, Samuel, Vernon L. Miller, and Dorothy P. Marquis. *Children's Sleep*. New York: Macmillan Company, 1933.

Report of the Commission on Obscenity and Pornography. New York: Bantam Books, 1970.

Rimberg, John. *The Motion Picture in the Soviet Union, 1918–1952: A Sociological Analysis*. New York: Arno Press, 1973.

Rosen, Marjorie. *Popcorn Venus*. New York: Coward, McCann and Geoghegan, 1973.

Rosten, Leo C. *Hollywood: The Movie Colony and the Movie Makers*. New York: Harcourt, Brace and Co., 1941.

Rotha, Paul. *The Film Till Now*. London: Spring Books, 1949.

Rotsler, William. *Contemporary Erotic Cinema*. New York: Random House, Ballantine Books, 1973.

Schickel, Richard. *The Disney Version*. New York: Avon Books, 1968.

———. *Movies: The History of an Art and an Institution*. New York: Basic Books, 1964.

———. *The Stars*. New York: Bonanza Books, 1962.

Schramm, Wilbur. *Responsibility in Mass Communication*. New York: Harper and Brothers, 1957.

Schumach, Murray. *The Face on the Cutting Room Floor*. New York: William Morrow and Co., 1964.

Seabury, William Marston. *The Public and the Motion Picture Industry*. New York: Macmillan Company, 1926; reprint ed., New York: Jerome S. Ozer, 1971.

Seldes, Gilbert. *The Great Audience*. New York: Viking Press, 1950.

Seligman, Ben B. *The Potentates: Business and Businessmen in American History*. New York: Dial Press, 1971.

Shain, Russell. *An Analysis of Motion Pictures About War Released by The American Film Industry, 1939–1970*. New York: Arno Press, 1976.

Shenton, Herbert. *The Public Relations of the Motion Picture Industry*. New York: Department of Research and Education, Federal Council of the Churches of Christ in America, 1931; reprint ed., New York: Jerome S. Ozer, 1971.

Shuttleworth, Frank K., and Mark A. May. *The Social Conduct and Attitudes of Movie Fans*. New York: Macmillan Company, 1933.

Sinclair, Andrew. *Era of Excess*. New York: Harper Colophon Books, 1962.

Smith, Richard. *Getting into Deep Throat*. Chicago: Playboy Press, 1973.

Stephenson, Ralph. *Animation in the Cinema*. 2nd ed. New York: A. S. Barnes and Co., 1973.

Stott, William. *Documentary Expression and Thirties America*. New York: Oxford University Press, 1973.

Strauss, Anselm. *The American City: A Sourcebook of Urban Imagery*. Chicago: Aldine Publishing Company, 1968.

Stuart, Fredric. *The Effects of Television on the Motion Picture and Radio Industries*. New York: Arno Press, 1975.

Thorp, Margaret. *America at the Movies*. New Haven: Yale University Press, 1939.

Turan, Kenneth, and Stephen F. Zito. *Sinema*. New York: Praeger Publishers, 1974.

Tyler, Parker. *The Hollywood Hallucination*. New York: Simon and Schuster, 1944.

———. *Magic and Myth of the Movies*. New York: Simon and Schuster, 1947.

Vardac, Nicholas. *From Stage to Screen*. Cambridge: Harvard University Press, 1949.
Vaughn, Robert. *Only Victims*. New York: G. P. Putnam's Sons, 1972.
Vizzard, Jack. *See No Evil*. New York: Simon and Schuster, 1970.
Wagenknecht, Edward. *The Movies in the Age of Innocence*. New York: Random House, Ballantine Books, 1971.
Walker, Alexander. *The Celluloid Sacrifice*. London: Michael Joseph, 1966.
———. *Stardom*. New York: Stein and Day Publishers, 1970.
Warner, W. Lloyd, and Paul S. Lunt. *The Social Life of a Modern Community*. New Haven: Yale University Press, 1941.
Westin, Alan F. *The Miracle Case: The Supreme Court and the Movies*. Inter-University Case Program No. 64. Alabama: The University of Alabama Press, 1961.
Wiebe, Robert H. *The Search for Order*. New York: Hill and Wang, 1967.
Williams, Raymond. *The Long Revolution*. New York: Harper and Row, 1965.
Wolfe, Glen J. *Vachel Lindsay: The Poet as Film Theorist*. New York: Arno Press, 1973.
Wolfenstein, Martha, and Nathan Leites. *Movies: A Psychological Study*. Glencoe: Free Press, 1950.
Young, Donald R. *Motion Pictures: A Study in Social Legislation*. Philadelphia: Westbrook Publishing Company, 1922; reprint ed., New York: Jerome S. Ozer, 1971.
Zierold, Norman. *The Moguls*. New York: Avon Books, 1972.
Zukor, Adolph. *The Public Is Never Wrong*. New York: G. P. Putnam's Sons, 1953.

Periodical Articles

Alpert, Hollis. "American Motion Picture: 1966 — View from the 28th Floor." *Saturday Review*, vol. 49, no. 51 (Dec. 24, 1966), pp. 17–19.
———. "The Lion Meows." *Saturday Review/World*, Jan. 26, 1974, pp. 56–57.
Ames, R. S. "The Screen Enters Politics." *Harper's*, vol. 171 (May, 1935), pp. 473–482.
Anast, Philip. "Differential Movie Appeals as Correlates of Attendance." *Journalism Quarterly*, vol. 44, no. 1 (1967), pp. 86–90.
"Anti-Block-Booking Bill Reported to Senate." *Christian Century*, vol. 56 (May 17, 1939), pp. 630–631.
"Anti-Trust Scenario." *Business Week*, no. 627 (Sept. 6, 1941), pp. 32–33.
Ardrey, Robert. "Hollywood: The Toll of the Frenzied Forties." *Reporter*, vol. 16 (Mar. 21, 1957), pp. 29–33.
———. "Hollywood's Fall Into Virtue." *Reporter*, vol. 16 (Feb. 21, 1957), pp. 13–17.
———. "What Happened to Hollywood?" *Reporter*, vol. 16 (Jan. 24, 1957), pp. 19–22.
"Are Movies the Opium of the People?" *Christian Century*, no. 64 (Jan. 8, 1947), p. 36.
Ayer, Douglas, Roy E. Bates, and Peter J. Herman. "Self-Censorship in the Movie Industry: An Historical Perspective on Law and Social Change." *Wisconsin Law Review*, no. 3 (1970), pp. 791–838.
"Baby Doll." *Commonweal*, vol. 65 (Jan. 11, 1957), pp. 371–372.
"Bank Night Bans." *Time*, Jan. 11, 1937, p. 55.
Barrett, Wilton A. "The Work of the National Board of Review." *Annals of the American Academy of Political and Social Science*, no. 128 (Nov., 1926), pp. 175–186.
Barry, Iris. "Why Wait for Posterity?" *Hollywood Quarterly*, vol. 1 (1946), pp. 131–137.
Batman, Richard Dale. "The Founding of the Hollywood Motion Picture Industry." *Journal of the West*, vol. 10 (Oct., 1971), pp. 609–623.
Benedict, John. "Movies are Redder than Ever." *American Mercury*, vol. 91 (Aug., 1960), pp. 3–23.
Benham, Albert. "The Movie as an Agency for Peace or War." *Journal of Educational Sociology*, vol. 12 (Mar., 1939), pp. 410–417.
Beranger, Clara. "The Cinema is Ready for College." *Theater Arts*, vol. 31, no. 1 (Jan. 1947), pp. 61–63.
Bergman, Mark. "Hollywood in the Forties Revisited." *Velvet Light Trap*, no. 5 (Summer, 1972), pp. 2–5.
Berman, Sam. "The Hays Office." *Fortune*, vol. 18 (Dec., 1938), pp. 68–72.
"Bid for Teens." *Business Week*, no. 1341 (May 14, 1955), p. 114.

"The Big Leer." *Time,* vol. 77 (June 9, 1961), pp. 55–56.

"Big Movie Year." *Business Week,* no. 702 (Feb. 13, 1943), pp. 37–38.

"The Birth of a New Art." *Independent,* Apr. 6, 1914, pp. 8–9.

"Black Movies." *Newsweek,* Oct. 23, 1972, pp. 74–81.

Blanchard, Paul. "Roman Catholic Censorship II: The Church and the Movies." *Nation,* vol. 166, no. 19, pt. 1 (May 8, 1948), pp. 499–502.

Bledsoe, William. "Revolution Came to Hollywood." *American Mercury,* vol. 49 (Feb., 1940), pp. 152–160.

Borneman, Ernest. "The Public Opinion Myth." *Harper's,* vol. 195 (May, 1945), pp. 30–40.

"Box-Office Appeal — After Tax is Not What It Seems." *U.S. News and World Report,* no. 42 (Feb. 8, 1957), pp. 128–131.

"Box-Office Buzzes Overseas." *Business Week,* no. 1836 (Nov. 7, 1964), p. 64.

Boyanowsky, Ehor D., Darren Newtson, and Elaine Walster. "Film Preferences Following a Murder." *Communication Research,* vol. 1, no. 1 (Jan., 1974), pp. 32–43.

Brady, Thomas A. "This Is Where the Money Went." *New Republic,* Jan. 31, 1949, pp. 12–15.

Brown, Stanley H. "Hollywood Rides Again." *Fortune,* vol. 74, no. 11 (Nov., 1966), pp. 181–182.

"Business Abroad — Battle of the Screen." *Fortune,* vol. 33, no. 3 (Mar., 1946), p. 200.

Carlson, Oliver. "The Communist Record in Hollywood." *American Mercury,* vol. 66, no. 290 (Feb., 1948), pp. 135–143.

"Censoring Movies." *Commonweal,* no. 74 (Mar. 31, 1961), p. 17.

"The Censors." *Time,* no. 63 (Jan. 11, 1954), p. 80.

"Censorship: Who Bans What." *Newsweek,* no. 57 (Feb. 13, 1961), pp. 89–90.

"Censorship of Motion Pictures." *Yale Law Review Journal,* vol. 48 (Nov., 1939), pp. 87–113.

Chambers, Robert W. "Need for Statistical Research." *Annals of the American Academy of Political and Social Science,* vol. 254 (Nov., 1947), pp. 169–172.

Champlin, Charles. "Can TV Save the Films?" *Saturday Review,* Dec. 24, 1966, p. 11.

"Chances the Movies Are Missing." *Christian Century,* vol. 54 (May 12, 1937), pp. 617–618.

Chandler, Alfred. "The Beginnings of 'Big Business.'" In *The Shaping of America,* edited by Richard M. Abram and Lawrence W. Levine, pp. 62–92. Boston: Little, Brown and Co., 1965.

Chandler, Edward H. "How Much Children Attend the Theatre." *Proceedings of the Child Conference for Research and Welfare.* New York: G. E. Stechert and Co., 1909, pp. 55–59.

———. "The Moving Picture Show." *Religious Education,* Oct., 1911, pp. 344–349.

Chappell, Fred. "Twenty-Six Propositions About Skin Flicks." In *Man and the Movies,* edited by W. R. Robinson, pp. 53–59. Baltimore: Penguin Books, 1969.

Chayefsky, Paddy. "Big Changes in Hollywood, Art Films — Dedicated Insanity." *Saturday Review of Literature,* vol. 40, no. 51 (Dec. 21, 1957), pp. 9–17.

"Cinema." *Time,* no. 68 (Dec. 24, 1956), p. 61.

Clancy, William P. "Censorship and the Court: Freedom of the Screen." *Commonweal,* vol. 59, no. 20 (Feb. 19, 1954), pp. 500–502.

"Cleavage and the Code." *Time,* no. 48 (Aug. 5, 1946), p. 50.

Clinard, Marshall B. "Secondary Community Influences and Juvenile Delinquency." *Annals of the American Academy of Political and Social Science,* vol. 255 (1948), pp. 42–54.

Cocks, Orrin G. "How a Neighborhood Can Improve Its Motion Picture Exhibitions." In *Proceedings,* National Conference of Social Work, 1921, pp. 340–343.

———. "The Motion Picture and the Upbuilding of Community Life." In *Proceedings,* National Conference of Social Work, 1919, pp. 311–313.

Coffin, T. E. "Television's Effects on Leisure-Time Activities." *Journal of Applied Psychology,* vol. 32 (1948), pp. 550–558.

Collier, John. "Censorship; and the National Board." *Survey,* Oct. 2, 1915, pp. 9–14.

493

―――. "The Motion Picture." *Proceedings of the Child Conference for Research and Welfare.* New York: G. E. Stechart and Co., 1910, pp. 108–118.

"Comeback — and Why." *Newsweek,* no. 44 (Sept. 13, 1954), p. 104.

Cooper, Eunice, and Helen Dinerman. "Analysis of the Film 'Don't Be a Sucker.'" *Public Opinion Quarterly,* vol. 15, no. 2, (1951), pp. 243–264.

Corliss, Richard. "The Legion of Decency." *Film Comment,* vol. 4; no. 4 (Summer, 1969), pp. 24–61.

Coughlan, Robert. "Now It Is Trouble that Is Supercolossal in Hollywood." *Life,* vol. 31 (Aug. 13, 1951), pp. 102–108.

Cousins, Norman. "Our Heroes." *Saturday Review of Literature,* vol. 24, no. 27 (Oct. 25, 1941), p. 10.

Craven, Thomas. "The Great American Art." *Dial,* vol. 81 (Dec., 1926), pp. 483–492.

Cressey, Paul F. "The Influence of Moving Pictures on Students in India." *American Journal of Sociology,* vol. 41, no. 3 (Nov., 1935), pp. 341–350.

Cressey, Paul G. "The Motion Picture as Informal Education." *Journal of Educational Psychology,* vol. 7 (1934), pp. 504–515.

―――. "The Motion Picture Experience as Modified by Social Background and Personality." *American Sociological Review,* vol. 3 (Aug., 1938), pp. 516–525.

Crichton, Kyle. "Hollywood Gets Its Teeth Kicked In." *Collier's* Jan. 9, 1943, pp. 34–35.

―――. "Hollywood Holocaust." *Collier's,* no. 111 (Feb. 13, 1943), pp. 16, 23.

Cripps, Thomas R. "The Death of Rastus: Negroes in American Films Since 1945." *Phylon,* vol. 28, pp. 267–275.

―――. "The Reaction of the Negro to the Motion Picture *Birth of a Nation.*" *Historian,* vol. 25 (1963), pp. 344–362.

Crowther, Bosley. "It's the Fans Who Make the Films." *New York Times Magazine,* June 24, 1945, p. 14.

―――. "Magic, Myth and Monotony." *TV Quarterly,* no. 4 (Fall, 1968), p. 52.

―――. "The Movies Follow the Flag." *New York Times Magazine,* Aug. 13, 1944, p. 18.

―――. "Seeing Things — 20° Cooler Inside." *Saturday Review of Literature,* vol. 28, no. 31 (Aug. 4, 1942), pp. 24–25.

―――. "The Strange Case of 'The Miracle.'" *Atlantic,* vol. 187 (Apr., 1951), pp. 35-39.

Currie, Barton W. "The Nickle Madness." *Harper's Weekly,* August 24, 1907, pp. 1246–1247.

Dale, Edgar. "On Miracles Come C.O.D." *Hollywood Quarterly,* vol. 3 (1948), pp. 82–85.

Dane, Clemence. "What is Love? Is It What We See in the Movies?" *Forum,* vol. 94 (Dec., 1935), pp. 335–338.

Dangerfield, George. "Time Muddles On." *New Republic,* no. 88 (Aug. 19, 1936), pp. 43–45.

Dawson, Anthony. "Motion Picture Economics." *Hollywood Quarterly,* vol. 3, (1948), pp. 217–240.

"Decency and Censorship." *Christian Century,* vol. 53 (July 29, 1936), pp. 1030–1032.

"Decoded: Hollywood Production Code." *Time,* vol. 72 (Nov. 3, 1958), p. 78.

de la Roche, Catherine. "That 'Feminine Angle.'" *Penguin Film Review,* no. 8 (Jan., 1949), pp. 25–34.

Denby, David. "Our Misanthropic Movies." *Atlantic Monthly,* vol. 228, no. 5 (Nov., 1971), pp. 144–148.

Diehl, Mrs. Ambrose A., "The Moral Effect of the Cinema on Individuals." *International Review of Educational Cinematography,* vol. 3 (1931), pp. 1123–1137.

"Dirty Joke." *Christian Century,* vol. 82 (Feb. 3, 1965), pp. 144–145.

"Divided Court Rewrites the Definition of Obscenity." *Congressional Quarterly,* June 23, 1973, pp. 1571–1572.

"Drama of the People." *Independent,* Sept. 29, 1910, pp. 713–715.

"Drive-Ins." *Time,* no. 38 (July 14, 1941), p. 66.

Dunne, Philip. "The Documentary and Hollywood." *Hollywood Quarterly,* vol. 1 (1946), pp. 166–172.

Eastman, Fred. "Chances the Movies are Missing." *Christian Century,* vol. 54 (May 12, 1936), pp. 617–618.

494

———. "Motion Pictures and American Culture." *Recreation*, vol. 40 (July, 1946), p. 228.

———. "Upgrading Home Town Movies." *Christian Century*, vol. 76 (Jan. 14, 1959), pp. 47–48.

———. "Your Child and the Movies." *Christian Century*, May 3, 10, 17, 24, 31, June 7, 14, 1933.

Eaton, Walter P. "The Menace of the Movies." *American Magazine*, Sept., 1913, p. 55.

———. "A New Epoch in the Movies." *American Magazine*, Oct., 1914, pp. 44, 55.

Elkin, Frederick. "The Psychological Appeal of the Hollywood Western." *Journal of Educational Sociology*, vol. 24, no. 2, (1950), pp. 72–86.

Ephron, Nora. "Women." *Esquire*, vol. 89, no. 4 (Feb., 1973), pp. 14–22.

Ernst, Morris. "Supercolossal: The Movies." *Atlantic Monthly*, vol. 166, no. 1 (July, 1940), pp. 17–28.

"Fade Out for Blockbuster Films?" *Business Week*, no. 1729 (Oct. 20, 1962), pp. 172–174.

Fadiman, William. "Hollywood: Shivering in the Sun." *New Republic*, vol. 162, no. 26 (June 27, 1970), pp. 17–19.

———. "Should American Films Be Subsidized?" *Saturday Review*, vol. 50, no. 31 (Aug. 5, 1967), pp. 14–17.

Farber, Stephen. "L.A. Journal." *Film Comment*, vol. 10, no. 6 (Nov.–Dec., 1974), pp. 2, 58.

Farrell, James T. "The Language of Hollywood." *Saturday Review of Literature*, vol. 27 (Aug. 5, 1944), pp. 28–32.

"Fateful Hour for the Movies." *Christian Century*, vol. 53 (May 27, 1936), p. 757.

Fearing, Franklin. "Influence of the Movies on Attitudes and Behavior." *Annals of the American Academy of Political and Social Science*, vol. 254 (Nov., 1947), pp. 70–79.

———. "Psychology and the Films." *Hollywood Quarterly*, vol. 2 (1947), pp. 118–121.

———. "The Screen Discovers Psychiatry." *Hollywood Quarterly*, vol. 1 (1946), pp. 154–158.

———. "Warriors Return: Normal or Neurotic?" *Hollywood Quarterly*, vol. 1 (1945), pp. 97–109.

———. "A Word of Caution for the Intelligent Consumer of Motion Pictures." *Quarterly of Film, Radio and Television*, vol. 6 (1952), pp. 129–142.

Fell, John L. "Dissolves by Candlelight." *Film Quarterly*, vol. 23, no. 3 (1970), pp. 22–34.

"Fever Chart for Hollywood." *American Magazine*, vol. 128 (Oct., 1939), pp. 67–74.

"Film Censorship: An Administrative Analysis." *Columbia Law Review*, vol. 39 (Dec., 1939), pp. 1383–1405.

"Film Exports Set Record." *Business Week*, June 26, 1937, p. 50.

"Film-making Gets Some Tight-fisted Angels." *Business Week*, Feb. 5, 1972, pp. 68–69.

"Film-Rating Fiasco." *America*, vol. 124 (May 29, 1971), p. 557.

"Films: Creative Chaos." *Newsweek*, Dec. 24, 1973, p. 40.

Finegan, Thomas E. "The Results of the Experiments with Eastman Classroom Films." *International Review of Educational Cinematography*, vol. 1 (1929), pp. 131–147.

Fiske, Marjorie, and Leo A. Handel. "Motion Picture Research: Content and Audience Analysis." *Journal of Marketing*, vol. 11, no. 2 (Oct., 1946), pp. 129–134.

"Flash in the Pan?" *Time*, no. 61 (Mar. 2, 1953), p. 90.

"For Movies—A Boom, But New Worries in Hollywood." *U.S. News and World Report*, no. 61 (Oct. 17, 1966), pp. 120–122.

"Fortune Survey: The People's Taste in Movies and Books." *Fortune*, vol. 39, no. 3 (Mar., 1949), pp. 39–40, 43–44.

Fox, M. S. "The Art of the Movies in American Life." *Journal of Aesthetics and Art Criticism*, vol. 3, no. 9–10 (1944), pp. 39–52.

Frakes, Margaret. "Why the Movie Investigation?" *Christian Century*, vol. 58 (Sept. 24, 1941), pp. 1172–1174.

Frank, Josette. "Chills and Thrills in Radio, Movies, and Comics." *Child Study*, Spring, 1948, pp. 42–48.

495

"Free the Movies Now." *Christian Century,* vol. 53 (Mar. 25, 1936), pp. 454-455.

Friedmann, N. L. "Some Sociological Notes on the Boom in Film Interest." *Youth and Society,* no. 2 (Mar., 1971), pp. 323-332.

Fulk, Joseph R. "The Effect on Education and Morals of the Moving Picture Shows." *Proceedings of the National Education Association Annual Meeting,* 1912, pp. 456-461.

Gans, Herbert J. "The Rise of the Problem-Film: An Analysis of Changes in Hollywood Films and the American Audience." *Social Problems,* vol. 11 (1964), pp. 327-336.

Gerbner, George. "An Institutional Approach to Mass Communications Research." In *Communication: Theory and Research,* edited by Lee Thayer, pp. 429-445. Springfield: Charles C. Thomas, 1967.

"Getting Them Back to the Movies." *Business Week,* no. 1364 (Oct. 22, 1955), p. 58.

"Give the Exhibitor a Chance." *Christian Century,* vol. 52 (June 19, 1935), pp. 819-821.

Goldstein, Sidney E. "The Motion Picture and Social Control." In *The Movies on Trial,* edited by William J. Perlman, pp. 206-231. New York: Macmillan Company, 1936.

Goldwyn, Samuel. "Hollywood in the Television Age." *Hollywood Quarterly,* vol. 4 (1950), pp. 145-151.

———. "Hollywood Is Sick!" *Saturday Evening Post,* vol. 213 (July 13, 1940), pp. 18-19.

Gordon, Jay E. "There's Really No Business Like Show Business." *Quarterly of Film, Radio and Television,* vol. 6 (1951), pp. 173-185.

Gorney, Sondra. "On Children's Cinema: America and Britain." *Hollywood Quarterly,* vol. 3 (1948), pp. 56-62.

Greene, Nelson L. "Motion Pictures in the Classroom." *Annals of the American Academy of Political and Social Science,* no. 217 (Nov., 1926), pp. 122-130.

Greene, Wesley H. "Ideas on Film — Midwest Takes the Lead." *Saturday Review of Literature,* vol. 32, no. 11 (Mar. 12, 1949), pp. 33-34.

Grierson, John. "Tomorrow the Movies I: Hollywood International." *Nation,* vol. 160, no. 1 (Jan. 6, 1945), pp. 12-14.

———. "Tomorrow the Movies II: Pictures Without Theaters." *Nation,* vol. 160, no. 2 (Jan. 13, 1945), pp. 37-39.

"Growth of Drive-Ins." *Commonweal,* vol. 65, no. 7 (Nov. 16, 1956), p. 166.

Guback, Thomas H. "Cultural Identity and Film in the European Economic Community." *Cinema Journal,* vol. 14, no. 1 (Fall, 1974), pp. 2-17.

Gundlach, Ralph H. "The Movies: Stereotypes or Realities?" *Journal of Social Issues,* vol. 3, no. 2 (1947), pp. 26-32.

Haley, Jay. "The Appeal of the Moving Picture." *Quarterly of Film; Radio and Television,* vol. 6 (1952), pp. 361-374.

Handel, Leo A. "Hollywood Market Research." *Quarterly of Film, Radio and Television,* vol. 7 (1953), pp. 304-309.

———. "The Social Obligation of Motion Pictures." *International Journal of Opinion and Attitude Research,* Dec., 1947, pp. 97-98.

———. "A Study to Determine the Drawing Power of Male and Female Stars Upon Movie-Goers of Their Own Sex." *International Journal of Opinion and Attitude Research,* vol. 2 (Summer, 1948), pp. 215-220.

Hansen, Harry L. "Hollywood and International Understanding." *Harvard Business Review,* vol. 25, no. 1 (Autumn, 1946), pp. 28-45.

Harmerz, Aljean. "How Do You Pick a Winner in Hollywood? You Don't." *New York Times,* April 29, 1973, Sec. 2, p. 1.

Harrison, P. S. "Give the Movie Exhibitor a Chance!" *Christian Century,* no. 52 (June 19, 1935), pp. 819-821.

Hawkins, Richard C. "Perspective on 3-D." *Quarterly of Film, Radio and Television,* vol. 7 (1952), pp. 325-334.

Hays, Will H. "Motion Pictures and Their Censors." *American Review of Reviews,* Apr., 1927, pp. 393-398.

Heindel, Richard H. "American Attitudes of British School Children." *School and Society,* vol. 46, no. 1200 (Dec. 25, 1936), pp. 838-840.

Hellmuth, William F., Jr. "The Motion Picture Industry." In *The Structure of American Industry*, edited by Walter Adams, pp. 360–402. New York: Macmillan Company, 1967.

Henry, Ralph L. "The Cultural Influence of the Talkies." *School and Society*, Feb. 2, 1929, pp. 149–150.

Herron, F. L. "Block-Booking." *International Review of Educational Cinematography*, vol. 4 (1932), pp. 597–603.

Hill, Gladwin. "Our Film Program in Germany II: How Far Was It a Failure?" *Hollywood Quarterly*, vol. 2 (1947), pp. 131–137.

Hodgins, Eric. "A Round Table on the Movies." *Life*, vol. 26 (June 27, 1949), pp. 90–110.

Holliday, Carl. "The Motion Picture and the Church." *Independent*, Feb. 13, 1913, pp. 353–356.

"Hollywood: The Big Leer." *Time*, vol. 77 (June 9, 1961), pp. 55–56.

"Hollywood: Fewer Stars, More Profits." *U.S. News and World Report*, no. 70 (Jan. 18, 1971), pp. 48–50.

"Hollywood: The Focus is Overseas." *Business Week*, no. 1310 (Oct. 9, 1954), pp. 158–160.

"Hollywood — A Postwar Record Breaker." *Business Week*, Dec. 7, 1946, p. 96.

"Hollywood: The Shock of Freedom in Films." *Time*, vol. 90 (Dec. 8, 1967), pp. 66–71.

"Hollywood and Radio." *Business Week*, Nov. 6, 1937, p. 27.

"Hollywood Goes Its Own Way." *Time*, no. 48 (Oct. 21, 1946), pp. 50, 52.

"Hollywood in Uniform." *Fortune*, vol. 25, no. 4 (April, 1942), pp. 92–95.

"Hollywood Learns How to Live with TV." *Business Week*, no. 1197 (Aug. 9, 1952), pp. 46–48.

"Hollywood Makes a Bid as New Broadcasting Center with 'Good News.'" *Newsweek*, no. 10 (Nov. 15, 1937), p. 25.

"Hollywood Meets Frankenstein." *Nation*, vol. 174, no. 26 (June 28, 1952), pp. 628–631.

"Hollywood Produces a New Alibi." *Christian Century*, vol. 64 (Feb. 5, 1947), p. 165.

"Hollywood Unions Say Too Many Films Shot Abroad." *Business Week*, no. 1433 (Feb. 16, 1957), p. 169.

"Hollywood Wows Wall Street." *Business Week*, May 11, 1946, p. 58.

"Hollywood's America — Real or Unreal?" *Scholastic*, no. 61 (Jan. 21, 1953), pp. 7–8.

"Hollywood's Clamor Boys." *American Mercury*, vol. 54 (Jan., 1942), pp. 85–92.

"Hollywood's Magic Mountain." *Fortune*, vol. 31, no. 2 (Feb., 1945), pp. 152–156.

"Hollywood's Press: Why the Stars Are in Your Eyes." *Newsweek*, no. 43 (Feb. 22, 1954), pp. 62–64.

Holmes, John Clellon. "15¢ Before 6:00 P.M.: The Wonderful Movies of 'The Thirties.'" *Harper's*, vol. 231 (Dec. 1965), pp. 51–55.

Holmes, John Haynes. "The Movies and the Community." In *The Movies on Trial*, edited by William J. Perlman, pp. 196–205. New York: Macmillan Company, 1936; reprinted, New York: Jerome S. Ozer, 1971.

Houseman, John. "Hollywood Faces the Fifties, Part I: The Lost Enthusiasm." *Harper's*, vol. 200, no. 1199 (Apr., 1950), pp. 50–59.

———. "How — And What — Does a Movie Communicate?" *Quarterly of Film, Radio and Television*, vol. 10 (1956), pp. 227–238.

———. "Today's Hero: A Review." *Hollywood Quarterly*, vol. 2 (1947), pp. 161–163.

Houston, Herbert S. "The Motion Picture and World Understanding." *Education*, vol. 64 (Mar., 1944), pp. 409–412.

———. "A Plan to Develop International Understanding Through Motion Pictures." *Education*, vol. 58 (May, 1938), pp. 560–561.

Houston, Penelope. "Hollywood." *Sight and Sound*, vol. 21 (Jan.–Mar., 1952), p. 137.

Hovland, Carl I. "Effects of the Mass Media of Communication." In *Handbook of Social Psychology*, edited by Gardner Lindzey, pp. 1062–1103. Reading: Addison-Wesley Publishing Company, 1954.

"How Are the Movies?" *Commonweal*, vol. 30 (Aug. 4, 1939), pp. 358–359.

"How Children Are Entertained." *Journal of Education*, Feb. 25, 1915, pp. 207–212.

"How Others See Us on Film." *America*, vol. 95 (Sept. 8, 1956), pp. 5–6.

"How to Run a Theater." *Time*, no. 42 (Nov. 22, 1943), pp. 94–95.

Howe, Frederic C. "Leisure for the Millions." *Survey*, vol. 31 (1914), pp. 415–416.

Howells, William Dean. "The Editor's Easy Chair." *Harper's*, Sept., 1912, pp. 634–637.

Hughes, Rupert. "Calamity with Sound Effects." *New Outlook*, Sept., 1933, pp. 21–26.

Hulett, J. E., Jr. "Estimating the Net Effect of a Commercial Motion Picture upon the Trend of Local Public Opinion." *American Sociological Review*, vol. 14, no. 2 (1949), pp. 263–275.

"The Image of the U.S." *Time*, no. 66 (Sept. 2, 1955), p. 22.

"Immorality, Crime and the Cinema." *International Review of Educational Cinematography*, vol. 2 (1930), pp. 319–334.

"Is There Any Future in Hollywood?" *Economist*, Feb. 28, 1970, pp. 52–53.

"Is This the End of Block-Booking?" *Christian Century*, no. 57 (Nov. 6, 1940), p. 1364.

"Jack Valenti Decries Confusion Caused by Supreme Court Ruling." *Boxoffice*, July 30, 1973, p. 4.

Jacobs, Lewis. "Experimental Cinema in America, 1921–1947." A supplement in *Rise of the American Film*, by Lewis Jacobs, pp. 543–582. New York: Teacher's College Press, 1968.

———. "World War II and the American Film." In *The Movies: An American Idiom*, edited by Arthur F. McClure, pp. 153–157. Rutherford: Farleigh Dickinson University Press, 1971.

Jarrico, Paul. "They Are Not So Innocent Abroad." *New Republic*, Jan. 31, 1949, pp. 17–19.

Jester, Ralph. "Hollywood and Pedagogy." *Journal of Educational Sociology*, vol. 12 (Nov., 1938), pp. 137–141.

Johnston, Eric. "Hollywood: America's Travelling Salesman." *Vital Speeches of the Day*, no. 23 (July 1, 1957), pp. 572–574.

Jones, Dorothy B. "Hollywood War Films." *Hollywood Quarterly*, vol. 1 (1945), pp. 1–19.

———. "Tomorrow the Movies III: Hollywood Goes to War." *Nation*, vol. 160, no. 4 (Jan. 27, 1956), pp. 93–95.

———. "Tomorrow the Movies IV: Is Hollywood Growing Up?" *Nation*, vol. 160, no. 5 (Feb. 3, 1945), pp. 123–125.

Jones, Harold E., and Herbert S. Conrad. "Rural Preferences in Motion Pictures." *Journal of Social Psychology*, vol. 1 (1930), pp. 419–423.

Joseph, Robert. "Our Film Program in Germany I: How Far Was It a Success?" *Hollywood Quarterly*, vol. 2 (1947), pp. 122–130.

Jump, Rev. Herbert A. "The Child's Leisure Hour — How It Is Affected by the Motion Picture." *Religious Education*, Oct., 1911, pp. 349–354.

Kael, Pauline. "Are Movies Going to Pieces?" *Atlantic Monthly*, vol. 214, no. 6 (Dec., 1964), pp. 61–66.

———. "The Creative Business." *New Republic*, vol. 155, no. 15 (Oct. 8, 1966), pp. 32–35.

———. "On the Future of the Movies." *New Yorker*, Aug. 5, 1974, pp. 43–58.

Kahn, Gordon. "One Psychological Moment, Please." *Atlantic Monthly*, vol. 178, no. 4 (Oct., 1946), pp. 135–137.

Kellogg, Arthur. "Minds Made by the Movies." *Survey Graphic*, May, 1933, pp. 245–250.

Kenny, Hubert A. "Going to School with the Movies." *American Mercury*, vol. 64 (Jan., 1946), pp. 36–42.

Kluckhohn, Clyde. "Have There Been Discernible Shifts in American Values During the Past Generation?" In *The American Style*, edited by Elting E. Morison, pp. 145–217. New York: Harper and Brothers, 1958.

Knebel, Fletcher. "Hollywood: Broke, and Getting Rich." *Look*, no. 34 (Nov. 3, 1970), pp. 50–52.

Knight, Arthur. "American Motion Picture: 1966 — Where Is the New Talent?" *Saturday Review*, vol. 49, no. 51 (Dec. 24, 1966), pp. 20–22.

———. "Dawn over Hollywood." *Theatre Arts*, vol. 34, no. 9 (Sept., 1950), pp. 21–27.

———. "Hollywood's Defense in Depth." *Reporter*, vol. 8 (June 9, 1953), pp. 32–34.

————. "Ideas on Film-Self-Expression." *Saturday Review of Literature*, vol. 33, no. 21 (May 27, 1950), pp. 38–40.

————. "What Golden Years?" *Saturday Review*, vol. 47, no. 35 (Aug. 29, 1964), pp. 169–171.

————. "Who's to Classify?" *Saturday Review*, vol. 49, no. 9 (Feb. 26, 1966), p. 42.

Koon, Cline M. "Motion Pictures in Education in the United States." *International Review of Educational Cinematography*, vol. 6 (1935), pp. 476–477.

Kornhauser, William. "The Theory of Mass Society." In *International Encyclopedia of Social Sciences*, vol. 10, pp. 58-64. New York: Macmillan and Free Press, 1968.

Kouwenhoven, John A. "The Movies Better Be Good!" *Harper's*, vol. 190 (May, 1945), pp. 534–540.

Kracauer, Siegfried. "Filming the Subconscious." *Theater Arts*, vol. 32, no. 2 (Feb., 1948), pp. 37–40.

————. "Hollywood's Terror Films: Do They Reflect an American State of Mind?" *Commentary*, vol. 2 (1946), pp. 132–136.

————. "National Types as Hollywood Presents Them." *Public Opinion Quarterly*, vol. 13, no. 1 (1949), pp. 53–72.

————. "Those Movies with a Message." *Harper's*, vol. 196 (June, 1948), pp. 567–572.

Kruse, William F. "The Motion Picture and the American School." *International Review of Educational Cinematography*, vol. 4 (1933); pp. 645–654.

Kubie, Lawrence S. "Psychiatry and the Films." *Hollywood Quarterly*, vol. 2 (1947), pp. 113–117.

Lanier, Henry W. "The Educational Future of the Moving Picture." *American Review of Reviews*, Dec., 1914, pp. 725–729.

Larson, Cedric. "The Domestic Motion Picture Work of the Office of War Information." *Hollywood Quarterly*, vol. 3 (1948), pp. 434–443.

"The Law: Censoring the Censors." *Time*, vol. 85 (Mar. 12, 1965), p. 72.

Lawson, W. P. "The Miracle of the Movie." *Harper's Weekly*, Jan. 2, 1915, pp. 7–9.

Lazarsfeld, Paul. "Audience Research in the Movie Field." *Annals of the American Academy of Political and Social Science*, vol. 254 (Nov., 1947), pp. 160–168.

Leary, Thomas B., and J. Roger Noall. "Entertainment: Public Pressures and the Law." *Harvard Law Review*, vol. 71, (1957), pp. 344–353.

"Legion of Decency and the Big Eight." *Christian Century*, vol. 57 (Mar. 20, 1940), p. 373.

"Legion of Decency Campaign Intensified." *Literary Digest*, vol. 118 (Dec. 22, 1934), p. 20.

Levien, Sonya. "New York's Motion Picture Law." *American City*, Oct., 1913, pp. 319–321.

"Liberty Bells in Hollywood." *Christian Century*, vol. 56 (Mar. 8, 1939), pp. 310–311.

Lounsbury, Myron O. " 'Flashes of Lightning': The Moving Picture in the Progressive Era." *Journal of Popular Culture*, vol. 3, no. 4 (1970), pp. 769–797.

Lowe, Herman A. "Washington Discovers Hollywood." *American Mercury*, vol. 60 (Apr., 1945), pp. 407–414.

Luther, Rodney. "Television and the Future of Motion Picture Exhibition." *Quarterly of Film, Radio and Television*, vol. 5 (1951), pp. 164–177.

Lyons, Timothy J. "Hollywood and World War I, 1914–1918." *Journal of Popular Film*, vol. I, no. 1 (Winter, 1972), pp. 15–29.

MacCann, Richard Dyer. "Hollywood Faces the World." *Yale Review*, vol. 51 (June, 1963), pp. 593–608.

McCreary, Eugene C. "Films and History: Some Thoughts on Their Interrelationship." *Societas*, Winter, 1971, pp. 51–66.

McDowell, Edwin. "The Critics Descend on Pornotopia." *Wall Street Journal*, May 15, 1973, p. 24.

MacGowan, Kenneth. "And So Into the Sunset . . ." *New Republic*, Jan. 31, 1949, pp. 23–24.

————. "A Change of Pattern." *Hollywood Quarterly*, vol. 1 (1946), pp. 148–153.

————. "The Screen's New Look — Wider and Deeper." *Film Quarterly*, vol. 11 (1956), pp. 109–130.

MacGregor, Ford H. "Official Censorship Legislation." *Annals of the American Academy of Political and Social Science,* no. 128 (Nov., 1926), pp. 163–174.

McGuire, W. "Attitudes and Opinions." *Annual Review of Psychology,* vol. 17 (1966), pp. 475–514.

MacKaye, Milton. "The Big Brawl: Hollywood vs. Television." *Saturday Evening Post,* vol. 224, Jan. 19, pp. 17–19; Jan. 26, p. 30; Feb. 2, 1952, p. 30.

McManus, John T., and Louis Kronenberger. "Motion Pictures, the Theater, and Race Relations." *Annals of the American Academy of Political and Social Science,* vol. 244 (March, 1946), pp. 152–159.

"Making the Movies into a Business." *Business Week,* June 23, 1973, p. 116.

Martin, Pete. "Tonight at Beachhead Bijou." *Saturday Evening Post,* vol. 217 (Aug. 12, 1944), pp. 20, 81–82.

Mayer, Arthur. "Hollywood Verdict: Gilt, but not Guilty." *Saturday Review,* Oct. 31, 1953, pp. 11–12.

———. "Premature Obituary: The Adventures of a Movie Theatre Operator." *Harper's,* vol. 189 (July, 1944), pp. 155–167.

Meccoli, Domenico. "Conglomerates Gobble Up Movies." *Successo,* vol. 12 (Mar., 1970), pp. 90–95.

"Men Behind Kung-Fooey." *Time,* June 11, 1973, p. 46.

"Menace of Adult Films." *America,* vol. 106 (Mar. 10, 1962), p. 747.

Merritt, Russell. "Nickelodeon Theaters: Building an Audience for the Movies." *AFI Report,* May, 1973, pp. 4–8.

Miller, Carl G. "Our Hollywood Competitor." *Education,* vol. 67 (Feb., 1947), p. 398.

Milliken, Carl E. "The Movie: Has It a Social Obligation?" In *Proceedings,* National Conference of Social Work, 1927, pp. 352–360.

Mirams, Gordon. "Drop That Gun." *Quarterly of Film, Radio and Television,* vol. 6 (1951), pp. 1–19.

"Motion Picture Films for the Schools to Be Selected from Hollywood Vaults." *School and Society,* vol. 46 (July 24, 1937), pp. 107–108.

"Motion Picture Research: Response Analysis." *Journal of Marketing,* vol. 11, no. 3 (Jan., 1947), pp. 273–280.

"Motion Pictures in the Schools." *School and Society,* vol. 42 (Oct. 12, 1935), pp. 498–499.

"Movie Censorship." *Life,* vol. 21 (Oct. 28, 1946), pp. 79–82.

"Movie Industry is Split over Why Business Is Better." *Business Week,* no. 1358 (Sept. 10, 1958), p. 54.

"Movie Manners and Morals." *Outlook,* vol. 113 (July 26, 1916), pp. 694–695.

"Moviemakers Bank on Willkie to Foil Propaganda Inquiry." *Newsweek,* no. 18 (Sept. 15, 1941), pp. 51–52.

"Moviemakers Look for Gold on the TV Screen." *Business Week,* no. 1338 (Apr. 23, 1955), pp. 154–156.

"Movies, the Big Flick Kick." *Look,* no. 29 (Mar. 9, 1965), pp. 17–28.

"Movies Are Brought to Judgement." *Christian Century,* Dec. 30, 1931, pp. 1647–1648.

"Movies Get New Moguls: Conglomerates Wooing Hollywood." *Business Week,* no. 2058 (Feb. 8, 1969), pp. 29–30.

"Movies Improve a Bit." *America,* vol. 100 (Dec. 20, 1958), p. 360.

"The Moving Picture and the National Character." *American Review of Reviews,* Sept., 1910, pp. 315–320.

Murray, James P. "Black Movies/Black Theater." *Drama Review,* vol. 116 (Dec., 1972), pp. 56–61.

Nelson, Donald M. "The Independent Producer." *Annals of the American Academy of Political and Social Science,* vol. 254 (Nov., 1947), pp. 49–57.

"The New Hollywood." *Time,* no. 69 (May 13, 1957), pp. 43–44.

"The New Industry." *Time,* no. 61 (May 4, 1953), p. 102.

"New Movie Code: Cleanup or Cover Up?" *Christian Century,* no. 93 (Oct. 25, 1968), pp. 5–8.

"New Techniques for Studying the Effectiveness of Films." *Journal of Marketing,* vol. 11, no. 4 (Apr., 1947), pp. 390–393.

North, C. J. "Our Foreign Trade in Motion Pictures." *Annals of the American Academy of Political and Social Science,* no. 128 (Nov., 1926), pp. 100–108.

Nye, Gerald P. "War Propaganda: Our Madness Increases as Our Emergency Shrinks." *Vital Speeches,* no. 7 (Sept. 15, 1941), pp. 720–723.

Olsen, Marvin E. "Motion Picture Attendance and Social Isolation." *Sociological Quarterly,* vol. 1 (1960), pp. 107–116.

Palmer, Charles. "Miracles Come C.O.D." *Hollywood Quarterly,* vol. 2 (1948), pp. 381–387.

———. "Reply to a Critic." *Hollywood Quarterly,* vol. 3 (1948), pp. 85–87.

"Panic in Paradise." *Time,* no. 50 (Sept. 22, 1947), p. 97.

"Pass the Neely Bill." *Christian Century,* vol. 57 (Feb. 21, 1940), pp. 240–241.

Patterson, Frances Taylor. "Bread and Cinemas." *North American Review,* vol. 246, no. 2 (Dec., 1938), pp. 259–266.

Patterson, Joseph Medill. "Nickelodeons." *Moving Picture World and View Photographer,* May 4, 1907, p. 149.

———. "The Nickelodeons, the Poor Man's Elementary Course in the Drama." *Saturday Evening Post,* Nov. 23, 1907, pp. 10–11, 38.

Paul, Elliot. "Of Film Propaganda." *Atlantic Monthly,* vol. 176, no. 3 (Sept., 1945), pp. 123, 127–128.

Peet, Creighton. "Hollywood at War, 1915–1918." *Esquire,* Sept. 1936, pp. 60–63, 109.

———. "Letter to Hollywood." *Outlook,* Dec. 17, 1930, 612–613.

———. "Our Lady Censors." *Outlook,* Dec. 25, 1929, pp. 645–647.

Pichel, Irving. "Areas of Silence." *Hollywood Quarterly,* vol. 3 (1948), pp. 51–55.

Pitken, Walter B. "Screen Crime vs. Press Crime." *Outlook and Independent,* July 29, 1931, pp. 398–399, 414.

Poffenberger, A. T. "Motion Pictures and Crime." *Scientific Monthly,* Apr., 1921, pp. 336–339.

Poster, William. "Movies. Hollywood Caters to the Middle Class: An Appraisal of Metro-Goldwyn-Mayer." *American Mercury,* vol. 73 (Aug., 1951), pp. 82–91.

Poussaint, Alvin F. "Cheap Thrills that Degrade Blacks." *Psychology Today,* vol. 7, no. 9 (Feb., 1974), pp. 22–26.

"Private Ratings of Motion Pictures as a Basis for State Regulation." *Georgetown Law Review,* vol. 59 (May, 1971), pp. 1205–1236.

"Propaganda or History?" *Nation,* vol. 153, no. 12 (Sept. 20, 1941), pp. 241–242.

Putnam, Harold. "The War Against War Movies." *Educational Screen,* vol. 22 (May, 1943), pp. 162–163, 175.

Quigley, Martin. "Importance of the Entertainment Film." *Annals of the American Academy of Political and Social Science,* vol. 254 (Nov., 1947), pp. 65–69.

Quirt, John. "The Movies Go International." *Exchange,* vol. 30 (June, 1969), pp. 8–13.

Raths, Louis E., and Frank N. Trager. "Public Opinion and 'Crossfire.' " *Journal of Educational Sociology,* vol. 21 (1948), pp. 345–368.

Rorty, James. "Dream Factory." *Forum,* vol. 94 (Sept., 1935), pp. 162–165.

Rosen, Irwin C. "The Effect of the Motion Picture 'Gentleman's Agreement' on Attitudes Toward Jews." *Journal of Psychology,* vol. 26 (1948), pp. 525–536.

Ross, Murray. "Labor Relations in Hollywood." *Annals of the American Academy of Political and Social Science,* vol. 254 (Nov., 1947), pp. 58–64.

Rosten, Leo. "Hollywood Revisited." *Look,* vol. 20 (Jan. 10, 1956), pp. 17–28.

———. "Movies and Propaganda." *Annals of the American Academy of Political and Social Science,* vol. 254 (Nov., 1947), pp. 116–124.

Rule, Phillip C. "Film Ratings: 1934 Revisited." *America,* May 29, 1971, pp. 570–572.

Schary, Dore. "Hollywood: Fade Out, Fade In." *Reporter,* vol. 16 (Apr. 18, 1957), pp. 20–25.

———. "Our Movie Mythology." *Reporter,* vol. 22 (Mar. 3, 1960), pp. 39–42.

Schechner, Richard. "Pornography and the New Expression." *Atlantic Monthly,* vol. 219, no. 1 (Jan. 1, 1967), pp. 74–78.

Schulberg, Budd. "Hollywood." *Holiday,* no. 5 (Jan., 1949), pp. 34–49.

"Screen Fans Organize to Bite the Hand that Feeds Them Double Features." *Newsweek,* no. 10 (Oct. 4, 1937), pp. 25–26.

"Script for Success." *Time*, vol. 73 (Apr. 27, 1959), p. 86.

Seldes, Gilbert. "Law, Pressure and Public Opinion." *Hollywood Quarterly*, vol. 1 (1946), pp. 422–426.

———. "The Movies Commit Suicide." *Harper's*, Nov., 1928, pp. 706–712.

———. "The Quicksands of the Movies." *Atlantic Monthly*, vol. 158, no. 4 (Oct., 1936), pp. 422–431.

———. "Screen and Radio." *Scribner's*, vol. 102, no. 1 (July, 1937), pp. 56–58.

Shain, Russell. "Hollywood's Cold War." *Journal of Popular Film*, vol. 3, no. 4 (Fall, 1974), pp. 334–350.

Shaw, Albert. "Will Hays: A Ten Year Record." *American Review of Reviews*, vol. 85 (March, 1932), pp. 30–31.

Shaw, Irwin. "Hollywood People." *Holiday*, vol. 5 (Jan., 1949), pp. 53–59.

Sinclair, Upton. "The Movies and Political Propaganda." In *The Movies on Trial*, edited by William J. Perlman, pp. 189–195. New York: Macmillan Company, 1936; reprint ed., New York: Jerome S. Ozer, 1971.

"6 N.E. States Plan Concerted Action in Pornography." *Variety*, July 25, 1973, p. 1.

Slout, William L. " 'Uncle Tom's Cabin' in American Film History." *Journal of Popular Film*, vol. 2, no. 2 (Spring, 1973), pp. 137–152.

"Small-Screen Hollywood." *Newsweek*, no. 50 (Dec. 16, 1957), p. 112.

Smythe, Dallas, et. al. "Portrait of a First-Run Audience." *Quarterly of Film, Radio and Television*, vol. 9 (1955), pp. 390–409.

Smythe, Dallas, Parker B. Lusk, and Charles A. Lewis. "Portrait of an Art-Theater Audience." *Quarterly of Film, Radio and Television*, vol. 9 (1955), pp. 28–50.

Soderbergh, Peter A. " 'Aux Armes': The Rise of the Hollywood War Film, 1916–1930." *South Atlantic Quarterly*, vol. 65 (1966), pp. 509–522.

———. "The Grand Illusion: Hollywood and World War II, 1930–1945." *University of Dayton Review*, vol. 5 (1968), pp. 13–22.

———. "On War and Movies: A Reappraisal." *Centennial Review*, vol. 11, no. 3 (Summer, 1967), pp. 405–418.

———. "The War Films." *Discourse: A Review of the Liberal Arts*, vol. 11, no. 1 (Winter, 1968), pp. 87–91.

Somers, Dale A. "The Leisure Revolution: Recreation in the American City, 1820–1920." *Journal of Popular Culture*, vol. 5, no. 1 (1971), pp. 125–143.

Sprachman, M., and M. Giller. "Uptown Cinema, Toronto." *Canadian Architect*, vol. 15 (Aug., 1970), pp. 26–30.

Stecker, Dora H. "Some Desirable Goals for Motion Pictures." In *Proceedings*, National Conference of Social Work, 1927, pp. 360–370.

Stelzle, Charles. "Movies Instead of Saloons." *Independent*, Feb. 28, 1916, p. 311.

Stern, Seymour. "The Birth of a Nation." *American Mercury*, Mar., 1949, p. 308.

Sugrue, Thomas. "The Newsreels." *Scribner's*, vol. 101, no. 4 (Apr., 1937), pp. 9–18.

Suskow, Ruth. "Hollywood Gods and Goddesses." *Harper's*, vol. 173 (July, 1936), pp. 189–200.

Susman, Warren I. "The Thirties." In *The Development of an American Culture*, edited by Stanley Coben and Lorman Ratner, pp. 179–218. Englewood Cliffs: Prentice-Hall, 1970.

Taylor, Frank J. "Big Boom in Outdoor Movies." *Saturday Evening Post*, vol. 229 (Sept. 15, 1956), pp. 31, 100–102.

Taylor, Ryland A. "Audiences and Movie Awards: A Statistical Study." *Journal of Broadcasting*, vol. 18, no. 2 (Spring, 1974), pp. 181–186.

Taylor, Winchell. "Secret Movie Censors." *Nation*, vol. 147, no. 2 (July 9, 1938), pp. 38–40.

"Television: Movies' Friend or Foe?" *U.S. News and World Report*, no. 26 (Jan. 7, 1949), p. 24.

"Tempest in a Hollywood Teapot." *Theatre Arts*, vol. 27 (Feb., 1943), pp. 71–72.

"Third Dimension: New Bait for Movie Box Office." *Business Week*, no. 1210 (Nov. 8, 1952), pp. 132–137.

Thompson, Blanche Jennings. "Clinics in Crime." *Commonweal*, vol. 29 (Apr. 14, 1939), pp. 686–687.

Thrasher, Frederic M. "Plan to Develop International Understanding Through Motion Pictures." *Education,* no. 58 (May, 1938), pp. 560–561.

———. "Sociological Approach to Motion Pictures in Relation to Education." *Education,* vol. 58 (Apr., 1938), pp. 467–473.

"Trouble in Paradise." *Time,* vol. 45 (Jan. 29, 1945), pp. 38–39.

Tudor, Andrew. "Film and the Measurement of Its Effects." *Screen,* vol. 10, no. 4–5 (1969), pp. 148–159.

"TV and Hollywood Sing a Duet." *Business Week,* no. 1911 (Apr. 16, 1966), pp. 106–108.

Twomey, John E. "Some Considerations on the Rise of the Art-Film Theater." *Quarterly of Film, Radio and Television,* vol. 10 (1956), pp. 239–247.

"The Ubiquitous Moving Picture." *American Magazine,* July, 1913, p. 102.

"U.S. Movie Exports Set Record." *Business Week,* June 26, 1937, pp. 50–51.

Valenti, J. "Motion Picture Code and the New American Culture." *PTA Magazine,* no. 61 (Dec., 1966), pp. 16–19.

Van Doren, Mark. "70,000,000 Americans." *Nation,* vol. 142, no. 3684 (Feb. 12, 1936), pp. 203–204.

"Vanishing Moviegoer." *Time,* vol. 71 (Feb. 10, 1958), p. 100.

Walsh, George E. "Moving Picture Drama for the Multitude." *Independent,* Feb. 6, 1908, pp. 306–310.

———. "Making Mature Movie Viewers." *America,* vol. 107 (Nov. 3, 1962), pp. 978–982.

———. "Of Ratings, Psychos, Etc." *America,* vol. 120 (Mar. 22, 1969), pp. 343–345.

Wanger, Walter F. "The Films: Forward from 1941." *Theater Arts,* vol. 25 (Sept., 1941), pp. 622–630.

———. "The O.W.I. and Motion Pictures." *Public Opinion Quarterly,* vol. 7, no. 1 (Spring, 1943), pp. 100–107.

———. "120,000 American Ambassadors." *Foreign Affairs,* vol. 18 (Oct., 1939), pp. 45–59.

———. "The Role of Movies in Morals." *American Journal of Sociology,* vol. 47 (Nov., 1941), pp. 378–383.

"War Hits Hollywood." *Business Week,* no. 544 (Feb. 3, 1940), pp. 49–50.

Warner, Harry P. "Television and the Motion Picture Industry." *Hollywood Quarterly,* vol. 2 (1946), pp. 11–18.

Wehberg, Hilla. "Fate of an International Film Institute." *Public Opinion Quarterly,* vol. 2 (July, 1938), pp. 483–485.

Weigall, Arthur. "The Influence of the Kinematograph upon National Life." *Nineteenth Century,* Apr., 1921, pp. 661–672.

Whelan, Russell. "The Legion of Decency." *American Mercury,* vol. 60 (June, 1945), p. 655–663.

White, E. B. "One Man's Meat." *Harper's,* vol. 179 (July, 1939), pp. 217–219.

Whitney, Simon N. "The Impact of Anti-Trust Laws: Vertical Disintegration in the Motion Picture Industry." *American Economic Review,* vol. 45 (May, 1955), pp. 491–498.

"Why We Need a Neely Bill." *Christian Century,* no. 57 (Apr. 10, 1940), p. 468.

Wiese, Mildred J., and Stewart G. Cole. "A Study of Children's Attitudes and the Influence of the Commercial Motion Picture." *Journal of Psychology,* vol. 21 (1946), pp. 151–171.

Williams, Barbara Morrow. "Filth vs. Lucre: The Black Community's Tough Choice." *Psychology Today,* vol. 7, no. 9 (Feb., 1974), p. 102.

Williams, John Elliot. "They Stopped at Nothing." *Hollywood Quarterly,* vol. I (1946), pp. 270–278.

Winter, Ella. "Hollywood Wakes Up." *New Republic,* no. 93 (Jan. 12, 1938), pp. 276–278.

Wirth, Louis. "The Social Sciences." In *American Scholarship in the Twentieth Century,* edited by Merle E. Curti, pp. 33–82. Cambridge: Harvard University Press, 1953.

Woodbury, Roy F. "Children and Movies." *Survey,* May 15, 1929, pp. 253–254.

"X." "Hollywood Meets Frankenstein." *Nation,* vol. 174 (June 28, 1952), pp. 628–631.

Young, Kimball. "Review of the Payne Fund Studies." *American Journal of Sociology,* Sept., 1935, pp. 250–255.

Zeisel, Joseph S. "The Workweek in American Industry, 1850–1956." In *Mass Leisure,* edited by Eric Larrabee and Rolf Meyersohn, pp. 145–153. Glencoe: Free Press, 1958.

Unpublished Material

Bernstein, Irving. "Hollywood at the Crossroads: An Economic Study of the Motion Picture Industry." Hollywood: A.F.L. Film Council, Dec., 1957. (Mimeographed.)

Bohn, Thomas. "An Historical and Descriptive Analysis of the 'Why We Fight' Series." Ph.D. dissertation, University of Wisconsin, 1968.

Drama Committee of the Twentieth Century Club. "The Amusement Situation in the City of Boston." Boston: Twentieth Century Club, 1910.

Fredericksen, Donald L. "The Aesthetic of Isolation in Film Theory: Hugo Munsterberg." Ph.D. dissertation, University of Iowa, 1973.

Giglio, Ernest David. "The Decade of the Miracle, 1952–1962: A Study in the Censorship of the American Motion Picture." D.SS. dissertation, Syracuse University, 1964.

Hutchins, Charles L. "A Critical Evaluation of Controversies Engendered by D. W. Griffith's *The Birth of a Nation.*" M.A. thesis, State University of Iowa, 1961.

Janes, Robert William. "The Legion of Decency and the Motion Picture Industry." M.A. thesis, University of Chicago, 1939.

Karimi, Amir Massoud. "Toward a Definition of the American Film Noir, 1941–1949." Ph.D. dissertation, University of Southern California, 1971.

Linden, Kathryn B. "The Film Censorship Struggle in the United States from 1926 to 1957, and the Social Values Involved." Ph.D. dissertation, New York University, 1972.

Motion Picture Producers and Distributors of America, Inc. "Authoritative Statements Concerning the Screen and Behavior." In the files of the Museum of Modern Art Film Library (no date).

Opinion Research Corporation. "The Public Appraises Movies." Princeton, 1957.

Perry, Donald L. "An Analysis of the Financial Plans of the Motion Picture Industry for the Period 1929 to 1962." Ph.D. dissertation, University of Illinois, 1966.

Phelan, John M., S.J. "The National Catholic Office for Motion Pictures: An Investigation of the Policy and Practice of Film Classification." Ph.D. dissertation, New York University, 1968.

Sargent, John A. "Self-Regulation: The Motion Picture Production Code, 1930–1961." Ph.D. dissertation, University of Michigan, 1963.

Schull, Claude A. "The Suitability of the Commercial Entertainment Motion Picture to the Age of the Child." Ph.D. dissertation, Stanford University, 1939.

Selby, Stuart A. "The Study of Film as an Art Form in American Secondary Schools." Ed.D. dissertation, Columbia University, 1963.

Short, Ray Leroy. "A Social Study of the Motion Picture." M.A. thesis, Iowa State University, 1916.

Suber, Howard. "The Anti-Communist Blacklist in the Hollywood Motion Picture Industry." Ph.D. dissertation, University of California, Los Angeles, 1968.

——. "The 1947 Hearings of the House Committee on Un-American Activities into Communism in the Hollywood Motion Picture Industry." M.A. thesis, University of California, Los Angeles, 1966.

Wilner, Daniel. "Attitude as a Determinant of Perception in the Mass Media of Communications: Reactions to the Motion Picture *Home of the Brave.*" Ph.D. dissertation, University of California, 1950.

Government Documents

Chicago. Motion Picture Commission. *Chicago Code, 1922.*

Chicago. Motion Picture Commission. *Report of the Commission, 1920.*

Massachusetts. *Number of Assessed Polls, Registered Voters.* Public Document No. 43, 1922.

U.S. Bureau of the Census. *Historical Statistics of the United States.* Washington: U.S.G.P.O., 1961.

U.S. Congress. House. Committee of Education. *Hearings, Proposed Federal Motion Picture Commission.* 69th Congress, 1st Session, 1926.

U.S. Congress. House. Subcommittee of the Committee on Interstate and Foreign Commerce. *Hearings, on H.R. 4757, H.R. 8877, and H.R. 6472, Motion Picture Films.* 74th Congress, 2nd Session, 1936.

U.S. Congress. Senate. Committee on the Judiciary. Subcommittee to Investigate Juvenile Delinquency. *Motion Pictures and Juvenile Delinquency, S. Rep. 2055.* 84th Congress, 2nd Session, 1956.

U.S. Surgeon-General's Scientific Advisory Committee on Television and Social Behavior. *Television and Growing Up: The Impact of Televised Violence.* Washington: U.S.G.P.O., 1972.

Index

mass media. *See* media
Martens, Charles H., 243–244
Martin, Olga G., 207
Marty, 356
Marvin, Henry N., 71 n.26
Mary Poppins, 450
Maryland, 119, 412
Massachusetts, 119, 167–169, 243
Massachusetts State Commission on Motion Pictures, 167
Maurois, André, 204
Maxim, Hudson, 66
May, Mark A., 222–223, 274
Mayer, Arthur, 371
Mayer, Louis B., 189, 295, 297
media, 3–9, 11–12, 202–203, 211–212, 266. *See also* magazines; newspapers; radio; television
Medium Cool, 435
Meet John Doe, 300
Mellett, Lowell, 307–309, 311
Melnick, David, 435
melodrama, 25
Merritt, Russell, 38, 49 n.54, 62–63
Methodist Episcopal General Conference, 154
Metrotone News, 189
Metzger, Radley, 443
Meyer, Russ, 443
MGM, 435–438
Michigan, 243
Mickey Mouse, 189
Middletown. *See* Muncie, Ind.
Midnight Cowboy, 435, 445
Midsummer Night's Dream, A, 181
Millard, Ruth, 146
Milliken, Carl E., 153, 176, 204, 250
Miracle, The, 404–408
Miracle decision. *See* Burstyn v. Wilson
Miracle on 34th Street, 414
Mississippi, 243
Mitchell, Alice Miller, 218–220, 263
Mix, Tom, 284
Moana of the South Seas, 189
Moley, Raymond, 172–173, 205–206, 226–227, 234, 238–239, 242, 245–246, 254, 272
Moon Is Blue, The, 409, 414–418
Mortal Storm, The, 299
Mortimer Mouse, 189
Moss, Frank, 111
Motion Picture, 177
Motion Picture Artists' Committee, 296
Motion Picture Association of America. *See* Motion Picture Producers and Distributors of America Inc.
Motion Picture Board of Trade, 156
Motion Picture Bureau. *See* Bureau of

Motion Pictures, Office of War Information
Motion Picture Committee Cooperating for National Defense, 307–309, 311, 321
Motion Picture Herald, 202
motion picture industry, 154–161, 197–203, 233–243, 253–256, 334–338; and communism, 393–396; control (*see* censorship; regulation); distribution practices, 13–14, 45, 275–284 (*see also* antitrust; block-booking; vertical integration); history, 26–34, 51–70, 185–186, 342–360, 428–457; statistics, 478, 480–481; and war (*see* war)
Motion Picture Patents Co., 33–34, 52–53, 55–58, 126. *See also* General Film Co.
Motion Picture Producers and Distributors of America Inc., 153, 164–182, 189–190, 200, 206, 226–228, 233–237, 240–244, 250, 272–273, 277, 282, 298, 337, 341, 375, 397–398, 415, 439–440, 455–456; Children's Film Library, 337; Code and Rating Administration, 441–443; Committee on Public Relations, 173–177, 236; Copyright Protection Bureau, 175–176; Production Code Administration Office (*see* Production Code Administration)
Studio Labor Relations Committee, 175–176, 237–238, 242
Motion Picture Production Code, 240–243, 247, 281, 382–383, 396–404, 413–421, 439–440, 465–469
Motion Picture Research Council, 220, 225, 228
motion pictures: abroad, 64, 68, 203–205, 283, 299, 302–303, 321–322, 324, 384–386; as art, 98–100, 377–379; audience (*see* audiences); content, 42–45, 62–65, 186–190, 317–321, 365–369; control of (*see* censorship; regulation); criticism, 97–98, 100, 195–196, 200, 335–336; early history, 24–33; influence of, 13–14, 64, 77–91, 95–100, 142–151, 210–229, 263, 265–275, 300–301, 321–322, 334–336, 369–375 (*see also* children; education); technology, 24–28, 33, 148–150, 185, 190–193, 195–197, 356–360, 431
Motion Pictures Not Guilty, 134
Motion Picture Stories, 56
Motion Picture Story Magazine, 56
motion picture theaters, 27–33, 51–52, 58–62, 82–83, 214, 260, 276, 354, 431, 477, 479. *See also* drive-ins
Moving Picture News, 101
Moving Picture World, 101
Mrs. Miniver, 300
Muncie, Ind., 49 n.59, 142–143, 262–263
Munsey's Magazine, 15